Bilingual Di

CW01501194

English-Gujarati
Gujarati-English
Dictionary

Compiled by
Sujata Basaria

STAR Foreign Language BOOKS

This Edition : 2024

Published by

STAR Foreign Language BOOKS

a unit of
Star Books
56, Langland Crescent
Stanmore HA7 1NG, U.K.
info@starbooksuk.com
www.bilingualbooks.co.uk

Printed in India at
Star Print-O-Bind, New Delhi-110 020

About this Dictionary

Developments in science and technology today have narrowed down distances between countries, and have made the world a small place. A person living thousands of miles away can learn and understand the culture and lifestyle of another country with ease and without travelling to that country. Languages play an important role as facilitators of communication in this respect.

To promote such an understanding, **STAR Foreign Language BOOKS** has planned to bring out a series of bilingual dictionaries in which important English words have been translated into other languages, with Roman transliteration in case of languages that have different scripts. This is a humble attempt to bring people of the word closer through the medium of language, thus making communication easy and convenient.

Under this series of *one-to-one dictionaries*, we have published almost 59 languages, the list of which has been given in the opening pages. These have all been compiled and edited by teachers and scholars of the relative languages.

Publishers

ONE TO ONE

Bilingual Dictionaries in this Series

English-Afrikaans / Afrikaans-English	Abraham Venter
English-Albanian / Albanian-English	Theodhora Blushi
English-Amharic / Amharic-English	Girun Asanke
English-Arabic / Arabic-English	Rania-al-Qass
English-Bengali / Bengali-English	Amit Majumdar
English-Bosnian / Bosnian-English	Boris Kazanegra
English-Bulgarian / Bulgarian-English	Vladka Kocheshkova
English-Burmese (Myanmar) / Burmese (Myanmar)-English	Kyaw Swar Aung
English-Cambodian / Cambodian-English	Engly Sok
English-Cantonese / Cantonese-English	Nisa Yang
English-Chinese (Mandarin) / Chinese (Mandarin)-Eng	Y. Shang & R. Yao
English-Croatian / Croatin-English	Vesna Kazanegra
English-Czech / Czech-English	Jindriska Poulova
English-Danish / Danish-English	Rikke Wend Hartung
English-Dari / Dari-English	Amir Khan
English-Dutch / Dutch-English	Lisanne Vogel
English-Estonian / Estonian-English	Lana Haleta
English-Farsi / Farsi-English	Maryam Zaman Khani
English-French / French-English	Aurélie Colin
English-Georgian / Georgina-English	Eka Goderdzishvili
English-Gujarati / Gujarati-English	Sujata Basaria
English-German / German-English	Bicskei Hedwig
English-Greek / Greek-English	Lina Stergiou
English-Hindi / Hindi-English	Sudhakar Chaturvedi
English-Hungarian / Hungarian-English	Lucy Mallows
English-Italian / Italian-English	Eni Lamllari
English-Japanese / Japanese-English	Miruka Arai & Hiroko Nishimura
English-Korean / Korean-English	Mihee Song
English-Latvian / Latvian-English	Julija Baranovska
English-Levantine Arabic / Levantine Arabic-English	Ayman Khalaf
English-Lithuanian / Lithuanian-English	Regina Kazakeviciute
English-Malay / Malay-English	Azimah Husna
English-Malayalam - Malayalam-English	Anjumol Babu
English-Nepali / Nepali-English	Anil Mandal
English-Norwegian / Norwegian-English	Samuele Narcisi
English-Pashto / Pashto-English	Amir Khan
English-Polish / Polish-English	Magdalena Herok
English-Portuguese / Portuguese-English	Dina Teresa
English-Punjabi / Punjabi-English	Teja Singh Chatwal
English-Romanian / Romanian-English	Georgeta Laura Dutulescu
English-Russian / Russian-English	Katerina Volobuyeva
English-Serbian / Serbian-English	Vesna Kazanegra
English-Sinhalese / Sinhalese-English	Naseer Salahudeen
English-Slovak / Slovak-English	Zuzana Horvathova
English-Slovenian / Slovenian-English	Tanja Turk
English-Somali / Somali-English	Ali Mohamud Omer
English-Spanish / Spanish-English	Cristina Rodriguez
English-Swahili / Swahili-English	Abdul Rauf Hassan Kinga
English-Swedish / Swedish-English	Madelene Axelsson
English-Tagalog / Tagalog-English	Jefferson Bantayan
English-Tamil / Tamil-English	Sandhya Mahadevan
English-Thai / Thai-English	Suwan Kaewkongpan
English-Tigrigna / Tigrigna-English	Tsegazeab Hailegebriel
English-Turkish / Turkish-English	Nagme Yazgin
English-Twi / Twi-English	Nathaniel Alonsi Apadu
English-Ukrainian / Ukrainian-English	Katerina Volobuyeva
English-Urdu / Urdu-English	S. A. Rahman
English-Vietnamese / Vietnamese-English	Hoa Hoang
English-Yoruba / Yoruba-English	O. A. Temitope

STAR Foreign Language BOOKS

English-Gujarati

A

a એક ek
a-1 *adj.* એ-1 A-1
aback *adv.* પાછળ paachhal
abandon *v.* છોડી દેવું chhodi devun
abandonment *n.* સ્વૈરાચાર svairaachar
abase *v.t.* નીચે ઉતારવું niche utaaravun
abash *v.* શરમાવવું sharamaavavun
abashed *adj.* શરમાયેલું sharamaayelun
abate *v.t.* ઓછું કરવું ochhu karvun
abattoir *n.* કતલખાનું katalkhaanun
abbreviate સંક્ષિપ્ત કરવું sankshipt karvun
abbreviation *n.* સંક્ષિપ્ત sankshipt
abdomen *n.* પેટ pet
abduct *v.t.* અપહરણ કરવું apaharan karvun
abduction *n.* અપહરણ apaharan
aberrance *n.* ઉન્માર્ગગામી unmaargagaamee
aberrant *n.* મનોવિકૃત manovikrut
abeyance *n.* મોકુફી mokufee
abhor *v.t.* તિરસ્કારવું tiraskarvun
abide *v.* નભાવી લેવું nabhaavi levu
abiding *prep.* ચિરસ્થાયી chirsthaayee
ability *n.* ક્ષમતા kshamata
abject *adj.* હલકું halakun
abjectness *n.* હલકાઈ halakaaee
abjuration *n.* ત્યાગ tyaag
abjure *v.* માન્યતા maanyataa
ablaze *adv.* ધગધગતું dhagadhagatun
able *adj.* કાર્યકુશળ kaaryakushal
abloom *adv.* ખીલેલી સ્થિતિમાં kheelelee sthitiman
ablush *adv.* શરમાતા શરમાતા sharamata sharamata
ablution *n.* સામાન્ય સ્નાન saamaanya snaan
abnormal *adj.* અસ્વાભાવિક asvaabhaavik
abode *n.* રહેઠાણ rahethan
abolish *v.t.* નાબૂદ કરવું naabud karvun
abolition *n.* નાબૂદી naabudi
abominable *adj.* ધૃણાસ્પદ dhrunaspad

abominate *v.t.* ધિક્કારવું dhikkaaravun
abort *v.* ગર્ભપાત કરવો garbhapaat karvo
abortion *n.* ગર્ભપાત gharbhapaat
abortive *adj.* ગર્ભપાત કરાવનારું garbhpaat karaavnarun
abound *v.* વિપુલ હોવું vipul hovun
about *adv.* આસપાસ aaspaas
abreast *adv.* સાથોસાથ, લગોલગ saathosaath, lagolag
abridge *v.t.* ટૂંકાવવું tunkaavavun
abroad *adv.* પરદેશમાં pardeshman
abrogate *v.t.* રદ કરવું rad karvun
abrupt *adj.* આકસ્મિક aakasmik
abruptness *n.* ઓચિંતાપણું ochintaapanun
abscond *v.* ફરાર faraar
absence *n.* ગેરહાજરી gerhaajaree
absent *adj.* ગેરહાજર gerhaajar
absolute *n.* અબાધિત abaadhit
absolve *v.t.* ક્ષમા kshamaa
absorb ક્ષમા આપવી kshamaa aapavee
absorbed મશગૂલ mashagool
absorption *n.* તલ્લીન થવું તે tallin thavun te
abstemious *adj* મિતાહારી mitaahari
abstemiousness *n.* મિત્તાહાર mittaahar
abstract *adj.* અમૂર્ત amoort
abstruse *adj.* ગૂઢ goodh
absurd *adj.* અસંગત asangat
absurdity *n.* અસંગતત asangatat
abundance *n.* વિપુલતા vipulataa
abundant *adj.* વિપુલ vipul
abuse *v.* ગાળ દેવી gaal devee
abusive *adj.* ગાળ દેનારું gaal denaarun
abyss *n.* ખાઈ khaaee
acacia *n.* શિંગોવાળું sheengovaalun
academic *adj.* તાત્ત્વિક taatvik
academy *n.* તાલીમની સંસ્થા taalimani sanstha
accede *v.* અધિકાર adhikaar
accelerate *v.* ગતિવધારવી gatee vadhaaravee
acceleration *n.* ગતિવર્ધન gateevardhan
accent *n.* ભાર દેવો bhaar devo
accept *v.* સ્વીકારવું svikaaravun

acceptable *adj.* સ્વીકારવા યોગ્ય svikaaravaa yogya

acceptance *n.* સ્વીકાર svikaar

access *n.* પ્રવેશ pravesh

accessary *n.* મળતિયો malatiyo

accessible *adj.* સુલભ sulabh

accession *n.* વધારો vadhaaro

accessory *adj.* વધારાનું vadhaaraanun

accident *n.* અકસ્માત akasmaat

accidental *adj.* અણધાર્યું anadhaaryun

acclaim *v.* વધાવવું vadhaavavun

acclimatize *v.* ટેવાઈ જવું tevaaee javun

accommodate *v.t.* સહાય કરવી sahaay karavi

accommodation *n.* સગવડ sagavad

accompany *v.t.* વળાવવું valaavavun

accomplice *n.* સહઅપરાધી saha aparaadhee

accomplish *v.* પૂરણ કરવું poorna karavun

accomplishment *n.* સમાપ્તિ samaapti

accord *v.t.* માન્ય કરવું maanya karvun

accordance *n.* મળતાપણું malataapanun

according *adv.* સુસંગત susangat

accost *v.* વિનંતિ કરવી veenanti karavee

account *v.t.* જવાબ આપવો javaab aapavo

accountable *adj.* જવાબદાર javaabdaar

accountancy *n.* નામું naamun

accountant *n.* હિસાબનીસ, મુનીમ hisabanis, muneem

accrue *v.t.* ઊપજવું oopajavun

accumulate *v.* સંચય થવો sanchay thavo

accuracy *n.* ચોકસાઈ, બારીકી chokasaaee, baarikee

accurate *adj.* ચોક્કસ, બરાબર chokkas, baraabar

accursed *adj.* તિરસ્કરણીય teeraskaaraniy

accusation *n.* આરોપ મૂકવો aarop mookavo

accuse *v.* દોષારોપણ કરવું doshaaropan karvun

accustom *v.t.* મહાવરો પાડવો mahaavaro paadavo

accustomed *adj.* રૂઢ, પ્રચલિત roodh, prachalit

ace *n.* એક્કો, સોગઠું aekko, sogathun

acerbate *v.* ચીદવવું chidavavun

acerbity *n.* કડવાશ, કટુતા kadavaash, katutaa

acetylene *n.* એસિટિલિન aesitilin

ache *v.t.* દુખવું, વેદના dukhavun, vedanaa

achieve *v.t.* પ્રાપ્ત કરવું praapt karavun

achievment *n.* પ્રાપૂર્તિ, સિદ્ધિ praapti, seeddhi

acid *adj.* તેજાબ tejaab

acidity *n.* ખટાશ, તેજાબિતા khataash, tejabitaa

acknowledge *v.* સ્વીકારવું svikaaravun

acknowledgement *n.* પહોંચ, પાવતી pahonch, paavati

acme *n.* શિખર shikhar

acne *n.* ફોલ્લીઓ, ખીલ folleeo, kheel

aconite *n.* વછનાગનો છોડ vachhavaanaagano chhod

acorn *n.* ઓકનું ફળ aokanun fal

acoustic *adj.* શ્રવણેન્દ્રિયીય shravanendariyeey

acquaint *v.t.* ને જાણ કરવી ne jaan karavee

acquaintance *n.* ઓળખીતું માણસ olakhitun maanas

acquiescence માન્યતા maanyataa

acquire *v.t.* મેળવવું melavavun

acquirement *n.* ઉપલબ્ધિ upalabdhi

acquisition *n.* સંપાદન sanpaadan

acquit *v.t.* દોષમુક્ત કરવું doshamukt karvun

acre *n.* એકર aekar

acrimony *n.* ઉગ્રતા, કઠોરતા ugrataa, kathorata

acrobat *n.* બજાણિયો bajaaniyo

across *adv.* એકબીજા પર આડું ekabijaa par aadun

act *n.* કાયદો kaayado

acting *adj.* અદાકારી, હંગામી adaakaaree, hangaamee

action *n.* મુકદ્દમો, કૃત્ય mukaddamo, krutya

active *adj.* સક્રિય sakriya

9

actively *adv.* ખંતપૂર્વક khantpoorvak

activity *n.* પ્રવૃત્તિ, કાર્યક્ષેત્ર pravrutti, kaaryakshetra

actor *n.* અભિનેતા, નટ abheeneta, nat

actual *adj.* ખરું, ચાલુ kharun, chaalun

actually *adj.* વાસ્તવિકપણે, ખરેખર vaastavikpane, kharekhar

actuate *n.* પ્રેરવું preravun

acuity *n.* અણિયાળાપણું aneeyaalaapanu

acumen *n.* સૂક્ષ્મભેદક દૃષ્ટિ sookshmabhedak drashtee

acute *dj.* બુદ્ધિમાન buddheemaan

acuteness *n.* કુશાગ્રતા kushaagrataa

adage *n.* કહેવત, સૂત્ર kahevat, sutra

adam *n.* બાવા આદમ baavaa aadam

adapt *v.t.* અનુકૂળ કરવું anukool karavun

adaptation *n.* અનુકૂલન, અનુરૂપતા anukoolan, anuroopataa

add *v.t.* ઉમેરવું umeravun

adder *n.* ઝેરી સાપ jheree saap

addicted નું વ્યસની nu vyasanee

additional *adj.* ઉમેરો, સરવાળો umero, saravaalo

address *v.t.* સંબોધન કરવું sanbodhan karavun

addressee સંબોધનધારક sanbodhandhaarak

adept *n.* ઉસ્તાદ ustaad

adequate *adj.* પૂરતું pooratun

adhere *v.t.* વળગી રહેવું valagee rahevun

adherent *n.* અનુષંગી anushangee

adhesion *n.* સંલગ્નતા sanlagnataa

adieu *n.* વિદાયવેળાની સલામ vidaayvelaani salaam

adjacent *adj.* નજીકનું, અડોઅડ najiknun, adoad

adjective *n.* (વ્યા) વિશેષણ (vya) veesheshan

adjectival *adj.* વિશેષણ યુક્ત visheshan yukt

adjoin *v.t.* જોડાયેલું હોવું jodaayelun hovun

adjourn *v.t.* સ્થગિત કરવું sthagit karavun

adjudge *v.t.* નિર્ણય કરવો nirnay karavo

adjudicate *v.t.* ચુકાદો આપવો chukaado aapavo

adjudication *n.* ચુકાદો chukaado

adjunct *n.* આશ્રિત, આધારિત aashrit, aadhaarit

adjure *v.t.* ભારપૂર્વક bhaarpoorvak

adjust *v.t.* ગોઠવવું gothavavun

adjustment *v.t.* ગોઠવણ gothavan

adjutant *n.* સમાદેશ મદદનીશ samaadesh madadanish

administer *v.t.* વહિવટ કરવો vahivat karavo

administration *n.* શાસન shaasan

administrator પ્રબંધક prabandhak

admirable *adj.* પ્રશંસાપાત્ર prashansaapaatra

admiral *n.* નૌસેનાપતિ nausenaapati

admiration *n.* આનંદાશ્ચર્ય aanandaashcharya

admire *v.t.* વખાણવું vakhaanavun

admirer *n.* પ્રશંસક, આશિક prashansak, aashik

admissible *adj.* ગ્રાહ્ય, સ્વીકાર્ય graahya, sveekaary

admission *n.* દાખલ કરવું daakhal karavun

admit *v.* દાખલ કરવું daakhal karavun

admittance *n.* પ્રવેશ, છૂટ pravesh, chhoot

admix *v.t.* ભેળવવું bhelavavun

admixiture *v.t.* ભેળવવાની ક્રિયા bhelavavaanee kriya

admonish *v.t.* પ્રેરવું, તાકીદ કરવી preravun, taakid karavee

admonition *n.* તાકીદ, શિખામણ taakid, shikhaaman

ado *n.* ધાંધલ, ખટપટ dhaandhal, khatapat

adolescence *n.* કિશોરાવસ્થા, તારુણ્ય kishoraavasthaa, taarunya

adolescent *adj.* કિશોર keeshor

adopt *v.t.* દત્તક લેવું dattak levun

adoration *n.* આરાધના, અંજલિ aaraadhanaa, anjalee

adore *v.t.* પ્રેમાદરપૂર્વક પૂજવું premaadarapoorvak poojavun

adorer *n.* પૂજક, આરાધક poojak, aaraadhak

adorn *v.t.* શણગારવું shanagaaravun

adrift *adv.* અસહાય, દયાપાત્ર asahaay, dayaapaatra

adroit *adj.* કુશળ, નિપુણ kushal, nipun

adulate *v.t.* ખુશામત કરવી khushaamat karavee

adult *n.* પુખ્ત વયનું pukht vayanun

adulterate *v.t.* ભેળસેળ કરવી bhelsel karavee

adulterer *n.* વ્યભિચારી vyabhichaaree

adultery *n.* વ્યભિચાર vyabhichaar

adumbrate *v.t.* પૂર્વચિહ્ન બતાવવું poorvchinha bataavavun

advance આગળ વધવું aagal vadhavun

advancement *n.* ઉન્નતિ, પ્રગતિ unnati, pragati

advantage *n.* લાભ laabh

advantageous *adj.* લાભપ્રદ, ફાયદાકારક laabhaprad, faayadaakaarak

advent *n.* આગમન aagaman

adventure *v.* સાહસ, જોખમ, saahas, jokham

adverb *n.* ક્રિયાવિશેષણ અવ્યય kriyaavishesan avyay

adversary *n.* પ્રતિસ્પર્ધી, હરીફ pratispardhee, harif

adverse *adj.* પ્રતિકૂળ,અશુભ pratikool, ashubh

advert *v.* વલણ ફેરવવું valan feravavun

advertise *v.* જાહેરાત કરવી jaaheraat karavee

advertisement *n.* જાહેરખબર jaaher khabar

advice *n.* સલાહ, ઉપદેશ salaah, upadesh

advisable *adj.* ભલામણ કરવા જેવું bhalaaman karavaa jevun

advise *v.* સલાહ આપવી salaah aapavee

advisory *adj.* સલાહકાર salaahkaar

advocacy *n.* હિમાયત, તરફદારી himaayat, tarafadaaree

advocate *v.* પક્ષકાર,હિમાયતી pakshakaar, himaayatee

adytum *n.* ગર્ભગૃહ, ગભારો garbhagruh, gabhaaro

adze *n.* સુતારનો વાંસલો sutaarno vaansalo

aegis *n.* રક્ષણ, આશ્રય rakshan, aashray

aerate *v.* ઓક્સિજનીકરણ oksijaneekaran

aerated *adj.* વાયુયુક્ત, વાયુમિશ્રિત vaayuyukt, vaayumishrit

aerial *adj.* વાયુવિષયક vaayuvishayak

aeriform *adj.* વાયુરૂપ, હલકું vaayuroop, halakun

aerodrome *n.* હવાઈ મથક havaaee mathak

aerogram *n.* બિનતારી સંદેશો beentaari sandesho

aeronaut *n.* વિમાનને લગતું vimaanane lagatun

aeroplane *n.* વિમાન, હવાઈ જહાજ vimaan, havaaee jahaaj

aesthetic *adj.* કદર કરનારું kadar karanaarun

aesthetics *n.* સૌંદર્ય શાસ્ત્ર saundarya shaastra

afar *adj.* દૂર, લાંબા અંતરે door, laanbaa antare

affable *adj.* મળતાવડું, સૌજન્યશીલ malataavadun, saujanyasheel

affair *n.* ઘટના ghatana

affect અસર કરવી asar karavee

affectation *n.* મિથ્યાડંબર mithya aadanbar

affected *adj.* કૃત્રિમ, ઢોંગી krutrim, dhongee

affection *n.* મમતા mamataa

affectionate *adj.* પ્રેમાળ premaal

affiance *n.* વેવિશાળ કરવું veveeshaal karavun

affidavit *n.* સોગંદનામું, પ્રતિજ્ઞાલેખ sogandnaamun, pratignaalekh

affilliate *v.* સદસ્ય બનાવવું sadasya banaavavun

affilliation *n.* સોબત, સમાગમ sobat, samaagam

affinity *n.* સગપણ sagapan

affirm *v.* નિશ્ચિતપણે કહેવું nishchitpane kahevun

affirmation *n.* દૃઢીકરણ dradhikaran

affirmative હકારાત્મક, ભાવદર્શક hakaaraatmak, bhaavdarshak

affix *v.* ચોડવું, બેસાડવું chodavun, besaadavun

afflatus *n.* કાવ્યાનુભૂતિ kaavyaanubhoote

afflict *v.* પીડવું, રિબાવવું pidavun, ribaavavun

affliction *n.* દુખનું કારણ, વેદના dukhanun kaaran, vedanaa

afflictive *adj.* દુ:ખોત્પાદક, પીડાકારી dukhotpaadak, pidaakaaree

affluence *n.* સંપત્તિ, સમૃદ્ધિ sampatti, samruddhi

affluent *adj.* ધનાઢ્ય, સાધનસંપન્ન dhanaadhy, saadhansampan

afflux *n.* અભિવાહ, પ્રવાહ abhivaah, pravaah

afford *v.* ગુંજાશ હોવી gunjaash hovee

afforest *v.* નું જંગલ બનાવવું nu jangal banaavavun

affray *n.* મારામારી, અશાંતિ maaraamaaree, ashaanti

affright *v.* બિવડાવવું, ચોંકાવવું bivadaavavun, chonkavavun

affront *n.* અપમાન કરવું apamaan karavun

afield *adv.* ખેતરમાં khetaraman

afire *adv.* બળતું, સળગતું balatun, salagatun

aflame *adv.* સળગતું, જ્વાલાગ્રસ્ત salagatun, jvaalaagrast

afloat *adv.* દરિયા પર dariya par

afoot *adv.* ચાલતું chaalatun

afore *prep.* સામે saame

afraid *adj.* ભયભીત, દ્વિધામાં bhayabheet, dvidhaamaan

afresh *adv.* ફરીથી, નવેસર fareethi, navesar

after *adv.* પાછળ paachal

after all *adv.* છેવટે, અંતે chhevate, ante

afternoon *n.* બપોર bapor

afterward *adv.* મોડેથી, આગળ જતાં modethi, aagal jatan

again *adv.* ફરી એકવાર, વળી faree ekavaar, valee

against *prep.* બદલામાં, મુકાબલે badalaamaan, mukaabale

agate *n.* ગોમેદ gomed

age *n.* ઉંમર, વય ummar, vay

aged *adj.* વૃદ્ધ, ઘરડું vruddha, gharadun

agency *n.* કચેરી kacheree

agenda *n.* કાર્યસૂચિ kaaryasoochi

agent *n.* કારભારી, આડતિયો kaarbhaari, aadatiyo

agglutinate *v.* જોડવું, જોડાવું jodavun, jodavun

aggrandize *v.* વ્યાપ વધારવો vyaap vadhaaravo

aggravate *v.* પરિસ્થિતિ બિગાડવી paristhitine bagaadavi

aggravation *n.* પરિસ્થિતિમાં બગાડો paristhitimaan bagaado

aggregate *v.* એકત્રિત, એકંદર ekatrit, ekandar

aggressive *adj.* આક્રમક, સ્વમતાગ્રહી aakramak, svamataagrahee

aggression *n.* અકારણ આક્રમણ akaaran aakraman

aggrieve *v.* નારાજ થવું naaraaj thavun

aghast *adj.* ભયભીત bhayabheet

agile *adj.* ઝડપી, ચપળ jhadapi, chapal

agitate *v.* ચળવળ ચલાવવી chalaval chalaavavi

agitation *n.* ચળવળ, વિરોધ chalval, virodh

agnostic *n.* અજ્ઞેયવાદી agneyvaadi

ago *adj.* પૂર્વે poorve

agog *adj.* ઉત્સુક utsuk

agonize *v.* અતિશય દુ:ખ દેવું atishay dukh devun

agrarian *adj.* કૃષિ krushi

agree *v.* સંમતિ આપવી sanmati aapavee

agreeable *adj.* મનપસંદ, અનુકૂળ manpasand, anukool

agreement *n.* સહમતી sahamatee

agrestic *adj.* ગ્રામીણ, અણઘડ graamin, anaghad

agricultural ખેતીવાડી khetivaadi

agriculture *n.* ખેતીવાડી, કૃષિવિજ્ઞાન khetivaadi, krushi vignaan

ague *n.* ટાઢિયો તાવ, ધ્રુજારી tadhiyo taav, dhrujaaree

ahead *adv.* આગળ, સામે, મોખરે aagal, saame, mokhare

aid *v.* સહાય કરવી sahaay karavee

ail *v.* માંદું હોવું maandun hovun

ailment *n.* માંદગી, બેચેની mandagee, bechenee

aim *n.* નિશાન, લક્ષ્ય, ઉદ્દેશ nishaan, lakshya, uddesh

air *n.* હવા havaa

aircraft *n.* હવાઈ જહાજ havaee jahaaj

airgun *n.* એરગન aergan

airline *n.* વિમાન કંપની vimaan kampani

airliner *n.* વિમાન vimaan

airmail *n.* હવાઈ ટપાલ havaaee tapaal

air-pump *n.* હવા પંપ havaa pamp

airship *n.* હવાઈ વહાણ havaaee vahaan

airtight *adj.* વાયુ પ્રતિબંધક vaayu pratibandhak

airy *adj.* હવા ઉજાસવાળું havaa ujaasvaalun

aisle *n.* માર્ગ maarg

akin *adj.* સગું, સમાન sagu, samaan

alabaster *n.* સફેદ પથ્થર safed patthar

alacrity *n.* ઉલટ, શીઘ્રતા oolat, shighrata

alamode *adv.* આધુનિક aadhunik

alarm *n.* ચેતવણી, સૂચના chetavani, soochana

alarming *adj.* ભયજનક bhayajanak

alarm ચેતવણી, સૂચના chetavanee, soochana

alas ઉદ્ગાર udagaar

albatross *n.* દરિયાઈ પક્ષી dariyaee pakshee

albeit *conj.* જોકે, યદ્યપિ joke, yadhyapee

albino હીન માણસ, ઢોર hin maanas, dhor

album *n.* અનેક ચીજોવાળી રેકર્ડ anek chijovaali rekard

albumen *n.* ઈંડાની સફેદી indaani safedi

alchemist *n.* કીમિયાગર keemiyaagar

alchemy *n.* કીમિયો keemiyo

alcohol *n.* મદ્યાર્ક, મદ્યસાર madyaark, madyasaar

alcoholic *n.* મદ્યાર્કવાળું madyarkvaalun

alcove *n.* બગીચામાં એકાંત બેઠક bagichaaman ekant bethak

alderman *n.* ઉપનગરાધ્યક્ષ upanagaraadhyaksh

ale *n.* દારૂ daaroo

alert *adj.* સાવધ કરવું saavadh karavun

alertness *n.* સાવધપણું saavadhapanun

algebra *n.* બીજગણિત bijaganit

algebrical *adj.* બીજગણિતવિષયક bijaganit vishayak

alias *adv.* ઉપનામ, ઉર્ફે, upanaam, urfe

alibi *adv.* અન્યત્ર હોવાની દલીલ anyatra hovaani dalil

alien *adj.* પારકું paarakun

alienable *adj.* પારકાપણું paarkaapanu

alienate *v.* સ્નેહ તોડવો sneh todavo

alienation *n.* જુદાઈ, ચિત્તભ્રમ judaaee, chittabhram

alight *v.t.* બળતું, પ્રદીપ્ત balatun, pradeept

alight *adj.* નીચે ઊતરવું niche ootaravun

align *v.t.* લાઈનદોરીમાં ગોઠવવું laaindorimaan gothavaavun

alike *adj.* સરખું, એ જ રીતે sarakhun, e ja rite

aliment *n.* આહાર, પુષ્ટિ આપવી aahaar, pushtee aapavi

alimentary *adj.* પૌષ્ટિક paushtik

alimony *n.* ખાધાખોરાકી khaadhaakhorakee

alive *adj.* જીવતું, સક્રિય jivatun, sakriy

all *adj.* બધા, સમગ્ર badhaa, samagra

allah *n.* અલ્લાહ allah

allay *v.* શાંત પાડવું shaant paadavun

allegation આક્ષેપ, આરોપ aakshep, aarop

allege *v.* આરોપ મૂકવો aarop mukavon

allegiance *n.* વફાદારી, રાજ્ય નિષ્ઠા vafaadaari, rajya neeshtha

allegorical *adj.* રૂપકાત્મક roopakaatmak

allegory *n.* રૂપક roopak

allergy *n.* અતડાપણું, વાયડાપણું atadaapanun, vaayadaapanun

alleviate *v.* શમન કરવું shaman karavun

alleviation *n.* શમન shaman

alleviative *adj.* શામક shaamak

alley *n.* સાંકડી ગલી saankadee galee

alliance *n.* સોબત, ગુણસાદૃશ્ય sobat, gunasaadrashya

allied *adj.* જોડાયેલું, મળતું jodaayelun, malatun

alligate *v.* જોડીને એક કરવું jodine ek karavun

alligator *n.* મગર, સુસવાટ magar, susavaat

alliteration વર્ણસગાઈ varnasagaaee

allocate *v.* ફાળવવું faalavavun

allocation *n.* ફાળવણી faalavanee

allopathy *n.* રોગ-વિરોધવાદ rog-virodhavaad

allot *v.* ફાળવવું faalavavun

allotment *n.* ફાળવણી faalavanee

allottee *n.* ફાળવાયેલી વ્યક્તિ faalavaayeli vyakati

allow *v.* પરવાનગી આપવી paravaanagi aapavi

allowable *adj.* માન્યતાને યોગ્ય maanyataane yogy

allowance *n.* વળતર, ભથ્થું valatar, bhaththun

alloy *n.* મિશ્રણ કરવું mishran karavun

all right *adv.* સુરક્ષિત surakshit

allure *v.* લલચાવવું, મોહિત કરવું lalachaavavun, mohit karavun

allurement *n.* લાલચ, મોહકતા laalach, mohakataa

alluring *n.* લલચાવવું lalachaavavun

allusion *n.* ઉલ્લેખ ullekh

allusive *adj.* સંકેતિક નિર્દેશ saanketik nirdesh

alluvial *adj.* કાંપવાળું kaanpavaalun

alluvium *adj.* કાંપ kaanp

ally *v.* સહાયકારી sahaaykaaree

almanac *n.* વાર્ષિક પંચાંગ vaarshik panchhang

almighty *adj.* સર્વશક્તિમાન, અતિશય sarvashaktimaan, ateeshay

almond *n.* બદામ badaam

almonry *n.* સદાવ્રત, અન્નક્ષેત્ર sadaavrat, annakshetr

almost *adj.* લગભગ, મોટે ભાગે lagabhag, motebhaage

alms *n.* ભિક્ષા, દાન bhikshaa, daan

aloe *n.* એળિયો aeliyo

aloes *n.* કુંવાર kunvaar

aloft *adv.* ઊંચે, તૂતક ઉપર oonche, tootak upar

alone *adj.* એકાકી, એકલદોકલ ekaakee, ekaladokal

along *adv.* આગળ, મોખરે aagal, mokhare

alongside *adv.* ની પડખે, બાજુમાં ni padakhe, baajuman

aloof *adv.* ઉદાસીન, છેટે, અળગું udaasin, chhete, alagun

aloud *adv.* મોટેથી, બુલંદ અવાજે motethee, buland avaaje

alp *n.* પર્વત શિખર parvat shikhar

alpha *n.* આલ્ફા aalfaa

alphabet *n.* ભાષાના મૂળાક્ષરો bhaashaana moolaksharo

alphabetical *adj.* ભાષાના મૂળાક્ષરો bhaashaana moolaksharo

already *adv.* અગાઉથી, પહેલાં agaauthee, pahelan

also *adv.* પણ pan

altar *n.* યજ્ઞવેદી yagnavedi

alter *v.* ફેરવવું, બદલવું feravavun, badalavun

alterable *adj.* પરિવર્તનીય parivartaneey

alteration પરિવર્તન parivartan

altercate *v.t.* વિવાદ કરવો vivaad karavo

alternate *adj.* વારાફરતી થતું vaaraafarati thatun

alternative *n.* વિકલ્પ vikalp

although *conj.* જોકે, યદ્યપિ joke, yadhyapee

altitude *n.* ઊંચાઈ oonchaaee

altogether *adj.* સંપૂર્ણપણે, એકંદરે sampoornpane, ekandare

altruism *n.* નિસ્વાર્થપણું neesvaarthapanun

alum *n.* ફટકડી fatakadee

aluminium *n.* એલ્યુમિનિયમ aelyuminiyam

alumnus *n.* ભૂતપૂર્વ વિદ્યાર્થી bhootapoorva vidyaarthee

always *adv.* હંમેશાં, સરવદા hanmesha, sarvada

am *v.t.* છું chhun

amain *adv.* શક્તથી, બળજોરીથી shaktithee, balajorithee

amalgam *n.* પારવણ paaravan

amalgamate *v.t.* મિશ્રણ કરવું mishran karavun

amalgamation *n.* મિશ્રણ mishran

amass *v.t.* એકઠું કરવું ekathun karavun

amateur *n.* જ્ઞાન કૌતુકી gyaan kautukee

amative *adj.* પૂરણયી, કામુક pranayee, kaamuk

amatory *adj.* શૃંગારિક shrungaarik

amaze *v.t.* આશ્ચર્યચકિત કરવું aashcharyachakit karavun

amazement *n.* આશ્ચર્યચકિત કરવું aashcharyachakit karavun

amazing *adj.* આશ્ચર્યકારક aashcharyakaarak

amazon *n.* બળવાન અથવા મલ્લ જેવી સ્ત્રી balavaan athava mall jevi stree

ambassador *n.* રાજદૂત, એલચી raajadoot, elachee

amber *n.* તૃણમણિ trunamanee

ambiguity *n.* દ્વઅર્થી, સંદિગ્ધ dviarthee, sandigdh

ambiguous *adj.* દ્વઅર્થી, અનિશ્ચિતાર્થ dviarthee, anishchitaarth

ambit *n.* હદ, ઘેરાવો had, gheraavo

ambitions *n.* પ્રબળ ઈચ્છા prabal eechchhaa

ambitious *adj.* અભિલાષા abhilaashaa

amble *v.* ઘોડાનીચાલ ghodaanee chaal

ambler *n.* ઘોડો ghodo

ambrosia *n.* અમૃત amrut

ambulance *n.* એમ્બ્યુલન્સ aembyulans

ambush *n.* છાપો, છુપાયેલું લશ્કર chhapo, chhupaayelun lashkar

ameliorate *v.t.* સુધારવું sudhaaravun

amelioration *n.* સુધારો sudhaaro

amen *n.* તથાસ્તુ, બેશક tathaastun, beshak

amenable *adj.* માને એવું, જવાબદાર maane evun, javaabadaar

amend *v.* ભૂલ સુધારવી bhool sudhaaravee

amendment *n.* સુધારો sudhaaro

amenity *n.* સુખકારકતા, સુખસગવડો sukhakaarakata, sukhasagavado

amethyst *n.* નીલમણિ, યાકૂત nilamanee, yaakoot

amiable *adj.* મળતાવડું malataavadun

amiability *n.* મળતાવડાપણું malataavadaapanun

amicable *adj.* મિત્રતાભર્યું mitrataabharyun

amicably *adv.* મૈત્રીપૂર્વક maitreepoorvak

amid *prep.* વચમાં vachaman

amiss *adj.* બગડેલું, અનુચિત bagadelun, anuchit

amity *n.* મિત્રતા mitrata

ammonia *n.* એમોનિયા, નવસા emoneeya, navasa

ammunition *n.* દારૂગોળો daroogolo

amnesty *n.* સર્વક્ષમા sarvakshama

among *prep.* ની વચ્ચે nee vachche

amorous *adj.* પ્રેમી, કામુક, રસિક premee, kamuk, rasik

amorphous *adj.* અવ્યવસ્થિત, વિલક્ષણ avyavasthit, vilakshan

amount *v.* કુલ જથો, પરિણમવું, રકમ kul jatho, parinamvun, rakam

amour *n.* પ્રણય કિસ્સો, ઈશ્ક pranay kisso, eeshk

amphibian *n.* ઉભયજીવી ubhayjeevee

amphi theatre *n.* શ્રોતાગૃહ, રંગભૂમિ shrotaagrah, rangbhoomee

ample *adj.* મોકળાશવાળું, ભરપૂર mokalaashavaalun, bharapoor

amplify *v.* વિસ્તારવું, પ્રસારવું vistaaravun, prasaaravun

amplification *n.* પ્રવર્ધન, પરિવર્ધન pravardhan, parivardhan

amplifier *n.* પરિવર્ધક, ધ્વનિવર્ધક parivardhak, dhvaneevardhak

amplitude *n.* કંપ વિસ્તાર kanp vistaar

amputate *n.v.* અંગ કાપવું ang kaapavun

amputation *n.* કાપી નાખવું તે kaapee naakhavun te

amuck *adv.* બેકાબૂ થઈને bekaboo thaeene

amulet *n.* માદળિયું, તાવીજ maadaleeyuun, taavij

amuse *v.* રમૂજ પમાડવી ramooj pamaadavee

amusing *adj.* રમૂજી, વિનોદી ramoojee, vinodee

anachronism *n.* કાલવ્યુત્ક્રમ, કાલદોષ kaalavyutkram, kaladosh

anaemia *n.* પાંડુરોગ, રક્તક્ષય paandurog, raktkshay

anagram *n.* વ્યસ્તાક્ષર શબ્દ vyastaakshar shabd

analogy *n.* સાદૃશ્યતા, અનુરૂપતા saadrashyata, anuroopata

analogous *adj.* સરખું, મળતું આવતું sarakhun, malatun aavatun

analyse *v.t.* મનોવિશ્લેષણ કરવું manovishleshan karavun

analysis *v.t.* મનોવિશ્લેષણ manovishleshan

analyst *n.* વિશ્લેષક vishleshak

analystical *adj.* પૃથક્કરણને લગતું pruthakkaranne lagatun

anarchy *n.* અરાજકતા, અવ્યવસ્થા araajakataa, avyavastha

anatomy *n.* શરીરરચના shareerrachana

anatomical *adj.* શરીરરચનાને લગતું shareerrachanane lagatun

anatomist *n.* શરીરરચનાવિદ્ shareerrachanaavid

ancestor *n.* પૂર્વજ poorvaj

ancestra *adj.* વડીલોપાર્જિત vadeelopaarjit

anchor *n.* લંગર, સ્થિર કરવું langar, sthir karavun

anchovy *n.* નાની માછલી naanee maachhalee

ancient *adj.* પુરાચીન, પુરાણું praacheen, puraanun

ancilliary *adj.* ગૌણ gauan

anecdote *n.* ટૂચકો tuchako,

anew *adv.* ફરીથી, નવેસરથી farithee, navesarathee

angel *n.* દેવદૂત, ફરસ્તિો devadoot, faristo

anger *n.* ગુસ્સો, ક્રોધ gusso, krodh

angle *n.* કોણ, ખૂણો, દૃષ્ટિકોણ kon, khuno, drashtikon

angler *n.* માછલાં પકડનાર maachhalaan pakadanaar

anglicize *v.* અંગ્રેજીમાં બોલવું angrejiman bolavun

anglo *n.* ગોરો માણસ goro maanas

anguish *n.* સંતાપ santap

angular *adj.* કોણવાળું konavaalun

animal *n.* જીવધારી, પ્રાણી jeevadhaaree, praani

animalcule *n.* પોરો poro

animate *v.* જીવતું, ચેતનવંતું jeevatun, chetanvantun

animated *adj.* જોસીલું, ચેતનવંતું joseelun, chetanvantun

animation *n.* પ્રાણસંચાર, જુસ્સો praanasanchaar, jusso

animism *n.* જીવવાદ, સર્વચેતનવાદ jivavaad, sarvchetanvaad

animosity *n.* વેર, શત્રુતા ver, shatruta

ankle *n.* પગની ઘૂંટી paganee ghoontee

annalist *n.* વર્ષાનુસાર, ઇતિહાસકાર varshaanusaar, eetihaasakaar

annals *n.* સાલવારી saalavaaree

annex *v.* ખાલસા કરવું khaalasaa karavun

annexe *n.* પુરવણી puravanee

annihilate *v.t.* સદંતર નાશ કરવો sadantar naash karavo

anniversary *n.* જયંતી, વર્ષગાંઠ jayantee, varshagaanth

annotate *v.t.* નોંધ ઉમેરવી nondh umeravi

annotation *n.* ટીકાટિપ્પણ tikaatippan

announce *v.t.* જાહેર કરવું jaaher karavun

announcement *n.* જાહેર નિવેદન, સંદેશો jaaher nivedan, sandesho

announcer *n.* ઉદ્ઘોષક udghoshak

annoy *v.t.* ત્રાસ આપવો traas aapavo

annoyance *n.* ત્રાસ, હેરાનગતિ traas, heraangati

annual *adj.* વાર્ષિક vaarshik

annually *adv.* દર વરસે dar varse

annuity *n.* વાર્ષિકી varshaasan, vaarshikee

annuitant *n.* વર્ષાસન મેળવનાર vaarshikee melavanaar

annul *v.t.* નાબૂદ કરવું naabood karavun

annulment *n.* નાબૂદી naaboodi

anodyne *n.* શામક shaamak

anoint *v.t.* તેલ ચોળીને અભિષિક કરવો tel choline abhishek karavo

anomalous *adj.* અનિયમિત, વિલક્ષણ aniyamit, vilakshan

anomaly *n.* અનિયમિત aniyamit

anonymity *n.* નામ વિનાનું, નનામું naam vinaanun, nanaamun

anonymous *adj.* નામ વિનાનું, નનામું naam vinaanun, nanaamun

anonymously *adj.* અનામ રહીને anaam raheene

another *adj.* બીજું, વધારાનું, જુદું biju, vadhaaranun, judun

answer *n.* પ્રત્યુત્તર, પ્રતિભાવ pratuttar, pratibhaav

answerable *adj.* જવાબદાર, ઉત્તરદાયી javaabadaar, uttaradaayee

ant *n.* કીડી kidee

antagonism *n.* વિરોધ, દુશ્મનાવટ virodh, dushmanaavat

antagonist *n.* વિરોધી, પ્રતિસ્પર્ધી virodhee, pratheespardhee

antagonistic *adj.* વિરોધ, દુશ્મનાવટ veerodhee, dushmanaavat

antarctic *adj.* દક્ષિણ ધ્રુવપ્રદેશનું daksheen dhruvapradeshanun

antecedent *adj.* પૂર્વેતિહાસ poorveteehaas

antechamber *n.* પ્રવેશખંડ praveshakhand

antedate *v.t.* પહેલાંની તારીખ લખવી pahelaannee taarikh lakhavee

antelope *n.* કાળિયાર, હરણ kaaleeyaar, haran

antenatal *adj.* પ્રસૂતિ પહેલાનું prasootee pahelaanun

anterior *adj.* અગ્રવર્તી, પૂર્વકાલીન agravartee, poorvakaalin

anteroom *n.* પ્રતીક્ષાલય pratikshaalay

anthem *n.* સ્તુતિગીત stutee git

anthology *n.* સાહિત્ય સંગ્રહ saahity sangrh

antic *n.* કઢંગો, બેડોળ kadhango, bedol

anticlimax *n.* પ્રતિસાંરાલંકાર, નિપાત pratisaaraalankaar, neepaat

antimony *n.* સુરમો suramo

antipathy *n.* તીવ્ર અણગમો, દ્વેષ tivr anagamo, dvesh

antiquarian *adj.* સંગ્રાહક sangraahak

antiquated *adj.* જુનવાણી, કાલગ્રસ્ત junavaani, kaalagrast

antique *adj.* જુનવાણી junavaanee

antiquities *n.* પ્રાચીન રીતરિવાજો praachin ritareevaajo

antiseptic *adj.* ચેપરોધક, જંતુનાશક cheprodhak, jantunaashak

anti-social *adj.* સમાજ વિરોધી samaaj veerodhee

antithesis *n.* વિરોધ, પ્રતિપક્ષતા veerodh, pratipakshata

antlers *n.pl.* ફાંટાયુક્ત શિંગડાઓ fantaayukt sheengadaao

antonym *n.* વિપર્યાય veeparyaay

anxiety *n.* ચિંતા, કાળજી chinta, kaalajee

anxious *adj.* ચિંતાતુર, ઉત્સુક chintatur, utsuk

any *adj.* કોઈ એક, કોઈપણ koee ek, koipan

anybody *pron.* કોઈપણ માણસ koipan maanas

anyhow *adv.* ગમે તે રીતે game te rite

anyone *pron.* ગમે તે game te

anything *pron.* એકાદ કોઈ ekaad koee

anyway *adv.* ગમે તેમ game tem

anywhere *adv.* ગમે ત્યાં game tyan

apace *adv.* જલદી, તાકીદે jaladee, taakide

apart *adv.* એક બાજુએ, જુદી રીતે ek baajue, judee rite

apartment *n.* ઓરડી, ખંડ, ફ્લેટ oradee, khand, flet

apartments *pl.* ઓરડાઓનો સમૂહ oradaaono samooh

apathetic *adj.* ઉદાસીન, રસહીન udaaseen, rasaheen

apathy *n.* લાગણીનો અભાવ laaganino abhaav

ape *n.* વાંદરાં જેવું પૂરાણી vaandara jevu praanee

aperture *n.* છિદ્ર chhidra

apex *n.* શરિબદ્ધિ shirobindu

aphorism *n.* સૂત્ર (મયકથન) sootra (mayakathan)

aphoristic *adj.* સૂત્ર (મયકથન) sootra (mayakathan)

aplary *n.* મધમાખી ઉછેર સ્થળ madhmaakhee ucher sthal

apiece *adv.* માથા દીઠ maatha deeth

aplomb *n.* આત્મવશિવાસ aatmavishvaas

apocryphal *adj.* શંકાસ્પદ. shankaaspad

apogee *n.* ઊંચામાં ઊંચું બદ્ધિ oonchaaman oonchun bindun

apologize માફી માગવી maafee maagavee

apologetic *adj.* માફી માગવાલાયક maafee maagavaalaayak

apology *n.* ક્ષમાયાચના kshamaayaachana

apoplexy *n.* સંન્યાસરોગ sanyaasrog

apoplectic *adj.* સંન્યાસરોગવાળો sanyaasrogavaalo

apostasy *n.* સ્વધર્મ ત્યાગ svadharm tyaag

apostate *n.* સ્વધર્મ ત્યાગી svadharm tyaagee

apostle *n.* સુધારાનો આગેવાન sudhaaraano aagevaan

apostrophe *n.* પ્રત્યયનું ચિહ્ન pratyayanu chinha

apothecary *n.* રસાયણશાસ્ત્રી rasaayanshaastree

apotheosis *n.* દેવીકરણ deveekaran

appal *v.t.* ભડકાવવું bhadakaavavun

apparatus *n.* પ્રયોગ સાધનો prayog saadhano

apparel *n.* વસ્તરો vastro

apparent *adj.* દેખીતું dekheetun

apparently *adv.* દેખીતી રીતે dekheetee reete

apparition *n.* આભાસ aabhaas

appeal *v.* વનિતી કરવી vinantee karavee

appear *v.* પ્રગટ થવું pragat thavun

appearance *n.* બહારનો વૈભવ bahaarano vaibhav

appeasement *n.* સંતુષ્ટ કરવું santusht karavun

appellant *n.* અપીલ કરનાર apeel karanaar

appellation *n.* પદવી padavee

append *v.* જોડવું jodavun

appendage *n.* ઉમેરેલી વસ્તુ umerelee vastu

appendicitis *n.* આંત્રપુચ્છનો સોજો aantrapuchchhano sojo

appendix *n.* આંત્રપુચ્છ aantrapuchchha

appertain *v.* ને લગતું ne lagatun

appetite *n.* ભૂખ bhookh

applaud *v.* વધાવવું vadhaavavun

applause *n.* અભિવાદન abhivaadan

apple *n.* સફરજન safarajan

applicable *adj.* લાગુ પડે એવું laagu pade evun

applicability *n.* પ્રયોજ્યતા prayojayataa

applicant *n.* અરજદાર arajadaar

application *n.* અરજી arajee

apply *v.i.* અરજી કરવી arajee karavee

appliance *n.* ઉપકરણ upakaran

appoint *v.t.* નિમણૂક કરવી. nimanook karavee

appointment *n.* નિમણૂક nimanook

apportion *v.t.* ભાગ કાઢી આપવો bhaag kaadhee aapavo

apposite *adj.* બંધબેસતું bandhabestun

appraisal *n.* મૂલ્ય નક્કી કરવું moolya nakkee karavun

appraiser *n.* મૂલવનાર moolavanaar

appraise *v.i.* મૂલ્યાંકન moolyankan

appreciate *v.t.* કદર કરવી kadar karavee

appreciation *n.* કદર kadar

appreciative *adj.* કદરદાનીવાળું kadardaaneevaalun

apprehend *v.t.* ધરપકડ કરવી dharapakad karavee

apprehension *n.* ધરપકડ dharapakad

apprehensive *adj.* શંકાસ્પદ shankaaspad

apprentice *n.* ધંધાની તાલીમ dhandhaanee taalim

apprenticeship *n.* કરારબદ્ધ ઉમેદવારી karaabaddha umedavaari

apprise *v.t.* ખબર આપવી khabar aapavee

approach *v.i.* સંપર્ક કરવો sanpark karavon

approachable *adj.* પહોંચાય એવું pahonchaay evun

approbation *n.* માન્યતા maanyataa

appropriate *adj.* યોગ્ય yogya

appropriately *adv.* બંધબેસતું bandhabesatun

appropriateness *n.* ઔચિત્ય aauchitya

appropriation *n.* બંધબેસતું bandhbesatun

approve *v.t.* બહાલી આપવી bahalee aapavee

approval *n.* મંજૂરી manjooree

approvingly *adv.* મંજૂરી આપતું manjooree aapatun

approver *n.* મંજૂર કરનાર manjoor karanaar

approximate *adj.* લગભગ lagabhag

approximately *adv.* લગભગ lagabhag

approximation *n.* અંદાજ andaaj

appurtenance *n.* આનુષંગિક પદાર્થ aanushangik padaarth

apricot *n.* જરદાળુ jaradaalu

apron *n.* બહિર્વસ્ત્ર bahirvastra

apt *adj.* યોગ્ય yogya

aptly *adv.* યથાયોગ્ય રીતે yathaayogya reete

aptness લાયકી laayakee

aptitude *n.* અભિરુચિ abhiruchi

aquarium *n.* માછલી ઘર maachhalee ghar

aquatic *adj.* જલીય jaleeya

aqueduct *n.* જળમાર્ગ નાળું jalamaarg naalun

aquiline *adj.* ગરુડ જેવું garud jevun

arable *adj.* ખેડાઉ khedaau

aramaic *n.* સીરિયાની ભાષા seeriyaanee bhaashaa

arbiter *n.* લવાદ lavaad

arbitrary *n.* મનસ્વી manasvee

arbitrate *v.t.* ઝઘડો પતાવવો jhagado patavavo

arbitration *n.* ઝઘડાની પતાવટ jhagadaani pataavat

arbitrator *n.* લવાદ lavaad

arboreal *adj.* વૃક્ષોને લગતું vrukshone lagatun

arboriculture *n.* ઝાડવાની ખેતી jhaadavaanee khetee

arbour *n.* કુંજ kunj

arc *n.* કમાન. kamaan

arcade *n.* તોરણમાલા toranamaalaa

archaeology *n.* પુરાતત્ત્વવિદ્યા puraatattvavidhya

archaeologist *n.* પુરાતત્ત્વવિદ્ puraatattvavidd

archaeological *adj.* પુરાતત્ત્વવિદ્યા –વિષયક puratattvavidhya-vishayak

archaic *adj.* પુરાચીન. pracheen

archaism *n.* આર્ષ પ્રયોગ. aarsh prayog

archer *n.* તીરંદાજ teerandaaj

archery *n.* તીરંદાજી teerandaajee

architect *n.* શિલ્પી, shilpee

architecture *n.* વાસ્તુશિલ્પ, vaastushilp

archives *n.* દફ્તરખાનું dafatarkhaanun

arctic *adj.* ઉત્તર ધ્રુવપ્રદેશ uttar dhruvapradesh

ardent *adj.* ઉત્સુક utsuk

ardour *n.* ઉત્સાહ utsaah

arduous *adj.* મુશ્કેલ mushkel

area *n.* ક્ષેત્રફળ kshetrafal

arena *n.* અખાડો akhaado

argosy *n.* મોટું જહાજ motun jahaaj

argue *v.i.* દલીલ કરવી daleel karavee

argument *n.* દલીલ daleel

argumentive *adj.* દલીલવાળું daleelvaalun

arid *adj.* શુષ્ક shushka

aright *adv.* યોગ્ય રીતે yogya reete

arise *v.i.* ઉત્પન્ન થવું utpann thavun

aristocracy *n.* અમીરશાહી ameerashaahee

aristocrat *n.* ઉમરાવ umaraav

aristocratic *adj.* અમીરી ameeree

arithmetic *n.* અંકગણિત ankaganit

arithmetical અંકગणितीय ankaganiteeya

arithmetician *n.* ગણિતશાસ્ત્રી ganitashaastree

ark *n.* કાયદાઓની પેટી kaayadaaonee petee

arm *n.* હાથ haath

arm-chair *n.* હાથાવાળી ખુરશી haathaavaalee khurashee

armament *n.* શસ્ત્રસંરંજામ shastrasanranjaam

armistice *n.* યુદ્ધવિરામ yuddhaviraam

armour *n.* બખતર bakhatar

armourer *n.* બખતર બનાવનાર bakhatar banaavanaar

armoury *n.* શસ્ત્રાગાર shastraagaar

army *n.* સેના senaa

aroma *n.* સુગંધ sugandh

aromatic *adj.* સુગંધિત sugandhit

arouse *v.t.* ઉશ્કેરવું ushkeravavun

arraign *v.t.* આરોપ મુકવો aarop mukavo

arrangement *n.* વ્યવસ્થા vyavasthaa

arrange *v.t.* વ્યવસ્થિત કરવું vyavasthit karavun

arrant *adj.* હડહડતું hadahadatun

array *v.t..* ઠાઠમાઠ thaathamaath

arrears *n.pl.* ચઢેલું કામ chadelun kaam

arrest *v.t.* ધરપકડ કરવી dharapakad karavee

arrival *n.* આગમન aagaman

arrive *v.i.* આવવું aavavun

arrogance *n.* અહંકાર ahankaar

arrogant *adj.* અહંકારી ahankaaree

arrow *n.* બાણ baan

arsenal *n.* શસ્ત્રાગાર shastraagaar

art *n.* કલા kalaa

artery *n.* ધમની dhamanee

artless *adj.* નખિાલસ nikhaalas

article *n.* લેખ lekh

articulate *v.t.* ઉચ્ચાર કરવો uchchaar karavo

artificial *adj.* કૃત્રિમ kutrim

aritillery *n.* તોપખાનું topkhaanun

artisan *n.* કારીગર kaareegar

artist *n.* કુશળ કારીગર kushal kaareegar

artistic *adj.* કલાત્મક kalaatmak

artistry *n.* કારીગરી kaareegaree

as *adv.* તરીકે tareeke

ascend *v.t.* ઊંચે જવું oonche javun

ascent *n.* ચડાણ chadaan

ascendancy *n.* વર્ચસ્વ varchasva

ascendant *adj.* ચડાણ chadaan

ascertain *v.t.* ખાતરી કરવી khaataree karavi

ascetic *n.* સંયમી sanyamee

ascribe *v.t.* ને આભારી ગણવું Ne aabhaaree ganavun

ascription *n.* કારણભૂત kaaranbhoot

ash *n.* રાખ raakh

ashamed *adj.* લજ્જિત lajjit

ashore *adv.* દરિયાકિનારો dariyaakinaaro

aside *adv.* એક બાજુએ ek baajue

ask *v.t.* પૂછવું poochhavun

askance *adv.* આડું aadun

askew *adv.* તીરછી નજરે teerachhee najare

asleep *adj.* ઊંઘી ગયેલું oonghee gayelun

asp *n.* નાનો ઝેરી સાપ nano jheree saap

asparagus *n.* શતાવરી shataavaree

aspect *n.* મોઢાપરનો ભાવ modhaaparano bhaav

aspen *n.* 'પૉપ્યુલર' ઝાડ 'poplar' jhaad

asperity *n.* કઠોરતા kathorataa

asperse *v.t.* ને લાંછન લગાડવું ne laanchhan lagaadavun

asphyxlate *v.t.* ગૂંગળાવવું goongalaavavaun

aspirant *n.* મહત્ત્વાકાંક્ષી mahattvaakaankshee

aspiration *n.* મહત્ત્વાકાંક્ષા mahattvaakaankshaa

aspire *v.i.* મનોકામના સેવવી manokaamana sevavee

ass *n.* ગધેડું gadhedun

assail *v.t.* પજવવું pajavavun

assailant *n.* હુમલાખોર humalaakhor

assassin *n.* ભાડૂતી ખૂની bhadooti khoonee

assassinate *v.t.* ખૂન કરવું khoon karavun

assassination *n.* હત્યા hatyaa

assault *v.t.* હુમલો કરવો humalo karavon

assay *v.t.* પૃથક્કરણ pruthakkaran

assemble *v.t.* એકત્ર કરવું ekatra karavun

assembly *n.* સભા sabhaa

assent *v.i.* માન્ય રાખવું maanya raakhavun

assert *v.t.* નિશ્ચયપૂર્વક કહેવું nishchayapoorvak kahevun

assertion *n.* દાવો રજૂ કરવો તે. daavo rajoo karavo te

assertive *adj.* આગ્રહી aagrahee

assertiveness *n.* દૃઢતા dradhataa

assess *v.t.* આકારણી કરવી aakaaranee karavee

assessment *n.* આકારણી aakaarani

assessor *n.* આકારણીકાર aakaaraneekaar

asset *n.* અસ્કયામત askayaamat

assiduous *adj.* ઉદ્યમી udyamee

assign *v.t.* મુકરર કરવું mukarar karavun

assignment *n.* સોંપણી sonpanee

assist *v.t.* મદદ કરવી madad karavee

assistance *n.* મદદ madad

assistant *n.* મદદનીશ madadaneesh

assize *n.* કાયદેસર કિંમત kaayadesar kinmat

associate *n.* જોડવું jodavun

association *n.* સંઘ સંસ્થા sangh sanstha

assort *v.t.* અનુકૂળ હોવું anukool hovun

assuage *v.t.* શમાવવું sharamaavavun

assume *v.t.* ધારણ કરવું dhaaran karavun

assumption *n.* સ્વીકૃત માન્યતા sveekrut maanyata

assure *v.t.* ખાતરી આપવી khaataree aapavee

assured *adj.* ખાતરીપૂર્વક khaatareepoorvak

assuredly *adj.* ખાતરીપૂર્વક khaatareepoorvak

assurance *n.* ખાતરી khaataree

asteroid *n.* ગ્રહ grah

asthma *n.* દમ dam

astir *adv.* ગતિમાન gatimaan

astonish *v.t.* આશ્ચર્ય પમાડવું aashchary pamaadavun

astound *v.t.* હેરત પમાડવું herata pamaadavun

astral *adj.* અપારથિવ apaarthiv

astray *adv.* અવળે રસ્તે avale raste

astride *adv.* પલાણીને. plaaneene

astringent *adj.* બંધક bandhak

astrologer *n.* ફલજ્યોતિષી falajyotishee

astrology *n.* ફલજ્યોતિષ falajyotish

astronomer *n.* ખગોળશાસ્ત્રી khagolashaastree

astronomy *n.* ખગોળશાસ્ત્ર khagolashaastra

astute *adj.* બાહોશ baahosh

asylum *n.* આશ્રય aashray

at *prep.* ખાતે khaate

atache *n.* નિરીશ્વરવાદ nireeshvaravaad

atheism *n.* નાસ્તિકવાદ naastikvaad

atheist *n.* નાસ્તિક વ્યક્તિ naastik vyakti

athlete *n.* રમતવીર ramatveer

athletic *adj.* વ્યાયામને લગતું vyaayaamne lagatun

athwart *prep.* તૂરાંસું traansun

atlas *n.* નકશાપોથી nakashaapothee

atmosphere *n.* વાતાવરણ vaataavaran

atmospheric *adj.* વાતાવરણને લગતું vaataavaranne lagatun

atom *n.* પરમાણુ paramaanu

atomic *adj.* પરમાણુને લગતું paramaanune lagatun

atone *v.t.* પ્રાયશ્ચિત કરવું praayashchit karavun

atonement *n.* પ્રાયશ્ચિત praayashchit

atop *adv.* મોખરે mokhare

atrocious *adj.* અત્યાચારી atyaachaaree

atrocity *n.* અત્યાચાર atyaachaar

atrophy *n.* શારીરિક કૃશતા shaareerik krushataa

attach *v.t.* બાંધવું baandhavun

attachment *n.* જોડાણ jodaan

attack *n.* હુમલો humalo

attain *v.t.* પ્રાપ્ત કરવું praapta karavun

attainable *adj.* પ્રાપ્ય praapya

attainment *n.* પ્રાપ્તિ praapti

attempt *n.* પ્રયત્ન prayatna

attend *v.t.* ધ્યાન આપવું dhyaan aapavun

attendance *n.* હાજરી haajaree

attendant *n.* સેવક sevak

attentive *adj.* સાવધાન saavadhaan

attest *v.t.* સાચું હોવા વિષે પ્રમાણપત્ર આપવું saachun hovaa vishe pramaanapatra aapavun

attic *n.* એથેન્સ, એટિકાનું ethens, etikaanun

attire *n.* પોશાક poshaak

attitude *n.* વલણ valan

attorney *n.* એટર્ની etarnee

attract *v.t.* આકર્ષવું aakarshavun

attraction આકર્ષણ aakarshan

attractive *adj.* આકર્ષક aakarshak

attribute *n.* કારણભૂત kaaranbhoot

auburn *adj.* રતાશપડતું rataashapadatun

auction *n.* લિલામી lilaamee

auctioneer *n.* લિલામ કરનાર lilaam karanaar

audacious *adj.* સાહસિક saahasik

audacity *n.* સાહસિકતા saahasikataa

audible *adj.* શ્રવ્ય shravya

audience *n.* શ્રોતા shrotaa

aud'it *n.* હિસાબ hisaab

auditor *n.* હિસાબ તપાસનીસ hisaab tapaasanees

audition *n.* હિસાબ તપાસણી hisaab tapaasanee

auditorium *n.* શ્રોતાપ્રેક્ષકગૃહ shrotaaprekshakagruh

auger *n.* શારડી shaaradee

aught *n.* કંઈક kaink

augment *v.t.* વધારવું vadhaaravun

augmentation *n.* વૃદ્ધિ vruddhi

augur *n.* ભવિષ્ય ભાખવું bhavishya bhaakhavun

august *adj.* ઑગસ્ટ મહિનો ogast mahino

aunt *n.* ફોઈ foee

aunty *n.* કાકી kaakee

aural *adj.* કાનને લગતું kaanane lagatun

auspice *n.* શકુન shakun

austere *adj.* સંયમી sanyamee

austerity *adj.* સંયમન sanyaman

austerely *adv.* સંયમિત sanyamit

authentic *adj.* વિશ્વાસપાત્ર vishvaasapaatra

authenticate *v.t.* પ્રમાણભૂત કરવું pramaanabhoot karavun

author *n.* લેખક lekhak

authority *n.* સત્તા satta

authoritative *n.* પ્રમાણભૂત pramaanhoot

atuhorize *v.t.* સત્તા આપવી sattaa aapavee

auto આત્મ–, સ્વત–, સ્વયં– aatma-, svat-, svayam-

autobiography *n.* આત્મચરિત્ર aatmacharitra

autocrat *n.* આપખુદ aapakhud

autocratic *adj.* આપખુદશાહી aapkhudshaahee

autograph *n.* પોતાના હસ્તાક્ષર potaanaa hastaakshar

automatic *adj.* સ્વયંચલન svayanchalan

automatically *adv.* સ્વયંચાલતિ svayanchaalit

automation *n.* સ્વયંચાલન svayanchaalan

automobile *n.* મોટરગાડી motargaadee

autonomy *n.* સ્વાયત્તતા svaayattataa

autonomous *adj.* સ્વાયત્ત svaayatt

autopsy *n.* શબપરીક્ષણ shabapareekshan

autumn *n.* પાનખર paankhar

autumnal *adj.* પાનખરનું paankharnun

auxiliary *adj.* સહાયક sahaayak

avail *v.i.* લાભ લેવો laabh levo

availability *n.* ઉપલબ્ધતા upalabdhataa

available *adj.* ઉપલબ્ધ upalabdh

avalanche *n.* હિમશિલા himshilaa

avarice *n.* લોભ lobh

avaricious *adj.* લોભી lobhee

avenge *v.t.* વેર વાળવું ver vaalavun

avenue *n.* સ્થળ sthal

aver *v.t.* વાજબી ઠરાવવું vaajabee tharaavavun

average *n.* સરેરાશ sareraash

averse *adj.* પ્રતિકૂળ pratikool

aversion *n.* પ્રતિકૂળ વલણ pratikool valan

avert *v.t.* ટાળવું taalavun

aviary *n.* પંખીઘર pankheeghar

aviation *n.* યાંત્રિક ઉડ્ડયન yaantrik uddayan

aviator *n.* વૈમાનિક vaimaanik

avid *adj.* ઉત્સુકતા utsukataa
avidity *n.* ઉત્સુક utsuk
avocation *n.* ધંધો dhandho
avoid *v.t.* થી દૂર રાખવું, thee door raakhavun
avoidance *n.* દૂર રહેવું door rahevun
avouch *v.t.* બાંયધરી આપવી baanyadharee aapavee
avow *v.t.* કબૂલ કરવું kabool karavun
avowal *n.* એકરાર ekaraar
await *v.t.* રાહ જોવી raah jovee
awake *v.t.* જાગવું jaagavun
award *n.* પુરસ્કાર puraskaar
aware *adj.* માહિતગાર maahitagaar
away *adv.* દૂર door
awe *n.* દહેશત daheshat
awesome *adj.* ભયાનક bhayaanak
awestruck *adj.* ગભરાયેલું gabharaayelun
awful *adj.* પૂરભાવી prabhaavee
awhile *adv.* ક્ષણભર kshanbhar
awkward *adj.* કઢંગુ kadhangu
awkwardly *n.* કઢંગી રીતે kadhangee reete
awkwardness *n.* કઢંગાપણું kadhangaapanun
awl *n.* મોચીનો સોયો mocheeno soyo
awning *n.* ચંદરવો chandaravo
awry *adj.* વાંકુંચૂકું vaankunchukun
axe *n.* કુહાડી kuhaadee
axis *n.* કલ્પિત ધરી kalpit dharee
axle *n.* ધરી dharee
ay *adv.* હા ha
aye હંમેશાં hanmeshaan
azure *adj.* નીલવર્ણ neelavarna

B

babble *v.t.* કાલું કાલું બોલવું kaalun kaalun bolavun
Babe *n.* બાળક baalak
baboon *n.* મોટું વાંદરું motun vaandarun
baby *n.* બાળક baalak
babyhood *n.* શૈશવ shaishav

bachelor *n.* કુંવારો kunvaaro
bacillus *n.* બેક્ટેરિયાનાં જંતું bekteriyaana jantun
back *n.* પાછલા ભાગમાં paachhalaa bhaagamaan
backbite *v.t.* નદિ કરવી ninda karavee
backbiter *n.* ચાડિયો chaadiyo
backbone *n.* કમરનું હાડકું kamarnun hadakun
background *n.* પૂર્વભૂમિકા poorvabhoomika
backing *n.* પીઠબળ peedhabal
backslide *v.i.* પાપમાં પડવું paapman padavun
backward *adj.* પછાત pachhaat
bacon *n.* ડુક્કરનું માંસ dukkaranu maans
bacterium *n.* સૂક્ષ્મ જંતુઓ sooksham jantun o
bacterial *adj.* જીવાણુ સંબંધી jeevaanu sambandhee
bacteriology *n.* જીવાણુ વિજ્ઞાન jeevaanu vigyaan
bad *adj.* ખરાબ kharaab
badge *n.* પદસૂચક બલ્લિો padasoochak billo
badger *n.* ભૂરા રંગનું ચોપગું પુરાણી bhoora rangnu chopagun praanee
badminton *n.* રમવાની એક રમત ramavaanee ek ramat
baffle *v.t.* ગૂંચવણમાં નાખવું goonchavanmaan naakhavun
bag *n.* થેલી theleekaravee
baggy *adj.* લટકતું latakatun
baggage *n.* સામાન saamaan
bagpipe *n.* બેગપાઈપ begapaaip
bail *n.* જામીન jaameen
bailiff *n.* બજાવણીદાર bajaavaneedaar
bait *n.* છટકું ગોઠવવું chhatakun gothavavun
baize *n.* ઊનનું જાડું કપડું oonnun jaadun kapadun
bake *v.t.* શેકવું shekavun
baker *n.* ભઠિયારો bhathiyaaro
bakery *n.* ભઠિયારખાનું bhathiyaarakhaanun
balance *n.* ત્રાજવું traajavun
balcony *n.* અટારી ataaree

bald *adj.* ટાલવાળું taalavaalun
bale ગાંસડી gaansadee
baleful *adj.* હાનિકારક haanikaarak
balk *v.t.* અટકાવવું atakaavavun
ball *n.* દડો dado
ballroom *n.* નૃત્યખંડ nrutyakhand
ballad *n.* પવાડો pavaado
ballast *n.* નીરમ neeram
ballet *n.* સંગીત નૃત્યનાટિકા sangeet nrutyanaatika
balloon *n.* ગુબ્બારો, gubbaaro
balloonist *n.* બલૂનમાં ઉડનાર balloonman udanaar
ballot *n.* મતપત્ર matapatra
ballot¶box *n.* મતપેટી matapetee
balm *n.* સુગંધીદાર દ્રવ્ય sugandheedaar dravya
balmy *adj.* બામનું baamanu
balustrade *n.* થાંભલીઓની હાર thanbhaleeoonee haar
bamboo *n.* વાંસ vaans
bamboozle *v.t.* મજાક કરવી majaak karavee
ban *v.t.* મનાઈ manaaee
banal *adj.* નીરસ niras
banana *n.* કેળું kelun
band *n.* બાંધવાનો લીરો baandhavaano leero
bandage *n.* પાટો paato
bandit *n.* બહારવટિયો bahaaravatiyo
bandolier *n.* કારતૂસનો પટો kaaratoosno pato
bandy *v.t.* આમ તેમ ફેંકવું aam tem fenkavun
bane *n.* આપત્તનું કારણ aapattinun kaaran
bang *v.t.* ધડાકો dhadako
bangle *n.* બંગડી bangadee
banish *v.t.* દેશનિકાલ કરવું deshnikaal karavun
banishment *n.* હદપારી hadapaaree
banister *n.* કઠેડો kadhedo
banjo *n.* ગિટારના જેવું એક વાદ્ય gitaarana jevun ek vaadhya
bank *n.* બેન્ક benk
banker *n.* બેંકનો વ્યવસ્થાપક bankano vyavasthapak

banking *n.* બેંક વ્યવસાય bank vyavasaay
bankrupt *n.* નાદાર બનાવવું naadaar banaavavun
bankruptcy *n.* નાદારી naadaaree
banner *n.* વાવટો vaavato
banns *n.* લગ્નની જાહેરાત lagnanee jaheraat
banquet *n.* પ્રીતિભોજન preetibhojan
banter *n.* વિનોદ vinod
banyan *n.* વડનું ઝાડ vadnu jhaad
baptism *n.* નામકરણવિધિ naamkaranvidhi
bar દાંડો daando
barb *n.* આંકડી aankadee
barbarian *n.* જંગલી jangalee
barbaric *adj.* અસંસ્કારી, જંગલી asanskaaree
barbarism *n.* જંગલિયત jangaliyat
barbarity *n.* હેવાનિયત hevaaniyat
barbarous *adj.* નિર્દય nirday
barber *n.* હજામ hajaam
bard *n.* ભાટ bhaat
bare *adj.* વસ્ત્રરહીન vastraheen
barefaced *n.* નિર્લજ્જ nirlajj
barely *adv.* ભાગ્યે જ bhagye ja
bareness *n.* નિવસ્ત્રાપણું nivastraapanun
barge *n.* શણગારેલી નૌકા shanagaarelee nauka
barium *n.* બેરિયમ beriyam
bark *n.* હોડી hodee
barely *n.* ભાગ્યે જ bhagye ja
barm *n.* ખમીર khameer
barn *n.* કોઠાર kothaar
barnaclen.بال શંખલું shrunkhalun
barometer *n.* બેરોમીટર beromeetar
baron *n.* ઉમરાવ વર્ગની એક પદવી umaraav vargnee ek padavee
baronet *n.* બેરોનેટ beronet
barony *n.* ઉમરાવની પદવી umaraavanee padavee
barque *n.* હોડી hodee
barrage *n.* બંધ bandh
barrel *n.* લાકડાનું પીપ laakadaanun peep
barren *adj.* ઉજ્જડ ujjad

barricade *n.* અવરોધ avarodh
barrier *n.* અવરોધ avarodh
barrister *n.* સનદી વકીલ sanadee vakeel
barrow *n.* હાથગાડી haathagaadee
barter *v.t.* વિનિમય vinimay
basal *adj.* પાયારૂપ paayaaroop
base *adj.* હલકું halakun
basement *n.* ભોંયરું bhonyarun
baseness *n.* અધમતા adhamataa
bashful *adj.* શરમાળ sharamaal
bashfulness *n.* શરમાળપણું sharamaalapanun
basic *adj.* પાયારૂપ paayaaroop
basil *n.* તુલસીનો છોડ tulaseeno chhod
basin *n.* નદીનો તટપ્રદેશ nadeeno tatapradesh
basis *n.* પાયો paayo
bask *v.t.* તડકે બેસવું tadake besavun
basket *n.* ટોપલી topalee
bass *n.* નીચા સૂરવાળું neechaa survaalun
bastard *n.* અનૌરસ anauras
baste *v.* ફટકારવું fatakaaravun
bastion બુરજ buraj
bat *n.* ચામાચીડિયું chaamaacheediyun
batch *n.* જૂથ jooth
bate *v.t.* ઘટાડવું ghataadavun
bath *n.* સ્નાન snaan
bathe *v.t.* નાહવું naahavun
bathos *n.* પૂરતિસારાલંકાર pratisaaraalankaar
baton *n.* લાકડી laakadee
battalion *n.* લશ્કરી ટુકડી lashkaree tukadee
batten *n.* પટ્ટી pattee
batter *n.* મારપીટ maarpeet
battery *n.* તોપખાનું topkhaanu
battle *n.* યુદ્ધ yuddha
battle-axe ઝઘડાખોર વૃધ્ધા. jhagadaakhor vrudhdha
bauble *n.* વિદૂષકની લાકડી vidushakanee laakadee
bawd *n.* વેશ્યા veshya
bawl *v.t.* રાડ પાડવી raad paadavee
bay *adj.* ખાડી khaadee
bayonet *n.* સંગીન sangeen
bazaar *n.* બજાર bajaar

be *v.i.* હોવું hovun
beach *n.* સમુદ્ર કિનારો samudr kinaaro
beacon *n.* ચેતવણીસૂચક chetavaneesoochak
bead *n.* માળાનો મણકો maalaano manako
beadle *n.* છડીદાર chhadeedaar
beak *n.* ચાંચ chaanch
beaker *n.* કટોરો katoro
beam *n.* લાકડાનો પાટડો lakadaano paatado
bean *n.* કઠોળનો દાણો katholano daano
bear *v.i.* ઉઠાવવું uthavavun
bearable *adj.* સહ્ય sahya
beard *n.* દાઢી daadhee
bearer *n.* સંદેશવાહક sandeshavaahak
bearing *n.* રીતભાત reetbhaat
beast *n.* પશુ pashu
beastly *adj.* ઘૃણાસ્પદ dhrunaaspad
beastliness *n.* હેવાન જેવું વર્તન hevaan jevun vartan
beat *v.t.* માર મારવો maar maaravo
beaten *p.p.* માર ખાધેલું maar khaadhelun
beatific *adj.* સુખી sukhee
beatify *v.t.* શણગારવું shanagaaravun
beatitude *n.* દિવ્યાનંદ divyaanand
beau *n.* ફાંકડો faankado
beauteous *adj.* સ્વરૂપવાન svaroopavaan
beautiful *adj.* સુંદર sundar
beautify *v.t.* સુશોભિત કરવું sushobhit karavun
beauty *n.* સૌંદર્ય saundarya
becall *v.t.* ગાળો દેવી gaalo devee
becalm *v.t.* શાંત પાડવું shaant paadavun
because *conj.* કારણકે kaaranke
beck *n.* ઇશારો eeshaaro
beckon *v.t.* ઇશારો કરવો eeshaaro karavo
become *v.i.* થવા માંડવું thavaa maandavun
becoming *adj.* શોભાસ્પદ shobhaaspad
bed *n.* પથારી pathaaree
bedaub *v.t.* રંગ ચોપડવો rang chopadavo
bedding *n.* પાથરણું paatharanun

bedeck *n.* શણગારવું shanagaaravun

bedew *v.* છંટકારવું chhantakaaravun

bedlam *n.* પાગલખાનું paagalakhaanun

bedlamite *n.* પાગલ paagal

bed-pan *n.* મળપાત્ર malapaatr

bed-rid પથારીવશ pathaareevash

bedouin *n.* રણવાસી આરબ ranavaasee aarab

bed-spread *n.* ચાદર chaadar

bedstead *n.* પલંગ palang

bee *n.* મધમાખી madhamaakhee

beech *n.* બીચ નામનું વૃક્ષ beech naamanun vruksh

beef *n.* ગોમાંસ gaumaans

bee-hive *n.* મધપૂડો madhapudo

bees-wax *n.* મીણ meen

beer *n.* જવનો શરાબ javano sharaab

beestings *n.* ખીરું khirun

beet *n.* બીટનો કંદ beetano kand

beetle *n.* વાંદો vaando

befall *v.t.* થવું thavun

befit *v.t.* યોગ્ય yogya

befool *v.t.* મૂરખ બનાવવું moorakh banaavavun

before *adj.* આગળ aagal

beforehand *adv.* અગાઉથી agaauthee

befoul *v.t.* ગંદુ કરવું gandu karavun

befriend *v.t.* મિત્રતા mitrataa

beg *v.t.* માગવું maagavun

beget *v.t.* સર્જન કરવું sarjan karavun

beggar *n.* ભિખારી bhikhaaree

beggarly *adj.* કંગાળ kangaal

beggary *n.* કંગાળિયત kangaaliyat

begging *n.* ભિક્ષાવૃત્તિ bhikshaavrutee

begin *v.t.* શરૂ કરવું, sharu karavun

beginning *n.* શરૂઆત sharooaat

begone *int.* ચાલ્યો જા chaalyo jaa

beguile *v.t.* ફસાવવું fasaavavun

begun *p.p.* ઉદ્ભવવું uddabhavavun

behalf *n.* વતી vati

behave *v.i.* વર્તવું vartavun

behaviour *n.* આચરણ aacharan

behead *v.t.* શરિચ્છેદ કરવો shirchchhed karavo

behest *n.* આજ્ઞા aagna

behind *prep.* પાછળ paachhal

behold *v.t.* નિરીક્ષણ કરવું nireekshan karavun

karavun

beholden *adj.* આભારી aabhaaree

behoof *n.* લાભ laabh

behove *v.t.* આવશ્યક હોવું aavashyak hovun

being *n.* હોવું hovun

belabour *v.t.* ઝૂડવું jhoodavun

belated *adj.* મોડું પડેલું modun padelun

belaud *v.t.* પ્રશંસા કરવી prashansa karavee

belay *v.t.* કસીને બાંધવું kaseene baandhavun

belch *v.t.* ઓડકાર ખાવો odakaar khaavo

beldam *n.* વંતરી vantaree

beleaguer *v.t.* ઘેરો ઘાલવો ghero ghaalavo

belfry *n.* ઘંટવાળો મિનારો ghantavaalo minaaro

belial *n.* દૈત્ય daitya

belie *v.t.* ખોટો ખ્યાલ આપવો khoto khyal aapavo

belief *n.* વિશ્વાસ vishvaas

believe *v.t.* માનવું maanavun

believer *n.* આસ્તિક aastik

belittle *v.t.* હલકું halakun

bell *n.* ઘંટ ghant

belle *n.* સૌન્દર્યરાણી saundaryaraanee

bellicose *adj.* યુધ્ધખોર yudhdhakhor

belligerent *adj.* યુદ્ધારૂઢ yuddhaaroodh

bellow *v.t.* ગરજવું garajavun

bellows *n.* ધમણ dhaman

belly *n.* પેટ pet

belong *v.t.* માલિકીનું હોવું maalikeenun hovun

belonging *n.pl.* અંગત માલમત્તા angat maalamatta

beloved *adj.* પ્રિય વ્યક્તિ priya vyakti

below *n.* નીચે neeche

belt *n.* પટો pato

belted *adj.* પટ્ટા વડે આવેષ્ટિત patta vade aaveshtit

bemoan *v.t.* શોક કરવો shok karavo

bemuse *v.t.* મૂંઝવણમાં નાખવું munjhavanman naakhavun

bench *n.* બાંકડો baankado

bend *n.* વાંકું કરવું vaanku karavun

beneath *prep.* થી ઉતરતા સ્થાને thee utarata sthane

benedick *n.* નવપરણિત વ્યક્તિ navaparineet vyakti

benediction *n.* આશીર્વાદ aasheervaad

benefaction *n.* ઉપકાર upakaar

benefactor *n.* દાતા daataa

benefice *n.* પરોપકાર paropakaar

beneficence *n.* દાનવૃતિ daanavrutee

beneficent *adj.* દયાળુ dayaalu

beneficial *adj.* લાભકારક laabhakaarak

benefit *n.* ફાયદો faayado

benevolence *n.* હિતકારીવૃત્તિ hitakaareevruti

benevolent *adj.* હિતકારી hitakaaree

benighted *adj.* અજ્ઞાનગ્રસ્ત agyaanagrast

benign *adj.* મોટા મનનું motaa mananun

benignant *adj.* ઉપકારક upakaarak

bent *n.* વલણ valan

benumb *v.t.* જડ બનાવવું jad banaavavun

benzoin *n.* લોબાન lobaan

bequeath *v.t.* વસિયતનામા દ્વારા આપવું vasiyatanaama dvaara aapavun

bequest *n.* વારસો vaaraso

bereave *v.t.* છીનવી લેવું chheenavee levun

bereavement *n.* વંચિત vanchit

berg *n.* બરફનો પહાડ barafano pahaad

berry *n.* બેરી beri

berth *n.* લંગરસ્થાન langarsthaan

beseech *v.t.* આજીજી કરવી aajeejee karavee

beseem શોભવું shobhavun

beset *v.t.* ઘેરી લેવું gheree levun

beside *prep.* બાજુએ baajue

besides *adv.* ઉપરાંત uparaant

besiege *v..t* બીજું ઘેરો ઘાલવો biju ghero ghaalavo

basmear *v.t.* ખરડવું kharadavun

besmirch *v.t.* ગંદુ કરવું gandu karavun

besom *n.* સાવરણો saavarano

bespatter *v.t.* ગાળો દેવી gaalo devee

bespeak *v.t.* કહી મૂકવું kahee mookavun

besprinkle *v.t.* ચોતરફ છાંટવું chotaraf chhantavun

best *adj.* સર્વોત્તમ sarvottam

bestial *adj.* પાશવી paashavee

bestir *v.t.* જાગ્રત jaagrut

bestow *v.t.* બક્ષિસ આપવી bakshis aapavee

bestowal *n.* પુરદાન pradaan

bestried *v.t.* પલાણીને બેસવું palaaneene besavun

bet *v.t.* શરત sharat

betake *v.t.* કોઈનો આશરો લેવો koeeno aasharo levo

betel *n.* નાગરવેલનું પાન. naagaravelanun paan

betel-nut *n.* સોપારી sopaaree

bethink *n.* યાદ કરવું yaad karavun

betide *v.i.* થવું thavun

betimes *adv.* વખતસર vakhatasar

betoken *v.t.* ની નિશાની હોવી nee nishaanee hovee

betray *v.t.* દગો દેવો. dago devo

betrayal *n.* દગો dago

betroth *v.i.* સગાઈ કરવી sagaaee karavee

better *adj.* બહેતર bahetar

betterment *n.* સુધારો sudhaaro

between *prep.* વચ્ચે vachche

beverage *n.* પીણું peenun

bevy *n.* સ્ત્રીઓનું વૃંદ streeonun vrund

beware *v.i.* ધ્યાન આપવું dyaan aapavun

bewilder *v.t.* ગુંચવવું gunchavavun

bewilderment *n.* ગભરાટ gabharaat

bewitch *v.t.* મુગ્ધ કરવું mugdh karavun

bewitchment *n.* વશીકરણ vasheekaran

beyond *prep.* પેલી પાર pelee paar

bi-annual વર્ષમાં બેવાર varshamaan bevaar

bias *n.* પૂર્વગ્રહ poorvagrah

bib *v.t.* દારૂ ઢીંચવો daaroo dheenchavo

bible *n.* ખ્રિસ્તિધર્મગ્રંથ khristi dharmagranth

bibliography *n.* ગ્રંથસૂચિ granthasoochi

bicameral *adj.* બે ગૃહોવાળું be grahovaalun

bicker *v.i.* ઝઘડવું jhagadavun

bickering *n.* જીભાજોડી jeebhaajodee

bicycle *n.* સાઇકલ saaeekal

bid *v.t.* બોલી બોલવી bolee bolavee

biddable *adj.* આજ્ઞાઆધારક aagnaadhaarak

bidder *n.* બોલી બોલનાર bolee bolanaar

bidding *n.* હરાજીમાં બોલી haraajeeman bolee

bide *v.* તકની રાહ જોવી takanee raah jovee

biennial *adj.* દ્વિવાર્ષિક dvivaarshik

bier *n.* ઠાઠડી thaathadee

bifurcate *v.t.* દ્વિભાજન કરવું dvibhaajan karavun

big *adj.* મોટું motun

bigot *n.* ધર્માંધ માણસ dhrmaandh maanas

bike *n.* મોટરસાઇકલ motarasaaeekal

bilateral *adj.* દ્વિપક્ષી dvipakshee

bile *n.* પિત્તપ્રકોપ pittaprakop

bilingual *adj.* દ્વિભાષી dvibhaashee

bill *n.* ભાલો bhaalo

billet *n.* બળતણનું લાકડું balatananun laakadun

billiards *n.* બલિયર્ડસ biliyards

billion *n.* અબજ abaj

billow *n.* મોટાં મોજાં motan mojan

bimonthly દ્વિમાસિક dvimaasik

bin *n.* ડબો dabo

binary *adj.* બેવડું bevadun

bind *v.t.* બાંધવું baandhavun

binder *n.* ચોપડીઓ બાંધનાર chopadeeo baandhanaar

binding *adj.* બંધનકારક bandhanakaarak

binocular *n.* દૂરબીન doorabeen

binomial *adj.* દ્વિપદી dvipadee

biographer *n.* જીવનચરિત્રકાર jeevanacharitrakaar

biography જીવનચરિત્ર jeevanacharitra

biology *n.* જીવવિજ્ઞાન jeevavigyaan

biologist જીવવિજ્ઞાની jeevavigyaanee

biped *n.* બેપગું પ્રાણી bepagun praanee

birch *n.* ભૂર્જવૃક્ષ bhurjvruksha

bird *n.* પક્ષી pakshee

birth *n.* જન્મ janma

birthday *n.* જન્મ તારીખ janma taareekh

birth-place *n.* જન્મ સ્થળ janma sthal

birth-right *n.* જન્મ અધિકાર janma adhikaar

biscuit *n.* બિસ્કિટ biskit

bisect *v.t.* ભાગ પાડવા bhaag paadava

bisector *n.* દ્વિભાજક dvibhaajak

bishop *n.* ધર્માધ્યક્ષ dharmaadhyksh

bison *n.* જંગલી ગાય jangalee gaay

bit *n.* ઓજાર ojaar

bite *v.t.* કરડવું karadavun

biting *adj.* દુઃખકારી dukhakaaree

bitter *adj.* કડવું kadavun

bitterness *n.* કટુતા katuta

bitumen *n.* ડામર daamar

bivalve *adj.* બે ઢાંકણાંવાળું be dhankananvaalun

bivouac *n.* ખુલ્લામાં નાખેલો પડાવ khullaaman naakhelo padaav

bizarre *adj.* ઉટપટાંગ utapataang

black *adj.* કાળુ kaalu

blacken *v.t.* કાળું કરવું kaalun karavun

blackguard *n.* દુરાચારી વ્યક્તિ duraachaaree vyakti

blacking *n.* કાળું પૉલિશ kaalun polish

blackish *adj.* કાળા રંગનું kaalaa rangnun

blackleg *n.* હડતાલ તોડનાર hadtaal todnaar

blackmail *n.* જાંસાચહ્દ્ધી jaansachidhdhee

blacksmith *n.* લુહાર luhaar

bladder *n.* મૂત્રાશય mootraashay

blade *n.* છરી chharee

blain *n.* ગૂમડું goomadun

blame *v.t.* દોષારોપણ doshaaropan

blanch *v.t.* સફેદ કરવું safed karavun

bland *adj.* વિનયી vinayee,

blandish *v.t.* ખુશામત કરવી khushaamat karavee

blank *adj.* કોરું karun

blanket *n.* કામળો kaamalo

blare તાણીને વગાડવું taaneene vagaadavun

blaspheme *v.t.* દેવનિંદા devnindaa

blasphemy *n.* ઈશ્વર નિંદા eeshvar ninda

blast *n.* ધડાકો dhadaako

blatant *adj.* હડહડતું hadahadatun

blaze *n.* રોશની roshanee

blazing *adj.* પ્રકાશતિ prakaashit

blazon *v.t.* કુળચિહ્નો વર્ણવવાં kulchinho varnavava

bleach *v.t.* સફેદીકરણ safedikaran

bleak *adj.* ઉજ્જડ ujjad

blear *adj.* ઝાંખી દ્રષ્ટિવાળું jhaankhee, drashtivaalun

bleat *v.t.* બકબક કરવી bakabak karavee

bleed *v.i.* લોહી નીકળવું lohee nikalavun

blemish *v.t.* કલંક લગાડવું kalank lagaadavun

blench *v.t.* ગભરાવું gabharavun

blend *v.t.* ભેળવવું bhelavavun

bless *v.t.* આશીર્વાદ આપવા aasheervaad aapava

blessed *adj.* આશીર્વાદ પ્રાપ્ત. aasheervaad praapt.

blessing *n.* આશીર્વાદ aasheervaad

blether *v.t.* વાહિયાત વાત vaahiyaat vaat

blight *v.t.* વનસ્પતિનો એક રોગ vanaspatino ek rog

blind *adj.* દ્રષ્ટિહીન drashtiheen

blindfold *adj.* આંખ મીચેલું aankh michelun

blindness *n.* અંધાપો andhaapo

blink *v.t.* પલકારા મારવા palakaara maarava

blinker *v.t.* ડાબલા daabala

bliss *n.* સ્વર્ગસુખ svargasukh

blissful *adj.* સુખાવહ sukhaavah

blister *n.* ફોલ્લો follo

blithe *adj.* મોજીલું mojeelun

blitzkrieg *n.* વીજઝીક આક્રમણ vijaleek aakraman

blizzard *n.* ભારે તોફાન bhaare tofan

bloat *v.t.* ફુલાવવું foolaavavun

block *n.* પથ્થરનો નક્કર ટુકડો pattarano nakkar tukado

blockade *n.* નાકાબંધી naakaabandhee

blockhead *n.* મૂરખ murkha

blond,blonde *adj.* આકર્ષક મહિલા. aakarshak mahila

blood *n.* લોહી lohee

bloodhound *n.* જાસુસી કુતરો jaasusee kutaro

blood-shed *n.* રક્તપાત raktapaat

blood-vessel *n.* રક્તવાહિની raktavaahinee

bloody *adj.* ખૂનખાર જંગ khoonakhaar jang

bloom *n.* સર્વશ્રેષ્ઠ તબક્કો, sarvashreshtha tabakko

blossom *n.* ફૂલ ખીલવાં fool kheelava

blot *v.t.* કલંક લગાડવું kalank lagaadavun

blotting-paper *n.* શાહીચૂસ કાગળ shaaheechoos kaagal

blouse *n.* બાંડી bandee

blow *v.t.* ફૂંકાવું foonkaavun

bludgeon *n.* દંડુકો danduko

blue *n.* વાદળી રંગ vaadalee rang

blueblood *n.* કુલીનતા kuleenata

blue-jacket *n.* નૌકાદળનો ખલાસી naukaadalano khalasee

blue-stocking *n.* વિદુષી vidushee

bluff *v.t.* આંખાબોલું aakhaabolun

blunder *v.t.* મૂરખામી કરવી murkhaamee karavee

blunt *adj.* જડ jad

blur *n.* ઝાંખપ jhankhap

blush *v.t.* મૂંઝવણ અનુભવવી munjavan anubhavavee

bluster *n.* ગરજવું garjavun

boa *n.* અજગર ajagar

boar *n.* જંગલી ડુક્કર jangalee dukkar

board *n.* લાકડાનું પાટિયું laakadaanun paatiyun

boarding *n.* છાત્રાલય chaatraalay

boast *n.* બડાઈ badaaee

boat *n.* હોડી hodee

boatswain *n.* નૌકાઅધિકારી naukaadhikari

bob *n.* લોલક પરનું વજન lolak paranun vajan

bobbin *n.* ફિરકી firakee

bode *v.t.* આગાહી કરવી aagahee karavee

bodice *n.* ચોળી cholee

bodily *adj.* શારીરિક shaareerik

body *n.* શરીર shareer

body-guard *n.* અંગરક્ષક angarakshak

bog *n.* કંપભૂમિ kanpbhoomi

bogie *n.* બોગી bogee

bogus *adj.* બનાવટી banaavatee

boil v. ઉકાળવું ukaalavun
boiler n. ચરુ charu
boisterous adj. તોફાની tofanee
bold adj. સાહસિક saahasik
boldness n. હિંમત hinmat
bolshevik n. રશિયાનો સામ્યવાદી rashiyaano saamyavadee
bolster n. લાંબો તકિયો laambo takiyo
bolt n. મોટો ખીલો moto kheelo
bomb n. બૉંબ bomb
bombard v.t. તોપમારો કરવો topamaaro karavo
bombast n. આડંબરી વાત aadanbaree vaat
bombastic adj. આડંબરયુક્ત aadanbarayukt
bonafide adj. સાચું saachun
bonafides n. શુભ દાનત shubh daanat
bond n. કરાર karaar
bondage n. ગુલામી gulaamee
bone n. હાડકું haadakun
bonnet n. ગોળ ટોપી gol topee
bone-setter n. હાડવૈદ haadavaid
bonfire n. વિજય સૂચક હોળી vijay soochak holee
bonny adj. પ્રસન્ન prasann
bonus n. બક્ષિસ bakshis
booby n. મૂરખ માણસ moorkh maanas
book n. પુસ્તક pustak
booking-office n. બુકિંગ કચેરી buking kacheree
bookish adj. વાચનનો શોખીન vaanchavano shokheen
book-keeper n. હિસાબનીસ hisaabanees
booklet n. નાનકડી ચોપડી naanakadee chopadee
bookseller n. પુસ્તકવિક્રેતા pustakavikreta
bookworm n. ગ્રંથકીટ granthkeet
boom v.t. તેજી tejee
boon n. કૃપા krupa
boor n. સંવેદનાહીન માનવ. sanvedanaaheen maanav
boorish adj. અસંસ્કારી વર્તાવ asanskaaree vartaav
boot n. જોડો jodo

booth v.t. કામચલાઉ દુકાન kaamachalaau dukaan
booty n. ઈનામ eenaam
borax n. ટંકણખાર tankankhaar
border n. સરહદ sarahad
bore v.t. કૂવો ખોદવો koovo khodavo
boredom n. કંટાળો kantaalo
born p.p. જન્મજાત janmajaat
borough v.t. મ્યુનસિપાલિટીવાળું શહેર myunisipaaliteevaalun shaher
borrow v.t. ઉછીનું લેવું uchheenun levun
bosh n. વાહિયાત વાત vaahiyaat vaat
bosom n. છાતી chhaatee
boss n. શેઠ sheth
botanist n. વનસ્પતિશાસ્ત્રી vanaspatishaastree
botany n. વનસ્પતિશાસ્ત્ર vanaspatishaastra
both prep. બન્ને banne
bother v.t. હેરાન કરવું heraan karavun
botheration n. માનસિક વ્યથા maanasik vyatha
bottle n. બાટલી baatalee
bottom n. તળિયું laliyun
bough n. ઝાડની ડાળી jhaadanee dalee
boulder n. ગોળ ખડક gol khadak
bounce v.t. કૂદકો koodako
bound n. પ્રદેશની સીમા pradeshnee seema
boundary n. સીમા seema
bounden adj. સ્થિર કરવું sthir karavun
boundless n. અમર્યાદા amaryaada
bountiful adj. ઉદાર udaar
bounty n. ઔદાર્ય audaarya
bouquet n. ફૂલોની કલગી foolonee kalagee
bourgeoisie n. મધ્યમ વર્ગ madhyam varga
bout n. કામનો સમય kaamano samay
bovine adj. મંદ mand
bow n. ધનુષ્ય dhanushya
bowler n. ગોલંદાજ golandaaj
bowels n.pl. આંતરડા aantarada
bower n. લતાકુંજ lataakunj
bowl n. વાટકો vaatako
bowling n. ગોલંદાજી golandaajee

box *n.* પેટી petee
boxing *n.* કુસ્તી kustee
boy *n.* છોકરો chhokaro
boycott *v.t.* બહિષ્કાર bahishkaar
boyhood *n.* બાળપણ baalapan
boyish *adj.* છોકરમત chokaramat
brace *n.* પટ્ટા patta
bracelet *n.* કંકણ kankan
brackish *adj.* જરાક ખારું jaraak khaarun
brag *v.t.* બડાઈ badaaee
braggart *n.* બડાઈખોર baadaaeekhor
braid *n.* ગૂંથેલા વાળ goonthela vaal
braille *v.t.* અંધલિપિ andhlipi
brain *n.* મગજ magaj
brainless *adj.* બુદ્ધિહીન buddhiheen
brainy *adj.* તીક્ષ્ણ બુદ્ધિવાળું teekshna buddhivaalun
brake *n.* ગીચ ઝાડી geech jhaadee
bramble *n.* કાંટાળો છોડ kaantaalo chhod
bran *n.* ભૂસું bhoosun
branch *n.* શાખા shaakhaa
brand *n.* મશાલ mashaal
brandish *v.i.* વીંઝવું veenjhavun
brand-new *adj.* નવું નક્કોર navun nakkor
brandy *n.* કડક દારૂ kadak daaroo
brass *n.* પિત્તળ pittal
brassier *n.* કમખો kamakho
bravado *n.* બહાદુરીનો દેખાવ bahaadureeno dekhaav
brave *adj.* શૂર shoor
bravo *int.* સરસ! શાબાશ ! saras!, shaabaash!
brawl *n.* કજિયો kajiyo
bray *v.t.* ગધેડાનું ભૂંકવું gadhedaanun bhoonkavun
braze *v.t.* રેણ કરવું ren karavun
brazen *n.* પિત્તળ જેવું pittala jevun
breach *n.* નિયમ ભંગ niyam bhang
bread *n.* પાઉરોટી paaunrotee
breadth *n.* પહોળાઈ paholaaee
break *v.t.* તોડવું todavun
breakage *n.* તૂટવું તે tutavun te
break-down *n.* અટકી પડવું atakee padavun

breakfast *n.* સવારનો નાસ્તો savaarano naasto
breakneck *adj.* ભયરૂપ bhayaroop
break-water બંધ bandh
breast *n.* સ્તન stan
breastplate *n.* છાતીનું બખતર chaateenu bakhatar
breath *n.* શ્વાસ svaas
breathe *v.t.* શ્વાસોચ્છ્વાસ કરવો svaasochchhaas karavo
breathing *n.* શ્વસનક્રિયા svasanakriya
breathless *adj.* હાંફતું haanfatun
breeches *n.* ચોરણો chorano
breed *v.t.* વંશવૃદ્ધિ કરવી vanshavruddhi karavee
breeding *n.* ઉછેર uchher
breeze *n.* મંદ સમીર mand sameer
breezy *adj.* હવાદાર havaadaar
brethren *n.* ભાઈબંધ bhaaeebandh
brevity *n.* સંક્ષેપ sankshep
brew *v.t.* દારૂ બનાવવો daaroo banaavavo
brevery *n.* દારૂનું કારખાનું daaroonun karakhanun
bribe *v.t.* લાંચ આપવી laanch aapavee
bribery *n.* લાંચ laanch
brick *n.* ઈટ eent
brick-bat *n.* રોડું rodun
brick-kiln *n.* ઈંટોનો ભઠ્ઠો eentono bhaththo
bricklayer *n.* કડિયો kadiyo
bridal *n.* લગ્નોત્સવ lagnotsav
bride *n.* નવવધૂ navavadhoo
bridgeroom *n.* કન્યાનો વર kanyaano var
bridge *n.* પુલ pul
bridle *n.* લગામ lagaam
brief *adj.* ટૂંકી નોંધ tunkee nonth
brig *n.* જહાજ jahaaj
brigade *n.* મોટી ટુકડી motee tukadee
brigadier *n.* બ્રિગેડનો વડો brigedno vado
brigand *n.* લૂંટારો loontaaro
brigandage *n.* લૂંટફાટ loontafaat
bright *adj.* ચળકતું chalakatun
brighten *v.t.* ચમકાવવું chamakaavavun
brilliance *n.* નામાંકિત naamaankit

brilliantine *n.* પ્રસાધન દ્રવ્ય prasaadhan dravya

brim *n.* પ્યાલો pyaalo

brimstone *n.* ગંધક gandhak

brine *n.* દરિયાનું પાણી dariyaanun paanee

bring *v.t.* લાવવું laavavun

brink *n.* કાંઠો kantho

briny *adj.* ખારા પાણીનું khaara paaneenun

brisk *v.t.* ચપળ chapal

bristle *n.* ટૂંકો બરછટ વાળ toonko barachhat vaal

british *adj.* બ્રિટિશ જનતા british janata

brittle *adj.* બરડ barad

broach *v.t.* કાણું પાડવું kaanun paadavun

broad *adj.* પહોળું paholun

broadcast *adj.* પ્રસારિત કરવું prasaarit karavun

broaden *v.t.* પહોળું કરવું paholun karavun

brocade *n.* ભરતકામવાળું કાપડ bharatakaamavaalun kaapad

brochure *n.* નાની પુસ્તિકા naanee pustikaa

broil *n.* કજિયો kajiyo

broker *n.* દલાલ dalaal

brokerage *n.* દલાલી dalaalee

bronze *n.* કાંસું kansun

brooch *n.* આંકડીવાળું ઘરેણું aankadeevalun gharenun

brood *v.t* ઈંડા સેવવાં eenda sevavan

brook *n.* સાંખવું saankhavun

broom *n.* સાવરણી saavaranee

broth *n.* માંસમચ્છીનું સૂપ maansamachcheenu soop

brothel *n.* વેશ્યાગૃહ veshyaagruh

brother *n.* સગો ભાઈ sago baaee

brotherhood *n.* બંધુત્વ bandhutva

brother-in-law *n.* સાળો saalo

brotherly *adj.* ભાઈચારો bhaaichaaro

brow *n.* કપાળ kapaal

browbeat *v.* ધમકાવવું dhamakaavavun

brown *adj.* છીંકણી chheenkanee

bruise *n.* છૂંદવું, chundavun

bruit *n.* અફવા afava

brunt *n.* આંચકો aanchako

brush *n.* કૂચડો koochado

brushwood *n.* ઝરડાંઝાંખરા jharadanjhaankhara

brushy *adj.* બરછટ barachhat

brusque *adj.* અસભ્ય asabhya

brutal *adj.* પાશવી. paashavee

brutality *n.* નિર્દયતા nirdayataa

brute *adj.* પશુસમાન pashusamaan

bubble *n.* પરપોટો parapoto

buck *n.* નર હરણ nar haran

buck up *v.t.* ઉતાવળ કરવી utaaval karavee

bucket *n.* ડોલ dol

buckle *n.* કડી kadee

buckram *n.* મીણિયું કાપડ meeniyun, kaapad

bud *n.* ફૂલની કળી fulanee kalee

budge *v.t.* ખસવું khasavun

budget *n.* અંદાજપત્ર andaajapatra

buff *n.* પીળું ચામડું peelun chaamadun

buffalo *n.* ભેંસ bhens

buffer *n.* પ્રતિરોધક pratirodhak

buffet *n.* તમાચો tamaacho

buffoon *n.* રંગલો rangalo

buffoonery વિદૂષક વેડા vidooshak vedaa

bug *n.* માંકણ maankan

buggy *n.* ઘોડાગાડી ghodaagaadee

bugle *n.* વાદળી ફૂલવાળો એક વેલો vaadalee fulovaalo ek velo

build *v.t.* બાંધવું baandhavun

building *n.* ઈમારત eemaarat

bulb *n.* ગોળો golo

bulge *n.v.i.* સુજી જવું, sujee javun

bulk *n.* મોટી સંખ્યામાં motee sankhyaaman

bulky *adj.* જથ્થામય jaththamay

bull *n.* આખલો aakhalo

bull-dog *n.* બુલડોગ buldog

bullet *n.* બંદૂકની ગોળી bandookanee golee

bulletin *n.* સત્તાવાર અહેવાલ sattaavaar ahevaal

bullion *n.* સોનાની લગડી sonanee lagadee

bullock *n.* બળદ balad

bully *v.t.* દાદાગીરી કરવી daadaageeree karavee

bulwark *n.* આડ aad

bump *n.* ટેકરો tekaro

bumper વિપુલ vipul

bumpkin *n.* ગામડિયો gaamadiyo

bun *n.* ગળી રોટી galee rotee

bunch *n.* ઝૂમખું jhoomakhun

bundle *n.* પોટલું, ભારી potalun, bhaaree

bunglow *n.* બંગલો banglo

bungle *v.t.* લોચો વાળવો locho vaalavo

bunk *n.* સૂવાનું પાટિયું soovaanun paatiyun

bunker *n.* ભોંયરું bhonyarun

bunting *n.* એક નાનું પક્ષી ek naanun pakshee

buoy *v.t.* બોયું boyun

buoyancy *n.* ઉમંગ umang

burden *n.* બોજો bojo

burdensome *adj.* બોજારૂપ bojaaroop

bureau *n.* કાર્યાલય kaaryaalay

bueaucracy *n.* નોકરશાહી nokarashaahee

bureaucrat *n.* અમલદાર amaldaar

burgher *n.* પરદેશી નાગરિક paradeshee naagarik

burglar *n.* ઘરફોડું gharafodun

burial *n.* દફન dafan

burlesque *n.* હાસ્યજનક નકલ haasyajanak nakal

burly *adj.* ખડતલ બાંધાનું khadatal baandhaanun

burn *v.t.* સળગવું salagavun

burning *adj.* સળગતું salagatun

burnish *v.t.* ઘસીને ચળકતું કરવું ghaseene chalakatun

burr *v.t.* ઘોઘરો સાદ ghoghharo saad

burrow *n.* બિલ bil

burst *v.t.* સ્ફોટ થવો sfot thavo

bury *v.t.* દફન કરવું dafan karavun

bus *n.* બસ bas

bush *n.* ઝાડ jhaad

bushel *n.* અનાજનું માપ annajnu maap

bushy *adj.* ગીચ ઊગેલું geech oogelun

business *n.* કારોબાર kaarobaar

busk *v.t.* પ્રવાસી નટ pravaasee nat

bust *n.* અર્ધમૂર્તિ ardhamoorti

bustle *v.t.* ઉતાવળ કરવી utaaval karavee

busy *n.* પ્રવૃત્ત pravrutt

but *adj.* પરંતુ parantun

butcher *n.* કસાઈ kasaaee

butler *n.* ખાનસામો khaanasaamo

butt *n.* બંદૂકનો કુંદો bandookano kundo

butter *n.* માખણ maakhan

butterfingered *adj.* ભારેહાથવાળું bharehaathvalun

butterfly *n.* પતંગિયું patangiyun

buttermilk *n.* છાશ chhaash

buttock *n.* કૂલો koolo

button *n.* બટન batan

buttress *n.* ટેકો teko

buxom *adj.* ભરાવદાર અંગવાળી bharavadaar angavaalee

buy *v.t.* ખરીદી કરવી khareedee karavee

buyer *n.* ખરીદનાર khareedanaar

buzz *v.t.* ગણગણાટ કરવો, ganaganaat karavo

by *adv.* નજીક najeek

by and by ધીમેધીમે dheemedheeme

by-corner *n.* છાનો ખૂણો chhaano khoono

by-end *n.* તરત જ tarat ja

by-gone *adj.* અતીત ateet

by-law *n.* પેટા કાયદો peta kaayado

by-name *n.* હુલામણું નામ hulaamanun naam

by-path *n.* આડવાટ aadvaat

by-product *n.* આડપેદાશ aadapedaash

bystander *adj.* દૂરથી જોનાર doorathee jonaar

by-word *n.* કહેવત kaheevat

bye-bye *n.* વિદાયવચન, સાહેબજી ! vidaayavachan, saahebajee !

C

cab *n.* ભાડાની મોટરગાડી bhaadaanee motaragaadee

cabal *n.* ચંડાળચોકડી chandaal chokadee

cabbage *n.* કોબી kobee

cabin *n.* લાકડાનું નાનું ઘર laakadaanun naanun ghar

cabinet *n.* મંત્રીમંડળ mantreemandal

cactus *n.* થોર thor

cadence *n.* સૂરનો આરોહ અવરોહ soorano aaroh avaroh

cadet *n.* લશ્કરી વદ્યિાર્થી lashkaree vidhyaarthee

cadge *v.i.* અવલંબન avalanmban

cafe *n.* નાસ્તાની દુકાન naastaanee dukaan

cage *n.* પાંજરું paanjarun

cajole મનાવવું manaavavun

cajolery *n.* પટામણી pataamanee

cake *n.* કેક kek

calabash *n.* કોળું kolun

calamitous *adj.* આપત્તજિનક. aapattijanak

calamity *n.* આપત્તિ aapatti

calcium *n.* કેલ્શયિમ kelsium

calculate *v.* ગણતરી કરવી ganataree karavaanee

calculation *n.* ગણતરી ganataree

caldron *n.* ચરુ charu

calendar *n.* પંચાંગ panchaang

calf *n.* ગાયનું બચ્ચુ gaaynun bachchun

calibre બંદૂકની નાળ bandooknee naal

calico *n.* સસ્તુ સુતરાઉ કાપડ sastu sutarau kaapad

calix *n.* પુષ્પકોશ pushpkosh

call *v.t.* બોલાવવું bolaavavun

calliper *n.* કેલપિર kelipar

calling *n.* ધંધો dhandho

callous *adj.* રીઢું reedhun

callow *adj.* બિનઅનુભવી binanubhavee

calm *adj.* સ્વસ્થ svastha

calmly *adv.* સ્વસ્થતાપૂર્વક svasthataapoorvak

calmness *n.* પ્રશાન્તિ prashaanti

calomel *n.* રેચક ઔષધ rechak, aushadh

caloric *n.* ઉષ્ણતાનો એકમ ushnataano ekam

calorie *n.* ઉષ્ણતાનો એકમ ushnataano ekam

calorimeter *n.* કેલરીમાપક યંત્ર kelareemaapak yantr

calumniate *v.t.* નિંદા કરવી neenda karavee

calumny *n.* નિંદા neenda

cambric *n.* ઝીણું કપડું jheenun kaapad

camel *n.* ઊંટ oont

camelopard *n.* જીરાફ jeeraaf

camera *n.* કેમેરા kemeraa

camouflage *n.* ઢાંકપિછોડો dhaankpichhedo

camp *n.* લશ્કરની છાવણી lashkaranee chhaavanee

campaign *n.* ઝુંબેશ jhunbesh

camphor *n.* કપૂર kapoor

canal *n.* નહેર naher

canard *n.* અફવા afava

cancel *v.* રદ કરવું rad karavun

cancer *n.* કર્ક (રાશી) kark (raashi)

candidly *adv.* સરળ ભાવે saral bhaave

candidate *n.* ઉમેદવાર umedavaar

candle *n.* મીણબત્તી meenabattee

candour *n.* નિખાલસતા nikhaalasata

candy *n.* એક મીઠાઈ ek meethaae

cane *n.* લાકડી laakadee

canine *adj.* કૂતરાને લગતું kootaraane lagatun

canister *n.* નાનું ડબલું naanun dabalun

canker *n.* ચાંદું chaandun

cannibal *n.* નરમાંસભક્ષી naramaansabhakshee

cannon *n.* તોપ top

cannonade *v.t.* અવરિત તોપમારો avirat topamaaro

canny *adj.* કરકસરિયું karakasariyun

canoe *n.* હોડકું hodakun

canon *n.* ઊંડી ખીણ oondee kheen

cant *n.* ઢાળવાળી સપાટી dhaalavaalee sapaatee

canteen *n.* નાસ્તાની દુકાન naastaanee dukaan

canter *n.* ચૌકચાલ chaukachaal

canto *n.* કાવ્યનો ખંડ kaavyano khand

cantonment *n.* લશ્કરી છાવણી lashkaree chhaavanee

canvas *n.* કંતાન kantaan

canvass *v.t.* પ્રચાર કરવો prachaar karavo

cap *n.* ટોપી topee

capable *adj.* ક્ષમતાવાળું kshamataavaalun

capacitate *v.t.* કાર્યક્ષમ બનાવવું kaaryaksham banaavavun

capacity *n.* ક્ષમતા kshamataa

caparison *n.* ઝૂલથી સજાવવું jhoolathee sajaavvun

cape *n.* બાંય વિનાનો ટૂંકો ઝભ્ભો. baany vinaano tunko jhabhbho

caper ઝંખરું zaankharun

capillary *n.* રક્તવાહિની raktavaahinee

capital *n.* રાજધાની raajadhaanee

capitalism *n.* મૂડીવાદ moodeevaad

capitalist *n.* મૂડીવાદી moodeevaadee

capitol *n.* જુપટિરનું મંદિર jupitaranun mandir

capitulate *v.i.* શરતી શરણાગતિ sharatee sharanaagati

capitulation *v.i.* શરતી શરણાગતિ sharatee sharanaagati

capon *n.* ખસી કરેલો કૂકડો khasee karelo kookado

caprice *n.* તરંગ tarang

capricious *adj.* તરંગી tarangee

capricorn *n.* મકર રાશિ makar raashi

capsize *v.t.* ઊંધું વળવું undhun valavun

capsule *n.* વનસ્પતિનો બીજકોષ vanaspatino beejakosh

captain *n.* કપ્તાન kaptaan,

caption *n.* મથાળું mathalun

captious છિદ્રાન્વેષી chhidraanveshee

captivate *v.* ચિત્ત હરી લેવું chitt haree levun

captive *n.* કેદી kedee

captivating *n.* મનોહર manohar

captivity *n.* બંધનાવસ્થા bandhanaavastha

captor *n.* બંદી કરનાર bandee karanaar

capture *v.t.* પકડી લેવું pakadee levun

car *n.* ગાડી gaadee

carat *n.* કેરેટ keret

caravan *n.* જાત્રાળુઓનો સંઘ jaatraauono sangh

caravanserai *n.* ઉતારો utaaro

carbon *n.* કાર્બન kaarban

carbuncle *n.* ઝેરી ગૂમડું jheree goomadun

carcass *n.* હાડપિંજર hadapinjar

card *n.* તારનો બ્રશ taarano brash

carder *n.* પીંજારો peenjaaro

cardamom *n.* ઈલાયચી eelaayachee

cardiac *adj.* હૃદયનું-ને લગતું rhadaynun-ne lagatun

cardinal *adj.* મધ્યવર્તી madhyavartee

care *v.t.* સંભાળ લેવી sanbhaal levee

career *n.* કારકીર્દિ kaarkeerdi

careful *adj.* કાળજીવાળું kaalajeevaalun

careless *adj.* અવિચારી avichaaree

caress *v.t.* ચુંબન chunban

careworn *n.* ચિંતાગ્રસ્ત chintaagrast

cargo *n.* માલ maal

carious *n.* સડો sado

carnage *n.* કત્લેઆમ katleaam

carnal *adj.* શારીરિક shaareerik

carnival *n.* મેળો melo

carnivorous *adj.* માંસાહારી પ્રાણીવર્ગ maansaahaaree praaneevarg

carol *v.t.* આનંદપૂર્વક ગાવું aanandapoorvak gaavun

carouse *v.i.* દારૂ ઢીંચવો daaroo dhinchavo

carpenter *n.* સુથાર suthaar

carpentry *n.* સુથારીનું કામ suthaareenun kaam

carpet *n.* પાથરણું paatharanun

carping *n.* દોષિક દૃષ્ટિ doshaik drashtee

carriage *n.* ગાડાભાડું gaadaabhaadun

carrier *n.* ઉપાડીને લઈ જનાર upaadeene laee janaar

carrion *n.* સડેલું માંસ sadelun maans

carrot *n.* ગાજર gaajar

carry *v.t.* ઊંચકીને લઈ જવું oonchakeene laee javun

cart *n.* ખટારો khataaro

cartage *n.* ગાડાભાડું gaadaabhaadun

cartel *n.* ઐક્ય aikya

cartilage *n.* કૂર્ચા foorcha

cartoon *n.* વ્યંગ્યચિત્ર vyangyachitr

cartridge *n.* કારતૂસ kaaratoos

carve *v.t.* કોતરવું kotaravun

cascade *n.* પાણીનો ધોધ paaneeno dhodh

case *n.* કોઈ ઘટનાનો દાખલો koe ghatanaano daakhalo

casement *n.* મજાગરાંવાળો ભાગ majaagaraanvaalo bhaag

cash *n.* રોકડ rokad

cashier *n.* કોષાધ્યક્ષ koshaadhyaksh

casino *n.* જુગારનો અડ્ડો jugaarno addo

cask *n.* દારૂનું પીપ daaroonun peep

casket *n.* ઝવેરાતની પેટી jhaveraatnee petee

casque *n.* માથાનું કવચ maathaanun kavach

cassock *n.* કાળો ઝભ્ભો kaalo jhabhbho

cast *v.t.* પડતું મુકવું padatun mukavun

castaway *n.* ભગ્નનૌકાનો યાત્રી bhgnanaukaano yatree

caste *n.* જ્ઞાત gnaati

castigate *v.t.* સજા કરવી sajaa karavee

castle *n.* મહેલ mahel

castor oil *n.* એરંડિયું erandiyun

castrate *v.t.* ખસી કરવી khasi karavee

casual *adj.* આકસ્મિક aakasmik

casually *adv.* પ્રસંગોપાત prasngopaat

casualty *n.* જાનહાનિ jaanhaani

cat *n.* બિલાડી bilaadee

cataclysm *n.* ઉત્પાત utpaat

Catalogue *n.* યાદી yaadee

cataract *n.* આંખનો મોતિયો. aankhano motiyo

catarrh *n.* સળેખમ salekham

catastrophe *n.* અચાનક આવેલી આપત્ત achaanak aavelee aapatti

catch *v.t.* પકડી લેવું pakadee levun

catechise *v.t.* પરીક્ષા લેવી pareeksha levee

catechu *n.* કાથો kaatho

categorical *adj.* સ્પષ્ટ spashta

category *n.* વર્ગ varg

cater *v.t.* ખાનપાનની વ્યવસ્થા khaanpaannee vyavastha

caterpillar *n.* ઈયળ eeyal

catgut *n.* વાજિંત્રનો તાર vaajintrno taar

cathedral *n.* મુખ્ય દેવળ mukhya deval

catheter *n.* નરશલાકા trashalaaka

catholic *n.* કેથલિક kethalik

cattle *n.* ઢોર dhor

caucus *n.* રાજકીય સમિતિ rajakeey samiti

caudle *n.* ગરમ કાંજી garam kanjee

cauldron *n.* ઉકાળવાનું મોટું વાસણ ukaalavaanun motun vaasan

cauliflower *n.* ફૂલગોબી foolagobee

causal *adj.* કારણદર્શક kaaranadarshak

cause *v.t.* કારણ kaaran

causeway *n.* પગદંડી pagadandee

caustic *adj.* આકરું aakarun

cauterize *v.t.* ની ઉપર ડામ દેવો nee upar daam devo

caution *n.* સાવધાની saavadhaanee

cautious *adj.* સાવધ saavadh

cavalcade *n.* ઘોડેસવારોનું સરઘસ ghodesavaaronun saraghas

cavalier *n.* તોછડું tarachhadun

cavalry *n.* ઘોડેસવાર સેના ghodesavaar senaa

cave *n.* ગુફા gufa

cavern *n.* કોતર kotar

cavity *n.* પોલાણ polaan

caw *n.* કાગડાનો 'કા' 'કા' અવાજ kaagadaano "ka" "ka" avaaj

cease *v.t.* બંધ કરવું bandh karavun

ceaseless *adj.* અવિરત avirat

cedar *n.* ગંધતરુ gandhataru

cede *v.t.* છોડી દેવું chhodee devun

ceiling *n.* છત chaat

celebrate *v.t.* ઊજવવું oojavavun

celebrated *adj.* પ્રસિદ્ધ prasiddh

celebration *n.* ધાર્મિક વિધિ dhaarmik vidhi

celebrity *n.* પ્રતિષ્ઠિત વ્યક્ત pratishthit vyakti

celerity *n.* ઝડપ jhadap

celestial *adj.* સ્વર્ગીય svargeey

celibacy *n.* બ્રહ્મચર્ય brahmcharya

celibate *adj.* અપરિણીત aparineet

cell *n.* કોષ kosh

cellar *n.* ભોંયરું bhonyarun

cellular *adj.* કોષોનું બનેલું koshonun banelun

celluloid *n.* એક જાતનું પ્લાસ્ટિક ek jaatnun plastik

cement *n.* સમિન્ટ ciment

cemetery *n.* કબરસ્તાન kabrastaan

cenotaph *n.* સ્મરણસ્તંભ smaranasthanbh

censor *n.* નિયંત્રણ niyantran

censurable *adj.* ઠપકાપાત્ર thapakaapaatra

censure *v.t.* નિંદા કરવી ninda karavee

census *n.* વસ્તી ગણતરી vastee ganataree

cent *n.* ડૉલરનો સોમો ભાગ dolarano somo bhaag

centenary *n.* શતાબ્દી shataabdee

centennial *adj.* શતાબ્દી ઉત્સવ shataabdee utsav

centigrade *adj.* સેન્ટિગ્રેડ sentigred

centipede *n.* કાનખજૂરો kaanakhajooro

central *v.t.* કેન્દ્રીય kendreeya

centralize *v.t.* કેન્દ્રીકરણ કરવું kendreekaran karavun

centre *n.* કેન્દ્ર kendra

centrifugal *adj.* કેન્દ્રાપગામી kendraapagaamee

centripetal *adj.* કેન્દ્રગામી kendragaamee

century *n.* શતાબ્દી shataabdee

ceramics *n.* માટીકામની કળા maateekaamanee kala

cereal *n.* ખાદ્ય પદાર્થ khaady padaarth

ceremony *n.* વિધિ vidhi

certain *adj.* નિશ્ચિત nishchit

certainly *adv.* ચોક્કસ chokkas

certificate *n.* પ્રમાણપત્ર pramaanapatra

certify *v.t.* પ્રમાણિત કરવું pamaanit karavun

cess *n.* ઉપકર upakar

cessation *n.* વિરામ viraam

cession *n.* હસ્તાંતર કરવું hastaantar karavun

cesspool *n.* ખાળકૂવો khaalakoovo

chafe *v.t.* ચીડવવું cheedavavun

chaff *n.* ધાનનું ફોતરું ghaananun fotarun

chaffer *v.i.* રકઝક કરવી rakajhak karavee

chagrin *n.* તીવ્ર સંતાપ teevr santaap

chain *n.* સાંકળ saankal

chair *n.* ખુરશી khurashee

chairman *n.* સભાપતિ sabhaapati

chaise *n.* બગી bagee

chalk *n.* ચોક chok

challenge *n.* પડકાર padakaar

chamber *n.* ઓરડી oradee

chamberlain *n.* વ્યવસ્થાપક vyavasthaapak

chambermaid *n.* દાસી daasee

chamois *n.* પહાડી હરણ pahaadee haran

champagne *n.* શેંપેન shempen

champion *n.* અનુયવતી લડનાર anyavatee ladanaar

chance *n.* તક tak

chancellor *n.* વિદ્યાપીઠનો કુલપતિ vidyaapeethano kulapatee

change *v.t.* ફેરફાર કરવો ferafaar karavo

changeable *adj.* પરિવર્તનશીલતા pareevartanasheelata

changeful *adj.* બદલી જાય તેવું badalee jaay tevun

changeling *n.* બદલી નાખેલું બાળક badalee naakhelun baalak

channel *n.* નાળું naalun

chant *n.* મેંદ ગીતનું સંગીત maid geetanun sangeet

chaos *n.* સંપૂર્ણ અવ્યવસ્થા sanpoorn avyavastha

chaotic *adj.* સાવ અસ્તવ્યસ્ત saav astvyast

chap *n.* છોકરો chokaro

chapel *n.* ખાનગી દેવળ khaanagee deval

chaplain *n.* દેવળનો ધર્મગુરુ devalno dharmaguru

chaplet *n.* મણકાની માળા manakaanee maala

chapter *n.* પુસ્તકનું પ્રકરણ pustakanun prakaran

char *v.t.* કોલસો કરવો kolaso karavo

character *n.* અક્ષર akshar

characteristic *adj.* લાક્ષણિકતા laakshanikata

characterize *v.t.* અમુક તરીકે વર્ણન કરવું amuk tareeke varnan karavun

charade *n.* ઉખાણું ukhaanun

charcoal *n.* લાકડાંનો કોલસો laakadaano kolaso

charge *n.* આરોપ aarop

chariot *n.* રથ rath

charioteer *n.* સારથિ saarathi

charitable *n.* દાન પર નભતું daan par

nabhatun

charity *n.* દાન daan

charm *n.* સૌન્દર્ય saundarya

charmer *n.* જાદુગર jaadugar

chart *n.* હકકપત્રક hakkapatrak

charter *n.* સનદવાળી સંસ્થાનું sanadavaalee sansthaanun

chary *adj.* કરકસરિયું karakasariyun

chase *v.t.* આકૃત ઉપસાવવી aakruti upasaavavee

chasm *n.* ખાઈ khaaee

chassis *n.* ગાડીની સાટી gaadeenee satee

chaste *adj.* ચારિત્ર્યશીલ chaaritryasheel

chasten *v.t.* કાબૂમાં આણવું kaboolamin aanavun

chastise ઠપકો આપવો thapako aapavo

chastity *n.* પાવિત્ર્ય paavitry

chat *v.i.* ગપ્પાં મારવાં gappan maravan

chateau *n,.* ફ્રેંચ હવેલી french havelee

chattel *n.* જંગમ મલિકત jangam milakat

chatter *v.i.* અર્થહનિ બોલવું arthhin bolavun

chatterbox *n.* કચકચાટ kachakachaat

chauffeur *n.* ડ્રાઇવર draaivar

chauvinism *n.* લડાયક સ્વદેશાભિમાન ladaayak svadeshaabhimaan

chawl *n.* ચાલી chaalee

cheap *adj.* સસ્તું sastun

cheapen *v.* સસ્તું કરવું sastun karavun

cheat *v.* છેતરવું chhetaravun

check *v.t.* નિયંત્રણમાં રાખવું niyantranaman raakhavun

checkmate *v.t.* હરાવવું haraavavun

cheek *n.* ઉદ્ધત ભાષણ uddhat bhaashan

cheer *n.* ઉત્સાહ utsaaah

cheerful *adj.* આનંદી aanandee

cheery *adj.* આનંદી aanandee

cheese *n.* ચીઝ cheejh

chemical *adj.* રસાયણશાસ્ત્રને લગતું rasaayanashaasrtane lagatun

chemicals *n.* રસાયણો rasaayano

chemist *n.* દવાઓ વેચનાર davaao vechanaar

chemistry *n.* રસાયણશાસ્ત્ર rasaayanashaastra

cheque *n.* ચેક chek

cherish *v.t.* આત્મસાન કરવું aatmasaan karavun

cheroot *n.* ચરૂટ chiroot

cherry *n.* ચેરી cheree

cherub *n.* દેવદૂત devadoot

chess *n.* શેતરંજ shetaranj

chest *n.* છાતી chhaatee

chew *v.t.* ચાવવું chaavavun

chic *adj.* અદ્યતનશૈલીનું adhyatanashaileenun

chick *n.* પક્ષીનું બચ્ચું paksheenun bachchun

chicken *n.* પક્ષીનું બચ્ચું paksheenun bachchun,

chicken-pox *n.* અછબડા achhabada

chide *v.t.* ઠપકો આપવો thapako aapavo

chief *adj.* મુખ્ય mukhya

chiefly *adv.* મુખ્યત્વે mukhyatve

chieftain *n.* ટોળીનો નાયક tolakeeno naayak

child *n.* બાળક baalak

children *n.* બાળકો baalako

childhood *n.* બચપણ bachapan

childish *adj.* બાલિશ baalish

childlike *adj.* નિર્દોષ nirdosh

chill *adj.* ઠંડું કરવું, thandun karavun

chilli *adj.* મરચું marachun

chilly *adj.* ઠંડું thandun

chime *n.* નો મેળ હોવો no mel hovo

chimera *n.* હાઉ haau

chimney *n.* ધુમાડિયું dhumaadiyun

chimpanzee *n.* ચપિાંજી chinpaanjhee

chin *n.* હડપચી hadapachee

china *n.* ચિનાઇ માટી chinaaee maatee

chinese *adj.* ચીની cheenee

chintz *n.* છીંટ chheent

chip *n.* છોડિયાં કાઢવાં chhodiya kaadhavan

chiromancy *n.* સામુદ્રિક વિજ્ઞાન saamudrik vignyaan

chirp *v.t.* ચીંચી કરવું cheencheen karavun

chisel *n.* છીણી chheenee

chit *n.* ચહિૂડી chiththee

chitchat *n.* ટોળટપ્પાં tolatappan

chivalrous *adj.* ધૈર્યયુક્ત સ્ત્રી dhairyayukt stree

chivalry *n.* ધૈર્યયુક્ત સૌરીદાક્ષણ્ય dhairyayuktdaakshiny

chloroform *n.* ક્લોરોફોર્મ kloroform

chocolate *n.* ચૉકલેટ chokalet

choice *n.* પસંદગી pasandagee

choir *n.* ગાયકવૃંદ gaayakavrund

choke *v.t.* ગૂંગળાવવું goongalaavavun

choler *n.* પિત્ત pitta

cholera *n.* કૉલેરા kolera

choleric *adj.* ચીડિયું cheediyun

choose *v.t.* પસંદ કરવું pasand karavun

chop *v.t.* કાપવું kaapavun

choral *adj.* વૃંદ ગાયેલું vrunde gaayelun

chord *n.* વીણાતાર veenaataar

chorister *n.* ગાયકવૃંદનો સભ્ય gaayakavrundno sabhya

chorus *n.* ગાયકવૃંદ gaayakavrund

christ *n.* ઈશુ ખ્રિસ્ત eeshu khrist

christen *v.t.* નામ પાડવું naam paadavun

christian *n.* ખ્રિસ્તી. khristee

christianity *n.* ખ્રિસ્તી ધર્મ khristee dharm

christmas *n.* નાતાલ naataal

chronic *adj.* લાંબી માંદગી laanbee maandagee

chronicle *n.* તવારીખ tavaareekh

chronological *adj.* કાલક્રમાનુસારી kaalakramaanusaaree

chronology *n.* સાલવારી saalavaaree

chronometer *n.* કાળ માપવાનું યંત્ર kaal maapavaanun yantra

chubby *adj.* હૃષ્ટપુષ્ટ hystpust

chuck *n.* મરઘીનો સાદ maragheeno saad

chuckle *n.* મંદહાસ્ય maandahaasy

chum *n.* લંગોટિયો મિત્ર langotiyo mitr

church *n.* ખ્રિસ્તી દેવળ khristee deval

church-yard *n.* દેવળનું ચોગાન devalanun chogaan

churn *v.t.* વલોવવું valovavun

cigar *n.* સિગાર sigaar

cigarette *n.* સિગારેટ sigaaret

cinchona *n.* ક્વિનીનનું ઝાડ kvineennu jhaad

cinema *n.* ચલચિત્રગૃહ chalachitragrah

cinnamon *n.* તજ taj

cipher *n.* અંકચિહ્ન ankachinha

circle *n.* વર્તુળ vartul

circuit *n.* પરિપથ paripath

circular *n.* ગોળાકાર golaakaar

circulate *v.t.* ફેરવવું feravavun

circulation *n.* પરિભ્રમણ paribhraman

circumcise *n.* સુન્નત કરવી sunnat karavee

circumference *n.* પરિધિ parigh

circumlocution *n.* ગોળ ગોળ બોલવું તે gol gol bolavuu te

circumscribe *v.* આંતરી લેવું aantaree levun

circumspect *adj.* સાવધ saavadh

circumspection *n.* સાવચેતી saavachetee

circumstance *n.* સાંપત્તિક સ્થિતિ saanpattik sthiti

circumvent *v.t.* છેતરવું chhetaravun

circus *n.* સરકસ sarkas

cistern *n.* પાણીની ટાંકી paaneenee taankee

citadel *n.* નગર – દુર્ગ nagar - durg

cite *v.t.* રજૂ કરવું rajoo karavun

citizen *n.* નાગરિક naagarik

citizenship *n.* નાગરિકત્વ naagarikatva

citron *n.* સાઈટ્રોન saitron

city *n.* શહેર shaher

civic *adj.* નાગરિકત્વનું naagariktvanun

civics *n.* નાગરિકશાસ્ત્ર naagarikashaastr

civil *adj.* મુલકી mulakee

civilian *n.* બિનલશ્કરી માણસ binalashkaree maanas

civility *n.* વિનય vinay

civilization *n.* સંસ્કૃતિ sanskruti

civilize *v.t.* સંસ્કારી બનાવવું sanskaaree banaavavun

civil war *n.* આંતરવિગ્રહ aantaravigrh

clack *v.t.* બકબક કરવી bakabak karavee

clad *p.p.* વસ્ત્રયુક્ત vastrayukt

claim *v.t.* દાવા daana

claimant *n.* ફરિયાદી fariyaadee

clairvoynce *n.* દીર્ઘદૃષ્ટિ deerghadrashti

clammy *adj.* ચિકણું chinkalun

clamour *n.* ધોંધાટ ghonghaat

clamorous *adj.* ધાંધલિયું dhaandhaliyun

clamp *n.* ચાપડો chaapado

clan *n.* કુળ kul
clansman *n.* કબીલો kabeelo
clang *v.t.* ખણખણવું khankhanvun
clap *v,t,* તાળીઓ પાડવી taaleeo paadavee
claps *n.* તાળીઓ taaleeo
clarification *n.* ખુલાસો khulaaso
clarify *v.t.* સ્પષ્ટતા કરવી spastata karavee
clarion *n.* જાગ્રત કરનાર અવાજ jaagrat karanaar avaaj
clash *v.t.* અથડામણ athadaaman
clasp *v.t.* ભેટવું bhetavun
class *n.* વર્ગ varga
classic *n.* ઉત્તમ uttam
classical *adj.* પ્રાચીન કલાકૃતિ praacheen kalaakruti
classify *v.t.* વર્ગીકરણ કરવું vargeekaran karavun
class-mate *n.* સહાધ્યાયી sahaadhyaayee
clatter *n.* ખણખણાટ khanakhanaat
clause *n.* જોગવાઈ jogavaaee
claw *n.* નહોર nahor
clay *n.* ચીકણી માટી cheenkanee maatee
clean *adj.* સ્વચ્છ svachchh
cleaner *n.* સ્વચ્છ કરનારું svachchh karanaarun
cleaning *n.* સફાઈ safaaee
cleanliness *n.* સ્વચ્છતા svachchhataa
cleanse *v.t.* સ્વચ્છ કરવું svachchh karavun
clear *adj.* સ્પષ્ટ spasht
clearance *n.* વિઘ્નનું નિવારણ vighnanun nivaaran
cleave *v.i.* ચોંટી રહેવું chontee rahevun
cleft *n.* ફાટ faat
clem *v.t.* નરમાશ naramaash
clemency *n.* ક્ષમા kshamaa
clement *adj.* દયાળુ dayaalu
clench *v.t.* મજબૂત પકડવું majaboot pakadavun
clergy *n.* ખ્રિસ્તી ધર્મોપદેશકો khristee dharmopadeshako
clergyman *n.* પાદરી paadaree
clerical *adj.* કારકૂની kaarkoonee
clerk *n* કારકુન kaarakun

clever *adj.* હોશિયાર honshiyaar
cleverness *n.* હોશિયારી honshiyaaree
clew *n.* દોરાનો દડો doraano dado
click *v.t.* ટકટક અવાજ કરવો takatak avaaj karavo
client *n.* ઘરાક gharaak
clientele *n.* ઘરાકો gharaako
cliff *n.* ઊભો ખડક oobhaa khadak
climate *n.* આબોહવા aabohava
climatic *adj.* આબોહવાઈ aabohavaaee
climax *n.* પરાકાષ્ઠા paraakaastha
climb *v.t.* ઉપર ચડવું upar chadavun
cling *v.t.* વળગી રહેવું valagee rahevun
clinic *n.* દવાખાનું davaakhaanun
clink *v.t.* ઘંટનો અવાજ કરવો ghantano avaaj karavo
clip *v.i.* મજબૂત પકડવું majaboot pakadavun
clipper *n.* ઝડપી વહાણ jhadapee vahaan
clipping *n.* કાપલી kaapalee
clique *n.* નાની ટોળી naanee tolee
cloak *n.* આચ્છાદન aachchhaadan
clock *n.* ઘડિયાળ ghadiyaal
clockwise *adj.* દક્ષિણાવર્ત dakshinaavart
clod *n.* માટીનું ઢેફું maateenun thefun
clog *n.* નડતર nadatar
cloister *n.* સાધુઓનો મઠ saadhuono math
close *v.t.* બંધ કરવું bandh karavun
closet *n.* કબાટ kabaat
closure *n.* સમાપ્તી samaaptee
clot *v.t.* ગંઠાઈ જવું ganthaaee javun
cloth *n.* કાપડ kaapad
clothe *v.t.* વસ્ત્ર પહેરવાં vastra paheravan
clothes *n.* કપડાં kapadan
cloud *n.* વાદળું vaadalun
cloudy *adj.* વાદળાંથી છવાયેલું vaadalaanthee chhavaayelun
clove *n.* લવિંગ laving
clown *n.* વિદૂષક vidooshak
cloy *v.t.* ઉબાવી નાખવું ubaavee naakhavun
club *n.* મંડળી mandalee

clue *n.* ચાવીરૂપ શબ્દો chaaveeroop shabdo

clumsy *n.* બેડોળ bedol

cluster *n.* ઝૂમખું jhumakhun

clutch *v.t.* આતુરતાથી પકડવું aaturataathee pakadavun

coach *n.* દરબારી ગાડી darabaaree gaadee

coachman *n.* ઘોડાગાડી હાંકનારો ghodaagaadee haankanaaro

coagulate *v.i.* થીજવું theejavun

coal *n.* કોલસો kaolaso

coalesce *v.i.* સંયુક્ત બનવું sanyukt banavun

coalition *n.* જોડાણ jodaan

coal-mine *n.* કોલસાની ખાણ kolasaanee khaan

coal-tar *n.* ડામર daamar

coarse *n.* બરછટ barachhat

coarsen *v.t.* અસભ્ય બનવું asabhya banavun

coast *n.* દરિયાકાંઠો dariyaakaantho

coat *n.* કોટ kot

coating *n.* રંગનો થર rangno thar

coaxal *adj.* સમાન ધરીવાળું samaan dhareevaalun

cobble *v.t.* ગોળ કાંકરી gol kaankaree

cobbler *n.* મોચી mochee

cobra *n.* એક જાતનો સાપ ek jaatano saap

cobweb *n.* કરોળિયાની જાળ karoliyaanee jaal

cocaine *n.* કોકેઇન kokain

cock *n.* કૂકડો kookado

cockade *n.* ફૂમતું foomatun

cockatoo *n.* કાકાકૌવા kaakaakauva

cockle *n.* કોકલ kokal

cockroach *n.* વંદો vando

cockscomb *n.* કૂકડાની કલગી kookadaanee kalagee

cock-sure *adj.* સર્વથા ચોક્કસ sarvatha chokkas

cocoa *n.* કોકોની ભૂકી kokonee bhookee

coconut *n.* નાળિયેર naaliyer

cocoon *n.* કોશેટો kosheto

cod *n.* કોડ માછલી kod maachhalee

coddle *v.t.* પંપાળવું panpaalavun

code *n.* કાયદાની સંહિતા kaayadaanee sanhita

codify *v.t.* સંહિતા બનાવવી sanhita banaavavee

co-education *n.* સહશિક્ષણ sahashikshan

coequal *adj.* બરોબરિયું barobariyun

coerce *v.t.* જબરદસ્તી કરવી jabaradastee karavee

coercion *n.* જબરદસ્તી jabaradastee

coercive *adj.* જબરદસ્તીપૂર્વક jabaradasteepoorvak

coeval *adj.* સમકાલીન samakaaleen

coexist *v.t.* સહઅસ્તિત્વ ધરાવવું sahaastitv dharaavavun

coffee *n.* કોફી kofee

coffer *n.* તિજોરી tijoree

coffin *n.* મડદાપેટી madadaapetee

cog *v.t.* દાંતા પાડવા daantaa paadavaa

cogent *adj.* સચોટ sachot

cogitate *v.t.* ચિંતન કરવું chintan karavun

cogitation *n.* મનમાં ઘોળવું તે manaman ghaolavun te

cognate *n.* સગોત્ર sagotr

cognition *n.* અનુભૂતિ anubhooti

cognizable *adj.* સગ્યાન sagyaan

cognizance *n.* સચેતના sachetana

cognizant *adj.* માહિતગાર maahitagaar

cognomen *n.* ઉપનામ upanaamm

cohabit *v.t.* સહનિવાસ કરવાં sahanivaas karavan

coheir *n.* સહવારસ sahavaaras

cohere *v.t.* સાથે ચોટી જવું saathe chotee javun

coherence *n.* સાથે ચોટી રહેવું saathe chotee rahevun

coherent *adj.* સાથે ચોટી રહેલું saathe chotee rahelun

cohesion *n.* સાથે વળગી રહેવું તે saathe valagee rahevun te

cohesive *adj.* સંયોગી sanyogee

coil *v.* તારનું ગૂંચળું taaranun goonchalun

coin *n.* સિક્કો sikko

coinage *n.* નાણાં - સિક્કા પાડવા તે naanun - sikka paadava te

coincide *v.i.* એકી વખતે થવું ekee vakhate thavun

coincidence *n.* સંયોગ sanyog

coincident *adj.* યોગાનુયોગ yogaanuyog

coir *n.* કાથી kaathee

coitus *n.* મૈથુન maithun

coke *n.* કોલસો kalaso

colander *n.* ગળણી galanee

cold *adj.* ઠંડું thandun

coldblooded *adj.* નિર્દયતાપૂર્વકનું nirdayataapoorvakavun

coldly *adv.* ભાવશૂન્ય રીતે bhaavashoony reete

colic *n.* પેટશૂળ petashool

collaborate *v.i.* સાથે કામ કરવું saathe kaam karavun

collapse *v.t.* પડી ભાંગવું તે padee baangavun te

collar *n.* ગળાપટ્ટી galaapattee

collarbone *n.* હાંસડી haansadee

collate *v.t.* વ્યવસ્થિત મૂકવું vyavasthit mookavun

collateral *adj.* સગોત્ર sagotra

colleague *n.* સહકાર્યકર sahakaaryakar

collect *v.t.* સંગ્રહ કરવો sangrah karavo

collection *n.* સંગ્રહ sangrah

collective *adj.* સામૂહિક saamoohik

collector *n.* ભેગું કરનારો bhegun karanaaro

college *n.* મહાવિદ્યાલય mahaavidhaala

collegian *n.* કૉલેજનો વિદ્યાર્થી kaolejano vidhyaarthee

collegiate *n.* મહાવિદ્યાલયને લગતું mahaavidhyaalayane lagatun

collide *v.t.* સામસામા અથડાવું saamasaama athadaavun

colliery *n.* કોલસાની ખાણ kolasaanee khaan

collision *n.* જોરદાર અથડામણ joradaar athadaaman

collocate *v.t.* નજીક મૂકવું najeek mukavun

collude *v.t.* કપટજાળ રચવી kapatjaal rachavee

collusion *n.* કપટજાળ kapatjaal

collyrium *n.* કાજળ kaajal

cologne *n.* સુગંધી પ્રવાહી sugandhee pravaahee

colon *n.* બૃહદ અંતર bruhadantra

colonial *adj.* વસાહતી vsaahatee

colonist *n.* વસાહતમાં વસનાર vasaahataman vasanaar

colonize *v.* વસાહત સ્થાપવી vasaahat sthaapavee

colony *n.* વસાહત vasaahat

colossal *adj.* પ્રચંડ prachanda

colossus *n.* વિશાળકાય vishaalakaay

colour *n.* રંગ rang

colt વછેરો vachhero

column *n.* સ્તંભ stanbh

coma *n.* મૂર્છા moorchha

comb *v.t.* કાંસકી kaansakee

combat *n.* લડાઈ ladaaee

combatant *n.* લડનાર ladanaar

come *n.* આવવું aavavun

combination *n.* સંયોગ sanyog

combine *n.* એક કરવું ek karavun

combustible *adj.* બળવાની ક્ષમતાવાળું balavaanee kshamataavaalun

combustion *n.* જ્વલન jvalan

come *v.i.* આવવું aavavun

comedian *n.* હસાવનાર વ્યક્તિ hasaavanaar vyakti

comedy *v.* પ્રહસન prahasan

comely *adj.* દેખાવડું dekhaavadun

comet *n.* ધૂમકેતુ dhoomaketu

comfort *n.* આરામ aaraam

comfortable *adj.* સુખદાયક sukhadaayak

comic *n.* મનોરંજન કરનારું manoranjan karanaarun

comity *n.* સૌજન્ય saujany

comma *n.* અલ્પવિરામ (,) alpaviraam (,)

command *n.* કાબૂ

commandant *n.* લશ્કરનો ઉપરી – સરદાર kaaboo

commander *n.* સેનાપતિ senaapati

commanding *adj.* વર્ચસ્વવાળું varchasvavaalun

commandment *n.* દૈવી આદેશ daivee aadesh

commemorate *v.t.* સ્મારક બનાવવું smaarak banaavavun

commemoration *v.t.* જાહેર સમરણોત્સવ jaaher smaranotsav

commencement *n.* શરૂ કરવું sharoo karavun

commend *v.t.* સોંપવું sonpavun

commendation *n.* સ્તુતિ stuti

commensurable *adj.* સમપરિમાણ samaparimaan

commensurate *n.* સમપ્રમાણ samapramaan

comment *n.* ટિપ્પણી tippanee

commentary *n.* ભાષ્ય bhaashya

commentator *n.* ટીકા કરવી teekaa karavee

commerce *n.* વાણિજ્યિક vaanijyik

commercial *adj.* આર્થિક લાભ માટે કરેલું aarthik laabh maate karelun

commination *n.* દૈવીસજા daiveesajaa

commingle *v.t.* ભેળવવું bhelavavun

commissariat *n.* ખોરાકનો પુરવઠો khoraakano puravatho

commission *n.* આયોગ aayog

commissioner *n.* પંચનો સભ્ય panchano sabhy

commit *v.t.* સોંપવું sonpavunn

commitment *n.* પ્રતિબદ્ધતા. pratibadhdhata

committal *n.* પ્રતિબદ્ધ. pratibadhdh

committee *n.* સમિતિ samiti

commodious *adj.* મોકળાશવાળું mokalaashvaalun

commodity *n.* ઉપયોગી વસ્તુ upayogee vastu

commodore *n.* કોમોડોર komodor

common *adj.* સામાન્ય saamaany

commoner *n.* સામાન્ય માણસ saamaanya maanas

commonplace *n.* વિશિષ્ટતા વિનાનું visheshata vinaanun

commonwealth *n.* રાષ્ટ્રસમૂહ raastrasamooh

commotion *n.* ખળભળાટ khalabhalaat

communicate *v.* સંપર્ક કરવો. sanpark karavo

communication *n.* પત્રવ્યવહાર, patravahevaar

communicative *adj.* મોકળા મનનું mokala mananun

communion *n.* પ્રભુભોજન prabhubhojan

communique *n.* સરકારી પત્રક sarakaaree patrak

communism *n.* સામ્યવાદ saamyavaad

communist *n.* સામ્યવાદી saamyavaadee

community *n.* સામુદાયિક saamudaayik

commute *v.* નિયમિત આવજા niyamit aavjaa

compact *n.* કરાર karaar

companion *n.* સાથી saathee

companionship *n.* સોબત sobat

company *n.* સોબત sobat

comparative *n.* તુલના tulanaa

compare *v.t.* તુલના કરવી tulana karavee

comparison *n.* સરખામણી sarakhaamaneenee

compartment *n.* ખંડ khand

compass *v.t.* હોકાયંત્ર hokaayantra

compassion *n.* કરુણા karunaa

compassionate *n.* દયાળુ dayaalu

compatible *adj.* સુસંગત susangat

compatriot *n.* દેશબંધુ deshabandhu

compeer *n.* બરોબરિયો barobariyo

compel *v.* ફરજ પાડવી faraj paadavee

compendious *adj.* સંક્ષિપ્ત sankshipt

compendium *n.* સંક્ષેપ sankshep

compensate *v.t.* વળતર આપવું valatar aapavun

compensation *n.* વળતર valatar

compete *v.i.* હરીફાઈ કરવી hareefaaee karavee

competence *n.* ક્ષમતા kshamataa

competent *adj.* પૂરતી લાયકાત pooratee laayakaat

competition *n.* હરીફાઈ hareefaaee

competitive *adj.* સ્પર્ધાત્મક spardhaatmak

competitor *n.* હરીફ hareef

compile *v.t.* સંગ્રહ કરવું sangrh karavun

compilation *n.* સંકલિત ગ્રંથ sankalit granth

compiler *n.* સંકલનકર્તા sankalanakarta

complacencency *n.* આત્મસંતોષ aatmasantosh

complacent *adj.* આત્મસંતુષ્ટ aatmasantushta

complain *v.t.* ફરિયાદ કરવી fariyaad karavee

complaint *n.* ફરિયાદ fariyaad

complaisance *n.* પરગજુ paragaj

complement *n.* પૂરણ pooran

complementary *adj.* પુરવણી કરનારુ pooravanee karanaarun

complete *v.t.* સંપૂર્ણ sanpoorn

completion *n.* સંપૂર્ણતા sanpoornataa

complex *adj.* જટિલ jateel

complexion *n.* અંગકાંતિ angakaanti

complexity *n.* આંટીઘૂંટી aanteeghoontee

compliance *n.* કબૂલ કરવું kabool karavun

complaint *adj.* ફરિયાદ fariyaad

complicate *v.t.* જટિલ બનાવવું jatil banaavavun

compliment *n.* અભિનંદન abhinandan

complimentary *n.* અભિનંદનાત્મક abhinandanaatmak

comply *v.t.* અનુસરવું anusaaravun

component *n.* ઘટક ghatak

comport *v.i.* અનુરૂપ હોવું anuroop havun

compose *v.t.* રચવું rachavun

composite *adj.* મિશ્ર mishra

composition *n.* મિશ્રણ mishran

compositor *n.* બીબાં ગોઠવનાર beeban gothavanaar

composure *n.* સ્વસ્થચિત્તતા svasthachittata

compound *v.t.* તડજોડ કરવી tadajod karavee

compounder *n.* કમ્પાઉન્ડર kampaaoondar

comprehend *v.t.* સમજવું samajavun

comprehensible *adj.* બુદ્ધિગ્રાહ્ય buddhigraahya

comprehension *n.* સમાવેશ samaavesh

comprehensive *adj.* વ્યાપક vyaapak

compress *v.t.* દાબવું daabavun

compressible *adj.* દબાવી શકાય તેવું dabaavee shakaay tevun

comprise *v.t.* –નું બનેલું હોવું nun banelun hovun

compromise *v.t.* તડજોડ કરવી tadajod karavee

comptroller *n.* નિયંત્રક niyantrak

controller નિયંત્રણ કરનાર niyantran karanaar

compulsion *n.* જબરદસ્તી jabaradastee

compulsory *adj.* ફરજિયાત farajiyaat

compunction *n.* દગદગો dagadago

compute *v.* ગણવું ganavun

computation *n.* ગણતરી ganataree

comrade *n.* સોબતી sobatee

comradership *n.* મિત્રતા mitrataa

con *v.i.* છેતરવું chhetaravun

concatenation *n.* જોડેલી સાંકળ jodelee saankal

concave *adj.* અન્તર્ગોલ antargol

conceal *v.t.* છુપાવવું chhupaavavun

concealment *n.* ગુપ્તતા guptataa

concede *v.t.* માન્ય કરવું maanya karavun

conceit *n.* ઉત્પ્રેક્ષા utprekshaa

conceited *adj.* અહંકારી ahankaaree

conceivable *adj.* કલ્પનીય kalpaneeya

conceive *v.t.* ગર્ભ ધારણ કરવો garbh dhaaran karavo

concentrate *v.* એકાગ્ર કરવું ekaagra karavun

concentration *n.* એકાગ્રતા ekaagrataa

concentric *adj.* એકકેન્દ્રી ekakendree

concept *n.* વિભાવના vibhaavana

conception *n.* ગર્ભધારણા garbhdhaarana

concern *v.t.* પ્રસ્તુત હોવું prastut hovun

concerning *prep.* –ને વિશે ne vishe

concert *n.* એકમત ekamat

concession *n.* સવલત savalat

conch *n.* શંખ shankh

conciliate *v.t.* પ્રસન્ન કરવું prasann karavun

conciliation સુલેહ suleh

concilliatory સમાધાન કરાવનારું samaadhaan karaavavun

concise *adj.* ટૂંકું toonkun

conclude *v.t.* સમાપન કરવું samaapan karavun

conclusion *n.* સારાંશ saaraansh

concoct *v.t.* ઉપજાવી કાઢવું upajaavee kaadhavun

concomitant *adj.* સહવર્તી sahavartee

concord *n.* સુમેળ sumel

concordance *n.* ઐક્ય aikya

concourse *n.* ભીડ bheed

concrete *adj.* વાસ્તવિક vaastavik

concubine *n.* રખાત rakhaat

concur *v.i.* એકમત થવું ekamat thavun

concurrence *n.* મતૈક્ય mataiky

concurrent *adj.* સહમત sahamat

condemn *v.t.* વખોડવું vakhodavun

condense *v.t.* ઘટ્ટ બનાવવું ghatt banaavavun

condescend અનુગ્રહ કરવો anugrh karavo

condign *adj.* યથાયોગ્ય yathaayogy

condiment *n.* મીઠું મસાલો meethun masaalo

condition *n.* શરત sharat

conditional *adj.* શરત બતાવનારું sharat bataavanaarun

condole *v.* સહાનુભૂતિ દાખવવી sahaanubhooti daakhavavee

condolence *n.* દિલાસો આપવો તે dilaaso aapavo te

condone *v.t.* દરગુજર કરવું daragujar karavun

conduce *v.t.* સહાય કરવી sahaay karavee

conducive *adj.* ઉપયોગી upayogee

conduct *v.t.* વર્તન vartan

conduction *n.* વીજળીનું વહન veejaleenun vahan

conductor *n.* વૃંદવાદન vrundavaadan

cone *n.* શંકુ shanku

confabulate *v.t.* ગપ્પાં મારવાં gappan maaravn

confection *n.* મીઠાઈ meethaaee

confederacy *n.* સંઘ sangh

confederate *adj.* જોડાયેલું jodaayelun

confederation સંઘ sangh

confer *v.t.* આપવું aapavun

conference *n.* પરિષદ parishad

confess *v.t.* કબૂલ કરવું kabool karavun

confession *n.* કબૂલાત kaboolaat

confidant *n.* વિશ્વાસપૂર્ણ vishvaasapoorn

confide *v.t.* ને સોંપણ કરવી ne sonpan karavee

confidence *n.* દૃઢ વિશ્વાસ dradh vishvaas

confident *adj.* આત્મવિશ્વાસવાળું aatmavishvaasavaalun

confidential *adj.* ખાનગી રાખવા જેવું khaanagee raakhavaa jevun

configuration *n.* રૂપરેખા rooprekhaa

confine *v.t.* મર્યાદામાં રાખવું maryaadaaman raakhavun

confinement *n.* અટકાયત atakaayat

confirm પુષ્ટિ આપવી pushti aapavi

confirmation *n.* પુષ્ટિ pushti

confiscate *v.t.* જપત કરવું japat karavun

confiscation *n.* જપત કરવું તે japat karavun te

conflagration *n.* દાવાનળ daavaanal

conflict *v.t.* લડત ladat

confluent *adj.* પ્રવાહક pravaahak

confluence *n.* સંગમ પામવો તે sangam paamavo te

conform *v.t.* રૂઢિનું પાલન કરવું roodhinun paalan karavun

confound *v.t.* ઉથલાવી દેવું uthalaavee devun

confront સામનો કરવો saamano karavo

confuse *v.t.* ગૂંચવી નાખવું goonchavee naakhavun

confusion *n.* ગૂંચવાડો goonchavaado

confute *v.t.* ખંડન કરવું khandan karavun

congeal *v.t.* થીજવું theejavun

congener *n.* સજાતીય sajaateey

congenial *adj.* સહાનુભૂતિશીલ sahaanubhootisheel

congenital *adj.* જન્મજાત janmajaat

congest *v.t.* ભરાવો કરવો bharaavo karavo

congestion ભરાવો bharaavo

congratulate *v.t.* અભિનંદન આપવા abhinandan aapava

congratulation અભિનંદન abhinandan

congregate *v.t.* ભેગુ થવુ bhegu thavun

congregation *n.* સભા sabhaa

congress પરિષદ parishad

congruence *n.* એકરાગ સુમેળ ekaraag, sumel

congruent સુસંગત susangat

conical શંકુના આકારનું shankuna aakaaranun

coniferous *adj.* શંકુઆકારના ફળવાળું shankuaakaarana falavaalun

conjecture *n.* અટકળ કરવી atakal karavee

conjoin *v.t.* જોડવું jodavun

conjugal *adj.* વૈવાહિક vaivaahik

conjugate *v.t.* ક્રિયાપદનાં કાળ kriyaapadanan kaal

conjunct *adj.* સંયુક્ત sanyukt

conjuction *n.* ઉભયાન્વયી અવ્યય ubhaavyavee avayav

conjure *v.t.* આજીજી કરવી aajeejee karavee

conjurer *n.* જાદુગર jaadugar

conk *n.* નાક naak

connate *adj.* સહજાત sahajaat

connect *v.t.* જોડવું jodavun

connection *n.* જોડાણ jodaan

connivance *n.* ચશ્મપોશી chashmaposhee

connive *v.t.* ચશ્મપોશી કરવી chashmaposhee karavee

connoisseur *n.* મર્મજ્ઞ marmagnya

connote *v.t.* અભિપ્રેત હોવું abhipret hovun

connubial *adj.* વૈવાહિક vaivaahik

conquer *v.t.* વિજયી થવું vijayee thavun

conquest *n.* જીત jeeta

conscience *n.* અંતરાત્માનો અવાજ. antaraatmaano avaaj

conscientious *n.* શુદ્ધ દાનતનું shuddh daanatanun

conscious *adj.* સચેત sachet

conscript *adj.* ફરજિયાત ભરતી કરેલું farajiyaat bharatee karaayelu

conscription *n.* ફરજિયાત ભરતી farajiyaat bharatee

consecrate *v.t.* પવિત્ર બનાવવું pavitra banaavavun

consecration *n.* સમર્પણ samarpan

consecutive *adj.* અનુક્રમિક anukramik

consent *v.i.* સંમત થવું, અનુમતિ sanmat thavun, anumati

consequent *adj.* નીપજેલું nipajelun

conservation *n.* સાચવણી saachavanee

conservative *adj.* રૂઢિચુસ્ત roodhichust

conserve *v.t.* સાચવવું saachavavun

consider *adj.* માન્યતા maanyataa

considerable *adj.* વિચારણીય vichaaraneeya

considerate *adj.* વિવેકબુદ્ધિવાળું vivekbudhivaalun

consideration *n.* વિચાર કરવા જેવી બાબત vichaar karava jevee baabat

consign *v.t.* સોંપવું sonpavun

consignee *n.* માલ લેનાર maal lenaar

consignment *n.* રવાના કરેલો માલ ravaana karelo maal

consist *v.t.* નું બનેલું હોવું nu banelun hovun

consistent *adj.* સુસંગત susangat

consistence *n.* સાતત્ય saatatya

consolation *n.* આશ્વાસન aashvaasan

console *v.t.* દિલાસો આપવો dilaaso aapavo

consolidate *v.t.* એક કરવું ne ek karavun

consols *n.pl.* સરકારી જામીનગીરીઓ sarakaaree jaameenageereeo

consonance *n.* એકરાગ ekaraag

consonant *adj.* વ્યંજન vyanjan

consort *n.* સહચર sahachar

conspicuous તરત નજરે પડતું tarataj najare padatun

conspiracy *n.* કાવતરું kaavatarun

conspire *v.t.* કાવતરું કરવું kaavatarun karavun

constable *n.* પોલીસનો સિપાઈ polisano sipaaee

constancy *n.* નિષ્ઠા nishthaa

constant અચળ achal

constellation *n.* નક્ષત્ર nakshatr

constipate *v.t.* કબજિયાત થવી kabajiyaat thavee

constipation *n.* કબજિયાત kabajiyaat

constituency *n.* મતવિસ્તાર matvistaar

constituent *adj.* ઘટક ghatak

constitute *v.t.* સ્થાપન કરવું sthaapan karavun

constitution *n.* રાજ્યબંધારણ raajyabandhaaran

constrain *v.t.* અવરોધ કરવો avarodh karavo

constraint *n.* અવરોધ avarodh

construct *v.t.* નિર્માણ કરવું nirmaan karavun

construction *n.* બાંધકામ baandhakaam

constructive *adj.* રચનાત્મક rachanaatmak

construe *v.* ભાષાંતર કરવું bhaashaantar karavun

consul *n.* મુખ્ય એલચી mukhy elachee

consulate *n.* વાણિજ્ય-દૂતાવાસ vaanijya dootaavaas

consult *v.t.* મસલત કરવી masalat karavee

consultation *n.* સલાહમસલત salaahamasalat

consume *v.t.* વાપરી નાખવું vaaparee naakhavun

consumer *n.* ઉપભોક્તા upabhokta

consummate *v.t.* પરિપૂર્ણ કરવું paripoorn karavun

consumption *n.* વપરાશ vaparaash

contact *n.* સંપર્ક sanpark

contagious *adj.* ચેપી chepee

contagion *n.* ચેપી રોગ chepee rog

contain *v.t.* માં અંદર હોવું maan andara hovun

contaminate *v.t.* દૂષિત કરવું dooshit karavun

contemplate *v.t.* મનમાં વિચારવું manamaan vichaaravun

contemporary *adj.* સમકાલીન samakaaleen

contempt *n.* અનાદર anaadar

contemptible *adj.* તિરસ્કારપાત્ર tiraskaarapaatra

contemptuous *adj.* નિંદાત્મક nindaatmak

contend *v.t.* દલીલ કરવી daleel karavee

content *n.* વિષય vishay

contention *n.* તકરારનો વિષય takaraarano vishay

contentment *n.* સમાધાન કરવું samaadhaan karavun

contest *n.* સ્પર્ધા spardhaa

context *n.* સંદર્ભ sandarbh

contiguity *n.* અડકતું adakatun

continence *n.* આત્મસંયમ aatmasanyam

confinent *n.* અટકાયત aatakaayat

continue *v.t.* ચાલુ રાખવું chaalu raakhavun

continuation *n.* ફરી ચાલુ થવું તે faree chaalu thavun

confort *v.t.* નિયમોનું પાલન કરવું niyamo nu paalan karavun

contour *n.* રૂપરેખા rooparekha

contra *prep.* વિરુદ્ધ viruddh

contraband *adj.* પરતબિંધતિ. pratibandhit

contraceptive *adj* ગર્ભનિરોધક garbhanirodhak

contract *n.* કરાર karaar

contraction *n.* સંક્ષિપ્ત રૂપ sankshipt roop

contradict થી વિસંગત હોવું thee visangat hovun

contradiction *n.* વિરોધાભાસ virodhaabhaas

contrary *v.t.* વિપરીત vipareet

contravene *v.t.* વિસંગત હોવું visangat hovun

contravention *n.* ઉલ્લંઘન ullanghan

contribute *v.t.* ફાળો આપવો faalo aapavo

contributor *n.* ફાળો આપનાર faalo aapanaar

contribution *n.* પ્રદાન. pradaan

contrite *adj.* પશ્ચાતાપી paschaataapee

contrition *n.* પશ્ચાયાત્તાપ pashchaayaattap

contrivance *n.* કુનેહથી ચલાવવું kunehathee chaalavun

contrive *v.t.* યોજવું yojavun

control *n.* નિયંત્રણ niyantran

controller *n.* નિયંત્રણ કરનાર niyantran karanaar

controversy *n.* વાદવિવાદ vaadavivaad
convalesce *v.t.* સાજા થવું saajaa thavun
convalescence *n.* સ્વાસ્થ્ય સુધારો svaastya sudhaaro
convection *n.* ઉષ્ણતાનયન ushnataanayan
convene *v.t.* આહવાન કરવું. aahavaan karavun
convener *n.* સંયોજક sanyojak
convenience *n.* અનુકૂળતા anukoolataa
convenient *adj.* સુલભ sulabh
convent *n.* સંન્યાસી મંડળ sanyaasee mandal
convention *n.* સભા sabhaa
converge *v.t.* કેન્દ્રગામી kendragaamee
convergent *adj.* નશ્ચિત બનિદ્ગામી nishchit bindugaamee
conversant *adj.* સારી રીતે પરિચિત saaree reete parichit
conversation *n.* વાર્તાલાપ vaartaalaap
converse *v.i.* વાતચીત કરવી vaatacheet karavee
conversion *n.* પરિવર્તન parivartan
convert *v.t.* ફેરવવું feravavun
convertible *adj.* પરિવર્તનક્ષમ parivartanaksham
convex *adj.* બહિગોળ bahigol
convey *v.t.* અભિવ્યક્ત કરવું abhivyakt karavun
conveyance *n.* તબદીલી tabadeelee
convict *v.t.* ગુનેગાર જાહેર કરવું gunegaar jaaher karavun
conviction *n.* ચુકાદો chukaado
convince *v.t.* —ને ખાતરી કરાવવી ne khaataree karaavavee
convocation *n.* પદવીદાન સમારંભ padaveedaan samaaranbh
convoke *v.t.* સભા બોલાવવી sabhaa bolaavavee
convoy *v.t.* રખવાળું કરવું rakhavaalun karavun
convulsion *n.* અટ્ટહાસ્ય attahaasya
coo *n.* હળવો ગણગણ અવાજ halavo ganagan avaaj
cook *n.* રસોઇયો rasoeeo
cooker *n.* કૂકર kookar
cookery *n.* રાંધણકળા raandhanakala

cool *adj.* શીતલ sheetal
coolie *n.* કૂલી koolee
coop *n.* મરઘાંનું પાંજરું maraghaannun paanjarun
cooper *n.* લાકડાનાં પીપ laakadaanan peep
co-operate *v.t.* સહકાર આપવો sahakaar aapavo
co-operation *n.* સહકાર sahakaar
co-opt *v.t.* સહવરણી કરવી sahavarani karavee
co-ordinate *v.t.* સહનર્દિશન sahanirdeshan
copartner *n.* ભાગીદાર bhaageedaar
cope *v.i.* —ને ડગલો પહેરાવવો ne dagalo paheraavavo
coping *n.* પાળી paalee
copious *adj.* વિપુલ vipul
copper *n.* પોલીસનો સિપાઇ poleesano sipaaee
coppice *n.* ઝાડી jhaadee
copula *n.* ક્રિયાપદનું રૂપ kriyaapadanun roop
copy *v.* અનુકરણ કરવું anukaran karavun
copyist *n.* અનુકરણ કરનાર anukaran karanaar
copyright *n.* કૉપીરાઇટ kopiraait
coquet *v.i.* નખરાબાજી nakharaabaajee
coquetry *n.* નખરાબાજી nakharaabaajee
coquette *n.* નખરેલ nakharel
coral *n.* પરવાળું paravaalun
cord *n.* પાતળું દોરડું paatalun doradun
cordate *adj.* હૃદયાકાર rhadayaakaar
cordial *adj.* મૈત્રીભર્યું maitreebharyun
cordon *n.* પોલીસોનો ઘેરો polisono ghero
core *n.* ગર્ભ garbh
cork *n.* બૂચના ઝાડ boochanaa jhaad
corn *n.* અનાજના દાણા anaajana daana
corner *n.* ખૂણો khoono
cornet *n.* કરનાઈ karanaaee
corollary *n.* અનુપંગી anushangee
corona *n.* તેજોવલય tejovalay
coronation *n.* રાજ્યાભિષેકની વિધિ raajyaabhishekanee vidhi

coroner *n.* અપમૃત્યુ-પરીક્ષક apmrutyu pareekshak

coronet *n.* નાનો મુગટ naano mugat

corporal *adj.* કોર્પોરલ korporal

corporate *adj.* કંપની kanpanee

corporation *n.* નિગમ nigam

corporeal *adj.* શરીરી shareeree

corps *n.pl.* લશ્કરી ટુકડી lashkaree tukadee

corpse *n.* લાશ laash

corpus *n.* મૃતદેહ mrutdeh

correct *v.t.* સુધારવું sudhaaravun

correction *n.* સુધારો sudhaaro

correlative *adj.* નિત્યસંબંધી nityasanbandhee

correspond *v.i.* પત્ર વ્યવહાર patra vyavhaar

correspondence *n.* પત્રવહેવાર patravahevaar

correspondent *n.* છાપાનો ખબરપત્રી chhaapaano khabarapatree

corridor *n.* રસ્તાવાળી પરસાળ rastaavaalee parasaal

corrigendum *n.* શુદ્ધિપત્ર shuddhipatr

corrigible *adj.* સુધારી શકાય એવું sudhaaree shakaay evun

corroborate *v.t.* સમર્થિત કરવું samarthit karavun

corroboration *n.* પુષ્ટિ pushti

corrode *v.t.* ખવાઈ જવું khavaaee javun

corrosion *n.* કાટ kaat

corrugate *v.t.* વાટા પાડવા vaata paadava

corrupt *adj.* લાંચિયું laanchiyun

corruption *n.* ભ્રષ્ટાચાર bhrashtaachaar

cosine *n.* કોટિજ્યા kotijya

cosmetic *n.* સૌંદર્યવર્ધક saundaryavardhak

cosmic *adj.* વૈશ્વીક vaishveek

cosmopolitan *n.* વિશ્વનાગરિક vishvanaagarik

cosmos *n.* બ્રહ્માંડ brahmaand

cost *n.* ખર્ચ kharch

costly *adj.* મોંઘું monghun

costume *n.* પહેરવેશ pahervesh

cosy *adj.* હૂંફાળું hoonfaalun

cot *n.* છાપરી chhaaparee

cote *n.* કોઢ kodh

coterie *n.* સામાજિક ટોળકી saamaajik tolakee

cottage *n.* નાનકડું ઘર naanakadun ghaar

cotton *n.* કપાસ kapaas

couch *n.* બાંકડો baankado

cough *n.* ઉધરસ udharas

council *n.* સ્થાનિક સ્વરાજસંસ્થા sthaanik svaraajasanstha

councillor *n.* પરિષદ - સભ્ય parishad sabhya

counsel *n.* વકીલ vakeel

counsellor *n.* સલાહ આપનાર salaah aapanaar

count *v.t.* ગણતરી કરવી ganataree karavee

countenance *n.* ચહેરા પરના ભાવ chaheraa parnaa bhaav

counter *n.* ટેબલ tebal

counteract *v.t.* પ્રતિક્રિયા આપવી pratikriya aapavee

counterfeit *v.t.* બનાવટી કરવું banaavatee karavun

counterfoil પહોંચ pahonch

countermand *n.* રદ કરવું rad karavun

counterpane *n.* ચાદર chaadar

countersign *v.t.* સામી સહી કરવી saamee sahee karavee

countless *adj.* અસંખ્ય asankhy

country *n.* દેશ desh

county પરગણો paragano

coup *n.* સફળ ચાલ safal chaal

couple *n.* સ્ત્રી અને પુરુષની જોડી stree ane purushanee jodee

couplet *n.* કાવ્યકણિકા kaavyakanika

coupon *n.* ચિઠ્ઠી chiththee

courage *n.* હિંમત hinmat

courageous *adj.* હિંમતવાન hinmatavaan

courier *n.* ખેપિયો khepiyo

course *n.* ગમનની દિશા gamananee disha

courser *n.* વેગીલો ઘોડો vegeelo ghodo

court *n.* ન્યાયમંદિર nyaayamandir

courteous *n.* વિનયી vinayee

courtesan *n.* ગણિકા ganika
courtesy *n.* સૌજન્ય saujany
courtier *n.* દરબારી darabaaree
courtmartial *n.* લશ્કરી અદાલત lashkaree adaalat
courtyard *n.* ખુલ્લો ચોક khullo chok
cousin *n.* પિતરાઈ pitaraaee
cove *n.* નાનો અખાત naano akhaat
covenant *n.* કરાર karaar
cover *n.* ઢાંકણું dhaankanun
covering *n.* આવરણ aavaran,
coverlet *n.* ચાદર chaadar
covert *n.* ગુપ્ત gupt
coverture *n.* સંશ્રય sanshraya
covet *v.t.* ઉત્કંઠા ધરાવવી utkanthaa dharaavavee
covetous *adj.* લોભી lobhee
cow *n.* ગાય gaay
coward *n.* બીકણ beekan
cowardice *n.* બીક beek
cowardly *adj.* ડરપોક darapok
coxcomb *n.* વરણાગિયો માણસ varanaagiyo maanas
coy *adj.* શરમાળ sharamaal
cozen *v.t.* છેતરવું chhetaravun
crab *n.* કરચલો karachalo
crack *v.t.* કડાકો કરવો kadaako karavo
cracker *n.* ફટાકડો fataakado
crackle *v.t.* તડતડવું tadatadavun
cradle *n.* પારણું paaranun
craft *n.* વિમાન vimaan
craftiness *n.* દગાબાજી dagaabaaj
craftsman *n.* શિલ્પી shilpee
crafty *adj.* લુચ્ચાઈપૂર્વક luchchaaeepoorvak
crag *n.* ઊભી ભેખડ oobhee bhekhad
cram *v.t.* છલોછલ ભરવું chhalochhal bharavun
crammer *n.* ગોખણપટ્ટી કરનારું gokhanapattee karanaarun
cramp *n.* હાથપગ ખેંચાવા haathapag khenchaava
crane *n.* બગલું bagalun
cranium *n.* ખોપરી khoparee
crank *n.* ધૂન dhoon
crash *n.* આકસ્મિક વધિવંસ aaksmik

vidhvans
crass *adj.* મૂરખ moorakh
crate *n.* મોટું ખોખું motun khokhun
crater *n.* જ્વાળામુખીનું મોઢું jvaalaamukheenun modhun
crave *v.t.* તીવ્ર ઇચ્છા ધરાવવી teevr eechchha dharaavavee
craving *n.* ઝંખના. jhankhana
craven *n.* ડરપોક માણસ darapok maanas
crawl *v.t.* ઘસડાતું સરકવું ghasadaatun sarakavun
crayon *n.* ચિત્રશલાકા chitrashalaakaa
craze *v.t.* દીવાનું બનાવવું deevaanun banaavavun
crazy *adj.* દીવાનું deevaanun
creak *v.i.* ચૂંચૂં અવાજ કરવો chun chun avaaj karavo
cream *n.* મલાઈ malaaee
crease *n.* કરચલી karachalee
create *v.t.* નિર્માણ કરવું nirmaan karavun
creation *n.* નિર્માણ nirmaan
creative *adj.* સર્જનાત્મક sarjanaatmak
creator *n.* નિર્માતા nirmaata
creature *n.* પ્રાણી praanee
creche *n.* ઘોડિયાઘર ghodiyaaghar
credence *n.* ભરોસો bharoso
credentials *n.pl.* ભલામણ પત્ર bhalaaman patra
credible *adj.* વિશ્વાસપાત્ર vishvaasapaatr
credibility *n.* વિશ્વાસપાત્રતા vishvaasapaatrata
credit સાખ saakh
creditable *adj.* પ્રશંસાપાત્ર prashansaapaatr
creditor *n.* લેણદાર lenadaar
credulity ભોળપણ bholapan
credulous *adj.* ભોળું bholun
creed *n.* પંથ panth
creek *n.* નાની ખાડી naanee khaadee
creep *v.i.* ભાંખોડિયે ચાલવું bhankhodiye chaalavun
creeper *n.* વેલો velo
cremate *v.t.* અગ્નિદાહ સંસ્કાર કરવો agnidaah sanskaar karavo

cremation *n.* અંતિમવિધિ antimvidhi

crescent *n.* અર્ધચન્દ્રાકાર ardhachandraakaar

crest *n.* કલગી kalagee

crestfallen *adj.* ઉદાસ udaas

crevice *n.* ફાટ faat

crew *n.* ખલાસીઓનો બેડો khalaaseeono bedo

crib *n.* કોઠાર kothaar

crick *n.* ચસક chasak

cricket *n.* ક્રિકેટ kriket

cricketer *n.* ક્રિકેટ રમનાર kriket ramanaar

crier *n.* બૂમ મારનાર boom maaranaar

crime *n.* ગુનો guno

criminal *adj.* ગુનેગાર gunegaar

criminology *n.* ગુનાવિજ્ઞાન gunaavignan

crimp *v.t.* ઝાલર લગાડવી jhaalar lagaadavee

cringe *v.i.* તાબે થવું. taabe thavun

cripple *n.* લંગડો langado

crisis *n.* કટોકટી katokatee

crisp *adj.* બરડ barad

criterion *n.* માપદંડ maapadand

critic *n.* ટીકાકાર teekaakaar

critical *n.* ટીકાત્મક teekaatmak

criticism *n.* ગુણદોષવિવેચન gunadoshavivechan

criticize *v.t.* ટીકા કરવી teeka karavee

critique *n.* વિવેચનાત્મક નિબંધ vivechanaatmak nibandh

croak *v.t.* ઘોઘરો અવાજ ghoghharo avaaj

crockery *n.* માટીના વાસણ maateena vaasan

crocodile *n.* મગર magar

crone *n.* કેદેથી વળી ગયેલી ડોશી kedethee valee gayelee doshee

crony *n.* જાની દોસ્ત jaanee dost

crook *v.i.* વાંકું કરવું vaanku karavun

crooked *adj.* વાંકું vaankun

crop *n.* ધાન્યનો પાક dhaanyano paak

crore *n.* કરોડ karod

cross *n.* વધસ્તંભ vadhastanbh

cross-bow *n.* ધનુષ્ય dhanushy

cross-examin *n.* ઊલટ તપાસ oolat tapaas

crossing *n.* ચોક chok

cross-road *n.* ચારરસ્તા chaararasta

cross-wise *adj.* કાટખૂણે છેદતું kaatakhoone chhedatun

crouch *v.t.* વળવું valavun

crow *n.* કૂકડાનો બોલ kookadaano bol

crow-bar *n.* લાંબો સળિયો laambo saliyo

crowd *n.* ટોળું tolun

crown *n.* તાજ taaj

crucial *adj.* નિર્ણાયક nirnaayak

crucible *n.* કુલ્લી kullee

crucifix *n.* ક્રૂસફિક્સ krucifix

crucify *v.t.* રિબાવવું ribaavavun

crucification *n.* ક્રૂસ સાથે જડી દેવું તે kros saathe jadee devun te

crude *adj.* શુદ્ધ કર્યા વિનાનું shuddh karya vinaanun

crudity *n.* કુદરતી દશાનું kudaratee dashaanun

cruel *adj.* નિર્દય nirday

cruelty *n.* નિર્દયતા nirdayata

cruet *n.* કાણાવાળી શીશી kaanaavaalee sheeshee

cruise દરીયાઈ સફર dareeyayee safar

cruiser *n.* યુદ્ધનૌકા yudhanaukaa

crumb *n.* નાનો ટૂકડો naano tukado

crumble *v.i.* ક્ષીણ થઈ જવું ksheen thai javun

crump *v.t.* ફટકો મારવો fatako maaravo

crumple *v.t.* કરચલીઓ પાડવી karachaleeo paadavee

crusade ધર્મયુદ્ધ dharmayuddh

crush *v.* ચગદવું chagadavun

crust *n.* ભૂપૃષ્ઠ bhooprushtha

crutch *n.* આધાર aadhaar

crux *n.* પ્રસ્તુત મુદ્દો prastut muddo

cry *adj..* વિલાપ vilaap

crypt *n.* ભોંયરું bhonyarun

cryptic *adj.* ગૂઢાર્થવાળું goodhaarthavaalun

cryptogram *n.* સંકેતલિપિનું લખાણ sanketalipinun lakhaan

crystal *n.* સ્ફટિક sfatik

crystalline *adj.* સ્ફટિકના જેવું સ્વચ્છ sfatikanaa jevun svachchh

crystalize *v.t.* સ્પષ્ટ થવું spasht thavun

cub *n.* સિંહનું બચ્ચું sinhanun bachchun
cube *n.* ધન ghan
cubit ક્યુબિટ kyubit
cuckoo *n.* કોયલ koyal
cucumber *n.* કાકડી. kaakadee
cud *n.* વાગોળવું તે vaagolavun te
cuddle *v.t.* પંપાળવું panpaalavun
cudgel *n.* ડંડૂકો dandooko
cue *n.* ઈશારો eeshaaro
culinary *adj.* રાંધવા માટેનું raandhavaa maatenun
cull *v.t.* વીણી કાઢવું તે veenee kaadhavun te
culminate *v.t.* પરાકાષ્ઠાએ પહોંચવું paraakaashthaae pahonchavun
culpable *adj.* દોષપાત્ર doshapaatra
culprit *n.* અપરાધી aparaadhee
cult *n.* ધાર્મિક સંપ્રદાય dhaarmik sanpradaay
cultivate *v.t.* ની ખેતી કરવી nee khetee karavee
cultivation *n.* ખેડ khed
cultivator *n.* ખેતીનું ઓજાર kheteenun ojaar
culture *n.* સંસ્કૃતિ sanskruti
culvert *n.* નાળું naalun
cumber *v.t.* અટકાવવું atakaavavun
cumbersome *adj.* અડચણરૂપ adachanaroop
cumbrous *n.* અડચણ કરનારુ adachan karanaaru
cumin *n.* જીરું jeerun
cumulative *adj.* સંચિત sanchit
cunning *adj.* લુચ્ચાઈ luchchaaee
cup *n.* પવાલું pavaalun
cupboard *n.* કબાટ kabaat
cupidity *n.* લાલસા laalasa
cupola *n.* નાનો ઘુમ્મટ naano ghummat
curriculum *n.* અભ્યાસક્રમ abhyaasakram
curry *v.t.* કઢી બનાવવી kadhee banaavavee
curse *n.* શાપ shaap
cursed *adj.* શાપિત shaapit
cursory *adj.* ઉતાવળિયું utaavaliyun

curt *adj.* અતિસંક્ષિપ્ત. ati sankshipta
curtail *v.t.* ટૂંકુ કરવું toonkun karavun
curtailment *n.* ઘટાડો ghataado
curtain *n.* પડદો padado
curtain-lecture *n.* કાન્તાબોધ kaantaabodh
curtly *adv.* તોછડાઈપૂર્વક tochhadaaeepoorvak
curtsey *n.* સ્ત્રીની સલામ streeni salaam
curvature *n.* વાંકવળાંકવાળી આકૃતિ vaankavalaankavaalee aakruti
curve *v.t.* વળાંક દેવો valaank devo
cushion *n.* તકિયો takiyo
cushy *adj.* આરામશીર aaraamasheer
custard-apple *n.* સીતાફળ seetaafal
custodian *n.* રખેવાળ rakhevaal
custom *n.* રિવાજ rivaaj
customary *adj.* રૂઢિ પર આધારિત roodhi par aadhaarit
customer *n.* ગ્રાહક graahak
cut *v.t.* કાપવું kaapavun
cuticle *n.* ત્વચા tvachaa
cutlass *n.* પહોળા પાનની તલવાર paholaa paan ni talavaar
cutler *n.* છરીચપ્પાં બનાવનાર chhareechappan banaavanaar
cycle *n.* ચક્ર chakra
cyclist *n.* સાયકલ સવાર saayakal savaar
cyclone *n.* ચક્રવાત chakravaat
cyclopaedia *n.* સર્વવિદ્યાસંગ્રહ gsarvavidhyaasangrah
cyclostyle *n.* નકલ nakal
cylinder *n.* નળાકાર કોઠી nalaakaar kothee
cylindrical *adj.* સિલિન્ડર આકારનું silindar aakaaranun
cymbal *n.* કરતાલ karataal
cynical *adj.* ઉપહાસ કરનારું upahaas karanaarun
cynosure *n.* માર્ગદર્શક તારો maargadarshak taaro
cypher *n.* શૂન્ય shoony
cyp ress *n.* સરુનું ઝાડ sarunun jhaad

D

dab *v.t.* હળવી થાપડ Halavee Thaapad
dabble *v.t.* છાંટા ઉડાડવા Chhaantaa Undaadavaa
dacoit *n.* ધાડપાડુ Dhaadpaadu
dacoity *n.* ધાડ Dhaad
dad *n.* પિતા Pitaa
daft *adj.* મૂરખ Moorkh
daffodil *n.* ડેફોડિલ defodil
dagger *n.* કટાર Kataar
daily *adj.* દૈનિક Dainik
dainty *n.* સ્વાદિષ્ટ Swaadishta
dairy *n.* ડેરી Deree
dais *n.* મંચ Manch
dale *n.* ખીણ Kheen
dalliance આળસુ aalasu
dally *v.t.* કામમાં ઢીલ કરવી Kaam maa dheel karavee
dam *n.* નદી પરનો બંધ Nadee parano bandh
damage *n.* હાનિ Haani
dame *n.* બાનુ baanu
damn *v.t.* ટીકા કરવી Teekaa karavee
damnable *adj.* ટીકાપાત્ર Teekaapaatra
damnation *n.* ચિરંતન નરકવાસ Chirantaran narakavaas
damned *adj.* તિરસ્કૃત Tiraskrut
damp *n.* ભેજ Bhej
damsel *n.* અપરણીત યુવતી aparaneet yuvatee
dance *v.t.* નૃત્ય કરવું nrutya karavun
dancer *n.* નૃત્ય કરનાર nrutya karanaar
dandle *v.t.* બાળકને રમાડવું bhaalakane ramaadavun
dandy *n.* વરણાગિયો. varanaagiyo
danger *n.* જોખમ jokham
dangerous *adj.* જોખમકારક jokhamakaarak
dangle *v.i.* લટકવું latakavun
daniel *n.* પ્રામાણિક ન્યાયાધીશ praamaanik nyaayadheesh
dank *adj.* ભીનું bheenu
dapple *n.* કાબરચીતરું kaabarcheetaru

dare *v.t.* સાહસ કરવું saahas karavun
dare-devil સાહસિક વ્યક્તિ saahasik vyakti
daring *adj.* સાહસ વૃત્તિ saahas vruti
dark *adj.* અંધારું andhaaru
darken *v.t.* અંધારું કરવું andhaaru karavun
darling *n.* પ્રિય priya
darn *v.t.* રફૂ કરવું rafoo karavun
dart *v.t.* ફેંકવું fenkavun
dash *v.t.* ઘસવું ghasavun
dashing *adj.* ભપકાવાળું bhapakaavaalu
dastard *n.* બદમાશ badmaash
data *n.* આધારભૂત માહિતી aadhaarbhoot maahitee
date *n.* તારીખ taareekh
dative *n.* સંપ્રદાન sampradaan
datum *n.* સ્વીકૃત હકીકત sveekrut hakeekat
daub *v.t.* લીપવું leenpavun
daughter *n.* દીકરી deekaree
daughter-in-law *n.* પુત્રવધૂ putravadhoo
daunt *v.t.* નાહિમ્મત કરવું naahimmat karavun
dauntless *adj.* નીડર needar
daw *n.* મૂરખ moorkh
dawdle *v.i.* આળસ રાખવી aalas raakhavee
dawn *v.i.* પરોઢ parodh
day *n.* દિવસ divas
day-break *n.* મળસકું malaskun
daze *v.t.* બાવરાપણું baavaraapanu
dazzle *v.t.* આંજવું aanjavun
deacon *n.* ગૌણ પાદરી gaun paadaree
dead *n.* મૃત mrut
deaden *v.t.* સંવેદનશૂન્ય કરવું samvedanshoonya karavun
dead letter *n.* અપ્રસ્તુત aprastut
deadly *adj.* જીવલેણ jeevalen
deaf *adj.* બહેરું baheru
deafen *v.t.* બધિર કરવું badhir karavun
deal *v.t.* સોદો. sodo
dealer *n.* વેપારી vepaaree
dealing *n.* લેવડદેવડ levadadevad
dean *n.* વિભાગનો વડો. vibhaagano vado

dear *adj.* પ્રિય priy
dearly *adv.* વહાલું vahaalu
dearth *n.* તંગી tangee
death *n.* મૃત્યુ mrutyu
debacle *n.* રકાસ rakaash
debar *v.t.* પ્રવેશ ન આપવો. pravesh na aapavo
debase *v.t.* મૂલ્ય ઘટાડવું moolya ghataadavun
debasement *n.* ગુણવત્તા ઘટાડવી gunavattaa ghataadavee
debatable *adj.* ચર્ચાપાત્ર charchaapaatra
debate *n.* ચર્ચા charcha
debauch *v.t.* અનૈતિક આચરણ કરવું anaitik aacharan
debauchery *n.* ભોગવિલાસ bhogavilaas
debenture *n.* ઋણપત્ર runapatra
debilitate *v.t.* કમજોર બનાવવું kamajor banaavavun
debility *n.* કમજોરી kamajoree
debit *v.t.* ઉધારવું udhaaravun
debonair *adj.* ખુશમિજાજ khushamijaaj
debris *n.* કાટમાળ kaatamaal
debt *n.* દેવું devun
debtor *n.* દેવાદાર devaadaar
decade *n.* દાયકો daayako
decadence *n.* પડતી padatee
decagon *n.* દશભુજ dashabhuj
decamp *v.i.* નાશી જવું naashee javun
decanter *n.* મદિરાપાત્ર madirapaatra
decapitate *v.t.* શિરચ્છેદ કરવો. shirachshed karavo
decay *v.i.* સડવું sadavun
decease *n.* મૃત્યુ mrutyu
deceased *adj.* મરહૂમ marahoom
deceit *n.* છેતરપિંડી chhetarapindee
deceitful *adj.* છેતરનારું chhetaranaaru
deceive *v.t.* છેતરવું chhetaravun
december *n.* ડિસેમ્બર december
deceny *n.* શિષ્ટાચાર shishtaachaar
decennial *adj.* દસવર્ષીય dasavarsheey
decent *adj.* શિષ્ટ shishta
decentralize *v.t.* વિકિન્દ્રિત કરવું vikendrit karavun
deception *n.* દગો dago

deceptive *adj.* ભ્રામક bhraamak
decide *v.t.* નિર્ણય કરવો nirnay karavo
decided *adj.* નિશ્ચિત nishchhtit
deciduous *adj.* પાનખર paanakhar
decimal *adj.* દશાંશ dashansh
decimetre *n.* એક દશાંશ મીટર ek dashaansh meetar
decipher *v.t.* અર્થ કરવો artha karavo
decision *n.* નિર્ણય nirnay
decisive *adj.* નિર્ણાયાત્મક nirnaayaatmak
deck *n.* હોડીનું તૂતક hodee nu tootak
declaim *v.t.* ભારપૂર્વક બોલવું bhaarpurvak bolavun
declaration *n.* જાહેરાત jaaheraat
declare *v.t.* જાહેર કરવું jaaher karavun
declension *n.* વિભક્તિરૂપાખ્યાન vibhaktee roopaakhyaan
decline *v.i.* ઇનકાર કરવો enakaar karavo
declivity *n.* ઢોળાવ dhodaav
decoction *n.* અર્ક કાઢવો ark kaadhavo
decompose *v.t.* સડવું sadavun
decorate *v.t.* શણગારવું shanagaaravun
decoration *n.* સજાવટ sajaavat
decorous *adj.* શોભાસ્પદ shobhaspad
decorum *n.* શિષ્ટાચાર shishtaachaar
decoy *v.t.* લલચાવવું lalachaavavun
decrease *n.* ઘટવું ghatavun
decree *n.* હુકમનામું hukamanaamu
decrepit *adj.* અશક્ત ashakt
decry *v.t.* વખોડવું vakhodavun
dedicate *v.t.* અર્પણ કરવું. arpan karavun
dedication *n.* સમર્પણ samarpan
dedicator *n.* સમર્પિત samarpit
deduce *v.t.* નિષ્કર્ષ કાઢવો nishkarsh kaadhavo
deduct *v.t.* બાદ કરવું baad karavun
deduction *n.* બાદ કરેલી રકમ baad karelee rakam
deductive *adj.* તાર્કિક taarkik
deed *n.* કૃત્ય krutya
deem *v.t.* ગણવું ganavun
deep *adj.* ઊંડુ oondu
deepen *v.t.* ઊંડું કરવું oondu karavun
deer *n.* હરણ haran

deface *v.t.* સૂરત બગાડવી soorat bagaadavee

defacto *v.t.* સત્તા રૂએ sattaa rooae

defaicate *v.t.*

defacation *n.* ઉચાપત uchaapat

defame *v.t.* બદનામ કરવું badanaam karavun

default *n.* કસૂર kasoor

defaulter *n.* કસૂરવાર kasooravaar

defeat *v.t.* પરાજય આપવો paraajay aapavo

defecate *v.t.* મળત્યાગ કરવો. malatyaag karavo

defect *n.* ખામી khaamee

defective *adj.* ખામીયુક્ત khaameeyukta

defence *n.* રક્ષણ rakshan

defenceless *adj.* રક્ષણહનિ rakshanhin

defend *v.* બચાવ કરવો bachaav karavo

defendant *n.* પ્રતિવાદી prativaadee

defender *n.* રક્ષક rakshak

defensive *adj.* રક્ષણાત્મક rakshanaatmak

defer *v.t.* મોકૂફ રાખવું mokoof raakhavun

deference *n.* સન્માન sanmaan

defiant *adj.* અવજ્ઞા કરનાર avagnaa karanaar

deficiency *n.* ઊણપ oonap

deficient *adj.* ઊણપવાળું oonapvaalu

deficit *n.* ખાધ khaadh

defile *v.t.* ગંદું બનાવવું gandu banaavavun

define *v.t.* વ્યાખ્યા કરવી vyaakhyaa karavee

definite *adj.* નિશ્ચિત કરવું nichhshit karavun

definition *n.* વ્યાખ્યા vyaakhyaa

deflagration *n.* ગરમીથી બળવું garamee thee balavun

deflate *v.t.* હવા કાઢવી havaa kaadhavee

deflect *v.t.* આડું ફંટાવું aadu fantaavun

deflower *v.t.* કૌમાર્યભંગ કરવો kaumayabhang karavo

deform *v.t.* વિકૃત કરવું vikrut karavun

deformation *n.* વિકૃત કરવું તે vikrut karavun te

deformity *n.* વક્રિત vikrutee

defraud *v.t.* છેતરવું chhetaravun

defray *v.* ખર્ચ ઉપાડવો kharch upaadavo

deft *adj.* નિપુણ nipun

defunct *adj.* કાલગ્રસ્ત kaalgrast

defy *v.i.* સામા થવું saamaa thavun

degenerate *v.i.* અધઃપતિત adhah patit

degeneration *n.* ભ્રષ્ટ થવું તે bhrasht thavun te

degradation *n.* માનભંગ maanbhang

degrade *v.t.* અધઃપાત કરવો adhahpaat karavo

degree *n.* પદવી padavee

deify *v.t.* દેવનું સ્થાન આપવું devanu sthaan aapavun

deign *v.t.* કૃપા કરવી krupaa karavee

deity *n.* દૈવી સ્વરૂપ daivee svaroop

deject *v.t.* ગમગીન બનાવવું gamageen banaavavun

dejection *n.* ગ્લાનિ glaani

dejected *adj.* હતોત્સાહિત hatosaahit karavun

delay *v.t.* વિલંબ vilamb

delectable *adj.* મજાનું majaanu

delegacy *n.* પ્રતિનિધિમંડળ pratinidhimandal

delegate *n.* સત્તા સોંપણી sattaa sonpanee

delegation *n.* પ્રતિનિધિમંડળ pratinidhimandal

delete *v.t.* છેકવું chhekavun

deliberate *v.t.* ઇરાદાપૂર્વકનું eraadaapurvakanu

deliberation *n.* ચર્ચાવિચારણા charchaavichaaranaa

delicacy *n.* નજાકત najaakat

delicate *adj.* નાજુક naajuk

delicious *adj.* સ્વાદિષ્ટ svaadisht

delict *n.* અપરાધ aparaadh

delight *n.* આનંદ આપવો aanand aapavo

delightful *adj.* આનંદપૂર્ણ aanandpoorn

delilah *n.* સુંદર પ્રેમિકા sundar premikaa

delineate *v.t.* રેખાચિત્ર દોરવું rekhaachitra doravun

delinquency *n.* ઉપેક્ષા upekshaa

deliquate *v.t.* પ્રમાદ કરવો pramaad karavo

deliquate *adj.* પ્રમાદી pramaadee

delirium *n.* ચિત્તભ્રમણા chittabhramanaa

deliver *v.t.* પ્રસૂત કિરાવવી prasooti karaavavee

deliverance *n.* મુક્તિ mukti

delivery *n.* પ્રસૂતિ prasooti

dell *n.* ઝાડીવાળું કોતર zaadeevaalu kotar

delta *n.* ત્રિકોણાકાર પ્રદેશ trikonaakaar pradesh

delude *v.t.* છેતરવું chhetaravun

deluge *n.* ઘોડાપૂર ghodaapoor

delusion *n.* ભ્રમણા bhramanaa

delve *v.* ખોદવું khodavun

demagogue *n.* લોકલાગણી બહેકાવનાર lokalaaganee bahekaavanaar

demand *v.t.* માગ કરવી maag karavee

demarcation *n.* સીમાંકન seemaankan

demean *v.t.* હલકું પાડવું halaku paadavun

demeanour *n.* રીતભાત reetabhaat

dement *v.t.* ઉન્મત્ત કરવું unmatt karavun

demerit *n.* દોષ dosh

demi *prep.* અપૂર્ણ aapoorn

demigod *n.* અર્ધદેવી ardhdevee

demise *n.* મૃત્યુ mrutyu

democracy *n.* લોકશાહી lokashaahee

democrat *n.* લોકશાહીનો સમર્થક lokshaaheeno samarthak

demoratic *adj.* લોકશાહી lokshaahee

demolish *v.t.* પાડી નાખવું paadee naakhavun

demon *n.* રાક્ષસ raakshas

demonstrate *v.t.* પ્રદર્શિત કરવું pradashit karavun

demonstration *n.* નિદર્શન nidarshan

demoralization *n.* નૈતિક અધ:પાત naitik adhahpaat

demur *v.i.* વાંધો ઉઠાવવો તે vaandho uthaavavo te

demure *adj.* પ્રતિષ્ઠિત pratishthit

demurrage *n.* વિલંબ શુલ્ક vilamb shulk

demy *n.* કાગળનો કદ kaagalno kad

den *n.* ગુફા gufaa

denature *n.* ગુણધર્મ ફેરફાર gundharma ferfaar

denial *n.* ઇનકાર enakaar

denizen *n.* રહેવાસી rahevaasee

denominate *v.t.* નામે કરવું naame karavun

denominator *n.* ભાજક bhaajak

denote *v.t.* સૂચક હોવું soochak hovun

denounce *v.t.* સખત નિંદા કરવી sakhat nindaa karavee

dense *adj.* ગીચ geech

density *n.* ગીચતા geechataa

dental *adj.* દંત્ય dantya

dentist *n.* દંતવૈદ્ય dantavaidya

dentistry *n.* દંતવિદ્યા dantyavidyaa

denture *n.* દાંતનું ચોકઠું daant nu chokathu

denudation *n.* વસ્ત્રાહરણ vastraaharan

denude *v.* નિવિસ્ત્ર કરવું nivastra karavun

denunciate *v.t.* નિંદા કરવી nindaa karavee

deny *v.t.* ઇનકાર કરવો enakaar karavo

depart *v.* રવાના થવું ravaana thavun

department *n.* વિભાગ vibhaag

departure *n.* વિદાય vidaay

depend *v.* આધાર રાખવો aadhaar raakhavo

dependable *n.* આધારભૂત aadhaarbhoot

dependant *n.* આશ્રિત aashrit

dependence *n.* પરાધીનતા paradheenataa

dependent *adj.* આધારિત aadhaarit

depict *v.t.* વર્ણન કરવું varnan karavun

depilation *n.* વાળ વગરનું vaal vagaranu

deplete *v.t.* ખાલી કરવું khaalee karavun

deplorable *n.* શોચનીય shochaneey

deplore *v.t.* શોક કરવો shok karavo

deplume *v.t.* છીનવી લેવી chheenavee levee

depopulate *v.t.* વસ્તી ઘટાડવી vastee ghataadavee

deport *v.t.* દેશપાર કરવું deshapaar karavun

deportation *n.* દેશનિકાલ deshanikaal

deportment *n.* ઢબ dhab

depose *v.* જુબાની આપવી. jubaanee aapavee

deposit *v.t.* જમા કરવું jamaa karavun

depositary *n.* અનામત રાખનાર anaamat raakhanaar

depostion *n.* જુબાની jubaanee

depositer *n.* થાપણદાર thaapandaar

depository જમા કરવાની જગ્યા jamaa karavun

depot *n.* વખાર vakhaar

deprave *v.t.* નીતિભ્રષ્ટ કરવું neetibhrast karavun

deprecate *v.* વખોડી કાઢવું vakhodee kaadhvun

depreciate *v.i.* કિંમત ઘટાડવી kimmat ghataadavee

depreciation *n.* ઘસારો ghasaaro

depredation *n.* લૂટફાટ loontfaat

depress *v.t.* નિરાશ કરવું niraash karavun

depression *n.* હવાનું દબાણ havaanu dabaan

deprive *v.* વંચિત રાખવું vanchit raakhavun

depth *n.* ઊંડાણ oondaan

deputation *n.* પ્રતિનિધિમંડળ pratinidhimandal

depute *v.t.* અવેજીમાં નીમવું avejeemaa neemavun

deputy *n.* મદદનીશ madadaneesh

derail *v.t.* ખડી પડવું khadee padavun

derange *v.t.* અવ્યવસ્થિત કરવું aavyavasthit karavun

derangement *n.* અવ્યવસ્થા aavyavasthaa

dereliction *n.* ઉપેક્ષા upekshaa

deride *v.t.* મશ્કરી કરવી. mashkaree karavee

derision *n.* ઉપહાસ upahaas

derivation *n.* મૂળ mool

derive *v.t.* મૂળ શોધવું mool shodavun

derogate *v.t.* મૂલ્ય ઘટાડવું moolya ghataadavun

derogatory *adj.* અપમાનજનક aapamaanajanak

derrick *n.* ડેરિક derik

derring *n.* સાહસિક saahasik

dervish *n.* ફકીર fakeer

descend *v.i.* ઊતરી આવવું ootaree aavavun

descendant *n.* વંશજ vanshaj

descent *n.* વંશ vansh

describe *v.t.* વર્ણન કરવું varnan karavun

description *adj.* વર્ણન varnan

descriptive *adj.* વર્ણનાત્મક varnaatmak

descry *v.t.* દૂરથી જોવું doorathee jovun

desecrate *v.t.* અપવિત્ર બનાવવું aapavitra banaavavun

desert *adj.* જંગલ jangal

deserter *n.* ભાગી જનાર સૈનિક bhaagee janaar sainik

desertion *n.* ત્યાગ tyaag

deserve *v.* ને માટે લાયક ne mate laayak

deservedly *adv.* યોગ્યતા પ્રમાણે yogyataa pramaane

deserving *adj.* લાયકાતવાળું laayakaatavaalu

desiderative *adj.* ઇચ્છાર્થક echhshaarthark

desideratum *n.* આવશ્યક વસ્તુ aavashyak vastu

design *v.t.* રૂપરેખા rooparekhaa

designate *v.t.* નિમણૂક કરવી nimanook karavee

designation *n.* હોદ્દો hoddo

designing *adj.* કાવતરાખોર kaavataraabaaj

desirable *adj.* ઇચ્છનીય echhchaneey

desire *v.t.* ઇચ્છા echhsha

desirous *adj.* ઇચ્છાવાળું echsavaalu

desist *v.i.* અટકવું atakavun

desk *n.* ટેબલ tebal

desolate *v.t.* વેરાન veraan

desolation *n.* વેરાન veraan

despair *v.t.* નિરાશ થવું niraash karavun

despatch *v.t.* પ્રેષિત કરવું preshit karavun

desperado *n.* મરણિયો maraniyo

desperate *adj.* મરણિયું maraniyu

despicable *n.* તિરસ્કારપાત્ર tiraskaarapaatra

despise *v.t.* તિરસ્કાર કરવો tiraskaar karavo

despite *n.* તેમ છતાં tem chhataa

despoil *v.t.* લૂંટવું loontavun

despond *v.t.* નિરાશ થવું niraash thavun

despondency *n.* હતાશા hataashaa

despondent *n.* નિરાશાપ્રેરક niraashaaprerak

despot *n.* નિરંકુશ રાજ્યકર્તા nirankush raajyakartaa

despotism *n.* સરમુખત્યારશાહી sarmukhtyaashahee

dessert *n.* ભોજન બાદ મિષ્ઠાનનું bhojan baad misthaan

destination *n.* ગંતવ્ય ganatavya

destine *v.t.* નીમવું, neemavun

destined *adj.* અગાઉથી નિર્ધારિત agaauthee niradhaarit

destiny *n.* નસીબ naseeb

destitute *adj.* નિરાધાર niraadhaar

destitution *n.* નિરાધારપણું niraadhaarapanu

destroy *v.t.* નાશ કરવું naash karavun

destroyer *n.* વિનાશકર્તા vinaashakartaa

destructible *adj.* નાશવંત naashavant

destruction *n.* વિનાશ veenash

destructive *adj.* વિનાશક vinaashak

desultory *n.* સાતત્ય વિનાનું saatatya vinaanu

detach *v.t.* અલગ કરવું aalag karau

detachment *n.* ટુકડી tukadee

detail *v.t.* વિગત આપવી vigat aaapavee

detain *v.* અટકાયત aatakaayat

detect *v.t.* શોધવું shodhavun

detective *n.* ગુનાશોધક gunaashodhak

detention *n.* અટકમાં રાખવું aatakmaa raakhvun

detenu *n.* અટકાયતી atakaayatee

deter *v.t.* નિરુત્સાહ કરવું nirutsaah karavun

deteriorate *v.i.* કથળવું kathalavun

determinate *n.* ચોક્કસ સ્વરૂપવાળું chokkas swaroopavaalu

determination *n.* નિર્ધાર nirdhaar

determine *v.t.* નિર્ધાર કરવો nirdhaar karavo

deterrent *adj.* પ્રતિબંધક pratibandhak

detest *v.t.* તિરસ્કાર કરવો. tiraskaar karavo

detestation *n.* નફરત nafarat

dethrone *v.t.* પદભ્રષ્ટ કરવું padbhrashta karavun

detract *v.t.* બાદ કરવું baad karavun

detraction *n.* બાદબાકી કરવી baadabaakee karavee

detriment *n.* અવરોધક aavarodhak

detrimental *adj.* નુકશાનકારક nukashaanakaarak

deuce *n.* શેતાન shetaan

devastate *v.* વેરાન કરવું veraan karavun

devastation *n.* વેરાન કરવું તે veraan karavun te

develop *v.t.* વિકસવું vikasavun,

development *n.* વિકાસ vikaas

deviate *v.t.* વિષયાંતર કરવું vishayaantar karavun

deviation *n.* વિષયાંતર vishayaantar

device *n.* સાધન saadhan

devil *n.* શેતાન shetaan

devilish *adj.* શેતાનનું shetaananu

devious *adj.* કપટી kapatee

devise *v.t.* વિચારી કાઢવું vichaaree kaadhavun

devisor *n.* વસિયતનામું બનાવનાર vasiyatanaamu banaavanaar

devoid *n.* મુક્ત mukt

devolve *v.t.* વારસામાં આવવું vaarasaamaa avavun

devote *v.t.* સમર્પણ કરવું samarpan karavun

devoted *adj.* સમર્પિત samarpit

devotee *n.* અનુયાયી aanuyaayee

devotion *n.* ભક્તિ bhakti

devotional ભક્તિમય bhaktimay

devour *v.t.* ભરખી જવું bharakhee javun

devout *adj.* શ્રદ્ધાળુ sraddhaalu

dew *n.* ઝાકળ zaakad

dewy *adj.* ઝાકળભીનું zaakadabheenu

dexterity *n.* કૌશલ્ય kaoshalya

dexterous *adj.* ચપળ chapal

diabetes *n.* મધુમેહ madhuprameh

diabolical *adj.* જંગલી jangalee

diadem *n.* મુગટ mugat

diagnose *v.t.* નિદાન કરવું nidaan karavun

diagnosis *n.* નિદાન nidaan

diagonal *adj.* ત્રાંસી લીટી transee leetee

diagram *n.* આકૃતિ aakruti

dial *n.* ટેલિફોનનો ચંદો telephone no chando

dialect *n.* લોકબોલી lokabolee

dialectic *n.* વિવાદશાસ્ત્ર vivaadshaastra

dialogue *n.* સંવાદ samvaad

diameter *n.* વ્યાસ vyaas

diametric *adj.* વ્યાસ સંબંધી vyaas sambamdhee

diamond *n.* હીરો heero

diaper *n.* બાળોતિયું baalotiyu

diaphanous *adj.* અતિશય પાતળું aatisay paatalu

diaphoretic *adj.* સ્વેદકારક svedakaarak

diaphragm *n.* પડદો padado

diarchy *n.* દ્વિમુખી રાજપદ્ધતિ drimukhee raajpaddhati

diarrhoea *n.* અતિસાર aatisaar

diary *n.* રોજનીશી rojaneeshee

diatribe *n.* કડવી ટીકા kadavee teekaa

dibble *n.* છોડ રોપવા chhod ropava

dice *n.* મંચ manch

dictate *v.t.* હુકમ કરવો hukam karavo

dictation *n.* લખાવેલું lakhaavelu

dictator *n.* સરમુખત્યાર sarmukhtyaar

diction *n.* બોલવાની શૈલી bolavaanee shailee

dictionary *n.* શબ્દકોશ shabdakosh

dictum *n.* સૂત્ર sootra

didactic *adj.* ઉપદેશાત્મક upadeshaatmak

die *v.t.* બીબું beebu

diehard *n.* કટ્ટર kattar

diesel *n.* ખનિજ તેલ khanij tel

diet *n.* પરહેજી પાળવી parahejee paalavee

dietary *n.* રોજનો આહાર rojano aahaar

differ *v.i.* અલગ પડવું alag padavun

difference *n.* મતભેદ matabhed

different *adj.* વિશિષ્ટ vishisht

differential તફાવત tafaavat

differentiate *v.t.* ભેદ હોવો bhed hovo

difficult *adj.* મુશ્કેલ mushkel

difficulty *n.* મુશ્કેલી mushkelee

diffidence *n.* આત્મવિશ્વાસનો અભાવ aatmavishvaas no abhaav

diffident *adj.* આત્મવિશ્વાસ વિનાનું aatmavishvaas no abhav

diffuse *v.t.* વિખેરવું vikheravun

diffusion *n.* વેર વિખેર થયેલું ver vikher thayelu

dig *v.t.* ખોદવું khodavun

digest *v.t.* ખોરાક પચાવવો khoraak pachaavavo

digestive *adj.* પાચક paachak

digestible *adj.* પચનીય pachaneeya

digestion *n.* પાચનશક્તિ paachanashakti

digit *n.* આંકડો aankado

dignified *adj.* સ્વાભિમાની svaabhimaanee

dignify *v.t.* ગૌરવ આપવું gaurav apaavavun

dignitary *n.* હોદ્દેદાર hoddedaar

dignity *n.* મોભો mobho

digress *v.t.* વિષયાંતર કરવું vishayaantar karavun

digression *n.* વિષયાંતર કરવું vishayaantar karavun

dike *n.* પાળ paal

dilapidate *v.t.* ખંડિયેર હાલત khandiyer haalat

dilapidation *n.* નાદુરસ્ત સ્થિતિ naadurast sthiti

dilate *v.t.* પહોળું કરવું paholu karavun

dilatory *adj.* મોડું કરવું modu karevun

dilemma *n.* ધર્મસંકટ dharmsankat

dilettante *n.* લલિતકલાઓનું શોખીન lalitkalaanu shokheen

diligence *n.* ખંત khant

diligent *n.* ખંતીલું khanteelu

dilute *v.t.* પાતળું કરવું paatalu karavun

diluvial *adj.* ઘોડાપૂર સંબંધિત ghodaapoor sambandhit

dim *adj.* નિસ્તેજ nistej

dimen *n.*

diminish *v.t.* ઓછું કરવું ochhu karavun

diminution *n.* ઘટાડો ghataado

diminutive *adj.* લઘુતા દર્શક laghutaa darshak

dimple *n.* ખંજન khanjan

din *n.* કોલાહલ kolaahal

dine *v.i.* જમવું jamavun

dingy *adj.* મેલું melu

dinner *n.* દિવસનું મુખ્ય ભોજન divas nu mukhya bhojan

dint *n.* ફટકો fatako

dip *v.t.* ડુબાડવું dubaadavun

diphtheria *n.* ડિપ્થેરીયા dipthereeyaa

diploma *n.* શિક્ષણનું પ્રમાણપત્ર shikshananu pramanpatra

diplomacy *n.* મુત્સદ્દીગીરી mutsaddigeeree

diplmat *n.* રાજદૂત raajdoot

diplmatic *adj.* રાજદ્વારી raajdvaaree

dire *adj.* ભયંકર bhayankar

direct *v.t.* સીધું seedhu

direction *n.* દિશા deesa

directly *adv.* સીધેસીધું seedheseedhu

director *n.* સંચાલક sanchaalak

directory *n.* ગ્રાહકોની યાદી graahakoni yaadee

dirge *n.* મરશિયો marshiyo

dirk *n.* એક જાતની લાંબી કટાર ek jaat nee lambee kataar

dirt *n.* ગંદકી gandakee

dirty *adj.* ગંદુ gandu

disability *n.* અક્ષમતા akshamataa

disable *v.t.* અક્ષમ aksham

disabuse *v.t.* આંખ ઉઘાડવી aankh ughaadavee

disadvantage *n.* ગેરલાભ geralaabh

disadvantageous *adj.* ગેરલાભ કરનારું geralaabh karanaaru

disaffection *n.* રાજકીય અસંતોષ raajkeey asantosh

disagree *v.t.* સંમત ન થવું sammat na thavun

disagreeble *adj.* અસંતુષ્ઠ asantushth

disallow *v.t.* નામંજૂર કરવું naamanjur karavun

disallowance *n.* અસ્વીકૃતિઓ asvikrutee

disappear *v.i.* અદ્રશ્ય થવું adrashya thavun

disappearance *n.* અદ્રશ્ય adrashya

disappoint *v.t.* નિરાશ થવું neeraash thavun

disappointment *n.* નિરાશા neeraasha

disapprobation *n.* નાપસંદગી. naapasandagee

disapproval *n.* નાપસંદગી naapasandagee

disapprove *v.t.* નામંજૂર કરવું naamanjoor karavun

disarm *v.t.* નિઃશસ્ત્ર કરવું; nishastra karavun

disarmament નિસ્ત્રીકરણ nishastreekaran

disarry *n.* ગૂંચવાયેલું gunchavaayelu

disaster *n.* હોનારત honaarat

disastrous *adj.* વિનાશક vinaashak

disavow *v.t.* નાકબૂલ કરવું naakabul karavun

disavowal *n.* નાકબૂલાત naakabulaat

disband *v.t.* વિખેરી નાખવું vikheree nakhavun

disbar *v.t.* સનદ રદ કરવી sanad rad karavee

disbelief *n.* વિશ્વાસ ના રાખવો vishvaash naa raakhavo

disbelieve *v.t.* વિશ્વાસ ના રાખવો vishvaash naa raakhavo

disburden *v.t.* બોજો ઉતારવો bojo utaaravo

disburse *v.t.* ચૂકવણું કરવું. chookavanu karavun

disc *n.* થાળી thaalee

discard *v.t.* ફેંકી દેવું fenkee devun

discern *v.t.* પારખવું paarakhavun

discernible *adj.* પારખી શકાય તેવું paarakhee shakaay tevun

discernment *n.* કળવું kalavun

discharge *v.t.* બરતરફ કરવું barataraf karavun

disciple *n.* શિષ્ય shishya

disciplinarian *n.* શિસ્તઆગ્રહી shista aagrahee

disciplinary *adj.* શિસ્તપાલનને લગતું shishtapaalanane lagatu

discipline *n.* શિસ્ત shisht

disclaim *v.t.* દાવો જતો કરવો daavo jato karavo

disclaimer *n.* જાહેર અસ્વીકૃતિ jaaher asveekrutee

disclose *v.t.* ઉઘાડું પાડવું ughaadu paadavun

disclosure *n.* પરદાફાશ pardaafaash

discomfit *v.t.* હરાવવું haraavavun

discomfort *n.* અસ્વસ્થતા asvasthataa

discompose *v.t.* અસ્વસ્થ asvasth

disconnect *v.t.* અલગ કરવું તે alag karavun te

disconsolate *adj.* ઉદાસ udaash

discontent *n.* અસંતોષ asantosh

discontented અસંતુષ્ટ. asantusht

discontinue *v.t.* બંધ કરવું bandh karavun

discord *n.* વિસંવાદિતા visamvaaditaa

discordant *adj.* વિસંવાદી visamvaadee

discount *n.* કિમતમાં કપાત kimmatmaa kapaat

discountenance *v.t.* નાપસંદ કરવું naapasand karavun

discourage *v.t.* નાહિંમત કરવું nahimmat karavun

discouraging *adj.* પ્રોત્સાહક proshaahak

discourse *n.* વાર્તાલાપ vaartaalaap

discourteous *adj.* અવિનયી avinayee

discourtesy *n.* અસભ્યતા asabhyataa

discover *v.t.* શોધી કાઢવું sodhee kaadhavun

discovery *n.* શોધ shodh

discredit *n.* નામોશી લગાડવી naamoshee lagaadavee

discreditable *adj.* અપયશકારક apayashakaarak

discreet *adj.* વિનમ્ર vinamra

discrepancy *n.* વિસંગતતા visangatataa

discretion *n.* મુનસફી munasafee

discretionary *adj.* મનસ્વી manasvee

discriminate *v.t.* ભેદ પાડવો bhed paadavo

discrimination *n.* ભેદભાવ bhedabhaav

discursive *adj.* વિષયાન્તર કરતું vishayaantar karavun

discuss *v.t.* ચર્ચા કરવી charchaa karavee

discussion *n.* ચર્ચા charchaa

disdain *v.t.* તિરસ્કાર કરવો tiraskaar karavo

disease *n.* રોગ rog

disembark *v.i.* કિનારે ઊતરવું kinaare utaravun

disembody *v.* વિઘટન કરવું vighatan karavun

disencumber *v.t.* વળગણ દૂર કરવું vadagan door karavun

disengage *v.t.* છૂટું કરવું chhootu karavun

disfavour *n.* નાપસંદગી naapasandagee

disfigure *v.t.* વિરૂપ કરવું viroop karavun

disfranchise *v.t.* મતાધિકાર રદ્દીકરણ mataadhikaar raddeekaran

disgorge *v.t.* ઓકી નાખવું aokee naakhavun

disgrace *n.* નામોશી લગાડવી naamoshee lagaadavee

disgrceful *adj.* શરમજનક sharamajanak

disgruntled *adj.* અસંતુષ્ટ asantusht

disguise *v.t.* વેષ પલટાવો vesh palatavo

disgust *n.* નફરત nafarat

dish *n.* રકાબી rakaabee

dishearten *v.t.* નાહિંમત કરવું nahimmat karavun

dishevelled *adj.* અસ્તવ્યસ્ત astavyast

dishonour *v.t.* બદનામ કરવું badanaam karavun

disillusion *v.t.* ભ્રમ દૂર કરવો bhram door karavo

disinclination *n.* અણગમો anagamo

disinfect *v.t.* ચેપરહિત કરવું. cheparahit karavun

disingenuous *adj.* કપટપૂર્વક kapatapoorvak

disinherit *v.t.* વારસહક લઈ લેવો. vaarasahak lai levo

disintegrate *v.t.* વિઘટન કરવું vighatan karavun

disinter *v.t.* દાટેલું કાઢવું daatelun kaadhavun

disinterested રસવિહીન rasaviheen

disjoin *v.t.* છૂટું પાડવું chhootu paadavun

disjoint *v.t.* સાંધામાંથી ખસવું saandhaamaathee khasavun

disk *n.* થાળી thaalee

dislike *v.t.* ન ગમવું n gamavun

dislocate *v.t.* સ્થાનભ્રષ્ટ કરવું sthaanbhrasht karavun

dislodge *v.t.* સ્થાનભ્રષ્ટ કરવું sthaanbhrasht karavun

disloyal *adj.* બેવફા bevafaa

dismal *adj.* ઉદાસ udaash

dismantle *v.t.* વેરવખિર કરવું veravikher karavun

dismay *v.t.* હિમ્મત ખોવી himmat khovee

dismember *v.t.* ભાગ કરવા bhaag karavaa

dismiss *v.t.* પદભ્રષ્ટ કરવું padabhrasht karavun

dismissal *n.* રુખસદ આપવી rukhasad aapavee

dismount *v.t.* ઉતારી દેવું utaaree padavun

disobedience *n.* અનાદર anaadar

disobedient *adj.* બળવાખોર balavaakhor

disobey *v.i.* હુકમ ન માનવો hukam naa maanavo

disorder *n.* ગેરવ્યવસ્થા geravyavsthaa

disorderly *adj.* અસ્તવ્યસ્ત astavyast

desorganize *v.t.* અસ્તવ્યસ્ત કરવું, astavyast karavun

disown *v.t.* નાકબૂલ કરવું naakabul karavun

disparage *v.t.* નિન્દા કરવી. nindaa karavee

disparity *n.* વિષમતા vishamataa

dispassionate *v.t.* નિષ્પક્ષ nishpaksh

dispatch *n.* રવાના કરવું ravaana kararu

dispel *v.t.* વખિરી નાખવું vikheree naakhavun

dispensable *adj.* બિનજરૂરી binajaruree

dispensary *n.* દવાખાનું davaakhaanu

dispense *v.t.* વહેંચવું vahenchavun

disperse *v.t.* વખિરાઈ જવું vikheraai javun

dispirit *v.t.* નિરુત્સાહ કરવું nirustaah karavun

displace *v.t.* પદભ્રષ્ટ કરવું padabhrastha karavun

displacement *n.* ખસેડવું khasedavun

display *v.t.* પ્રદર્શન કરવું pradarshan karavun

displease *v.t.* નાખુશ કરવું nakhush karavun

displeasure *n.* નામરજી naamarajee

disport *v.t.* મોજમજા કરવી mojamajaa karavee

disposal *n.* નિકાલ nikaal

dispose *v.t.* નિકાલ કરવો. nikaal karavo

dispose of *v.t.* વેચી દેવું vechee devun

disposition *n.* સ્વભાવ svabhaav

dispossess *v.t.* કબજામાંથી લેવું kabajaamaa levun

disproportion *n.* અપ્રમાણસર apramaansar

disprove *v.* ખોટું પુરવાર કરવું khotu puravaar karavun

disputeble *adj.* વિવાદાસ્પદ vivaadaaspad

disputant *n.* વિવાદ કરનાર vivaad karanaar

disputation *n.* દલીલયુક્ત ચર્ચા daleelayukt charchaa

dispute *v.t.* વિવાદ vivaad

disqualify ગેરલાયક geralaayak

disquiet *v.t.* અસ્વસ્થતા asvasthataa

disquisition *n.* વિવરણ viravaran

disregard *v.t.* ઉપેક્ષા કરવી upekshaa karavee

disrelish *n.* અણગમો anagamo

disrepute *n.* બેઆબરૂ beaabaroo

disrespect *v.t.* અનાદર anaadar

disrobe *v.t.* કપડાં ઉતારવાં kapadaa utaaravaa

disrupt *v.t.* ચૂરેચૂરા કરવા choorechooraa karavaa

disruption *n.* ખોરવી નાંખવું khoravee naakhavun

dissatisfaction *n.* અસંતોષ asantosh

dissatisfy *v.t.* અસંતુષ્ટ કરવું asantusht karavun

dissect *v.t.* પૃથક્કરણ કરવું pruthakkaran karavun

dissection *n.* પૃથક્કરણ pruthakkaran

dissemble *v.* છુપાવવું chhupaavavun

disseminate *v.t.* ચોમેર વિખેરવું chomer vikheravun

dissension *n.* ઝઘડો zagado

dissent *v.t.* સંમતિના આપવી sammatee naa aapavee

dissentient *n.* મતભેત ધરાવતું matabhet dharaavatu

dissertation *n.* સવિસ્તાર પ્રબંધ savistaar prabandh

disservice *n.* કુસેવા kusevaa

dissimilar *adj.* ભિન્ન bhinn

dissimulation *n.* ઢોંગ dhong

dissipate *v.* ઉડાડી દેવું udaadee devun

dissipated *adj.* વિઘટિત vighatit

dissipation *n.* ભોગવિલાસ bhagavilaas

dissociate *v.t.* ઉડાઉ udaaoo

dissoute *adj.* ભ્રમિત કરવું bhramit karavun

dissolve *v.t.* ઓગાળવું ogaadavun

dissonance બેસૂરાપણું besooraapanu

dissuade *v.t.* સમજાવવું samajaavavun

distaff *n.* તકલી takalee

distance *n.* અંતર antar

distant *adj.* દૂરનું dooranu

distaste *n.* અરુચિ anagamo

distasteful *adj.* બેસ્વાદ beswaad

distemper *n.* ડિસ્ટેમ્પર distampar

distend *v.t.* ફુલાવવું fulaavavun

distill *v.t.* નિસ્યંદિત કરવું nisyandit karavun

distiller *n.* દારૂ ગાળનાર daaru gaalanaar

distinct *adj.* સ્પષ્ટ spasht

distinction *n.* તફાવત tafaavat

distinctive *adj.* લાક્ષણિક laakshanik

distinguish *v.t.* ભેદ કરવો bhed karavo

distinguished *adj.* નામાંકિત naamaankit

distort *v.t.* વિકૃત કરવું vikrut karavun

distortion *n.* વિકૃતિ vikruti

distract *v.t.* ધ્યાનભંગ કરવો dhyaanabhang karavo

distraction *n.* ચિત્તક્ષોભકારક chittakshobhakaarak

distrain *v.t.* માલ જપ્ત કરવો. maal japt karavo

distraint *n.* માલની જપ્તી maalanee japtee

distress *n.* માનસિક પીડા maansik peedaa

distressful *adj.* ચિંતાજનક chintaajanak

distribute *v.* વહેંચવું vahenchavun

distribution *n.* વહેંચણી vahenchanee

district *n.* જિલ્લો. jillo

distrust *v.t.* અવિશ્વાસ avishvaas

distrustful *adj.* શંકાવાળું shankaavalu

disturb *v.t.* અસ્વસ્થ કરવું asvastha karavun

distrubance *n.* ખલેલ khalel

disunion *n.* જુદા પડવું judaa paadavun

disunite *v.t.* અલગ કરવું alag karavun

divider *n.* ભાગ પાડનાર bhaag paadanaar

divination *n.* ભવિષ્ય જાણવું bhavishya jaanavun

divine *adj.* દૈવિક daivik

divinity દેવત્વ devatva

divisible *adj.* ભાગી શકાય એવું bhaagi shakaay tevun

division વહીવટી વિભાગ vaheevatee vibhaag

divisor *n.* ભાજક bhaajak

divorce *v.t.* છૂટાછેડા chootaachhedaa

divulge *v.t.* ઉઘાડું પાડવું ughaadu paadavun

dizzy *adj.* તમ્મર tammar

do *v.t.* કામ કરવું kaam karavun

docile *adj.* કહ્યાગરું kahyaagaru

docility *n.* સાલસપણું saalasapanu

dock *n.* ગોદી godee

docket *n.* સારસૂચિ saarsoochee

dockyard *n.* જહાજવાળો jahaajavaado

doctor *n.* તબીબ tabeeb

doctrinaire *n.* હઠાગ્રહી hathaagrahee

doctrine *n.* સિદ્ધાંત siddhaant

document *n.* દસ્તાવેજ dastaavej

documentary *aj.* દસ્તાવેજને લગતું dastaavejne lagatu

dodge *v.t.* દાવપેચ daavpech

doe *n.* હરણની માદા. harananee maadaa

doer *n.* કોઇ કામ કરનાર koi kaam karnaar

doff *v.t.* ટોપી ઉતારવું topee utaaravee

dog *n.* કૂતરો kootaro

dogged *adj.* ચીવટવાળું chivatvaalu

dogma *n.* ધાર્મિક સદ્ધિધાંત dhaarmik siddhaant

dogmatic *adj.* ધમંડી ghamandee

dogmatize *v.t.* ઠસાવવું dhasaavavun

doings *n.* કરતૂતો kartooto

doldrums *n.* સ્થગતિ sthagit

dole *n.* ખેરાત kheraat

doleful *adj.* ઉદાસ udaas

doll *n.* ઢીંગલી dheengalee

dollar *n.* અમેરિકાનું ચલણ amerikanu ek chalan

dolorous *adj.* દુઃખદ dukhad

dolour *n.* દુઃખ dukh

dolphin *n.* દરિયાઇ માછલી dariyaaee maachhalee

doit *n.* સંવનન samvanan

domain *n.* કાર્યક્ષેત્ર karyakshetra

dome *n.* ધુંમટ ghoommat

domestic *adj.* ઘરેલુ gharelu

domesticate પાળવું paalavun

domicile *n.* અધિવાસ adhivaas

dominant *adj.* વર્ચસ્વવાળું varchasvavaalu

dominate *v.t.* વર્ચસ્વ ધરાવવું varchasva dharaavatu

domineer *v.t.* હું પદન દર્શાવવું hun padun darshaavavun

dominic *n.* ડૉમનિકિ સંપ્રદાયનું dominik sampradaayanu

dominion *n.* તાબાનો મુલક taabaano mulak

don *v.t.* કપડા પહેરવા kapadaa paheravaa

donate *v.t.* દાન કરવું daan karavun

donation *n.* દાન daan

done *n.* કરેલું karelun

donee *n.* દાન સ્વીકારનાર daan sweekarnaar

donkey *n.* ગધેડુ gadhedu

donor *n.* દાતા daataa

doom *v.t.* વિનાશ vinaash

doomsday *n.* કયામતનો દિવસ kayaamat no divas

door *n.* દરવાજો darvaajo

doorkeeper *n.* દ્વારપાળ dvaarpaal

dormant *adj.* ગુલામ gulaam

dormouse *n.* ઉંદરની એક જાત undar nee ek jaat

dose *n.* દવાની માત્રા davaanee maatraa

dost *v.t.* તે te

dot *n.* ટપકું tapaku

dotage *n.* ઘડપણની નબળાઇ ghadapanni nabalaayee

dotard *n.* વૃદ્ધ vrudhh

dote *v.i.* નબળા મનવાળું nabalaa manvaalu

dotish *adj.* નબળું nabalu

double *n.* બમણું bamanu

double-cross *n.* દગો dago

double-dealer *n.* દાઘવાળુ daaghvaalu

doubt *n.* શંકા shankaa

doubtful *adj.* શંકાશીલ shankaasheel

douche *n.* પિચકારી મારવી pichakaaree maaravee

dough *n.* ગૂંદેલી કણક goondelee kanak

doughty *adj.* બહાદૂર bahaadoor

dove *n.* કબૂતર kabootar

dovetail *v.t.* સાંધો કરવો saandho karavo

dowager *n.* વિધવા vidhavaa

dowdy *n.* નસિતેજ nistej

dower *n.* વિધવાદાય vidhavaadaay

down *n.* નીચે neeche

downcast *adj.* હતાશ hataash

downfall ધોધમાર વરસાદ dhodhamaar varsaad

downhill *n.* ઢોળાવવાળું dholaavavaalu

downpour *n.* ધોધમાર વરસાદ dhodhamaar varasaad

downright *adj.* સંપૂર્ણપણે sampurnpane

downstairs *adv.* નીચેના માળનું neechenaa maalanu

downtrodden *adj.* કચડાયેલું kachadaayelu

downward *adj.* નીચેની જગ્યાએ neechenee jagyaae

downy *adj.* સુંવાળું suvaalu

dowry *n.* દહેજ dahej

doze *v.t.* ઘેનમાં હોવું ghenamaa hovun

dozen *n.* બારનો જુમલો baarano jumalo

drab *n.* નીરસ neeras

draft *n.* મુસદ્દો musaddo

draftsman *n.* મુસદ્દો ઘડનાર musaddo ghadanaar

drag *v.t.* ઘસડવું ghasadavun

dragon *n.* રાક્ષસ raakshas

dragoon *n.* ઘોડદળનો સૈનિક ghodadalano sainik

drain *v.t.* પ્રવાહીનો નિકાલ pravaaheeno nikaal

drainage *n.* ગટરવ્યવસ્થા gataravyavasthaa

drake *n.* નર બતક nar batak

dram *n.* દારૂનો ઘૂંટ daaroono ghoont

drama *n.* નાટક naatak

dramatic *adj.* નાટકીય naatakeey

dramatis personae *n.* નાટકના કલાકારો naatakana kalaakaaro

dramatist *n.* નાટ્યકાર naatyakaar

dramatize *v.t.* નાટક કરવું naatak karavun

drape *v.t.* વ્યવસ્થિત ગોઠવવું vyavsthit gothavavun

draper *n.* કાપડિયો. kaapadiyo

drat *v.t.* હેરાન કરવું heraan karavun

draught *v.t.* દુષ્કાળ dushkaal

draw *v.t.* ખેંચવું khenchavun

drawback *n.* ખામી khaamee

drawer *n.* ખેંચનાર khenchanaar

drawe *n.* નાણા ચુકવનાર naana chukavanaar

drawing *n.* રેખાકૃતિ rekhaakrutee

drawing room *n.* ચિત્રરૂમ chitraroom

dread *n.* ભયાનક bhayaanak

dreadful *n.* ભયાનક bhayaanak

dream *n.* સ્વપ્ન swapn

dreary *adj.* સૂનકાર soonkaar

dregs *n.* કાદવ kaadav

drench *v.t.* તરબોળ કરવું tarbol karavun

dress *v.t.* કપડાં પહેરવા kapadaa paheravaa

dressing *n.* મલમપટ્ટી malampattee

drew ખેંચવું khenchavun

drift *v.i.* ઘસડાવવું ghasadaavavun

drill *n.* શારડી shaaradee

drink *v.t.* પીવું peevun

drinkable *adj.* પીવાલાયક peevaalaayak

drip *v.i.* ટીપાં પાડવાં teepaa paadavaa

drive *n.* હાંકવું haankavun

drivel *n.* વાહિયાત vaahiyaat

driver *n.* વાહનચાલક vaahanachaalak

drizzel *v.i.* ઝરમર વરસાદ zaramar varasaad

droll *adj.* રમૂજી ramoojee

drollery *n.* મશ્કરી mashkaree

drone *n.* નર મધમાખી nar madhamaakhee

droop *v.i.* નીચે વળવું neeche valavun

drop *v.t.* ટીપા પાડવા teempa paadavaa

dropsy *n.* જલોદર jalodar

dross *n.* કચરો kacharo

drought *n.* દુકાળ dukaal

drove *v.t.* ઢોરનું ટોળું dhoranu tolu

drown *v.t.* ડૂબવું doobavun

drowsy *adj.* ઘેનમા ghenamaa

drowsiness *n.* તંદ્રા tandraa

drudge *n.* મજૂર majoor

drudgery *n.* ગધ્ધાવૈતરું gaddhaavaitaru

drug *n.* દવા davaa

druggist *n.* દવાવાળો. davaavaalo

druid *n.* સેલ્ટ ધર્મગુરુ selt dharmaguru

drum *n.* નગારું nagaaru

drummer *n.* ઢોલચી dholachee

drunken *adj.* દારૂ પીધેલ daaru peedhel

drunkard *n.* દારૂડિયો. daarudiyo

drunkenness *n.* દારૂની આદત daarunee aadat

dry *adj.* શુષ્ક shushk

dryad *n.* વનપરી vanaparee

dryness *n.* શુષ્કતા shuskataa

dry-shod *n.* કોરા પગવાળું koraa pagavaalu

dual *adj.* બેવડું bevadu

dub *v.t.* ચિત્રપટનુ ભાષાંતર chitrapatnu bhaashaantar

dubiors *adj.* શંકાસ્પદ shankaaspad

duck *n.* બતક batak

duckling *n.* બતકનું બચ્ચું batakanu bacchu

duct *n.* નળી nalee

ductile *adj.* કહ્યાગરું kahyaagaru

dudgeon *n.* ક્રોધ krodh

due *adj.* લેણું lenun
duel *n.* યુદ્ધ yuaddh
duet *n.* યુગલગીત yugal geet
duffer *n.* ડફોળ dafol
dug *n.* આંચળ aanchal
duke *n.* ઉમરાવ umaraav
dukedom *n.* ઉમરાવનો મોભો
  umaraavano mobho
dulcet *adj.* મધુર madhur
dull *adj.* ઝાંખું zankhu
dullard *n.* મંદબુદ્ધિમાણસ
  mandabuddhi maanas
duly *adv.* વખતસર vakhatasar
dumb *adj.* મૂંગું moongu
dumb-bells *adj.* મુરૂખ murkh
dummy *n.* ડમી damee
dump *n.* ઢગલો કરવો dhagalo karavo
dumpy *adj.* ઠીંગણું thinganun
dunce *n.* ઠોઠ નિશાળિયો thoth
  nishaadiyo
dune *n.* ઢૂવો. dhoovo
dung *n.* છાણ chhaan
dungeon *n.* અંધારકોટડી andhaar
  kotadee
dupe *n.* છેતરવું chhetaravun
duplex *adj.* બે માળવાળું be maalvaalu
duplicate *v.t.* પ્રતિકૃતિરૂપ pratikrutiroop
duplicator *n.* નકલ કરનાર nakal
  karanaar
duplicity *n.* કપટભાવ kapatabhaav
durable *adj.* ટકાઉ takaau
durability *n.* ટકાઉપણું takaaupanu
durance *n.* કેદ ked
duration *n.* ટકવું તે takavun te
during *prep.* દરમિયાન daramiyaan
dusk *n.* સંધ્યાનો સમય sandyaano
  samay
dust *n.* ધૂળ dhool
duster *n.* ઝાપટિયું zaapatiyu
dusty *adj.* ધૂળવાળું dhoolvaalu
dutch *n.* નેધરલેન્ડનું nedharlendanu
dutiable *adj.* જકાત વેરાનેપાત્ર jakaat
  veraane paatra
dutiful *adj.* કરતવ્યનિષ્ટ kartavyanisht
duty *n.* ફરજ faraj
dwarf *n.* વામન vaaman
dwarfish *adj.* નાનું naanu

dwell *v.i.* રહેવું rahevun
dwelling *n.* ઘર ghar
dwindle *v.i.* ઘટવું ghatavun
dyad *n.* યુગલ yugal
dye *v.t.* રંગ કરવો rang karavo
dyer *n.* રંગ કરનાર rang karanaar
dying *adj.* અંતકાળ antakaal
dynamic *adj.* જોમવાળું jomavaalu
dynamite *n.* સ્ફોટક પદાર્થ sfotak
  padaarth
dynamo *n.* ડાયનેમો dayanemo
dynasty *n.* વંશ vansh
dysentery *n.* મરડો marado
dyspepsia *n.* અપચો apacho
dyspeptic *adj.* પાચનરોગી
  paachanarogee
dysuria *n.* પેશાબમાં તકલીફ peshabama
  takalif

E

each *adj.* દરેક darek
eager *adj.* આતુર aatur
eagerly *adv.* આતુરતાપૂર્વક
  aaturtaapoorvak
eagerness *n.* આતુરતા aaturtaa
eagle *n.* ગરુડ garud
eagle-eyed *adj.* તીક્ષ્ણ દ્રષ્ટિ tikshna
  drushti
eaglet *n.* ગરુડનું બચ્ચુ garudanu
  bachchu
ear *n.* કાન kaan
early *adj.* નિયત સમય પહેલાનું niyat
  samay pahelaanu
earn *v.t.* કમાવું kamaavun
earnest *adj.* આતુર aatur
earnestly *adv.* આતુરતાપૂર્વક
  aaturataapoorvak
earnestness *n.* આતુરતા aaturtaa
earnings *n.* કમાણી kamaanee
earth *n.* પૃથ્વી pruthavee
earthen *adj.* માટીનું maateenu
earthenware *n.* માટીના વાસણ
  maateenaa vaasan

earthly *adj.* દુન્યવી dunavayee
earthquake *n.* ધરતીકંપ dharateekamp
earthy *adj.* દુન્યવી dunvayee
ease *n.* આરામ aaram
easement *n.* પડોશહક્ક padoshakka
easily સરળતાથી saralataathee
east *n.* પૂરવ purva
easter *n.* ઇસ્ટર istar
eastern *adj.* પૂરવનું poorvanu
easterly *adj.* પૂરવ તરફનું poorva
    tarafanu
eastward *adj.* પૂરવ દિશા poorv dishaa
easy *adj.* સરળ saral
easychair *n.* આરામદાયક ખુરશી
    aaraamadaayak khurashee
eat *v.t.* ખાવું khaavun
eaten ખાધેલું khaadelu
eatable *adj.* ખાદ્ય વસ્તુ khaadya vastu
ebb *n.* ઓટ aot
ebonite *n.* વલ્કેનાઇઝની પ્રકૃમિ
    valkenaaizanee prakriyaa
ebony *n.* કઠણ અને ભારે kathan ane
    bhaare
ebullient *adj.* ઊકળતું ookalatu
ebullition *n.* ઊભરો oobharo
eccentric *adj.* તરંગી tarangee
ecclesiastic *n.* ધર્મોપદેશક
    dharmopadesh
ecciesiastical *adj.* ચર્ચ સાથે જોડાયેલું
    charch saathe jodaayelu
echo *n.* પડધો padagho
eclat *n.* ફતેહ fateh
eclipse *n.* ગ્રહણ grahan
economical *adj.* કરકસર કરનારું
    karakasar karanaaru
economics *n.* અર્થશાસ્ત્ર arthashaastra
economist *n.* અર્થશાસ્ત્રી
    arthashaastree
economize *v.t.* કરકસર કરવી karakasar
    karavee
economy *n.* અર્થતંત્ર arthatantra
ecstasy *n.* પરમાનંદ paramaanand
eczema *n.* ખરજવું kharajavun
edacious *adj.* ખાઉધરું khaudharu
eddy *n.* વમળ vamal
eden *n.* દાંત વિનાનું daant vinaanu
edge *n.* ધાર dhaar

edible *adj.* ખાદ્ય khaadya
edict *n.* રાજઆજ્ઞા raajaagnaa
edifice *n.* ઇમારત emaarat
edify *v.t.* સુધારવું sudhaaravun
edit *v.t.* સંપાદન કરવું sanpaadav karavun
edition *n.* આવૃત્તિ aavrutee
editor *n.* સંપાદક sampaadak
editorial *adj.* તંત્રીલેખ tantreelekh
educate *v.t.* કેળવણી આપવી kelavanee
    aapavee
educated *adj.* શક્ષિત shikshit
education *n.* શક્ષિણ shikshan
educational *adj.* શૈક્ષણિક shaikshanik
educationist *n.* કેળવણીકાર
    kelavaneekaar
educative *adj.* શૈક્ષણિક shaikshanik
educe *v.t.* બહાર કાઢવું bahaar kadhavun
efface *v.t.* ભૂસી નાખવું bhoonsee
    naakhavun
effect *n.* અસર asar
effective *adj.* પ્રભાવશાળી
    prabhaavashaalee
effectual *adj.* સાર્થક saarthak
effeminate *adj.* બાયલું baayalu
effervesce *v.i.* ઊભરાવું ubharaavun
effete *adj.* નબળું nabalu
efficacious *adj.* ગુણકારક gunkaarak
efficacy *n.* કાર્યક્ષમતા
    kaaryakshamataa
efficient *n.* કાર્યક્ષમ kaaryaksham
effigy *n.* નનામી nanaamee
efflorescence *n.* મોર આવવાવાળું mor
    aavavaavaalu
effluent *adj.* બહાર વહી જતું bahaar
    vahee jatu
effort *n.* પ્રયત્ન prayatna
effrontery નઇરતા nidarataa
effulgent *adj.* તેજસ્વી tejasvee
effulgence *n.* તેજસ્વિતા tesasvitaa
effuse *v.t.* ઊભરો oobharo
effusion *n.* ઊભરો oobharo
effusive *adj.* વહેતું vahetu
egg *n.* ઈંડું indu
ego *n.* અહં aham
egocentric *adj.* અહંકેન્દ્રી
    ahamakendree

egoism *n.* અહંભાવ ahamabhaav

egotism *n.* આપવડાઈ aapavadaai

egotist *adj.* આપવડાઈવાળો aapavadaaivaalo

egregious *adj.* આઘાતજનક aaghaatajanak

egress *n.* બહાર જવું bahaar javun

eh *int.* ઉદ્દગાર udagaar

eight આઠ aath

eighteen *adj.* અઢાર adhaar

eighth *adj.* આઠમો aathamo

eightieth *adj.* એંશીમું aesheemu

eighty *adj.* એંશી aenshee

either *adj.* બેમાંથી કોઈ એક bemaathee koye ek

ejaculate *v.t.* ઓચિંતું ochintun

ejaculation *n.* ઉદ્દગાર કાઢવો udagaar kaadhavo

eject *v.t.* બહાર ફેંકવું bahaar fenkavun

eke *v.t.* ઘટ પૂરવી ghat pooravee

elaborate *adj.* ઝીણવટભર્યું zeenavatbharyu

elapse *v.t.* વીતવું veetavun

elastic *adj.* સ્થિતિસ્થાપક sthitisthaapak

elasicity *n.* સ્થિતિસ્થાપકતા sthitisthaapakataa

elate *v.t.* ઉત્તેજતિ uattejit

elation *n.* ઉત્તેજના uattejanaa

elbow *n.* કોણી konee

elder *adj.* મોટી ઉંમરનું motee uamarnu

eldest *adj.* જ્યેષ્ઠ jayeshtha

elderly *adj.* પૂરોઢ praudh

elect *v.t.* ચૂંટવું choontavun

elction *n.* ચૂંટણી choontanee

elective *n.* ચૂંટણી નિયુક્ત choontanee niyukt

elector *n.* મતદાર matdaar

electorate *n.* મતદારયાદી matdaar yaadee

electrical *n.* વીજળીક veejaleek

electrician *n.* વદ્યિુતશાસ્ત્રી vidyutshastree

electricity *n.* વીજળી veejalee

electrify *v.t.* વદ્યિુતકિરણ vidhytikaran

electrocution *n.* વીજળી દ્વારા મોત veejalee dvaaraa mot

electron *n.* મૂળભૂત ઘટક moolabhoot

dhatak

elegance *n.* લાલિત્ય laalitya

elegant *adj.* ભવ્ય bhavya

elegy *n.* શોકગીત shokgeet

element *n.* તત્ત્વ tattvaa

elemental *adj.* મૂળભૂત moolabhoot

elementary *adj.* પ્રાથમકિ praathamik

elephant *n.* હાથી haathee

elephantine *adj.* કદાવર kadaavar

elevate *v.t.* ઉન્નત કરવું unnnat karavun

elevation *n.* ઊંચે ચડાવવું uanche chadaavavun

elevator *n.* લિફ્ટ lift

eleven *adj.* અગિયાર agiyaar

eleventh *adj.* અગિયારમુ agiyaaramu

elf *n.* વેતાળયું vetiyu

elfin *adj.* ઠિંગુજીઓને લગતું thingujeeaone lagatu

elicit *v.t.* માહિતી કઢાવવી maahitee kadhavavee

elide *v.t.* શબ્દલોપ shabdalop

eligible *adj.* હકદાર hakadaar

eligibility *n.* પાત્રતા paatrataa

eliminate *v.t.* દૂર કરવું door karavun

elimination *n.* નાબૂદી naaboodee

elision *n.* પદલોપ padalop

elite *n.* ચુનંદો વર્ગ chunando varg

elixir *n.* અમૃત amrut

elk *n.* સાબર saabar

ellips *n.* અંડાકૃત andaakrutee

ellipsis *n.* અધ્યાહાર adyaahaar

elocution *n.* વકતૃત્વ vakatrutva

elocutionist *n.* વકતૃત્વકળાવાન vakatrutvakalaavaan

elongate *v.t.* લંબાવવું lambaavavun

elope *v.i.* સહપલાયન કરવું sahapalaayan karavun

eloquence *n.* વકતૃત્વ vakatrutva

eloquent *adj.* વાક્પટુતા vaakapatutaa

else *adj.* અન્યથા anyathaa

elsewhere *adv.* બીજે કોઈ ઠેકાણે bijee koi thekaade

elucidate *v.t.* સમજાવવું samajaavavun

elucidation *n.* સ્પષ્ટીકરણ spashtikaran

elude *v.t.* હોશિયારીથી ટાળવું hoshiyaareethee taalavun

elusion *n.* પલાયનયુક્તિ palaayanayuktee

elusive *adj.* છેતરનારું chhetarnaarun

elysium *n.* સ્વર્ગ svarg

emaciate *v.t.* પાતળું બનાવવું paatadu banaavavun

emaciation *n.* પાતળું બનાવવું તે paatadu banaavavy te

emanate *v.t.* માંથી નીકળવું maathee neekadavun

emanation *n.* બહાર નીકળવું તે bahaar neekadavun te

emancipate *v.t.* બંધનમુક્ત કરવું bandhanmukta karavun

emancipation *n.* બંધનમુક્તિ bandhan mukti

emasculate *v.t.* ખસી કરવું khasee karavun

embankment *n.* બાંધ baandh

embargo *n.* મનાઈહુકમ manaaihookam

embark *v.t.* વહાણમાં ચડાવવું vahaanamaa chadaavavun

embarrass *v.t.* શરમિંદુ થાય તેમ કરવું sharmindu thaay tem karavun

ebmarrassment *n.* શરમિંદગી sharmindagee

embassy *n.* રાજદૂતાલય raajadootaalay

embattle *v.t.* કિલેબંધી કરવી kilebandhee karavee

embed *v.t.* ભેગું કરવું bhegu karavun

embellish *v.t.* સુશોભિત કરવું sushobhit karavun

embellishment *n.* સુશોભન sushobhan

ember *n.* ચિનગારી. chingaaree

embezzle *v.t.* ઉચાપત કરવી uchaapat karavee

embitter *v.t.* કડવું બનાવવું kadavun banaavavun

emblazon *v.t.* શણગારવું shanagaaravun

emblem *n.* પ્રતીક prateek

emblematic *adj.* પ્રતીક prateek

embodiment *n.* મૂર્તસ્વરૂપ moortasvaroop

embody *v.t.* સ્વરૂપ હોવું svaroop aapavun

embolden *v.t.* મજબૂત બનાવવું majaboot banaavavun

emboss *v.t.* નકશી કરવી nakashee karavee

embrace *v.t.* ભેટવું bhetavun

embroidery *n.* ભરતકામ bharatakaam

embryo *n.* ગર્ભ garbha

embryonic *adj.* ગર્ભ garbha

emendation *n.* પાઠ સંશોધન paath sansodhan

emerald *n.* નીલમ neelam

emerge ઉદ્દ્ભવવું udabhavavun

emergence *n.* ઉભરવું ubharavun

emergency *n.* કટોકટી katokatee

emergent *adj.* બહાર પાડનારું baraar paadanaaru

emeritus *adj.* નિવૃત્ત nivrutta

emetic *adj.* ઊલટીકારક દવા oolateekaarak davaa

emigrant નિર્ગામી nirgaamee

emigrate *v.t.* નિર્ગમન nirgaman

emigration *n.* સ્થળાંતર sthadaantar

eminence પ્રખ્યાત prakhyaat

eminet *adj.* જાસૂસી jaasoosee

emissary *n.* જાસૂસ jaasoos

emission *n.* ઉત્સર્જન utsarajan

emit *v.t.* બહાર કાઢવું bahaar kaadhavun

emmet *n.* કીડી. keedee

emolument *n.* મળતર malatar

emotion *n.* મનોભાવ manobhaav

emotional *adj.* ભાવનાશીલ bhaavanaasheel

emperor *n.* સમ્રાટ samraat

emphasis *n.* પ્રાધાન્ય praadhaanya

emphasize *v.t.* ભાર મૂકવો. bhaar mookavo

emphatic *adj.* ભારપૂર્વકનું bhaarapoorvakanu

empire *n.* સામ્રાજ્ય saamraajya

empirical *adj.* પ્રયોગમૂલક prayogamoolak

emplane *v.t.* વિમાનમાં ચડવું vimaanama chadavun

employ *v.t.* કામમાં લેવું kaamamaa levun

employed *n.* નિયોજિત niyojit

employee *n.* કર્મચારી karmachaaree

employer *n.* નોકરીદાતા nokareedaataa

employment *n.* રોજગારી rojagaaree

emporium *n.* બજાર bajaar

empower *v.t.* સત્તા આપવી sattaa aapavee

empress *n.* સામ્રાજ્ઞી saamraagnee

emptiness ખાલીપણુ khaaleepanu

empty *adj.* ખાલી khaalee

emulate *v.t.* સ્પર્ધા કરવી spardhaa karavee

emulation *n.* સ્પર્ધા spardhaa

emulous *adj.* સ્પર્ધાપ્રેરિત spardhaaprerit

enable *v.t.* સમર્થ કરવું samarth karavun

enact *v.t.* કાયદો ઘડવો kaayado ghadavo

enamel *n.* કાચના જેવો એક પદાર્થ kaachanaa jevo ek padaarth

enamour *v.t.* મોહિત કરવું moheet karavun

encage *v.t.* પાંજરામાં પૂરવું paajaraamaa poorvun

encamp *v.t.* છાવણી કરવી chhaavanee naakhavee

encampment *n.* છાવણી chaavanee

encase ખોખામાં મૂકવું khokhaamaa mukavun

encashment *n.* વટાવવું vataavavun

enchain *v.t.* સાંકળ વડે બાંધવું saakad vade baandhavun

enchant *v.t.* જાદુ કરવું jaadu karavun

enchantment *n.* કામણ કરવું kaaman karavun

enchanter *n.* જાદૂગર jadoogar

enclave *n.* વિદેશી થાણું videshee thaanu

encloseure *n.* વાડો vaado

encomium *n.* ઔપચારિક વખાણ aupachaarik vakhaan

encompass *v.t.* ઘેરવું dheravun

encounter *v.t.* અથડામણ athadaaman

encourage *v.t.* ઉત્તેજન આપવું uttejan aapavun

encroach *v.t.* અતિક્રમણ કરવું atikraman karavun

encumber *v.i.* અડચણ કરવી adachan karavee

encumbrance *n.* ભાર bhaar

encyclopedia *n.* જ્ઞાનકોશ gnaankosh

end *n.* છેડો chhedo

endanger જોખમમાં નાખવું jokhamama naakhavun

endear *v.t.* પ્રિય બનાવવું priya banaavau

endearment *n.* વહાલ કરવું vahaal karavun

endeavour *v.t.* કોશિશ koshish

endless *adj.* અનંત anant

endow *v.t.* સત્તા આપવી sattaa aapavee

endowment *n.* ગુણવત્તા gunavattaa

endurance *n.* સહનશક્તિ sahanashaktee

endure *v.t.* સહન કરવું sahan karavun

enema *n.* બસ્તિક્રિયા bastikriya

enemy *n.* દુશ્મન dushman

energetic *adj.* જુસ્સાવાળું jussaavaalu

energize *v.t.* પ્રોત્સાહિત કરવું protasaahit karavun

energy *n.* જુસ્સો jusso

enervate *v.t.* નિર્બળ બનાવવું nirbal banaavavun

enfeeble *v.t.* કમજોર બનાવવું kamajor banaavavun

enforce *v.t.* લાદવું laadavun

enfranchize *v.t.* વેચાણ પરવાનો લેવો vechaan parvaano levo

engage *v.t.* વચનબદ્ધ થવું vachanabadhh thavun

engagement *n.* ની સાથે ગૂંથાઈ જવું nee saathe goonthai javun

engender *v.t.* પેદા કરવું pedaa karavun

engine *n.* ગતિપ્રેરક યંત્ર gatiprerak yanta

engineer *n.* ઈજનેર ejaner

engirdle *v.t.* ની ફરતે વર્તુળ બનાવવું nee farate vartul banaavavun

english *adj.* અંગ્રેજી ભાષા angrejee bhaashaa

engraft *v.t.* માં દાખલ કરવી maa daakhal karavun

engrain *v.t.* પાકો રંગ દેવો paako rang devo

engrave *v.t.* કોતરવું kotaravun

engraving *n.* છાપેલી આકૃતિ chhaapelee aakrute

engulf *v.t.* ઘેરી લેવું dheree levun

enhance *v.t.* વધારવું vadhaarvun

enigma *n.* કોયડો koyado

enjoin *v.t.* આજ્ઞા કરવી aagnaa karavee

enjoy *v.t.* આનંદ માણવો aanand maanavo

enjoyment *n.* આનંદ aanand

enkindle *v.t.* સળગાવવું sadagaavavun

enlace *v.t.* ઘેરી લેવું dheree levun

enlarge *v.t.* વિસ્તૃત કરવું vistrut karavun

enlighten *v.t.* બોધ આપવો bodh aapavo

enlightenment *n.* બોધ આપવો bodh aapavo

enlist *v.t.* યાદી બનાવવી yaadee banaavavee

enliven *v.t.* સજીવન કરવું sajeevan karavun

enmity *n.* વેર ver

ennoble *v.t.* ને ઉમરાવ બનાવવો ne umaraav banaavavo

enormity *n.* ઘોર અપરાધ dhor aparaadh

enormous *adj.* પ્રચંડ prachand

enogh *adj.* પૂરતું pooratu

enounce *v.t.* ઉચ્ચાર કરવો. uchchaar karavo

enquire *v.t.* તપાસ કરવી tapaas karvee,

enrage *v.t.* ગુસ્સે કરવું gusse karavun

enrapt *v.t.* અત્યંત આનંદિત કરવું atyant aananadit karavun

enrapture *v.t.* અત્યંત આનંદિત કરવું atyant aananadit karavun

enrich *v.t.* સમૃદ્ધ થવું samruddh thavun

enrol *v.* પત્રકમાં નામ નોંધવું patrak maa naam nodhavun

enshrine *v.t.* સંઘરવું sangharavun

enshrond *v.t.* આચ્છાદન કરવું aaschhadan karavun

ensign *n.* નિશાની nishaanee

enslave *v.t.* ને ગુલામ બનાવવું ne gulaam banaavavun

ensue *v.i.* પાછળથી થવું paasadthee thavun

ensuing *adj.* આગામી aagaamee

ensure *v.t.* ખાતરી કરવી khaataree karavee

entail *v.t.* આવશ્યક બનાવવું aavashyak banaavavun

entangle જાળમાં ફસાવવું, jaalamaa fasaavavun

entente *n.* મિત્રતાની સમજૂતી mitrataanee samajootee

enter *v.t.* દાખલ થવું daakhal thavun

enterprise *n.* ઉદ્યોગસાહસ udyog saahas

entertain *v.t.* મનોરંજન કરવું manoranjan karavun

entertainment *n.* મનોરંજન manoranjan

enthral *v.t.* મોહિત કરવું mohit karavun

enthrone *v.t.* ગાદી પર બેસાડવું gaadee par besaadavun

enthusiasm *n.* ઉત્સાહ utsaah

enthusiast *adj.* ઉત્સાહી utsaahee

entice *v.t.* લલચાવવું lalachaavavun

enticing *adj.* આકર્ષક aakarshak

entire *adj.* સંપૂર્ણ sampoorn

entitle *v.t.* મથાળું આપવું mathaadu aapavun

entity *n.* એકમ ekam

entomb *v.t.* કબરમાં દાટવું kabaramaa daatavun

entomology જંતુશાસ્ત્ર jantushastra

entrails *n.pl.* આંતરડાં aantardaa

entrance *n.* પ્રવેશદ્વાર praveshdvaar

entrap *v.t.* પાંજરામાં પકડવું paanjaraamaa pakadavun

entreat *v.t.* આજીજી કરવી aajeejee karavee

entreaty *n.* આજીજી aajeejee

entrench *v.t.* કિલ્લેબંધી કરવી killebandhee karavee

entrust *v.t.* ભરોસે મૂકવું bharose mookavun

entry *n.* પ્રવેશ pravesh

entwine *v.t.* વીંટળાઈ જવું veentadaai javun

entwist *v.t.* આમળવું aamadavun

enumerate *v.t.* ગણતરી કરવી ganataree karavee

enumeration *n.* ગણતરી ganataree

enunciate *v.t.* જાહેર કરવું jaaher karavun

enunciation *n.* જાહેરાત jaaheraat

envelop *v.t.* વીંટવું veentavun
envelope *n.* પરબીડિયું parabeediyu
envenom *v.t.* ઝેર નાખવું zer nankhavun
enviable *adj.* અદેખાઈ આવે એવું adekhaai aave evun
envious *adj.* ઈર્ષ્યાળુ ershaadu
environ *v.t.* ની ફરતે વર્તુળ nee farate vartul
environment *n.* વાતાવરણ vaataavaran
envisage *v.t.* ધ્યાનમાં લેવું dhyaanman levun
envoy *n.* રાજદૂત raajdoot
envy *n.* અદેખાઈ asekhaee
enwrap *v.t.* વીંટવું veentavun
eon *n.* ખૂબ જ અચોક્કસ સમય khoob j achokkas samay
ephemeral *adj.* ક્ષણભંગુર kshanbhangur
epic *n.* મહાકાવ્ય mahaakaavya
epicure *n.* સવાદિયું માણસ savaadiyu maanas
epicurean *n.* ભોગવાદી bhogavaadee
epidemic *n.* રોગચાળો rogachaado
epigram *n.* ટુચકો tuchako
epigraph *n.* શિલાલેખ shilaalesh
epilepsy *n.* વાઈ vaai
epileptic *adj.* ફેફસાનો રોગી fefasaano rogee
episode *n.* પ્રકરણ prakaran
epistle *n.* પત્રના રૂપમાં કાવ્ય patranaa joop maa kaavya
epitaph *n.* સમાધિલેખ samaadhilekh
epithet *n.* ગુણવાચક વિશેષણ gunavaachak visheshan
epitome *n.* સાર saar
epitomize *v.t.* સાર કાઢવો saar kaadhavo
epoch *n.* યુગ yug
equal *adj.* સમાન samaan
equality *n.* સરખાપણું sarakhapanu
equalize *v.t.* સરખું બનાવવું sarakhu banaavavun
equanimity *n.* સ્વસ્થતા svasthataa
equate *v.t.* સરખાપણું ગણવું sarakhapanu ganavun
equation *n.* સમીકરણ sameekaran
equator *n.* વિષુવવૃત્ત vishuvavrut

equatorial *adj.* વિષુવવૃત્તયિ vishuvavruttiy
equilateral *adj.* સમભુજ samabhuj
equilibrium *n.* સમતોલપણું samatolapanu
equinox *n.* સંપાત sanpaat
equip *v.t.* સજ્જ કરવું sajj karavun
equipage *n.* આવશ્યક સાજસરંજામ aavashyak saajasarnjaam
equipoise *n.* સમતુલા samatulaa
equitable *adj.* વાજબી vaajabee
equitation *n.* અશ્વારોહણ ashvaarohan
equity *n.* સમાનતા samaanataa
equivalence *n.* સમાનાર્થ samaanaarth
equivalent *adj.* સમાનાર્થ samaanaarth
equivocal *adj.* દ્વિઅર્થી dviarthee
equivocate દ્વિઅર્થી બોલવું dviarthee bolavun
era *n.* યુગ yug
eradicate *v.t.* નિર્મૂલ કરવું nirmool karavun
erase *v.t.* ભૂંસી નાખવું bhoonsee naakhavun
eraser *n.* રબર rabar
erasure *n.* ભૂંસી નાખવું તે bhoonsee naakhavun te
ere *adv.* પૂર્વે poorve
erect *v.t.* ટટાર કરવું tattaar karavee
erection *n.* ટટાર tattar
erode *v.t.* ઘસી કાઢવું ghasee kaadhavun
erosion *n.* ધોવાણ dhovaan
erotic *adj.* શૃંગારિક shrungaarik
err *v.i.* ભૂલ કરવી bhool karavee
errand *n.* સંદેશ sandesh
erratic *adj.* ચંચળ chanchal
erratum *n.* છાપભૂલ chhaapbhool
erroneous *adj.* ભૂલભરેલું bhoolabharelu
error *n.* ભૂલ bhool
eruidite *adj.* પ્રકાંડ પંડિત prakaand pandeet
erudition *n.* પાંડિત્ય paanditya
erupt *v.t.* ફાટી નીકળવું faatee nikalavun
eruption *n.* ફાટવું faatavun
escape *v.t.* ટાળવું taalavun
eschew *v.t.* ટાળવું taalavun
escort *v.t.* વળાવવું valaavavun

esoteric *adj.* ખાનગી khaanagee
especial *adj.* વશિષ vishesh
espial *n.* જાસૂસી jaasoosee
espionage *n.* જાસૂસી jaasoosee
esplanade *n.* સપાટ મેદાન sapaat medaan
espouse *v.t.* પરણવું paranavun
espousal *n.* લગ્ન lagna
espy *v.t.* નજરે પડવું najare padavun
essay *v.t.* નિબંધ nibandh
essence *n.* તથ્ય sattva, tathya
essential *adj.* આવશ્યક aavashyak
establish *v.t.* સ્થાપવું sthaapavun
establishment *n.* સ્થાપન કરવું તે sthaapan karavun te
estate *n.* મલિકત milakat
esteem *n.* ચાહના chaahanaa
estimate *v.t.* અંદાજ કાઢવો andaaj kaadavo
estimation *n.* અંદાજ andaaj
estrange *v.t.* મતિરભાવ ગુમાવવો. mitrabhaav gumaavavo
etcetera *adj.* વગેરે vagere
etch *v.t.* કોતરકામ કરવું kotarkaam karavun
eternal *adj.* શાશ્વત shaashvat
eternity *n.* શાશ્વતી shaashvatee
ether *n.* આકાશ aakaash
etherial *adj.* અમૂર્ત amoort
ethic *adj.* નૈતિક સદ્ધિધાનતો naitik sinddhaant
ethics *n.* નીતિશાસ્ત્ર neetishaashtra
etiquette *n.* રીતભાત reetbhaat
etymology *n.* વ્યુત્પત્તિશાસ્ત્ર vyatpateeshaashtra
eulogy *n.* પ્રશંસા prasansaa
eunuch *n.* કનિન્નર kinnar
eureka *n.* મનપસંદ manapasand
european *n.* યુરોપને લગતું. uropane lagatu
evacuate *v.t.* ખાલી કરવું khaalee karavun
evade *v.t.* થી નાસી જવું thee naasee javun
evaluate *v.t.* મૂલ્યાંકન કરવું moolyaankan karavun
evanescent *adj.* વલીન veelin

evaporate *v.t.* બાષ્પીભવન થવું baashpeebhavan thavun
evasion *n.* ઉડાઉ જવાબ udaau javaab
evasive *adj.* ઉડાઉ udaau
eve *n.* સંધ્યાકાળ, sandyaakaal
even *adj.* કાયમી kaayamee
even *adv.* સમાન samaan
evening *n.* સાંજ saanj
event *n.* બનાવ banaav
eventide *n.* સાંજ saanj
eventual *adj.* આખરનું aakharanu
ever *adv.* નિત્ય nitya
everlasting *adj.* સદાને માટે sadaane maate
evermore *adv.* સદાને માટે sadaane maate
evidence *n.* પુરાવો puraavo
evident *adj.* સ્પષ્ટ spasht
evil *adj.* દુષ્ટ dusht
evince *v.t.* રસ દર્શાવવો ras darshaavavo
evoke *v.t.* ભાવ જગાડવો. bhaav jagaadavo
evolve *v.t.* વિકસિત કરવું vikasit karavun
evolution *n.* ઉત્ક્રાંતિ utkraanti
ewe *n.* ઘેટી ghetee
ewer *n.* ચંબૂ chamboo
exact *adj.* ચોક્કસ chokkas
exactly *adv.* તદ્દન બરાબર taddan baraabar
exaggerate *v.t.* અતિશયોક્તિ કરવી atishayokti karavee
exaggeration *n.* અતિશયોક્તિ atishayokti
exalt *v.t.* પ્રશંસા કરવી prashansaa karavee
examination *n.* પરીક્ષા pareekshaa
examine *v.t.* પરીક્ષા કરવી pareeksha karavee
examinee *n.* પરીક્ષાર્થી pareekshaarthee
examiner *n.* પરીક્ષક pareekshak
example *n.* ઉદાહરણ udaaharan
exanimo *adj.* સ્નેહપૂર્વક snehapoorvak
exasperate ચીડવવું, cheedavavun
excavate ખોદવું khodavun
exceed *v.t.* વટાવી જવું vataavee javun

excel *v.t.* ચડી જવું chadee javun

excellence *n.* શ્રેષ્ઠતા shreshthataa

excellency *adj.* સન્માન સૂચક ખિતાબ sanmaanjanak khitaab

excellent *adj.* ઉત્કૃષ્ટ utakrusht

except *prep.* નો અપવાદ કરવો no apavaad karavo

exception *n.* અપવાદ apavaad

exceptionable *adj.* વાંધાસ્પદ vaandhaspad

excerpt *n.* અવતરણ કરવું avataran karavun

excess *n.* અત્યંત atyant

excessive *adj.* વધારે પડતું vadhaare padatu

exchange *v.t.* આદાનપ્રદાન aadaanpradaan

exchequer *n.* તિજોરી tijoree

excise *n.* જકાત jakaat

excite *v.t.* ઉશ્કેરવું ushkervun

excitement *n.* ઉત્તેજના uttejanaa

exclaim *v.i.* બોલી ઉઠવું bolee uthavun

exclamation *n.* ઉદ્‌ગાર udagaar

exclude *v.t.* બાકાત રાખવું baakaat raakhavun

exclusive *adj.* એકમાત્ર, અનન્ય ekamaatra, ananya

excommunicate *v.t.* બહિષ્કાર કરવો bahishkaar karavo

excoriate *v.t.* છાલ ઉખેડવી chhaal ukhedavee

excrement *n.* વિષ્ટા vishtaa

excruciate *v.t.* આનંદ પર્યંતન aanand paryatan

exculpate *v.t.* દોષમુક્ત કરવું doshamukt karvun

excursion *n.* સહેલગાહ sahelagaa

excuse *n.* માફી maafee

execrate *v.t.* ધિક્કારવું dhikkaaravun

execute *v.t.* નો અમલ કરવો no amal karavo

execution *n.* દેહાંતદંડ dehaantdand

executioner *n.* જલ્લાદ jalllaad

executive *n.* વ્યવસ્થાપક vyavasthaapak

executor *n.* વહીવટકર્તા vaheevatakartaa

executrix *n.* અમલ કરનાર સ્ત્રી amal karanaar stree

exemplar *n.* નમૂનો, દાખલો namoono ., daakhalo

exemplary *adj.* ઉદાહરણીય udaaharaneey

exempt *v.t.* માફી આપવી maafee aapavee

exemption *n.* માફી maafee

exercise *n.* કસરત kasarat

exert *v.t.* ક્રિયાશીલ કરવું kriyasheel karvun

exertion *n.* પ્રયત્ન prayatna

exhale *v.t.* શ્વાસ છોડવો swaash chhodavo

exhalation *n.* ઉચ્છવાસ uchchhavaas

exhaust *v.t.* ખલાસ કરવું khalaas karvun

exhaustion *n.* થકાવટ thakaavat

exhibit *v.t.* પ્રદર્શન કરવું pradarshan karvun

exhibition *n.* પ્રદર્શન pradarshan

exhilarate *v.t.* આનંદિત કરવું aanandit karvun

exhort *v.t.* સલાહ આપવી salaah aapavee

exhume *v.t.* ખોદી કાઢવું khodee kaadhavun

exigency *n.* તાકીદની જરૂરિયાત taakeedanee jarooreeyaat

exigent *adj.* અલ્પ alp

exiguous *adj.* બારીક baareek

exile *v.t.* દેશવટો deshavato

exist *v.i.* હોવું hovun

existence *n.* અસ્તિત્વ astitva

exit *n.* વિદાય vidaay

exodus *n.* હિજરત heejarat

exorable *adj.* વિનવણીથી સમજાવી શકાય તેવું vinavaneethee samajaavee kakaay tevun

exorbitant અતિશય ateeshay

exorcize *v.t.* વળગણમાંથી મુક્તિ valaganamaathee mukti

exotic *adj.* વિચિત્ર vichitra

expand *v.t.* ફેલાવવું felaavavun

expanse *n.* મોટો વિસ્તાર moto vistaar

expansion *adj.* વિસ્તરણ vistaran

expansive *adj.* વિસ્તરણક્ષમ vistaranksham

exparte *adj.* એક પક્ષી ek pakshi

expatriate *v.t.* દેશનિકાલ કરવું deshnikaal karavun,

expect *v.t.* ધારવું dhaaravun

expectant *adj.* અપેક્ષા રાખી રહેલ apekshaa raakhee rahel

expectation *n.* ધારણા dhaaranaa

expediency *n.* અનુકૂળતા anukudataa

expedient *adj.* લાભદાયી laabhadaayee

expedite *v.t.* તાકીદે કરવું taakeede karavun

expedition *n.* સહેતુ પ્રવાસ sahetu pravaash

expel *v.t.* બહાર કાઢવું bahaar kaadhavun

expend *v.t.* ખરચવું kharchvun

expenditure ખર્ચ kharch

expensive *adj.* મોંઘું mondhu

experience *n.* અનુભવ anubhav

experiment *v.* પ્રયોગ prayog

expert *adj.* નિપુણાત nishnaat

expiate *v.t.* સુધારવું sudhaaravun

expire *v.t.* નો અંત આવવો no ant aavavo

expiry *n.* સમાપ્તિ samaapti

explain *v.t.* સમજાવવું samajaavavun

explanation *n.* ખુલાસો khulaaso

explicable *adj.* ખુલાસા લાયક khulaasaa laayak

explicit *adj.* સ્પષ્ટપણે કહેલું spashtapane kahelu

explode *v.t.* સ્ફોટ કરવો sfot karavo

exploit *v.* શોષણ કરવું shoshan karavun

exploration શોધખોળ shodakhol

explore *v.t.* ની તપાસ કરવી nee tapaash karavee

explorer *n.* શોધક shodhak

explosion *n.* વિસ્ફોટ visfot

explosive *adj.* સ્ફોટક sfotak

exponent *n.* નમૂનો namoono

export *v.t.* નિકાસ nikaas

expose *v.t.* છતું કરવું chhatu karavun

exposition *n.* વિવરણ vivaran

expostulate *v.i.* કાન ઉઘાડવા kaan ughaadavaa

exposure *n.* ખુલ્લું કરવું khullun karavun

expound *v.t.* સવિસ્તર રજૂ કરવું savistar rajoo karavun

express *v.t.* ખૂબ વેગવાળું khoob vegavaalu

expression *n.* અભિવ્યક્તિ abhivyakti

expulsion *n.* હકાલપટ્ટી hakaalapattee

expunge *v.t.* છેકી નાખવું chhekee naakhavun

exquisite *adj.* અતિસુંદર atisundar

extant *adj.* હજી વિદ્યમાન hajee vihyamaan

extemporaneous *n.* તૈયારી વિના taiyaaree vinaa

extempore *adv.* તત્કાળ રજૂ tatkaal raju

extend *v.t.* ફેલાવવું felaavavun

extension *n.* લંબાવવું lambaavavun

extensive *adj.* વ્યાપક vyaapak

extent *n.* પરિમાણ parimaan

extenuate *v.t.* ઓછું કરવું ochhun karavun

exterior *adj.* બહારનું bahaaranu

exterminate *v.t.* નાશ કરવો. naash karvo

external *adj.* બાહ્ય baahya

extinct *adj.* હોલવાઈ ગયેલું holavaai gayelu

extinction *n.* હોલવાવું holavaavun

extinguish *v.t.* નાશ કરવો naash karavo

extirpate *v.t.* ઉચ્છેદવું uchchhedavun

extirpation ઉચ્છેદન uchchhedan

extol *v.t.* ગુણ ગાવા gun gaava

extort *v.t.* ખંડણી ઉઘરાવવી khandalee ugharaavavee

extra *adj.* વધારાનું vadhaaraanu

extract *n.* અર્ક કાઢવો ark kaadhavo

extraction *n.* કુળ kul

extraneous *adj.* બહારનું bahaaranu

extraordinary *adj.* અસાધારણ asaadhaaran

extravagance સ્વૈરપણું svairapanu

extravagant *n.* ઉડાઉ udaau

extreme *adj.* અત્યંત atyant

extremely *adv.* અત્યંત atyant

extremist *n.* કટ્ટરવાદી kattaravaadee

extremity છેડો, છેડાનું chhedo, chhedaanu

extricable *adj.* ગૂંચ ઉકેલવી goonch ukelavee

extricate *v.t.* ગૂંચ ઉકેલવી goonch ukelavee

extrinsic *adj.* અંગભૂત નહિ એવું angabhoot nahee tevun

extrude *v.t.* બહાર ધકેલવું bahaar dhakelavun

exuberance *n.* પુષ્કળ pushkal

exuberant વિપુલ vipul

exude *v.t.* માંથી નીકળવું manthee neekalavun

exudation *n.* ઝરણ zaran

exult *v.t.* અતિઆનંદિત થયેલ atee aanandit thayel

exultation *n.* અતિઆનંદ થવો atee aanand thavo

eye *n.* આંખ aankh

eyeball *n.* આંખની કીકી aankh nee keekee

eyebrow *n.* ભમ્મર bhammar

eye-glasses *n.* ચશ્મા chasmaa

eyelash *n.* પાંપણ paanpad

eyelid *n.* પોપચું popachu

eyesight *n.* નજર najar

eyesore *n.* આંખની કણી aankhanee kanee

eye-wash *n.* છેતરપિંડી chhetarapindee

eye-witness *n.* પ્રત્યક્ષદર્શી pratyakshadarshee

eyrie *n.* ઊંચે વસવાટ unche vasavaat

F

fable *n.* બોધવાળી પુરાણીકથા bodhavaalee praaneekathaa

fabric *n.* કાપડ kaapad

fabircate ઉપજાવી કાઢવું upajaavee kaadhavun

fabrication *n.* બનાવટ banaavat

facade *n.* મોખરાનો ભાગ mokharaano bhaag

face *n.* ચહેરો chahero

facet *n.* પાસું paasu

facetious *adj.* ટીખળ teekhal

facia *n.* દુકાનદારનું પાટિયું dukaanadaar nu paatiyu

facial *adj.* ચહેરાનું chaheraanu

facile *adj.* સહેલું saheluu

facilitate *v.t.* સુવિધા કરી આપવી suvidhaa karee aapavee

facility *n.* સુવિધા suvidhaa

facsimile *n.* આબેહૂબ નકલ aabehoob nakal

fact *n.* હકીકત hakeekat

faction *n.* પક્ષ paksh

factor *n.* પરિબળ paribal

factory *n.* કારખાનું kaarakaanu

faculty *n.* શિક્ષક shikshak

fad *n.* લહેર laher

fade *v.i.* કરમાવ karamaav

faded *adj.* કરમાવું karamaavun

fag *v.t.* વૈતરું તૂટેલ છેડો. vaitaru, tootel chhedo

fag-end *n.* અંત ભાગ ant bhaag

fall *v.i.* નીચે પડવું neeche padavun

falling *n.* પડતું padatu

fain *adv.* ખુશ khush

faint *adj.* બેભાન bebhaan

fair *adj.* મેળો melo

fairly *adv.* યોગ્ય રીતે yogya reete

fairy *n.* પરી paree

faith *n.* શ્રદ્ધા shraddhaa

faithful *adj.* વફાદાર vafaadaar

faithless *adj.* શ્રદ્ધાવિહીન shraddhaaviheen

fake *n.* નકલ કરવી nakal karavee

falcon *n.* બાજ પક્ષી baaj pakshee

fall *v.i.* નીચે પડવું neeche padavun

fallacy *n.* તર્કદોષ tarkdosh

fallible *adj.* ભૂલને પાત્ર bhulane paatra

fallow *n.* પડતર padatar

FALSE *adj.* ભૂલભરેલું bhoolabharelu

falsify *v.t.* ચેડાં કરવાં chedan karavaan

falsity *n.* ભૂલભરેલું bhoolabharelu

falter *v.i.* લથડવું lathadavun,

fame *n.* કીર્તિ keerti

familiar *adj.* સુપરિચિત suparichit

familliarity પરિચિતતા parichitataa

familiarize *v.t.* પરિચિત કરવું parichit karavun

family *n.* કુટુંબ kutumb
famine *n.* દુકાળ dukaal
famish *v.t.* ભૂખ્યાં થવું bhookhyaan thavun
famous *adj.* પ્રખ્યાત prakhyaat
fan *n.* પંખો pankho
fanatic *adj.* ધર્માંધ dharmaandh
fanaticism *n.* ધર્માંધતા dharmaandhataa
fanciful શેખચલ્લી shekhachallee
fancy *adj.* કલ્પના kalpanaa
fane *n.* દેવાલય devaalay
fang *n.* સાપનો ઝેરી દાંત saapano zeree taant
fantastic *adj.* અસાધારણ asaadhaaran
fantasy *n.* દિવાસ્વપ્ન divaasvapna
far *adj.* દૂરનું dooranu
farce *n.* પ્રહસન prahasan
fare *n.* ભાડું bhaadu
farewell *n.* વિદાય vidaay
farm *n.* ખેતર khetar
farmer *n.* ખેડૂત khedoot
farming *n.* ખેતી khetee
farrago *n.* શંભુમેળો. shambumelo
farrier *n.* લુહાર luhaar
farther *adj.* વધારે દૂર vadhaare door
fascinate *v.t.* આકર્ષવું aakarashavun
fascination *n.* મંત્રમુગ્ધ કરવું mantamugdh karavun
fascism *n.* ફાસીવાદ faaseevaad
fashion *n.* શૈલી shailee
fast *adj.* ઉપવાસ કરવો upavaash karavun
fastidious *adj.* ચોખલિયું chokhaliyun
fastness *n.* દૃઢતા dradhataa
fat *adj.* ચરબી charabee
fatal *adj.* જીવલેણ jeevalen
fatalism *n.* પ્રારબ્ધવાદ praarabdhaavaad
fatalist *n.* પ્રારબ્ધવાદી praarabdhavaadee
fatality *n.* મરણાંક maranaank
fate *n.* નિયતિ niyatee
father *n.* પિતા pitaa
father-in-law *n.* શ્વસુર shvasur
fatherland *n.* સ્વદેશ svadesh
fatherly *adj.* પિતૃ તુલ્ય pitrutulya

fathom *n.* આકલન કરવું aakalan karavun
fathomless *adj.* અગાધ aghaad
fatique *n.* થકાવટ thakaavat
fatness *n.* સ્થૂળતા sthrudataa
fatten *v.t.* પુષ્ટ કરવું pusht karavun
fatty *adj.* ચરબી જેવું charabee jevun
fatuous *adj.* જડ jad
fault *n.* દોષ dosh
faultless *adj.* દોષ રહિત dosharahit
faulty *adj.* દોષયુક્ત doshayukt
fauna *n.* પ્રાણીસૃષ્ટિ praaneesrushti
favour *n.* ચાહના chaahanaa
favourable *adj.* સદ્દભાવવાળું sadabhavanaavaalu
favourite *n.* પસંદગીનું pasandageenu
favouritism *n.* જૂથનો પક્ષપાત joothano pakshapaat
fawn *n.* હરણનું બચ્ચું harananu bachchu
fealty *n.* વફાદારી vafaadaaree
fear *n.* ભય bhay
ferful *adj.* બીકણ beekan
fearless *adj.* નિર્ભય neerbhay
fearlessness નિર્ભયતા neerbhayataa
feasibility શક્ય shakya
feasible શક્ય shakya
feather પીંછું peenchhu
february *n.* ફેબ્રુઆરી મહિનો. february maheeno
fecundate *v.t.* ફલિત કરવું faleet karavun
fecundity *n.* ફળદ્રુપતા faladrupataa
federal *adj.* સમવાયી samavaayee
federate *v.t.* એકત્ર કરવું aekatra karavun
federation *n.* સંઘરાજ્ય sandharaajya
fee *n.* શુલ્ક shulk
feeble *adj.* નબળુ nabalu
feed *v.t.* ખવડાવવું khavadaavavun
feeder *n.* રેલવેની શાખા railway nee shakhaa
feel *v.t.* અનુભવવું anubhavavun
feeling *n.* લાગણી laaganee
feign *v.t.* ઝાંખું zaankhu
feint *n.* ઢોંગ કરવો dhong karavo
felicitate *v.t.* સન્માનિત કરવું sanmaanit karavun
felicitations *n.pl.* સન્માન sanmaan

felicitous યોગ્ય yogya
felicity *n.* આનંદદાયક સ્વભાવ aanandadaayak svabhaav
feline *adj.* બિલાડીના કુળનું પુરાણી biladeena kulanu praanee
fell *adj.* નીચે પાડવું neeche paadavun
fellow *n.* સમોવડિયો samovadiyo
fellowship *n.* અધ્યેતાવૃત્તિ adhyetavrutti
felon *n.* મહાઅપરાધ mahaaaparaadh
felonious *adj.* મહાઅપરાધી mahaaaparaadhee
felony *n.* મહાઅપરાધ mahaaaparaadh
felt *n.* બનાતનું કાપડ banaatnu kaapad
feminine *adj.* સ્ત્રીલિંગ streeling
femoral *adj.* થાપાનું thaapaanu
fen *n.* ભેજવાળી નીચાણવાળી જમીન bejavaalee neechaanavaalee jameen
fence *n.* વાડ vaad
fencing *n.* વાડ vaad
fend *v.t.* ખાળવું khaadavun
feral *adj.* જંગલી jangalee
ferment *n.* આથો aatho
fermentation *n.* આથો ચઢાવવો aatho chadaavavo
fern *n.* અપુષ્પ વનસ્પતિ apushpa vanaspatee
ferocious *adj.* વિકરાળ vikaraad
ferocity વિકરાળતા vikaraadataa
ferret *n.* ખોળી કાઢનારું khodee kaadhanaaru
ferry *n.* ઘાટનૌકા ghaatanaukaa
ferryman *n.* નાવિક naavik
fertile *adj.* ફળદ્રુપ faladrup
fertility *n.* ફળદ્રુપતા faladrupataa
fertilize *v.t.* ફળદ્રુપ બનાવવું faladrup banaavavun
fervency *n.* ચળકાટ chalakaat
fervent *adj.* ગરમ garam
fervid ચળકતું chalakatu
fervour *n.* જુસ્સો jusso
festal *adj.* મિજબાનીને લગતું mijabaaneene lagatu
fester *v.t.* પાકવું paakavun
festival *n.* તહેવાર tahevaar
festive *adj.* ઉજાણી ujaanee

festivity *n.* આનંદ પ્રમોદ aandapramod
festoon *n.* તોરણ toran
fetch *v.t.* લઈ આવવું laee aavavun
fete *n.* સન્માનવું sanmaanavun
fetish *n.* જડપૂજા jadapooja
fetters *n.* હાથકડી haathakadee
feud *n.* ઝઘડો zaghado
feudal *adj.* જાગીરને લગતું jaageerne lagatun
feudatory *n.* ખંડિયું khandiyu
fever *n.* તાવ taav
feverish *adj.* તાવનાં લક્ષણોવાળું taavanaa lakshanavaalu
few *adj.* નહીવત naheevat
fiance *n.* વાગ્દત્તા vaagdatta
fiasco *n.* સંપૂર્ણ નિષ્ફળતા sampoorn nishfalataa
fiat *n.* હુકમ kookam
fib *n.* ગપ્પું gappu
fibre *n.* તંતુ tantu
fickle *adj.* ચંચળ chanchal
fiction *n.* કલ્પિત વાત kalpit vaat
fictious *adj.* કાલ્પનિક kaalpanik
fiddle *n.* વાયોલિન vaayolin
fiddler *n.* વાદ્ય વગાડનાર vaadya vagaadanaar
fidelity *n.* વફાદારી vafaadaaree
fidget *v.i.* બેચેની bechenee
fie ધિક્કારવાચક ઉદ્ગાર dhikkaravaachak udagaar
fief *n.* નિયંત્રણક્ષેત્ર niyantran kshetra
field *n.* ખેતર khetar
fiend *n.* શેતાન shetaan
fierce *adj.* ક્રૂર kroor
fiercely *adj.* હિંસક hinsak
fiery *adj.* ઉગ્ર ugra
fife *n.* વાંસળી vaansanee
fifteen *adj.* પંદરમું pandarmu
fifth *adj.* પાંચમું paanchamu
fiftieth *adj.* પચાસમું pachaasamu
fifty *adj.* પચાસ pachaas
fig *n.* અંજીર anjeer
fight *v.t.* લડવું ladavun
figment *n.* કલ્પનાનો તુક્કો. kalpanaano tukko
figure *n.* આકૃતિ aakrutee
filament *n.* તાર taar

filch *v.t.* તફડંચી કરવી tafadanchee karavee

file *n.* ફાઈલ file

filial *adj.* સંતાન જેવું santaan jevun

filiation *n.* વંશાનુક્રમ vanshaanukram

fill *v.t.* ભરવું bharavun

fillip *n.* ટકોરો takoro

filly *n.* વછેરી vachheree

film *n.* ચિત્રપટ chitrapat

filter *v.t.* ગળણી galanee

filth *n.* ગંદવાડ gandavaad

fin *n.* માછલીની પાંખ maachaleenee paankh

final *adj.* નિર્ણાયક niranaayak

finality *n.* સમાપ્તિ samaapti

finance *n.* નાણાંવ્યવસ્થા naanavyavathaa

financial *adj.* નાણાકીય naanaakiy

financier *n.* નાણાં ધીરનાર naana dheeranaar

find *v.t.* શોધવું shodhavun

fine *adj.* દંડ dand

finery *n.* ભભકાદાર પોશાક bhabhakaadaar poshaak

finesse *n.* કુનેહ, ચાલાકી kuneh, chaalaakee

finger *n.* આંગળી aangalee

finish *v.t.* અંત ant

finite *adj.* મર્યાદિત maryaadit

finny *adj.* માછલીને લગતું maachhaleene lagatu

fir *n.* ચીડનું વૃક્ષ cheednu vruksh

fire *n.* આગ aag

fire-arm *n.* શસ્ત્રો shastro

fire-brigade *n.* આગ હોલવનાર ટુકડી aag holavanaar tukadee

fire-pan *n.* તાવડી taavadee

fire-place *n.* ચૂલો. choolo

fire-proof *adj.* ખામીરહિત khameeraheet

firewood *n.* બળતણના લાકડા balatananaa laakadaa

fireworks *n.* આતશબાજી aatashabaajee

firm *adj.* મક્કમ makkam

firmness *n.* મક્કમતા makaamataa

firmament *n.* ઉગતો સિતારો. ugato sitaaro

first *adj.* પહેલું pahelu

first aid *n.* પ્રાથમિક સારવાર praathamik saaravaar

firth *n.* સમૂહનો ફાંટો. samoohano faanto

fiscal *adj.* રાજકોષીય raajakosheey

fish *n.* માછલી maachhalee

fisherman *n.* માછીમાર maachheemaar

fishery *n.* મત્સ્યઉદ્યોગ matsyaudhog

fishy *adj.* શંકાશીલ shankaasheel

fissure *n.* ચિરાડ chiraad

fist *n.* મુઠ્ઠી muththee

fistula *n.* ભગંદર bhagandar

fit *adj.* વાઈ vaaee

fitness *n.* તંદુરસ્તી tandurastee

fitter *n.* કારીગર kaareegar

five *adj.* પાંચ paanch

fix *v.t.* બેસાડવું besaadavun

fixture *n.* જડિત વસ્તુ jadit vastu

fizz *n.* સણસણવું sanasanavun

fizzle *v.i.* સણસણવું sanasanavun

flabby *adj.* નરમ naram

flaccid *adj.* નિર્બળ nirbal

flag *n.* ધ્વજ dhvaj

flagon *n.* દારૂ ભરવાનું પાત્ર daaroo bharavaanu paatra

flagrant *adj.* ઉઘાડું udhaadu

flake *n.* નરમ પડ naram pad

flambeau *n.* મશાલ mashaal

flamboyant *n.* ભભકાદાર bhabhakaadaar

flame *n.* જ્યોત jyot

flamingo *n.* સુરખાબ surakhaab

flameable *adj.* જ્વલનશીલ jvalanasheel

flannel *n.* સુંવાળું ઊની કાપડ sunvaadi unee kaapad

flap *v.t.* પાંખ ફફડાવવી paankh fafadaavavee

flare *v.t.* ઝબૂકવું zabukavun

flash *n.* ઝબકારો zabakaaro

flask *n.* પ્રયોગશાળાની બાટલી prayogashaalaanee baatalee

flat *adj.* ફ્લેટ પ્રકારના આવાસ flat prakaaranaa aavaas

flatter *v.* ખુશામત khushaamat

flatterer *n.* ખુશામતિયો khushaamatiyo

flattery *n.* ખુશામત કરવી khushaamat karavee

flaunt *v.i.* રોફ઼ મારવો rof maaravo

flavour *n.* લહેજત lahejat

flaw *n.* દોષ dosh

flax *n.* અળસીનો છોડ alaseeno chhod

flay *v.t.* સખ્ત ટીકા કરવી sakhat tikaa karavee

flea *n.* ચાંચડ chaanchal

fleck *n.* ડાઘો daagho

fledge *v.t.* રૂંવાટીથી યુક્ત કરવું ruvaateethee yukt karavun

flee *v.i.* નાસી જવું naasee javun

fleece *n.* કાતરેલું kaatarelu

fleecy *adj.* કાતરેલું kaatarelu

fleer *v.i.* મશ્કરી mashkaree

fleet *v.i.* કાફ઼લો kaafalo

flesh *n.* પુષ્ટતા pushtataa

fleshy *adj.* હૃષ્ટપુષ્ટ rushtapusht

flexibility *n.* લવચીકતા lavacheekataa

flexible *adj.* લવચીક lavacheek

flexure *n.* વળાંક valaank

flick *n.* હળવો ઝપાટો halavo zapaato

flicker *v.t.* ટમટમવું tamatamavun

flight *n.* ઉડાણ undaan

flimsy *adj.* ક્ષણભંગુર kshanabhangur

flinch *v.i.* પાછુ હઠવું paasu hatavun

fling *v.t.* ધસવું dhasavun

flint *n.* ચકમકનો પથ્થર chakamakano paththar

flip *v.t.* ટપલી tapalee

flippancy *n.* છોકરવાદી chhokarvaad

flippant *adj.* બનિગંભીરતા binaganbheerataa

flirt *v.t.* પ્રણયચેષ્ટા કરવી pranayacheshta karavee

flirtation *v.* પ્રણયચેષ્ટા કરવી pranayacheshta karavee

flit *v.t.* રહેઠાણ બદલવું rahethan badalavun

float *v.i.* તરવું taravun

flock *n.* મોટું ટોળું motu todu

flog *v.t.* ફટકારવું fatakaaravun

flogging *n.* ચાબુકથી મારવું chaabukthee maravun

flood *n.* પૂર poor

floor *n.* મજલો majalo

flora *n.* વનસ્પતિસૃષ્ટી vanaspatee srushtee

floral *adj.* વનસ્પતિને લગતું vanaspatine lagatun

florescence *n.* ફૂલો આવવાનો સમય foolo aavavaano samay

florid *adj.* અલંકારપ્રચુર alanakaaraprachur

florist *n.* માળી maalee

flounce *n.* આંચકો. aanchako

flounder *v.t.* તરફડિયાં મારવાં tadafadeeya maaravaa

flour *n.* આટો aato

flourish *v.* ફાલવું faalavun

flout *v.t.* તરછોડવું tarachhodavun

flow *v.i.* વહેવું vahevun

flower *n.* ફૂલ fool

flowerpot *n.* ફૂલોની ક્યારી foolonee kyaaree

flowery *n.* વિપુલ ફૂલોવાળું vipul foolovaalu

fluctuate *v.t.* ચઢઊતર કરવી chadautar karavee

fluctuation *n.* ચઢઊતર chadautar

flue *n.* ઉષ્ણતાવાહક નળી ushnataavaahak nalee

fluency અસ્ખલતિતા askhalitatataa

fluent *adj.* અસ્ખલતિ askhalit

fluid *n.* પ્રવાહી pravaahee

fluke *n.* ક્રૃમિ krumee

flunk *n.* નિષ્ફળ કરવું nishfal karavun

flunkey *n.* સિપાઈ sipaaee

flurry *n.* ગરબડ garabad

flush *n.* તાજગી taajagee

flute *n.* વાંસળી vaansadee

flutter *n.* પાંખો ફફડાવવી pankha fafadaavavee

flux *n.* ભરતી bharatee

fly *n.* માખી maakhee

foal *n.* ઘોડાનું વછેરું ghodanu vachheru,

foam *n.* ફીણ feen

fob *n.* નાનું ખીસું naanu kheesu

focal *adj.* કેન્દ્રનું kendranu

focus *n.* કિરણસંપાત બિંદુ keeranasampaat bindu

fodder *n.* સૂકું ઘાસ suku ghaas

foe *n.* દુશ્મન dushman

foetus *n.* ગર્ભ garbh

fog *n.* ધુમ્મસ dhummas

fogy *n.* ધુમ્મસવાળું dhummasavaadu

foible *n.* દોષ dosh

foil *v.t.* વરખ varakh

foist *v.t.* જબરદસ્તી કરવી jabaradastee karavee

fold *n.* ઘેટાંનો વાડો ghetaano vaado

folk *n.* વિશિષ્ટ વર્ગના લોકો vishisht varg naa loko

folksong *n.* લોકગીત lokageet

follow *v.t.* અનુસરવું anusaravun

following *n.* નિમ્નલિખિત nimnalikhit

folly *n.* મૂર્ખતા moorkhataa

foment *v.t.* શેકવું shekavun

fomentation *n.* શેકવું shekavun

fond *adj.* ભાવનાશીલ bhaavanaasheel

fondle *v.t.* પંપાળવું panpaadavun

font *n.* જલપાત્ર jalapaatra

food *n.* ખોરાક khoraak

fool *n.* મૂર્ખ moorkh

foolhardy *adj.* અતિસાહસિક atee saahasik

foolish *adj.* બેવકૂફીભરેલુ bevakoofeebharelu

foot *n.* પગ pag

football *n.* ફૂટબોલ footbol

footwear *n.* પગરખાં pagarakhaa

foothold પકડ pakad

footing સુરક્ષિત જગ્યા surakshit jagyaa

footman *n.* ગણવેશધારી નોકર ganaveshadhaaree nokar

footnote *n.* પાદટીપ paadateep

footpath *n.* પગદંડી pagadandee

footprint *n.* પગલાની છાપ pagalaanee chhaap

footstep *n.* પાદચિહ્ન paadachinha

fop *n.* છેલછબીલો chhelachhabeelo

for ને માટે ne maate

forage *n.* વિપુલ આહાર vipul aahaar

foray *n.* હુમલો humalo

forbear *n.* ધીરજ dheeraj

forbearance ધીરજ રાખવી dheeraj raakhavee

forbid *v.t.* મનાઈ કરવી manaaee karavee

force *n.* બળ bal

forceps *n.* શસ્ત્રવિદ્યનો ચીપિયો shatravidyaano cheepiyo

forcible *adj.* જબરદસ્તીવાળું jabaradasteevaalu

ford *n.* તીર્થ teerth

fore *adj.* સામેની બાજુ saame nee baaju

forebode *v.t.* અગાઉથી સૂચના agaauthee soochanaa

forecast *v.t.* અનુમાન કરવું anumaan karavun

forefather *n.* પૂર્વજ poorvaj

forego *v.t.* પહેલાં જવું pahelaaa javee

forehead *n.* કપાળ kapaal

foreign *adj.* પરદેશ paradesh

foreigner *n.* વિદેશી videshee

foreman *n.* મુખ્ય કારીગર mukya kaareegar

foremost *adj.* શ્રેષ્ઠ shresht

foresee *v.t.* આગળથી જોવું aagadathee jovun

foresight *n.* દૂરંદેશી doorandeshee

forest *n.* જંગલ jangal

forestall *v.t.* બીજા કરતા પહેલા કરવું beja karata pahela karavun

foretell ભવિષ્ય ભાખવું bhavishya bhaakavun

forever *adv.* હંમેશાં, સતત hammesha, satat

foreword *n.* પ્રસ્તાવના prastaavanaa

forefeiture *n.* જતું કરવું jatu karavun

forge *n.* બનાવટી દસ્તાવેજ banaavatee dastavej

forgery *n.* છેતરપીંડી chhetarapindee

forge *v.t.* ધીમે ધીમે આગળ વધવું dheeme dheeme aagal vadhavun

forgetful *adj.* ભુલકણું bhulakanu

forgive *v.t.* ક્ષમા કરવી kshamaa karavee

forgiveness *n.* ક્ષમા kshamaa

forgiving *adj.* ક્ષમા કરવી kshamaa karavee

fork *n.* દાંતાવાળું ઓજાર daantaavaalu aojaar

forlorn *adj.* તજી દીધેલું tyajee deethelu

form *n.* સ્વરૂપ svaroop

formal *adj.* વિધિપૂર્વકનું vidhipoorvakanu

formality *n.* ઔપચારિકતા aaupachaarikataa

formation *n.* રચના rachana

former *adj.* ભૂતપૂર્વ bhootapoorv

formerly *adv.* અગાઉ agaunu

formidable *adj.* ભયાનક bhayaanak, jabaru

formula *n.* નુસખો nusakho

formulate *v.t.* ઘડવું ghadavun

forsake ત્યાગ કરવો tyaag karavo

forsooth *adv.* ખરેખર kharekhar

forswear સમ ખાઈને છોડવું sama khaaine chhodavun

fort *n.* કિલ્લો killo

forte *n.* વિશેષ આવડત vishesh aavadat

forth *adv.* હવે પછી have pachhee

forthwith *adv.* તત્કાળ tatkaal

fortieth *adj.* ચાળીસમો chaalisamo

fortification *n.* કિલ્લેબંધી kilebandhee

fortify *v.t.* પોષક તત્ત્વો ઉમેરવાં poshak tatto umeravaa

fortitude *n.* હિંમત himmat

fortnight *n.* પખવાડિયું pakhavaadiyu

fortress *n.* ગઢ gadh

fortuitous સંજોગવશાત્ sanjogovasaat

fortunate *adj.* નસીબદાર naseebadaar

fortune *n.* ભાવિ bhaavee

fortune-teller *n.* ભવિષ્ય કહેનાર bhavishya kahenaar

forty *adj.* ચાળીસ chaalis

forum *n.* ચર્ચા સ્થાન charchaasthaan

forward *adv.* આગળનું aagalanu

fossil *n.* અવશેષ avashesh

foster *v.t.* ઉછેરવું uchheravun

foul *adj.* નિયમવિરુદ્ધ niyamaviruddh

found *v.t.* સ્થાપવું sthaapavun

foundation *n.* સ્થાપના sthaapanaa

founder *n.* સ્થાપક sthaapak

foundling *n.* ત્યજી દેવાયેલું બાળક tyajee devaayelu baalak

fountain *n.* ફુવારો foovaaro

four *n.* ચાર chaar

fourteen *n.* ચૌદ chaud

fourth *adj.* ચોથો ભાગ chotho bhaag

fowl *n.* મરઘું maraghu

fowler *n.* શિકારી shikaaree

foundry *n.* ધાતુકામનું કારખાનું dhaatukaamanu kaarakhanu

fount *n.* ઝરો zaro

fox *n.* શિયાળ shiyaal

fracas *n.* બોલાચાલી balaachaalee

fraction *n.* અપૂર્ણાંક apoornaak

fracture *n.* અસ્થિભંગ asthibhang

fragile *adj.* ક્ષણભંગુર kshanabhangur

fragment *n.* ટુકડો tukado

fragrance *n.* સુગંધ sugandh

fragrant *adj.* સુગંધી sugandhee

frail *adj.* નાજુક naajuk

frailty *n.* નબળાઈ nabadaai

frame *n.* તકતી taktee

franchise *n.* મતાધિકાર mataadhikaar

frank *adj.* નિખાલસ nikhaalas

frankness *n.* નિખાલસતા nikhaalasataa

frantic *adj.* મરણિયું maraniyun

fraternal *adj.* ભ્રાતૃભાવ bhaatrubhaav

fraternity *n.* ભાઈચારો bhaatrutva, bhaaichaaro

fratricide *n.* ભ્રાતૃભગિનીનો હત્યારો bhaatrubhagineeno hatyaaro

fraud *n.* કૌભાંડ kaubhaand

fray *n.* બોલાચાલી bolaachaali

freak *n.* તરંગ tarang, lahereepanu

free *adj.* સ્વતંત્ર svatantra

freebooter *n.* ચાંચિયો. chaanchiyo

freedom *n.* સ્વતંત્રતા svatantrataa

freehold *n.* અમર્યાદા સત્તા amaryaad satta

free-thinker *n.* મુક્ત વિચારક mukta vichaarak

free trade *n.* મુક્ત વેપાર mukta vepaar

freeze *v.i.* થીજવવું theejavavun

freezing *adj.* થીજે છે તે તાપમાન theeje chhe te taapamaan

freight *n.* માલભાડું maalabhaadu

frenzy *n.* ઝનૂન zanoon, unmaad

frequent *adj.* વારંવાર થતું vaaramavaar thatu

fresco *n.* ભીંતચિત્ર bheentachitra

fresh *adj.* તાજું taaju

fret *v.t.* સુશોભિત કરવું sushobhit karavun

fretwork *n.* કોતરકામ kotarkaam

friar *n.* ભિક્ષુક bheekshuk
friction *n.* ઘર્ષણ dharshan
friday *n.* શુક્રવાર shukravaar
friend *n.* મિત્ર mitra
friendly *adj.* માયાળું maayaalu
freindship *n.* મિત્રતા mitrataa
frigate *n.* યુદ્ધજહાજ yuddhhajahaaj
fright *n.* ધ્રાસકો dhraasko
frighten *v.t.* બિવડાવવું bivadaavavun
frigid *adj.* ઠંડું thandu
frigidity *n.* અતિશય ઠંડક atishay
    thandak
fringe *n.* બાહ્ય સીમા baahya seemaa
frisk *v.i.* નાચવું naachavun
fritter *v.t.* માંસના ટુકડા maansanaa
    tukadaa
frivolity *n.* વ્યર્થતા vyarthatha
frivolous *adj.* વ્યર્થ vyarth
frock *n.* ફરાક faraak
frog *n.* દેડકો dedako
from *prep.* માંથી maanthee
front *v.i.* મોખરાની બાજુ mokharaanee
    baaju
frontier *n.* સીમા seema
frontispiece *n.* મુખચિત્ર mukhachitra
frost *n.* ઝાંકળ zaankad
froth *n.* ફીણ બહાર કાઢવું feen bahaar
    kaadhavun
frown *v.t.* ભવાં ચડાવવાં bhavaa
    chadaavavaa
fructify *v.i.* ફળીભૂત થવું faleebhoot
    thavun
frugal *adj.* કરકસરિયું karakasariyu
fruit *n.* ફળ fal
fruiterer *n.* ફળોનો વેપારી falono
    vepaaree
fruition *n.* ફળપ્રાપ્તિ falapraapapti
frustrate *v.t.* નિરાશ થવું neeraash
    thavun
frustration *n.* હતાશા hataashaa
fry *v.t.* તળવું talavun
frying-pan *n.* તાવડી taavadee
fuel *n.* બળતણ balatan,
fugitive *adj.* ભાગેડું bhaagedu
fulcrum *n.* આલંબ aalamb

fulfil *v.t.* પરિપૂરણ કરવું paripoorn
    karavun
fulgent *adj.* તીવ્ર ઓજાશ tivra aojash
full *adj.* પૂરેપૂરું ભરેલું poorepooru
    bharelu
fulminate *v.i.* વિસ્ફોટ કરવો visfot
    karavo
fulsome *adj.* કંટાળાજનક kantaanajanak
fumble *v.i.* ફાંફાં મારવાં faafaa maaravaa
fume *n.* ધુમાડો, ગુસ્સો dhumaado,
    gusso
fumigation *n.* શુદ્ધીકરણ
    shuddheekaran
fun *n.* મનોરંજન, આનંદ manoranjan,
    aanand
function *v.i.* કાર્ય કરવું kaarya karavun
functionary *n.* હોદ્દેદાર hoddedaar
fund *n.* ભંડોળ bhandol
fundamental *adj.* મૂળભૂત moolabhoot
funeral *n.* અંતમિક્રયા antimakriyaa
fungus *n.* ફૂગ foog
funk ગભરાટ gabharaat
funnel *n.* ગળણી galanee
funny *adj.* રમૂજી ramoojee
fur *n.* ઉન un
furious *adj.* ખિજાયેલું khijaayelu
furl *v.t.* સંકેલવું sankelavun
furlough *n.* લાંબી રજા lambhee rajaa
furnace *n.* ભઠ્ઠી bhaththee
furnish *v.t.* પૂરું પાડવું pooru paadavun
furniture *n.* રાચરચીલું raacharacheelu
furrow *n.* ચાસ chaas
further *adv.* વધુમાં vadhuma
turtherance *n.* બઢતી bhadhatee
furtive *adj.* ચોરીછૂપીથી કરેલું
    choreechhoopeethee karelu
fur *n.* ઉન un
furious *adj.* રોષિત roshit
fuse *v.t.* ગરમી આપી ઓગાળવું garamee
    aapee aogaalavun
fusion *n.* સંયોજન sanyojan
fuss *n.* ધાંધલ dhaandhal
futility *n.* નકામું nakaamun
future *n.* ભાવિ bhaavi

G

gab *n.* લવારો lavaaro

gabble *n.* બકબક કે લવારો bakabak ke lavaaro

gad *n.* ભટકવું bhatakavun

gadfly *n.* બગાઈ bagaaee

gag *v.t.* ચૂપ બેસાડવું choop besaadavun

gage *n.* બાંયધરી baanyadharee

gaily *adv.* આનંદ aanand

gain *v.t.* મેળવવું melavavun

gainsay *v.t.* ઇનકાર કરવો eenakaar karavo

gait *n.* ચાલવાની ઢબ chaalavaanee dhab

gala *n.* આનંદનો પ્રસંગ aanandano prasang

galaxy *n.* આકાશગંગા aakaashaganga

gale *n.* જોરદાર પવન joradaar pavan

gall *n.* કડવાશ, નફટાઈ kadavaash, vafataaee

gallant *adj.* બહાદુર bahaadur

gallantry *n.* શૌર્ય shaury

galleon *n.* યુદ્ધનૌકા yuddhanauka

gallery *n.* બાલ્કની baalkanee

galley *n.* સૂપડી soopadee

gallop *v.i.* છલંગો મારતા દોડવું chhalango maarata dodavun

gallows *n.* ફાંસીનો માંચડો faanseeno maanchado

gamble *v.i.* દ્યુત કે જુગાર રમવો dhut ke jugaar ramavo

gambol *n.* કૂદકો, ઠેકડો koodako, thekado

game *n.* રમત ramat

gamester *n.* જુગારી jugaaree

gander હંસ hans

gang *n.* કેદીઓની ટોળી kedeeonee tolee

gangway *n.* મધ્યપથ madhyapath

gaol *n.* કેદખાનું kedakhaanun

gaoler *n.* જેલર jelar

gap *n.* તફાવત tafaavat

gape બગાસું ખાવું bagaasu khaavun

garage *n.* ગેરેજ gerej

garb *n.* પહેરવેશ paheravesh

garbage *n.* ગંદકી, ગંદુ સાહતિય gandakee, gandu saahity

garden *n.* બગીચો bageecho

gardener *n.* માળી maalee

gardening *n.* બગાયત પ્રવૃતિ bagaayat pravruti

gargle *v.t.* કોગળો કરવો kogalo karavo

garland *n.* હાર, તોરણ haar, toran

garlic *n.* લસણ lasan

garment *n.* વસ્ત્ર vastr

garner *n.* અનાજનું કોઠાર anaajanun kothaar

garnish *v.t.* શણગારવું shanagaaravun

garret *n.* કાતરિયું kaatariyun

garrison *n.* રક્ષક સૈન્ય rakshak sainya

garrulous *adj.* વાતોડિયું vaatodiyun

gas *n.* વાયુ vaayu

gascon *n.* ડંફાશિયું માણસ danfaashiyun maanas

gasconade *n.* ડંફાશ danfaash

gasolene *n.* પેટ્રોલ petrol

gasometer *n.* ગેસોમીટર gesomeetar

gasp *v.t.* હાંફવું haanfavun

gastric *adj.* પેટને લગતું petne lagatun

gate *n.* દરવાજો daravaajo

gateway *n.* દરવાજાવાળો પ્રવેશમાર્ગ daravaajaavaalo praveshamaarg

gather *v.t.* ભેગુ કરવું bhegu karavun

gathering *n.* સંમેલન sanmelan

gaudy *adj.* ભપકાવાળું bhapakaavaalun

gauge *v.t.* માનદંડ maanadand

gaunt *adj.* પાતળું paatalun

gauntlet *n.* મોટું મોજું motun mojun

gauze *n.* ઝીણું કાપડ zinun kaapad

gay *adj.* સમલિંગકામી samalingakaamee

gaze *v.t.* તાકીને જોવું taakeene jovun

gear *n.* ગીયર giyar

gelatine *n.* જીલેટિન jiletin

geld *n.* ખસી કરવું khasee kravun

gem *n.* રત્ન ratna

gender *n.* શબ્દની જાતિ–લિંગિ shabdanee jaatee - ling

genealogy *n.* વંશાવળી vanshaavalee

general *adj.* સાધારણ saadhaaran

generalissimo *n.* સરસેનાપતિ sarasenaapati

generalize સામાન્ય રૂપ આપવું saamaany roop aapavun

generally *adv.* સામાન્ય અર્થમાં saamaany arthaman

generate *v.t.* પેદા કરવું peda karavun

generation *n.* પ્રજનન prajanan

generosity *n.* ઉદારતા udaaratan

generous *adj.* ઉમદા umada

genesis *n.* ઉત્પત્તિ utpati

genial *adj.* સૌમ્ય. saumya

genital *adj.* જનનેન્દ્રિયો સંબંધી jananedriyo sanbandhee

genitive *n.* છઠ્ઠી વિભક્તિ chhaththee vibhakti

genius *n.* પ્રતિભાસંપન્ન માણસ pratibhaasanpann maanas

genteel *adj.* સુશીલ susheel

gentility *n.* સામાજિક શ્રેષ્ઠતા saamaajik shreshthata

gentle *adj.* વિનયશીલ vinayasheel

gentleman *n.* સદ્‌ગૃહસ્થ sadgrahasth

gentry *n.* મધ્યમ વર્ગના લોકો madhyam vargana loko

genuine *adj.* અસલ asal

genus *n.* પ્રકાર prakaar

geography *n.* ભૂગોળ bhoogol

geology *n.* ભૂસ્તરશાસ્ત્ર bhoostarashaastra

geometry *n.* ભૂમિતિ bhoomiti

germ *n.* સૂક્ષ્મજીવ sookshmajeev

germicide *n.* જંતુનાશક jantunaashak

germinate *v.i.* અંકુર ફૂટવો ankur footavo

gestation *n.* ગર્ભધારણ garbhadhaaran

gesticulate *v.t.* અંગચેષ્ટા કરવી angacheshta karavee

get *v.t.* મેળવવું melavavun

geyser *n.* ગરમ પાણીનો ઝરો garam paaneeno jharo

ghastly *adj.* ભયાનક bhayaanak

ghost *n.* પ્રેતાત્મા pretaatma

ghostly *adj.* ભૂતના જેવું bhootanaa jevun

giant *n.* રાક્ષસ raakshas

gibbet *n.* વધસ્તંભ vadhastanbh

gibe *v.i.* કટાક્ષ kataaksh

giddy *adj.* ચંચળ chanchal

gift *n.* દેણગી denagee

gifted *adj.* પ્રતિભાસંપન્ન pratibhaasanpann

gigantic *adj.* રાક્ષસી raakshasee

giggle *v.i.* કૃત્રિમ હસવું kutrim hasavun

gild *v.i.* સોનાનો ઢોળ ચડાવવો sonaano dhol chadaavavo

gill *n.* ચૂંઈ choonee

gin *v.t.* ફાંસો faanso

ginger *n.* આદુ aadu

gipsy *n.* રખડુ જાતનું માણસ rakhadu jaatnun maanas

giraffe *n.* જિરાફ jiraaf

gird *v.t.* ઘેરવું gheravun

girder *n.* પાટડો paatado

girdle *v.* કમરપટો બાંધવો kamarapato baandhavo

girl *n.* છોકરી chhokaree

girth *n.* ઘોડાના જીતનો પટો ghodaana jeetano pato

gist *n.* નષ્કિર્ષ nishkarsh

give *v.i.* મંજૂરી આપવી manjooree aapavee

glacier *n.* હિમનદી himanadee

glad *adj.* સંતુષ્ટ santusht

gladden *v.t.* રાજી raajee

gladiator *n.* યોદ્ધો yoddho

glamour *n.* આકર્ષક સૌન્દર્ય aakarshak saundary

glance *n.* ઉતાવળો દ્રષ્ટિક્ષેપ utaavalo drashtikshep

gland *n.* ગ્રંથી granthee

glare *n.* ઝગમગવું jhagamagavun

glass *n.* કાચ kaach

glasses *n.pl.* કાચ kaach

glaucoma *n.* એક નેત્રરોગ ek netrarog

glaze *v.t.* ઓપ દેવો op devo

gleam *n.* ક્ષણિક પ્રકાશ kshaneek prakaash

glean *v.t.* વીણવું neenavun

glee *n.* આનંદ aanand

gleet *n.* રસી rasee

glen *n.* સાંકડી ખીણ saankadee kheen

glib *adj.* સત્યાભાસી satyaabhaasee

glide *v.i.* એંજિન વિના ઉડવું enjin vina udavun

glimmer *v.i* આંખો પ્રકાશ jhankho

prakaash
glimpse *n.* ઝાંખી કરવી jhaankhee karavee
glitter *v.* ચળકવું chalakavun
gloat *v.i.* કગિલાવું kingalavun
globe *n.* ધન વર્તુલ ghan vartul
gloom *n.* અંધારું andhaarun
gloomy *adj.* અંધારાવાળું andhaaraavaalun
glorify *v.t.* મહત્તા વધારવી mahatta vadhaaravee
glorious *adj.* ભવ્ય bhavy
glory *n.* કીર્તિ keerti
gloss *n.* ભ્રામક bhraamak
glossary *n.* પારિભાષિક શબ્દકોશ paaribhaashik shabdakosh
glove *n.* મુષ્ટિયોદ્ધાનું હાથમોજું mushtiyoddhaanun haathamojun
glow *v.i.* ધખધખવું dhakhadhakhavun
glow-worm *n.* આગિયો aagiyo
glucose *n.* ગ્લુકોઝ glukoz
glue *n.* ગુંદર gundar
glum *adj.* ગમગીન gamageen
glutton *n.* ખાઉધરો khaaudharo
glycerine *n.* ગ્લિસિરીન glisareen
gnash *v.t.* કકડાવવા kakadaavava
gnat *n.* મચ્છર machchhar
gnaw *v.t.* કોતરી ખાવું kotaree khaavun
gnomon *n.* સૂચક soochak
go *v.i.* જવું javun
goad *n.* અંકુશ ankush
goal *n.* લક્ષ્ય lakshy
goat *n.* બકરો bakaro
gobble *v.t.* ઉતાવળે ખાવું utaavale khaavun
go-between *n.* મધ્યસ્થીથનાર madhystheethanaar
goblet *n.* પ્યાલો pyaalo
goblin *n.* તોફાની પિશાચ tofaanee pishaach
god *n.* પરમેશ્વર parameshvar
goddess *n.* દેવી devee
godly *adj.* ધાર્મિક dhaarmik
godown *n.* વખાર vakhaar
godsend *n.* પરમ સૌભાગ્ય param saubhaagy
goggle *v.t.* ટગરટગર જોવું tagaratagara

jovun
gold *n.* સોનું sonun
golden *adj.* સોનાનું sonaanun
goldsmith *n.* સોની sonee
golf *n.* ગોલ્ફની રતમ golfanee ramat
gong *n.* ઝાલર jhaalar
gonorrhoea *n.* પરમિયો paramiyo
good *adj.* લાયક laayak
goo·bye આવજો aavajo
goodwill *n.* ભલમનસાઈ bhalamanasaaee
googly *n.* ગૂગલી googlee
goose *n.* હંસ hans
gore *n.* ગંઠાયેલું પૂરવાહી gandhayelun pravaahee
gorge *n.* સાંકડી ખીણ saankadee kheen
gorgeous *adj.* ભપકાદાર bhapakaadaar
gory *adj.* ખૂનરેજીવાળું khoonarejeevaalun
gospel *n.* સંદેશ sandesh
gossamer *n.* તુષારજાલક tushaarajaalak
gossip *n.* ગપ્પાં gappan
gouge *n.* ફરસી farasee
gout *n.* સંધિવા sandhiva
govern *v.i.* રાજ્ય કરવું raajy karavun
government *n.* સરકાર sarakaar
governor *n.* રાજ્યપાલ raajyapaal
gown *n.* ઝભ્ભો jhabhbho
grab *v.t.* આંચકી લેવું aanchakee levun
grace *n.* આકર્ષકતા aakrshakata
graceful *adj.* લાલિત્યપૂર્ણ laalityapoorn
gracious *adj.* કૃપાળુ krupaalu
gradation *n.* ગુણવત્તા gunavatta
grade *n.* દરજ્જો darajjo
graduate *n.* સ્નાતક snaatak
gradual *adj.* ક્રમિક kramik
graft *n.* કલમ kalam
grain *n.* અનાજનો દાણો anaajano daano
gram *n.* ચણો chano
grammar *n.* વ્યાકરણશાસ્ત્ર vyaakaranashaastr
grammatical *adj.* વ્યાકરણ અનુસારનું vyaakaran anusaaranun
gramme *n.* ગ્રામ gram
gramophone *n.* ગ્રામોફોન gramophon

granary *n.* ધાન્ય ભંડાર dhaanya bhandaar

grand *adj.* સર્વોચ્ચ કક્ષાનું sarvochch kakshaanun

grandchild *n.* પૌત્ર pautra

grandeur *n.* ઊંચુ પદ oonchun pad

grandfather *n.* દાદા daadaa

grandiose *adj.* ભવ્ય bhavya

granite *n.* અડદિયો પથ્થર adadiyo paththar

grant *n.* માન્ય કરવું maany karavun

grape *n.* દ્રાક્ષ draaksh

graph *n.* આલેખ aalekh

grapple *v.i.* બાઝંબાઝી કરવી baajhanbaajhee karavee

grasp *n.* મજબૂત પકડવું majaboot pakadavun

grass *n.* ઘાસચારો ghaasachaaro

grate *n.* સગડી sagadee

grateful *adj.* કૃતજ્ઞ krutagn

gratification *n.* સંતૃપ્ત કરવું santrupt karavun

gratify નું મન સાચવવું nun man saachavavun

grating *n.* જાળીનો કઠેરો jaaleeno kathero

gratis *adv.* મૂલ્ય વિનાનું mooly vinaanun

gratitude *n.* કૃતજ્ઞતા krutagnata

gratuity *n.* નિવૃતિલાભ nivrutilaabh

grave *n.* કબર kabar

gravel *n.* પથરી patharee

gravitation *n.* ગુરુત્વાકર્ષણ gurutvaakarshan

gravity *n.* ગુરુત્વાકર્ષણ gurutvaakarshan

gray *adj.* વાદળાથી છવાયેલું vaadalaathee chhavaayelun

graze *v.t.* ચરવું charavun

grease *v.t.* ઊંજણ તરીકે oojan tarike

great *adj.* વિસ્તીર્ણ vistirn

greatness *n.* શ્રેષ્ઠતા shreshthata

greed *n.* દ્રવ્યલોભ dravyalobh

greediness *n.* લોભ lobh

greedy *adj.* અતિલોભી atilobhee

green *adj.* લીલા રંગનું leela ranganun

greenery *n.* હરિયાળી hariyaalee

greet *v.i.* નમસ્કાર કરવા namaskaar karava

greeting *n.* શુભેચ્છા. shubhechchha

gregarious *adj.* જૂથચારી joothadhaaree

grey *adj.* સીસાના રંગનું seesaana ranganun

grid *n.* જાળી jaalee

grief *n.* શોક shok

grievance *n.* તકરારનો મુદ્દો takaraarano muddo

grieve *v.t.* દુભાવવું dubhaavavun

grievous *adj.* દુઃખદાયક dukhadaayak

grill *n.* જાળીની સગડી jaaleenee sagadee

grim *adj.* નિર્દય nirday

grimace *n.* મોંનો ચાળો monno chaalo

grin *v.t.* આનંદ વિનાનું હાસ્ય aanand vinaanun haasy

grind *v.t.* દળવું dalavun

grip *n.* મજબૂત પકડ majaboot pakad

grisly *adj.* ઘૃણાસ્પદ dhrunaaspad

grit *n.* કાંકરી kaankaree

groan *v.i.* કણસવું kanasavun

grocer *n.* મોદી modee

groom *n.* રાવત raavat

groove *n.* પૂરણાલી pranaalee

grope *v.i.* ફંફોસવું fanfosavavun

gross *n.* ૧૨ ડઝન, (૧૪૪નંગ) 12 dajhan, (144 nang)

grotesque *adj.* વિસંગત visangat

grotto *n.* ગુફાના જેવી રચના gufaana jevee rachana

ground *n.* ક્ષેત્ર kshetr

ground floor *n.* ભોંયતળિયાનો મજલો bhonyataliyaano majalo

groundless *n.* નિષ્કારણ nishkaaran

groun·nut *n.* મગફળી magafalee

groundwork *n.* મૂળભૂત સિદ્ધાંત moolabhoot siddhaant

group *n.* જૂથ jooth

grove *n.* વૃક્ષરાજિ vruksharaaji

grow *v.t.* ઊગવું oogavun

growl *n.* ઘુરકવું ghurakavun

growth *n.* વિકાસ vikaas

gruel *n.* કાંજી kaanjee

gruesome *adj.* ભયંકર કંટાળાજનક bhayankar kantaalaajanak

grumble *v.i.* બબડવું તે babadavun te
guarantee *n.* જામીનખત jaameenakhat
guard *v.t.* ચોકી chokee
guardian *n.* સંરક્ષક sanrakshak
guava *n.* જામફળ jaamafal
guerrila *n.* છાપામાર યુદ્ધ chhaapaamaar yuddh
guess *v.t.* આશરાથી કહેવું aasharaathee kahevun
guest *n.* મહેમાન mahemaan
guidance *n.* માર્ગદર્શન maargadarshan
guide *v.t.* માર્ગદર્શક maargadarshak
guild *n.* મહાજન mahaajan
gullet *n.* ગળું galun
guilt *n.* દોષ dosh
guilty *adj.* ગુનાહિત gunaahit
guise *n.* વેશ vesh
gulf *n.* અખાત akhaat
gulp *v.t.* ગટગટાવવું gatagataavavun
gum *n.* ગુંદર gundar
gun *n.* બંદૂક bandook
gunner *n.* તોપચી topachee
gunpowder *n.* દારુગોળો daarugolo
gunny *n.* ગુણપાટ gunapaat
gurgle *v.t.* કોગળા કરવા kogala karava
gush *v.t.* વિપુલ પ્રવાહ vipul pravaah
gust *n.* ઝાપટું zapatun
gusto *n.* લિજ્જત lijjat
gut *n.* જઠર jathar
gutter *n.* પરનાળ paranaal
guttural *n.* કંઠસ્થાનીય kanthasthaaneey
guzzle *v.t.* ઠાંસવું thansavun
gymkhana *n.* વ્યાયામશાળા vyaayaamshaalaa
gymnasium *n.* અખાડો akhaado
gypsy *n.* રખડુ rakhadun
gyrate *v.i.* ચકરાવો લેવો chakaravo levo
gyroscope *n.* ધ્રુણાક્ષસ્થાપી dhrurnaakshasthaapee
gyrus *n.* ગૂંચળું goonchalun

H

habiliment *n.* સાધન સામગ્રી saadhan saamagree
habit *n.* ટેવ tev
habitable *n.* વસવાટ યોગ્ય vasavaat yodya
habitation *n.* નિવાસ nivaas
habitual *adj.* રીઢું reedhun
hack *v.t.* લાત મારવી laat maaravee
hackney *n.* અતિસામાન્ય atisaamaanya
hades *n.* નરક narak
haemorrhage *n.* રક્તસ્રાવ raktastraav
haggard *adj.* જંગલી દેખાતું jangalee dekhaatun
haggle *v.i.* રકઝક કરવી rakazaka karavee
hall *n.* ઓરડો orado
hair *n.* વાળ vaal
hairy *adj.* વાળ જેવી વસ્તુવાળું vaal jevee vastuvaalun
hale *adj.* નિરોગી nirogee
half *n.* અડધો ભાગ adadho bhaag
half-brother *n.* સાવકા ભાઈ - બહેન saavaka bhaaee bahen
hall *n.* ઓરડો orado
hallo હેલો helo
hallucination *n.* આભાસ aabhaas
halt *v.i.* મુકામ mukaam
halter *n.* મોરડી moradee
hamlet *n.* નાનકડું ગામડું naanakadun gaamadun
hammer *n.* હથોડી hathodee
hammock *n.* ઝોળી jholee
hamper *n.* કરંડિયો karandiyo
hand *n.* હાથ haath
handbill *n.* છાપેલ હસ્તપત્રક chhaapel hastapatrak
handbook *n.* માહિતી પુસ્તિકા maahitee pustika
handcuffs *n.* હાથકડી haathakadee
handful *n.* મુઠ્ઠી (ભર) muththee (bhar)
handicap *n.* સંપ્રતિબંધ હરીફાઈ sanpratibandh hareefaaee

handicraft *n.* હસ્તઉદ્યોગ hastaudhyog

handkerchief *n.* હાથરૂમાલ haatharoomaal

handle *n.* હાથો haatho

handsel *n.* પ્રથમ વક્રિય pratham vikray

handsome *adj.* રૂપાળુ roopalun

handwriting *n.* હસ્તાક્ષર hastaakshar

handy *adj.* સુલભ sulabh

hang *v.t.* ટાંગવું taangavun

hanger *n.* જલ્લાદ jallaad

hank *n.* ઊનની આંટી oonanee aantee

hanker *v.i.* ઝંખવું zankhavun

hap *n.* સંજોગો sanjogo

haphazard *adj.* આકસ્મિક aakasmik

happen *v.i.* અચાનક બનવું achaanak banavun

happily *adv.* સદભાગ્યે sadabhaagye

happiness *n.* પ્રસન્નતા prasannata

happy *n.* નસીબદાર naseebadaar

harangue *n.* આવેશયુક્ત ભાષણ aaveshayukta bhaasan

harass *n.* પજવવું pajavavun

harbinger *n.* અગ્રદૂત agradoot

harbour *n.* બંદર bandar

hard *adj.* મહેનતનું mahenatanun

harden *v.i.* સખત બનાવવું sakhata banavavun

hardly *adv.* કઠોરપણે kathorapane

hardship *n.* ભૂખમરો bhookhamaro

hardware *n.* ધાતુનો સામાન dhaatuno samaan

hare *n.* સસલું sasalun

harem *n.* બૈરાનો ઓરડો bairaano orado

hark *v.i.* સાંભળવું saanbhalavun

harm *n.* નુકશાન nukashaan

harmony *n.* એકવાક્યતા ekavaakyata

harmonious *adj.* સુસંગત susangat

harmonium *n.* વાજાની પેટી vaajaanee petee

harness *n.* ઘોડાને સાજ ghodaane saaj

harp *n.* વીણા veena

harpoon *n.* ભાલો bhaalo

harrow *v.t.* લાગણી દુભવવી. laaganee dubhavavee

harsh *adj.* કર્કશ karkash

hart *n.* હરણનો નર haranano nar

harvest *n.* કાપણી લણણીની મૌસમ kaapanee lananeenee mausam

has *v.i.* કચુંબર kachunbar

haste *n.* ઉતાવળ utaaval

hasty *adj.* ઉતાવળું utaavalun

hat *n.* ટોપો topo

hatch *v.t.* બારણું baaranun

hatchet *n.* કુહાડી kuhaadee

hate *v.* −નો તીવ્ર દ્વેષ કરવો no teevr dvesh karavo

hatred *n.* તિરિસ્કાર tiraskaar

haughty *adj.* ઘમંડી ghamandee

haul *v.t.* ઘસડવું ghasadavun

haunt *v.t.* વળગવું valagavun

have *v.t.* −ની કબજામાં − હોવું nee kabajaaman - hovun

haven *n.* આશ્રયસ્થાન aashrayasthaan

havoc *n.* અણધારી આપત્તિ. anadhaaree aapatti

haw *n.* હોથોર્ન'નો ટેટો hothorn'no teto

hawk *n.* બાજ પક્ષી baaj pakshee

hawker *n.* ફેરિયો. fefiyo

hay *n.* ઘાસની ગંજી ghaasanee ganjee

hazard *n.* આકસ્મિક ઘટના aakasmik ghatana

haze *n.* ધુમ્મસ dhummas

hazel *adj.* હળવો બદામી રંગ halavo badaamee rang

he નર જાત nar jaati

head *n.* માથું maanthun

headache *n.* માથાનું દરદ maathaanun darad

heading *n.* શીર્ષક sheershak

headland *n.* ભૂશિર bhooshir

headlong *adv.* આંધળુંકિયું aandhalunkiyun

headman *n.* મુખી mukhee

headquarters પ્રવૃત્તનું કેન્દ્ર. pravruttinun kendr

headman *n.* મુખી mukhee

headstrong *adj.* દુરાગ્રહી duraagrahee

headway *n.* પ્રગતિ pragati

heal *v.t.* સાજુંસમું થવું saajunsamun thavun

health *n.* તંદુરસ્તી tandurastee

healthy *adj.* તંદુરસ્ત tandurast

heap *n.* ઢગલો dhagalo
hear *v.t.* સાંભળવું saanbhalavun
hearing *n.* સુનાવણી sunaavanee
hearken *v.i.* ધ્યાનપૂર્વક સાંભળવું.
  dhyaanapoorvak saanbhalavun
hearsay *n.* અફવા afava
hearse *n.* મડદાગાડી madadaagaadee
heart *n.* હૃદય rhaday
hearten *v.t.* હિંમત આપવી hinmat
  aapavee
heartfelt *adj.* ખરા દિલનું kharaa
  dilanun
hearth *n.* ચૂલો. choolo
hearty *adj.* ખુશમિજાજ khushamijaaj
heat *n.* ઉષ્ણતા ushnata
heated *adj.* ઉત્તેજિત uttejit
heath *n.* ઝાંખરા zankharaa
heathen અપ્રબુદ્ધ–માણસ aprabuddh
  - maanas
heave *v.t.* નિસાસો નાંખવો nisaaso
  nankhavo
heaven *n.* સ્વર્ગ svarg
heavy *n.* ખૂબ વજનદાર khoob
  vajanadaar
hectic *adj.* પ્રક્ષુબ્ધ prakshubdh
hedge *n.* ઝાડવાની વાડ jhaadavaanee
  vaad
heed *v.t.* ધ્યાનમાં લેવું dhyaanaman
  levun
heedful *adj.* કાળજી kaalajee
heel *n.* પગની એડી paganee edee
hefty *adj.* કદાવર kadaavar
heifer *n.* ન વિયાયેલી ગાય na viyaayelee
  gaay
height *n.* શિખર shikhar
heighten *v.* અતિશયોકિત કરવી
  atishayokti karavee
heinous *adj.* ભયાનક bhayaanak
heir *n.* વારસ vaaras
helicopter *n.* હેલિકોપ્ટર helicoptar
helium *n.* હિલીયમ hileeyam
hell *n.* નરક narak
helm *n.* સુકાન sukaan
helmet *n.* શિરસ્ત્રાણ shirastaan
helmsman *n.* સુકાની sukaanee
help *n.* મદદ madad
helpful *adj.* સહાયકારી sahaayakaaree

hem *n.* કાપડની કિનાર kaaapadnee
  kinaar
hemisphere *n.* ગોળાર્ધ golaardh
hemlock *n.* એક ઝેરી વનસ્પતિ ek jheree
  vanaspati
hemorrhage *n.* રક્તસ્ત્રાવ raktastraav
hemp *n.* શણ shan
hen *n.* મરઘી maraghee
hen-packed *adj.* પત્નીને આધિન
  patneene aadhin
hence *adv.* અહીંથી aheenthee
henceforth *adv.* હવેથી havethee
her *pro* તેણીનું teneenun
herald *n.* અગ્રદૂત agradoot
herb *n.* કાષ્ઠૌષધિ kaashthaushadhee
herbage *n.* ઔષધિઓ aushadhio
herculean *n.* મહામુશ્કેલ.
  mahaamushkel
herd *n.* ધણ dhan
here *adv.* અહીં aheen
hereditary *adj.* વંશપરંપરાથી મળતું
  vanshaparanparaathee malatun
herewith *adv.* આ સાથે aa saathe
heritage *n.* સંસ્કૃતિનો વારસો.
  sanskrutino vaaraso
heretic *adj.* પાખંડી paakhandee
hermitage *n.* આશ્રમ aashram
hernia *n.* સારણગાંઠ saaranagaanth
hero *n.* પરાક્રમી પુરુષ paraakramee
  purush
heroism *n.* શૌર્ય shaury
heroin *n.* ઘેનની દવા ghenanee davaa
heron *n.* બગલાની એક જાત. bagalaanee
  ek jaat
hesitate *v.i.* નામરજીવાળું હોવું
  naamarajeevaalun hovun
hesitating *adj.* અચકાવવું achakaavavun
hesitation *n.* અચકાતું achakaatun
hessian *n.* ગુણપાટ goonapaat
heterodox *adj.* પાખંડી paakhandee
heterogeneous ભિન્ન લક્ષણવાળું bhinn
  lakshanavaalun
hew *v.t.* વાઢવું vaadhavun
hexagon *n.* ષટ્કોણ shatakon
hiccup *n.* હેડકી hedakee
hidden *p.p.* અદ્રશ્ય adrashy
hide *v.t.* છુપાવવું chhupaavavun

hideous *adj.* બિહામણું bihaamanun

hierarchy *n.* સ્તરીકરણ stareekaran

hierogtyph ધર્મગુરુઓનું રાજ્ય dharmaguruonun raajy

higgle *v.i.* ભાવ વિષે રકઝક કરવી bhaav vishe rakajhak karavee

high *adj.* આત્યંતિક aatyantik

highway *n.* ધોરી માર્ગ dhoree maarg

hike *n.* પગપાળા પર્યટન pagapaala paryatan

hilarity *n.* મસ્તીખોરી masteekhoree

hill *n.* ટેકરી tekaree

hillock *n.* ટેકરી tekaree

hilt *n.* મૂઠ mooth

hind *n.* રાતી raatee

hinder *v.t.* અટકાવવું atakaavavun

hindrance *n.* અડચણ adachan

hinge *n.* મજાગરાં majaagaran

hint *n.* આડકતરી સૂચના aadakataree soochana

hip *n.* કુલો kulo

hippopotamus *n.* જળઘોડો. jalaghodo

hire *v.t.* ભાડે રાખવું bhaade raakhavun

hireling *n.* ભાડૂતી માણસ bhaadootee maanas

his *pro.* ષષ્ઠવિભક્તિનું રૂપ. shashthivibhaktinun roop

hiss *v.t.* સિસકારો કરવો sisakaaro karavo

historic *adj.* ઐતિહાસિક aitihaasik

history *n.* ઇતિહાસ eetihaas

hit *v.t.* મારવું maaravun

hitch *n.* અડચણ adachan

hither *adv.* આ બાજુએ આવેલું aa baajue aavelun

hitherto *adv.* અત્યાર સુધી atyaar sudhee

hive *n.* મધપૂડો madhapoodo

hoard *n.* ભેગો કરેલો જથ્થો bhego karelo jaththo

hoarse *adj.* બેઠેલો અવાજ bethelo avaaj

hoary *adj.* જૂનું પુરાણું joojun puraanun

hobby *n.* શોખ shokh

hockey *n.* ગેંડીદડો gendeedado

hog *n.* સૂઅર sooar

hoist *v.t.* ઉઠાવવું udhaavavun

hold *v.* પકડી રાખવું pakadee raakhavun

hole *n.* ગાબડુ, દર, રાફડો gaabadun

holiday *n.* ઉજાણીનો દિવસ ujaaneeno divas

holiness *n.* પવિત્રતા pavitrata

hollow *n.* પોલું polun

holy *adj.* પવિત્ર. pavitr

homage *n.* સત્કાર satkaar

home *n.* રહેવાનું ઘર rahevaanun ghar

homely *adj.* કદરૂપું kadaroopun

homicide *n.* મનુષ્ય વધ. manushy vadh

homogeneous *adj.* સજાતીય sajaatiy

honest *adj.* પ્રામાણિક praamaanik

honesty *n.* પ્રમાણિકપણું praamaanikapanun

honey *n.* મધ madh

honeycomb *n.* મધપૂડો madhapoodo

honeymoon *n.* મધુમાસ madhumaas

honorarium *n.* માનદ વેતન maanad vetan

honorary *adj.* માનદ maanad

honour *adj.* સત્યનિષ્ઠા satyanishtha

honourable *n.* માનનીય maananeey

hood *n.* પદવીદર્શક વસ્ત્ર padaveedarshak vastr

hoodwink *v.t.* કપટ કરવું kapata karavun

hoof પગની ખરી paganee kharee

hook *n.* આંકડો aankado

hooligan *n.* મવાલી mavaalee

hoot *v.i.* હુર્યો બોલાવવો huryo bolaavavo

hop *v.i.* ઠેકડા મારવા dhekada maravan

hope *n.* આશા aasha

horde *n.* રખડુ જમાતનું ટોળુ rakhadu jamaatanun tolun

horizon *n.* ક્ષિતિજ kshitij

horn *n.* શિંગડુ shingadu

hornet *n.* ભમરો bhamaro

horoscope *n.* જન્માક્ષર janmaakshar

horrible *adj.* આઘાતજનક aaghaatajanak

horrid *adj.* અપ્રિય apriy

horrify *v.t.* ગભરાવવું gabharaavavun

horripilation રોમાંચ romaanch

horror *n.* કમકમાટી kamakamaatee

horse *n.* અશ્વ ashv

horseman *n.* ઘોડેસવારીમાં કાબેલ ghodesavaareeman kabel

horticulture *n.* બાગકામ baagakaam

hose *n.* પગનું લાંબું મોજું paganun laanbun mojun

hosiery *n.* ગૂંથેલી ચીજો goonthelee cheejo

hospitable *adj.* અતિથિસત્કાર કરનારું atithisatkaar karanaarun

hospital *n.* રુગ્ણાલય rugnaalay

hospitality *n.* આતથ્ય aatithy

host *n.* સમુદાય samudaay

hostage *n.* બંદી bandee

hostel *n.* છાત્રાલય chhaatraalay

hostile *adj.* શત્રુતાવાળું shatrutaavaalun

hostility *n.* શત્રુતા shatruta

hot *adj.* ઉત્સાહી utsaahee

hound *n.* શિકારી કૂતરો shikaaree kutaro

hour *n.* કલાક kalaak

hourly *adj.* દર કલાકે બનતું dar kalaake banatun

house *n.* ઘર ghar

household *n.* ઘરગથ્થું gharghatthun

housemaid *n.* નોકરડી nokaradee

housewife *n.* ગૃહિણી gruhinee

hovel *n.* છાપરું chhaaparun

hover *v.i.* અનિશ્ચિત રહેવું anirnit rahevun

how *adv.* કેવી રીતે kevee reete

howdah *n.* અંબાડી anbaadee

however *adv.* ગમે તે રીતે game te reete

howitzer તોપ top

howl *v.t.* કારમી ચીસ kaaramee chees

hubbub *n.* કોલાહલ kolaahal

huddle *v.t.* ભીડ કરવી bheeda karavee

hue *n.* રંગ rang

hug *v.t.* પકડી રાખવું pakadee raakhavun

huge *adj.* પ્રચંડ prachand

hull *n.* ફોતરું fotarun

hum *v.i.* ગણગણાટ ganaganaat

human *adj.* માનવોચિત maanavochit

humane *n.* સંસ્કારિતાસંવર્ધક sanskaarita sanvardhak

humanity *n.* પરોપકારિતા paropakaarita

humble *adj.* વિનયશીલ vinayasheel

humbug *n.* ધતિંગ dhating

humdrum *n.* જડ jad

humid *adj.* ભીનાશવાળું bheenaashavaalun

humidity *n.* ભીનાશ bheenaash

humiliate *v.* હલકું પાડવું halakun paadavun

humility *n.* દીનતા deenata

humorist વિનોદી vinodee

humorous *n.* હાસ્યોત્પાક hasyotpaak

humour *n.* હાસ્યજનકતા haasyajanakata

hump *n.* વિષાદ vishaad

hundred *n.* સો so

hunger *n.* ભૂખ bhookh

hungry *adj.* ભૂખ્યું bhookhyun

hunt *v.t.* શિકાર કરવો shikaar karavo

hunter *n.* શિકારી shikaaree

hurdle *n.* અવરોધ avarodh

hurl *v.t.* જોરથી ફેંકવું jorathee fenkavun

hurrah *int.* જયજયકાર jayajayakaar

hurricane *n.* વાવાઝોડું vaavaajhodun

hurry *v.t.* ઉતાવળ કરવી utaaval karavee

hurt *v.t.* નુકશાન કરવું nukashaan karavun

husband *n.* પતિ pati

husbandry *n.* કૃષિ krushi

hush *v.t.* ચૂપ રાખવું choop raakhavun

husk *n.* છાલાં chhaalan

hut *n.* ઝૂંપડી jhoonpadee

hybrid *adj.* વર્ણસંકર varnasankar

hydrant *n.* મોટો નળ moto nal

hydraulic *adj.* હાયડ્રોલિક hayadrolic

hydrogen *n.* હાઈડ્રોજન haidrojan

hydrophobia *n.* હડકવા hadakava

hydrous *adj.* પાણીવાળું paaneevaalun

hyena *n.* તરસ taras

hygiene *n.* આરોગ્ય શાસ્ત્ર aarogy shaastr

hymn *n.* ભજન bhajan

hyperbole *n.* અતિશિયોક્તિ atishayokti

hyphen *n.* સંયોગ ચિહ્ન sanyog chinh

hypnotism *n.* સંમોહનવિદ્યા sanmohanavidhya

hypocrisy *n.* મિથ્યાચાર mithyaachaar

hypocrite *adj.* વેષધારી veshadhaaree

hypotenuse *n.* કર્ણ karn

hypothesis *n.* પૂર્વધારણા purvadhaarana

hypothetical *adj.* પૂર્વપક્ષાત્મક poorvapakshaatmak

hysteria *n.* વાઈ vaaee

hysteric *adj.* હિસ્ટેરીયાગ્રસ્ત histereeyaagrasta

i *pro.* પુરુષવાચક સર્વનામ purushavaachak sarvanaam
ice *n.* બરફ baraf
iceberg *n.* તરતો બરફનો પહાડ tarato barafano pahaad
ice-cream *n.* ઠારેલી દૂધમલાઈ thaarelee doodhamalaaee
icicle *n.* બરફની પાટ barafanee paat
icon *n.* બાવલું baavalun
iconoclast *n.* મૂર્તભંજક moortibhanjak
icy *adj.* ઠંડું dhandun
idea *n.* યોજના yojana
ideal *adj.* આદર્શ aadarsh
idealist *n.* આદર્શવાદી. aadarshavaadee
idealize *v.t.* આદર્શરૂપ બનાવવું aadarshroop banaavavun
identical *adj.* તદ્દન એના જેવું જ taddan ena jevun ja
identify *v.t.* ઓળખવું olakhvun
identity *n.* એકત્વ ekatv
idiom *n.* રૂઢિપ્રયોગ roodhee prayog
idiomatic *adj.* રૂઢિપ્રયુક્ત roodheeprayukt
idiosyncracy *n.* વ્યક્તિગત વશિષ્ટિતા vyaktigat vishishtata
idiot *n.* જડબુદ્ધિમાણસ jadabuddhi maanas
idle *adj.* આળસુ aalasu
idler *n.* પ્રમાદી માણસ pramaadee maanas
idleness *n.* પ્રમાદ pramaad
idol *n.* મૂર્તિ moorti
idolater *n.* મૂર્તિપૂજક moortipoojak
idolatry *n.* મૂર્તિપૂજા moortipooja
idolize *v.t.* ની અતિશય પ્રીતિ nee atishay preetee
idyll *n.* ગોપકાવ્ય gopakaavy
idyllic નૈસર્ગિક naisargik
if *conj.* જો jo

igneous *adj.* અગ્નિકૃત agnikrut
ignite *v.t.* સળગાવવું salagaavavun
ignition *n.* સળગવાની પ્રક્રિયા salagavaanee prakriya
ignoble *adj.* નીચી પાયરીનું neechee paayareenun
ignominy *n.* ગેરઆબરૂ geraaabaroon
ignorance *n.* અજ્ઞાન agnaan
ignorant *adj.* અજ્ઞાન agnaan
ignore *v.t.* ની અવગણના કરવી nee avaganana karavee
ill *adj.* માંદું maandun
illation *n.* તારવણી taaravanee
illative *adj.* પરિણામસૂચક parinaamasoochak
ill-bred *adj.* અસંસ્કારી asanskaaree
illegal *adj.* ગેરકાયદેસર gerakaayadesar
illegible *adj.* ઉકેલે નહી તેવું ukele naheen tevun
illegitimate *adj.* ગેરકાયદે, gerakaayade
illiberal *adj.* કંજૂસ kanjoos
illicit *adj.* ગેરકાયદે, નિષિદ્ધ gerakaayade
illmitable *adj.* અમર્યાદ amaryaad
illiteracy *n.* નિરક્ષરતા niraksharata
illiterate *adj.* નિરક્ષર abhan, nirakshar
illness *n.* માંદગી maandagee
illogical *adj.* ન્યાય વિરુદ્ધ nyaay viruddh
illuminate *v.t.* પ્રકાશિત કરવું prakaashit karavun
illumination પ્રકાશિત કરવું તે prakaashit karavun te
illumine દીવો કરવો deevo karavo
illusion *n.* ભ્રમ bhram
illusive *adj.* માયાવી maayaavee
illustrate *v.t.* સમજાવવું samajaavavun
illustration *n.* ઉદાહરણ udaaharan
illustrious *adj.* પ્રસિદ્ધ prasiddh
image *n.* માનસિક ચિત્ર maanasik chitr
imaginable *adj.* કલ્પનીય kalpaneey
imaginary *n.* કાલ્પનિક kaalpanik
imagination *n.* કલ્પનાશક્તિ kalpanaashakti
imaginative *adj.* કલ્પક kalpak
imagine *v.t.* ની કલ્પના કરવી nee kalpana karavee

imbecile *adj.* નબળા મનનું nabala manunun

imbibe *v.t.* ચૂસી – શોષી લેવું choosee - shoshee levun

imbrue *v.t.* કલંકિત કરવું kalankit karavun

imbue *v.t.* પૂરેરતિ કરવું prerit karavun

imitable *adj.* અનુકરણક્ષમ anukaranaksham

imitate *v.t.* નકલ કરવી nakal karavee

imitation *n.* અનુકરણ anukaran

immaculate *adj.* નિષ્કલંક nishkalank

immanent *adj.* વિશ્વવ્યાપી vishvavyaapee

immaterial *adj.* અમૂર્ત amoort

immature *adj.* અપૂરોઢ aparipakv, apraudh

immaturity અપરિપક્વતા, અપૂરોઢત્વ apraudhatv

immeasurable *adj.* અમાપ amaap

immediate *adj.* તાત્કાલિક taatkaalik

immediately *adv.* તત્કાળ tatkaal

immemorial *adj.* અતિપ્રાચીન atipraacheen

immense *adj.* વિશાળ vishaal

immerse *v.t.* બોળવું bolavun

immethodical *adj.* અવ્યવસ્થિત avyavasthit

immigrant *n.* દેશાગત deshaagat

immigrate *v.t.* દેશાગમન કરવું deshaagaman karavun

imminent *adj.* નિકટવર્તી nikatavartee

immobile *adj.* અચલ achal

immoderate *adj.* અતિશય atishay

immodest *adj.* ઉદ્ધત uddhat

immolate *v.t.* બલિદાન આપવું balidaan aapavun

immoral *adj.* વ્યાભિચારી vyaabhichaaree

immortal *adj.* અવિસ્મરણીય avismaraneey

immortalize *v.t.* ચિરંજીવ કરવું chiranjeev karavun

immovable *adj.* અણનમ ananam

immune રોગના ચેપથી મુક્ત rogana chepathee mukt

immunity *n.* રોગપ્રતિકારકતા rogapratikaarakataa

immutable *adj.* અવિકારી avikaaree

imp *n.* મસ્તીખોર masteekhor

impact *n.* અસર asar

impair *v.t.* ને ઈજા પહોંચાડવી ne eeja pahonchaadavee

impale *v.t.* શૂળીએ ચડાવવું shooleee chadaavavun

impalpable *adj.* અગોચર agochar

imparity *n.* અસમાનતા asamaanata

impark *v.t.* વાડામાં પૂરવું vaadaaman pooravun

impart –નો ભાગ આપવો no bhaag aapavo

impartial *adj.* નિષ્પક્ષપાતી nishpakshapaatee

impasse *n.* મડાગાંઠ madaagaanth

impassioned ખૂબ ઉત્સાહી khoob utsaahee

impassive *adj.* ભાવના વિનાનું bhaavana vinaanun

impatience *n.* અસહિષ્ણુતા asahishnuta

impatient *adj.* અસહિષ્ણુ asahishnu

impeach રાજદ્રોહનો ઠપકો આપવો raajadraahano thapako aapavo

impede *v.t.* અડચણ કરવી adachan karavee

impediment *n.* નડતર nadatar

impel *v.t.* આગળ ચલાવવું aagal chalaavavun

impend *v.t.* લટકતું હોવું latakatun hovun

impending આસન્ન aasann

impenetrable અપ્રવેશ્ય apraveshy

imperative *adj.* આજ્ઞાવાચક aagnaavaachak

imperceptible *adj.* અદ્રશ્ય adrashy

imperfect *adj.* અપૂરણ apoorn

imperial *adj.* બાદશાહી baadashaahee

imperialism *n.* સામ્રાજ્યવાદ saamraajyavaad

imperil *v.t.* જોખમમાં નાખવું jokhamaman naakhavun

imperious *adj.* મનસ્વી manasvee

imperishable અવિનાશી avinaashee

impersonal *adj.* વ્યક્તિનિરપેક્ષ vyakti nirapeksh

impersonate *v.t.* હોવાનો ઢોંગ કરવો hovaano dhong karavo

impertinent *adj.* અપ્રસ્તુત aprastut

impervious *adj.* અભેદ્ય abhedhy

impetuous *adj.* અવિચારીપણાથી વર્તતું avichaareepanaathee vartavun

impetus *n.* ગતિઆપનારું જોર gati aapanaarun jor

impiety *n.* અધાર્મિકતા adhaarmikata

impish *adj.* તોફાની tofaanee

implacable *adj.* દુરારાધ્ય duraaraadhy

implant મનમાં ઠસાવવું manaman thasaavavun

implement *n.* યોજનાનો અમલ કરવો yojanaano amal karavo

implicate *v.t.* માં સંડોવવું maan sandovavun

implication *n.* સૂચિતાર્થ ધ્વન્વાર્થ soochitaarth dhvanvaarth

implicit *adj.* અભિપ્રેત abhipret

implied *adj.* સૂચિત soochit

implore *v.t.* આજીજી કરવી aajeejee karavee

imply *v.t.* ઇશારો કરવો eeshaaro karavo

impolite *adj.* અસભ્ય asabhy

import *v.t.* આયાત કરવું aayaat karavun

importance *n.* અગત્યતા agatyata

important *n.* મહત્ત્વનું mahatvanun

importunity *n.* આગ્રહી aagrahee

impose *v.t.* છેતરીને લેવડાવવું chhetareene levadaavavun

imposing *adj.* રૂઆબદાર rooaabadaar

imposition ઉપર હાથ મૂકવા તે upar haath mookava te

impossible *adj.* અશક્ય ashakya

impost *n.* વેરો vero

impostor ઢોંગી dhongee

impotent *adj.* વીર્યહીન veeryaheen

impoverish *v.t.* ગરીબ બનાવવું gareeb banaavavun

impracticable *adj.* અવ્યવહાર્ય avyavahaary

imprecate *v.t.* ને શાપ દેવો ne shaap devo

impregnable *adj.* અજેય ajey

impregnate *v.t.* સગર્ભા બનાવવું sagarbha banaavavun

impress પૂરભાવ કે અસર prabhaav ke asar

impression *n.* છાપ chhap

impressive *adj.* પૂરભાવી prabhaavee

imprison *v.t.* કેદમાં નાખવું kedaman naakhavun

improbable *adj.* અવિશ્વસનીય avishvasaneey

improbity *n.* અપ્રામાણિકતા apraamaanikata

improper *adj.* અચોક્કસ achokkas

impropriety *n.* અયોગ્યતા ayogyata

improve *v.* સુધારવું sudhaaravun

improvement *n.* સુધરવુ sudharavun

imprudent અવિચારી avichaaree

impudent *adj.* બેશરમ besharam

impugn *v.t.* વાંધો ઉઠાવવો vaandho uthaavavo

impulse લાગણીનો આવેગ laaganeeno aaveg

impulsion *n.* પ્રોત્સાહન protsaahan

impunity *n.* સજામુક્તિ sajaamukti

impure *adj.* અશુદ્ધ ashuddh

imputation *n.* ને નામે લખવું ne naame lakhavun

impute *v.t.* ને નામે લખવું ne naame lakhavun

in *prep.* માં maan

inability અક્ષમતા akshamata

inaccessible *adj.* પહોંચ બહારનું pahonch bahaaranun

inaccurate *adj.* અચોક્કસ achokkas

inadequate *adj.* અપૂરતું apooratun

inadmissible *adj.* અગ્રાહ્ય agraahy

inadvertent *adj.* નહિતુ nihetu

inane *adj.* ખાલી khaalee

inapplicable *adj.* અનુપયુક્ત anupayukt

inapt *adj.* અકુશળ akushal

inaptitude અકુશળ akushal

inattentive *adj.* દુર્લક્ષ durlaksh

inaudible *adj.* સંભળાય નહિએવું sanbhalaay nahi evun

inaugural *adj.* ઉદ્ઘાટન સમયનું uddghaatan samayanun

inaugurate *v.t.* ઉદ્ઘાટન કરવું uddghaatan karavun

inauguration *n.* ઉદ્ઘાટન uddghaatan

inborn *adj.* જન્મજાત janmajaat

incalculable *adj.* ગણાય નહિ એવું ganaay nahi evun

incandescence *n.* તાપદીપ્ત taapadeept

incandescent *adj.* તાપદીપ્ત taapadeept

incantation જાદુટોણો jaadutono

incapable *adj.* અસમર્થ asamarth

incapacitate *v.t.* નિષ્ક્રિય કરવું nishkriya karavun

incarcerate *v.t.* કેદમાં પુરવું kedaman puravun

incarnate *v.t.* મૂર્તિમંત બનાવવું moortimant banaavavun

incase *v.t.* ના કસિસામાં naa kissaaman

incendiary *adj.* સળગાવનારું salagaavanaarun

incense *n.* ધૂપ dhoop

incentive *adj.* પ્રોત્સાહક protsaahak

inception *n.* આરંભ aaranbh

incessant *n.* વારંવાર થતું vaaranvaar thatun

inch *n.* ફૂટનો બારમો ભાગ footano baaramo bhaag

incident *n.* ઘટના ghatana

incision *n.* ઉપર કાપ મૂકવો upar kaap mookavo

incite *v.t.* ઉશ્કેરવું ushkeravun

incivility *n.* અવિનય avinay

inclination *n.* વલણ valan

incline *v.t.* ઢોળાવ namavun, dholaav

inclosure *n.* બિડાણ bidaan

include *v.t.* સમાવેશ કરવો samaavesh karavo

inclusion *n.* સમાવેશ samaavesh

incognito *n.* વેશધારી veshadhaaree

income *n.* આવક aavak

income-tax *n.* આવકવેરો aavakavero

incomparable *adj.* અજોડ ajod

incompatible *adj.* અસંગત asangat

incompetent *adj.* અક્ષમ aksham

incomplete અધૂરું adhoorun

incomprehensible *adj.* અકળ akal

inconceivable *adj.* અકલ્પ્ય akalpy

inconclusive *adj.* અનિર્ણિત anirnit

incongruous *adj.* મૂર્ખામી ભરેલું moorkhaamee bharelun

inconsiderate *n.* અવિવેકી avivekee

inconsistent *adj.* પરસ્પર વિરોધી paraspar virodhee

inconstant *adj.* અનિયમિત aniyamit

incorporate *v.t.* નિગમ બનાવવું nigam banaavavun

incorrect *adj.* ખોટું khotun

incorrigible *adj.* સુધરે નહિ એવું sudhare nahi evun

increase *v.t.* વધવું vadhavun

increasingly *adv.* વધારે પ્રમાણમાં vadhaare pramaanaman

incredible *adj.* આશ્ચર્યજનક aashcharyajanak

increment *n.* વધારો vadhaaro

incriminate *v.t.* આરોપમાં સંડોવાવું aaropaman sandovaavun

inculcate *v.t.* ઠસાવવું dhasaavavun

incumbent *adj.* પદધારી padadhaaree

incur *v.t.* ખર્ચ કરવો kharcha karavo

incurable *adj.* રીઢું (માણસ) reedhun (maanas)

incursion *n.* ઓચિંતો હુમલો ochinto humalo

indebted *adj.* ઉપકૃત upakrut

indecency *n.* અશોભનીયતા ashobhaneeyata

indecent *adj.* અશ્લીલ ashleel

indecisive *adj.* અનિર્ણાયક anirnaayak

indeed *adj.* અલબત્ત alabatt

indefatigable *adj.* અથાક athaak

indefensible *adj.* ગેરવાજબી geravaajabee

indefinite *adj.* અનિશ્ચિત anishchit

indelible કાયમનું kaayamanun

indemnity *n.* નુકસાની nukasaanee

indent *v.t.* માં ખાંચા પાડવા maan khaancha paadava

indenture *n.* સહીસિક્કાવાળું કરારનામું saheesikkaavaalun karaaranaamu

independence *n.* આઝાદી aajhaadee

independent *adj.* સ્વતંત્ર svatantr

indestructible *n.* અવિનાશી avinaashee

index *n.* કક્કાવાર સૂચિ kakkaavaar soochee

indian *n.* હિન્દનો વતની hindano vatanee

indicate *v.t.* – નું સૂચક ચિહ્ન હોવું nun soochak chinh hovun

indict *v.t.* આરોપ મુકવો aarop mukavo

indifferent *adj.* પક્ષપાત વિનાનું pakshapaat vinaanun

indigenuous *adj.* તળપદું talapadun

indigent *adj.* જરૂરીયાતવાળું jarooreeyaatavaalun

indigestion *n.* અપચો aapacho

indignation *n.* પુણ્યપ્રકોપ પામેલું તે punyaprakop paamelun te

indignity *n.* અયોગ્ય વર્તન ayogya vartan

indigo *n.* ઘેરો વાદળી રંગ ghero vaadalee rang

indirect *adj.* પરોક્ષ paroksh

indiscreet *adj.* અવિચારી avichaaree

indispensable *adj.* અનિવાર્ય anivaary

indisposition *n.* સહેજ માંદગી sahej maandagee

indistinct *adj.* અસ્પષ્ટ aspasht

individual *n.* વ્યક્તિગત vyaktigat

individuality *n.* વ્યક્તિત્વ vyaktitv

indolence *n.* આળસ aalas

indolent *adj.* આળસું aalasun

indomitable *adj.* અણનમ ananam

indoor *adj.* મકાનની અંદરની makaananee andaranun

indoors *adv.* મકાનની અંદર makaananee andar

indorse *v.t.* શેરો મારવો shero maaravo

induce *v.t.* લલચાવવું lalachaavavun

inducement *n.* લલચ lalach

induction *n.* આકર્ષવું તે aakarshavun te

inductive પ્રમાણ નિર્ધારિત pramaan nirdhaarit

indulge *v.t.* રીઝવવું reejhavavun

indulgence *n.* આપેલ વિશેષહક aapel visheshahak

indulgent *adj.* અનુગ્રહશીલ amugrahasheel

industrial *adj.* ઔધોગિક audhyogik

industrious *adj.* ઉદ્યમી udhyamee

industry *n.* ઉદ્યમ udhyam

inedible *adj.* અભાદ્ય akhaadhy

ineffable *adj.* અવર્ણનીય avarnaneey

ineffective *adj.* બિનઅસરકારક binaasarakaarak

ineligible *adj.* અયોગ્ય ayogy

inept *adj.* બિન–કુશળ bin-kushal

inequality *n.* વિષમતા vishamata

inert *adj.* ચેતનવિહીન chetanaviheen

inertia *n.* નિષ્ક્રિયતા nishkriyata

inevitable *adj.* અવશ્યંભાવી avashyanbaavee

inexcusable *adj.* અક્ષમ્ય akshamy

inexhaustible અખૂટ akhoot

inexorable *adj.* નિષ્ઠુર kathor

inexpedient *adj.* અનુચિત anuchit

inexplicable *adj.* સુઝે નહી તેવું suze nahee tevun

infallible *adj.* અચૂક achook

infamous *adj.* કુખ્યાત kukhyaat

infamy *n.* અપકીર્તિ apakeerti

infancy *n.* બાલ્યાવસ્થા baalyaavastha

infant *n.* શિશુ (સાત વરસથી નાનું) shishu (saat varasathee naanun)

infanticide *n.* બાળહત્યા baalahatya

infantile *adj.* બાળક સંબંધી baalak sanbandhee

infantry પાયદળ paayadal

infatuate *v.t.* મોહિત કરવું mohit karavun

infect *v.t.* ચેપ લગાડવો chep lagaadavo

infection *n.* ચેપ chep

infectious *adj.* ચેપી chepee

infer *v.t.* અનુમાન કરવું anumaan karavun

inference *n.* અનુમાન anumaan

inferior *adj.* ગૌણ gaun

inferiority *n.* હીનતા heenata

infernal *adj.* શેતાની setaanee

infest *v.t.* ઉપદ્રવ કરવો upadrav karavo

infidel *n.* અશ્રદ્ધાળું ashraddhaalun

infinite *n.* અમર્યાદ amaryaad

infinitesimal *adj.* અતિસૂક્ષ્મ atisookshm

infirm *adj.* અસ્થિર asthir

infirmity *n.* નબળાઈ nabalaaee

inflame *v.* ઉશ્કેરવું ushkeravun

inflammable *adj.* જ્વલનશીલ jvalanasheel

inflammation *n.* બળતરા balatara

inflation *n.* ફુગાવો fugavo

inflection *n.* વિભક્તિપ્રત્યય vibhakti pratyay

inflexible *adj.* જિદ્દી jiddee

inflict *v.t.* લાદવું laadavun

influence *n.* પ્રભાવ પાડવો prabhaav paadavo

influential *adj.* વગદાર vagadaar

influenza *n.* તાવ taav

influx *n.* અંદર વહેવું તે andar vahevun te

inform *v.t.* જણાવવું janaavavun

informal *adj.* અનૌપચારિક anaupachaarik

information *n.* જાણકારી jaanakaaree

infringe *v.t.* ભંગ કરવો bhang karavo

infuriate ગુસ્સે કરવું gusse karavun

infuse *v.t.* મનમાં ઉતારવું manaman utaaravun

ingenious *adj.* યુક્તિબાજ yuktibaaj

ingenuity *n.* બુદ્ધિશાળી buddhishaalee

ingenuous *adj.* નિખાલસ nikhaalas

ingot *n.* ધાતુનો ઢાળિયો dhaatuno dhaaliyo

ingraft *v.t.* કલમ આરોપણ kalam aaropan

ingratitude *n.* કૃતઘ્નતા krutaghnata

ingredient *n.* ઘટક દ્રવ્ય ghatak dravy

inhabit *v.t.* વસવું vasavun

inhabitant *n.* રહીશ raheesh

inhale *v.t.* સૂંઘવું soonghavun

inherent *n.* સ્વાભાવિક svaabhaavik

inherit *v.t.* વારસામાં મળવું vaarasaaman malavun

inhibition *n.* નિયંત્રણ niyantrin

inhuman *n.* ઘાતકી ghaatakee

inimical *adj.* શત્રુતાવાળું shatrutaavaalun

inimitable *adj.* અદ્વિતીય. adviteey

iniquitous *adj.* દુષ્ટ dusht

initial *n.* શરૂઆતનું sharooaatanun

initiate શરૂઆત કરવી sharooaat karavee

initiative *n.* પહેલવૃત્તિ pahelavrutti

inject *v.t.* દાખલ કરવું daakhal karavun

injunction *n.* મનાઈ manaaee

injure *v.t.* નુકસાન કરવું nukasaan karavun

injury *n.* નુકસાન nukasaan

injustice *n.* અન્યાય anyaay

ink *n.* શાહી shaahee

inkling *n.* આછો ખ્યાલ aachho khyaal

ink-pot *n.* શાહીનો ખડીયો shaaheeno khadeeyo

inlay *v.t.* જડવું jadavun

inlet *n.* સાંકડી ખાડી saankadee khaadee

inmate *n.* સહવાસી sahavaasee

inn *n.* પથિકાશ્રમ pathikaashram

innate *adj.* સહજ sahaj

inner *adj.* અંદરનું andaranun

innings *n.* વારો vaaro

innkeeper *n.* વીશીવાળો veesheevaalo

innocent *adj.* નિર્દોષ nirdosh

innocuous *adj.* નિરુપદ્રવી nirupadravee

innovate *v.t.* ફેરફાર કરવા ferafaar karava

innumerable *adj.* અગણિત asankhy

inoculate રસી મુકવી rasee mukavee

inopportune *adj.* અપ્રાસંગિક apraasangik

inordinate *adj.* અપરિમિત aparimit

inquest *n.* અપમૃત્યુ તપાસ apamrutyu tapaas

inquire *v.i.* પૂછવું poochhavun

inquiry પૂછપરછ poochhaparachh

inquisition *n.* અદાલતી તપાસ adaalatee tapas

inquisitive *adj.* કુતૂહલવાળું kutoohalavaalun

inroad *n.* અતિક્રમણ atikraman

insane *adj.* ગાંડુ gaandu

inscribe *v.t.* અક્ષર કોતરવાં akshar kotaravan

inscription *n.* શિલાલેખ shilaalekh

inscrutable *adj.* ગૂઢ goodh

insect *n.* જંતુ jantu

insecure *adj.* અસુરક્ષિત asurakshit

insensible ચેતનાહિન chetanaahin

insert *v.t.* –માં ઘાલવું maan ghaalavun

inside *n.* અંદરની બાજુની જગ્યા andaranee baajunee jagya

insight *n.* સૂક્ષ્મદ્રષ્ટિ sookshmadrashti

insignificant *adj.* બિનમહત્ત્વનું binamahattvanun

insincere *adj.* નિષ્ઠાહીન nishthaaheen

insist *v.i.* −નો આગ્રહ કરવો no aagrah karavo

insistence *n.* આગ્રહ aagrah

insolence *n.* અપમાનકારકતા apamaanakaarakata

insolent *adj.* તોછડું tochhadun

insoluble *adj.* અદ્રાવ્ય adraavya

insolvency *n.* નાદારી naadaaree

insolvent *adj.* નાદાર naadaar

insomnia *n.* અનદ્રિા(રોગી) anidra (rogee)

inspect *v.t.* બારીકાઇથી જોવું baareekaaeethee jovun

inspection *n.* બારીકાઇથી જોવું તે baareekaaeethee jovun te

inspector *n.* નરિીક્ષક nireekshak

inspiration *n.* એકદમ સ્ફુરેલો વચિાર ekadam sfurelo vichaar

inspire *v.t.* પ્રેરણા આપવી prerana aapavee

instable *adj.* અસ્થરિ asthir

install *v.t.* સ્થાપન કરવુ sthaapan karavun

installation *n.* સ્થાપના sthaapan

instalment *n.* હપતો hapato

instance *n.* ઉદાહરણ udaaharan

instant *n.* તાકીદનું taakeedanun

instantaneous *adj.* ક્ષણવારમાં − થતું kshanavaaraman - thatun

instantly *adv.* એકદમ. ekadam

instead *adv.* બદલામાં badalaaman

instigate *v.t.* ઉશ્કેરવું ushkeravun

instigation *n.* ઉશ્કેરણી ushkeranee

instil *v.t.* ટીપે ટીપે ભરવું teepe teepe bharavun

instinct *n.* સ્વયંસ્ફૂરતિ svayansfoorti

instinctive *adj.* સ્વયંસ્ફૂરતિ svayansfoorti

institute *n.* સ્થાપન કરવું sthaapan karavun

institution *n.* સંસ્થા sanstha

instruct *v.t.* −ને ખબર આપવી ne khabar aapavee

instruction *n.* આદેશો aadesho

instrument *n.* સાધન saadhan

insubordinate *adj.* માથાભારે maathaabhaare

insufficient *adj.* અપર્યાપ્તતા aparyaaptata

insulate *v.t.* અલગ પાડવું alag paadavun

insult *n.* અપમાન apamaan

insuperable *adj.* અનુલ્લંઘનીય anullanghaneey

insurance *n.* વીમો veemo

insure *v.t.* વીમો ઉતરાવવો veemo utaraavavo

insurgent *n.* બળવો કરનાર balavo karanaar

insurmountable *adj.* દુસ્તર dustar

insurrection *n.* બળવો balavo

intact *adj.* અસ્પૃષ્ટ asprusht

intangible *adj.* અગોચર agochar

integer *n.* પૂર્ણાંક poornaank

integral *adj.* અભનિ્ન abhinna

integrate *v.t.* પૂરણ કરવું poorn karavun

integration *n.* એકત્રીકરણ ekatreekaran

integrity *n.* અખંડતિતા akhanditata

intellect *n.* બુદ્ધિ buddhi

intellectual *n.* બૌદ્ધકિ bauddhik

intelligence *n.* બુદ્ધિ buddhi

intelligent *adj.* હોશયિાર hoshiyaar

intelligible *adj.* બુદ્ધગિ્રાહ્ય buddhigraahy

intend *v.t.* ધારવું dhaaravun

intense *adj.* જોશીલું josheelun

intensity *n.* ઉત્કટતા utkatata

intent *adj.* હેતુ hetu

intention *n.* હેતુ hetu

intentional ઇરાદાપૂર્વક કરેલું eeraadaapoorvak karelun

intercept *v.t.* અટકાવવું atakaavavun

interchange *v.t.* વનિમિય vinimay

intercourse *n.* મૈથુન maithun

interdict *v.t.* પૂરતબિંધ pratibandh

interest વ્યાજ vyaaj

interesting *adj.* મનોરંજક manoranjak

interfere *v.i.* માં દખલ કરવી maan dakhal karavee

interference *n.* દખલ dakhal

interim *n.* કામચલાઉ kaamachalaau

interior *adj.* આંતરકિ aantarik

interject *v.t.* આડું નાંખવું aadun nankhavun

interjection *n.* ઉદ્દગાર uddagaar

interlink v.t. પરસ્પર જોડવું paraspar jodavun

interlocution n. પરિષદ parishad

intermarriage n. આંતરજ્ઞાતીય વિવાહ aantaragnaateey vivaah

intermediate adj. વચ્ચે આવનાર (વસ્તુ) vachche aavanaar (vastu)

intermingle v.t. મિશ્રણ કરવું mishran karavun

intermittent adj. સતત ચાલું satat chaalun

internal આત્મલક્ષી aatmalakshee

international adj. આન્તરરાષ્ટ્રીય aantararaashtriy

interpellation n. કામમાં દાખલ kaamaman daakhal

interpret v.t. અર્થ કરવો artha karavo

interpretation અર્થઘટન arthaghatan

interpreter n. દુંભાષિયો dubhaashiyo

interrogate v.t. તપાસ કરવી tapaas karavee

interrogation n. તપાસ tapaas

interrupt v.t. ની આડે આવવું nee aade aavavun

interruption n. રોકવું rokavun

intersect v.t. છેદીને જવું chhedeene javun

interstice ફાટ faad

intertwine v.t. વીંટળાઈ જવું veentalaaee javun

interval n. વિરામ viraam

intervene દરમ્યાનગીરી કરવી daramyaanageeree karavee

intervention n. દરમ્યાનગીરી daramyaanageeree

interview n. મુલાકાત mulaakaat

intestate adj. બિનવસિયતી binvasiyatee

intestines n.pl. આંતરડું aantaradun

intimacy n. ઘરોબો dharobo

intimate v.t. તદ્દન અંગત taddan angat

intimation n. જાણ jaan

intimidate v.t. બિવડાવવું bivadaavavun

into prep. માં રસ ધરાવનારું maan ras dharaavanaarun

intolerable adj. અસહ્ય asahy

intolerence n. અસહિષ્ણુતા asahishnuta

intoxicant adj. માદક maadak

intoxicate v.t. છાકટું કરવું chhaatakun karavun

intractable adj. હઠીલું hatheelun

intransitive adj. અકર્મક akarmak

intrepid adj. બહાદુર bahaadur

intricacy n. જટીલતા jateelataa

intricate adj. ગૂંચવણ ભરેલું goonchavan bharelun

intrigue n. કાવતરું kaavatarun

intrinsic adj. અંતર્ભૂત angabhoot

introduce v.t. ઓળખાણ કરાવવી olakhaan karaavavee

introduction n. પ્રસ્તાવના prastaavan

introspection n. આત્મનિરિક્ષણ aatmanireekshan

intrude v.t. –માં ઘાલવું maan ghaalavun

intuition n. અન્તર્દ્દષ્ટિ antardashti

inundate v. રેલમછેલ કરવું relamachhel karavun

inundation n. રેલમછેલ કરવું તે relamachhel karavun te

inure v.t. –ની ટેવ – મહાવરો – પાડવો nee tev - mahaavaro - paadavo

invade v.t. અતિક્રમણ કરવું atikraman karavun

invalid adj. ઘેર રવાના કરવું gher ravaana karavun

invalidate v.t. રદ કરવું rad karavun

invaluable adj. અમૂલ્ય amooly

invariable અવિકારી avikaaree

invasion n. અતિક્રમણ atikraman

invective નિંદાત્મક ભાષણ nindaatmak bhaashan

invent v.t. નિર્માણ કરવું nirmaan karavun

inventor n. નવનિર્માતા navanirmaata

inventory n. માલયાદી maalayaadee

inverse adj. ઊલટું oolatun

invert v.t. ઉલટાવવું ulataavavun

invest ની પાછળ ખર્ચ કરવું nee paachhal kharch karavun

investigate v.t. કાળજીપૂર્વક તપાસવું kaalajeepoorvak tapaasavun

investment n. રોકેલાં નાણાં rokelan naana

invidious adj. અરોચક arochak

invigorate *v.t.* માં પ્રાણ પૂરવો maan praan pooravo

invincible *adj.* અજેય ajey

inviolable ભ્રષ્ટ ન કરાય એવું bhrsht na karaay evun

invisible *adj.* અદૃશ્ય adrshy

invitation *n.* આમંત્રણ aamantran

invite *v.t.* આમંત્રણ આપવું aamantran aapavun

invoice *n.* ભરતિયું bharatiyun

invoke *v.t.* આહવાન કરવું aahavaan karavun

involve *v.t.* સામેલ કરવું saamela karavun

inward અંદર આવેલું andar aavelun

irascible *adj.* ગરમ મિજાજવાળું garama mijaajavaalun

ire *n.* ક્રોધ krodh

irenic *adj.* શાંતિવાચ્છું shaantivaachchhun

iris *n.* આંખની કીકી aankhanee keekee

irk *v.t.* થકવી નાંખવું thakavee naankhavun

irksome કંટાળાજનક kantaalaajanak

iron *n.* લોઢું lodhun

ironic વ્યંગ્યાત્મક vyangyaatmak

irony *n.* વક્રોક્તિ vakrokti

irradiate *v.t.* ઉપર પ્રકાશવું upar prakaashavun

irrational *adj.* બુદ્ધિહીન buddhiheen

irregular *adj.* બદલાતું badalaatun

irregularity *n.* અસમતા asamata

irrelevant *adj.* અપ્રસ્તુત aprastut

irreparable *adj.* સુધારી ન શકાય તેવું sudhaaree na shakay tevun

irresistible *adj.* બળવાન balavaan

irresolute *adj.* દૃઢ નિશ્ચય વિનાનું dradh nishchay vinaanun

irresponsible *adj.* બેજવાબદાર bejavaabadaar

irretrievable *adj.* કાયમનું ગુમાવેલું kaayamanun gumaavelun

irrevocable *adj.* અટલ atal

irrigate *v.t.* સિંચાઈ કરવી sinchaaee karavee

irrigation *n.* સિંચાઈ sinchaaee

irritate *v.t.* ચીડવવું cheedavavun

irruption *n.* સ્ફોટ sfot

is *v.i.* છે chhe

isle *jn.* (બહુધા નાનો) ટાપુ (bahudha naano) taapu

island *n.* ટાપુ taapu

islet *n.* નાનો ટાપુ naano taapu

isolate *v.t.* રોગીને અલગ રાખવો rogeene alag raakhavo

issue *n.* પરિણામ parinaam

isthmus *n.* સંયોગી ભૂમિ sanyogee bhoomi

it *pro* તે te

italics *n.pl.* ઈટાલિક અક્ષરો itaalik aksharo

itch *n.* ખજવાળ khajavaal

its *pro.* તેનું tenun

item *n.* બાબત baabat

itinerary *n.* પ્રવાસનો માર્ગ pravaasano maarg

ivory *n.* હાથીદાંત haatheedaant

ivy *n.* વેલો velo

J

jab *v.t.* ભોંકવું bhonkavun

jabot *n.* ઝાલર zaalar

jack *n.* ઊંટડો oontado

jackal *n.* શિયાળ shiyaal

jackass *n.* મૂરખમાણસ moorkhamaanas

jackdaw *n.* જંગલી કાગડો jangalee kaagado

jacket *n.* જાકીટ jaakeet

jade *n.* દૂબળું ઘોડું doobalun ghodun

jail *n.* કેદખાનું kedakhaanun

jam *n.* ચગદવું chagadavun

jamboree *n.* ઉજાણી ujaanee

janitor *n.* દરવાન daravaan

january *n.* જાન્યુઆરી મહિનો. jaanyuaaree mahino

jar *n.* કર્કશ અવાજ કરવો karkash avaaj karavo

jargon *n.* શુદ્ધ ભાષા shuddha bhaasaa

jasmine *n.* ચમેલી chamelee

jaundice *n.* કમળો. kamalo

jaunt *n.* આનંદ પર્યટન aanand parytan
jaunty *adj.* આડંબરી aadanbaree
javelin *n.* ભાલો bhaalo
jaw *n.* લૌકિ વાત laukik vaat
jay *n.* નલિકંઠ જેવું પંખી nilakanth jevun pankhee
jealous *adj.* ઈર્ષાળું eershaalun
jealousy *n.* ઈર્ષા eersha
jeer *v.t.* ટોણાં મારવા tonan maarava
jelly *n.* ફળનો મુરબ્બો falano murabbo
jeopardize *v.t.* જોખમમાં નાખવું. jokhamaman naakhavun
jeopardy *n.* જોખમ jokham
jerk *n.* આંચકો aanchako
jerkin *n.* ટૂંકું જાકિટ toonku jaakit
jersey *n.* ગૂંથેલું જાકિટ gunthelun jaakit
jest *n.* રમૂજ ramooj
jester *n.* વિદૂષક vidooshak
jet *n.* ફુવારો foovaaro
jetty *n.* ઓવારો ovaaro
jew *n.* યહૂદી yahoodee
jewel *n.* રત્ન ratn
jeweller *n.* ઝવેરી. jhaveree
jewellery *n.* ઝવેરાત. jhaveraat
jibe કટાક્ષ kataaksh
jilt *n.* તરછોડવું tarachodavun
jingle *n.* ઝણકાર jhanakaar
job *n.* રોજિંદુ કામ rojindun kaam
jobber *n.* છૂટક કામ કરનાર chhutak kaam karanaar
jockey *n.* જોકી jokee
jocular *adj.* મશ્કરું mashkarun
jocund *adj.* ખુશમિજાજી khushamijaajee
jog *v.t.* કોણીનો હળવો ગોદો koneeno halavo godo
join *v.t.* જોડવું jodavun
joint *n.* જોડાણ jodaan
jointer *n.* સાંધો saandho
jointure *n.* સ્ત્રીધન streedhan
joke *n.* રમૂજ ramooj
jollity *n.* ઉલ્લાસ ullaas
jolly *adj.* ખુશ મિજાજ khush mijaaj
jolt *v.t.* આંચકો મારવો. aanchako maaravo
jot *n.* અતિ સૂક્ષ્મ ભાગ ati sookshm bhaag

jotting *n.* યાદી yaadee
journal *n.* રોજમેળ rojamel
journalism *n.* પત્રકારત્વ patrakaaratv
journalist *n.* પત્રકાર patrakaar
journey *n.* પ્રવાસ pravaas
jovial *adj.* મોજીલું mojilun
joy *n.* હરખ harakh
joyful *adj.* ખુશ. khush
joyous *adj.* ઉલ્લાસી ullaasee
jubilant *adj.* હરખઘેલું. harshghelun
jubilee *n.* જયંતી jayantee
judge *n.* ન્યાયાધીશ nyaayaadheesh
judgement *n.* ચુકાદો chukaado
judicious *adj.* વિવેકપૂરણ vivekapoorn
jug *n.* કૂંજો koonjo
juggler *n.* જાદૂગર jaadoogar
juice *n.* ફળ અથવા માંસનો રસ. fal athava maansano ras
juicy *adj.* રસદાર rasadaar
jumble *v.t.* ગોટાળો કરવો gotaalo karavo
jump *v.t.* ઓચિંતો ઉછાળો. ochinto uchhaalo
junction *n.* સંગમસ્થાન sangamasthaan
juncture *n.* સમય–બિંદુ samay - bindu
jungle *n.* વન. van
junior *adj.* નાની ઉમરનું naanee unmaranun
junket *n.* ઉજાણી ujaanee
jupitor *n.* ગુરુ ગ્રહ guru grah
jurisdiction *n.* અધિકારક્ષેત્ર. adhikaarakshetr
jurisprudence *n.* કાયદાશાસ્ત્ર kaayadaashaastr
jurist *n.* કાયદાશાસ્ત્રી. kaayadaashaastree
jury *n.* જૂરીનો સદસ્ય jooreeno sadasy
just *adj.* વાજબી vaajabee
justice *n.* ન્યાયાધીશ nyaayaadheesh
justification વાજબીપણું vaajabeepanun
justify *v.t.* ઉચિત ઠેરવવું uchita theravavun
jut *v.t.* આગળ ધસી જવું. aagal dhasee javun
jute *n.* શણ. shan
juvenile *adj.* કિશોર kishor

juvenility *n.* શિશુનો અપરાધ. shishuno aparaadh

juxtaposition *n.* સમીપતા. sameepata

K

kale *n.* એક જાતની કોબી ek jaatanee kobee

kaleidoscope આકૃતિદર્શક aakrutidarshak

kaleidoscopic *adj.* કેલીડોસ્કોપ keleedoskop

kangaroo *n.* કાંગારૂ kaangaaroo

kedge *n.* નાનું લંગર naanun langar

keel *n.* નૌતાલ nautaal

keen *adj.* તીક્ષ્ણ teekshn

keep *v.* ઉછેરવું uchheravun

keeping *n.* કબજો kabajo

keg *n.* નાનકડું પીપ naanakadun peep

ken *v.t.* જ્ઞાન મર્યાદા gyaan maryaada

kennel *n.* શ્વાનગૃહ shvaanagruh

kerchief *n.* હાથરૂમાલ haatharoomaal

kernel *n.* કોપરૂં koparoo

kerosene *n.* ઘાસલેટ ghaasalet

kettle *n.* કિટલી kitalee

key *n.* ચાવી chaavee

kick *v.i.* —ને લાત મારવી ne laat maaravee

kid *n.* લવારું lavaarun

kiddy *n.* બાળક baalak

kidnap *v.t.* અપહરણ કરવું તે. apaharan karavun te

kidney *n.* મૂતરપિંડ mootrapind

kill *v.t.* મારી નાખવું maaree naakhavun

kiln *n.* ભઠ્ઠી bhaththee

kin *n.* વંશ vansh

kind *n.* જાત jaati

kindle *v.t.* સળગાવવું salagaavavun

kindness *n.* સદ્‌વ્યવહાર saddavyavahaar

kindred *adj.* સજાતીય sajaateey

kine *n.* ગાયો gaayo

king *n.* રાજા raaja

kingdom *n.* રાજ્ય raajy

kinsman *n.* લોહીના સંબંધીઓ loheena sanbandheeo

kiss *n.* ચુંબન chunban

kit *n.* સાજસરંજામ saajasaranjaam

kitchen *n.* રસોડું rasodun

kite *n.* પતંગ patang

kith *n.* સ્નેહીજનો sneheejano

kitten *n.* બિલાડીનું બચ્ચું bilaadeenun bachchun

kleptomania *n.* ચોરવાનો રોગ choravaano rog

knack *n.* કરામત karaamat

knapsack *n.* થેલો thelo

knave *n.* બદમાશ badamaash

knavery *n.* બદમાશી badamaashee

knead *v.t.* માલિશ કરવું maalish karavun

knee *n.* ઢીંચણ dheenchan

kneel *v.i.* ઘૂંટણિયે પડવું ghoontaniye padavun

knell *n.* મૃત્યુઘંટ mrutyughant

knickers *n.* સ્ત્રીની ચડ્ડી streenee chaddee

knife *n.* છરી chharee

knight *n.* સરદાર saradaar

knit *v.t.* ગૂંથવું goonthavun

knob *n.* મૂઠ mooth

knock *v.t.* ટકોરો મારવો takoro maaravo

knot *n.* ગાંઠ gaanth

knotty *adj.* ગાંઠોગાંઠોવાળું gaanthogaanthovaalun

know *v.t.* —ની ઓળખાણ હોવી nee olakhaan hovee

knowingly *adv.* જાણીજોઈને jaaneejoeene

knowledge *n.* જ્ઞાન gnaan

knuckle વેઢો vedho

koran *n.* કુરાન kuraan

kosher *n.* ખરૂં kharun

kukri *n.* કટાર kataar

L

label *n.* કાપલી kaapalee

labial *adj.* ઓઠોનું othonun

laboratory *n.* પ્રયોગશાળા. prayogashaala

laborious *adj.* મહેનતુ mahenatanun

labour *n.* મજૂર majoor

labyrinth *n.* ભુલભુલામણી bhulabhulaamanee

lace *n.* જોડાની દોરી jodaanee doree

lacerate *v.t.* ચીરવું cheeravun

lack *n.* ન્યૂનતા nyoonata

lackey *n.* ખુશામતિયો. khushaamatiyo

laconic *adj.* સૂત્રમય. sootramay

lactometer *n.* દુગ્ધમાન dugdhamaan

lad *n.* જુવાનિયો. juvaaniyo

ladder *n.* સીડી seedee

lade *p.p.* લાદવું laadavun

lading *n.* લાદેલું laadelun

ladle *n.* કડછી kadachhee

lady *n.* સ્ત્રી stree

lag *n.* બહુ ધીમે જવું bahu dheeme javun

lagoon *n.* ખારાપાણીનું સરોવર khaaraapaaneenu sarovar

lair *n.* બોડ bod

lake *n.* તળાવ. talaav

lamb *n.* ઘેટાનું બચ્ચું ghetaanun bachchun

lame લંગડું langadun

lament *v.t.* દુઃખ વ્યક્ત કરવું dukh vyakt karavun

lamentation *n.* વિલાપ vilaap

lamp *n.* દીવો deevo

lampoon *n.* કટાક્ષવાળું – લખાણ kataakshavaalun - lakhaan

lance *n.* ઘોડેસવારનો ભાલો ghodesavaarano bhaalo

lancer *n.* ઘોડાદળનો સિપાઈ ghodaadalano sipaai

lancet *n.* શસ્ત્રવૈદ્યનું શસ્ત્ર shastravaidyanun shastra

land *v.t.* જમીન jameen

landing *n.* રમણું ramanun

lan·mark *n.* સીમાચિહ્ન seemaachinha

landscape *n.* બગીચાકામ bageechaakaam

lane *n.* સાંકડો રસ્તો saankado rasto

language *n.* ભાષ bhaashaa

languid મંદ mand

languish *v.i.* તીવ્રતા ગુમાવવી teevrata gumaavavee

languor *n.* સુસ્તી sustee

lank *adj.* સુકલકડી sukalakadee

lantern *n.* ફાનસ faanas

lap *n.* ખોળો kholo

lapidary *n.* નકશીકાર nakasheekaar

lapse *n.* નજીવી ભૂલ najeevee bhool

larboard *n.* લારબોર્ડ laarabord

larceny *n.* ચોરી choree

lard *n.* ડુક્કરની ચરબી dukkaranee charabee

large *adj.* વિશાળ vishaal

largese *n.* બક્ષિસ bakshis

lark *n.* ચંડોળ chandol

larva *n.* ઈયળ eeyal

lash *n.* આંખની પાંપણ aankhanee paanpan

lass *n.* છોકરી. chhokaree

lassitude *n.* સુસ્તી sustee

lasso *n.* ગાળિયો gaaleeyo

last *adj.* છેલ્લુ chhellu

lasting *adj.* અસ્તિત્વમાં રહેવું astitvaman rahevun

latch *n.* બારણાની ખીંટી baaranaanee kheentee

late *adv.* મોડું modun

latent *adj.* અવ્યક્ત avyakt

lateral *adj.* બાજુનું baajunun

lathe *n.* ખરાદ kharaad

lather *n.* સાબુનું ફીણ saabunun feen

latitude *n.* અક્ષાંશ akshaansh

latrine *n.* પાયખાનું paayakhaanun

latter *adj.* તાજેતરનું taajetaranun

lattice *n.* જાફરી jaafaree

laud *v.t.* વખાણ – કરવા vakhaan - karava

laudable *adj.* વખાણવાલાયક vakhaanavaalaayak

laudanum *n.* અફીણનો અર્ક afeenano ark

laudatory *adj.* પ્રશંસાત્મક prashansaatmak

laugh *v.t.* હસવું hasavun

laughter *n.* હાસ્ય haasy

launch *v.t.* ફેંકવું fenkavun

laundry *n.* ધોલાઈઘર dholaaighar

gumaavavee

lava *n.* લાવા laavaa
lavatory *n.* કમોડ kamod
lave *v.t.* ધોવું, નહાવવું dhovun, nahaavun
lavish *adj.* ભરપૂર bharapoor
law *n.* કાનૂન kaanoon
lawful *adj.* કાયદેસર kaayadesar
lawn *n.* ઝીણું કાપડ zinnu kaapad
lawyer *n.* વકીલ vakeel
lax *adj.* શિથિલ shithil
laxative *adj.* સારક (દવા) saarak (dava)
laxity *n.* શિથિલતા shithilataa
layer *n.* પટ્ટો:સ્તર:પડ pattohastarahapad
layman *n.* સામાન્ય માનવી saamaanya maanavee
laziness *n.* પ્રમાદ pramaad
lazy *adj.* આળસુ aalasu
lea *n.* ખેડવાલાયક જમીન khedavaalaayak jameen
lead *v.t.* દોરવું doravun
leader *n.* આગેવાન aagevaan
leaf *n.* પાંદડું paandadun
leaflet *n.* ચોપાનિયું chopaaniyun
league *n.* સંઘ sangh
leak *n.* ચૂવો choovo
leakage *n.* ચૂવું તે choovo te
lean *v.t.* વલણ હોવું valan hovun
leaning *n.* વલણ valan
leap *n.* કૂદવું koodavun
learn *v.t.* ભણવું bhanavun
learned *adj.* વિદ્વાન vidvaan
learning *n.* ભણતર bhanatar
lease *n.* ગણોતપટો ganotapato
least *adj.* લેશમાત્ર leshamaatr
leather *n.* ચામડું chaamadun
leave *v.t.* રજા પરવાનગી rajaa paravaanagee
leaven *n.* ખીરું kheerun
lecture *n.* ભાષણ bhaashan
ledger *n.* હિસાબની ખાતાવહી hisaabanee khaataavahee
lee *n.* આશારો aasharo
leech *n.* જળો jalo
leer *n.* કામી kaamee
left *adj.* ડાબી બાજુનું daabee baajunun
leg *n.* પગ pag
legacy *n.* વારસો. vaaraso

legal *adj.* કાયદેસરનું kaayadesaranun
legalize *v.t.* કાયદેસર કરવું, kaayadesar karavun
legation *n.* એલચી અને તેના માણસો elachee ane tena maanaso
legend *n.* મુદ્રાલેખ mudraalekh
legendary *adj.* પૌરાણિક pauraanik
legible *adj.* સુવાચ્ય suvaachy
legion *n.* મોટી સંખ્યા motee sankhya
legislate *v.t.* કાયદો ઘડવો kaayado ghadavon
legislation કાયદા ઘડવા તે kaayada ghadava te
legislator *n.* કાયદા ઘડનાર kaayada ghadanaar
legislature *n.* રાજ્યની ધારાસભા raajyanee dhaaraasabha
legitimate *adj.* ઔરસ auras
legume *n.* વટાણા vataana
leisure *n.* નવરાશ navaraash
leman *n.* માશૂક maashook
lemon *n.* લીંબુ leenbu
lemonade *n.* લીંબુનું શરબત leenbunun sharabat
lend *v.t.* ઉછીનું આપવું uchheenun aapavun
length *n.* લંબાઈ lanbaaee
lengthen *v.t.* લાંબુ કરવું laanbu karavun
lens *n.* ચશ્મા chashma
lentil *n.* મસૂરનો દાણો masoorano daano
leopard *n.* દિપડો dipado
leper *n.* (રક્ત)પીતિયો (rakt)peetiyo
leprosy *n.* રક્તપિત્ત raktapitt
less *adj.* આટલું બધું નહઈ aatalun badhun nahi
lesson *v.i.* બોધપાઠ bodhapaath
lest *conj.* કદાચને kadaachane
let *v.t.* અટકાવવું atakaavavun
lethal *adj.* જીવલેણ jeevalen
lethargy *n.* ગાફેલપણું gaafelapanun
letter *n.* અક્ષર akshar
levant *adj.* પૂર્વ ભૂમધ્ય પ્રદેશ poorv bhoomadhy pradesh
levee *n.* મહેમાનોનો મેળાવડો mahemaanono melaavado
level *n.* સપાટી sapaatee
lever *n.* ઉચ્ચાલક uchchaalak

levity *n.* આછકલાપણું aachhakalaapanun

levy *v.t.* ફરજિયાત ઉઘરાણું farajiyaat ugharaanun

lewd *adj.* અશ્લીલ ashleel

lexicographer *n.* કોશરચના કરનાર kosharachana karanaar

lexicon *n.* શબ્દકોશ shabdakosh

liability *n.* જવાબદાર હોવું તે javaabadaar hovun te

liable *adj.* જવાબદાર javaabadaar

liar *n.* જૂઠું બોલનારો joothun bolanaaro

libel *n.* બદનક્ષી badanakshee

liberal *adj.* ઉદાર udaar

liberate *v.t.* મુક્ત કરવું mokt karavun

libertine *n.* વિષયસંપટ માણસ vishayasanpat maanas

liberty *n.* સ્વાધીનતા svaadheenata

libidinous *adj.* લંપટતા ને લગતું lanpatata ne lagatun

library *n.* ગ્રંથાલય granthaalay

licence *n.* પરવાનગી paravaanagee

licentiate *n.* પદવીધર padaveeghar

licentious *adj.* વ્યભિચારી vyabhichaaree

lick *v.t.* ચાટી નાખવું chaatee naakhavun

lid *n.* આંખનું પોપચું aankhanun popachun

lie *n.* જૂઠું joothun

liege *n.* સ્વામી svaamee

lieu *n.* – ને બદલે ne badale

lieutenant *n.* લેફ્ટનન્ટ leftanant

life *n.* જીવન jeevan

lifelike *adj.* આબેહૂબ aabehoob

lift *v.t.* ઊંચુ કરવું oonchun karavun

light *n.* પ્રકાશ prakaash

lighten *v.t.* હળવું કરવું halavun karavun

lighthouse *n.* દીવાદાંડી divaadaandee

lightning *n.* વિજળી vijalee

like *v.t.* ના જેવું naa jevun

likelihood *n.* શક્યતા shakyata

likewise *adv.* એ જ પ્રમાણે e ja pramaane

liking *n.* અભિરુચિ abhiruchi

lily *n.* કમળનું ફૂલ kamalanu fool

limb *n.* સૂરૂષનો વશિષ્ટ કોર sooryano vishisht kor

lime *n.* ચૂનો choono

lime-light *n.* પ્રસદ્ધિનો ચળકાટ prasiddhino chalakaat

limit *n.* સીમા seema

limp *v.i.* લંગડાવું langadaavun

line *n.* લીટી leetee

lineage *n.* વંશ vansh

lineal *adj.* વંશપરંપરાગત vanshaparanparaagat

lineament *n.* લક્ષણ lakshan

linear *adj.* રેખીય rekheey

linen *n.* શણનું કાપડ shananun kaapad

liner *n.* ઉતારુ વિમાન utaaru vimaan

linger *v.t.* ઢીલ કર્યા કરવી dheel karya karavee

lingual *adj.* વાણીનું vaaneenun

linguist *n.* ભાષાશાસ્ત્રી bhaashaashaastree

liniment *n.* ચોપડવાનું ઓસડ chopadavaanun osad

link *v.t.* બાહુમાં બાહુ પરોવવા baahooman bahoo parovava

linseed *n.* અળસી aalasee

lint *n.* શણિયાનો પાટો કાપડ shaniyaano paato kaapad

lion *n.* સિંહ sinh

lip *n.* હોઠ hoth

liquefy *v.t.* ઓગાળવું ogalavun

liquid *n.* પ્રવાહી pravaahee

liquidate *n.* કરજ ભરપાઈ karaj bharapaaee

liquidation *n.* કરજનો ફડચો karajano fadacho

liquor *n.* દારૂ daaroo

lisp *v.i.* તોતડું બોલવું totadun bolavun

list *n.* સૂચિ soochi

listen *v.i.* ધ્યાનપૂર્વક સાંભળવું dhyaanapoorvak saanbhalavun

listless *adj.* ઉદાસીન udaaseen

literacy *n.* સાક્ષરતા saaksharata

literal *adj.* અક્ષરે અક્ષરનું akshare aksharanun

literally *adv.* શાબ્દિક અર્થ અનુસાર shaabdik artha anusaar

literary *adj.* સાહિત્યપ્રેમી saahityapremee

literate *adj.* શિક્ષિત shikshit

literature *n.* સાહિત્ય saahity
lithograph *n.* શિલાછાપ shilaachhaap
litigate *v.t.* દાવો માંડવો daavo
maandavo
litigation *n.* દાવો daavo
litter *n.* અટારો ataaro
little *adj.* નાનકડું naanakadun
live *adj.* જીવંતું jeevatun
livelihood *n.* આહાર aahaar
lively *adj.* ચેતનવંતું chetanavantun
liver *n.* પિત્તાશય pittaashay
livery *n.* ગણવેશ ganavesh
live-stock *n.* પશુધન pashudhan
living *n.* આજીવિકા aajeevika
lizard *n.* કાચિંડો kaachindo
load *n.* બોજો bojo
loadstar *n.* પથદર્શક pathdarshak
loadstone *n.* આકર્ષક વસ્તુ
aakarshak vastu
loaf *n.* પાંઉરોટી paanurotee
loaves *v.t.* રોટી બનાવવી rotee
banaavavee
loafer *n.* સ્વૈરવિહારી svairavihaaree
loan *v.t.* ઉછીની રકમ uchheenee rakam
loath *adj.* નાખુશ naakhush
loathe *v.t.* નફરત – તિરસ્કાર કરવો nafarat
- tiraskaar karavo
loathsome *adj.* ઘૃણાસ્પદ dhrunaaspad
lobby *n.* ઓસરી osaree
lobe *n.* કાનની બૂટ kaananee boot
lobster *n.* સાંઢિયો saandhiyo
local *adj.* સ્થાનિક sthaanik
locality *n.* સ્થાન sthaan
locate *v.t.* –ની જગ્યા જણાવવી nee
jagya janaavavee
loch *n.* સરોવર sarovar
lock *n.* વાળની લટ vaalanee lat
locket *n.* તાવીજ taaveej
lock-up *n.* કાચું કેદખાનું kaachun
kedakhaanun
locomotion *n.* હાલચાલ haalachaal
locus *n.* કક્ષા kaksh
locust *n.* તીડ teed
lodge *n.* બંગલી bangalee
lodging *n.* ભાડાની ઓરડી bhaadaanee
oradee
lofty *adj.* મિજાજી mijaajee

log *n.* ઘાતાંક ghaataank
logic *n.* તર્કશાસ્ત્ર tarkashaastr
loin *n.* કમર kamar
lone *adj.* એકલું ekalun
lonely *adj.* એકલું પડેલું ekalun padelun
lonesome *adj.* સૂનકાર soonakaar
long *adj.* દીર્ઘ deergh
longevity *n.* દીર્ઘાયુષ્ય deerghaayushy
longing *n.* મહત્વાકાંક્ષા
matatvaakankshaa
longitude *n.* રેખાંશ rekhaansh
look *v.t.* જોવું jovun
look after *v.t.* કાળજી રાખવી kaalajee
raakhavee
looking-glass *n.* અરીસો areeso
look-out *n.* ચોકી chokee
loom *n.* વણવાનો સંચો vanavaano
sancho
loop *n.* આંકડો aankado
loop-hole *n.* છટકબારી chhatakabaaree
loose *adj.* શિથિલ shithil
loosen *v.t.* ઢીલું કરવું dheelun karavun
lop *v.t.* ઝાડની ડાળી ડાળખાં કાપવાં
jhaadanee daalee daalakhan
kaapavan
loquacious *n.* વાતોડિયું vaatodiyun
lord *n.* સામંત saamant
lore *n.* માન્યતા maanyataa
lorn *adj.* એકલવાયું ekalavaayun
lorry *n.* ખટારો khataaro
loose *v.t.* ઢીલું કરવું dheelun karavun
loss *n.* ખોટ khot
lost *adj.* ગુમાવેલું gumaavelun
lot *n.* હસ્સો hisso
lotion *n.* દવા davaa
lottery *n.* નસીબની કસોટી naseebanee
kasotee
lotus *n.* કમળ. kamal
loud *adj.* બુલંદ buland
lounge *v.i.* નવરા બેસવું navara besavun
louse *n.* હલકટ માણસ. halakat maanas
lout *n.* ગમાર. gamaar
love *n.* પ્રેમ prem
love-lady *n.* પ્રેયસી preyasee
lovely *adj.* રોચક rochak
lover *n.* પ્રેમી premee
love-sick *adj.* પ્રેમાંધ premaandh

low *adj.* અલ્પ alp
lower *v.t.* હલકું પાડવું halakun paadavun
lowland *n.* નીચાણવાળો પ્રદેશ neechaanavaalo pradesh
loyal *adj.* રાજનિષ્ઠ raajanishth
loyalty *n.* રાજનિષ્ઠા raajanishtha
lubricate *v.t.* ઊંજવું oonjavun
lucid *adj.* વ્યવસ્થિતતા. vyavasthitata
lucifer *n.* દીવાસળી deevaasalee
luck *n.* નસીબ naseeb
luckily *adv.* સદ્ભાગ્યે sadabhaagye
lucrative *adj.* લાભકારક laabhakaarak
ludicrous *adj.* હાસ્યાસ્પદ haasyaaspad
luggage *n.* મુસાફરનો સામાન musaafarano saamaan
lukewarm *adj.* કોકરવાયું kokaravaayun
lull *v.t.* સુવાડવું suvaadavun
lullaby *n.* હાલરડું haalaradun
lumbago *n.* કટિવા kativa
lumber *n.* નકામો સામાન nakaamo saamaan
luminary *n.* તેજસ્વી tejasvee
luminous *adj.* તેજસ્વી tejasvee
lump *n.* સોજો sojo
lunacy *n.* ગાંડપણ gaandapan
lunar *adj.* ચંદ્રને લગતું chandrane lagatun
lunatic *adj.* દીવાનું deevaanun
lunch *n.* શિરામણ shiraaman
lung *n.* ફેફસું. fefasun
lurch *n.* –નમી પડવું namee padavun
lure *v.t.* લાલચાવવું laalachaavavun
lurid *adj.* સનસનાટીભર્યું sanasanaateebhryun
lurk *v.i.* છુપાવું chhupaavun
luscious *adj.* કામોત્તેજક kaamottejak
lust *n.* વિષયસેવન vishayasevan
lustre *n.* પ્રભા prabha
lustrous *adj.* ચમકતું chamakatun
lusty *adj.* તંદુરસ્ત tandurast
lute *n.* તંતુવાદ્ય tantuvaadya
luxuriant *adj.* અતિઅલંકારી atialankaaree
luxurious *adj.* સુખસગવડવાળું sukhasagavadavaalun
luxury *n.* એશઆરામની વસ્તુ eshaaaraamanee vastu

lyric *n.* લેખકની ભાવનાઓ lekhakanee bhaavanaao

ma *n.* બા baa
ma'am *n.* મેડમ medam
macaroni *n.* વરણાગિયો. varanaagiyo
mace *n.* ગદા gada
machination *n.* ચાલબાજી. chaalabaajee
machine *n.* યંત્ર yantr
machinery *n.* સંચાની રચના sanchaanee rachana
macrocosm *n.* બ્રહ્મંડ branmaad
mad *adj.* પાગલ paagal
madam *n.* મેડમ medam
madcap *n.* ગાંડિયું gaaniyun
madden *v.t.* ગાંડુ બનાવવું gaandu banaavavun
made *p.p.* કર્યું karyun
madhouse *n.* પાગલખાનું paagalakhaanun
madness *n.* પાગલપણું paagalapanun
magazine *n.* સામાયિક saamaayik
maggot *n.* એક જાતનો કીડો ek jaatano keedo
magic *n.* જાદુ jaadu
magician *n.* જાદુગર jaadugar
magistrate *n.* દંડનાયક dandanaayak
magnanimity *n.* મોટા મનપણું mota manapanun
magnanimous *adj.* મોટા મનનું mota mananun
magnate *n.* ધુરંધર dhurandhar
magnesium *n.* મેગ્નેશિયમ megnesiyam
magnet *n.* લોહચુંબક lohachunbak
magnetic *adj.* લોહચુંબકનું lohachunbakanun
magnetism *n.* પ્રભાવી prabhaavee
magnificent *adj.* ભવ્ય bhavy
magnifier *n.* આવર્ધક aavardhak
magnify *v.t.* અતિશયોક્તિ કરવી atishayokti karavee

magnitude *n.* મોટાપણું motaapanun

maid *n.* કુમારિકા kumaarika

maiden *n.* કુમારી kumaaree

mail *n.* ટપાલ tapaal

main *adj.* સૌથી મહત્વનું sauthee mahatvanun

mainland *n.* ભૂખંડ bhookhand

mainstay *n.* મુખ્ય આધાર mukhy aadhaar

maintain *v.t.* દુરસ્ત રાખવું durast raakhavun

maintenance *n.* ભરણપોષણ bharanaposhan

maize *n.* મકાઈ makaaee

majestic *adj.* ભભકાદાર bhabhakaadaar

majesty *n.* ભવ્યતા bhavyata

major *n.* મુખ્ય mukya

majority *n.* બહુમતી bahumatee

make *v.t.* બનાવવું banaavavun

maker *n.* સરજનહાર sarajanahaar

malady *n.* માંદગી maandagee

malaria *n.* ટાઢિયો તાવ taadhiyo taav

malcontent *adj.* નારાજ naaraaj

male *n.* નરજાતિનું narajaatinun

malediction *n.* શાપ shaap

malefactor *n.* અપરાધી. aparaadhee

malevolent *n.* અદેખાઈ adekhaaee

malice *n.* દ્વેષભાવ dveshabhaav

malicious *adj.* કુંભાવવાળું kunbhaavavaalun

malign *adj.* હાનિકારક haanikaarak

malignant *adj.* ખારીલું khaareelun

malignity *n.* અતિદુષ્ટ ati dusht

mall *n.* વૃક્ષાચ્છાદિત માર્ગ vrukshaachchhaadit maarg

malleable *adj.* કેળવાય એવું kelavaay evun

mallet *n.* હથોડો hathodo

malt *n.* જવ jav

maltreat *v.t.* દુર્વ્યવહાર કરવો durvyavhaar karavo

mamma *n.* (બાલભાષામાં) મા. (baalabhaashaaman) ma

mammal *n.* સસ્તન પ્રાણી. sastan praanee

mammon *n.* કુબેર kuber

mammoth *n.* પ્રચંડ prapanch

man *n.* માનવજાતિ maanavajaati

manacle *n.* હાથકડી haathakadee

manage *v.t.* વ્યવસ્થાપન કરવું vyavasthaapan karavun

management *n.* વ્યવસ્થા vyavastha

manageable *adj.* વ્યવસ્થાપ્ય vyavasthaapya

mandate *n.* આદેશ aadesh

mandible *n.* જડબાનું હાડકું jadabaanun haadakun

mandoline *n.* એક તંતુવાદ્ય ek tantuvaadh

mane *n.* કેશવાળી keshavaalee

manganese *n.* મેંગેનિઝ mengeniz

manger *n.* ગમાણ. gamaan

mangle *v.t.* સંચો sancho

mango *n.* કેરી keree

mania *n.* ગાંડપણ gaandapan

maniac *adj.* ગાંડું gaandun

manifest *v.t.* દેખીતું dekheetun

manifestation પ્રકાશન prakaashan

manifesto *n.* જાહેરનામું jaahernaamu

manifold *n.* અનેકગણુ anekaganu

manikin *n.* ઠિંગુજી thingujee

manipulate *v.t.* ચેડાં કરવા chedaan karavaa

mankind *n.* માનવજાતિ maanavajaati

manly *adj.* મરદના ગુણવાળું maradana gunavaalun

manner *n.* શિષ્ટાચાર shishtaachaar

mannerly *adj.* સભ્ય sabhy

manoeuvre *n.* દાવપેચ, વ્યૂહ daavapech, vyooh

manor *n.* જાગીર jaageer

mansion *n.* મોટું મકાન motun makaan

mantle *n.* ઢાંકણું dhaankanun

manual *adj.* હાથ વતી કરેલું haath vatee karelun

manufactory *n.* નિર્માણ શાળા nirmaan shaala

manufacture *v.t.* ઉત્પાદન કરવું utaadan karavun

manumit *v.t.* મુક્તિ આપવી mukti aapavee

manure *n.* છાણ chhaan

manuscript *n.* હસ્તલિખિત hastalikhit

many *adj.* સંખ્યાબંધ sankhyaabandh

map *n.* નકશો. nakasho
mar *v.t.* નુકશાન કરવું nukashaan karavun
maraud *v.t.* ધાડ પાડવી dhaad paadavee
marble *n.* આરસપહાણ aarasapahaan
march *v.t.* હદ had
mare *n.* ઘોડી ghoodee
margarine *n.* માર્જરિન maarjarin
margin *n.* હાંસિયો haansiyo
marginal *adj.* ભાગ્યે જ પૂરતું bhaagye ja pooratun
marigold *n.* ગલગોટો. galagoto
marine *adj.* દરિયાનું dariyaanun
mariner *n.* નાવિક. naavik
marital *adj.* વૈવાહિક vaivaahik
maritime *adj.* દરિયાઈ dariyaai
mark *n.* ચિહ્ન chinha
marked *adj.* અંકિત ankit
market *n.* બજાર bajaar
marketable *adj.* વેચાણયોગ્ય vechaanayogy
marking *n.* ઓળખાણનું પ્રતીક olakhaananun prateek
marksman *n.* નિશાનબાજ nishaanabaaj
maroon *n.* મરૂણ marun
marquis *n.* માર્કવિસ markvis
marrow *n.* મજ્જા majja
marry *v.t.* લગ્ન કરવા lagna karavaa
mars *n.* મંગળનો ગ્રહ mangalano grah
marsh *n.* કળણ kalan
marshal *n.* માર્શલ maarshal
mart *n.* બજાર bajaar
martial *adj.* લડાયક. ladaayak
martin *n.* માર્ટિન પક્ષી maartin pakshee
martyr *n.* શહીદ shaheed
martyrdom *n.* શહાદત shahaadat
marvel *n.* અદ્દભુત વસ્તુ addabhut vastu
marvellous *adj.* અદ્દભુત addabhut
mascot *n.* સારી વ્યક્તિ saaree vyakti
masculine *adj.* નરજાતનું narajaatinun
mash *v.t.* અનાજનો લોચો anaajno locho
mask/masque *n.* બુરખાધારી વ્યક્તિ burakhaadhaaree vyakti
mason *n.* કડિયો. kadiyo
mass *n.* સમૂહ samooh

massacre *n.* હત્યાકાંડ hatyaakaand
massage *n.* માલિશ કે ચંપી maalish ke chanpee
massive *adj.* સામૂહિક saamoohik
massy *adj.* વજનદાર vajanadaar
mast *n.* દેવદાર devadaar
master *n.* નિયંત્રક niyantrak
masterpiece *n.* ઉત્કૃષ્ટ કલાકૃતિ utkrushta kalaakruti
mastery *n.* વર્ચસ્વ varchasv
masticate ચાવવું chaavavun
mat *n.* ચટાઈ chataaee
match *n.* દીવાસળી. deevaasalee
matchless *adj.* અદ્વિતીય. adviteey
mate *n.* (શહે)માત (કરવી). (sheh) maat (karavee)
material *n.* ભૌતિક bhautik
materialism *n.* જડવાદ jadavaad
materialize *v.t.* મૂર્ત રૂપ આપવું moort roop aapavun
maternal *adj.* માતૃપક્ષનું સગું maatrupakshanun sagun
maternity *n.* માતૃત્વ maatrutv
mathematics *n.* ગણિતશાસ્ત્ર. ganitashaastr
matinee *n.* મેટિની metinee
matricide *n.* માતૃહત્યા. maatruhatya
matriculation *n.* યુનિવર્સિટીમાં પ્રવેશ yunivarsitiman pravesh
matrimony *n.* દાંપત્યાવસ્થા daanpatyaavastha
matrix *n.* ગર્ભાશય garbhaashay
matron *n.* ગૃહમાતા gruhamaataa
matter *n.* ભૌતિક પદાર્થ દ્રવ્ય bhautik padaart dravy
mattock *n.* તીકમ. teekam
mattress *n.* ગાદલું gaadalun
mature *adj.* પરિપક્વ paripakv
maturity *n.* પરિપક્વતા paripakvata
maturation *n.* પૂર્ણ વિકાસ poorn vikaas
maudlin *adj.* વેવલું vevalun
mausoleum *n.* સ્મૃતિસ્તંભ smruti stanbh
maxim *n.* નિયમ niyam
maximum *n.* મહત્તમ mahattm

mayor *n.* મહાનગરપાલિકાનો પ્રમુખ mahaanagarapaalikano pramukh

maze *n.* ભુલભુલામણી bhulabhulaamanee

me *pro.* મને mane

meadow *n.* ઘાસવાળી જમીન ghaasavaalee jameen

meagre *adj.* અલ્પ. alp

meal *n.* અનાજનો દળેલો લોટ. anaajano dalelo lot

mealy *adj.* લોટવાળું lotavaalun

mean *v.t.* નીચી કક્ષાનું neechee kakshaanun

meander *n.* વાંકોચુકો રસ્તો vaankochuko rasto

meaning *n.* અર્થપૂરણ સૂચક arthapoorn soochak

meanness *n.* દુરાચાર duraachaar

means સાધન saadhan

meantime *adv.* વચગાળાનો સમય vachagaalaano samay

measure *n.* માપ maap

measurement *n.* પરિમાણ parinaam

meat *n.* પૂરાણીનું માંસ praaneenun maans

mechanic *n.* મકિનિક mikenik

mechanical *adj.* યંત્રશાસ્ત્રનું yantrashaastranun

mechanics *n.pl.* યંત્રશાસ્ત્ર yantrashaastr

mechanism *n.* યંત્રરચના yantrarachanaa

medal *n.* પદક padak

medallist *n.* ચન્દ્રક વિજિતા chandrak vijeta

meddle *v.i.* હસ્તક્ષેપ કરવો hastkshep karavo

meddlesome *adj.* હસ્તક્ષેપી hastkshepee

medial *adj.* મધ્યમા આવેલું madhyaman aavelun

median *n.* મધ્યગા madhyaga

mediate *v.i.* મધ્યસ્થી કરવી madhyasthee karavee

medical *adj.* વૈદકનું vaidakanun

medicate *v.t.* ઉપચાર કરવો upachaar karavo

medicine *n.* દવા dava

medicinal *adj.* દવાનું davaanun

mediocre *adj.* મધ્યકોટિ madhyakotik

mediocrity *n.* સામાન્ય માણસ saamaanya maanas

meditate *v.t.* ચિંતન કરવું chintan karavun

meditation *n.* ધ્યાન ધરવું dhyaan dharavun

medium *n.* માધ્યમ maadhyam

medley *n.* શંભુમેળો shanbhumelo

meed *n.* યોગ્ય બદલો yogy badalo

meek *adj.* આજ્ઞાંકિત aagnaankit

meet *v.t.* ઉચિત uchit

meeting *n.* ચર્ચાનો મેળાવડો charchaano melaavado

megaphone *n.* મેગાફોન megaafon

megrim *n.* આધાશીશી aadhaasheeshee

melancholy *n.* વિષાદ vishaad

meliorate *v.t.* ઉન્નત કરવું unnat karavun

mellow *adj.* કોમલ komal

melodious *adj.* રાગોત્પાદક raagotpaadak

melody *n.* સુસ્વરસંગીત susvarasangeet

melon *n.* તરબૂચ tarabooch

melt *v.t.* લુપ્ત કરવું lupt karavun

member *n.* મંડળીનો સભ્ય mandaleeno sabhy

membrane *n.* અન્તસ્તવચા antastvacha

memento *n.* સંભારણું sanbhaaranun

memoir *n.* સ્મરણકથા smaranakathaa

memorable સંસ્મરણીય sansmaraneey

memorandum *n.* અનૌપચારિક પત્ર anaupachaarik patr

memorial *v.i.* સ્મરણ કરાવનારું smaran karaavanaarun

memorize *v.t.* યાદ કરવું yaad karavun

memory *n.* સ્મરણશક્તિ smaranashakti

men *n.* પુરૂષો puroosho

menagerie *n.* પશુવાડો pashuvaado

mend *v.t.* સુધારવું sudhaaravun

mendacious *adj.* અપ્રામાણિક વ્યક્તિ apraamaanik vyakti

mendicant *n.* ભિક્ષુક bhikshuk

menial *adj.* હલકું halakun

menses *n.pl.* માસિક maasik

mensuration *n.* ક્ષેત્રમાપન kshetramaapan

menstruation *n.* માસિક સ્ત્રાવ થવો તે maasik straav thavo te

mental *adj.* માનસિક વિકૃતિથી પીડિત maanasik vikrutithee peedit

mentality *n.* માનસિકવૃત્તિ maanasikavrutti

menthol *n.* મેન્થોલ menthol

mention *v.t.* કશાકનો ઉલ્લેખ કરવો kashaakano ullekh karavo

mentor *n.* સલાહકાર salaahakaar

menu *n.* ભોજનપત્રક bhojanapatr

mercantile *adj.* વેપાર કરનારું vepaar karanaarun

mercenary *adj.* ભાડૂતી bhaadootee

merchandize *n.* વેપારની ચીજવસ્તુઓ vepaaranee cheejavastuo

merchant *n.* વેપારી vepaaree

merchantman *n.* માલવાહક જહાજ maalvaahak jahaaj

merciful *adj.* દયાશીલ dayaasheel

merciless *adj.* નિર્દય nirday

mercury *n.* પારો paaro

mercy *n.* ક્ષમાશીલતા kshamaasheelata

mere *adj.* તળાવ talaav

merely માત્ર maatr

merge *v.t.* બીજામાં વિલીન કરવું beejaaman vileen karavun

merger *n.* વિલીનીકરણ vileeneekaran

meridian *n.* યામ્યોત્તર વૃત્ત yaamyottar vrutt

merit *n.* લાયકાત laayakaat

meritorious *adj.* પ્રશંસાપાત્ર prashansaapaatr

mermaid *n.* મત્સ્ય કન્યા matsy kanya

merriment *n.* મોજમજા mojamaja

merry *adj.* હસતું hasatun

mesh *v.t.* જાળમાં પકડવું jaalaman pakadvun

mess *n.* ગંદવાડ gandavaad

message *n.* સંદેશો sandesho

messenger *n.* સંદેશવાહક sandeshavaahak

messiah *n.* તારણહાર taaranhaar

metal *n.* કપચી kapachee

metallic *adj.* ધાતુનું dhaatunun

metaphor *n.* અલંકાર alankaar

mete *v.t.* વહેંચી આપવું vahenchee aapvun

meteor *n.* ઉલ્કા ulka

meteorology *n.* હવામાનશાસ્ત્ર havaamaanashaastr

meter *n.* માપક maapak

methinks *v.i.* મને લાગે છે કે mane laage chhe ke

method *n.* પદ્ધતિ paddhati

methodical *n.* પદ્ધતિસરનું paddhatisaranun

meticulous *adj.* અતિ ચોક્કસ ati chokkas

metonymy *n.* ઉપલક્ષણ upalakshan

metre *n.* દશાંશમાપન dashaanshamaapan

metropolis *n.* મુખ્ય શહેર mukhy shaher

mettle *n.* હિંમત hinmat

mew *v.i.* જળકૂકડી jalakookadee

mewl *v.i.* ધીમે ધીમે રડવું dhime dhime radavun

mica *n.* અબરખ abarakh

mice *n.pl.* ઉંદરડાં undardaa

microbe *n.* જીવાણું jeevaanun

microcosm *n.* નાની પ્રતિમા naanee pratimaa

microphone *n.* ધ્વનિવર્ધક યંત્ર dhvanivardhak yantr

microscop *n.* સૂક્ષ્મદર્શક યંત્ર sookshmadarshak yantr

mid *adj.* વચલું vachalun

midday *n.* બપોર bapor

middle *adj.* મધ્યમ કોટિનું madhyam kotinun

middleman *n.* આડતીયો aadateeyo

midget *n.* સૂક્ષ્મ વસ્તુ sukshma vastu

midnight *n.* મધ્યરાત્ર madhyaraatr

midst *n.* મધ્યભાગ madhyabhaag

midway *adv.* અધવચ્ચે adhavachche

midwife *n.* દાઈ daaee

midwifery *n.* સુયાણી કામ suyaanee kaam

mien *n.* માણસનો દેખાવ maanasano dekhaav

might *n.* સાધનસંપત્તિ saadhanasanpatti

mighty *adj.* જોરાવર joraavar

migrant *n.* સ્થળાંતર કરનારું sthalaantar karanaarun

migrate *v.t.* સ્થળાંતર કરવું sthalaantar karavun

migration *n.* સ્થળાંતર sthalaantar

migratory *adj.* યાયાવર yaayaavar

mikado *n.* જાપાનનો બાદશાહ jaapaanano baadashaah

milage *n.* અંતર antar

mike *n.* ધ્વનિવર્ધક યંત્ર dhvanivardhak yantr

milkman *adj.* દૂધવાળો. doodhavaalo

mild *adj.* સૌમ્ય saumy

mildew *n.* ફૂગ foog

mildness *n.* સૌમ્યતા saumyata

mile *n.* માઈલ, ૧૭૬) વાર maaeel, 176) vaar

milestone *n.* માર્ગસૂચક સ્તંભ maargasoochak stanbh

militant *adj.* લડાયક ladaayak

military *adj.* લશ્કરી lashkaree

militate *v.t.* –ની વિરુદ્ધ nee viruddh

militia *n.* લશ્કરી દળ lashkaree dal

milk *n.* દૂધ doodh

milkmaid *n.* ગોવાલણ govaalan

milky *adj.* ડહોળાયેલું daholaayelun

milky way *n.* આકાશગંગા aakaashaganga

mill *n.* દળવાની ઘંટી dalavaanee ghantee

millennium સુવર્ણયુગ suvarnayug

miller *n.* ઘંટીવાળો ghanteevaalo

millet *n.* બાજરી baajaree

milliard *n.* એક અબજ ek abaj

million *n.* દસ લાખ das laakh

millionaire *n.* લખપતિ lakhapati

mimic *n.* ચાળા પાડનાર chaala paadanaar

minaret *n.* મિનારો minaaro

mince *v.t.* છુંદો કરવો chhundo karavo

mind *n.* મન man

mindful *adj.* –ની ફિકર કરનાર nee fikar karanaar

mine *n.* મારું maarun

miner *n.* ખાણિયો khaaniyo

mineral *n.* ખનિજ khanij

mineralogy *n.* ખનિજ (ધાતુ) વિદ્યા khanij (dhaatu) vidhya

mingle *v.t.* એકત્ર કરવું ekatr karavun

miniature *n.* લઘુચિત્ર laghuchitr

minikin *n.* વહાલું માણસ vahaalun maanas

minim *n.* સંગીતનો એક સૂર sangeetano ek soor

minimize *v.t.* ઘટાડવું ghataadavun

minimum *n.* અલ્પતમ alpatam

minister *n.* પ્રધાન pradhaan

ministry *n.* પ્રધાન મંડળ pradhaan mandal

minor *adj.* સગીર sageer

minority *n.* સગીરપણું sageerapanun

minstrel *n.* મધ્યયુગીન ગાયક madhyayugeen gaayak

mint *n.* ફૂદીનો foodeeno

minus *n.* ઋણ સંખ્યા roon sankhya

minute *n.* મિનીટ mineet

minx લુચ્ચી છોકરી luchchee chhokaree

miracle *n.* ચમત્કાર chamatkaar

miraculous *adv.* અલૌકિક alaukik

mirage *n.* દ્રષ્ટિભ્રમ drashtibhram

mire *n.* કાદવ kaadav

mirror *n.* દર્પણ darpan

mirth *n.* હાસ્યવિનોદ haasyavinod

misanthrope *n.* માનવદ્વેષી maanavadveshee

misadventure *n.* દુસાહસ dusaahas

misapply *v.t.* દુરૂપયોગ કરવો durupayog karavo

misapprehend *v.t.* ગેરસમજ કરવી gerasamaj karavee

misapprehension *n.* ગેરસમજ gerasamaj

misappropriate *v.t.* ઉચાપત કરવી. uchaapaat karavee

misbegotten *adj.* અધમ. adham

misbehave *v.t.* અયોગ્ય વર્તવું ayogy vartan

misbelief *n.* ખોટું મંતવ્ય khotun mantavy

miscarriage *n.* કસુવાવડ kasuvaavad

miscarry ગેરવલ્લે જવું geravalle javun

miscellaneous *adj.* વિવિધ જાતનું vividh jaatanun

miscellany *n.* શંભુમેળો. shanbhumelo

mischance *n.* દુર્દેવી ઘટના durdevee ghatana

mischief *n.* ઉપદ્રવ upadrav

mischievous *adj.* ઉપદ્રવી upadravee

misconduct *n.* વ્યભિચાર vyabhichaar

miscreant *n.* દુર્જન. durjan

misdeed *n.* દુષ્કર્મ. dushkarm

misdirect *v.t.* ગેરમાર્ગે દોરવું geramaarge doravun

miser *n.* કંજૂસ. kanjoos

miserable *adj.* કંગાળ kangaal

misery *n.* કંગાલિયત kangaaliyat

misfortune *n.* દુર્દેવી ઘટના durdevee ghatana

misgive *v.t.* સંશય પેદા કરવો sanshay pedaa karavo

misgiving દહેશત. daheshat

misguide *v.t.* ગેરમાર્ગે દોરવું germaarge doravun

mishap *n.* દુર્ઘટના durghatana

misinterpret *v.t.* –નો ખોટો અર્થ કરવો no khoto arth karavo

misjudge *v.t.* ખોટો ન્યાય કરવો khoto nyaay karavo

mislay *v.t.* આડુંઅવળું મૂકવું aaduaavalun moonkavun

mislead *v.t.* ભમાવવું. bhamaavavun

mismanage *v.t.* ગેરવ્યવસ્થાપન. geravyavasthaapan

misnomer *n.* ખોટું નામ khotun naam

misogamy *n.* વિવાહદ્વેષ vivaahadvesh

misogyny *n.* સ્ત્રીદ્વેષ. streedvesh

misplace *v.t.* ખોટી જગ્યાએ મૂકવું khotee jagyaae mookavun

misprint *n.* ખોટું છાપવું. khotun chhaapavun

mispronounce –નો ખોટો ઉચ્ચાર કરવો no khoto uchchaar karavo

misrepresent *v.t.* ખોટી રજૂઆત કરવી khotee rajooaat karavee

misrule *n.* કુશાસન kushaasan

miss *n.* ચૂકવું chookavun

missile *n.* પ્રક્ષેપાસ્ત્ર prakshepaastr

missing *adj.* નહિ જડતું nahi jadatun

mission *n.* જીવનલક્ષ્ય. jeevanalakshy

missionary *n.* ધર્મપ્રસારકમંડળ સંબંધી dharmaprasaarakamandal sanbandhee

mist *n.* ધુમ્મસ dhummas

mistake *v.t.* ભૂલ કરવી bhool karavee

mister *n.* શેઠ sheth

mistress *n.* શેઠાણી shethaanee

mistrust *n.* શંકા shanka

misty *adj.* ઝાંખળવાળું jhaankalavaalun

misunderstanding *n.* ગેરસમજ gerasamaj

misuse *v.t.* દુરુપયોગ કરવો durupayog karavo

mite *n.* અતિસૂક્ષ્મ જંતુ. ati sookshm jantu

mitigate *v.t.* શાંત પાડવું shaant paadavun

mitre *n.* મુગટ mugat

mix *v.t.* મિશ્રણ કરવું mishran karavun

mixture *n.* મિશ્રણ mishran

mizzle *v.t.* ઝરમર ઝરમર વરસવું jharamar jharamar varasavun

moan *v.i.* ઊંડી આહ oondee aah

moat *n.* કિલ્લો killo

mob *n.* અવ્યવસ્થિત ટોળું avyavasthit tolun

mobile *v.t.* ખસેડી શકાય એવું khasedee shakaay evun

mobilize *v.t.* ગતિશીલ બનાવવું gatisheel banaavavun

mock *n.* ઠઠ્ઠામશ્કરી thaththaamaskaree

mockery *n.* ઠેકડી thekadee

mode *n.* પ્રચલિત પ્રથા prachalit pratha

model *n.* નમૂનો namoono

moderate *n.* સાધારણ saadhaaran

moderation *n.* સમધારણકાર્ય samadhaaranakaary

modern *adj.* આધુનિક aadhunik

modesty *n.* નમ્રતા namrata

modicum *n.* અલ્પમાત્રા alpamaatra

modification *n.* ફેરફાર ferafaar

modify *v.t.* ફેરફાર કરવા. ferafaar karava

modish *adj.* છટાદાર. chhataadaar

modulate *v.t.* સમાયોજન કરવું samaayojan karavun

mofussil *adj.* મુફસલિ mufasil
moiety *n.* અર્ધો ભાગ. ardho bhaag
moil *v.t.* વૈતરું કરવું vaitarun karavun
moist *adj.* ભેજવાળું bhejavaalun
moisture *n.* ભેજ bhej
molasses *n.* ગોળની રસી golanee rasee
mole *n.* શરીર પરનો તલ. shareer parano tal
molecular *n.* પરમાણુ સંબંધી paramaanun sanbandhee
molest *v.t.* ઉપદ્રવ કરવો upadrav karavo
mollify *v.t.* ઉપશમન કરવું. oopashaman karavun
molten *adj.* પીગળેલું. peegalelun
moment *n.* ક્ષણ kshan
momentary *adj.* ક્ષણિક kshanik
momentous *adj.* ઘણું મહત્ત્વનું ghanun mahattvanun
momentum *n.* સંવેગ sanveg
monarch *n.* સર્વસત્તાધીશ શાસક sarvasattaadheesh shaasak
monarchy *n.* રાજાશાહી raajaashaahee
monastery *n.* મઠ math
monetary *adj.* નાણાકીય naanaakeey
money *n.* પૈસા paisa
moneyed *adj.* પૈસાદાર paisaadaar
mongoose *n.* નોળિયો. noliyo
monitor *v.t.* દેખરેખ રાખવી dekharekha raakhavee
monk *n.* મઠવાસી. mathavaasee
monkey *n.* વાંદરો vaandaro
monocular *adj.* એક આંખવાળું ek aankhavaalun
monogamy *n.* એક પત્નીત્વ ek patneetva
monogram *n.* આદ્યાક્ષરી મુદ્રા. aadhyaaksharee mudra
monopolist *n.* એકાધિકારનો સમર્થક ekaadikaarano samarthak
monopolize *v.t.* એકાધિકાર મેળવવો. ekaadikaar melavavo
monopoly *n.* એકાધિકાર. ekaadikaar
monotheism *n.* એકેશ્વરવાદ ekeshvaravaad
monotonous *adj.* એકધારું ekadhaarun
monotony *n.* વૈવિધ્યહીનતા vaividhyaheenataa

monsoon *n.* ચોમાસું chomaasun
monster *n.* રાક્ષસ raakshas
monstrous બિહામણું bihaamanun
montage *n.* મોન્ટાજ montaaj
month *n.* મહિનો mahino
monthly *adj.* માસિક maasik
monument *adj.* સ્મૃતિચિહ્ન. smrutichinh
monumental *n.* સ્મારક સ્વરૂપનું smaarak svaroopanun
mood *n.* મનની સ્થિતિ mananee sthiti
moon *n.* ચન્દ્ર chandr
moor *n.* ખરાબાનો પટ kharaabaano pat
moot *v.t.* પુરાચીન ધારાસભા praachin dhaaraasabhaa
mop *n.* કુચડો kuchado
mope *v.i.* ઉદાસ થવું udaas thavun
moral *n.* નીતિમત્તા neetimatta
morale *n.* ચારિત્ર્યબળ chaaritryabal
moralist *n.* સદાચારી. sadaachaaree
morality *n.* નૈતિકતા naitikata
moralize *v.i.* નીતિનો ઉપદેશ neetino upadesh
morass *n.* કળણ kalan
moratorium *n.* દેવા મોકૂફી devaa mokoofee
morbid *adj.* માંદલું. maandalun
mordant *adj.* ખૂંચે તેવું khoonche tevun
more *adj.* વધારે vadhaare
moreover તદુપરાંત. taduparaant
morgue *n.* શબઘર shabaghar
morning *n.* સવાર savaar
morning star *n.* શુક્રનો તારો shukrano taaro
morose *adj.* ઉગ્ર સ્વભાવવાળું ugr svabhaavavaalun
morphia *n.* અફીણનો અર્ક afeenano ark
morrow *n.* પછીનો દિવસ pacheeno divas
morsel *n.* કોળિયો koliyo
mortal *adj.* પ્રાણઘાતક. praanaghaatak
mortality *n.* મરણનું પ્રમાણ marananun pramaan
mortar *n.* એક નાની તોપ ek naanee top
mortgage *n.* ગીરો geero
mortgagee *n.* ગીરો લેનાર geero lenaar

mortification *n.* ઇન્દ્રિયદમન કરવું તે eendriyadaman karavun te
mortify *v.t.* ઇન્દ્રિયદમન કરવું eendriyadaman karavun
mosaic *n.* લાદીચિત્ર laadeechitra
mosque *n.* મસ્જિદ masjid
mosquito *n.* મચ્છર machchhar
moss *n.* શેવાળ shevaal
most *adj.* મોટામાં મોટો ભાગ motaaman moto bhaag
mostly *adv.* ઘણું કરીને ghanun kareene
mote *n.* રજકણ rajakan
moth *n.* કીટક keetak
mother *n.* મા maa
mother-in-law *n.* સાસુ saasun
motif *n.* પ્રધાનતત્ત્વ pradhaanatattv
motion *n.* પ્રસ્તાવ prastaav
motionless *adj.* નિશ્ચલ nishchal
motive *n.* પ્રવર્તક pravartak
motor *n.* ચાલકયંત્ર chaalakayantr
motto *n.* મુદ્રાલેખ mudraalekh
mould *v.t.* ઘાટ આપવો ghaat aapavo
mound *n.* માટીનો ઢગલો maateeno dhagalo
mount *v.t.* જડવું jadavun
mountain *n.* પર્વત parvat
mountaineer *n.* કુશળ પર્વતારોહક kushal parvataarohak
mourn *v.t.* વિલાપ કરવો. vilaap karavo
morning *n.* સવાર savaar
mouse *n.* ઉંદર undar
moustache *n.* મૂછ moochh
mouth *n.* મોઢું moodhun
mouthful *n.* કોળિયો koliyo
mouthpiece *n.* મુખપત્ર mukhapatra
movable *adj.* અસ્થિર asthir
move *v.t.* હલાવવું halaavavun
movement *n.* આંદોલન aandolan
mover *n.* ચાલનાર chaalnaar
movie *n.* ચિત્રપટ chitrapat
mow *v.t.* ઘાસ વાઢવું ghaas vaadhavun
much *adj.* ઘણું ghanun
muck *n.* છાણ chhaan
mucus *n.* લાળ laal
mud *n.* કાદવ kaadav
muddle *v.t.* ગૂંચવણમાં નાખવું goonchavanaman naakhavun

muddy *adj.* કાદવવાળું. kaadavavaalun
muffler *n.* ગલપટ્ટો. galapatto
mug *n.* ગોખણિયો વિદ્યાર્થી gaukhaniyo vidhyaarthee
mule *n.* વર્ણસંકર સંતાન varnasankar santaan
multifarious *adj.* વૈવિધ્યવાળું vaividhyavaalun
multiform *adj.* બહુરૂપી bahuroopee
multiple *n.* બહુવિધ બહુલ. bahuvidh bahul
multiplication *n.* ગુણાકાર gunaakaar
multiplicity *n.* બહુવિધતા bahuvidhata
multiply *v.t.* અનેક ઘટકો વાળું anek ghatako vaalun
multitude *n.* મોટી સંખ્યા motee sankhya
mum મૌન maun
mumble *v.i.* અસ્પષ્ટપણે બોલવું aspashtapane bolavun
mummery *n.* હાસ્યાસ્પદ વિધિ haasyaaspad vidhi
mummy *n.* મા maa
mumps *n.* ગાલપચોળિયાં gaalapacholiyan
munch *v.t.* વાગોળવું vaagolavun
mundane *adj.* આ દુનિયાનું aa duniyaanun
municipal *adj.* નગરપાલિકાનું nagarapaalikaanun
municipality *n.* નગરપાલિકા nagarapaalika
munificent *adj.* પરોપકારી. paropakaaree
munition *n.* દારૂગોળો daaroogolo
murder *n.* મનુષ્યવધ manushyavadh
murderous *adj.* ખૂની khoonee
murky *adj.* ઘોર અંધારાવાળું ghor andhaaraavaalun
murmur *n.* ગણગણાટ ganaganaat
muscle *n.* સ્નાયુ snaayu
muscular *adj.* સ્નાયુબધ્ધ snaayubadhdh
muse *v.i.* ધ્યાન ધરવું dhyaan dharavun
museum *n.* સંગ્રહાલય sangrahaalay
mushroom *n.* બિલાડીનો ટોપ bilaadeeno top

music *n.* સંગીત sangeet
musician *n.* સંગીતશાસ્ત્રી sangeetashaastree
musk *n.* કસ્તૂરી kastooree
musket *n.* બંદૂક bandook
musketeer *n.* બંદૂકવાળો સિપાઈ bandookavaalo sipaaee
muslin *n.* મલમલ malamal
must *v.* દ્રાક્ષનો રસ draakshano ras
mustard *n.* રાઈ raaee
muster *v.t.* એકત્ર કરવું ekatra karavun
musterroll *n.* હાજરી પત્રક haajaree patrak
mutable *adj.* પરિવર્તનશીલ parivartanasheel
mutation *n.* પરિવર્તન ફેરફાર. parivartan ferafaar
mute *adj.* ચૂપ choop
mutilate *v.t.* ઈજા પહોંચાડવી eeja pahonchaadavee
mutilation *n.* અંગછેદન angachhedan
mutineer *n.* બંડ કરનાર band karanaar
mutinous *adj.* બંડખોર balavaakhor, bandakhor
mutiny *n.* બંડ band
mutt *n.* ગફલત કરનાર gafalat karanaar
mutter *v.t.* ગણગણવું ganaganavun
mutton *n.* ઘેટાંબકરાંનું માંસ. ghetanbakaraannun maans
mutual *adj.* અન્યોન્ય anyony
muzzle *n.* નાળચું naalachun
my *pro.* મારૂ maaree
myopia *n.* ટૂંકી દૃષ્ટિ toonkee drashti
myriad *n.* ઘણી મોટી સંખ્યા ghanee motee sankhya
myrobaian *n.* આમળું maamalun
myrrh *n.* સુગંધીદાર પરફ્યુમ sugandheedaar parafyum
myrtle *n.* મેંદી mendee
myself *pro.* મારી જાતે. maaree jaate
mysterious *adj.* રહસ્યમય. rahasyamay
mystery *n.* ગૂઢ બાબત goodh baabat
mystify *v.t.* રહસ્યમય બનાવવું rahasyamay banaavavun
myth *n.* પુરાચીન દંતકથા praacheen dantakatha
mythological *adj.* પૌરાણિક pauraanik

mythology *n.* પુરાણવદ્યા puraanavidhya

nab *v.t.* પકડી પાડવું. pakadee paadavun
nadir *n.* અધઃસ્વસ્તિક adhahasvastik
nag *n.* ટટ્ટુ tattu
nail *n.* નખ nakha
naive *adj.* નિષ્કપટ nishkapat
naked *adj.* વસ્ત્રહીન vastraheen
name નામ naam
nameless *adj.* અનામિક anaamik
namesake *n.* નામરાશિ naamaraashee
nap *n.* ઝોકું jhokun
nape *n.* ગરદન. garadan
napkin *n.* રૂમાલ roomaal
narcissism *n.* અહંપ્રેમ ahanprem
narcotic *adj.* ઘેનની દવા ghenanee davaa
narrate *v.t.* વર્ણવવું varanavavun
narration *n.* વર્ણન varnan
narrative *adj.* વાર્તાના રૂપનું vaartaana roopanun
narrow *adj.* સાંકડું saankadun
narrowly *adv.* મુશ્કેલીથી mushkeleethee
narrow-minded *adj.* સંકુચિત sankuchit
nasal *adj.* નાકનું naakanun
nascent *adj.* તાજું અસ્તિત્વમાં આવતું taajun astitvaman aavatun
nasty *adj.* બીભત્સ beebhats
natal *adj.* જન્મથી. janmathee
nation *n.* રાષ્ટ્ર raashtra
national *adj.* રાષ્ટ્રનું raashtranun
nationalism *n.* રાષ્ટ્રીયતા raashtreeyata
nationality *n.* રાષ્ટ્રિકત્વ. raashtrirakatv
nationalize *v.t.* રાષ્ટ્રની માલિકીનું raashtranee maa[ikeenun
native *n.* મૂળનું moolanun
nativity *n.* જન્મપત્રિકા. janmapatrika
natty *adj.* વ્યવસ્થિત vyavashit

natural *adj.* કુદરતનું kudaratanun

naturally સ્વાભાવિક રીતે svaabhaavik reete

nature *n.* પ્રકૃતિસ્વભાવ prakrutisvabhaav

naught *n.* કંઈ નહિ kanee nahi

naughty *adj.* તોફાની tofaanee

nausea *n.* સૂગ soog

nauseate *v.t.* ધૃણા–સૂગ પેદા કરવી dhruna - soog peda karavee

nauseous *adj.* સૂગ–ચીતરી ચડે એવું soog - cheetaree chade evun

nautch *n.* નાચ naach

nautical *adj.* દરિયાઇ dareeyaaee

naval *adj.* યુદ્ધનૌકાઓનું yuddhanaukaaonun

nave *n.* મધ્યવીથિ madhyaveethi

navel *n.* નાભિ naabhi

navigable *adj.* નાવ્ય naavya

navigate *v.t.* દરિયો ખેડવો dariyo khedavo

navigation *n.* નૌકાનયન naukaanayan

navy *n.* નૌકાસૈન્ય naukaasainy

nay *adj.* એટલું જ નહિ etalun ja nahi

near *adv.* નજીકના સંબંધવાળું najeekana sanbandhavaalun

nearly *adv.* લગભગ lagabhag

neat *adj.* સ્વચ્છ svachchh

neatly *adv.* સરસ રીતે saras reete

neatness *n.* વ્યવસ્થિતપણું sughadata

nebula *n.* નિહારિકા nihaarika

nabulous *adj.* ધૂંધળું doondhalun

necessary *adj.* અનિવાર્ય anivaary

necessitous *adj.* ગરજવાળું. garajavaalun

necessity *n.* અનિવાર્ય આવશ્યકતા anivaary aavashyakata

neck *n.* ગરદન garadan

necklace *n.* માળા maala

necromancy *n.* ભવિષ્યવાણી વિદ્યા bhavishyavaanee vidyaa

necropolis સ્મશાન smashaan

nectar *n.* અમૃત amrut

need *n.* જરૂર jaroor

needful *adj.* જરૂરી jarooree

needle *n.* સોય soy

needs *n.pl.* જરૂરીયાતો jarooriyato

needy *adj.* ગરજવાળું garajavaalun

nefarious *adj.* દુષ્ટ dusht

negative *adj.* નકારસૂચક nakaarasoochak

neglect *v.t.* અનાદર કરનાર annadar karanaar

negligence *n.* બેદરકારી bedarakaaree

negligent *adj.* બેદરકાર bedarakaar

negligible *adj.* ઉપેક્ષણીય upekhaneey

negotiable *adj.* વાટાઘાટપાત્ર vaataaghaatpaatra

negotiate *v.t.* વાટાઘાટ કરવી vaataaghaat karavee

negotiation *n.* વાટાઘાટ vaataaghaat

negro *n.* હબસી. habasee

neigh *v.t.* હણહણવું hanahanavun

neighbour *n.* પાડોશી paadoshee

neighbourhood પાડોશ paadosh

neighbouring *adj.* પાડોશનું paadoshanun

neighbourly સદ્ભાવયુક્ત વર્તનવાળું sadabhaavayukt vartanavaalun

neither *adv.* બેમાંથી એકે નહિ bemaanthee eke nahi

nerve *n.* જ્ઞાનતંતુ gnaanatantu

nervous *adj.* ગભરાટિયું gabharaatiyun

nescient *adj.* અજાણ ajaan

nest *n.* પક્ષીનો માળો paksheeno maalo

nestle *v.i.* સોડમાં રહેવું sodaman rahevun

nestling *n.* પંખીનું બચ્ચુ pankheenun bachchu

net *n.* જાળ jaal

nether *adj.* નીચે આવેલું. neeche aavelun

neural *adj.* મજ્જાતંતુનું – સંબંધી. majjaatantunun - sanbandhee

neuralgia *n.* મજ્જાતંતુનું દરદ majjaatantunnun darad

neurosis *n.* માનસિક અસ્વસ્થતા maanasik asvasthata

neuter *adj.* નપુંસક લિંગનું napunsak linganun

neutral *adj.* નિષ્પક્ષપાત nishpakshapaat

neutralize *v.* તટસ્થીકૃત tatastheekrut

never *adv.* ક્યારેય નહિ kyaarey nahi

nevermore *adv.* ભવિષ્યમાં કદી નહિ bhavishyaman kadee nahi

nevertheless *adv.* તેમ છતાં tem chhatan

new *adj.* નવું navun

news *n.* સમાચાર samaachaar

newsmonger *n.* બાતમીદાર baatamidaar

newspaper *n.* વર્તમાન પત્ર vartamaan patr

next *prep.* પાસેમાં પાસેનું paaseman paasenun

nib *n.* કલમની ટાંક kalamanee taank

nibble *v.t.* કરડી ખાવું તે karadee khaavun te

nice *adj.* મૈત્રીવાળું maitreevaalun

nicely *adv.* સરસ રીતે saras reete

nicety *n.* ચોકસાઈ chokkasaaee

niche *n.* ગોખલો gokhalo

nick *n.* ખાંચ khaanch

nickel *n.* કલાઈ kalaai

nickname *n.* ખીજનું નામ kheejanun naam

nicotine *n.* નિકોટિન nikotin

niece *n.* ભત્રીજી bhatreejee

niggard *n.* કંજૂસ kanjoos

nigger *n.* હબસી habasee

nigh *adj.* (–ની) નજીક (nee) najeek

night *n.* રાત raat

nightfall *n.* સંધ્યાકાળ sandhyaakaal

nightingale *n.* કોયલ koyal

nightly *adj.* દરરોજ રાતે થતું dararoj raate thatun

nightmare *n.* નઠારું સપનું nathaarun sapanun

nil *n.* શૂન્ય shoonya

nimble *adj.* ચપળ chapal

nine *adj.* નવ nav

ninefold *adj.* નવગણું navaganun

nineteen *n.* ઓગણીસ. oganees

ninetieth *adj.* નેવુમું, નેવુમો અંશ nevumun, nevumo ansh

ninety *n.* નેવું. nevun

ninny *n.* મૂર્ખમાણસ moorkhamaanas

ninth *adj.* નવમો (ભાગ). navamo (bhaag)

nip *n.* દારૂનો ઘૂંટડો daaroono ghoontado

nipple *n.* કુચાગ્ર kuchaagr

nit *n.* લીખ leekh

nitrate *n.* નાઈટ્રેટ naaitret

nitre *n.* સુરોખાર surokhaar

no *adj.* નહિ nahi

nobility *n.* ખાનદાની khaanadaanee

noble *adj.* ઉચ્ચ ચારિત્ર્યવાળું uchch chaaritryavaalun

nobleman *n.* ઉમરાવ umaraav

nobody *n.* કોઈ નહિ koee nahi

nocturnal નિશાચર nishaachar

nod *v.t.* માથું ડોલાવવું maathun dolaavavun

noddle *n.* માથું maathun

node *n.* ગ્રહની કક્ષા grahanee kaksha

noise *n.* શોરબકોર shorabakor

noiseless *adj.* નિરવ nirav

noisy *adj.* શોરબકોર કરનારું shorabakor karanaarun

nomad *n.* રખડનાર rakhadanaar

nomadic *adj.* રખડનાર rakhadanaar

nomenclature *n.* નામકરણ naamakaran

nominal *adj.* કેવળ નામમાં રહેલું keval naamaman rahelun

nominate નિમણૂક કરવી nimanook karavee

nomination *n.* નિમણૂક કરવી તે nimanook karavee te

nominative *n.* પ્રથમાવિભક્તિનું prathamavibhaktinun

nominator *n.* નિમણૂક કરનાર nimanook karanaar

nominee *n.* નીમેલું માણસ neemelun maanas

none *adj.* કોઈ યે નહિ koee ye nahi

nonsense *n.* મૂર્ખામીભર્યું moorkhaameebharyun

nook *n.* એકાન્ત ખૂણો ekaant khoono

noon *n.* બપોર bapor

noose *n.* ફાંસો faanso

norm *n.* માન્ય થયેલો નમુનો maany thayelo namuno

normal *adj.* સામાન્ય saamaany

north *n.* ઉત્તર દિશા uttar disha

northern *adj.* ઉત્તરનું uttaranun

northward *adj.* ઉત્તરાભિમુખ uttaraabhimukh

nose *n.* નાક naak

nose-bag *n.* તોબરો tobaro
nostril *n.* નસકોરું nasakorun
not *adv.* નહિ nahi
notable *adj.* નોંધપાત્ર nondhapaatr
notary *n.* નોટરી notaree
notch *n.* ખાંચો khaancho
note *n.* ચલણી નોટ chalanee not
noteworthy *adj.* નોંધપાત્ર nondhapaatr
nothing *n.* કશું નહિ kashun nahi
notice *n.* તાકીદ taakeed
notification *n.* —ને સૂચના ne soochana
notify *v.t.* —ને તાકીદ આપવી ne taakeed aapavee
notion *n.* કલ્પના kalpana
notorious *adj.* કુવિખ્યાત kuvikhyaat
nought *n.* શૂન્ય soony
noun *n.* સંજ્ઞા sangna
nourish *v.t.* પોષવું poshavun
nourishing *adj.* પોષણકારક poshanakaarak
novel *n.* નવલકથા navalakatha
novelist *n.* નવલકથાકાર navalakathaakaar
novelty *n.* નવાઈની વસ્તુ navaaeenee vastu
novice *n.* શિખાઉ માણસ shikhaau maanas
now *adv.* હાલ haal
nowadays *adv.* આજકાલ. aajakaal
nowhere *adv.* કોઈ પણ જગ્યામાં નહિ koee pan jagyaaman nahi
noxious *adj.* હાનિકારક haanikaarak
nozzle *n.* ટોટી totee
nuclear *adj.* અણુકેન્દ્રીય anukendreey
nucleus *n.* અણુ anu
nude *adj.* વસ્ત્રહીન vastraheen
nugget *n.* કાચું સોનું kaachun sonun
nuisance *n.* ઉપદ્રવકારક વસ્તુ upadravakaarak vastu
null *adj.* ભાવશૂન્ય bhaavashoony
nullify *v.t.* બિનઅસરકારક બનાવવું binaasarakaarak banaavavun
numb *adj.* સંવેદનાશૂન્ય sanvedanaashoony
number *n.* આંકડો aankado
numerical *adj.* સંખ્યા વાચક sankhya vaachak

numeration *n.* ગણતરી ganataree
numerator *n.* અંશ ansh
numerous *adj.* સંખ્યાબંધ sankhyaabandh
numismatic *n.* સિક્કા sikka
nun *n.* સંન્યાસિની (ખ્રિસ્તી) sannyaasinee (khristee)
nunnery *n.* સંન્યાસિનીઓની જમાત sannyaasineeonee jamaat
nuptial *adj.* લગ્નવિધિનું lagnavidhinun
nurse *n.* પરિચારિકા parichaarika
nursinghome *n.* ખાનગી ઇસ્પિતાલ khaanagee ispitaal
nursery *n.* ધરુવાડી dharuvaadee
nurture *n.* પાલનપોષણ paalanaposhan
nut *n.* કોટલાવાળું બીજ kotalaavaalun beej
nu¶crackers *n.* સૂડી soodee
nutrition *n.* પોષણ poshan
nutritious *adj.* કૌવત આપનાર kauvat aapanaar
nutshell *n.* કાચલી kaachalee
nymph *n.* એક પૌરાણિક દેવતા ek pauraanik devata

oaf *n.* અણઘડ anaghad
oak *n.* ઓક ok
oakum *n.* દોરડાના ફૂચા doradaanaa koochaa
oar *n.* હલેસું halesun
oarsman *n.* હલેસાં મારનાર halesan maaranaar
oasis *n.* રણદ્વીપ ranadveep
oat *n.* ઓટ ot
oath *on* પ્રતિજ્ઞા pratigna
obduracy *n.* કઠોરતા kathorata
obdurate *adj.* દૂરાગ્રહી duraagrahee
obedience *n.* આજ્ઞાનુસરણ aagnaanusaran
obedient *adj.* કર્તવ્યતત્પર kartavyatatpar
obeisance નમસ્કાર namaskaar

obelisk *n.* સમારક સ્તંભ smaarak stanbh

obesity *n.* મેદવૃદ્ધિ medavruddhee

obey *v.t.* નું કહ્યું કરવું nun kahyun karavun

obit *n.* મરણતિથિ maranatithi

obituary *adj.* મૃત્યુનોંધ mrutyunondh

object *n.* કર્મ karm

objection *n.* વાંધો vaandho

objectionable *adj.* વાંધાભરેલું vaandhaabharelun

objective *adj.* વાસ્તવિક vaastavik

oblation *n.* બલિ bali

obligate *v.t.* ફરજ પાડવી faraj paadavee

obligation *n.* અહેસાન ahesaan

obligatory *adj.* બંધનકારક bandhanakaarak

oblige *v.t.* ઉપકાર કરવો upakaar karavo

obliging *adj.* પરોપકારી paropakaaree

oblivious ભુલાવનારું bhulaavanaarun

obnoxious *adj.* વાંધાભરેલું vaandhaabharelun

obscene *adj.* અશ્લીલ ashleel

obscenity *n.* અશ્લીલતા ashleelata

obsecure *adj.* અસ્પષ્ટ aspasht

obsecurity *n.* ઝાંખપ jhaankhap

obsequies *n.* અન્ત્યવિધિ antyavidhi

observance *n.* અનુષ્ઠાન anushthaan

observation *n.* અવલોકન avalokan

observatory *n.* વેધશાળા vedhashaala

observe *v.t.* તપાસવું tapaasavun

obsess *v.t.* વળગવું valagavun

obsolete *adj.* કાલગ્રસ્ત kaalagrast

obstacle *n.* અંતરાય antaraay

obstinacy *n.* હઠીલાપણું hatheelaapanun

obstinate *adj.* હઠીલું hatheelun

obstruct *v.t.* ની આડે આવવું nee aade aavavun

obstruction *n.* અવરોધ avarodh

obtain *v.t.* મેળવવું melavavun

obtrude *v.t.* પરાણે વળગાડવું paraane valagaadavun

obtuse *adj.* બૂઠું boothun

obverse *adj.* સિક્કાનો મુખભાગ sikkaano mukhabhaag

obviate *v.t.* અંતરાયરહિત કરવું antaraayarahit karavun

obvious *adj.* દેખીતું dekheetun

occasion *n.* પ્રસંગવશાત્ prasangavashaat

occasional *adj.* પ્રાસંગિક praasangik

occident *n.* પાશ્ચાત્ય દેશો paashchaaty desho

occidental *adj.* પાશ્ચાત્ય paashchaaty

occult *adj.* રહસ્યમય rahasmay

occupancy *n.* કબજો kabajo

occupant કબજેદાર kabajedaar

occupation *n.* કબજો કરવાની પ્રક્રિયા kabajo karavaanee prakriya

occupy *v.t.* નો કબજો લેવો no kabajo levo

occur *v.i.* સૂઝવું soojhavun

occurrence *n.* થવું તે thavun te

ocean *n.* મહાસાગર mahaasaagar

octagon *n.* અષ્ટકોણ ashtakon

octave *n.* અષ્ટક ashtak

octroi *n.* જકાત jakaat

ocular *adj.* આંખે જોઈ શકાય એવું aankhe joee shakaay evun

odd *adj.* અસાધારણ asaadhaaran

oddity *n.* વિચિત્રતા vichitrata

ode *n.* ઉચ્ચ કોટિનું ઊર્મિકાવ્ય uchch kotinun oormikaavy

odious *adj.* તિરસ્કારપાત્ર tiraskaarapaatr

odium *n.* ફિટકાર fitakaar

odour *n.* સુગંધ sugandh

off *adv.* આઘે aadhe

offal *n.* કચરો kacharo

offence *n.* મર્યાદાભંગ maryaadaabhang

offend *v.i.* મર્યાદાભંગ કરવો maryaadaabhang karavo

offensive *adj.* આક્રમણાત્મક aakranaatmak

offer *v.t.* કહેણ kahen

offering *n.* આહુતિ aahuti

off-hand *adv.* તોછડું tochhadun

office *n.* કાર્યાલય kaaryaalay

officer *n.* સરકારી અમલદાર sarakaaree amaladaar

official *adj.* અધિકારની રૂએ કરેલું adhikaaranee rooe karelun

officiate *v.t.* ફરજ બજાવવી faraja bajaavavee

offset *n.* ફાંટો faanto
offshoot *n.* ફૂટતો ફણગો footato fanago
offspring *n.* ઓલાદ olaada
often *adv.* વારંવાર vaaranvaar
oh *int.* અરેરે ! arere !
oil *n.* તેલ tel
oil-cake *n.* ખોળ khol
oil-cloth *n.* મીણિયું meeniyun
oil-painting *n.* તેલ ચિત્ર tail chitr
oily *adj.* ચીકણું cheekanun
ointment *n.* ઊટણું oontanun
old *adj.* વયોવૃદ્ધ vayovruddh
olfactory *adj.* સૂંઘવાનું soonghavaanun
oligarchy *n.* અલ્પજનસત્તાક રાજ્ય alpajanasattaak raajy
olive *n.* ઓલિવનું ઝાડ olivanun jhaad
olympic *adj.* ઓલિમ્પિક olimpik
omen *n.* શુકન shukan
ominous *adj.* અશુભ ashubh
omission છોડી દેવું chhodee devun
omit *v.t.* છોડી દીધેલી બાબત chhodee deedhelee baabat
omnipotent *adj.* સર્વશક્તિમાન sarvashaktimaan
omnipresent સર્વવ્યાપી sarvvyaapee
omniscient *adj.* સર્વજ્ઞ. sarvagn
oncoming *adj.* નજીક આવતું najeek aavatun
on *adv.* ઉપરનું uparanun
once *adv.* એકવાર ekavaar
one *adj.* એકલું ekalun
onerous *adj.* ભારરૂપ bhaararoop
oneself *pro.* પોતે pote
one-sided *adj.* પક્ષપાતી pakshapaatee
onion *n.* ડુંગળી dungalee
only *adj.* એકનું એક ekanun ek
onslaught *n.* ભીષણ આક્રમણ. bheeshan aakraman
onto *pre.* વ્યક્ત vyakti
ontology *n.* પંચીકરણવિદ્યા pancheekaranavidya
onus *n.* જવાબદારી javaabadaaree
onward *adv.* આગળનું aagalanun
ooze *v.i.* ગળવું galavun
opacity *n.* અપારદર્શકતા apaaradarshakata
opal *n.* લસણિયો. lasaniyo

opaque *adj.* અપારદર્શક apaaradarshak
open *adj.* ઉઘાડું ughaadun
open-hearted *adj.* નિખાલસ nikhaalas
opening *n.* આરંભ aaranbh
opera *n.* સંગીત નાટક sangeet naatak
operate *v.t.* ચલાવવું chalaavavun
operation *n.* ક્રિયા kriya
operative *adj.* અમલમાં ચાલુ amalaman chaalu
operator *n.* પ્રચાલક prachaalak
opine *v.t.* અભિપ્રાય વ્યક્ત કરવો abhipraay vyakt karavo
opinion *n.* અભિપ્રાય abhipraay
opium *n.* અફીણ afeen
opponent *n.* પ્રતિપક્ષી pratipakshee
opportune *adj.* સમયોચિત samayochit
opportunist *n.* તકસાધુ takasaadhu
opportunity *n.* તક tak
oppose *v.t.* —ના વિરોધમાં મૂકવું naa virodhaman mookavun
opposite *adj.* વિરોધી virodhee
opposition *n.* વિરોધ virodh
oppress *v.t.* અતિશય ભાર વડે દબાવવું. atishay bhaar vade dabaavavun
oppression *n.* જુલમ julam
oppressive *adj.* જુલ્મી julmee
oppressor *n.* જુલમ કરનાર julam karanaar
opprobrious *adj.* બદનામી કરનારું badanaamee karanaarun
opprobrium *n.* અપકીર્તિ apakeerti
optic *n.* દૃષ્ટિનું drashtinun
optical *adj.* દૃષ્ટિનું સંબંધી drashtinun sanbandhee
optician *n.* ચશ્મા બનાવનાર chashma banaavanaar
optics *n.* નેત્રવિદ્યા netravidya
optimism *n.* સર્વશુભવાદ sarvashubhavaad
optimist *n.* સૌભાગ્યવાદી saubhaagyavaadee
option *n.* વિકલ્પ vikalp
optional *adj.* વૈકલ્પિક vaikalpik
opulence ધનિકતા dhanikata
opulent *adj.* પૈસાદાર paisaadaar
or *conj.* અથવા athava
oracle *n.* દેવવાણી devavaanee

oral *adj.* મૌખિક maukhik
orange *n.* નારંગી naarangee
oration *n.* ભાષણ bhaashan
orator *n.* વક્તા vakta
oratory *n.* વક્તૃત્વકળા vakatrutvakala
orb *n.* વર્તુળાકાર બિંબ vartulaakaar binb
orbit *n.* ગ્રહની ભ્રમણકક્ષા grahanee
   bhramanakaksha
orchard *n.* ફળઝાડની વાડી
   falajhaadanee vaadee
orchestra *n.* વાદકવૃંદ vaadakavrund
ordeal *n.* કસોટી kasotee
order *n.* ક્રમ kram
orderly *adj.* સુવ્યવસ્થિત suvyavasthit
ordinal *adj.* ક્રમવાચક (સંખ્યા)
   kramavaachak (sankhya)
ordinance *n.* વટહુકમ vatahukam
ordinary *adj.* સાધારણ saadhaaran
ordinate *n.* યથાક્રમ yathaakram
ordnance *n.* તોપખાનું topakhaanun
ore *n.* કાચી ધાતુ kaachee dhaatu
organ *n.* શરીરની ઇન્દ્રિય shareeranee
   eendriy
organic *adj.* શરીરનાં ઇન્દ્રિયોનું
   shareeranan eendriyonun
organism *n.* સજીવ રચના sajeev
   rachanaa
organization *n.* સંગઠિત સંસ્થા
   sangathith sanstha
organize *v.t.* તંત્રબદ્ધ કરવું tantrabaddh
   karavun
orient *adj.* પૂર્વ દિશાનું poorva
   dishaanun
oriental *adj.* પૂર્વનો માણસ poorvano
   maanas
orifice *n.* પ્રવેશ માર્ગ pravesh maarg
origin *n.* ઊગમ oogam
original *adj.* અસલનું asalanun
originate *v.t.* નવું ઉત્પન્ન કરવું navun
   utpann karavun
orion *n.* મૃગશીર્ષ mrugasheersh
ornament *v.t.* શણગારવું shanagaaravun
ornamental શોભાવનાર shobhaavanaar
ornate *adj.* અતિઅલંકૃત. atialankrut
orphan *n.* અનાથ બાળક anaath baalak
orphanage *n.* અનાથાશ્રમ
   anaathaashram

orpiment *n.* હરતાલ harataal
orthodox *adj.* સનાતની sanaatanee
oscillate *v.i.* દોલન dolan
oscillation *n.* દોલન dolan
osier *n.* નેતર netar
osseous *adj.* હાડકાવાળું haadakaavaalun
ostensible *adj.* તથાકથિત tathaakathit
ostentation *n.* આડંબર aadanbar
ostentatious *adj.* આડંબરી aadanbaree
ostracism *n.* સમાજબહિષ્કાર
   samaajabahishkaar
ostrich *n.* શહામૃગ shahaamrug
other *adj.* બીજું beejun
otherwise *adv.* બીજી રીતે beejee reete
otter *n.* જળબિલાડી jalabilaadee
ounce *n.* ઔંશ aunsh
our *adj.* આપણું aapanun
oust *v.t.* ની જગ્યા લઈ લેવી nee jagya
   laee levee
out *adv.* કોઈ જગ્યાથી દૂર koee
   jagyaathee door
outbid *v.t.* ઊંચી બોલી લગાવવી oonchee
   bolee lagaavavee
outbreak *n.* ઉત્પાત utpaat
outburst *n.* ભાવનાનો ઉદ્રેક
   bhaavanaano udrek
outcast *adj.* બહિષ્કૃત bahishkrut
outcome *n.* પરિણામ prinaam
outcry *n.* બુમરાણ bumaraan
outdo *v.t.* ને પાછળ પડવું ne paachhal
   padavun
outdoor *adj.* બહાર કરવાનું bahaar
   karavaanun
outfit *n.* આવશ્યક સાજસામગ્રી
   aavashyak saajasaamagree
outhouse *n.* ઉપગૃહ upagruh
outing *n.* મજા ખાતર કરેલો પ્રવાસ maja
   khaatar karelo pravaas
outlandish અપરિચિત aparichit
outlaw *n.* બહારવટિયો bahaaravatiyo
outlay *n.* મૂડીરોકાણ moodeerokaan
outlet *n.* નિકાલ nikaal
outlive *v.t.* વધુ જીવવું vadhu jeevavun
outlook *n.* દૃષ્ટિબિંદુ drashtibindu
outlying *adj.* દૂરસ્થ doorasth
outnumber સંખ્યામાં ચઢિયાતું
   sankhyaman chadiyaatun

outpost *n.* દૂરની વસાહત. dooranee vasaahat

output *n.* માલનું ઉત્પાદન maalanun utpaadan

outrage *v.t.* અત્યાચાર કરવો ayaachaar karavo

outrageous અત્યાચારભર્યું atyaachaarabharyun

outright *adv.* સંપૂર્ણપણે sanpoornapane

outset *n.* શરૂઆત sharooaat

outside *n.* બહારની બાજુ bahaaranee baaju

outsider *n.* પારકો paarako

outskirt *n.* પરિસર parisar

outspoken *adj.* સ્પષ્ટવક્તા spashtavakta

outstanding *adj.* આગળ પડતું aagal padatun

outward *adv.* બહારનું bahaaranun

outweigh *v.t.* વજનમાં વધવું vajanama vadhavun

outwit *v.t.* બુદ્ધિમાં ચડિયાતું buddhiman chadiyaatun

oval *adj.* અંડાકાર andaakaar

ovary *n.* અંડાશય andaashay

ovation *n.* ઉત્સાહભર્યો આવકાર utsaahabharyo aavakaar

oven *n.* ભઠ્ઠી bhaththee

over *prep.* ઉપર upar

overawe *v.t.* બિવડાવી નાખવું bivadaavee naakhavun

overburden *v.t.* વધુ પડતો ભાર vadhu padato bhaar

overcast *v.t.* વાદળાંથી ઢંકાયેલું vaadalaanthee dhankaayelun

overcharge *v.t.* વધુ પડતી કિંમત vadhu padatee kinmat

overcoat *n.* પહેરવાનો મોટો ડગલો. paheravaano moto dagalo

overcome *v.t.* —ની ઉપર પ્રભુત્વ મેળવવું nee upar prabhutv melavavun

overdo *v.t.* અતિરેક કરવો atirek karavo

overdraw *v.t.* વધુ પડતો ઉપાડ vadhu padato upaad

overflow *n.* ઉપરથી વહેવું uparathee vahevun

overhear *v.t.* છાનમાના સાંભળવું chhaanamaana saanbhalavun

overjoy *v.t.* અતિશય હરખાયેલું atishay harakhaayelun

overlay *v.t.* ઉપર ચડાવવું upar chadaavavun

overlook ઊંચે ઠેકાણેથી જોવું oonche thekaanethee jovun

overpower *v.t.* હરાવવું haraavavun

overrule *v.t.* નામંજૂર કરવું naamanjoor karavun

oversee *v.t.* દેખરેખ રાખવી dekharekha raakhavee

overseer *n.* દેખરેખ રાખનાર dekharekh raakhanaar

oversight *n.* દૂરલક્ષ durlaksh

overt *adj.* ખુલ્લું khullun

overtake આગળ નિકળી જવું aagal nikalee javun

overthrow *v.t.* ગબડાવી દેવું gabadaavee devun

overture *n.* પૂરાસ્તાવિક સંગીત. praastaavik sangeet

overturn *n.* ઉથલાવી પાડવું uthalaavee paadavun

overweening *adj.* ઘમંડી ghamandee

overwhelm *v.t.* દાટવું daatavun

overwork *n.* અતિશ્રમ. atishram

ovum *n.* રજોગોલ rajogol

owe *v.t.* —નું ઋણી હોવું nun roonee hovun

owing *prop.* ના દેવા naa deva

owl *n.* ઘુવડ ghuvad

own *adj.* પોતાનું potaanun

owner *n.* માલિક maalik

ox *n.* બળદ balad

oxide *n.* ઓક્સાઇડ oksaaid

oxygen *n.* પ્રાણવાયુ praanavaayu

oyster *n.* મોતીની છીપ moteenee chheep

ozone *n.* ઓઝોન ozon

P

pace *n.* ડગલું dagalun
pacific *adj.* પ્રશાંત prashaant
pacification *n.* સાંત્વન આપવું saantvan aapavun
pacify *v.t.* શાંત પાડવું shaant paadavun
pack *n.* પોટલું potalun
package *n.* પોટલું potalun
packet *n.* પડીકું padeekun
pad *n.* ગાદી gaadee
paddle *v.t.* હલેસાં મારવા halesan maaravan
paddy *n.* ક્રોધાવેશ krodhaavesh
padlock *n.* છૂટું તાળું chhoontun taalun
pagan *n.* મૂર્તિપૂજક moortipoojak
paganism *n.* મૂર્તિપૂજા moortipooja
page *n.* હોટલનો બાળ નોકર hotalano baal nokar
pageant *n.* જાહેર ઉત્સવ jaaher utsav
pagoda *n.* પેગોડા pengodaa
pail *n.* ડોલ dol
pain *n.* પીડા peeda
painstaking *adj.* ખંતીલું khanteelun
paint *v.t.* રંગ લગાડવો rang lagaadavo
painter *n.* ચિત્રકાર chitrakaar
pair *n.* જોડી jodee
palace *n.* રાજમહેલ raajamahel
palankeen *n.* પાલખી paalakhee
palatable *adj.* સ્વાદિષ્ટ svaadisht
palatal *adj.* તાળવાનું taalavaanun
palate *n.* તાળવું taalavun
palatial *adj.* ભવ્ય bhavy
pale *adj.* ફિક્કું fikkun
paleness *n.* ફિક્કાશ fikkaash
palette *n.* રંગમિશ્રણ પાટી rangamishran paatee
palfrey *n.* શાંત ઘોડો shaant ghodo
paling *n.* ખૂંટાની વાડ khoontaanee vaad
pall *n.* કફન kafan
palliate *v.t.* નરમ પાડવું naram padavun
palliation *n.* ઉપશમન upashaman
pallid *adj.* નિસ્તેજ nistej
pallor *n.* ફીકાશ feekaash

palm *n.* હથેલી hathelee
palmist *n.* હસ્તરેખાશાસ્ત્રી hastarekhaashaastree
palmistry *n.* હસ્તરેખાશાસ્ત્ર hastarekhaashaastr
palmy *adj.* સમૃદ્ધ samruddh
palpable પ્રગટ ઇંદ્રિયગમ્ય pragat eendriyagamy
palpitate *v.i.* ધબકવું dhabakavun
palpitation *n.* ધબકારો dhabakaaro
palsy *n.* લકવો lakavo
palter *v.t.* વાત ઉડાવવી vaat udaavavee
paltry *adj.* નિરર્થક nirarthak
pamper *n.* પંપાળવું panpaalavun
pamphlet *n.* પત્રિકા patrika
pan *n.* તવો tavo
panacea *n.* અક્સીર ઇલાજજ્ઞઉપાય akseer eelaajagnaupaay
pane *n.* બારીનો કાચ baareeno kaach
panegyrize *v.t.* પ્રશસ્તિ લિખવી prashasti lakhavee
pang *n.* માનસિક સંતાપ maanasik santaap
panic *n.* ગભરાટ gabharaat
pannier *n.* છાલકું chhalakun
panoply *n.* પૂરણ બખ્તરજ્ઞકવચ poorn bakhtaragnakavach
panorama *n.* વિશાળ દ્રષ્ય vishaal drashy
pant *v.t.* હાંફવું haanfavun
pantaloon *n.* મશ્કરો mashkaro
pantheism *n.* સર્વેશ્વરવાદ sarveshvaravaad
panther *n.* દિપડો dipado
pantry *n.* કોઠાર kothaar
pants *n.* પાયજામો paayajaamo
pap *n.* સ્તનાગર staanaagr
papa *n.* પિતા pita
papal *adj.* પોપનું popanun
paper *n.* કાગળ kaagal
papist *n.* પોપસમર્થક popasamarthak
par *n.* સમાન samaan
parable *n.* બોધવાર્તા bodhavaarta
parachute *n.* હવાઈ છત્રી havaaee chhatree
parade *n.* નિદર્શન nidarshan
paradise *n.* સ્વર્ગ svarg

paradox *n.* અસંગત વાત asangat vaat
passable *adj.* ઠીકઠીક thikathik
passage *n.* અવરજવર માર્ગ avarajavar maarg
passenger *n.* પ્રવાસી pravaasee
passer *n.* વટેમાર્ગુ vatemaargu
passion *n.* આવેશ aavesh
passionate *adj.* કામી kaamee
passive નિષ્ક્રિય nishkriy
passport *n.* પાસપોર્ટ paasaport
past *adv.* વીતી ગયેલું veetee gayelun
paste *v.t.* લૂગદી loogadee
pasteurize *v.t.* પેશ્ચ્યુરાઇઝ peshchyuraaiz
pastime *n.* મનોરંજન manoranjan
pastry *n.* પેસ્ટ્રી pestree
pasturage ગોચર gochar
pasture *n.* ચરો charo
pat *n.* થાબડવું thaabadavun
patch *n.* થીગડું theegadun
patent *n.* પેટન્ટ petant
paternal *adj.* પિતૃપક્ષનું pitrupakshanun
paternity *n.* પિતૃપરંપરા pitruparanpara
path *n.* પગદંડી pagadandee
pathetic *adj.* કરુણાજનક karunaajanak
pathos *n.* કરુણરસ karunaras
patience *n.* સહનશીલતા sahanasheelata
patient *adj.* ધીરજવાળું dheerajavaalun
patiently *adv.* શાંતિથી shaantithee
patriarch *n.* કુલપતિ kulapita
patrician *n.* કુળવાન માણસ kulavaan maanas
patricide *n.* પિતૃહત્યા pitruhatya
patrimony *n.* વારસો vaaraso
patriot *n.* દેશભક્ત deshabhakt
patriotism *n.* દેશદાઝ deshadaajh
patriotic *adj.* દેશાભિમાનવાળું deshaabhimaanavaalun
patrol *adj.* ચોકી પહેરો chokee pahero
patron *n.* પુરસ્કર્તા puraskarta
patronage *n.* મુરબ્બીવટ murabbeevat
patronize *v.t.* ને આશ્રય આપવો ne aashray aapavo
patter *v.i.* ઉતાવળથી બોલવું તે utaavalathee bolavun te
pattern *n.* અનુકરણીય નમૂનો anukaraneey namoono

paucity *n.* અછત achhat
pauper *n.* દરિદ્ર daridr
pauperism *n.* દરિદ્રતા daridrata
pause *v.t.* જરા થોભવું jara thobhavun
pave *v.t.* ચીરાબંધી કરવી cheeraabandhee karavee
pavement *n.* ફરસબંધી farasabandhee
pavillion *n.* રજવાડી શમિયાનો rajavaadee shamiyaano
paw *n.* પ્રાણીનો પંજો praaneeno panjo
pawn ગીરે મૂકેલી વસ્તુ geere mukelee vastu
pawnee *n.* ગીરોદાર geerodaar
pay *v.t.* પૈસા ચૂકવવા paisa chookavava
payable *adj.* આપી શકાય એવું aapee shakaay evun
payee *n.* નાણાં લેનાર nanan lenaar
payment *n.* ચુકવણી chukavanee
pea *n.* વટાણો vataano
peace *n.* શાંતિ shaanti
peaceful *adj.* શાંતતાવાળું shaantataavaalun
peacock *n.* મોર mor
peahen *n.* ઢેલ dhel
peak *n.* ક્ષીણ થવું ksheen thavun
pearl *n.* મોતી motee
peasant *n.* ખેડૂત khedoot
peasantry *n.* ખેડૂતવર્ગ khedootavarg
pebble *n.* ગોળ લીસો કાંકરો gol leeso kaankaro
peccable *adj.* પાપવૃત્તિવાળું paapavruttivaalun
peck *v.t.* ચાંચ મારવી chanch maaravee
peckish *adj.* ભૂખ્યું bhookhyun
peculation *n.* ઉચાપત uchaapaat
peculiar *adj.* વિચિત્ર. vichitr
peculiarity *n.* વિલક્ષણતા vilakshanata
pedagogue *n.* શાળાના શિક્ષક shaalaana shikshak
pedal *adj.* પગનું કે પગોનું paganun ke pagonun
pedant *n.* દંભી danbhee
pedantry *n.* મિથ્યા પાંડિત્ય mithya paandity
peddle *v.t.* ફેરિયાનો ધંધો કરવો feriyaano dhandho karavo

pedestal *n.* થાંભલાની કુંભી thaanbhalaanee kunbhee

pedestrian *n.* પગે ચાલતું page chaalatun

pedigree *n.* વંશાવળી vanshaavalee

pedlar *n.* ફેરિયો feriyo

peel *v.t.* છોલવું chholavun

peep *v.i.* ડોકીયું કરવું dokeeyun karavun

peer *n.* ડોકિયાં કરવા dokiyan karava

peerage *n.* ઉમરાવો umaraavo

peerless *adj.* અદ્વિતીય aditeey

peevish *adj.* રિસાળ risaal

peg *n.* ખીલો kheelo

pekoe *n.* ચાની જાત chaanee jaat

pelf *n.* સંપત્તિ sanpatti

pelican *n.* જળકુકડી jalakukadee

pellet *n.* ગોળી golee

pellmell *adj.* અસ્તવ્યસ્ત astavyast

pellucid *adj.* તદ્દન નિર્મળ taddan nirmal

pelt *n.* ખાલ khaal

pen *n.* કલમ kalam

penal *adj.* સજાને પાત્ર sajaane paatr

penalty *n.* દંડ કે બીજી કોઈ સજા dand ke beejee koee saja

penance *n.* પ્રાયશ્ચિત praayashchit

pencil *n.* સિસાપેન sisaapen

pendant *adj.* પેન્ડન્ટ pendant

pending *adj.* નિકાલ થાય ત્યાં સુધી nikaal thaay tyan sudhee

pendulum *n.* ઘડિયાળનું લોલક ghadiyaalanun lolak

penetrate *v.t.* પ્રવેશ કરવો pravesh karavo

penetration *n.* પ્રવેશ pravesh

peninsula *n.* દ્વીપકલ્પ dveepakalp

penitence *n.* પસ્તાવો pastaavo

penitent *adj.* પસ્તાવો કરનાર pastaavo karanaar

penknife *n.* નાનું ચપ્પુ naanun chappu

pennant *n.* પતાકા pataaka

penniless *adj.* નિરાધાર niraadhaar

pension *n.* નિવૃત્તિવેતન nivrutti vetan

pensioner *n.* નિવૃત્તિવેતન પામનાર nivrutti vetan paamanaar

pensive *adj.* ચિન્તાગ્રસ્ત chintaagrast

pent *adj.* પૂરી દીધેલું pooree deedhelun

pentagon *n.* પંચકોણ panchakon

penultimate *adj.* ઉપાન્ત્ય upaanty

penumbra *n.* ઉપચ્છાયા upachhaaya

penurious *adj.* નિર્ધન nirdhan

penury *n.* કંગાલિયત kangaaliyat

peon *n.* પટાવાળો pataavaalo

people *n.* વ્યક્તિઓનું જૂથ vyaktionun jooth

pepper *n.* કાળામરી kaalaamaree

perambulator *n.* બાબાગાડી baabaagaadee

perceive ઇન્દ્રિય દ્વારા જાણવું eendriy dvaara jaanavun

percentage *n.* ટકાવારી takaavaaree

perceptible ઇન્દ્રિયગમ્ય eendriyagamy

perception *n.* ગ્રહણશક્તિ grahanashakti

perceptive *adj.* સમજ શક્તિવાળું samaj shaktivaalun

perch *n.* પંખીનું વિરામ સ્થાન pankheenun viraam sthaan

perchance *adv.* કદાચ kadaach

percolate *v.i.* નીતરવું neetaravun

percussion *n.* આઘાત aaghaat

perdition *n.* અધોગતિ adhogati

peremptory *adj.* નિશ્ચયાત્મક nishchayaatmak

perennial *adj.* આખું વરસ ટકનારું aakhun varas takanaarun

perfect *adj.* ખામી વિનાનું khaamee vinaanun

perfection *n.* સંપૂર્ણતા sanpoornata

perfidious *adj.* વિશ્વાસઘાતી vishvaasaghaatee

perfidy *n.* વિશ્વાસઘાત vishvaasaghaat

perforate *v.t.* કાણાં પાડવાં kaanan paadavun

perforce જબરદસ્તીથી jabaradasteethee

performance *n.* કામગીરી બજાવણી kaamageeree bajaavanee

perfume *n.* સુવાસ suvaas

perfumer *n.* સરૈયો. saraiyo

perfumery *n.* સુગંધી પદાર્થો sugandhee padaartho

perfunctory *adj.* બેદરકારીથી કરેલું bedarakaareethee karelun

perhaps *adv.* કદાચ kadaach

peri *n.* આસપાસનું aasapaasanun

peril *n.* જોખમ jokham

perilous *adj.* જોખમી jokhamee

perimeter *n.* પરિમિતિ parimiti

period *n.* અવધિ avadhi

periodic *adj.* નિયતકાલીન niyatakaaleen

periodical *adj.* નિયતકાલીન niyatakaaleen

perish *v.t.* નાશ પામવું naash paamavun

perishable જલદી બગડે એવું jaladee bagade evun

perjure *v.t.* ખોટા સોગન લેવા khota sogan leva

perjury ખોટી જુબાની khotee jubaanee

permanence *n.* સ્થાયિત્વ sthaayitv

permanent *n.* કાયમી kaayamee

permanently *v.t.* સ્થાયી રૂપ sthaayee roop

permissible *adj.* પરવાનગી પાત્ર paravaanagee paatr

permission *n.* પરવાનગી paravaanagee

permit *v.t.* પરવાનગી દેવી paravaanagee devee

permutation *n.* અદલાબદલ adalaabadal

pernicious *adj.* વિનાશક vinaashak

peroration *n.* વ્યાખ્યાનનું સમાપન vyaakhyaananun samaapan

perpendicular *adj.* ટટ્ટાર tattaar

perpetrate *v.t.* ખોટું કામ કરવું khotun kaam karavun

perpetual *n.* કાયમનું kaayamanun

perpetuate કાયમી બનાવવું kaayamee banaavavun

perpetuity *n.* ચિરસ્થાયીપણું chirasthaayeepanun

perplex *v.t.* વ્યાકુળ કરવું vyaakul karavun

perplexity *n.* વ્યગ્રતા vyagrata

perquisite *n.* હકસાઈ hakasaaee

persecute *v.t.* દમન કરવું daman karavun

persecution *n.* સિતમ sitam

perseverance *n.* સતત પ્રયાસ satat prayaas

persist મંડ્યા રહેવું mandya rahevun

persistent *adj.* ખંતીલું khanteelun

person *n.* વ્યક્તિ vyakti

personage મહત્ત્વવનું માણસ mahattvanun maanas

personal *adj.* વ્યક્તિગત vyaktigat

personality *n.* વ્યક્તિત્વ vyaktitv

personally *adj.* પોતાને વિષે potaane vishe

personate *v.t.* છદ્મનામ ધારણ chhadmanaam dhaaran

personification *n.* વ્યક્તિકરણ vyaktikaran

personnel *n.* કર્મચારી વર્ગ karmachaaree varg

perspective *adj.* યથાર્થદર્શન ચિત્ર yathaarthadarshan chitr

perspicuity *n.* સુસ્પષ્ટતા suspashtata

perspiration *n.* પરસેવો. parasevo

perspire *v.i.* પરસેવો છૂટવો parasevo chhootavo

persuade *v.* ખાતરી કરાવવી khaataree karaavavee

persuation *n.* સમજાવટ samajaavat

persuasive *adj.* સચોટ sachot

pert *adj.* અવિનયી avinayee

pertinacious *adj.* દુરાગ્રહી duraagrahee

pertinacity દુરાગ્રહ duraagrah

pertinence *n.* ઔચિત્ય auchity

pertinent *adj.* પ્રસંગાનુરૂપ. prasangaanuroop

perturb ક્ષોભમાં નાખવું kshobhaman naakhavun

perturbation *n.* ક્ષોભમાં નાખવું તે kshobhaman naakhavun te

perusal *n.* અધ્યયન adhyayan

peruse *v.t.* ધ્યાનપૂર્વક વાંચવું dhyaanapoorvak vaanchavun

pervade *v.t.* પ્રસરવું prasaravun

perverse *adj.* અડિયલ adiyal

perversion *n.* વિપરીતતા vipareetata

pervious *adj.* પ્રવેશક્ષમ praveshaksham

pessimism *n.* નિરાશાવાદ niraashaavaad

pessimist *n.* નિરાશાવાદી niraashaavaadee

pest ઉપદ્રવકારક માણસ upadravakaarak maanas

pester *v.t.* જીવ ખાવો jeev khaavo

pestilence *n.* મહામારી mahaamaaree

pestle *n.* સાંબેલું saanbelun

pet *adj.* લાડકવાયું laadakavaayun

petal *n.* પુષ્પદલ pushpadal

petite *adj.* નાજુક naajuk

petition *n.* અરજ araj

petrify *v.t.* પથ્થર જેવું કરવું paththar jevun karavun

petrol *n.* પેટ્રોલ petrol

petticoat *n.* ચણિયો chaniyo

pettish *adj.* ચીઢિયું cheedhiyun

pettiness *n.* ક્ષુદ્રતા kshudrata

petty *adj.* ક્ષુદ્ર kshudr

petulance *n.* કચકચિયું kachakachiyun

petulant *adj.* ચીડ cheed

pew *n.* દેવળની બેઠક devalanee bethak

phantasm *n.* ભ્રમ bhram

phantastic *adj.* માયાવી maayaavee

phantasy *n.* કલ્પના kalpana

phantom *n.* ભૂત bhoot

pharmaceutical *adj.* ઔષધ નિર્માણ aushadh nirmaan

pharmacy *n.* ઔષધાલય aushadhaalay

pharos *n.* દીવાદાંડી deevaadaandee

phase *n.* વિકાસનો તબક્કો vikaasano tabakko

phenomenal *adj.* વિલક્ષણ vilakshan

phenomenon *n.* અસાધારણ વ્યક્તિ asaadhaaran vyakti

phial *n.* નાની શીશી. naanee sheeshee

philander *v.i.* પ્રેમ ચેષ્ટા કરવી prem cheshtaa karavee

philanthropic *adj.* પરોપકારી paropakaaree

philatelic *n.* ટપાલ ટિકિટ સંગ્રહ tapaal tikit sangrah

philogist *n.* ભાષાવિદ્દ bhaashaavidd

philology *n.* ભાષાવિજ્ઞાન bhaashaavignaan

philosopher *n.* તત્ત્વજ્ઞાની tattvagnaanee

philosophic *adj.* તત્ત્વજ્ઞાનને લગતું tattvagnaanane lagatun

philosophy *n.* તત્ત્વજ્ઞાન tattvagnaan

philter *n.* વશીકરણ vasheekaran

phoenix *n.* અદ્વિતીય વ્યક્તિ adviteey vyakti

phone *n.* ટેલિફોન telifon

phonetic *adj.* ઉચ્ચારશાસ્ત્રીય uchchaarshaastreey

phonetics *n.pl.* ઉચ્ચારશાસ્ત્ર uchchaarashaastr

phonograph *n.* ફોનોગ્રાફ fonograaf

phonology *n.* ધ્વનિશાસ્ત્ર. dhvanishaastr

phosphoric *adj.* ફોસ્ફરિક fosfaric

phosphorus *n.* ફોસ્ફરસ fosfaras

photograph *n.* તસવીર tasaveer

photographer *n.* તસવીરકાર tasaveerakaar

photography *n.* ફોટોગ્રાફી. fotograafee

photometer *n.* પ્રકાશમાપક. prakaashamaapak

phrase *n.* શબ્દ સમૂહ shabd samooh

phraseology *n.* શબ્દશૈલી shabdashailee

phrenology *n.* મસ્તકવિદ્યા mastikvidyaa

phthisis *n.* ફેફસાનો ક્ષયરોગ fefasaano kshayarog

physic *n.* વૈદક vaidak

physical *adj.* ભૌતિક bhautik

physician *n.* વૈદ vaid

physics *n.* ભૌતિક વિજ્ઞાન bhautik vignaan

physiognomy *n.* સામુદ્રિક વિજ્ઞાન saamudrik vignaan

physiology *n.* શરીર ક્રિયા વિજ્ઞાન shareer kriya vignaan

physique *n.* શરીરનો બાંધો shareerno baandho

pianist *n.* પિયાનોવાદક piyaanovaadak

piano *n.* પિયાનો piyaano

pick *v.t.* વીણી કાઢવું તે veenee kaadhavun te

pickaxe *n.* તીકમ teekam

picket *n.* અણીદાર ખૂંટો aneedaar khoonto

pickle *n.* સરકો sarako

pickpocket *n.* ખિસ્સાકાતરુ માણસ khissaakaataru maanas
picnic *n.* ઉજાણી ujaanee
pictorial *adj.* સચિત્ર sachitr
picture *n.* ચિત્ર chitr
pie *n.* કચોરી kachoree
piece *n.* ટુકડો tukado
pier *n.* થાંભલો thaanbhalo
pierce *v.t.* —ને ભોંકવું ni bhonkavun
piety *n.* ધાર્મિકતા dhaarmikata
pig *n.* ડુક્કર dukkar
pigeon *n.* કબૂતર kabootar
pigheaded *adj.* અડિયલ adiyal
pigeon-hole *n.* કબૂતરખાનું kabootarakhaanun
pigment *n.* રંગદ્રવ્ય rangadravy
pigmy *n.* ઠીંગૂજી theengoojee
pike *n.* ભાલો bhaalo
pile *n.* ઢગલો dhagalo
piles *n.* હરસનું દરદ harasanun darad
pilfer *v.t.* તફડંચી કરવી tafadanchee karavee
pilferage *n.* તફડંચી tafadanchee
pilgrim *n.* જાત્રાળુ jaatraalun
pilgrimage *n.* તીર્થયાત્રા teerthayaatra
pill *n.* દવાની ટીકડી davaanee teekadee
pillar *n.* સ્તંભ stanbh
pillion *n.* વાહનની પાછળની બેઠક vaahananee paachaalnee bethak
pillow *n.* ઓશિકું oshikun
pilot *n.* સુકાની sukaanee
pilotage *n.* નૌચાલન nauchaalan
pimp *n.* ભડવો bhadavo
pimple *n.* ખીલ. kheel
pin *n.* ટાંકણી taankanee
pincers *n.* પકડવાનું ઓજાર pakadavaanun ojaar
pinch *v.t.* ચીમટી ખણવી, cheematee khanavee
pine *n.* ઝૂરવું jhooravun
pine-apple *n.* અનેનાસ anenaas
pinion *n.* પક્ષીની પાંખ paksheenee paankh
pink *n.* ગુલાબી gulaabee
pinnacle *n.* શિખર shikhar
pint *n.* પિન્ટ pint
pioneer *n.* અગ્રેસર agresar

pious *adj.* ધાર્મિક dhaarmik
pip *n.* ફળનું બીજ falanun beej
pipe *n.* વાંસળી જેવું વાદ્ય vaansalee jevun vaady
pipette *n.* પિપેટ pipet
piquancy *n.* તમતમાટ tamatamaat
piquant *adj.* તીખું તમતમતું teekhun tamatamatun
pique *v.t.* ને માનભંગ કરવો ne maanabhang karavo
piracy *n.* ચાંચિયાગીરી chaanchiyaageeree
pirate *n.* દરિયાઈ લૂટારો dariyaaee lootaaro
piratical *adj.* ચાંચિયાગીરી chaanchiyaagiri
piss *n.* મૂતર mootar
pistol *n.* તમંચો tamancho
piston *n.* પિસ્ટન pistan
pit *n.* ફળનો ઠળિયો falano thaliyo
pitch *n.* ડામર daamar
pitcher *n.* કુંજો kunjo
pith *n.* ગર gar
pithy *adj.* સારગર્ભ saaragarbh
pitiable *adj.* દયાપાત્રજનક dayaapaatrajanak
pitiful *adj.* દયાજનક dayaajanak
pitiless *adj.* દયાહીન dayaaheen
pittance *n.* અલ્પ જથ્થો alp jaththo
pity *n.* દયા daya
pivot *n.* ખીલો kheelo
pivotal *adj.* મહત્ત્વશીલ mahatvasheel
placard *n.* ભીંત પત્ર bheent patr
place *n.* સ્થળ sthal
placid *adj.* સૌમ્ય saumy
placidity *n.* સૌમ્યતા saumyata
plagiarism *n.* સાહિત્યચોરી saahityachoree
plagiarize *v.t.* સાહિત્યિક ચોરી કરવી saahityik choree karavee
plague *n.* ભારે ઉપદ્રવ bhaare upadrav
plaid *n.* કાંબળો kaanbalo
plain *adj.* સ્પષ્ટ spasht
plainly *adv.* સ્પષ્ટતાપૂર્વક spashtataapoorvak
plaint *n.* ફરિયાદ fariyaad

plaintiff *n.* ફરિયાદી fariyaadee
plaintive *adj.* શોકાતુર shokaatur
plait *n.* પાટલી paatalee
plan *n.* યોજેલો ઘાટ yojelo ghaat
plane *adj.* સમતળ samatal
planet *n.* ગ્રહ grah
plank *n.* પાટિયું paatiyun
plant *n.* વનસ્પતિનો રોપ vanaspatino rop
plantain *n.* કેળ kel
plantation *n.* ઉદ્યાન udyaan
plash *n.* ખોબોચિયું khobochiyun
plaster *n.* મલમ malam
plastic *adj.* પ્લાસ્ટિક plastik
plate *n.* પાતળું પતરું paatalun patarun
plateau *n.* ઉચ્ચપ્રદેશ uchchapradesh
platform *n.* મંચ manch
platinum *n.* પ્લેટિનમ pletinam
platitude *n.* સામાન્ય મંતવ્ય saamaany mantavy
platonic *adj.* પ્લાટોને લગતું plaatone lagatun
platoon *n.* પાયદળની ટુકડી paayadalanee tukadee
plaudit *n.* વાહવા vaahava
plausible *adj.* સત્યાભાસી satyaabhaashee
play *n.* રમત ramat
player *n.* ખેલાડી khelaadee
playful *adj.* રમતિયાળ ramatiyaal
playground *n.* રમતનું મેદાન ramatanun medaan
playhouse *n.* નાટકશાળા naatakashaala
playmate *n.* ગોઠિયો gothiyo
plaything *n.* રમકડું ramakadun
plea *n.* દલીલ daleel
plead *v.i.* કારણ બતાવવું kaaran bataavavun
pleader *n.* વકીલ vakeel
pleasant *adj.* સુખકારક sukhakaarak
pleasantry મશ્કરી mashkaree
please *v.t.* –ને આનંદ આપવો ne aanand aapavo
pleasure *n.* સંતોષ santosh
plebiscite *n.* સાર્વમત saarvamat
pledge *n.* ગીરો મુકેલી વસ્તુ geero mukelee vastu

plenary *adj.* સંપૂર્ણ sanpoorn
plentiful *adj.* ભરપૂર bharapoor
pleonasm *n.* શબ્દબાહુલ્ય shabdabaahuly
plethora *n.* અતિશયતા atishayataa
pliability *n.* મૃદુ સ્વભાવ mrudu svabhaav
pliable *adj.* મૃદુ સ્વભાવનું mrudu svabhaavanun
pliers *n.* સાણસી saanasee
plight *n.* દશા dasha
plinth *n.* પરથાર parathaar
plod *v.i.* ધીમે કામ કરવું dheeme kaam karavun
plot *n.* જમીનનો ટુકડો jameenano tukado
plough *v.i.* હળ hal
pluck *v.t.* ખેંચી કાઢવું khenchee kaadhavun
plucky *adj.* પાણીદાર paaneedaar
plug *n.* ડૂચો doocho
plum *n.* કાળીસુકી દ્રાક્ષ kaaleesukee draaksh
plumage *n.* પક્ષીનાં પીછાં paksheenan peenchhan
plumb *n.* કડિયાનો ઓળંબો kadiyaano olanbo
plumber *n.* પ્લમ્બર plambar
plume *n.* પીછું peenchhun
plummet *n.* ઓળંબાવાળી દોરી olanbaavaalee doree
plump *adj.* ગોળમટોળ golamatol
plunder *v.t.* લૂંટીને લઈ જવું loonteene laee javun
plunge *v.i.* બોળવું bolavun
pluperfect *adj.* સંપૂર્ણભૂતકાળ sanpoornabhootakaal
plural *adj.* બહુવચન bahuvachan
plurality *n.* અનેકત્વ anekatv
plus *n.* અધિક adhik
plutocracy *n.* ધનિકવર્ગ dhanikavarg
pluvial *adj.* વરસાદનું varasaadanun
ply *v.t.* ગડી gadee
pneumatic *adj.* હવાવાળું havaavaalun
pneumatics *n.* વાયુશાસ્ત્ર vaayushaastra

pneumonia *n.* ફેફસાંનો સોજો fefasaanno sojo
pock *n.* ફોલ્લો. follo
pocket *n.* ખીસું kheesun
pod *n.* સીગ seeng
poem *n.* કાવ્ય kaavy
poesy *n.* કવિતા kavita
poet *n.* કવિ kavi
poetaster *n.* જોડકણાંજોડું jodakanaanjodun
poetic *adj.* કાવ્યાત્મક kaavyaatmak
poetical *adj.* કાવ્યમાં રચેલું kaavyaman rachelun
poetry *n.* કાવ્યસૌન્દર્ય kaavyasaundary
poignant મર્મભેદક marmabhedak
point *n.* બિંદુ bindu
pointed *adj.* અણિયાળું aniyaalun
poison *n.* ઝેર jher
poisonous *adj.* ઝેરી jheree
poke *n.* ગોદો મારવો godo maaravo
polar *n.* ધ્રુવનું પાસેનું dhruvanun paasenun
pole *n.* સોટો soto
polemic *adj.* વિવાદાસ્પદ vivaadaaspad
pole-star *n.* માર્ગદર્શક વસ્તુ maargadarshak vastu
police *n.* પોલીસ સિપાઈ polees sipaaee
policeman *n.* પોલીસ કર્મચારી polisa karmachaaree
police-station *n.* પોલીસથાણું. poleesathaanun
policy *n.* નીતિ neeti
polish *v.t.* ચળકતું કરવું chalakatun karavun
polished *adj.* ચકચકિત chakachakit
polite *adj.* સૌજન્યવાળું saujanyavaalun
politeness *n.* સભ્યતા sabhyata
politic *n.* વ્યવહારનિપુણ vyavahaaranipun
political *adj.* રાજકીય raajakeey
politician *n.* રાજનીતિજ્ઞ raajaneetign
politics *n.* રાજકારણ raajakaaran
polity *n.* રાજ્યવ્યવસ્થાતંત્ર raajyavyavasthaatantr
poll *n.* મતદાન matadaan
pollen *n.* ફૂલમાંનો પરાગ foolamaanno paraag

poll-tax *n.* જજિયાવેરો jajiyaavero
pollute *v.t.* દૂષિત કરવું dooshit karavun
pollution *n.* પ્રદૂષણ pradushan
poltroon *n.* કાયર kaayar
polyandry *n.* બહુપતિપ્રથાવાળું bahupatneeprathaavaalun
polygamy *n.* બહુપત્નીત્વ bahupatneetva
polygon *n.* બહુભૂજ આકૃતિ bahubhooj aakruti
polytechnic *n.* કલાભવન kalaabhavan
pomegranate *n.* દાડમ daadam
pomp *n.* વૈભવ vaibhav
pompous ભપકાદાર bhapakaadaar
pond *n.* તળાવ talaav
ponder *v.t.* –નો વિચાર કરવું. no vichaar karavun
ponderous *adj.* વજનદાર vajanadaar
poniard *n.* નાની કટાર naanee kataar
pony *n.* ટટ્ટુ tattu
pool *n.* નદીનો ધરો. nadeeno dharo
poor *adj.* દયાપાત્ર dayaapaatr
pop *v.i.* એકદમ aekdam
pope *n.* પોપ pop
popinjay *n.* ફાંકડો માણસ faankado maanas
poplin *n.* પોપલિન poplin
poppy *n.* ખસખસનો છોડ khasakhasano chhod
populace *n.* આમ જનતા aam janata
popular *n.* લોકપ્રિય lokapriy
popularity *n.* લોકપ્રિયતા lokapriyata
popularize *v.* લોકપ્રિય બનાવવું lokapriy banaavavun
populate –માં વસાહત કરવી maan vasaahat karavee
population *n.* વસ્તીનું પ્રમાણ vasteenun pramaan
populous *n.* ગીચવસ્તીવાળું geechavasteevaalun
porcelain *n.* પોર્સેલિન porselin
porch *n.* દ્વારમંડપ dvaaramandap
porcupine *n.* શાહુડી. shaahudee
pore *n.* છિદ્ર chhidr
pork *n.* ડુક્કરનું માંસ dukkaranun maans
porous *adj.* છિદ્રોવાળું chhidrovaalun

porridge *n.* રાબ raab
porringer *n.* તાંસળું taansalun
port *n.* બંદર bandar
portable *adj.* સુવાહ્ય suvaahya
portal *n.* દરવાજો daravaajo
portend *v.t.* ભાવિસૂચક bhaavi choochak
portent *n.* શકુન કે અપશુકન shakun ke apashukan
porter *n.* દરવાન daravaan
portfolio *n.* જોસદાન josadaan
portico *n.* દ્વારમંડપ dvaarmandap
portion *n.* ભાગ bhaag
portly *adj.* જાડું jaadun
portmanteau *n.* પાકીટ paakeet
portrait *v.t.* આબેહૂબ વર્ણન aabehoob varnan
pose *v.t.* ઢોળ કરવો dol karavo
poser *n.* કોયડો koyado
position *n.* સ્થિતિ sthiti
positive *n.* નિશ્ચયાત્મક nishchayaatmak
possess *n.* ની માલિકીનું હોવું nee maalikeenun hovun
possession *n.* કબજો kabajo
possessive *adj.* માલિકીનું maalikeenun
possessor *n.* મલિક maalik
possibility *n.* શક્યતા shakyata
possible *adj.* શક્ય shaky
possibly *adv.* શક્ય હોય ત્યાં સુધી shaky hoy tyan sudhee
post *n.* સ્તંભ stanbh
postage *n.* ટપાલનું લવાજમ tapaalnun lavaajam
postal *adj.* ટપાલનું tapaalanun
pos¶date *v.t.* પાછળની તારીખ લખવી paachalnee taareekh lakhavee
poster *n.* મોટું છાપેલું ચિત્ર motun chhaapelun chitr
posterity *n.* વંશજો vanshajo
postman *n.* ટપાલી tapaalee
postmortem *adv.* મરણોત્તર maranottar
postpone *v.t.* મુલતવી રાખવું mulatavee raakhavun
postprandial *adj.* ભોજન પછીનું bhojan pachheenun

postscript *n.* તાજા કલમ taaja kalam
postulate *n.* ગૃહીત સદ્ધિદ્ધાન્ત gruheet siddhaant
posture *n.* અંગસ્થિતિ angasthiti
posy *n.* પુષ્પગુચ્છ pushpaguchchh
pot *n.* વાસણ vaasan
potable પી શકાય એવું pee shakaay evun
potato *n.* બટાકો. bataako
pot-belly *adj.* ઢૂંઢાળું doondaalun
potency *n.* તાકાત taakaat
potent *adj.* બળવાન balavaan
potentate *n.* શાસક shaasak
potential *adj.* સંભવનીય sanbhavaneey
potentiality *adj.* શક્યતા shakyata
pother *n.* શોરબકોર shorabakor
potion *n.* દવાનો ઘૂંટડો davaano ghoontado
potter *n.* વેઠ ઉતારવી veth utaaravee
pottery *n.* કુંભારકામ kunbhaarakaam
pouch *n.* નાનકડી કોથળી naanakadee kothalee
poulter *n.* મરઘા વેચવાવાળો maraghaa vechavaavaalo
poultry *n.* મરઘા ઉછેર maraghaa uchher
pounce *v.t.* હુમલો કરવો humalo karavo
pour *v.* વહેવું vahevun
poverty *n.* ગરીબાઈ gareebaaee
powder *n.* ભૂકી bhookee
power *n.* ક્રિયાશક્તિ kriyaashakti
powerful *adj.* ખૂબ બળવાન khoob balavaan
powerless *adj.* શક્તિહીન shaktiheen
pox *n.* ઉપદંશ upadansh
practicable *n.* વહેવારું vahevaarun
practical *adj.* વ્યાવહારિક vyaavahaarik
practically *adv.* વહેવારની દ્રષ્ટિથી vahevaaranee drashtithee
practice *n.* અભ્યાસ abhyaas
practise *v.t.* –નો મહાવરો કરવો no mahaavaro karavo
practitioner *n.* વૈદ્યકીય vaidyakeey
pragmatic *adj.* વ્યાવહારિક દ્રષ્ટીવાળું vyaavahaarik drashteevaalun
praise *v.t.* વખાણ કરવાં vakhaan karavan

praiseworthy *adj.* વખાણવા જોગ vakhaanava jog

prank અડપલું adapalun

prate *v.i.* લવારો કરવો lavaaro karavo

prattle *n.* બકવાટ bakavaat

pray *v.i.* પ્રાર્થના કરવી praarthana karavee

prayer *n.* પ્રભુપ્રાર્થના prabhupraarthana

preach *v.t.* ધર્મોપદેશ આપવો dharmopadesh aapavo

preamble *n.* આમુખ aamukh

precarious *adj.* અનિશ્ચિત anishchit

precaution *n.* સાવચેતી saavachetee

precede *v.t.* મહત્ત્વ mahattv

precedence અગ્રેસરત્વ agresaratv

precedent *n.* પૂર્વ આધાર poorv aadhaar

preceding *adj.* અગાઉનું agaaunun

precept ઉપદેશ upadesh

preceptor *n.* નિર્દેશક nirdeshak

precinct *n.* પરિસર parisar

precious *adj.* મહામૂલું mahaamoolun

precipice *n.* ભેખડ bhekhad

precipitation *n.* અવક્ષેપ avakshep

preciptous *n.* સીધા ઢોળાવ જેવું seedha dholaav jevun

precis *n.* સંક્ષેપ sankshep

precise *n.* ચોક્કસ શબ્દોવાળું chokkas shabdovaalun

precision *n.* ચોકસાઇ chokasaaee

preclude *n.* અશક્ય બનાવવું ashaky banaavavun

precocious *n.* પ્રૌઢ praudh

precognition *n.* પૂર્વજ્ઞાન poorvagnaan

preconceive *v.t.* પૂર્વધારણા કરવી purvadhaarnaa karavee

preconception પૂર્વધારણા poorvadhaarana

precursor *n.* પૂર્વચિહ્ન poorvachinh

precursory *adj.* અણસારા anasaara

predatory *n.* લૂંટફાટ કરનારું loontafaat karanaarun

predecessor *n.* પૂર્વગામી poorvagaamee

predestinate *v.t.* અગાઉથી નયિત કરવું agaauthee niyat karavun

predetermine *v.t.* પૂર્વનિશ્ચિતિ purvanishchit

predicament *n.* દુર્દશા durdasha

predict *v.t.* ભવિષ્ય ભાખવું bhavishy bhaakhavun

prediction *n.* ભવિષ્ય bhavishy

predilection *n.* પક્ષપાત pakshapaat

predominance *n.* —નું વર્ચસ્વ હોવું nun varchasv hovun

pre-eminent *adj.* સર્વોત્તમ sarvottam

pre-emption *v.t.* અગ્રક્રયાધિકાર agrakrayaadhikaar

pre-exist *v.t.* પૂર્વઅસ્તિત્વ purvaastitva

preface *n.* પ્રસ્તાવના prastaavana

prefactory *adj.* પ્રસ્તાવના સંબંધી prastaavana sanbandhee

prefer *v.t.* પસંદ કરવું pasand karavun

preferable *adj.* વધુ ઇચ્છવા યોગ્ય vadhu eechchhava yogy

preference *n.* પહેલી પસંદગી pahelee pasandagee

preferential *adj.* અગ્રાધિકાર agraadhikaar

prefix *n.* ઉપસર્ગ upasarg

pregnancy *n.* સગર્ભાવસ્થા sagarbhaavastha

pregnant *adj.* સગર્ભા sagarbha

prehension *n.* પકડવાની શક્તિ pakadavaanee shakti

prehistoric *adj.* પ્રાગૈતિહાસિક praagaitihaasik

prejudge *v.t.* વહેલો નિર્ણય કરવો vahelo nirnay karavo

prejudice *n.* પૂર્વગ્રહ poorvagrah

prejudicial *adj.* પૂર્વગ્રહયુક્ત poorvagrahayukt

prelate *n.* જાહેર વ્યાખ્યાન jaaher vyaakhyaan

preliminary *adj.* પ્રાસ્તાવિક praastaavik

prelude *n.* પ્રાસ્તાવિક કરવું praastaavik karavun

premature *adj.* ઉતાવળિયું utaavaliyun

premeditate *v.t.* પૂર્વવિચાર કરવો purvavichaar karavo

premeditation *n.* અગાઉથી વિચારવું agaauthee vichaaravun

premier *adj.* અગ્રેસર agresar

premises *n.pl.* પરિસર parisar

premium *n.* બક્ષિસ bakshees

premonition *n.* પૂર્વાભાસ poorvaabhaas

premonitory *adj.* પૂર્વસૂચક purvasoochak

pre-occupancy *n.* પૂર્વકબજો purvakabajo

pre-occupy *v.t.* અગાઉથી કબજો agaauthee kabajo

prepaid *adj.* પહેલાથી ચૂકવેલું pahelaathee chukavelun

preparative *adj.* પ્રારંભિક તૈયારી praaranbhik taiyaaree

preparation *n.* પૂર્વતૈયારી purvataiyaaree

prepare *v.t.* તૈયાર કરવું taiyaar karavun

prepay *v.t.* અગાઉથી આપવું agaauthee aapavun

preponderate *v.i.* વધારે ભારે હોવું vadhaare bhaare hovun

preposition નામયોગી અવ્યય naamayogee avyay

prepossess *v.t.* પૂર્વાધિકાર purvaadhikaar

preposterous *adj.* બુદ્ધિથી વિરુદ્ધ buddhithee viruddh

pre-requisite *n.* પૂર્વાપેક્ષિત બાબત poorvaapekshit baabat

prerogative *n.* વિશિષ અધિકાર vishesh adhikaar

presage *v.t.* અગાઉથી જોવું agaauthee jovun

prescribe *v.t.* નિયત કરવું niyat karavun

prescript *n.* ફતવો fatavo

prescription *n.* નિર્ધારણ nirdhaaran

presence *n.* હાજરી haajaree

present *adj.* હાજર haajar

present *n.* ભેટ bhet

presently *adv.* હમણાં hamanan

preservation *n.* સુરક્ષિત રાખવું surakshit raakhavun

preserve *v.t.* સંરક્ષણ કરવું sanrakshan karavun

preside *v.t.* અધ્યક્ષસ્થાન લેવું adhyakshasthaan levun

presidency પ્રમુખપદની અવધિ pramukhapadanee avadhi

president *n.* અધ્યક્ષ adhyaksh

presidential *adj.* પ્રમુખપદને લગતું pramukhapadane lagatun

press *v.t.* દાબવું daabavun

pressing *adj.* તાકીદનું taakeedanun

pressure *n.* દબાણ dabaan

prestige *n.* પ્રતિષ્ઠા pratishtha

presume *v.t.* ગૃહીત ધરવું gruheet dharavun

presumption *n.* અહંકાર ahankaar

presumptuous *adj.* બેઅદબ beadab

pretence *n.* આડંબર aadanbar

pretend *v.t.* ડોળ કરવો dol karavo

pretender *n.* વેષધારી veshadhaaree

pretermit *n.* અવગણવું avaganavun

preternatural *adj.* અસાધારણ asaadhaaran

pretext *n.* બહાનું bahaanun

prettiness *n.* સુંદરતા sundarata

pretty *adj.* રૂપાળું roopaalun

prevail *v.t.* પ્રવર્તવું pravartavun

prevailing *adj.* પ્રબળ prabal

prevalence *n.* પ્રચલિત prachalit

prevalent *n.* સાર્વત્રિક saarvatrik

prevaricate *v.t.* ઉડાઉ જવાબો આપવા udaau javaabo aapava

preventive *adj.* પ્રતિબંધક pratibandhak

previous *adj.* પહેલાંનું pahelaannun

prey *n.* શિકાર shikaar

price *n.* કિંમત kinmat

priceless *adj.* અમૂલ્ય amooly

prick *v.t.* ભોંકવું bhonkavun

prickle *n.* કંટક kantak

prickly *adj.* કાંટાળું kaantaalun

prickly *heat* કાંટાદાર kaantaadaar

pride *n.* ગર્વ garv

priest *n.* પુરોહિત purohit

priestly *adj.* પુરોહિતના જેવું purohitana jevun

prim *adj.* અક્કડવર્તનવાળું akkadavartanavaalun

primarily *adv.* મુખ્યત્વે mukhyatve
primary અસલ. asal
prime *adj.* સૌથી મહત્ત્વનું sauthee mahattvanun
primer *n.* બાળપોથી baalapothee
primitive *adj.* પુરાચીન praacheen
primordial *adj.* તદ્દન શરૂઆતનું taddan sharooaatanun
primrose *n.* આછો પીળો રંગ aachho peelo rang
primus *n.* સ્ટવની એક જાત stavanee ek jaat
prince *n.* રાજકુંવર raajakunvar
princely *adj.* વૈભવશાળી vaibhavashaalee
princess *n.* રાજકન્યા raajakanya
principal *adj.* સૌથી મહત્ત્વનું sauthee mahattvanun
principality *n.* રાજ્ય raajya
principle *n.* સદ્દિધાન્ત siddhaant
print *v.t.* છાપવું chaapavun
printer *n.* છાપખાનાવાળો. chhaapakhaanaavaalo
printing *n.* છાપકામ chhaapakaam
printing press *n.* છાપવાનું યંત્ર chhaapavaanun yantr
prior *adj.* અગાઉનું agaaunun
priority *n.* અગ્રતા agrata
prism *n.* સમપાશ્રવ samapaashrv
prison *n.* કારાગૃહ kaaraagrah
prisoner *n.* કેદી kedee
pristine *adj.* પુરાચીન praacheen
prithee *int.* કૃપા કરીને krupaa kareene
privacy *n.* ખાનગી khaanagee
private *n.* અંગત angat
privately *adv.* અંગત રીતે angat reete
privation *n.* હાલાકી haalaakee
privy *adj.* ગુપ્ત gupt
prize *n.* ઈનામ eenaam
probability *n.* શક્યતા shakyata
probably *adj.* ઘણું કરીને ghanun kareene
probate *n.* મૃત્યુપત્રની સાબતી mrutyupatranee saabitee
probation *n.* શિખાઉપણાનો તબક્કો shikhaaupanaano tabakko

probationary *adj.* અજમાયસી ajamaayasee
probe *v.t.* તપાસ કરવી tapaas karavee
probity *n.* પ્રામાણિકતા praamaanikata
problem *n.* કૂટપ્રશ્ન kootaprashn
problematic *adj.* સમસ્યારૂપ samasyaaroop
procedure *n.* કાર્યપ્રણાલી. kaaryapranaalee
proceed *v.i.* આગળ વધવું aagal vadhavun
proceeding *n.* વર્તનૂક vartanook
proceeds *n.* વકરો vakaro
process *n.* કરવાની રીત karavaanee reet
procession *n.* વરઘોડો. varaghodo
proclaim *v.t.* જાહેર કરવું jaaher karavun
proclamation *n.* જાહેરાત jaaheraat
proclivity *n.* કુદરતી વલણ kudaratee valan
procrastinate *v.t.* ઢીલ કર્યા કરવી dheel karya karavee
procrastination *n.* લાસરિયાપણું laasariyaapanun
procreate *v.t.* પેદા કરવું peda karavun
proctor *n.* કુલાનુશાસક kulaanushaasak
procure *v.t.* પ્રયાસ કરીને પ્રાપ્ત કરવું prayaas kareene praapt karavun
prod *v.t.* ઘોંચવું ghonchavun
prodigal *adj.* ઉડાઉ udaau
prodigality *n.* ઉડાઉગીરી udaaugeeree
prodigious *adj.* વિલક્ષણ vilakshan
prodigy *n.* આશ્ચર્યકારક વસ્તુ aashcharyakaarak vastu
produce *v.t.* આગળ દેખાડવું aagal dekhaadavun
product *n.* ઉત્પાદન utpaadan
production *adj.* ઉત્પન્ન કરવું utpann karavun
productive *adj.* ઉત્પાદક utpaadak
profane *v.t.* અપવત્રિ apavitr
profess *v.t.* પોતાની લાગણી જાહેર કરવું potaanee laaganee jaaher karavun
profession *n.* ધંધોરોજગાર dandhorojagaar
professional *adj.* કોઈ વ્યવસાયનું koee vyavasaayanun

professor *n.* વિદ્યાપીઠનો અધ્યાપક vidyaapithano adhyaapak

proffer *v.t.* આપવાનું કહેવું aapavaanun kahevun

proficiency *n.* કૌશલ્ય kaushaly

proficient *adj.* નિષ્ણાત nishnaat

profit *v.t.* નફો કરવો nafo karavo

profitable *adj.* લાભદાયક laabhadaayak

profligate *adj.* દુરાચારી duraachaaree

profound *adj.* ગહન gahan

profuse *adj.* પુષ્કળ pushkal

profusion *n.* વિપુલતા vipulata

prog *n.* મુસાફરીનું ભાતું musaafareenun bhaatun

progenitor *n.* પૂર્વગામી poorvagaamee

progeny *n.* ફલશ્રુતિ falashruti

prognosis *n.* રોગનિદાન roganidaan

prognostic *adj.* પૂર્વસૂચક poorvasoochak

prognosticate *v.i.* આગાહી કરવી aagaahee karavee

programme *n.* કાર્યક્રમ kaaryakram

progress *n.* પ્રગતિ pragati

progression *n.* પ્રગતિ pragati

progressive *adj.* પ્રગતિશીલ pragatisheel

prohibit રોકવું rokavun

prohibition *n.* મનાઈનો હુકમ manaaeeno hukam

project *n.* યોજવું yojavun

projectile *n.* તોપનો ગોળો. topano golo

projection *n.* મૂરતકલ્પના moortakalpana

proletariat *n.* મજૂરવર્ગ majooravarg

prolific *adj.* ફલપ્રદ falaprad

prolix *adj.* લંબાણવાળું lanbaanavaalun

prolixity *n.* લંબાણઅંકટાળાજનક lanbaanakantaalaajanak

prologue *n.* પૂરાકકથન praakakathan

prolong *v.t.* લંબાવવું lanbaavavun

promenade *n.* જાહેરમાં વિહાર jaaheraman vihaar

prominent *adj.* આગળ પડતું aagal padatun

promiscuous *adj.* સંમિશ્રિતા sanmishrata

promise *n.* વચન vachan

promising *adj.* આશાસ્પદ aashaaspad

promissory *adj.* વચનવાળું vachanavaalun

promote *v.t.* મહત્ત્વ વધારવું mahattv vadhaaravun

promotion *n.* પદવૃદ્ધિ padavruddhi

prompt *adj.* તત્પર tatpar

promulgate *v.t.* પ્રસિદ્ધ કરવું prasiddh karavun

promulgation *n.* ઢંઢેરો dhandhero

prone *adj.* અધોમુખ adhomukh

pronoun *n.* સર્વનામ. sarvanaam

pronounce *v.t.* ઉચ્ચારવું uchchaaravun

pronunciation *n.* ઉચ્ચારણ uchchaaran

proof *n.* પુરાવો puraavo

propaganda *n.* ભ્રામક માહિતી bhraamak maahitee

propagandist *n.* પ્રચારક prachaarak

propagate *v.t.* –નો પ્રચાર કરવો ni prachaar karavo

propel *v.t.* હાંકવું haankavun

propensity વલણ valan

proper *adj.* અનુકૂળ anukool

properly *adv.* યોગ્ય રીતે yogy reete

property *n.* સ્થાવર મિલકત sthaavar milakat

prophecy *n.* ભાવીની આગાહી bhaaveenee aagaahee

prophesy *n.* ભવિષ્ય કહેવું bhavishy kahevun

prophet *n.* પેગંબર peganbar

prophetic *adj.* ભવિષ્યવેત્તાને લગતું bhavishyavettaane lagatun

prophylactic *adj.* સંકટ પ્રતિબંધક sankat pratibandhak

propitiate *v.t.* મનાવવું manaavavun

propitiation *n.* મનાવવું તે manaavavun te

propitious *adj.* પયમતાવાળું payamataavaalun

proportional *adj.* પ્રમાણસરનું pramaanasaranun

proposal *n.* પ્રસ્તાવ prastaav

propose *v.t.* દરખાસ્ત મુકવી darakhaast mukavee

proposition *n.* દરખાસ્ત darakhaast

propound *v.t.* વિચારણા માટે મૂકવું vichaaranaa maate mukavun

proprietary *adj.* મલિકત ધરાવનાર milakat dharaavanaar

proprietor *n.* માલિક maalik

propriety *n.* શિષ્ટાચાર shishtaachaar

prorogation *n.* સત્રસમાપ્તિ satrasamaapti

prorogue *v.t.* સત્ર સમાપ્ત કરવું satra samaapt karavun

prosaic *adj.* નીરસ neeras

proscribe *v.t.* દેશનિકાલ કરવું deshanikaal karavun

proscription *n.* પ્રતિબંધ pratibandh

prose *n.* ગદ્ય gady

prosecute *v.t.* પગલાં ભરવા pagalan bharavaan

prosecution *n.* ફરિયાદપક્ષ fariyaadapaksh

prosecutor *n.* વકીલ vakeel

proselyte *n.* વટલાયેલો vatalaayelo

prosody *n.* પિંગળશાસ્ત્ર pingalashaastr

prospect *n.* માનસિક ચિત્ર maanasik chitr

prospective *adj.* અપેક્ષિત apekshit

prospectus *n.* માહિતીપત્રક maahiteepatrak

prosper *v.t.* આબાદ થવું aabaad thavun

prosperity *n.* સમૃદ્ધિ samruddhi

prosperous *adj.* શુભ shubh

prostitute વેશ્યા veshya

prostitution *n.* વેશ્યાવૃતિ veshyaavruti

prostrate *v.t.* પગે પડવું page padavun

protagonist *n.* કથાનાયક kathaanaayak

protect *v.t.* સુરક્ષિત રાખવું surakshit raakhavun

protection *n.* રક્ષણ rakshan

protective *n.* સંરક્ષક sanrakshak

protector *n.* રક્ષક rakshak

protectorate *n.* રક્ષિત રાજ્ય rakshit raajya

protege *n.* રક્ષિત માણસ rakshit maanas

protest *v.t.* વાંધો ઉઠાવવો vaandho uthaavavo

protestant *n.* સુધારાવાદી ખ્રિસ્તી sudhaaraavaadee khristee

protocol *n.* નયાચાર nayaachaar

protoplasm *n.* જીવરસ jeevaras

prototype *n.* આદર્રૂપ aadiroop

protract *v.t.* લાંબું કરવું laanbun karavun

protraction *n.* લંબાણ lanbaan

protractor *n.* કોણમાપક konamaapak

protrude *v.t.* બહાર નીકળવું bahaar neekalavun

protuberance *n.* સોજો sojo

proud *adj.* અભિમાની abhimaanee

prove *v.t.* સિદ્ધ કરવું siddh karavun

provender *n.* ઘાસચારો ghaasachaaro

proverb *n.* કહેવત kahevat

proverbial *adj.* કહેવતરૂપ બનેલું kahevataroop banelun

provide *v.t.* —ને માટે તૈયારી ne maate taiyaaree

provided *conj.* એવી શરતે કે evee sharate ke

providence *n.* પરમેશ્વર parameshvar

provident *adj.* કરકસરિયું karakasariyun

providential *adj.* નસીબદાર naseebadaar

province *n.* પ્રાન્ત praant

provincialism *n.* પ્રાન્તિક praantik

provision *n.* તજવીજ કરવી tajaveej karavee

provisional તત્કાલીન tatkaaleen

proviso *n.* પરંતુક parantuk

provocation *n.* ગુસ્સાનું કારણ gussaanun kaaran

provoke *v.t.* ઉશ્કેરવું ushkeravun

prow *n.* વહાણનો મોરો vahaanano moro

prowess *n.* વીરતા veerata

proximate *adj.* પાસેમાં પાસેનું paaseman paasenun

proximity *n.* સાન્નિધ્ય saannidhy

proximo *adj.* આવતા મહિનાનું aavata mahinaanun

proxy *n.* અવેજી avejee

prude *n.* વાણીમાં અતિચોખલિયું vaaneeman ati chokhaliyun

prudence *n.* ડહાપણ dahaapan

prudent *n.* સાવધ saavadh

prudery *n.* ઠાવકાઈ thaavakaaee

prune *v.t.* ઘાટ આપવો ghaat aapavo

prurient *adj.* કામાતુર kaamaatur

pry *v.t.* ખોદણી કરવી khodanee karavee

psalm *n.* પ્રાર્થનાગીત praarthanaageet

pseudo *n.* કૃતરિમ krutrim

pseudonym *n.* ઉપનામ upanaam

pshaw *int.* છટ્ઠછટ્ઠૂ chhatoochhatoo

psyche *n.* આત્મા aatma

psychic *adj.* માનસિક maanasik

psychological *adj.* માનસશાસ્ત્રીય maanasshaastreeya

psychology *adj.* મનોવિજ્ઞાન manovignaan

puberty *n.* પ્રજનનક્ષમ અવસ્થા prajananaksham avastha

public *adj.* સાર્વજનકિ saarvajanik

publication *n.* પ્રસદિ્ધ કરવું તે prasiddh karavun te

publicity *n.* પ્રસદિ્ધિ prasiddh

publish *v.t.* પ્રકાશતિ કરવું prakaashit karavun

publisher *n.* ચોપડીઓનો પ્રકાશક chopadeeono prakaashak

pudding *n.* પુડગિ puding

puddle *n.* ખાબોચિયું khaabochiyun

puerile *adj.* બાલશિ baalish

puerility *n.* બાલશિતા baalishata

puff *n.* ફૂંક foonk

pug *n.* નાનું કૂતરું naanun kootarun

pugilist *n.* મુષ્ઠિયોદ્ધો mushthiyoddho

pugnacious *adj.* કજયિાખોર kajiyaakhor

pugnacity કજયિાખોર સ્વભાવ kajiyaakhor svabhaav

puisne *adj.* દરજ્જામાં ઊતરતું darajjaaman ootaratun

puissant *adj.* શક્તિશાળી shaktishaalee

puke *v.t.* ઊલટી કરવી oolatee karavee

pule *v.t.* શીશુંનું રુંદન sheeshunun rundan

pull *v.t.* તાણવું taanavun

pulley *n.* ગરગડી garagadee

pulmonary *adj.* ફેફસાંને લગતું fefasaanne lagatun

pulp *n.* ગર gar

pulpit *n.* વ્યાસપીઠ vyaasapeeth

pulpy *v.t.* ગરયુક્ત garayukt

pulse *n.* નાડીનો ધબકારો naadeeno dhabakaaro

pulverize *v.t.* નો ભૂકો કરવો no bhooko karavo

pump *n.* પંપ panp

pumpkin *n.* કોળું kolun

pun *n.* શબ્દશ્લેષ shabdashlesh

punch *n.* મુક્કો mukko

punctilious *adj.* રીતભાતમાં ચોક્કસ reetabhaataman chokkas

punctual *n.* સમયસાવધ samayasaavadh

punctuality *n.* સમયપાલન samayapaalan

punctuate *v.t.* વિરામચહિ્ન મુકવું viraamachinya mukavun

punctuation *n.* વિરામચહિ્ન viraamchinha

punctur માં કાણું પાડવું maan kaanun paadavun

pungency *n.* તીખાશ teekhaash

pungent *adj.* તીખું teekhun

punish *v.t.* સજા કરવી saja karavee

punishable *adj.* શક્ષિાપાત્ર shikshaapaatr

punishment *n.* સજા saja

punitive *adj.* શક્ષિાત્મક shikshaatmak

punster *n.* શબ્દશ્લેષ કરનારો. shabdashlesh karanaaro

punt *v.i.* હોડી hodee

puny *adj.* દૂબળું doobalun

puppy *n.* કુરકુરિયું kurakuriyun

pupil *n.* શષિ્ય shishy

puppet *n.* કઠપૂતળી kathapootalee

purblind *adj.* ઝાંખી દૃષ્ટવિાળું jhaankhee drashtivaalun

purchase *v.t.* ખરીદી khareedee

pure *adj.* શુદ્ધ shuddh

purgative *adj.* રેચક દવા rechak dava

purgatory *n.* પાપ વમિુક્તિસ્થાન paap vimukti sthaan

purge *n.* પાપ વમિુક્તિ paap vimukti

purification *n.* શુદ્ધીકરણ shuddheekaran

purify *v.t.* શુદ્ધ કરવું shuddh karavun

puritan *n.* ધાર્મકિ dhaarmik

purity *n.* પવત્રિ્ય pavitry

purl *v.i.* ખળખળ વહેવું khalakhal vahevun

purple *adj.* જાંબુડયિો રંગ jaanbudiyo rang

purpor *n.* આશય બતાવવો aashay bataavavo

purposely *adj.* હેતુપૂર્વક hetupoorvak

purr *v.i.* પુર અવાજ pur avaaj

purse *n.* બટવો batavo

purse-proud *adj.* ધનગર્વિત dhanavargit

purse-strings ખર્ચ ઉપર કાબૂ kharach upar kaaboo

pursuance *n.* અનુસરણ anusaran

pursue *v.t.* પાછળ પડવું paachhal padavun

pursuit *n.* પીછો peechho

purulent *adj.* પરુવાળું paruvaalun

purvey *v.t.* ખોરાક આપૂર્તિ khoraak aapurti

purveyance *n.* પુરવઠો puravatho

purview *n.* દૃષ્ટિમર્યાદા drashti maryaada

pus *n.* પરુ paru

push *v.t.* ધકેલવું dhakelavun

pusillanimous *adj.* બીકણ beekan

put મૂકવું mookavun

putrefaction *n.* કોવાઈ જવું kovaaee javun

putrid *adj.* કોવાયેલું kovaayelun

putrefy *v.t.* કોવડાવવું kovadaavavun

putsch *n.* વિદ્રોહ vidroh

putty *n.* લાપી laapee

puzzle *v.t.* ગૂંચવવું gunchavavun

pygmy *n.* ઠીંગૂજી theengoojee

pyorrhoea *n.* દાંતનો પરુનો રોગ daantano paruno rog

pyramid *n.* પરિમિડ piraamid

pyre *n.* ચિતા chita

pyrotechnic *adj.* દારૂખાના જેવું daarookhaana jevun

python *n.* અજગર ajagar

quack *v.i.* બતકનો અવાજ batakano avaaj

quackery *n.* ઊંટવૈદું oontavaidun

quadrangle *n.* ચતુર્ભુજ આકૃતિ chaturbhuj aakruti

quadrant *n.* ચતુષ્ભાગ chatushbhaag

quadratic *adj.* વર્ગસમીકરણ vargasameekaran

quadrennial *adj.* ચતુવાર્ષિક chatuvaarshik

quadrilateral *adj.* ચતુર્ભુજ chaturbhuj

quadrillion *n.* એક કરોડ પરાર્ધ ek karod paraardh

quadruped *n.* ચોપગું પશુ chopagun pashu

quadruple *n.* ચાર ભાગવાળું chaar bhaagavaalun

quaff *v.i.* ગટગટાવવું gatagataavavun

quagmire *n.* કળણ kalan

quail *n.* ક્વેઈલ kveil

quaint *adj.* વિલક્ષણ vilakshan

quake *v.i.* કંપવું kanpavun

qualification *n.* લાયકાત laayakaat

qualified *adj.* લાયક laayak

qualify *v.t.* લાયકાત કેળવવી laayakaat kelavavee

qualitative *adj.* ગુણધર્મની દૃષ્ટિએ gunadharmanee drashtee

quality *n.* ગુણધર્મ gunadharm

qualm *n.* ઉલાળો ulaalo

quandary *n.* મૂંઝવણ moonjhavan

quantitative *n.* પરિમાણવાચક parimaanavaachak

quantity *n.* જથો jatho

quantum *n.* આવશ્યક પરિણામ aavashyak parinaam

quarantine *n.* સંસર્ગનનિષેધ sansarganishedh

quarrel *v.i.* કજિયો કરવો kajiyo karavo

quarrelsome *adj.* કજિયાખોર kajiyaakhor

quarry *n.* પથ્થરની ખીણ paththaranee kheen

quarter *n.* ચોથો ભાગ chotho bhaag

quarterly ત્રૈમાસિક traimaasik

quartz *n.* કાચમણિ kaachamani

quasi *adv.* કેમ જાણે kem jaane

quatrain *n.* ૪ લીટીનો શ્લોક 4 leeteeno shlok

quaver *n.* ધ્વનીનું કંપન dhvaneenun kanpan

quay *n.* કૃત્રિમ ડક્કો. kutrim dakko

quayage *n.* ડક્કાવેરો dakkaavero

queasy *adj.* પાપભીરું paapabheerun

queen *n.* રાજાની પત્ની raajaanee patnee

queenly *adj.* રાણીના જેવું raaneena jevun

queer *adj.* વચિત્ર vichitr

quell *v.t.* કચડી નાખવું kachadee naakhavun

quench *v.t.* ઓલવવું olavavun

querist *n.* પ્રશ્ન પૂછનાર prashn poochhanaar

query *n.* પ્રશ્ન prashn

quest *n.* શોધખોળ shodhakhol

question *n.* પ્રશ્ન prashn

questionable *adj.* સંશયાત્મક sanshayaatmak

queue *n.* કતાર kataar

quick *adj.* સ્ફૂર્તિલું sfoortilun

quicken *v.t.* સચેત થવું sachet thavun

quickness *n.* ચાલાકી chaalaakee

quicklime *n.* કળીચૂનો kaleechoono

quicksilver *n.* પારો paaro

quid *n.* તમાકુની ગોળી tamaakunee golee

quiddity *n.* સારતત્વ saaratatv

quidnunc *n.* વાતોડિયો vaatodiyo

quiescent *adj.* સુપ્ત sushupt

quiet *v.t.* શાંત કરવું shaant karavun

quietly *adv.* શાંતિપૂર્વક shaantipoorvak

quietude *n.* નિરાંત niraant

quietus *n.* મરણ maran

quill *n.* પીછું peenchhun

quilt *n.* ગોદડું godadun

quinary *adj.* પાંચગણું paanchaganun

quinine *n.* ક્વિનાઈન kvinaain

quinsy *n.* કાકડાનો સોજો kaakadaano sojo

quintessence *n.* સારતત્ત્વ saaratattv

quip *n.* મહેણું mahenun

quire *n.* કાગળનો ઘા kaagalano ghaa

quirk *n.* વાકછળ vaakachhal

quit *v.t.* -નો ત્યાગ કરવો no tyaag karavo

quite *adv.* તદ્દન taddan

quittance *n.* ઋણમુક્તિ roonamukti

quiver બાણનો ભાથો. baanano bhaatho

quixotic *adj.* તરંગિતતા tarangitata

quiz *n.* કોયડો koyado

quizzical *adj.* રમૂજી ramoojee

quoin *n.* મકાનનો ખૂણો makaanano khuno

quondam *adj.* ભૂતપૂર્વ bhootapoorv

quota *n.* નિયત હિસ્સો niyat hisso

quotation *n.* અવતરણ avataran

quote *v.* -નકલ કરવી nakal karavee

quoth *n.* હું - તે - તેણી - બોલ્યું hun - he - henee - bolyun

quotidian *adj.* હંમેશનું hanmeshanun

quotient *n.* ભાગાકારનું ફળ bhaagaakaaranun fal

R

rabbit *n.* સસલું sasalun

rabble તોફાની ટોળું tofaanee tolun

rabid *adj.* બેલગામ belagaam

rabies *n.* કૂતરાનો હડકવા kootaraano hadakava

race *n.* સ્પર્ધા spardhaa

race-course *n.* ઘોડદોડ ghodadoa

racial *adj.* વંશ જાતિનું vansh jaatinun

rack *n.* ઘોડી ghodee

racket *n.* કોલાહલ kolaahal

racketeering *n.* ધૂતારાગીરી dhootaraageeree

racy *adj.* ઉત્સાહ utsaah

radial *adj.* કિરણ સંબંધી kiran sanbandhee

radiance *n.* પ્રકાશ prakaash

radiant *adj.* દીપ્તિમાન deeptimaan

radiate *v.t.* કિરણોત્સર્જન kiranotsarjan

radiation *n.* કિરણોત્સર્ગ kiranotsarg

radical *adj.* મૂળગત moolagat

radio *n.* રેડિયો rediyo

radiogram *n.* રેડિયોગ્રામ rediyogram

radiology *n.* વિકિરણ ચિકિત્સાવિજ્ઞાન vikiran chikitsaavignaan

radish *n.* મૂળો. moolo
radium *n.* રેડિયમ rediyam
radius *n.* ત્રિજ્યા trijyaa
raffle *n.* વહેંચણી vahenchanee
raft *n.* તરાપો taraapo
rafter *n.* છાપરાની વળી chhaaparaanee valee
rag *n.* ચીથરું cheetharun
rage *n.* ક્રોધાવેશ krodhaavesh
ragamuffin *n.* ગંદું માણસ gandu maanas
ragged *adj.* ચીથરેહાલ cheentharehaal
raid *n.* છાપો chhaapo
rail *n.* કઠેરો kathero
railing *n.* રેલના પાટા relana paata
raillery *n.* વિનોદ vinod
railway *n.* રેલવે relve
raiment *n.* પોશાક poshaak
rain *n.* વરસાદ varasaad
rainbow *n.* મેઘધનુષ meghadhanush
rainfall *n.* વરસાદ varasaad
raingauge *n.* વર્ષામાપક યંત્ર varshaamaapak yantr
rainy *adj.* ચોમાસાનું chomaasaanun
raise ઊભું કરવું oobhun karavun
raisin *n.* સૂકી દ્રાખ sookee darakh
rake *n.* પંજેટી panjetee
rakish *n.* લંપટ lanpat
rally *v.t.* રેલી reli
ram *n.* ઘેટો gheto
ramble *v.i.* સ્વૈરવિહાર કરવો svairavihaar karavo
ramification *n.* વિભાજન vibhaajan
ramify *v.t.* વિભાગીકરણ vibhaagikaran
rammer *n.* મોગરી mogaree
ramp *v.i.* ઢાળવાળો માર્ગ dhaalavaalo maarg
rampage *n.* ક્રોધાવેશ krodhaavesh
rampant ઉરછૃંખલ urachhunkhal
rampart *n.* રક્ષણ rakshan
rancid *adj.* ખોરું khorun
rancorous *adj.* દ્વેષીલું dvesheelun
rancour *n.* દ્વેષ dvesh
rand *n.* પગરખાંની સગતળી pagarakhaannee sagatalee
random *adj.* અવ્યવસ્થિત avyavasthit
randy *adj.* કામાતુર kaamaatur

range *v.t.* હારબંધ ગોઠવવું haarabandh gothavavun
ranger *n.* જંગલનો રક્ષક jangalano rakshak
rank *n.* હારબંધ સૈનિકો haarabandh sainiko
rankle મનમાં સાલવું manamaan saalavun
ransack લૂટવું loontavun
ransom *n.* ખંડણી khandanee
rant *n.* ધમાલિયો બકવાસ dhamaaliyo bakavaas
rap *n.* હળવી ટાપલી halavee taapalee
rapacious *adj.* લોભી lobhee
rapacity *n.* લૂટારુવૃત્તિ lootaaruvrutti
rape *n.* બળાત્કારે સ્ત્રીસંભોગ balaatkaare streesanbhog
rapid *adj.* વેગીલું vegeelun
rapidity *n.* ઝડપ jhadap
rapier *n.* જમૈયો jamaiyo
rapine *n.* લૂટફાટ lootafaat
rapport *n.* એકરાગ ekaraag
rapprochement *n.* સુલેહ suleh
rapt *adj.* તલ્લીન talleen
rapture *n.* અત્યાનંદ atyaanand
rare અસામાન્ય asaamaany
rerefy *v.t.* પાતળું કરવું paatalun karavun
rarely *adv.* જવલ્લે જ javalle ja
rarity *n.* વિરલ વસ્તુ viral vastu
rascal *n.* બદમાશ badamaash
rascality *n.* બદમાશી badamaashee
rase *v.t.* ધ્વંશ કરવો dhvansh karavo
rash *adj.* અતિઅધીરું ati adheerun
rasp *n.* કાનસનો અવાજ kaanasano avaaj
raspberry *n.* કરમદા karamada
rat *n.* ઉંદર undar
ratable *adj.* દર લાયક dar laayak
rate ભાવ bhaav
rather *adv.* વધુ સાચું કહીએ તો vadhu saachun kaheee to
ratification *n.* અનુસર્મથન anusarmathan
ratify *v.t.* અનુસર્મથન કરવું anusarmathan karavun
ratio *n.* ગુણોત્તર gunottar

ratiocination n. તર્કના નિયમોનું પાલન tarkana niyamonun paalan

ration n. સીધુંસામાન seedhunsaamaan

rational adj. સમજશક્તિવાળું samajashaktivaalun

rationale તાર્કિ આધાર taarkik aadhaar

rationalist n. સમજદાર samajadaar

rattle v.i. ખડખડાટ કરવો khadakhadaat karavo

ravage n. પાયમાલી paayamaalee

rave v.i. ઉત્સાહપૂર્વક આલોચના utsaahapoorvak aalochana

ravel v.t. ગૂંચવવું goonchavavun

raven n. જંગલી કાગડો jangalee kaagado

ravenous લૂંટફાટ કરનારું loontafaat karanaarun

ravine n. કોતર kotar

ravish v.t. બળાત્કાર કરવો balaatkaar karavo

ravishment n. સંભોગ sanbhog

raw adj. રાંધ્યા વિનાનું raandhya vinaanun

ray n. પ્રકાશનું કિરણ prakaashanun kiran

rayon n. રેયોન reyon

raze v.t. જમીનદોસ્ત કરવું jameenadost karavun

razor n. અસ્તરો. astro

reach v.t. વિસ્તરવું vistaravun

react v.i. –નો પ્રત્યાઘાત no praanaghaat

reaction n. પ્રતક્રિયા pratikriya

reactionary adj. પ્રત્યાઘાતી વ્યક્તિ pratyaaghaatee vyakti

read v.t. મોટેથી વાંચવું motethee vaanchavun

readable adj. સુવાચ્ય suvaachy

reader n. વાંચનપોથી vaanchanapothee

readiness n. શીઘ્રતા sheeghrata

reading n. વાંચન vaanchan

readjust v.t. ફરીથી ગોઠવવું fareethee gothavavun

ready adj. સજ્જ sajj

readymade adj. તાત્કાલિક ઉપયોગ માટેનું taatkaalik upayog maatenun

real adj. વાસ્તવિક vaastavik

realism n. વાસ્તવવાદ vaastavavaad

realistic adj. વાસ્તવલક્ષી vaastavalakshee

reality n. વાસ્તવિકતા vaastavikata

realization n. અર્થગ્રહણ કરવો arthagrahan karavo

realize v.t. સ્પષ્ટપણે જાણવું spashtapane jaanavun

really adv. ખરેખર kharekhar

realm n. ક્ષેત્ર kshetr

ream n. કાગળના ૨) ઘા kaagalana 2) ghaa

reap v.i. લણવું lanavun

reaper n. લણનાર વ્યક્તિ lananaar vyakti

reappear v.i. ફરી દેખા દેવી faree ekha devee

rear n. પાછળનું paachalanun

rearm v.t. ફેરશસ્ત્રીકરણ ferashastreekaran

rearrange v.t. પુનર્રચના કરવી punarrachana karavee

reason n. કારણ kaaran

reasonable adj. વિવેકી vivekee

reasoning n. દલીલ daleel

reassign v.t. પરત સોંપવું parat sonpavun

reassure v.t. ફેરખાતરી આપવી ferakhaataree aapavee

reave v.t. પડાવી લેવું padaavee levun

rebate v.t. ઓછું કરવું ochhun karavun

rebel n. બળવાખોર balavaakhor

rebellion n. બળવો balavo

rebound n. પ્રત્યાઘાત pratyaaghaat

rebuff n. ધુતકારવું dhutakaaravun

rebuke v.t. ઠપકો આપવો thapako aapavo

rebut v.t. ખંડન કરવું khandan karavun

recalcitrant adj. હઠીલું hatheelun

recall n. બરતરફી baratarafee

recant v.t. સ્વમત ખંડન કરવું svamat khandan karavun

recantation n. સ્વમત ખંડન svamat khandan

recapitulate v.t. સંક્ષેપમાં કહેવું sankshepaman kahevun

recapture *v.t.* ફરીથી પકડવું fareethee pakadavun

recast *v.t.* નવો આકાર આપવો navo aakaar aapavo

recede *v.ti.* પાછા હઠવું paachha hathavun

receipt *n.* રસીદ raseed

receive *v.t.* સ્વીકારવું sveekaaravun

receiver *n.* સ્વીકારનાર sveekaaranaar

recension *n.* પાઠભેદ paathabhed

recent *adj.* તાજેતરનું taajetaranun

recently *adv.* હમણાં હમણાં hamanan hamanan

receptacle *n.* બારદાન baaradaan

reception *n.* સ્વાગતસમારંભ svaagatasamaaranbh

receptive *adj.* ગ્રહણશીલ grahanasheel

recess *n.* વિશ્રાન્તિનો સમય vishraantino samay

recipe *n.* નુસખો. nukhaso

recipient *n.* ગ્રહણ કરનાર grahan karanaar

reciprocal *adj.* વ્યુત્ક્રમ vyutkram

reciprocate *v.t.* પરસ્પર વિનિમય paraspar vinimay

reciprocity *v.t.* આદાનપ્રદાન વૃત્તિ aadaanapradaan vrutti

recital *n.* ગાયન કાર્યક્રમ gaayan kaaryakram

recitation ગાયન gaayan

recite *v.t.* મુખપાઠ કરવો mukhapaath karavo

reckless *adj.* અવિચારી avichaaree

reckon *v.t.* ગણતરી કાઢવી ganataree kaadhavee

reckoning *n.* ગણતરી ganataree

reclaim *v.t.* નવપ્રાપ્ત કરવું navapraapt karavun

reclamation *n.* નવપ્રાપ્તિ navapraapti

recline *v.t.* અઢેલવું adhelavun

recluse *n.* એકાંતવાસી ekaantavaasee

recognition *n.* ઓળખ olakh

recognizance *v.t.* મુચરકો mucharako

recoil *v.i.* આંચકો ખાવો aanchako khaavo

recollect *v.t.* સાંભરવું saanbharavun

rocollection *n.* સ્મરણશક્તિ smaranashakti

recommend *n.* ભલામણ કરવી bhalaaman karavee

recommendation *n.* ભલામણ bhalaaman

recompense *n.* વળતર valatar

reconcile *v.t.* સમાધાન કરાવવું samaadhan karaavavun

reconciliation *n.* મનમેળ manamel

recondite *adj.* ગહન grahan

reconnaissance જાસૂસી પૂર્વેક્ષણ jasoosee purvekshan

reconnoitre *v.t.* જાસૂસી પૂર્વેક્ષણ કરવું jasoosee purvekshan karavun

reconstitute *v.t.* પુનર્રચના કરવી punarrachana karavee

record *n.* નોંધવહી nondhavahee

recorder *n.* અધિકૃત નોંધણીદાર adhikrut nondhaneedaar

recount *v.t.* વિગતવાર કહેવું vigatavaar kahevun

recoup *v.t.* ભરપાઈ કરવું bharapaai karavun

recourse *n.* આશ્રય aashray

recover *v.t.* પાછું મેળવવું paachhun melavavun

recoverable *adj.* વસૂલાતપાત્ર vasulaatpaatra

recovery *n.* વસૂલાત vasoolaat

recreant *adj.* બાયલું baayalun

recreate *v.t.* મનોરંજન કરવું manoranjan karavun

recreation *n.* વિનોદ vinod

recruit *v.t.* ભરતી કરવી bharatee karavee

rectangle *n.* સમચોરસ આકૃતિ samachoras aakruti

rectangular *adj.* સમચોરસ આકારનું samachoras aakaaranun

rectification *n.* સુધારો sudhaaro

rectify શુદ્ધ કરવું shuddh karavun

rectitude *n.* પ્રામાણિકતા praamaanikata

rector *n.* રેક્ટર rectar

recumbent અઢેલીને બેઠેલું adheleene bethelun

recuperate *v.t.* ફરી તંદુરસ્ત થવું faree tandurast thavun

recur *v.i.* ફરીથી યાદ આવવું fareethee yaad aavavun

recurrence *n.* પુનરાવૃત્તિ punaraavrutti

recurrent *adj.* આવર્તક aavartak

red *adj.* લોહી કે અંગારા જેવું lohee ke angaara jevun

redaction *n.* પુનઃસંસ્કરણ punahsansaran

redden *v.t.* લાલ કરવું કે થવું laal karavun ke thavun

reddish *adj.* રાતું raatun

redeem *v.t.* અદા કરવું adaa karavun

redeemer *n.* ઇશુ ખ્રિસ્ત eeshu khrist

redemption *n.* પાપથી મુક્તિ paapathee mukti

redness *n.* લાલાશ laalaash

redolent *adj.* નું તીવ્રપણે સૂચક nu teevrapane soochak

redoubt *n.* નાની કિલ્લેબંધી naanee killebandhee

redoubtable *adj.* બળવાન balavaan

redress *v.t.* પાછું સરખું કરવું paachhu sarakhun karavun

reduce *v.t.* ઘટાડવું ghataadavun

reducible *adj.* પરિવર્તનક્ષમ parivartanksham

reduction *n.* પાયરી ઉતાર paayaree utaar

redundant અનાવશ્યક anaavashyak

reduplicate *v.t.* પુનરાવર્તન કરવું punaraavartan karavun

reed *n.* સુષિરવાદ્ય sushiravaady

reef *n.* ખડકની કરાડ khadaknee karaad

reefy *adj.* ખડકાળ khadakaal

reek *n.* દુર્ગંધ durgandh

reel *n.* ફીરકી feerakee

refection *n.* અલ્પાહાર alpaahaar

refectory *n.* ભોજનશાળા bhojanashaala

refer *v.t.* સંદર્ભ આપવો. sandarbh aapavo

referee *n.* લવાદ lavaad

reference સંદર્ભ sandarbh

referendum *n.* સર્વમત sarvamat

refine *v.t.* ચોખ્ખું કરવું chokhkhun karavun

refined *adj.* સંસ્કારી sanskaaree

refinement *n.* સંસ્કાર sanskaar

refinery *n.* રિફાઇનરી refaainaree

reflect *v.t.* પ્રતિબિંબ પાડવું pratibinb paadavun

reflection *adj.* પરાવર્તન paraavartan

reflective *n.* પ્રતિબિંબ પાડનારું pratibinb paadanaarun

reform *v.* સુધારવું sudhaaravun

reformation *n.* નવરચના navarachana

reformatory સુધારણા કરનારું sudhaarana karanaarun

reformer *n.* સુધારક sudhaarak

refract *v.t.* વક્રીભવન કરવું vakreebhavan karavun

refraction *n.* પ્રત્યાવર્તન pratyaavartan

refractory *adj.* હઠીલું hatheelun

refrain *v.i.* ધ્રુવપદ dhruvapad

refresh *v.t.* તાજું કરવું taajun karavun

refreshing *adj.* તાજગી આપનારું taajagee aapanaarun

refreshment *n.* ઉપાહાર upaahaar

refrigerate *v.t.* થિજાવવું thijaavavun

refrigerator *n.* શીતભવન sheetabhavan

refuge *n.* આશ્રય aashray

refugee *n.* શરણાર્થી sharanaarthee

refulgence *n.* તેજસ્વિતા tejasvita

refund *v.t.* પાછું આપવું paachhun aapavun

refusal *n.* ઇનકાર eenakaar

refuse *v.t.* અસંમતિ દર્શાવવી asanmati darshaavavee

refutation *n.* રદિયો radiyo

refute *v.t.* રદિયો આપવો radiyo aapavo

regain *v.t.* પાછું મેળવવું paachun melavavun

regal *adj.* બાદશાહી baadashaahee

regale *n.* મિજબાની આપવી mijabaanee aapavee

regalia *n.* રાજચિહ્નો raajachinho

regard *v.t.* બારીકાઇથી જોવું baareekaaeethee jovun

regarding *prep.* —ની બાબતમાં nee baabataman

regardless *adj.* બેદરકાર bedarakaar

regency *n.* રાજ પૂરતનિધિનું પદ raaj pratinidhinun pad

regenerate *v.t.* પુનર્જીવતિ કરવું punarjeevit karavun

regeneration *n.* પુનર્જીવન punarjeevan

regent *n.* કારભારી kaarabhaaree

regicide *n.* રાજહત્યા raajahatya

regime *n.* શાસનપદ્ધતિ shaasanapaddhati

regimen *n.* ઉપચાર upachaar

regiment *n.* રેજમિન્ટ rejiment

regina *n.* ગાદીનશીન રાણી gaadeenasheen raanee

region *n.* પ્રદેશ pradesh

register *n.* નોંધપોથી nondhapothee

registrar *n.* નોંધણી અધિકારી nondhanee adhikaaree

registration *n.* નોંધણી. nondhanee

registry *n.* નોંધણી કચેરી nondhanee kacheree

regnal *adj.* રાજ્ય અમલનું raajy amalanun

regress *v.i.* પાછા જવાની વૃત્તિ paachha javaanee vrutti

regression *n.* પીછેહઠ peechhehath

regret *v.t.* ખેદ કરવો khed karavo

regular *n.* નિયમિત niyamit

regularity *n.* નિયમિતતા niyamitata

regularize *v.t.* નિયમસર કરવું niyamasar karavun

regulate *v.t.* નિયમબદ્ધ કરવું niyamabaddh karavun

regulation *n.* કાનૂન kaanoon

regulator *n.* નિયમનકાર niyamankaar

rehabilitation *n.* પુનર્વસવાટ punarvasavaat

rehearsal *n.* પૂર્વપ્રયોગ poorvaprayog

rehearse *v.t.* પૂર્વપ્રયોગ કરવો poorvaprayog karavo

reign *v.t.* રાજ કરવું raaj karavun

reimburse *v.t.* ભરપાઇ કરવું bharapaaee karavun

rein *n.* લગામ lagaam

reindeer *n.* હરણ haran

reinforce *v.t.* બળવત્તર કરવું balavattar karavun

reinforced બલીકૃત baleekrut

reinforcement *n.* પ્રબલીકરણ prabaleekaran

reins *n.* મૂત્રપિંડ mootrapind

reinstate *v.t.* મૂળ સ્થિતિમાં આવવું mool sthitiman aavavun

reinsure *v.t.* ફરી વીમો ઉતરાવવો faree veemo utaraavavo

reinvest *v.t.* ફરીથી નાણુ રોકવું fareethee naanun rokavun

reiterate *v.t.* પુનરુચ્ચારણ કરવું punarurachaaran karavun

reiteration પુનરુચ્ચારણ. punarurachaaran

reive *v.i.* લૂંટી લેવું lootee levun

reject *v.t.* રદ કરવું rad karavun

rejection *n.* અસ્વીકાર asveekaar

rejoice *v.t.* ને આનંદ થવો ne aanand thavo

rejoicing *n.* આનંદ પ્રમોદ aanand pramod

rejoin *v.t.* પ્રત્યુત્તર આપવો pratyuttar aapavo

rejoinder *n.* પ્રત્યુત્તર pratyuttar

rejuvenate *v.i.* કાયાકલ્પ કરવો. kaayaakalp karavo

rejuvenation|દ|ઝ કાયાકલ્પ kaayaakalp

relate *v.t.* બયાન કરવું bayaan karavun

related સંબંધિત sanbanshit

relating *adj.* ની સાથે સંબંધિત nee saathe sanbandhit

relation *n.* સંબંધ sanbandh

relationship *n.* વહેવાર vahevaar

relative *n.* સગું sagun

relax *v.t.* શિથિલ થવું shithil thavun

relaxation *n.* વિશ્રાંતિ vishraanti

relay *n.* બદલી ટુકડી badalee tukadee

release *v.t.* છૂટું કરવું chootun karavun

relegate *v.t.* ઉતરતી કક્ષામાં મૂકવું utaratee kakshaaman mookavun

relegation *n.* અન્યને કરેલી સોંપણી anyane karelee sonpanee

relent *v.t.* કૂણા પડવું koona padavun

relentless *n.* નિર્દય nirday

relevance *n.* સુસંગતતા susangatata

relevant *adj.* સુસંગત susangat

reliability *n.* વિશ્વસનીયતા vishvasaneeyata

reliable *adj.* વિશ્વસનીય vishvasaneey

reliance *n.* વિશ્વાસ vishvaas

relic *n.* સ્મૃતિચિહ્નો smrutichinho

relict *n.* અવશષ્પિટ avashisht

relief *n.* રાહત raahat

relieve *v.t.* ને રાહત આપવી ne raahat aapavee

reliever *n.* છૂટું કરનાર chootun karanaar

religion *n.* ધર્મ dharm

religiose *adj.* ધર્મઘેલું dharmaghelun

religious *adj.* ધાર્મિક dhaarmik

relinquish ત્યાગ કરવું tyaag karavun

relish *n.* શોખ shokh

reluctance *n.* અનિચ્છા anichchha

reluctant *adj.* અનિચ્છાવાળું anichchaavaalun

rely *v.i.* અવલંબન avalanban

remain *v.t.* બાકી રહેવું baakee rahevun

remainder *n.* શેષભાગ sheshabhaag

remains *n.* અવશેષો avashesho

remand *v.t.* રિમાન્ડ rimaand

remark *v.t.* અવલોકન કરવું avalokan karavun

remarkable *adj.* અસાધારણ asaadhaaran

remedy *n.* ઈલાજ eelaaj

remember *v.t.* યાદ રાખવું yaad raakhavun

remembrance *n.* સ્મૃતિ smruti

remind *v.t.* સ્મરણ કરાવવું smaran karaavavun

reminder *n.* સ્મૃતિપત્ર smrutipatr

reminiscence *n.* સંભારણું sanbhaaranun

reminiscent *adj.* સૂચક soochak

remiss *adj.* બેપરવા beparava

remission *n.* માફી maafee

remit *v.t.* માફ કરવું maaf karavun

remittance *n.* મોકલેલા પૈસા mokalela paisa

remittent *adj.* ઓસરી જનારું osaree janaarun

remnant *n.* બચેલો ભાગ bachelo bhaag

remonstrance વાંધો vaandho

remonstrate *v.i.* વાંધો ઉઠાવવો vaandho uthaavavo

remorse *n.* પશ્ચાતાપ pashchaataap

remote *adj.* દૂરના સંબંધવાળું doorana sanbandhavaalun

remount *v.t.* ફરી સવાર થવું faree savaar thavun

removal *n.* સ્થળાંતર sthalaantar

remove *v.t.* દૂર કરવું door karavun

remunerate મહેનતાણું આપવું mahenataanun aapavun

remuneration *n.* મહેનતાણું mahenataanun

remunerative *adj.* લાભદાયી laabhadaayee

renal *adj.* મૂત્રપિંડ સંબંધી mootrapind sanbandhee

rend *v.t.* ચીરવું cheeravun

render *v.t.* બદલામાં આપવું badalaaman aapavun

rendering *n.* ભાષાંતર bhaashaantar

rendezvous *n.* સંકેતસ્થાન sanketasthaan

renegade *n.* પક્ષપલટું pakshapalatun

renew *v.t.* નવીકરણ કરવું naveekaran karavun

renewal *n.* નવીકરણ naveekaran

renounce જતુ કરવું jatu karavun

renovate *v.t.* જીર્ણોદ્ધાર કરવો jeernoddhaar karavo

renown *n.* ખ્યાતિ khyaati

renowned *adj.* સુવિખ્યાત suvikhyaat

rent *n.* ચીરો cheero

rental *n.* ભાડું bhaadun

renunciation સ્વૈચ્છીક પરિત્યાગ svaichchheek parityaag

repair *v.t.* સમારકામ કરવું samaarakaam karavun

repairable *adj.* મરામત યોગ્ય maraamat yogya

reparation *n.* સમારકામ samaarakaam

repartee *n.* હાજર જવાબ haajar javaab

repast *n.* ભોજન bhojan

repatriate *v.t.* સ્વદેશ ગમન svadesh gaman

repay *v.t.* પરત ચૂકવવું parat chookavavun

repeal *v.t.* રદ કરવું rad karavun
repeat *v.t.* ફરી બોલવું faree bolanun
repeatedly વારંવાર vaaranvaar
repel *v.t.* પાછું ધકેલવું paachhun dhakelavun
repent *v.t.* પ્રશ્ચાતાપ કરવો. prashchaataap karavo
repentance *n.* પ્રશ્ચાતાપ prashchaataap
repentant *adj.* પ્રશ્ચાતાપ કરનાર prashchaataap karanaar
repercussion પ્રત્યાઘાત pratyaaghaat
repertory *n.* ઉપરોક્ત ગીત uparokt geet
repetition *n.* પુનરાવર્તન punaraavartan
repine *v.i.* દુઃખી થવું dukhee thavun
replace *v.t.* બદલવું badalavun
replenish *v.t.* ફરી ભરીદેવું faree bhareedevun
replete *adj.* છલોછલ ભરેલું chhalochhal bharelun
replica *n.* પ્રતકૃતિ pratikruti
replication *n.* આબેહૂબ નકલ aabehoob nakal
reply *n.* જવાબ આપવો javaab aapavo
report *v.t.* અહેવાલ આપવો ahevaal aapavo
reporter *n.* ખબરપત્રી khabarapatree
repose *v.t.* વિશ્વાસ મૂકવો. vishvaas mookavo
repository *n.* સંગ્રહસ્થાન sangrahasthaan
reprehend *v.t.* ઠપકો આપવો thapako aapavo
reprehensible *adj.* દોષપાત્ર doshapaatr
reprehension *n.* દોષ dosh
represent પ્રતિનિધિત્વ કરવું pratinidhitv karavun
representation *n.* રજૂઆત rajooaat
representative *n.* દ્રષ્ટાંતરૂપ drashtaantaroop
repress *v.t.* દબાવી રાખવું dabaavee raakhavun
repression *n.* દાબ daab
reprieve *n.* સજા મોકૂફી sajaa mokoofee
reprimand સખત ઠપકો આપવો sakhat thapako aapavo

reprint *v.t.* પુનર્મુદ્રણ punarmudran
reprisal *n.* બદલો badalo
reproach *n.* વઢવું vadhavun
reproachful *adj.* નિંદાત્મક nindaatmak
reprobate *adj.* ધિક્કારવું dhikkaaravun
reprobation *n.* ધિક્કાર dhikkaar
reproduce *v.t.* પુનરુત્પાદન કરવું punarutpaadan karavun
reproduction *v.t.* પ્રતિકૃતિ pratikruti
reproof *n.* ઠપકો thapako
reproval *n.* ઠપકો thapako
reprove ઠપકો આપવો. thapako aapavo
reptile *n.* સરિસૃપ sarisrup
republic *n.* પ્રજાસત્તાક prajaasattaak
republican *adj.* પ્રજાસત્તાક prajaasattaak
republish *v.t.* પુનઃપ્રકાશિત કરવું punahprakaashit karavun
repudiate *v.t.* અસ્વીકાર કરવો asveekaar karavo
repugnance *n.* અણગમો anagamo
repugnant *adj.* અણગમતું anagamatun
repulse *v.t.* પાછું હઠાવવું paachhun hathaavavun
repulsion *n.* તીવ્ર અણગમો teevr anagamo
repulsive *adj.* અણગમો પેદા કરનારું anagamo peda karanaarun
reputable *adj.* આદરપાત્ર aadarapaatr
reputation *n.* પ્રતિષ્ઠા pratishtha
repute *n.* આબરૂ aabaroo
reputed *adj.* નામાંકિત naamaankit
request *v.t.* વિનંતી કરવી vinantee karavee
requiem *n.* શાંતિપ્રાર્થના shaanti praarthanaa
require *v.t.* ની જરૂર હોવી nee jaroor hovee
requirement *n.* આવશ્યકતા aavashyakta
requisite *adj.* જરૂરી jarooree
requisition *n.* લખિત માગણી likhit maaganee
requital *n.* ઈનામ eenaam
requite *v.t.* બદલો આપવો badalo
rescind *v.t.* રદબાતલ કરવું radabaatal karavun

rescission *n.* વિલય vilay
rescue *v.t.* બચાવવું bachaavavun
research *n.* સંશોધન sanshodhan
resemblance *n.* અણસાર anasaar
resemble *v.t.* —ના જેવું હોવું naa jevun hovun
resent *v.t.* માઠું લાગવું maanthun laagavun
resentment *n.* મનદુઃખ manadukh
reservation *n.* આરક્ષણ aarakshan
reserve *v.* અનામત રાખવું anaamat raakhavun
reserved *adj.* અલગ રાખેલું alag raakhelun
reside *v.i.* —માં નિહિત હોવું maan nihit hovun
residence *n.* રહેવાની જગ્યા rahevaanee jagya
resident *n.* રહેવાસી rahevaasee
residential *adj.* આવાસી aavaasee
residual *adj.* બાકી રહેલું baakee rahelun
residue *n.* બચેલો શેષ ભાગ bachelo shesh bhaag
resign *v.t.* નિવૃત્ત થવું nivrutt thavun
resignation *n.* રાજીનામું આપવું તે raajeenaamun aapavun te
resilience *n.* સ્થિતિસ્થાપકતા sthitisthaapakata
resin *n.* રાળ raal
resist *v.t.* નો પ્રતિકાર કરવો no pratikaar karavo
resistible *adj.* પ્રતિકારક્ષમ pratikaaraksham
resolute *adj.* અડગ adag
resolution *n.* નિર્ધાર nirdhaar
resolve *v.t.* નિર્ધાર કરવો nirdhaar karavo
resonance *n.* પડઘો padagho
resonant *adj.* અનુનાદ કરનારું anunaad karanaarun
resort *v.i.* આશરો લેવો aasharo levo
resound *v.i.* પડઘો પડવો padagho padavo
resource *n.* સાધનસામગ્રી saadhanasaamagree
resourceful *adj.* સાધનસંપન્ન saadhanasanpann

respect *n.* આદર aadar
respectable *adj.* આદરણીય aadaraneey
respectful *adj.* અદબવાળું adabavaalun
respecting *prep.* —ની બાબતમાં nee baabataman
respective *adj.* પોતપોતાનું potapotaanun
respetively સાપેક્ષ રીતે saapeksh reete
respiration *n.* શ્વાસોચ્છ્વાસ shvaasochchhaas
respire *v.t.* શ્વાસ લેવો shvaas levo
respite *n.* મહેતલ mahetal
resplendent *adj.* ઝળહળતું jhalahalatun
respond *v.t.* જવાબ આપવો javaab aapavo
respondent *n.* પ્રતિવાદી prativaadee
response *n.* પ્રતિક્રિયા pratikriya
responsibility *n.* જવાબદારી javaabadaaree
responsible *adj.* જવાબદાર javaabadaar
rest *n.* આરામ aaraam
restaurant *n.* ભોજનાલય bhojanaalay
restitution *n.* નુકશાન ભરપાઈ nukashaan bharapaaee
restive *adj.* રઘવાયું raghavaayun
restless *adj.* નિદ્રાહીન nidraaheen
restoration *n.* પુનઃપ્રસ્થાપના punahaprasthaapana
restore *v.t.* પુનઃસ્થાપના કરવી punahasthaapana karavee
restrain *v.t.* અટકાવવું atakaavavun
restraint *n.* અટકાવ atakaav
restrict *v.t.* પ્રતિબંધ મૂકવો. pratibandh mookavo
restriction *n.* પ્રતિબંધ pratibandh
restrictive *adj.* પ્રતિબંધક pratibandhak
resultant *adj.* પરિણામરૂપી parinaamaroopee
resume *v.i.* ફરી શરૂ કરવું faree sharoo karavun
resumption *n.* પુનઃગ્રહણ punahagrahan
resurrect *v.t.* પુનઃજીવિત કરવું punhajeevit karavun
resurrection *n.* પુનર્જીવન punarjeevan

retail *v.i.* છૂટક વેચાણ કરવું chhotak vechaan karavun

retailer *n.* છૂટક વેચાણકાર chootak vechaankaar

retain *v.t.* કબજામાં રાખવું kabajaaman raakhavun

retainer *n.* અનુયાયી anuyaayee

retaliate *v.t.* વેર વાળવું ver vaalavun

retaliation *n.* વેર ver

retaliative *adj.* વેરને લગતું verane lagatun

retard *v.t.* ગતિ અવરોધવી gati avarodhavee

retch *v.t.* ઓકારી આવવી okaaree aavavee

retention *n.* મળાવરોધ malaavarodh

retentive *adj.* રાખવાની વૃત્તિવાળું raakhavaanee vruttivaalun

reticence મૌન maun

reticent *adj.* ઓછાબોલું ochhaabolun

retina *n.* નેત્રપટલ netrapatal

retinue *n.* પરિચારક વર્ગ parichaarak varg

retire *v.i.* નિવૃત્ત થવું nivrutt thavun

retired *adj.* નિવૃત nivrut

retirement *n.* નિવૃત્તિ nivrutti

retort *v.t.* બદલો વાળવો badalo vaalavo

retouch *n.* સુધારવું sudhaaravun

retrace *v.t.* પાછા જવું paachaa javun

retract *v.t.* પાછું ખેંચવું paachhun khenchavun

retreat *v.i.* પાછું હટવું paachhun hatavun

retrench *v.t.* છટણી કરવી chhatanee karavee

retrenchment *n.* છટણી chhatanee

retribution *n.* યોગ્ય શિક્ષા yogy shiksha

retrograde *v.t.* પાછળ લઈ જનારું paachhal laee janaarun

retrogress *v.i.* અધઃપતન થવું adhahapatan thavun

return *v.i.* પાછું આવવું paachhun aavavun

reunion *n.* સ્નેહસંમેલન snehasanmelan

reunite *v.t.* ફરી એકત્ર આણવું faree ekatr aanavun

reveal *v.t.* પ્રગટ કરવું pragat karavun

revel *v.t.* આનંદ માણવો aanand maanavo

revelation *n.* દૈવી સાક્ષાત્કાર daivee saakshaatkaar

revelry *n.* ધમાચકડી dhamaachakadee

revenge *v.t.* વેરની વસૂલાત veranee vasoolaat

revengeful *adj.* કીનાખોર keenaakhor

revenue *n.* વાર્ષિક આવક vaarshik aavak

reverberate *v.t.* પડઘો પડવો padagho padavo

reverberation *n.* પરાવર્તન paraavartan

revere *v.t.* પૂજવું poojavun

reverend *adj.* પૂજ્ય pooj

reverent *adj.* આદરયુક્ત aadarayukt

reverie *n.* કલ્પનાતરંગ kalpanaatarang

reversal *n.* ઊલટોક્રમ oolatokram

reverse *v.t.* વિપરીત અસર કરવી vipareet asar karavee

revert *v.i.* પૂર્વ સ્થિતિએ જવું poorv sthitie javun

review *n.* ફેરતપાસણી feratapaasanee

reviewer *n.* સમાલોચક samaalochak

revile *v.t.* નિંદા કરવી ninda karavee

revision *n.* સુધારવું તે sudhaaravun te

revise *n.* ફરી જોઈ જવું faree joee javun

revival *n.* પુનઃજીવન punahjeevan

revive *v.t.* પુનઃજીવિત કરવું punahjeevit karavun

revocable *adj.* રદ કરવા પાત્ર rad karava paatr

revocation *n.* રદ કરવું તે rad karavun te

revoke *v.t.* પાછું ખેંચી લેવું paachhun khenchee lavun

revolt *v.t.* બળવો કરવો balavo karavo

revolution *n.* રાજ્યક્રાંતિ raajyakraanti

revolutionary *adj.* ક્રાંતિકારક kraantikaarak

revolutionist *n.* ક્રાંતિવાદી kraantivaadee

revolutionize ક્રાંતિ લાવવી kranti laavavee

revolve *v.t.* મનમાં ઘોળ્યા કરવું manaman gholya karavun

revolver *n.* રિવોલ્વર rivolvar
revulsion *n.* નફરત nafarat
reward *n.* બક્ષિસ bakshis
rhapsodist *n.* ઉત્સાહી વક્તા utsaahee vaktaa
rhapsody *n.* અસંબદ્ધ વ્યાખ્યાન asanbaddh vyaakhyaan
rhetoric *n.* અલંકારશાસ્ત્ર alankaarashaastr
rhetorical *adj.* અતિશિયોક્તિવાળું atishayoktivaalun
rhinoceros *n.* ગેંડો gendo
rhyme *n.* અનુપ્રાસ anuprasaar
rhythm *n.* લય lay
rhythmic તલબદ્ધતા talabaddhata
rib *n.* પાંસળી paansalee
ribald *n.* હલકટ halakat
ribaldry *n.* બીભત્સ વાણી beebhats vaanee
riband *n.* ફીત feet
rice *n.* ચોખા chokha
rich *n.* પૈસાદાર paisaadaar
richness *n.* વિપુલતા vipulata
rick *n.* ઘાસની ગંજી ghaasanee ganjee
rickets *n.* બાળકોનો સુકતાન રોગ baalakono sukataan rog
rickety *adj.* ખખડી ગયેલું khakhadee gayelun
ricksha *n.* રક્ષિા rikshaa
rid *v.t.* મુક્ત કરવું mukt karavun
riddance *n.* છુટકારો chhutakaaro
riddle *n.* ઉખાણું ukhaanun
ride *v.t.* ઘોડા પર બેસવું ghoda par besavun
rider *n.* ઘોડા પર બેસનાર ghoda par besanaar
ridge *n.* સાંકડી ટોચ saankadee toch
ridicule *n.* ઉપહાસ upahaas
ridiculous *adj* હાસ્યાસ્પદ haasyaaspad
riding *n.* ઘોડેસવારી ghodesavaaree
rife *adj.* પ્રચલિત prachaleet
rifle *n.* રાઈફલ raaifal
riff-raff *n.* રઝળતા લોકો rajhalata loko
rift *n.* તરાડ taraad
rig *v.t.* ચાલાકી કરવી chaalaakee karavee
right *adj.* ઉચિત uchit
right angle *n.* કાટખૂણો kaatakhoono

righteous *adj.* પ્રામાણિક praamaanik
rightful *adj.* હકનું hakanun
rigid *adj.* અક્કડ akkad
rigidity *n.* કડકાઈ kadakaaee
rigorous *adj.* આકરું aakarun
rigour *n.* સખતાઈ sakhataaee
rill *n.* વહેળિયું vaheliyun
rim *n.* કિનાર kinaar
rime *n.* ઝાકળ jhaakal
rimy *adj* ઝાકળવાળું jhaakalavaalun
rind *n.* છાલ chhaal
ring *n.* વીંટી veentee
ringlet *n.* લટકતા વાળની લટ latakata vaalanee lat
ringmaster *n.* રિંગમાસ્ટર ringamaastar
ringworm *n.* દાદર daadar
rinse *v.t.* વીંછળવું veenchhaalavun
riot *n.* હુલ્લડ hullad
riotous *adj.* તોફાની tofaanee
rip *v.t.* ફાડી નાખવું faadee naakhavun
ripe *adj.* પરિપક્વ paripakv
ripen *v.t.* પાકવું paakavun
ripple *n.* પાણીનો ખળભળાટ paaneeno khalabhalaat
rise *v.t.* ઊભા થવું oobha thavun
risible *adj.* હસનારું hasanaarun
rising *n.* બળવો. balavo
risk *n.* જોખમ jokham
risky *adj.* જોખમ ભરેલું jokham bharelun
rite *n.* વ્રતપાલન vratapaalan
rituals *adj.* વિધિપૂર્વકનું vidhipoorvakanun
rival *n.* હરીફ hareef
rivalry *n.* હરીફાઈ hareefaaee
rive *v.t.* ફાડવું faadavun
river *n.* નદી nadee
riverside *n.* નદીકાંઠાનો પ્રદેશ nadeekaanthaano pradesh
rivet *n.* રિવટ rivet
rivulet *n.* નાનકડી નદી naanakadee nadee
road *n.* રસ્તો rasto
roam *v.i.* રખડવું rakhadavun
roan *n.* કાબરચીતરું kaabaracheetarun
roar *n.* ગર્જના garjana
roaring *adj.* ગર્જનારું garjanaarun

151

roast *v.t.* દેવતા પર શેકવું devata par shekavun

rob *v.t.* લૂંટવું loontavun

robber *n.* લૂંટારો loontaaro

robbery *n.* લૂંટ loont

robe *n.* ઝભ્ભો jhabhbho

robin *n.* રોબિન robin

robot *n.* મનુષ્યાકૃતિ યંત્ર manushyaakruti yantr

robust *adj.* ખડતલ khadatal

rock *n.* ખડક khadak

rocket *n.* રૉકેટ roket

rocking-chair *n.* ઝૂલાખુરશી jhoolaakhurashee

rock-oil *n.* ખનિજ તેલ khanij tel

rock-salt *n.* સિંધાલૂણ sindhaaloon

rocky *adj.* ખડકાળ khadakaal

rodent *adj.* ખિસકોલી khisakolee

rodomontade *adj.* બડાશ badaash

roe *n.* નાનું હરણ naanun haran

rogue *n.* બદમાશ badamaash

roguery *n.* બદમાશી badamaashee

roguish *adj.* બદમાશ badamaash

role *n.* નિયતકાર્ય niyatakaary

roll *v.t.* ગબડતાં જવું તે gabadatan javun te

roll-call *n.* હાજરી haajaree

roller *n.* વેલણ velan

romance *n.* રોમાંચક (કલ્પિત) ઘટનાઓ. romaanchak (kalpit) ghatanao

romantic *adj.* અદ્ભુત રસવાળું addabhut rasavaalun

romp ધિંગામસ્તી dhigaamastee

rood *n.* ઈશુનો ક્રૂસ eeshuno kroos

roof *n.* મકાનનું છાપરું makaananun chhaaparun

rook *n.* કાળું kaalun

room *n.* ઓરડો orado

roomy *adj.* મોકળાશવાળું. mokalaaashavaalun

roost *n.* પક્ષીનું વિશ્રાન્તિસ્થાન paksheenun vishraantisthaan

root *n.* મૂળિયું mooliyun

rope *n.* દોરડું doradun

rosary *n.* ગુલાબવાડી gulaabavaadee

rose *n.* ગુલાબનો છોડ gulaabano chhod

roseate *adj.* ગુલાબી રંગનું gulaabee ranganun

rosette *n.* રોસેટ roset

rosin *n.* રાજન raajan

rostrum *n.* વ્યાખ્યાન મંચ vyaakhyaan manch

rosy *adj.* આશાવાળું aashaavaalun

rot *v.i.* કહોવડાવવું kahovadaavavun

rotary *adj.* વારાફરતી કરનારું vaaraafaratee karanaarun

rotate *v.i.* કક્ષામાં ફરવું kakshaaman faravun

rotation *n.* ક્રમાનુસાર kramaanusaar

rotative *adj.* આવર્તક aavartak

rote *n.* ગોખણપટ્ટી gokhanapattee

rotten *adj.* મૂર્ખામીભરેલું moorkhaameebharelun

rotund *adj.* ભરાવદાર bharaavadaar

rotunda *n.* ગોળ ઓરડો gol orado

rough *n.* ખરબચડું kharabachadun

round *adj.* ગોળ gol

rouse *v.t.* પ્રવૃત્ત થવું pravrutt thavun

rout *n.* નાસભાગ naasabhaag

route *n.* માર્ગ maarg

routine *n.* નિયમિત niyamit

rove *v.t.* રઝળવું rajhalavun

rover *n.* દરિયાઈ લૂંટેરો dariyaaee luntero

row *n.* પંક્તિ pankti

rowdism *n.* શોરબકોર shorabakor

rowdy *adj.* ધાંધલિયું dhaandhaliyun

royal *adj.* રાજવી raajavee

royalist *n.* રાજાનો પુરસ્કર્તા raajaano puraskartaa

royalty *n.* રાજવીઓ raajaveeo

rub *v.t.* ઘસવું ghasavun

rubber *n.* રબર rabar

rubbish *n.* કચરો khacharo

rubble *n.* રોડાં rodan

rubstone *n.* સરાણનો પથ્થર saraanano paththar

ruby *n.* માણેક maanek

ruck *v.t.* કરચલી પડવી karachalee paadavee

rudder *n.* વહાણનું સુકાન vahaananun sukaan

ruddy *adj.* સુરખીદાર surakheedaar

rude *adj.* સાદું saadun

rudeness *n.* તોછડાઈ tochhadaaee

rudiment *n.* મૂળ તત્ત્વો mool tattvo

rudimentary *adj.* મૂળારંભનું moolaaranbhanun

rue *v.t.* નો અફસોસ કરવો no afasos karavo

ruffian *n.* બદમાશ badamaash

ruffle *v.t.* અસ્વસ્થ કરવું asvasth karavun

rug *n.* ગાદલું gaadalun

rugged *adj.* ખરબચડું kharabachadun

ruin *n.* પતન patan

ruinous *adj.* વિનાશક vinaashak

ruins *n.* અવશેષો avashesho

rule *v.t.* નિયમ niyam

ruler *n.* રાજકર્તા raajakarta

ruling *adj.* પ્રચલિત prachaleet

rum *n.* રમ ram

rumble *v.t.* ગડગડાટ કરવો gadagadaat karavo

ruminate *v.t.* વાગોળવું vaagolavun

rumination *n.* વાગોળવાની ક્રિયા vaagolavaanee kriya

rummage *v.t.* ખોળાખોળ કરવી kholaakhol karavee

rummy *n.* વિલક્ષણ vilakshan

rumour *n.* અફવા afava

rump *n.* પ્રાણી કે માણસના કૂલા praanee ke maanasana koola

run *v.t.* દોડવું dodavun

runagate *n.* રખડું માણસ rakhadun maanas

runaway *n.* ભાગેડું માણસ bhaagedun maanas

rung *n.* સીડીનું પગથિયું seedeenun pagathiyun

runlet *n.* નાનું ઝરણું naanun jharanun

runner *n.* ખેપિયો khepiyo

running *adj.* દોડ dod

rupee *n.* રૂપિયો roopiyo

rupture *v.t.* ફાટવું faatavun

rural *adj.* ગામડાનું gaamadaanun

ruse *n.* પ્રપંચ prapanch

rush *v.i.* ધસવું ghasavun

russet *adj.* ભૂરું bhoorun

rust *n.* કાટ kaat

rustic *adj.* ગામઠી gaamathee

rusticate *v.t.* ગામડામાં રહેવું gaamadaaman rahevun

rustle *v.i.* ખડખડાટ khadakhadaat

rusty *adj.* કટાયેલું kataayelun

rut *n.* ચીલો cheelo

ruth *n.* અનુકંપા anukanpa

ruthless *n.* નિષ્ઠુર nishthur

rye *n.* એક જાતનું અનાજ ek jaatanun anaaj

ryot *n.* ભારતીય ખેડૂત "રૈયત" bhaarateey khedoot "raiyat"

S

sabbath *n.* સબાથ sabaath

sable *adj.* ગમગીન. Gamageen

sabotage *n.* ઈરાદાપૂર્વકની ભાંગફોડ Iraadaapurvak bhaangfod

sabre *n.* તલવાર Talavaar

sac *n.* અનૃતસ્તુવચાની કોથળી Antastvachaanee kothalee

saccharin *n.* ખૂબ ગળ્યું Khub galyun

sack *n.* હાંકી કાઢવું haankee kaadhavun

sackcloth *n.* ગૂણપાટ goonapaat

sacrament *n.* ખ્રિસ્તી વિધિ khristee vidhi

sacred *adj.* પવિત્ર Pavitra

sacrifice *v.t.* બલિદાન આપવું balidaan aapavun

sacrificial *adj.* બલિદાનને લગતું balidaan ne lagatun

sacrificer *n.* બલિદાન આપનાર balidaan aapanaar

sacrilege *n.* અપવિત્ર કરવું apavitra karavun

sacrilegious *n.* નાસ્તિક naastik

sacrosanct *adj.* રક્ષિત rakshit

sad *adj.* દુઃખી Dukhee

sadden *v.t.* દુઃખી થવું – કરવું. Dukhee Thavu - Karvu

saddle *n.* જીન Jeen

saddler *n.* જીનગર Jeengar

sadism *n.* પરપીડનવૃત્તિ Parpeedanvruti

sadly *adv.* દુઃખદ Dukhad

sadness *n.* દુઃખ Dukh
safe *adj.* સહીસલામત Saheesalaamat
safeguard *n.* સંરક્ષણ વ્યવસ્થા Sanrakshan vyavsthaa
safety *n.* સલામતી Salaamatee
saffron *n.* ભગવું Bhagavu
sag *v.* વાંકું વળવું Vaanku Valvu
sagacious *adj.* ડાહ્યું, ચતુર Daahyu, Chatur
sagacity *n.* ડહાપણ Dahaapan
sage *n.* ડાહ્યું Dahyu
sago *n.* સાબુદાણા Saabudaanaa
sail *v.t.* વહાણનાં બધાં સઢ Vahaanna badhaa sadh
sailing *n.* વહાણમાં મુસાફરી Vahaanmaa musaafaree
sailor *n.* ધંધાદારી ખારવો Dhandhaadaaree khaarvo
saint *n.* સંત sant
saintly *adj.* સંત જેવું Sant jevun
sake *n.* અમુકને ખાતર Amukne Khaatar
salable *adj.* વેચવા લાયક Vechvaa laayak,
salad *n.* સલાડ salaad
salary *n.* પગાર Pagaar
sale *n.* વેચાણ vechaan
salesman *n.* વેચાણકર્તા vechaanakartaa
salient *adj.* આગળ પડતું Aagal Padtun
saline *adj.* મીઠાવાળું Meethaavaalun
saliva *n.* લાળ Laal
salivate *v.t.* લાળ પેદા કરવી laal pedaa karavee
sallow *adj.* વિલાનો છોડ vilaano chhod
sally *n.* ઠઠ્ઠા Thaththaa
salmon *n.* સેલમન માછલી selaman maachalee
saloon *n.* દીવાનખાનું Deevaankhaanu
salt *n.* મીઠું Meethun
saltish *adj.* સાધારણ ખારું Saadhaaran Khaarun
saltpetre *n.* સૂરોખાર Soorokhaar
salubrious *adj.* આરોગ્યદાયક Aarogyadaayak
salutary *adj.* લાભદાયક Laabhdaayak
salutation *n.* સલામ Salaam
salute *v.t.* સ્વાગત કરવું Swaagat karvun

salvation *n.* આત્મોદ્ધાર Aatmodhdhaar
salve *n.* દિલિને સહારો આપવો Dilne Sahaaro Aapvo
salver *n.* થાળ Thal
salvo *n.* તોપમારો topamaaro
same *adj.* એક સરખું Ek Sarakhun
sameness *n.* સરખાપણું Sarkhaapanun
sample *n.* નમૂનો namoonao
sanctify *v.t.* ને પવિત્ર કરવું Ne Pavitra karvun
sanction *n.* મંજૂરી manjooree
sanctity *n.* સાધુતા Saadhutaa
sanctuary *n.* દેવળ Deval
sand *n.* રેતી Retee
sandal *n.* ચંપલ Champal
sandal-wood *n.* ચંદનનું લાકડું Chandannu Laakdun
sane *adj.* સાબૂત મનનું Saaboot Mannu
sanguine *adj.* લોહીના જેવું રાતું Loheena jevun Raatu
sanitary *adj.* સ્વચ્છ Swachchh
sanitation *n.* આરોગ્ય અને સ્વચ્છતા Aarogya ane Swachchhtaa
sanity *n.* મનનું સાબૂતપણું Mananun Saabootpanun
sap *n.* ભૂગર્ભસુરંગ Bhoogarbhsurang
sapid *adj.* લહેજતદાર Lahejatdar
sapience *n.* વિવેકબુદ્ધિ Vivekbudhdhi
sapient *adj.* ડાહ્યું daahyu
sapling *n.* રોપો Ropo
sapphire *n.* ઈન્દ્રનીલ મણિ Indraneel Mani
sappy *adj.* જીવનરસવાળું Jeevanrasvaalu
saracen *n.* આરબ Aarab
sarcasm *n.* મર્મવચન Marmvachan
sarcastic *adj.* કટું કે કડવું Katun ke Kadvun
sarcophagus *n.* પથ્થરની કબર pattharanee kabar
sardonic *adj.* કડવી મશ્કરીવાળું Kadvee mashkareevaalu
sash *jn.* ખેસ khes
sat *p.t.* શનિવારનું સંક્ષિપ્ત Shanivaarnu sankshipt
satan *n.* શેતાન Shetaan

satanic *adj.* શેતાનના જેવું Shetaannaa Jevun

satchel *n.* વિદ્યાર્થીનું દફ્તર Vidhyaartheenu Daftar

sateen *n.* સાટીન saateen

satellite *n.* ઉપગ્રહ upahrah

satiate *v.t.* સંતુષ્ટ કરવું santusht karavun

satiety *n.* આતતૃપ્તિ Aattrupti

satin *n.* સાટીન saateen

satire *n.* ઉપહાસ upahaas

satirist *n.* ઉપહાસકાર uphaaskaar

satirize *v.t.* ઉપહાસ કરવો uphaas karavo

satisfaction *n.* સંતોષ Santosh

satisfactory *adj.* સંતોષકારક Santoshkaarak

satisfy *v.t.* સંતુષ્ટ કરવું santusht karavun

satrap *n.* પરશિયાનો ગવર્નર parshiano gavarnar

saturate સારી પેઠે ભીજવવું Saari pethe bheejvvun

saturation *n.* પૂરેપૂરું ભરી દેવું તે Poorepoorun bharee devun te

saturday *n.* શનિવાર Shanivaar

saturn *n.* રોમનો કૃષિદેવ romano krushidev

satyr *n.* હવસખોર માણસ havasakhor maanas

sauce *n.* ચટણી Chatnee

saucer *n.* રકાબી rakaabee

saucy *adj.* ઉદ્ધત Udhdhat

saunter *n.* આરામથી ચાલવું Aaraamthee chaalvun

sausage *n.* કુલમો kulamo

savage *adj.* અણસુધરેલું Ansudhrelu

savanna *n.* ઘાસનું જંગલ ghaasanu jangal

savant *n.* અતિવિદ્વાન માણસ Ati vidhvaan maanas

save બચાવવું Bachaavvu

saving *n.* શરતી Shartee

saviour *n.* બચાવનાર Bachaavnaar

savour *n.* સ્વાદ Swaad

savoury *n.* લહેજતદાર Lahejatdaar

saw *n.* જૂની કહેવત Joonee kahevat

sawdust *n.* લાકડાંનો વહેર Laakdaano vaher

sawyer *n.* લાકડાં વહેરનાર Laakdaan Vahernaar

say *v.t.* કહેવું Kahevun

saying *n.* ઉક્તિ Ukti

scabbard *n.* મ્યાન Myaan

scaffold *n.* ફાંસીનો માંચડો Fanseeno Manchdo

scaffolding *n.* પાલખ paalakh

scald *n.* પાણીથી દાઝવું paaneethee daazavun

scale *n.* ભીંગડા Bheengdaa

scalene *adj.* વિષમભુજ Vishambhuj

scall *n.* માથાનો ખોડો Maathaano khodo

scalp *n.* ખોપડીની ચામડી khopadeenee chaamadee

scamp *n.* હરામખોર Haraamkhor

scamper *v.t.* પલાયન કરવું palaayan karavun

scan *v.t.* ઝીણી તપાસ કરવી zeenee tapaas karavee

scandal *n.* નિંદા Nindaa

scandalize *v.t.* દુભાવવું dubhaavavun

scandalous *adj.* શરમભરેલું Sharambharelu

scant *adj.* માંડ પૂરતું Maand Poortu

scanty *adj.* ઓછું Ochhun

scapegoat *n.* હોળીનું નાળિયેર Holeenu naaliyer

scapegrace *n.* હરામખોર Haraamkhor

scar *n.* જખમની નિશાની Jakhamnee nishaani

scarce *adj.* અપૂરતું Apoortu

scarcely *adv.* ભાગ્યે જ Bhaagye j

scarcity *n.* અછત Achhat

scare *n.* ભડકાવી મારવું Bhadkaavee maarvu

scarecrow *n.* ચાડિયો chaadiyo

scarf *n.* ગલપટ્ટો galapatto

scarp *n.* આકરો ઢાળ aakaro dhaal

scathe *v.t.* સાજું નરવું Saaju Narvun

scatter *v.t.* ચોમેર વેરવું chomer veravun

scavenger *n.* રસ્તો સાફ કરનાર Rasto Saaf karnar

scene *n.* ઘટના સ્થળ Ghatnaa sthal

scenery *n.* રંગભૂમિના દૃશ્યો Rangbhuminaa drashyo

scent *n.* સોડમ Sodam

sceptic *n.* નાસ્તિક Naastik

scepticism *n.* સંશયવાદ Sanshayvaad
sceptre *n.* રાજદંડ Raajdand
schedule *n.* વગિતવારનું નોંધપત્રક Vigatvaarnu Nondhpatrak
scheme *n.* યોજના Yojnaa
schism *n.* મતભેદ matabhed
scholar *n.* વદ્દિધાન મહાપંડતિ Vidhvaan mahaapandit
scholarly *adj.* વદ્દિધતાભર્યુ Vidhvtaabharyu
scholarship *n.* વદ્દિવતા Vidhvtaa
scholastic *adj.* શક્ષિણ સંબંધી shikshan sanbandhee
school *n.* શાળા Shaalaa
schooling *n.* શાળાશક્ષિણ Shaalaashikshan
sciatica *n.* રાંઝણ કે રાંઝણી Raanzan ke Ranzanee
science *n.* વज्ञાન vigyaan
scientific *adj.* વૈज्ञાનકિ vaigyaanik
scientist *n.* વज्ञાનશાસ્ત્રનો અભ્યાસી Vigyaanshaastrano abhyaasee
scimitar *n.* કટાર Kataar
scintillate *v.i.* ચળકવું Chalkvun
sciolist *n.* લેભાગુ માણસ lebhaagu maanas
scion *n.* પોતે પાંગરીને Pote paangreene
scissors *n.* કાતર Kaatar
scoff *v.t.* તુષ્કારવું Tushkaarvu
scold *v.t.* સખત ઠપકો આપવો Sakhat thapko aapvo
scoop *n.* પાવડો paavado
scope *n.* ગુંજાશ gunjaash
scorch *v.t.* શેકી નાખવું Shekee naakhvun
score *n.* છેકો Chheko
scorer *n.* ગણતરીકાર ganatareekaar
scorn *v.t.* ધક્કિાર Dhikkar
scornful *adj.* તરિસ્કારવાળું Tirskaarvaalun
scorpion *n.* વીછી Veenchhee
scot *n.* કરવેરો Karvero
scotfree *adj.* કરવેરામાંથી મુક્ત Karveraamaathee mukt
scoundrel *n.* હરામખોર Haraamkhor
scour *v.t.* ઘસીને સાફ કરવું ghaseene saaf karavun

scourge *n.* ચાબુક Chaabuk
scout *n.* બાલવીર baalaveer
scowl *v.t.* તોબરો ચડાવવો Tobro chadaavvo
scramble *v.t.* ઝડપથી આગળ વધવું zadapathee aagal vadhavun
scrap *n.* ટુંકડો Tunkdo
scrape *v.t.* છોલી કાढ़वुं Chholee kaadhvu
scratch *n.* ઉઝરડાં પાડવા Uzardan paadvaa
scrawl *v.t.* ઘસડવું Ghasdavun
scream *n.* ચીસ પાડવી chees paadavee
screech *n.* તીણી ચીસ teenee chees
screen *n.* પડદો Paddo
screw *n.* પેચ Pech
scribble *v.t.* દમ વનિાનु લખાણ Dam vinaanu lakhaan
scribbler *n.* ક્ષુદ્ર લેખક Kshudra lekhak
scribe *n.* લહયિો lahiyo
scrip *n.* પાકટિ Pakit
script *n.* હસ્તાક્ષર Hastaakshar
scripture *n.* ગ્રંથ granth
scroll *n.* નામાવલि naamaavali
scrotum *n.* અંડકોષ Andkosh
scrub *v.t.* બહુ જોરથી ઘસવું Bahu jorthee ghasvun
scrutinize *v.t.* ઝીણવટથી જોવું કે તપાસવું Zinvatthi jovun ke tapaasvun
scuffle *n.* ધक्કામुક्की dhakkamukki
scull *n.* હલેસાંની જોડમાંનું એક Halensanee jodmaanu ek
sculptor *n.* શલ્પી Shilpee
sculpture *n.* શલ्पकला Shilkalaa
scum *n.* પ્રવાહી પદાર્થ પર બાઝતો મેલ Pravahee padaarth par baazto mel
scurf *n.* ખોડો Khodo
scurrilous *adj.* ગાળો ભાંડનારું Gaalo bhaandnaaru
scurvy *n.* હલકટ halkat
scythe *n.* વલિાયતી દાતરડું vilaayatee daatardu
sea *n.* દરયિો Dariyo
seaboard *n.* દરયિાકાંઠાનો પ્રદેશ Dariyaakathaano pradesh
seal *n.* સીલ માછલી seel maachhalee

seam *n.* સીવણ Seevan

seaman *n.* ખારવો Khaarvo

seamster *n.* સઈ Sai

seamstress *n.* દરજણ Darjan

sear *v.t.* તપાવેલા લોઢા વડે ડામ દેવો Tapaavelaa lodhaa vade daam devo

search *v.t.* શોધવું Shodhvun

searching *adj.* તપાસ tapaas

searover *n.* ચાંચિયો Chaanchiyo

season *n.* ઋતુ rutu

seasonable *adj.* સમયાનુરૂપ samayaanuroop

seasoned *adj.* ઋતુ, મોસમ Rutu Mosam

seal *n.* બંધ કરવું bandh karavun

secede *v.i.* કોઈ ધર્મસંઘ Koi dharmsangh

secession *n.* જુદું પડવું તે Judu padvu te

seclude *v.t.* એકાંતમાં મૂકવું Ekantman mookvu

seclusion *n.* એકાન્ત જગ્યા Ekaant Jagyaa

second *adj.* બીજું Beeju

secondary *adj.* ઓછા મહત્ત્વનું Ochha mahatvnu

secrecy *n.* ગુપ્ત રાખવું તે Gupta raakhvun te

secret *n.* ગુપ્ત Gupta

secretary *n.* મંત્રી Mantree

secretariate *n.* સચિવાલય Sachivaalay

secretary *n.* સચિવ sachiv

secrete છુપાવવું Chhupaavvun

secretion *n.* નિસ્સરણ Nisaran

secretive *adj.* ગોપનીય gopaneey

sect *n.* સંપ્રદાય Sampradaay

sectarian *adj.* સાંપ્રદાયિક Saampradaayik

section *n.* કાપી કાઢેલો ભાગ Kaapee kaadhelo bhaag

sector *n.* ક્ષેત્ર kshetra

secular *adj.* બિનસાંપ્રદાયિક Binsaampradaayik

secure *adj.* સલામત salaamat

security *n.* સલામતી Salaamatee

sedan *n.* મ્યાનો myaano

sedate *adj.* શાંત Shaant

sedative *adj.* ઉપશામક upashaamak

sedentary *adj.* બેસતું Bestu

sedge *n.* ઘાસ ghaas

sediment *n.* નિક્ષેપ nikshep

seditious *adj.* બળવો balavo

seduce *v.t.* શીલભંગ માટે લલચાવવું sheelbhang maate lalachaavavun

seduction *n.* ભ્રષ્ટ કરવું કે થવું તે Bhrast karvun ke thavun te

seductive *adj.* ખોટે રસ્તે લઈ જનારું Khote raste lai janaarun

sedulous *adj.* ખંતીલું Khanteelun

see જોવું jovun

seed *n.* બી bee

seedling *n.* બીમાંથી ઉછરેલો છોડ Beemathi uchhrelo chhod

seek *v.t.* શોધવું Shodhvun

seem *v.i.* ઉપર ઉપરથી દેખાવું Upar uparthi dekhaavu

seeming *adj.* દેખીતું dekheetun

seemly *adj.* છાજતું Chhajtu

seepage *n.* ઝમવું તે Zamvun te

seer *n.* જોનારો Jonaaro

seesaw *n.* અનિયમિત ગતિ aniyamit gati

seethe *n.* ઉકાળવું Ukaalvun

segment *n.* અંશ ansh

segregate *v.t.* વિભાજન કરવું vibhaajan karvun

segregation *n.* વિભાજન vibhaajan

seigneur *n.* સરંજામદાર sarnjaamadaar

seismal *adj.* ધરતીકંપનું dharateekanpnun

seismograph *n.* સીસ્મોગ્રાફ sismograf

seize *v.t.* જપ્ત કરવું japt karvun

seizure *n.* જપ્તી jatpee

seldom *adj.* ભાગ્યે જ Bhaagye j

select *v.t.* પસંદ કરવું pasand karvun

selection *n.* પસંદ કરવું તે Pasand karvun te

selective *adj.* પસંદગીપાત્ર pasandageepaatra

selector *n.* વિશિષ્ટ Vishisht

self *n.* પંડ Pand

self-centred *adj.* સ્વાર્થી Swaarthee

self-confidence *n.* આત્મ વિશ્વાસ Aatma vishvaas

self-control *n.* સ્વ અંકુશ sw ankush

self-denial *n.* મન મારવું તે man maarvu te

self-esteem *n.* સ્વાભિમાન swaabhimaan

selfish *n.* સ્વાર્થી Swaarthee

selfishness *n.* સ્વાર્થપણું Swaarthpanu

self-respect *n.* સ્વાભિમાન Swabhimaan

selfsame *n.* એ જ E J

sell *v.t.* વેચવું Vechvun

semaphore *n.* સેમફોર semafor

semblance *n.* સાદ્રશ્ય saadrashya

semen *n.* વીર્ય Veerya

semester *n.* એક સત્ર ek satra

semi *adj.* અર્ધ ardha

seminal *adj.* વીર્ય સંબંધી veerya sanbandhee

seminar *n.* ચર્ચામંડળ Charchaamandal

seminary *n.* પાદરીની શાળા paadareenee shaalaa

senate *n.* ધારાસભા dhaaraasabhaa

senator *n.* સેનેટનો સદસભ્ય Senetno sadsabhya

send *v.t.* ને મોકલવું Ne mokalvun

send off *n.* વિદાય Vidaay

senescent *adj.* ઘરડું થયેલું Ghardun thayelun

senile *adj.* વૃદ્ધાવસ્થાદર્શી vrudhhaavasthaadarshee

senility *n.* ઘડપણની નબળાઈ Ghadpannee nablaai

senior *adj.* ઉપરી uparee

seniority *n.* જ્યેષ્ઠતા Jayeshthtaa

sensation *n.* સંવેદના Samvednaa

sense *n.* ચેતના chetanaa

senseless *n.* સાવ મૂરખ Saav murkh

sensibility *n.* સંવેદનક્ષમતા Samvedankshamtaa

sensible *adj.* સમજુ Samju

sensitive *adj.* સંવેદનશીલ Samvedansheel

sensorial *adj.* સંવેદનાવાહક Samvednavaahak

sensorium સંવેદનાસ્થાન Samvedanaasthaan

sensual *n.* વિષયાસક્ત Vishyaasakt

sensualism *n.* વિષયાસક્ત વૃત્તિ Vishyasakt vruti

sensuality *n.* વિષયાસક્તિ Vishyasakti

sentence *n.* વાક્ય Vaakya

sentiment *n.* લાગણી Laagnee

sentimental *adj.* લાગણીવશ Laagneevash

sentinel *n.* સંતરી Santree

sentry *n.* ચોકીદાર Chokeedaar

separable *adj.* વિભાજ્ય vibhaajya

separate *v.t.* નોખું Nokhun

separately *n.* અલગથી Alagthee

separation *n.* વિભાજન vibhaajan

sepoy *n.* હિન્દી લશ્કરી સિપાઈ Hindi lashkree sipaai

sepsis *n.* કોહ Koh

september *n.* સપ્ટેમ્બર મહિનો Saptembar mahino

septennial *adj.* સપ્તવાર્ષિક Saptvaarshik

septic *adj.* કહોવાણ કરે એવું Kahovaan kare evun

sepulchre *n.* કબર Kabar

sepulture *n.* દફન Dafan

sequacious *adj.* આજ્ઞાનુવર્તી Aagnaanuvartee

sequel *n.* અનુગામી anugaamee

sequence *n.* અનુક્રમ Anukram

sequester *v.i.* જુદું કાઢવું કે કરવું Judun kaadhvun ke karvun

sequestration *n.* તાત્પૂરતી જપ્તી Taatpoortee japtee

seragilo *n.* અન્તઃપૂર કે જનાનખાનું Anthpur ke Janaankhaanun

seraph *n.* દેવદૂત devadoot

sere *adj.* કરમાયેલું Karmaayelun

serene *adj.* સ્વચ્છ Swachchh

serenity સ્વચ્છતા Swachchhtaa

serf *n.* વૈતરો Vaitro

serfdom *n.* ખેતગુલામી Khetgulaamee

serge *n.* ઊની કાપડ oonee kaapad

serial *adj.* પંક્તિ Pankti

sericulture *n.* કોશેટા ઉછેર koshetaa ucher

series *n.* શ્રેણી Shrenee

serious *adj.* વિચારશીલ Vichaarsheel

seriousness *n.* ગંભીરતા Gambheerta

sermon *n.* ધાર્મિક પૂરવચન dhaarmik pravachan

serpent *n.* સર્પ Sarp

serpentine *adj.* સાપના જેવું Saapnaa jevun

serum *n.* લોહીનો પ્રવાહી અંશ loheeno pravaahee ansh

servant *n.* નોકર Nokar

serve *v.t.* સેવા કરવી sevaa karavee

service *n.* નોકરી Nokree

serviceable *adj.* ઉપયોગી Upyogee

servile *adj.* ગુલામી વૃત્તનું Gulaamee vrutinun

servility *n.* ગુલામી દશા Gulaamee dashaa

servitor *n.* ચાકર Chaakar

servitude *n.* ગુલામી Gulaamee

sesame *n.* તલ tal

session *n.* બેઠક Bethak

sesspool *n.* ખાળકૂવો Khalkoovo

set *v.t.* સજ્જ sajj

setback *n.* પૂરગતમાં વિઘ્ન Pragtimaan vighn

setting *n.* રચના rachanaa

settle *v.t.* ઠરીઠામ થવું Thareethaam thavun

settlement *n.* પતાવટ Pataavat

settler *n.* વસાહતી vasaahatee

seven *adj.* સાત Saat

sevenfold *adj.* સાતગણું Saatganun

seventeen *adj.* સત્તર Sattar

seventh *adj.* સાતમું saatmun

seventieth *adj.* સત્તરમું sattarmun

seventy *adj.* સત્તિરમું Sittermun

sever *v.t.* ભાગ પાડવા કે પડવા Bhaag paadvaa ke padvaa

several *adj.* કેટલાક Ketlaak

severally *adj.* અલગ અલગ Alag alag

severance *n.* વિચ્છેદન vichchhedan

severe *adj.* કડક Kadak

severity *n.* કડકાઈ Kadkaai

sew *v.t.* સીવવું Sivvun

sewage *n.* શહેર Shaher

sewer *n.* મળમૂત્ર લઈ જવાની મોરી Malmootra lai javaanee moree

sewing *n.* સીવવાનાં કપડાં Seevvaanaan kapdaan

sex *n.* લિંગ Ling

sextant *n.* ખૂણામાપક khoonaamaapak

sexual *adj.* લૈંગિક Laingik

shabby *adj.* જીર્ણશીર્ણ Jirnasheerna

shackle *v.t.* બેડી bedee

shade *n.* છાયા Chhaayaa

shadow *n.* પડછાયો Padchhaayo

shadowy *adj.* પડછાયા જેવું Padchhaayaa jevun

shady *adj.* છાયાવાળું Chhaayaavaalun

shaft *n.* દાંડો Daando

shag *n.* બરછટ વાળનો જથ્થો Barchhat vaalno jaththo

shaggy *adj.* જાડા બરછટ વાળવાળું Jaadaa Barchhat vaalvaalun

shake *v.t.* હલાવવું કે હાલવું Halaavvun ke haalvun

shall *adv.* હશે hashe

shallow *asj.* છીછરું Chhichhrun

sham *n.* ઢોંગ Dhong

shamble *v.i.* લથડિયાં ખાતાં ચાલવું Lathdiyaan khaataan chaalvun

shame *n.* શરમ Sharam

shameful *adj.* શરમ આવે એવું Sharam aave evun

shameless *adj.* બેશરમ Besharam

shampoo *v.t.* શેમ્પૂ shempoo

shank *n.* પગનો નળો pagano nalo

shanty *n.* ઝૂંપડી Zoompdee

shape *n.* આકાર Aakaar

shapeless *adj.* બેડોળ Bedol

shapely *adj.* ઘાટદાર Ghaatdaar

share *n.* હિસ્સો Hisso

shareholder *n.* ભાગીદાર Bhaageedaar

shark *n.* શાર્ક shark

sharp *adj.* તીક્ષ્ણ teekshna

sharpen *v.t.* ધારદાર કરવું dhaaradaar karavun

shatter *v.t.* પૂરેપૂરો નાશ કરવો Poorepooro naash karvo

shave *v.t.* વાળ ઉતારવા Vaal utaarva

shawl *n.* શાલ ઓઢવી કે ઓઢાડવી Shaal odhvee ke odhaadvee

she *pr.n.* તેણી Tenee

sheaf *n.* પૂળી Poolee

shear *v.t.* વાઢવું vaadhvun

shears *n.pl.* કાતર kaatar

sheath *n.* ચુસ્ત આવરણ Chust aavran
shed *n.* પાડી નાખવું Paadi naakhvun
sheen *n.* ચળકાટ Chalkaat
sheep *n.* ઘેટું Ghetun
sheep-cote *n.* ઘેટાંનો વાડો Ghetanno vaado
sheepish *n.* શરમાળ Sharmaal
sheer *adj.* સંપૂરણ Sampoorna
sheet *n.* ચાદર Chaadar
shee¶anchor *n.* લંગર langar
shelf *n.* છાજલી chhajalee
shell *n.* બીજનું કોચલું Beejnun kochlun
shelter *n.* રક્ષણ Rakshan
shelve છાજલીઓ chhaajaleeo
shepherd *n.* ભરવાડ Bharvaad
sherbet *n.* શરબત Sharbat
shield ઢાલ Dhaal
shift *v.i.* ખસવું Khasvun
shimmer *n.* ઝબુંકવું zabunkavun
shin *n.* પગનો નળો pagano nalo
shine *v.t.* પ્રકાશવું Prakaashvun
shinning *adj.* ઝગારા મારતું Zagaaraa maartun
shinto *n.* શનિટો અનુયાયી shinto anuyaayee
shiny *adj.* સ્વચ્છ Swachcha
ship *n.* વહાણ Vahaan
shipmate *n.* સહપ્રવાસી sahapravaasee
shipment *n.* નિકાસ nikaas
shipping *n.* વહાણવટું vahaanvatun
shipwreck *n.* જહાજનો નાશ jahaajno naash
ship-yard *n.* જહાજ રોકાય તે જગ્યા Jahaaj rokaay te jagyaan
shire *n.* પરગણું કે જિલ્લો Parganun ke Jillo
shirk *v.t.* કામચોર થવું Kaamchor thavun
shirt *n.* ખમીસ Khamees
shirting *n.* શર્ટનું કાપડ shartanun kaapad
shirty *adj.* ચિડાયેલું Chidanyelun
shiver *v.t.* ધ્રૂજવું Dhroojvun
shoal *n.* ટોળું Tolun
shock *n.* આંચકો aanchako
shocking *adj.* આઘાતજનક Aaghaatjanak
shoe *n.* પગરખું Pagrkhun

shoe-black *n.* પોલિશ કરનાર છોકરો Polish karnaar chhokro
shoe-maker *n.* મોચી Mochee
shoot *n.* ગોળી મારવી golee maaravee
shooting *n.* ગોળીબાર goleebaar
shop *n.* દુકાન Dukaan
shopping *n.* બજાર કરવું તે Bajaar karvun te
shore *n.* ટેકો Teko
short *n.* નાનું Naanun
shortage *n.* અછત Achhat
shortcoming *n.* નિષ્ફળતા nishfalataa
short cut *n.* ટૂંકો રસ્તો Toonko rasto
shorten *v.t.* ટૂંકાવવું Toonkaavvun
shortly *adv.* ટૂંકમાં Toonkmaa
shorts *n.* અર્ધ પાટલૂન Ardh paatloon
shot *n.* ધૂપછાંવ Dhoopchhanv
should *v.t.* થવું જોઈએ thavun joiye
shoulder *n.* બરડાનો ઉપરનો ભાગ Bardaano uparno bhaag
shout *v.i.* રાડ કે બૂમ પાડવી Raad ke boom paadvee
shove *v.t.* હડસેલો Hadselo
shovel *n.* પાવડો paavado
show *n.* જવા દેવું Javaa devun
shower *v.t.* વરસવું varasavun
showery *adj.* વરસાદી varasaadee
showy *adj.* દેખાવડું dekhaadavun
shrapnel *n.* શ્રાપનેલ shrepanel
shred *n.* નાનો ટુકડો naano tukado
shrew *n.* છછુંદર Chhachhundar
shrewd *adj.* વિચક્ષણ Vichakshan
shrewish *adj.* વઢકણું Vadhknun
shrick *n.* ચીસ Chees
shrill *adj.* તીણું Teenun
shrine *n.* અસ્થિ, ઇ. અવશેષોની પેટી Asthi e avsheshonee petee
shrink સંકોચાવું sankochaavun
shroud *n.* વીટવાની ચાદર Vintvaanee chaadar
shrub *n.* ઝાડવું(થડ વિનાનું) Zaadvun (Thad Vinaanun)
shrug *v.t.* અણગમો બતાવવો anagamo bataavavo
shudder *v.i.* ધ્રૂજવું Dhroojvun
shuffle *v.t.* ઘસડાતાં ચાલવું Dhasdaataa chaalvun

shun *v.t.* દૂર કરવું Door karvun

shunt *v.t.* એક બાજુએ વાળવું Ek baajue vaalvuun

shut *v.t.* બંધ કરવું કે થવું Bandh karvun ke thavun

shutter *n.* કમાડ kamaad

shuttle *n.* વણકરનો કાંઠલો Vankarno kanthlo

shuttlecock *n.* બેડમિન્ટનનું ફૂલ bedamintannun fool

shy *v.i* શરમાવવું sharamaavavun

sibilant *adj.* સકારવાળું Sakaarvaalun

sick *adj.* માંદું Maandun

sicken *v.t.* માંદું પડવું maandun padavun

sickle *n.* દાતરડું Daatrdun

sickly *adj.* માંદલું Maandlun

sickness *n.* માંદગી Maandgee

side *n.* બાજુ Baaju

sidelong બાજુનું Baajunun

sidewise *adv.* બાજુ પ્રમાણે Baaju pramaane

siding *n.* સાઇડિંગ saaiding

siege *n.* ઘેરો ghero

sieve *n.* ચાળણી Chaalnee

sift *v.t.* ચાળણી વતી ચાળવું Chaalnee vatee chaalvun

sigh *v.i.* ઊંડો શ્વાસ Undo shwaas

sight *n.* દૃષ્ટિ Drusti

sightly *adj.* પ્રેક્ષણીય Prekshneey

sign *n.* નિશાનીવાળું Nishaaneevaalun

signal *n.* સંકેત sanket

signatory *n.* દસ્તાવેજ Dastaavej

signature *n.* સહી Sahee

signboard *n.* નામનું પાટિયું Naamnun paatiyun

signet *n.* સિક્કો Sikko

significance *n.* આશય Aashay

significant *adj.* અર્થવાળું Arthvaalun

significantly *adj.* અર્થપૂરણ રીતે Arthpoorn reete

signification ચોક્કસ અર્થ કે આશય Chokkas arth ke aashay

signify *v.t.* પ્રતીક હોવું prateek hovun

signor *n.* સાઇનોર sainor

signpost *n.* પથદર્શક પાટિયા pathadarshak paatiya

silence *n.* નીરવતા Neeravtaa

silent *adj.* શાંત shaant

silica *n.* સલિકા silika

silk *n.* રેશમી કાપડ Reshmee kaapad

silken *n.* રેશમનું Reshamnun

silkworm *n.* રેશમનો કીડો Reshamno keedo

silly *adj.* મૂરખ Moorkh

silo *n.* ચારા સંગ્રહસ્થાન chaaraasangrahasthaan

silt *n.* કાંપ kaanp

silvan *adj.* વનવાળું Vanvaalun

silver *n.* ચાંદી Chaandee

silvery ચળકતું chalakatun

simian *n.* એપ કે મંકી (વાંદરો) Ep ke mankee (Vaandro)

similar *adj.* —ના જેવું કે સરખું Naa jevun ke sarkhun

similarity *n.* સામ્ય Saamya

similarly *adv.* એ જ રીતે કે પ્રકારે E j reete ke prakaare

simile *n.* તુલના tulanaa

similitude *n.* સ્વાંગ Swaang

simmer *v.t.* ઉકળતું રાખવું ukalatun raakhavun

simper *v.i.* મુરખાઈભર્યું સ્મિત murkhaaibharyu smit

simple *adj.* સરળ saral

simpleton *n.* મૂરખો Moorkho

simplicity *n.* સાદાઈ Saadaai

simplify *v.t.* સાદું બનાવવું Saadun bannaavvun

simply *adj.* સહેલાઈથી Sahelaaithee

simulate *v.t.* ઢોંગ કરવો dhong karavo

simulation *adj.* ઢોંગ dhong

simultaneous *adj.* એક સાથે ek saathe

sin *n.* પાપ Paap

since *adv.* થી અત્યાર સુધી Thee atyaar sudhee

sincere *adj.* નિષ્કપટ nishkapat

sincerely *adv.* ખરા દિલથી Kharaa dilthee

sincerity *n.* નિષ્કપટી naishkapatee

sine *n.* જ્યા (ભૂમિતિ-ત્રિકોણમિતિ) Jya (Bhoomiti- Trikonmiti)

sinecure *n.* બેઠાખાઉ નોકરી bethaakhaau nokaree

sinew *n.* અસ્થિબંધન Asthibandhan

sinewy *adj.* અસ્થિબંધન ધરાવનાર asthibandhan dharaavanaar

sinful *adj.* પાપ કરનારું paap karanaarun

sing *v.i.* ગાવું Gaavun

singer *n.* ગાયક Gaayak

single *adj.* ફક્ત એક જ Fakta ek j

singly *adv.* એક પછી એક Ek pachhee ek

singular *adj.* અસામાન્ય Asaamaanya

singularity *n.* એકલું હોવાપણું Eklun hovaapanun

sinister *n.* અશુભ(નું સૂચક) Ashubh (nun soochak)

sink *v.i.* ધીમે ધીમે પડવું Dheeme dheeme padvun

sinless *adj.* નિષ્પાપ Nishpaap

sinuous *adj.* અનેક વળાંકોવાળું Anek valaankovaalun

sip *v.t.* ઘૂંટડો ભરવો ghoontado bharavo

siphon *n.* ખાલી કરવું khaalee karavun

sir *n.* સાહેબ saheb

sire *n.* પિતા Pitaa

siren *n.* ભયંકર મોહક સ્ત્રી Bhayankar mohak stree

sirrah *n.* સરાહ saraah

sister *n.* સગી બહેન Sagee bahen

sisterhood *n.* ભગિનીત્વ bhaginitva

sister-in-law *n.* નણંદ Nanand

sisterly *adj.* સગી બહેન જેવું Sagee bahen jevun

sit *v.i.* બેસવું besavun

sitting *n.* બેઠક bethak

situate અમુક જગ્યાએ મૂકવું Amuk jagyaaye mookvun

situation *n.* આસપાસના સંજોગો Aaspaasnaa sanjogo

six *adj.* છ (ની સંખ્યા, ૬) chh (ni sankhyaa, 6)

sixfold *adj.* છગણું Chh ganun

sixteen *n.* સોળ (ની સંખ્યા, ૧૬) Sol (ni sankhyaa 16)

sixteenth *adj.* સોળમું, સોળમો ભાગ Solmun, Solmo bhag

sixth *adj.* છઠ્ઠું Chhaththun

sixtieth *adj.* સાઠમું saathamun

sixty *adj.* સાઠ (ની સંખ્યા, ૬૦) Saath (ni sankhya, 60)

size *n.* પરિમાણ Parimaan

sizzle *v.i.* ગણગણાટ ganaganaat

skate *n.* સ્કેટ માછલી sket maachalee

skein *n.* કોકડું kokadun

skeleton *n.* હાડપિંજર Haadpinjar

sketch *n.* ખરડો Khardo

skiff *n.* નાની હોડી naanee hodee

skilful *adj.* કુશળ Kushal

skill *n.* કુશળતા Kushaltaa

skilled *adj.* કુશળ kushal

skim મલાઈ ઉતારવી malaai utaaravee

skimmer *n.* મલાઈ ઉતારનાર malaai utaarnaar

skin *n.* ચામડી Chaamdee

skindeep *adj.* ઉપરછલ્લું Uparchhallu

skip *v.i.* આમતેમ કૂદકા મારવા Aamtem koodka maarvaa

skipping *n.* કૂદકા koodakaa

skipper *n.* કપ્તાન Kaptaan

skirmish *n.* અચાનક અથડામણ Achaanak athdaaman

skirt *n.* ચણિયો chaniyo

skit *n.* નકલ nakal

skull *n.* ખોપરી Khopree

skulk ભરાઈ રહેવું Bharaai rahevun

sky *n.* આકાશ Aakaash

skylark *n.* ચંડોળ પક્ષી Chandol pakshee

sky-scraper *n.* ગગનચુંબી ઇમારત Ganchumbee imaarat

slab *n.* સ્તર star

slabber *v.i.* લાળ ઝરવી Laal zarvee

slack *adj.* આળસુ Aalsu

slacken *v.t.* ઢીલું Dheelun

slackness *n.* શિથિલતા Shithiltaa

slake *v.t.* છિપાવવી Chhipaavvee

slam *v.t.* પછાડવું pachhadavun

slander *n.* બદગોઈ Badgoi

slanderer *n.* નિંદા કરનારું માણસ Nindaa karnaarun maanas

slang *n.* અપશબ્દ ઉચ્ચારવા Apshabd uchchaarvvaa

slant *adj.* કતરાતું Katraatun

slap *n.* થપાટ કે તમાચો મારવો Thapaat ke tamaacho maarvo

slash *n.* કોરડા વડે ફટકારવું Kordaa vade fatkaarvun

slat *n.* ચપટી પટ્ટી chapatee pattee
slate *n.* સ્લેટ slet
slater *n.* સ્લેટર sletar
slattern *n.* ગંધાતી સ્તૂરી gandhaatee stree
slaughter *n.* કતલ katal
slaughter-house *n.* કતલખાનું Katalkhaanu
slave *n.* ગુલામ Gulaam
slaver *n.* ગુલામોનો વેપારી gulaamono vepaaree
slavery *n.* ગુલામી(ની દશા) Gulaamee(nee dashaa)
slavish *adj.* ગુલામીની વૃત્તિવાળું Gulaameenee vrutivaalun
slay *v.t.* મારી નાખવું Maaree naakhvun
sledge *n.* સ્લેજ slej
sleek *adj.* લીસું Leesun
sleep *n.* ઊંઘ Ungh
sleeper *n.* ઊંઘતું માણસ Unghtun maanas
sleepless *adj.* ઊંઘ વિનાનું Ungh vinaanun
sleepy *adj.* ઊંઘે ઘેરાયેલું Unghe gheraayelun
sleet *n.* અર્ધઓગળેલો બરફ ardhaogalelo baraf
sleeve *n.* બાંય baany
sleigh *n.* બરફગાડી barafagaadee
sleight *n.* હોશિયારી Hoshiyaaree
slender *adj.* પાતળું Paatlun
slice *n.* ભાગ Bhaag
slide *v.t.* સરકવું sarakavun
slight *adj.* લગીર Lageer
slightingly *adj.* અવજ્ઞા કે ઉપેક્ષાપૂર્વક Avagnya ke upekshaapoorvak
slim *adj.* પાતળું Paatlun
slime *n.* ચીકણો પદાર્થ cheekano padaarth
slimy *adj.* અધમ Adham
sling *n.* ઝોળી Zolee
slip *v.t.* લપસી જવું lapasee javun
slipper *n.* સ્લિપર sliper
slippery *n.* લપસણું Lapasanun
slit *v.t.* ફાટ Faat
sliver *v.t.* લાકડાની ફાડ Laakdaanee faad
slobber *n.* લાળ ટપકવી કે પાડવી Laal tapkvee ke paadvee

slogan *n.* સૂત્રોચ્ચાર sootrochchaar
sloop *n.* નાનું વહાણ naanun vahaan
slop *n.pl.* ઢોળવું Dholvun
slope *n.* ઢાળ કે ઢોળાવ વાળી જમીન Dhaal ke dholaavvaalee jameen
sloppy *adj.* ભીનું થયેલું Bheenun thayelun
slot *n.* કાણું Kaanun
sloth *n.* આળસ Aalas
slothful *adj.* પ્રમાદી Pramadee
slough *n.* કાંચળી kaanchalee
sloven *n.* મેલું Melun
slovenly *adj.* એદી Edee
slow *adj.* ધીમું Dheemun
slowly *adv.* ધીમે ધીમે Dheeme Dheeme
slug *n.* સખત ફટકો મારવો Sakhat fatko maarvo
sluggard *n.* આળસુનો પીર Aalsuno peer
sluggish *adj.* મંદ Mand
sluice *n.* કૃત્રિમ નહેર krutrim naher
slum *n.* ઝૂંપડપટ્ટી zoopadapattee
slumber *n.* ઊંઘ લેવી Ungh levee
slump *n.* મંદી mandee
slur *n.* અસ્પષ્ટ ઉચ્ચાર aspashta uchchaar
slut *n.* ફૂવડ નાર Fuvad naar
sly *adj.* કાવતરાબાજ Kaavtraabaaj
smack *n.* કોઈ પદાર્થની સોડમ Koi padaarthnee sodam
small *adj.* નાના કદનું Naanaa kadnu
smallness *n.* નાનાપણું Naanaapanun
smart *adj.* હોશિયાર Hoshiyaar
smash *v.t.* ભૂકો કરવો bhooko karavo
smear *v.t.* ધબ્બો લગાડવો dhabbo lagaadavo
smell *n.* ઘ્રાણેન્દ્રયિ Ghranendriya
smelly *adj.* દુર્ગંધવાળું Durgandhvalun
smelt *v.t.* સ્મેલ્ટ માછલી slemt maachhalee
smile *v.i.* હસવું Hasvun
smiling *adj.* મલકાતું Malkaatun
smirk *n.* મૂર્ખતાભર્યું Moorkhtaabharyun
smite *v.i.* મારવું Maarvun
smith *n.* ધાતુ કામ કરનાર Dhaatu kaam karnaar

smithy *n.* લુહારની કોઢ Luhaarnee kodh

smoke *n.* ધુમાડો Dhumaado

smoker *n.* ધૂમ્રપાન કરનાર Dhoomrapaan karnaar

smoky *adj.* ધુમાડાવાળું Dhumaadaavaalun

smooth *adj.* સરખું Sarkhun

smoothen *v.t.* લીસું કરવું Leesun karvun

smoothly *adv.* સીધી રીતે Seedhee reete

smother ગૂંગળાવવું Goonglaavvvun

smoulder *v.i.* જ્વાળાવગર સળગવું jvaalaa vagar salagavun

smouldering *adj.* ધૂંધવાતું Dhoondhvaatun

smudge *n.* ડાઘો Daagho

smug *n.* સ્વસંતોષી Svasantoshee

smuggle *v.t.* દાણચોરી કરવી daanchoree karavee

smuggling *n.* દાણચોરી Daanchoree

smut *n.* કાજળ કે મેશનો પોપડો Kaajal ke meshno popdo

snack *n.* નાસ્તો Naasto

snaffle *n.* પાતળી લગામ paatalee lagaam

snail *n.* ગોકળગાય gokalagaay

snake *n.* સાપ Saap,

snap *n.* ઝડપી છબી Zadpee chhabee

snappish *adj.* ચીઢિયું Cheedhiyun

snare *n.* પાશ Paash

snarl *v.i.* ગૂંચ Goonch

snatch *n.* આંચકવું aanchakavun

sneak *v.i.* હલકટ Halkat

sneer *v.t.* તિરસ્કારદર્શક હાસ્ય Tirskaardarshak haasya

sneeze *v.i.* છીંક ખાવી તે Chhink khaavee te

snide *adj.* નકલી Naklee

sniff *v.i.* નસકોરા બોલાવવા nasakoraa bolaavavaa

snip *v.t.* કાતરવું Kaatrvun

snivel *n.* આંખમાં આંસુ આવવાં તે Aankhmaa aansu aavvaan te

snob *n.* દંભી Dambhee

snobbery *n.* દંભ Dambh

snooze ઝોકું ખાવું Zonku khaavun

snore *v.i.* ઘોરવું તે Ghorvun te

snort *v.t.* ક્રોધનો સુસવાટો Krodhno susvaato

snot *n.* લીંટ Leent

snout *n.* સૂંઢ soondh

snow *n.* બરફ Baraf

snowy *n.* બરફ આચ્છાદતિ Baraf aachchhaadit

snub *v.* ઉતારી પાડવું Utaaree paadvun

snuff *n.* છીંકણી chheenkanee

snuffle *v.i.* સરડકો બોલાવવો કે ભરવો Sardko bolaavvi ke bharvo

snug *adj.* ટાઢ તડકાથી સુરક્ષિત Taadh tadkaathee surkshit

so *adj.* આમ Aam

soak *v.t.* બરાબર પલાળવું baraabar palaalavun

soap *n.* ને સાબુ દેવો કે લગાડવો Ne saabu devo ke lagaadvo

soapy *n.* સાબુ જેવું Saabu jevun

soar *v.i.* ઊંચે ઊડવું Unche Udvun

sob *v.i.* ડૂસકું Dooskun

sober *adj.* ઠરેલ tharel

sobriety *n.* શુદ્ધ વિવેક Shudhdh Vivek

sobriquet *n.* મશ્કરીનું Mashkareenun

sociable *adj.* મળતાવડું Maltaavdun

social *adj.* સમાજમાં રહેનારું Samaajmaan rahenaarun

socialism *n.* સમાજવાદ Samaajvaad

society *n.* સામાજિક જીવનપદ્ધતિ Saamaajik jeevanpadhdhati

sociology *n.* સમાજશાસ્ત્ર Samaajshaastra

sock *n.* મોજું mojun

socket *n.* ખાડો Khaado

sod *n.* હરિયાળી(નો ટુકડો) Hariyaalee(no tukdo)

soda *n.* અણગમતો માણસ anagamato maanas

sodium *n.* સોડીયમ sodiam

sofa *n.* સોફા sofaa

soft *adj.* નરમ Naram

soften *v.i.* પોચું કરવું pochun karavun

softly *adj.* નરમાશપૂર્વક Narmaashpoorvak

soil *n.* મેલું કરવું Melun karvun

soiree *n.* સાંજનો મેળાવડો Saanjno melaavdo

sojourn *n.* મુકામ mukaam

sojourner *n.* મહેમાન Mahemaan

solace *n.* દિલાસો delaaso

solar *adj.* સૂર્યનું Sooyanun

solarium *n.* સૌરચિકિત્સાલય saurachikitsaalaya

solder *v.t.* રેણ કરવું ren karavun

soldier *n.* લશ્કરનો સિપાઈ Lashkarno sipaai

soldiery *n.* સિપાઈવર્ગ Sipaaivarg

sole *n.* પગરખાનું તળિયું Pagarkhaanun taliyun

solely *adv.* ફક્ત Fakt

solemn *adj.* વિચારપૂર્વક vichaarpoorvak

solemnity *n.* વિચાર કરાવે એવું Vichaar karaave evun

solemnize *v.t.* વિધિપૂર્વક ઉજવણી vidhipoorvak ujavanee

solicit *v.t.* ફરી ફરી માગવું Faree faree maagvun

solicitation *n.* આજીજી કરવી તે Aajeejee karvee te

solicitor *n.* વકીલ vakeel

solicitous *n.* ઉત્સુક Utsuk

solicitude *n.* ચિંતા Chintaa

solid *adj.* સ્થિર આકારનું Sthir aakaarnun

solidarity *n.* એકતા Ektaa

solidify *v.t.* કઠણ બનાવવું Kathan banaavvun

solidity *n.* સ્થિર આકાર Sthir aakaar

soliloquize *v.i.* સ્વગત ભાષણ કરવું Swagat bhaashan karvun

soliloquy *n.* સ્વગતોક્તિ svagatokti

solitariness *n.* એકલતા Ekltaa

solitary *adj.* એકલું (રહેતું) Eklun (rahetun)

solitude *n.* એકાંતવાળી જગ્યા Ekaantvaalee jagyaa

solo *n.* એકાકી ekaakee

solstice *n.* સંક્રાંતિ sankraanti

solubility *n.* દ્રાવ્ય Dravya

soluble *adj.* દ્રાવ્ય draavya

solution *n.* વિલયન Vilayan

solve *v.t.* ખુલાસો કે ઉકેલ કરવો Khulaaso ke ukel karvo

solvent *adj.* દ્રાવક Dravak

sombre *adj.* કાળું Kalun

some *adj.* કેટલુંક Ketlunk

somebody *n.* કોઈ એક માણસ Koi ek maanas

somehow *adv.* કોઈપણ રીતે Koipan reete

someone *n.* કોઈ એક Koi ek

something *n.* કોઈ વસ્તુ Koi Vastu

sometime *adj.* ક્યારેક ક્યારેક Kyaarek kyaarek

somewhere *adv.* ક્યાંક Kyank

somnambulism *n.* નિદ્રાભ્રમણ Nindrabhraman

somniferous *adj.* ઊંઘ લાવનારું Ungh laavnaarun

somniloquist *n.* ઊંઘમાં બડબડનાર વ્યક્તિ unghman badbadnaar vyakti

somnolent *adj.* અર્ધનિદ્રિત Ardhnindrit

son *n.* પુત્ર Putra

song *n.* કંઠસંગીત Kanthsangeet

songster *n.* ગાયક Gaayak

songatress *n.* ગાયિકા Gaayikaa

son-in-law *n.* જમાઈ Jamaai

sonnet *n.* સોનેટ sonet

sonorous *adj.* પ્રભાવી Prabhaavee

soon *adv.* થોડા જ વખતમાં Thodaa j vakhatmaan

soot *n.* મેશ Mesh

soothe *n.* શાંત કે નરમ પાડવું Shaant ke naram paadvun

soothe *v.t.* શમાવવું Shamaavvun

soothsay *v.t.* ભવિષ્ય ભાખવું Bhavishyaa bhaakhvun

soothsayer *n.* ભવિષ્ય કહેનાર Bhavishyaa kahenaar

sooty *n.* મેશનું કે મેશના જેવું Meshnun ke meshnaa jevun

sophism *n.* ખોટી દલીલ Khotee daleel

sophist *n.* ખોટો યુક્તિવાદ કરનાર Khooto yuktivaad karnaar

sophisticate *v.t.* દુનિયાદારીમાં કુશળ Duniyaadaareeman kushal

sophistry *n.* ભ્રામક દલીલ bhaamak daleel

sorcerer *n.* જાદુટોણો કરનાર ભૂવો Jaadutono karnaar bhoovo

sorcery *n.* જાદુટોણાની ક્રિયા
Jaadutonaanee kriyaa
sordid *adj.* મેલું Melun
sore *n.* વેદનાથી પીડિત Vednaathee
peedit
sorely *adv.* સખત રીતે Sakhat reete
soreness *n.* દર્દ Dard
sorority મહિલા સંઘ mahilaa sangh
sorrel *adj.* આછા છીકણી રંગનું aachhaa
chhinkanee rangnun
sorrow *n.* શોક Shok
sorrowful શોકાતુર Shokaatur
sorry *adj.* કશાક માટે દિલગીર Kashaak
maate dilgeer
sort *n.* જાત Jaat
sos *n.* મદદ માટે પોકાર Madad maate
pokaar
sot *n.* પાકો દારૂડિયો Paako daarudi
sottish *adj.* પાકા દારૂડિયા જેવું Paakaa
daarudiyaa jevun
soul *n.* આત્મા Aatmaa
sound *n.* અવાજ Avaaj
soup *n.* રસો Raso
sour *adj.* ખટાશવાળું Khataashvaalun
source *n.* ઉગમસ્થાન Ugamsthaan
sourness *n.* ખટાશ Khataash
souse *v.t.* અથાણામાં નાખવું
Athaanaaman naakhvun
south *n.* દક્ષિણ દિશા Dakshin dishaa
soutÅeast *adj.* આગ્નેય દિશાનું Aagney
dishaanun
southern *adj.* દક્ષિણમાં Dakshinmaan
southward દક્ષિણ દિશા તરફ Dakshin
dishaa taraf
soutÅwest *n.* નૈઋત્ય દિશા Nairutya
dishaa

sovereign *n.* સર્વોપરિ Sarvopari
sovereignty *n.* સર્વોપરિતા Sarvoparita
soviet *n.* સોવિયેત soviyet
sow *n.* બી રોપવું Bee ropvun
sow *v.t.* ડુક્કરની માદા Dukkarnee
maadaa
space *n.* અંતરિક્ષ Antriksh
spacious *adj.* જગ્યાની છૂટવાળું
Jagyaanee chootvaalun
spade *n.* ખોદવાનું ઓજાર Khodvaanun
ojaar
span *n.* વિસ્તાર vistaar
spangle *n.* આભલું Aabhlun
spaniel *n.* સ્પેનીયલ કુતરૂં spenial
kutarun
spank ઝડપથી હાંકવું zadapathee
haankavun
spar *n.* મજબૂત વાંસ Majboot vaans
spare *v.t.* ફાજલ પાડવું faajal paadavun
sparing *adj.* કરકસરિયું Karkasriyun
spark *n.* તણખો Tankho
sparkle *v.i.* તણખા ફેંકવા tanakhaa
fenkavaa
sparkish *n.* રંગીલું Rangeelun
sparrow *n.* ચકલી Chaklee
sparse *adj.* છૂટુંછવાયેલું
chhootunchhavaayelun
spasm *n.* તાણ Taan

spatter *v.t.* છાંટા ઉડાડવા chhantaa
udaadavaa
spay *v.t.* બીજાશયો કાઢવા beejaashayo
kaadhavaa
speak *v.i.* બોલવું Bolavun
speaker *n.* બોલનાર Bolnaar
spear *n.* ભોંકવું bhonkavun
special *adj.* વિશિષ્ટ vishishta
specialist *n.* કોઈ ખાસ કામના નિષ્ણાત
Koi khaas kaamnaa nishnat
speciality *n.* વિશિષ્ટ ગુણ કે લક્ષણ
Vishisht gun ke lakshan
specialize *v.t.* તજજ્ઞ હોવું tajagya
hovun
specially ખાસ કરીને Khaas kareene
specie *n.* રોકડા નાણાં કે સિક્કા Rokdaa
naanaan ke sikka
species *n.* જાતિ jaati
specific *adj.* નિશ્ચિત Nishchit
specification *n.* વિગતવાર વર્ણન
Vigatvaar varanan
specify *v.t.* સ્પષ્ટતા કરવી spashtataa
karavee
specimen નમૂનો Namoono
specious સુફિયાણું sufiyaanu
speck *n.* નાનકડો ધબ્બો Naankdo
dhabbo

speckle *n.* કશાકનો નાનો ભાગ kashaakano naano bhaag

specs *n.pl.* ચશ્મા Chasmaa

spectacle *n.* જાહેર તમાશો Jaaher tamaasho

spectator *n.* પ્રેક્ષક Prekshak

spectral *adj.* ભૂત જેવું Bhoot jevun

spectre *n.* ભૂત Bhoot

spectrum *n.* વર્ણપટ્ટ varnapatta

speculate કલ્પના કરવી kalpanaa karavee

speculation *n.* સટ્ટો કરવો Satto karvo

speculative *adj.* કાલ્પનિક kaalpanik

speculator *n.* કલ્પના કરનાર kalpanaa karanaar

speech *n.* બોલવાની ક્રિયા Bolvaanee kriyaa

speechless *adj.* અવાક Avaak

speed *n.* ઉતાવળ Utaaval

speedy *adj.* ઝડપી Zadpee

spell *v.i.* જાદુનો મંત્ર Jaaduno mantra

spelling *n.* જોડણી સ્પર્ધાની રમત Jodnee spardhaanee ramat

spelter *n.* જસત Jasat

spencer *n.* ટૂંકો કોટ toonko kot

spend *v.t.* ખરચવું Kharchvun

spendhrift *n.* ઉડાઉ વ્યક્તિ Udaau vyakti

sperm *n.* નરનું વીર્ય Narnun veerya

spew *v.t.* ઊલટી કરવી કે થવી Ultee karvee ke thavee

sphere *n.* ગોળો Golo

spherical *adj.* ગોળાકાર Golaakaar

spheroid *n.* ગોળીય પદાર્થ goleeya padaarth

spice *n.* મસાલાની ચીજ Masaalaanee cheej

spicy *adj.* સનસનાટીવાળું Sansanaateevaalun

spicer *n.* તેજાનો કે સમૂહગત રીતે Tejaano ke samoohgat reete

spigot *n.* પીપનો ડાટો Peepno daato

spike *n.* તીક્ષ્ણ અણી Teekshan anee

spill *v.i.* ઢોળવું Dholvun

spillway *n.* નીક neek

spin *n.* સૂતર કાંતવું Sootar kaantvun

spinal *adj.* કરોડ કે પૃષ્ઠવંશનું karod ke prushtvanshnun

spindle *n.* કાંતવાની તૂરાક Kaantvaanee traak

spine *n.* કરોડ Karod

spineless *adj.* પૃષ્ઠવંશ વિનાનું Prushthvansh vinaanun

spinner *n.* સુતર કાંતનાર sutar kaantanaar

spiral *n.* સર્પલિ sarpil

spire *n.* મિનારો minaaro

spirit *n.* જુસ્સો jusso

spirited *adj.* પાણીદાર Paaneedaar

spirited *adj.* તેજસ્વી Tejsvee

spiritual *adj.* આત્મા સંબંધી Aatmaa sambandhee

spiritualism *n.* પ્રેતાત્માને લગતું pretaatmaane lagatun

spirituality *n.* આધ્યાત્મિકતા Aadhyaatmiktaa

spirituous *adj.* મદ્યાર્કવાળું Madhyaarkvalun

spit *v.t.* સળિયો saliyo

spite *n.* દ્વેષ Dwesh

spiteful *adj.* અસૂયાપ્રેરિત Asooyaaprerit

spittle *n.* મુખરસ Mukhras

spittoon *n.* થૂંકદાની Thoonkdaanee

splash *v.t.* છાંટા ઉડાડવા chhantaa udaadavaa

spleen *n.* બરોળ Barol

spleeny *adj.* રસિાળ Risaal

splendent *adj.* ઝળહળતું Zalhaltun

splendid *adj.* વિશાળ Vishaal

splendour *adj.* વૈભવ Vaibhav

splice *v.t.* લગ્નગ્રંથિથી જોડવું તે Lagnagranthithee jodaavun te

splint પાતળી ચીપ Paatlee cheep

split *v.t.* ફાટ પાડવી faat paadavee

spoil *n.* નકામું nakaamun

spoke *n.* પૈડાનો આરો Paidaano aaro

spokesman *n.* કોઈની વતી બોલનાર Koinee vatee bolnaar

spoliate *v.t.* લૂંટફાટ કરવી Loontfaat karvee

spoliation *n.* લૂંટ Loont

sponge *n.* વાદળી vaadalee

sponger *n.* વાદળી એકતર કરનાર vaadalee ekatra karanaar

sponsor *n.* ધર્મપિતા Dharmpitaa

spontaneous *adj.* સ્વયંસ્ફૂર્ત Swayamsfoort

spook *n.* ભૂત Bhoot

spool *n.* ફરકડી farakadee

spoon *n.* ચમચો Chamcho

sporadic *adj.* અહીંતહીં Aheen taheen

sport *n.* ઠાઠમાઠ બતાવવા Thaathmaath bataavvaa

sportive *adj.* રમતિયાળ Ramtiyaal

sportsman *n.* રમતવીર ramataveer

sportsmanship *n.* ખેલદિલી Kheldilee

spot *n.* અમુક કે ચોક્કસ સ્થળ કે જગ્યા Amuk ke chokkas sthal ke jagyaa

spotless *adj.* પૂરેપૂરું સ્વચ્છ Pooreepoorun swachchh

spotted *adj.* ટપકાંવાળું, તલકાવાળું Tapkaanvaalun, Talkaavaalun

spouse *n.* પતિ અથવા પત્ની Pati athvaa patnee

spout *n.* ટોટી Totee

sprawl *v.i.* લાંબા થઈને સૂવું laanbaa thaine soovun

spray *n.* ફુવારો Fuvaaro

spread *v.t.* ફેલાવવું Felaavvun

sprig *n.* નાનો ખીલો naano kheelo

sprightly *adj.* ઉલ્લાસવાળું Ullasvaalun

spring *n.* વસંતઋતુ vasantrootu

sprinkle *v.t.* પ્રવાહી ઇ. છાંટવું Pravaahee e chhantvun

sprinkling *n.* છંટકાવ chhantakaav

sprite *n.* અડપલાં કરનારું ભૂત Adaplaan karnaarun bhoot

sprout *n.* વધવા માંડવું Vadhvaa maandvun

spruce *adj.* ઠીક ઠીક પોશાક પહેરેલું Theek theek poshaak paherelun

spruce *n.* ચકોર chakor

spry *adj.* ચપળ Chapal

spume *n.* ફીણ આવવું Feen aavvun

spumy *adj.* ફીણવાળું આવવું Feenvaalun aavvun

spur *n.* પ્રેરક વસ્તુ Prerak vastu

spurious *adj.* બનાવટી Banaavatee

spurn *v.t.* તિરસ્કૃત tiraskrut

spurt *v.i.* અચાનક વહેવું achaanak vahevun

sputter *v.i.* મોંમાંથી લાળ પાડવી Monmaanthee laal paadvee

sputum *n.* લાળ Laal

spy *n.* જાસૂસી કરનાર Jasoosee karnaar

squabble *n.* નજીવી બાબતમાં કજિયો Najeevee baabtmaan kajiyo

squad *n.* ટુકડી tukadee

squalid *adj.* ગંદું Gandun

squall *n.* એકદમ ઊઠેલું વંટોળ Ekdam uthelun vantol

squander છૂટે હાથે વેરવું chhoote haathe veravun

square *n.* સમચોરસ Samchoras

squash *v.t.* છૂંદવું Chhoondvun

squat *v.t.* ઊકડું બેસવું Ukdoon besavun

squeak *n.* નાનકડી ચીસ Naankdee chees

squeal *v.t.* લાંબી ચીસ પાડવી laanbee chees paadavi

squeamish *n.* જરામાં કંટાળે એવું Jaraamaa kantaale evun

squeeze *v.t.* કચડવું Kachdvun

squib *n.* સુરસુરિયું surasuriyun

squint *v.i.* બાડી નજર થવી baadee najar thavee

squire *n.* જમીનદાર Jameendaar

squirrel *n.* ખિસકોલી khisakolee

stab *v.t.* જખમી કરવું jakhamee karavun

stability *n.* સ્થિરતા Sthirta

stable *n.* હાલે નહિ એવું Haale nahee evun

stack *n.* ઘાસની ગંજી ghaasanee ganjee

stadium *n.* સ્ટેડિયમ stediyam

staff *n.* હથિયાર Hathiyaar

stag *n.* સાબર કે હરણનો નર Saabar ke haranno nar

stage *n.* ઊંચી બેઠક Unchee bethak

stagger *v.i.* લથડિયાં ખાવા lathadiyaan khaavaa

stagnant *adj.* વહેતું નહિ એવું Vahetun nahi evun

stagnate *v.i.* વહેતું બંધ હોવું કે થવું Vahetun bandh hovun ke thavun

staid *adj.* ઠરેલ અને શાણું Tharel ane shaanun

stain *n.* રંગ બગાડવો Rang bagaadvo

stainless *adj.* ડાઘ વિનાનું Daagh vinaanun

stair *n.* નિસરણી nisaranee

staircase *n.* દાદરો Daadro

stake *n.* અણિયાળો થાંભલો aniyaalo thaanbhalo

stale *adj.* ઊતરી ગયેલું Utaree gayelun

stalk *n.* છોડની દાંડી Chhodnee daandee

stall *n.* દુકાન Dukaan

stallion *n.* ખસી કર્યા વિનાનો ઘોડો Khasee karyaa vinaano ghodo

stalwart *adj.* જબરું Jabrun

stamen *n.* ફૂલમાંનો નરકેસર Foolmaano narkesar

stamina *n.* જોમ Jom

stammer *v.i.* તોતડું બોલવું totadun bolavun

stamp *v.t.* પગ ઠોકવો Pag thokvo

stampede *v.i.* નાસભાગ કરવી naasabhaag karavee

stanch *adj.* વહેતું બંધ કરવું vahetun bandh karavun

stand *v.i.* ઊભા હોવું Ubhaa hovun

standard *n.* માનદંડ Maandand

standardize *v.t.* સુયોગ્ય કરવું suyogya karavun

standing *adj.* સ્થાયી Sthayee

stannary *n.* કલાઈની ખાણ Kalaainee khaan

stannic *adj.* કલાઈનું કે તેને લગતું Kalaainun ke tene lagtun

stanza *n.* કાવ્યનો શ્લોક Kaavyano shlok

staple *n.* મુખ્ય જણસ mukhya janas

star *n.* તારો Taaro

starboard *n.* જમણું jamanun

starch *n.* સ્ટાર્ચ staarch

stare *v.i.* એકીટસે જોવું ekeetase jovun

stark *adv.* વેરાન Veraan

starry *adj.* તારા જેવું (તેજસ્વી) Taaraa jevun (tejswi)

start *v.t.* પ્રવાસ શરૂ કરવો Pravaas sharoo karvo

startle *v.t.* આઘાત પહોંચાડવો aaghaat pahonchaadavo

starvation *n.* ભૂખમરો bhookhamaro

starve *v.i.* ભૂખ મરો Bhookh maro

starving *adj.* ક્ષુધાપીડિતી Kshudhaa peeditee

state *n.* સ્થિતિ Sthiti

stately *adj.* ભવ્ય Bhavya

statement *n.* નિવેદન Nivedan

statesman *n.* રાજનીતિમાં કુશળ પુરુષ Raajneetiman kushal purush

statesmanship *n.* રાજનીતિજ્ઞતા Raajneetignyataa

static *v.t.* સ્થિત Sthit

statics *n.* સ્થિર બળોનું શાસ્ત્ર sthir balonun shaastra

station *n.* થાણું Thaanun

stationary *adj.* સ્થિર Sthir

stationer *n.* લેખન સાહિત્ય વેચનાર Lekhan saahitya vechnaar

stationery *n.* લેખનસાહિત્ય સામગ્રી Lekhan Saahitya saamgree

statistical *adj.* આંકડાને લગતું aankadaane lagatun

statistics *n.* આંકડાકીય માહિતી aankadaakeeya maahitee

statuary *n.* મૂર્તિઓનું Moortionun

statue *n.* મૂર્તિ કે બાવલું Moorti ke baavlun

stature *n.* શરીરની ઊંચાઈ shareernee oonchaai

status *n.* કાનૂની સ્થિતિ kaanoonee sthite

statute *n.* કાયદો kaayado

statutory *adj.* કાયદેસર kaayadesar

staunch *adj.* વફાદાર vafaadaar

stave *n.* વાંકવાળું પાટિયું vaankvaalun paatiyun

stay *v.t.* ટેકો Teko

stead *n.* જગ્યા Jagyaa

steadiness *n.* સ્થિરતા Sthirtaa

steady *v.* દૃઢ Drudh

steal *v.t.* ચોરી કરવી Choree karvee

stealth *n.* ચોરીચૂપકી Choreechoopkee

stealthy *adj.* ચોરીથી કરેલું choreethee karelun

steam *n.* વરાળ Varaal

steamer *n.* આગબોટ Aagbot

steel *n.* પોલાદ Polaad

steelyard વજનકાંટો vajankaanto

steep *adj.* પલાળવું Palaalvun

steeple *n.* શિખર shikhar
steerage *n.* હંકારવું hankaaravun
steersman *n.* વહાણ ઇ.નો સુકાની Vahaan e no. sukaanee
stellar *adj.* તારાઓનું Taaraaonun
stem *n.* ઝાડ ઇ.નો મુખ્ય ભાગ Zaad e no mukhya bhaag
stench *n.* દુર્ગંધ Durgandh
stencil *n.* આકૃતિવાળું કાગળ aakrutivaalu kagal
stenograph *n.* લઘુલિપિનો અક્ષર laghulipino akshar
stenographer *n.* લઘુલિપિ લેખક laghulipi lekhak
stenography *n.* લઘુલિપિ લેખન laghulipi lekhan
stentorian *adj.* ખૂબ મોટો Khoob moto
step *v.i.* કદમ કે ડગલું ભરવું Kadam ke daglun bharvun
step-brother *n.* સાવકો કે ઓરમાન ભાઈ Saavko ke ormaan bhaai
step-father *n.* સાવકા પિતા Saavkaa pitaa
step-son *n.* સાવકું બાળક Saavkun baalak
steppe *n.* વિસ્તીર્ણ મેદાન visteerna medaan
stepping-stone *n.* વૃદ્ધિ સહાયક vrudhdhi sahaayak
stereoscope *n.* ત્રિમિતિદર્શક Trimitidarshak
stereotype *n.* કાયમનો ઠસ્સો Kaayano thasso
stereotyped *adj.* નિશ્ચિત સ્વરૂપનું Nischit swaroopnun
sterile *adj.* અનુપજાઉ Anupjaau
sterility *n.* વાંઝિયું Vaanziyun
sterilize જંતુરહિત કે વંધ્ય બનાવવું Janturahit je vyandhy banaavvun
sterling *n.* બ્રિટિશ નાણાનું નાણામાં British naanaanun ne naanaaman
stern *n.* સખત Sakhat
stet *v.t.* સુધારા રદ કરવા sudhaaraa rad karavaa
stethoscope *n.* સ્ટેથોસ્કોપ stethoskop
stew *v.t.* બાફવું baafavun
steward *n.* કારભારી Kaarbhaari

stewardess *n.* પરિચારિકા parichaarikaa
stick *n.* વીંધવું Veendhvun
stickler *n.* ચોકસાઈ Chokksaai
sticky *adj.* ચોંટે એવું Chonte evun
stickiness *n.* ચીકાશ Chikaash
stiff *adj.* વળે નહિ એવું Vale nahi evun
stiffen *v.t.* કઠણ Kathan
stiffness *n.* અકડાઈ કે મગરૂરી Akdaai, Magroori
stifle *v.t.* ગૂંગળાવવું goongalaavavun
stigma *n.* કલંક Kalank
stigmatize *v.t.* લાંછન લગાડવું laanchhan lagaadavun
stile *n.* પગથિયાં pagathiyan
still *adj.* દારૂ ગાળવાનું સાધન daaroo gaalavaanun saadhan
silently ચુપચાપ chupchaap
stilt *n.* ડોળઘાલુ Dolghaalun
stilted *adj.* આડંબરવાળું Aadambarvaalun
stimulant ઉદ્દીપક uddipak
stimulate *v.t.* ઉત્તેજના કે સ્ફૂર્તિ આપવી Uttejna ke sfoorti aapvee
stimulation ઉત્તેજના કે સ્ફૂર્તિ Uttejna ke sfoorti
stimulus *n.* પ્રેરણા Prernaa
sting *n.* કટુતા Katutaa
stingless *n.* ડંખરહિત Dankhrahit
stinging *adj.* તીક્ષ્ણ Teekshan
stingy *adj.* કંજૂસ Kanjoos
stink *n.* ગંધાવું Gandhaavun
stint *v.t.* ખાવાનું ઇ. પૂરતું ન આપવું Khaavaanun e poortun na aapvun
stipend *n.* પગાર Pagaar
stipendiary *adj.* પગારદાર Pagaardaar
stipulate *v.t.* નિશ્ચિત Nischit
stipulation *n.* ઠરાવ Tharaav
stipulator *n.* બોલી કે શરત કરનાર Bolee ke sharat karnaar
stir *v.i.* જરા ખસવું કે ખસેડવું Jaraa khasvun ke khasedvun
stirring *adj.* ઉત્તેજક Uttejak
stirrup *n.* ઉત્તેજિત કરવું Uttejit karvun
stitch *n.* સોયનો ટાંકો Soyno taanko
stithy *n.* એરણ Eran
stock *n.* વેપારી પેઢીનું ભંડોળ Vepaaree pedheenun bhandol

stockade *n.* કિલ્લેબંધી killebandhee

stocking *n.* મોજું mojun

stoic *n.* ભારે સંયમી Bhare saymee

stoicism *n.* ધૈર્યવાળો Dhairyvaalo

stoker *n.* ભઠ્ઠી ચાલક bhaththee chaalak

stolid *adj.* સુસ્ત Sust

stomach *n.* પેટ Pet

stone *n.* પથ્થર Paththar

stony *adj.* વિપુલ પથ્થરવાળું Vipul paththarvaalun

stooge *n.* તાબાનું માણસ Tambaanub maanas

stook *n.* પૂળા બાંધવા poolaa baandhavaa

stool *n.* હાથા વગરની બેઠક haathaa vagaranee bethak

stoop *v.t.* નમવું namavun

stop *v.t.* અટકાવવું Atkaavvun

stoppage *n.* બંધ કરવું bandh karavun

stopper *n.* ડાટો Daato

stopple બૂચથી બંધ કરવું boochthee bandh karavun

store *n.* વિપુલતા Vipultaa

storehouse *n.* કોઠાર Kothaar

store-keeper *n.* કોઠારી Kothaaree

storey *n.* મકાનનો માળ કે મજલો Makaanno mal ke majo

stork *n.* બગલો bagalo

storm *n.* હવાનું તોફાન Havaanun tofaan

stormy *adj.* તોફાન મચાવનારું Tofaan machaavnaarun

story *n.* માળ Maal

stout *adj.* બહાદુર Bahaadur

stove *n.* ચૂલો choolo

stow *v.t.* સામાન ગોઠવવો saamaan gothavavo

straggle *v.i.* વેરાઈ જવું Veraai javun

straggler *n.* વિખુટો પડેલો vikhuto padelo

straight *adj.* રેખા Rekhaa

straighten *v.t.* સીધું કરવું કે થવું Seedhun karvun ke thavun

straightway તાબડતોબ Taabadtob

strain *v.t.* તણાવ tanaav

strained અસ્વાભાવિક Aswaabhaavik

strait *n.* સાંકડું Saankdu

straiten સખત કે તંગ કરવું Sakhat ke tang karvun

straitened *n.* તંગ Tang

strand *n.* ખરાબે ચડવું Kharaabe chadvun

stranded *adj.* અસહાય Asahaay

strange *adj.* પરદેશી Pardeshee

strangeness *n.* અસ્વાભાવિકતા Aswabhaaviktaa

stranger *n.* અપરિચિત Aparichit

strangle *v.t.* ગળુ દબાવવું galu dabaavavun

strangury *n.* મૂત્રાવરોધ Mootravrodhak

strap *n.* ચામડા ઈ.નો બકલવાળો પટો Chaamda e no bakalvaalo pato

strapping *adj.* હૃષ્ટપુષ્ટ hrushtapushta

strate *n.* યુદ્ધકળાને લગતું Yudhdhakalaane lagtun

stratagem *n.* યુક્તિપ્રયુક્તિ Yuktiprayukti

strategical *adj.* વ્યૂહાત્મક Vyuhaatmak

strategy *n.* વ્યૂહરચના vyooharachanaa

stratify *v.t.* સ્તરબદ્ધ કરવું starabaddh karavun

straw *n.* સૂકું Sookun

strawberry *n.* સ્ટ્રોબેરી stroberi

stray *v.i.* રખડવું Rakhdvun

streak *n.* રેખા rekhaa

steaky *adj.* રેખાંકિત Rekhaankit

stream *n.* પાણીનો પૂરવાહ Paneeno pravaah

streamer *n.* પતાકા pataakaa

streamlet *n.* નાનું ઝરણું Naanun zarnun

street *n.* શેરી મહોલ્લો Sheree maholllo

streetwalker *n.* વેશ્યા veshyaa

strength *n.* સામર્થ્ય Saamrthya

strengthen *v.t.* મજબૂતાઈ Majbootaai

strenuous *adj.* ઘણી મહેનત કરનારું Ghanee mahenat karnaarun

stress *n.* દબાણ Dabaan

strew *v.t.* વેરવું veravun

stricken *adj.* રોગ, દુઃખ, ઈ.થી પીડિત Rog, Dukh e thee peedit

strict *adj.* ચોક્કસ Chokkas

strictness *n.* કઠોરતા Kathortaa

stricture *n.* સખત ટીકા Sakhat teeka

stride *v.t.* ડાંફ Daamf
strife *n.* સંઘર્ષ Sangharsh
strike *v.t.* આઘાત પહોંચાડવો Aaghaat pahochaadvo
striking *adj.* જોઈ શકાય એવું Joi shakaay evun
string *n.* દોરીઓ Doreeo
stringent *adj.* કડક Kadak
stringy *adj.* દોરી જેવું Doree jevun
strip *v.t.* કાપડા કાઢવા kapadaa kaadhavaa
stripe *n.* ચારિત્ર્ય Chaaritrya
stripling *n.* ઊગતો જુવાનિયો Ugto juvaaniyo
strive *v.t.* મથવું Mathvun
stroke *n.* દોહવું Dohvun
stroll *v.i.* રસળવું Rasalvun
strong *adj.* બળવાન Balvaan
stronghold *n.* ગઢ Gadh
strop *n.* લટપટિયું Latpatiyun
structure *n.* રચના Rachnaa
struggle *v.t.* કઠિન પરિશ્રમ Kathin parishram
strumpet *n.* વેશ્યા Veshyaa
strut *v.i.* ઠસ્સો Thasso
strychnine *n.* ઝેરકચોલું Zerkacholun
stub *n.* બીડી, પેન્સલિ ઇ.નું ઠૂંઠું Beedee, pensil e nu thoonthoo
stubble *n.* લણી લીધેલું ખેતર Lanee leedhelun khetar
stubborn *adj.* હઠીલું Hatheelun
stubbornness *n.* દુરાગ્રહ Duragrah
stubby *adj.* ઠૂંઠદાર thoontadaar
student *n.* વિદ્યાર્થી Vidhyaarthee
studied *adj.* જાણીબૂજીને કરેલું Janeeboojeene karelun
studio *n.* સ્ટૂડિયો studiyo
studious *adj.* અભ્યાસી Abhyaasee
study *n.* વિદ્યાભ્યાસ Vidhyaabhyaas
stuff *n.* નકામો બકવાટ Nakaamo bakvaat
stuffing *n.* ભરતી bharti
stuffy *adj.* હવાઉજાસ વિનાનું Havaaujaas vinaanun
stultify *v.t.* −નું પરિણામ ધોઈ નાખવું Nun parinam dhoi naakhvun
stumble *v.i.* ગોથું ખાવું Gothun khaavu

stump *n.* સ્ટમ્પ stamp
stumpy *adj.* ઠીગણું અને જાડું Thingnun ane jaadun
stun *v.t.* બેભાન કરવું bebhaan karavun
stunt *v.t.* વશિષ્ટ પ્રયત્ન Vishisht praytna
stunted *adj.* અધૂરિયું Adhooriyun
stupe *n.* ગરમપાણીનો શેક garamapaaneeno shek
stupefy *v.t.* બેવકૂફ બનાવવું bevakoof banaavavun
stupendous *adj.* અજબ Ajab
stupid *adj.* બેભાન અવસ્થામાં Bebhaan avasthaamaan
stupidity *n.* મંદબુદ્ધિ Mandbudhdhi
stupor *n.* બેહોશી Behoshee
sturdy ખડતલ Kharatal
stutter *v.i.* તડાવું તે Tadaavun te
sty *n.* ભૂંડનો વાડો bhoondano vaado
stygian *adj.* નારકી Naarkee
style *n.* શૈલી shailee
stylish *adj.* ફેશનેબલ Feshanebal
suasion *n.* સલાહસૂચના salaahasoochan
suasive *adj.* ઉપદેશાત્મક Updeshaatmak
suave *adj.* વિવેકી Vivekee
suavity *n.* વિવેકીપણું Vivekeepanun
sub નીચે Neeche
subaltern *adj.* હાથ નીચેનું Hath neechenu
sub-committee *n.* ઉપ સમિતિ Up samiti
sub-divide *v.t.* પેટાભાગ Petaabhaag
sub-division *n.* ઉપ વિભાગ Up vibhaag
subdue તાબે કરવું Taabe karvun
subject *adj.* વિષય vishay
subjection *n.* નું આજ્ઞાંકિત Nun Aagnyankit
subjective *adj.* આત્મલક્ષી Aatmalakshee
subjugate *v.t.* તાબામાં આણવું Taabaamaan aanvun
subjunctive *adj.* સંશય sanshay
sublet *v.t.* આડભાડે આપવું Aadbhaade aapvun
sublimate *v.t.* શુદ્ધ કરવું Shudhdh karvun
sublimation *n.* ઊર્ધ્વપાતન

sublime *adj.* ઊંચું Unchun

sublimity *n.* ઉદાત્તતા Udattata

sublunary *adj.* ચંદ્રની નીચેનું Chandranee neechenun

submarine *adj.* સબમરિન sabamarin

submerge *v.t.* ડુબવું dubavun

submerse *v.t.* ડુબાડવું Dubaadvun

submersion *n.* ડૂબ doob

submission *n.* રજૂ કરવું કે થવું તે Rajoo karvun ke thavun te

submissive *n.* તાબે થનારું Tabbe thanaarun

submit *v.t.* તાબે થવું Taabe thavun

subnormal *adj.* મંદબુદ્ધિ mandbuddhi

subordinate *n.* હાથ નીચેનું Haath nichenun

subscriben. ✍ લવાજમ lavaajam

subscript *adj.* સબસ્ક્રિપ્ટ sabaskript

subscription *n.* લવાજમ Lavaajam

subsequent *adj.* તરત પાછળનું Tarat paachhalnun

subsequently *adv.* પાછળથી Paachhalthee

subservient *adj.* આજ્ઞાકારી Aagnyaakaaree

subside *v.i.* ઓસરી જવું Osree javun

subsidiary *adj.* સહાયક Sahayak

subsidize *v.t.* આર્થિક મદદ કરવી Aarthik madad karvee

subsidy *n.* આર્થિક સહાય aarthik sahaay

subsist *v.t.* અસ્તિત્વ ધરાવવું Astitva dharaavvun

subsistence *n.* જીવતા રહેવું તે Jeevtaa rahevun te

subsoil *n.* અવભૂમિ avabhoomi

substance *n.* સારતત્ત્વ Saartatva

substantial *adj.* પૈસાદાર Paisadaar

substantiate *v.t.* પુષ્ટિ કરવી pushti karavee

substantive *n.* સ્વતંત્ર અસ્તિત્વવાળું Swatantra astitvvaalun

substitute *n.* અવેજી Avejee

substitution *n.* બદલો badalo

substratum *n.* નીચેનો થર Neecheno

thar

subtenant *n.* પેટા ભાડૂત Petaa bhaadoot

subtend *v.t.* ચાપની સામે હોવું chaapnee saame hovun

subterfuge બહાનું bahaanun

subterranean *adj.* ભૂમિ નીચેનું Bhoomi neechenun

subtile *adj.* તરકટી Tarkatee

subtle *adj.* નાજુક Naajuk

subtract *v.t.* બાદ કરવું Baad karvun

subtraction *n.* બાદબાકી Badbaakee

suburb *n.* ઉપનગર Upnagar

suburban *adj.* ઉપનગરોનું Upnagaronun

subvention *n.* સરકારી મદદ sarakaaree madad

subversion ઊંધું વાળવું કે ઉથલાવવું તે Undhun valvun ke uthlaavvun te

subversive *adj.* વિધ્વંસક Vidhvansak

subway *n.* ભૂગર્ભ માર્ગ bhoogarbh maarg

succeed *v.t.* સફળ થવું safal thavun

success *n.* સફળતા Safaltaa

successful *adj.* વિજયી Vijyee

succession *n.* ક્રમશઃ આવવું તે Kramash aavvun te

successive *adj.* અનુગામી anugaamee

successor *n.* વારસ Vaaras

succinct *adj.* ટૂંકું Toonku

succour *v.t.* અણીને વખતે કરેલી મદદ Anine vakhte karelee madad

succulent *adj.* રસદાર, જાડાં અને માવાવાળાં પાંદડાંવાળી Rasdaar, Jaadan ane maavaavaalan paanddaanvaalee

succumb હારી જવું Haree javun

suck *n.* ચૂસવું Choosvun

suckle *v.t.* ધવડાવવું Dhavdaavvun

suckling *n.* બચ્ચું bachchun

sudden *adj.* ઓચિંતું Ochintu

suddenly *adv.* એકાએક Ekaaek

suddenness *n.* તુવરા Twaraa

sudorific *adj.* સ્વેદકારી svedakaaree

suds *n.* સાબુનું ફીણ Saabunun feen

sue *v.t.* અદાલતમાં દાવો માંડવો Adaalatman daavo mandvo

suffer v.t. દરદ Darad
sufferance n. મૂક સંમતિ Mook, Sammati
suffering n. દુઃખ dukh
suffice v.t. ને માટે પૂરતું હોવું Ne maate poortun hovun
sufficiency n. પૂરતું Poortun
sufficient adj. જોઈએ તેટલું Joie tetlun
suffix v.t. પૂરતઃયય prayay
suffocate v.t. ગૂંગળાવવું Goonglaavvun
suffocation n. ગૂંગળામણ Goonglaaman
suffrage n. રાજકીય મતાધિકાર Raajkeey mataadhikaar
suffuse ફેલાવું felaavun
sugar n. ખાંડ Khaand
sugarcane n. શેરડી Sherdee
suggest v.t. વિચાર Vichaar
suicidal આત્મઘાતી Aatmaghaatee
suicide n. આત્મહત્યા Aatmhatyaa
suit v.i. વિશિષ પહેરવેશ vishesh paheravesh
suitability n. અનુકૂળતા Anukooltaa
suitable adj. બંધબેસતું Bandhbeshtun
suitably adv. યોગ્ય Yogya
suite n. ઓરડા Ordaa
suitor n. અનુનય કરનાર Anunay karnaar
sulk v.i. ગુસ્સે થવું Gusse thavun
sulky adj. રિસાયેલું Risaayelun
sullen adj. ચડિયેલું Chodaayelun
sully v.t. કલંકિત કરવું kalankit karavun
sulphate n. ગંધકામ્લના ક્ષારવાળું Gandhkaamlnaa ksharvaalun
sulphur n. ગંધક Gandhak
sulphurous adj. ગંધકના જેવું Gandhaknaa jevun
sulphury adj. ગંધકના જેવું Gandhaknaa jevun
sultry adj. ઉકળાટવાળું ukalatavaalun
sum n. સંક્ષેપ Sankshep
summarize v.t. નો સંક્ષેપકરવો કે હોવો No sankhep karvo ke hovo
summary adj. ટૂંકો હેવાલ Toonko hevaal
summer n. ઉનાળો Unaalo
summit n. ટોચ Toch
summon v.t. એકત્ર બોલાવવું Ektra bolaavvun

summons n. સમનૂસ samans
sumpter n. ભારવાહક ઘોડો bhaaravaahak ghodo
sumptuary adj. ખરચને લગતું Kharachne lagtun
sumptuous adj. ભારે કીમતી Bhaare kimti
sun n. સૂર્ય Soorya
sun-bath n. સૂર્યસ્નાન કરવું Sooryasnaan karvun
sunbeam n. સૂર્યકિરણ Soorakiran
sunday n. રવિવાર Ravivaar
sun-dial n. છાયાયંત્ર chhaayaayantra
sundry adj. જાતજાતનું પરચૂરણ Jaatjaatnun parchooran
sunflower n. સૂરજમુખી ફૂલ Soorajmukhee fool
sunk p.p. સ્થગતિ મૂડી Sthagit moodee
sunken adj. ડૂબેલું Doobelun
sunny adj. સૂર્યપ્રકાશવાળું Sooryaprakaashvaalun
sunrise n. સૂર્યોદયનો સમય Sooryodayno samay
sunshine n. સૂરજની જેમ ચળકતું Soorajnee jem chalktun
sup v.t. વાળુ કરવું Vaalun karvun
super adj. વધારાનું માણસ Vadhaaraanun maanas
superadd v.t. અધિકાધિક કરવું Adhikaadhik karvun
superannuate v.t. જૂનું થઈ જવું joonun thai javun
superannuation n. નિવૃત્તવિતન Nivrutti vetan
superb adj. ભવ્ય Bhavya
superficial adj. છીછરું chheechharun
superfine adj. અતિ ઉચ્ચ પ્રકારનું Ati uchcha prakaarnun
superfluous adj. જરૂર કરતાં વધારે Jaroor kartaan vadhaare
superfluity n. ખપ કરતા વધારાનું Khap kartaa vadhaaraanun
superhuman adj. અતિમાનુષી Atimaanushee
superintend દેખરેખ રાખવી dekharekha raakhavee

superintendence સંચાલન Sanchaalan

superintendent *n.* દેખરેખ રાખનાર Dekhrekh raakhnaar

superior *adj.* ઊંચી જાતનું Unchee jaatnun

superiority *n.* ચઢિયાતાપણું Chadhiyaataapanun

superlative *adj.* ઉચ્ચતમ માત્રાનું Uchchattam maatranun

superman *n.* અતિમાનવ Atimaanav

supernal *adj.* દિવ્ય Divya

supernatural *adj.* કુદરતના કાયદાથી પર Kudratnaa kaaydaathee par

superscribe *v.t.* ઉપર લખવું upar lakhavun

supersede *v.t.* ની જગ્યા લેવી Nee Jagya levee

superstition *n.* ખોટી માન્યતા Khotee maanyataa

superstitious *adj.* વહેમી Vahemee

superstructure *n.* ઈમારત કે વહાણનો ઉપલો ભાગ Imaarat ke vahaan uplo bhaag

supervention *n.* વધિનરૂપે આવવું vidhnaroope aavavun

supervise *v.t.* નજર રાખવી najar raakhavee

supervision *n.* નિરીક્ષણ nireekshan

supervisor *n.* નિરીક્ષક nireekshak

supine *adj.* સુસ્ત Sust

supper *n.* દિવસનું છેલ્લું ભોજન Divasnu Chhellu bhojan

supplant *v.t.* ની જગ્યા લેવી Nee jagyaa levee

supple *adj.* કોમળ komal

supplement *n.* વધારો Vadhaaro

supplementary *adj.* વધારાનું Vadhaaranu

suppliant *adj.* આજીજી કરનાર Aajiji karnaar

supplicate *v.t.* અરજ કરવી araj karavee

supply *v.t.* આપૂર્તિ કરવી aapoorti karavee

support *n.* ટેકો આપવો Teko aapvo

supportable *adj.* આધાર આપવા જોગ Aadhar aapvaa jog

supporter *n.* સમર્થક samarthak

suppose *v.t.* માનવું Maanvun

supposition *n.* માની લીધેલી વસ્તુ Maanee leedhelee vastu

suppository *n.* ગુદામાં નાંખવાની સોગટી gudaamaan naakhavaanee sogati

suppress દાબી દેવું Daabee devun

suppression *n.* જાહેર ન થવા દેવું Jaaher na thavaa devun

suppurate *v.i.* માં પરુ થવું Maan paru thavu

supreme *adj.* સર્વોપરી Sarvoparee

surcharge *v.t.* વધારાનો બોજો Vadhaaraano bojo

sure *adj.* નિશ્ચિત nishchit

surely *adv.* ખાતરીપૂર્વક Khaatreepoorvak

surf *n.* મોટું મોજું motun mojun

surface *n.* કોઈ વસ્તુનો બહારનો ભાગ Koi vastuno bahaarno bhaag

surfeit *n.* ખાવા પીવામાં અતિરિક Khaavaa peevaamaan atirek

surge *n.* મોજાંનો ઉછાળો Mojanno uchhalo

surgeon *n.* શસ્ત્રવૈદ્ય Shastravaidhya

surgery *n.* શસ્ત્રક્રિયા Sasrakriya

surgical *adj.* શસ્ત્રવૈદક Shastravaidak

surly *adj.* અસભ્ય Asabhya

surmise *v.t.* અનુમાન Anumaan

surmount જીતવું Jeetvun

surname *n.* અટક Atak

surpass *v.t.* ચડિયાતું બનવું chadiyaatun banavun

surpassing *adj.* ચડિયાતું chadiyaatun

surplus *n.* ફાજલ faajal

surprise *n.* આશ્ચર્ય aashcharya

surprising *adj.* વિલક્ષણ Vilakshan

surrender *v.t.* સોંપી દેવું Sonpee devun

surreptitious *adj.* ચોરીથી કરેલું Choreethee karelun

surround *v.t.* ચોતરફ ફરી વળવું chotaraf faree valavun

surroundings *n.* વીંટી લેનારું Veentee lenaarun

surtax *n.* વધારાનો કર Vadhaaraano kar

surveillance *n.* દેખરેખ Dekhrekh

survey *v.t.* મોજણી mojanee

surveyor *n.* મોજણીદાર Mojneedaar
survival *n.* ઉત્તરજીવિતા uttarajeevita
survive *n.* બચી જવું bachee javun
survivor *n.* ઉત્તરજીવી uttarjeevee
susceptible *adj.* ગ્રહણક્ષમ Grahanksham
suspect *v.t.* શંકા કરવી shankaa karavee
suspend ટાંગવું Tangvun
suspense *n.* અનિશ્ચિત સ્થિતિ Anischit sthiti
suspension *n.* સ્થગિતતા Sthagitta
suspicious *n.* સંશયાસ્પદ Sanshayaspad
sustain *v.t.* નો ભાર ઝીલવો કે ખમવો No bhaar zilvo ke khamvo
sustenance *n.* ગુજરાન Gujaran
suture *n.* તાંતવ સંધિ taantav sandhi
suzerain *n.* સરંજામદાર Saranjaamdaar
suzerainty *n.* શાસન વર્ચસ્વ Shaashan varchswa
swab *n.* પોતું potun
swag *n.* ચોરીનો માલ Choreeno maal
swagger *v.i.* ડોળ Dol
swain જુવાન ગામડિયો Juvaan gaamdiyo
swallow *n.* કોળીયો koleeyo
swamp *n.* ભેજવાળી પોચી જમીન Bhejvaalee pochee jameen
swampy *adj.* જળબંબોળ jalabanbol
swan *n.* રાજહંસ Raajhans
swank *n.* ડોળ કે દેખાવ કરવો Dol je dekhaav karvo
swap *n.* વિનિમય કરવો vinimay karavo
sward *n.* ટૂંકું ઘાસ Toonkun ghaas
swarm *n.* સમુદાય samudaay
swarthy *adj.* કાળું પડેલું Kaalu padelun
swash *v.t.* પાણી ઉડાડવું Paani udaadvun
swath *n.* ઘાસનો પટો ghaasno pato
swathe લૂગડામાં વીંટવું Loogdaaman vintvun
sway *v.t.* અસ્થિરપણે ઝૂલવું Asthirpane zoolvun
swear *v.t.* સોગન લેવી Sogan levee
sweat *n.* પરસેવો Parsevo
sweater *n.* ઊની સ્વેટર Unee swetar
sweaty *adj.* પરસેવો Parsevo
sweep *v.i.* ઝાડુ મારવું zaadu maaravun

sweeping *n.* ખૂબ વ્યાપક Khoob vyaapak
sweet *adj.* ગળ્યું Galyun
sweets *n.* મનોરંજક Manoranjak
sweeten *v.t.* ગળ્યું કરવું galyun karavun
sweetheart *n.* પ્રિયા અથવા પ્રતમિ Priya athvaa pratim
sweetmeat *n.* બજારુ મીઠાઈનું ચકતું Bajaaru meethainu chaktu
sweetness *n.* મીઠાઈભર્યુ Mithaaibharyu
swell *v.i.* વધવું Vadhvun
swelling *n.* સોજો Sojo
swerve *v.i.* બાજુએ ખસવું baajue khasavun
swift *adj.* ઉતાવળું Utaavalun
swiftness *n.* શીઘ્ર ગતિ Shighra, Gati
swim *v.i.* તરે તેમ કરવું Tare tem karvun
swindle *v.t.* છેતરવું Chhetrvun
swindler *n.* ઠગ Thag
swine *n.* ડુક્કર Dukkar
swing *v.t.* ઝૂલવું Zoolvun
swinge *v.t.* મારવું Maarvun
swirl *v.i.* વંટોળિયો Vantoliyo
switch *n.* વીજળીના તાર Veejleenaa taar
swivel *n.* ભંવરકડી Bhanvarkadee
swoon *v.i.* મૂર્છા પામવી moorchhaa paamavee
swoop *v.t.* તરાપ મારવી taraap maaravee
swop *n.* અદલાબદલ કે વિનિમય કરવો Adlaabadal ke vinimay karvo
sword *n.* તલવાર Talvaar
swordsman *n.* તલવાર બહાદુર Talvaar bahaadur
sybarite *n.* વિલાસી અને સ્ત્રૈણ માણસ Vilaasee ane strain maanas
sycophancy *n.* ખુશામત Khushaamat
sycophant *n.* ખુશામતિયો Khushaamatiyo
syllable *n.* શબ્દાંશ shabdaansh
syllabus *n.* અભ્યાસક્રમ Abhyaskram
syllogism *n.* સાધ્ય પ્રમાણ Saadhya pramaan
sylph *n.* વાયુદેવતા Vaayudevtaa
sylvan *adj.* વનનું Vannun
symbol *n.* સંકેતચિહ્ન Sanketchinh
symbolical *adj.* સંકેતચિહ્ન Sanketchinh

symmetrical *adj.* સમપ્રમાણ
Sampramaan
symmetry *n.* સમમતિ samamiti
sympathetic *adj.* સહાનુભૂતિવાળું
sahaanubhootivaalun
sympathize *v.i.* સહાનુભૂતિ થિવી
sahaanubhooti thavee
sympathy *n.* સહાનુભૂતિ sahaanubhooti
symphony *n.* સંગીતરચના
sangeetarachanaa
symposium *n.* ચર્ચા પરિષદ Charchaa
parishad
symptom *n.* લક્ષણ Lakshan
synchronism *n.* સહકાલનિતા
Sahlaalintaa
synchronize *v.t.* સમકાલિક કરવું કે થવું
Samkaalik karvun ke thavun
synchronous *adj.* સમકાલિક
samakaalik
syndicate *n.* સંઘ sangh
synod *n.* ધર્મસભા dharmasabhaa
synonym *n.* સમાનાર્થક શબ્દ
Samaanaarthak Shabd
synonymous *adj.* સમાનાર્થક
Samanarthak
synopsis *n.* સારાંશ Saraansh
syntax *n.* વાક્યરચના કે તેના નિયમો
Vakyarachna ke tena niymo
synthesis *n.* સંશ્લેષણ sanshleshan
synthetic *adj.* વાક્યરચના કે તેના નિયમો
Vaakyarachnaa ke tenaa niyamo
syphillis *n.* ઉપદંશ ગરમીવાળું Updwansh
garmeevalun
syringe *n.* પિચિકારી મારવી કે વતી
છાંટવું Pichkaaree maarvee ke vati
chhatvun
system *n.* સમગ્ર કે આખી વસ્તુ Samgra
ke aakhee vastu
systematic *adj.* પદ્ધતિસરનું
Padhdhateesarnun
systematize *v.t.* વ્યવસ્થિત બનાવવું
vyavasthit banaavavun
systole સંકોચન sankochan

T

tab *n.* ટેબ teb
tabby *n.* બિલાડી bilaadee
tabernacle *n.* યહૂદી પ્રાર્થના તંબૂ
yahoodee praarthana tanboo
table *n.* મેજ, ટેબલ mej, teble
tableau શોભાયાત્રા shobhaayaatraa
tablet *n.* કોતરેલા લખાણવાળી તકતી
kotrelaa lakhaanvalee taktee
tabloid *n.* છાપાની નાની આવૃત્તિ
chhapaanee naanee avrutti
taboo *n.* નિષેધ nishedh
tabor *n.* નાનકડું ઢોલ. naanakdoo dhol
tabular સારણીબદ્ધ saaraneebaddh
tach *n.* ચોપડો chopado
tacit *adj.* કહ્યા કે બોલ્યા વિના સૂચિત
kahyaa ke bolyaa vinaa soochit
taciturn *adj.* ઓછાબોલું ochaabolu
tack *n.* ખીલી kheelee
tackle *n.* બાથ ભીડવી baath bheedvee
tact *adj.* આવડત aavdat
tactful *adj.* કુનેહવાળું koonehvalu
tactician *n.* યુક્તિબાજ yuktibaaj
tactics *n.* યુક્તિ yukti
tactile *adj.* પર્શેન્દ્રિયનું ને લગતું
pashendriyan, ne lagatu
tadpole *n.* દેડકાનું બચ્ચું dedakaanun
bachchun
tag *n.* દોરી doree
tail *n.* પૂછડી poochadee
tailor *n.* દરજી; darjee
tailoress *n.* દરજી કામ કરતી મહિલા
darjee kaam kartee mahilaa
taint *n.* ડાઘો daagho
taintless *adj.* નિષ્કલંક nishkalank
take *v.t.* ઝાલવું jhaalvu
talc *n.* અભ્રક abhark
talent *n.* વિશિષ્ટ આવડત vishishta
aavdat
talented *adj.* પ્રતિભાશાળી
pratibhaashalee
talk *v.i.* બોલવું bolavu
talkative *adj.* વાતોડિયું vaatodiyu

talker *n.* બોલકણો માણસ bolakno maanas

talkies *n.* બોલતી ફિલ્મો bolatee filmo

tall *adj.* અત્યુક્તિવાળું antyuktivaalu

tallow *n.* કઠણ ચરબી kathan charabee

tally *v.t.* હિસાબ hisaab

talon *n.* શિકારી પક્ષીનો નહોર shikaree paxeeno nahor

tamable *adj.* વશમાં કરી શકાતો vashmaa karee shakaato

tamarind *n.* આમલી (નું ઝાડ). aamlee (nu jhaad)

tambour *n.* ઢોલ dhol

tambourine *n.* નાની ઢોલકી naanee dholkee

tame *adj.* દમ વગરનું, પામર dam vagar nu paamar

tamper *v.i.* નાહક માથું મારવું naahak maathu maarvu

tan *n.* ચામડું કમાવવું chaamadun kamaavavun

tang *n.* છરી chharee

tangent *n.* સ્પર્શ રેખા sparsh rekhaa

tangibility *n.* પરશનીયતા parshneeyataa

tangible *adj.* વાસ્તવિક vaastavik

tangle *v.t.* ગૂંચવવું goonchavavu

tank *n.* મોટી ટાંકી motee taanki

tankard *n.* દારૂનું પાત્ર daarunun paatra

tanker *n.* ટેન્કર tenkar

tanner *n.* ચામડિયો chaamadiyo

tantalize *v.t.* ટળવળાવવું talavalaavavun

tantamount *adj.* એના જેવું જ enaa jevuj j

tantrum *n.* લાગણીનો સ્ફોટ laagneeno sfot

tap *v.t.* નળની ટોટી nalnee totee

tape *n.* સાંકડી પટ્ટી saankdee pattee

taper *n.* પાતળી મીણબત્તી paatlee minbattee

tapestry *n.* નકશીદાર કાપડ nakasheedaar kaapad

tapis *n.* ભારે કાપડ bhaare kaapad

tapster *n.* શરાબખાનાનો નોકર sharaab khaanano nokar

tar *n.* ડામર daamar

tardiness *n.* મંદી mandee

tardy *adj.* ધીમું dheemu

target *n.* નિશાન nishaan

tariff *n.* દર કોષ્ટક dar koshtak

tarn *n.* પર્વતમાંનું નાનું સરોવર. parvatmaanu nanu sarovar

tarnish *v.t.* ઝાંખું jhankhu

tarpaulin *n.* તાડપત્રી taadapatree

tarry *adj.* ડામર ચોપડેલું. daamar chopdelu

tart *adj.* ખાટું khaatu

tartar *n.* છારી chhaaree

tartuffe *n.* પાખંડી paakhandee

task *n.* સોંપેલું કામ sonpelu kaam

tassel *n.* ફૂમતું foomatun

taste *v.t.* સ્વાદ swaad

tasteful *adj.* સારી અભિરુચિવાળું saaree abhiruchivaalu

tasteless *adj.* કશા સ્વાદ વિનાનું kashaa swaadvinany

tasty *adj.* સ્વાદિષ્ટ swaadishta

tatter *n.* ચીથરું cheentharun

tattle *v.t.* નકામા ગપાટા મારવા nakaama gapaataa maarvaa

tattler *n.* બડાઈખોર nadaaeekhor

tattoo *n.* છૂંદણું chhoondnun

taunt *n.* ટોણો tono

taurus *n.* આખલો aakhlo

taut *adj.* ખેંચેલું khenchelu

tautological *adj.* પુનરાવર્તન punaraavartan

tautology *n.* પુનરોક્તિ punarokti

tavern *n.* વીશી veeshee

taw *v.t.* લખોટીની એક જૂની રમત lahoteenee ek junee ramat

tawdry *adj.* દેખાઉ અને ભભકાદાર dikhaaoo ane bhabhakaadaar

tawny *adj.* પીળચટું pilchattu

tax *n.* કર kar

taxable *adj.* કરપાત્ર karpaatra

taxation *n.* કર બેસાડવા કે ભરવા તે. kar besaadvo ke bharvo te

taxi *n.* ભાડે ફરતી મોટર ગાડી bhaade fartee motor gaadee

tea *n.* ચાનો છોડ chaano chhod

teach *v.t.* શીખવવું sheekhavavun

teacher *n.* શિક્ષક sheexak

teaching *n.* શિક્ષકનું કામ-ધંધો sheexak no kaam dhandho teak *n.* સાગ saaga

teal *n.* પનકૂકડી panakookadee

team *n.* ટુકડી tukadee

te¡poy *n.* ટીપોઇ teepoy

tear *n.* અશ્રુ ashru

tease *v.t.* મશ્કરી કરીને ચીડવવું mashkaree kareene cheedavvun

teat *n.* આંચળ aanchal

technic *n.* યંત્રોદ્યોગશાસ્ત્ર yantrodhyogashaastra

technical કોઇ વશિષ્ટ કળા koi vishishta kalaa

technicality *n.* વશિષ્ટ લક્ષ્પँણ vishishta lakshan

technician *n.* તકનિકીવીદ્ takanikeevid

technique *n.* તકનકિ takanik

technology *n.* પ્રૌદ્યોગિકી prodhyogikee

ted *v.t.* ટેડ ted

tedious *adj.* કંટાળાભરેલું kantaalaabharelun

tedium *n.* કંટાળો kantaalo

teem *v.t.* ઉભરાવવું ubharaavavun

teens *n.pl.* 13થી 19ની ઉમર 13thee 19nee umar

teeth *n.pl.* દાંત daanta

teethe *v.t.* દાંત આવવા,દૂધિયા દાંત daanta aavavaa, doodhiyaa daanta

teetotaller *n.* મદ્યત્યાગી madyatyaagee

tele *prep.* દૂર door

telegram *n.* તાર taar

telegraph *n.* તારયંત્ર taarayantra

telegraphic *adj.* તારનું taarnun

telegraphy *n.* ટેલગિરાફ્ફી teligraafee

telepathy *n.* મનથી વિચારોની આપ-લે manathee vichaaronee aaple

telephone *n.* ટેલિફ઼ોન telifon

teleprintery *n.* ટેલપ્રિનટ્રી teliprinaree

telescope *n.* દૂરબીન doorbeena

telescopic *adj.* ટેલસિ઼ક઼ોપ teliskop

television *n.* દૂરદર્શનનો સટ dooradarshanno set

tell કહેવું kahevun

teller *n.* મતગણક mataganak

telling *adj.* પરિમાણકારક paricaanakaarak

tele-tale *n.* માહતિી આપવી maahitee aapvee

temerity *n.* ધૃષ્ટતાા dhrushtataa

temper *n.* મિજાજ mijaaj

temperament *n.* સામાન્ય સ્વભાવ saamaanya svabhaav

temperance *n.* મતિાચાર mitaachaar

temperate *adj.* અતરિક ટાળનારું atireka taalnaaru

temperature *n.* તાપમાન taapamaan

tempered *adj.* સ્વભાવ svabhaav

tempest *n.* વાવાઝોડું vaavaazodun

tempestuous *n.* તોફાની tofaanee

temple *n.* મંદરિ. mandir

tempo *n.* તાલ taal

temporary *adj.* કામચલાઉ kaamchalaau

temporize *v.i.* અનુકૂળ થવું anukool thavun

tempt *v.t.* લલચાવવું lalachaavavun

temptation *n.* પ્રલોભન pralobhan

tempter પ્રલોભક pralobhak

ten *adj.* દસ das

tenable *adj.* તર્કસંગત tarkasangat

tenacious *adj.* મક્કમ makkam

tenacity *n.* મક્કમતા makkamataa

tenancy *n.* ભોગવટો bhogavato

tenant *n.* ઘરનો ભાડૂત gharano bhaadoot

tenantry *n.* ગણોતિયાઓ ganotiyaao

tend *v.t.* અમુક દિશામાં જવું amuka dishaamaa javun

tendency *n.* ઝોક jhok

tender *v.t.* આપવાનું કહેવું aapavaanu kahevu

tenderness *n.* કોમળતા komalataa

tendon *n.* કંડરા kandaraa

tendril *n.* વાળો તંતુ vaalo tantu

tenement *n.* રહેવાનું મકાન rahevaanu makaan

tenet *n.* કોઇ પક્ષ કે સંપ્રદાયનો મત koi paksha ke sampradaayano mat

tenfold *adj.* દસડવું dasadavun

tennis *n.* ટેનસિ tenis

tenon *v.t.* (લાકડાનું) સાલ. (laakadaanu) saal

tenor *n.* સમયગાળો samayagaalo

tense *adj.* તાણીને ખેંચેલું taaneene khenchelun

tension *n.* માનસિક તાણ maanasik taan

tent *n.* તંબૂ tamboo

tentacle *n.* પ્રાણીની મૂંછ praaneenee moonchh

tentative *adj.* પ્રયોગાત્મક prayogaatmak

tented *adv.* માથે છાંયાવાળું maathe chaanyaavaalun

tenth *adj.* દસમું. dasamu

tenuous *adj.* પાતળું paatalun

tergal *adj.* વાંસાનું કે તેને લગતું vaansaanu ke tene lagatun

term *n.* અમુક મર્યાદિત સમય amuka maryaadita samay

termagant *adj.* વઢકણી સ્ત્રી vadhakanee stree

terminal *adj.* સત્રાંત santraat

terminate *v.t.* અંત લાવવો anta laavavo

terminable *n.* અંત લાવી શકાય એવું anta laavee shakaaya aevun

terminology *n.* પરિભાષા paribhaashaa

terminal *n.* સત્રાંત satraant

termite *n.* ઉધઈ udhaaee

tern *adj.* દરિયાઈ અબાબીલ dariyaai abaabeel

ternate *adj.* તૂરણના સમૂહનો સેટ trana naa samoohno set

terra *n.* ધરતી dhartee

terrace *n.* ઊંચાણવાળો જમીનનો સમતલ પટો oochaanvalo jameenno samtal pato

terrafirma *n.* સૂકી જમીન sookee jameen

terrestrial *adj.* ધરતી કે પૃથ્વીનું dharatee ke pruthaveenun

terrible *n.* ભયજનક bhayajanak

terrific *adj.* ભયંકર bhayankar

terrify *v.t.* ભયભીત કરવું bhayabheet karavun

territorial *adj.* પ્રાદેશિક praadeshik

territory *n.* પ્રદેશ pradesh

terror *n.* થથરી જવાય એવો ભય thatharee javaaya aevo bhay

terrorism *n.* આતંકવાદ aatankavaad

terrorize *v.t.* ભયભીત કરી નાખવું bhayabeeta karee naakhavun

terse *adj.* સંક્ષિપ્ત sankshipt

tertian *adj.* એકાંતરિયો તાવ aekaantariyo taava

test *n.* કસોટી kasotee

testament *n.* મૃત્યુપત્ર mrutyupatra

testamentary *adj.* મૃત્યુપત્રનું mrutyupatranu

testator *n.* મૃત્યુપત્ર કરનાર mrutyupatra karanaar

testicle *n.* અંડકોષ andakosh

testify *v.t.* સાક્ષી – પુરાવો – આપવો saakshee, puravo aapavo

testimonial *n.* પ્રમાણપત્ર pramaanapatra

testimony *n.* પુરાવો puravo

testy *n.* ચીડિયું cheediyun

tetanus *n.* ધનુર્વા dhanurvaa

tether *n.* બાંધવાનું દોરડું baandhvaanun doradun

tetrad *n.* ટારનું જૂથ taarnu jooth

tetrahedron *n.* ચાર સપાટી chaar sapaatee

text *n.* મૂળ શબ્દ mool shabd

tex¶book *n.* પાઠયપુસ્તક paathayapustak

textile *adj.* વણાટનું vanaatanu

textual *adj.* મૂળ પાઠનું moola paathanu

texture *n.* વણાટ vanaat

than *conj.* અપેક્ષા apekshaa

thank —નો આભાર – પાડ માનવો no aabhaar, -paada maanavo

thankful *adj.* કૃતજ્ઞ krutagyana

thankless *adj.* પાડ ન માનનારું paada na maananaarun

that *pro.* પેલું pelun

thatch *v.t.* છાપરા માટેનાં છાજ chaaparaa maatenaa chhaaj

thaumatur *n.* થૌમાતુર thaumatur

thaumatge *n.* ચમત્કાર chamatkaar

thaw *v.t.* ઓગળવું ogalavun

theatre *n.* નાટ્યગૃહ naatyagruha

thee *pro.* કર્મની વિભક્તિ karmanee vibhakti

theft *n.* ચોરી. choree

their તેમનું temanu

theism *n.* આસ્તિક aastik

theist *n.* ઈશ્વરવાદી ishvaravaadee

them તેમને temane

theme *n.* વિષય વસ્તુ vishay vastu

then *adv.* તે વખતે te vakhate

thence *adv.* ત્યાંથી tyaanthee

theo *pref.* ઈશ્વર અથવા દેવ ishvara athavaa deva

theocracy *n.* ધર્મશાસન dharmashaasan

theodolite *n.* ખૂણા માપક khoonamaapak

theologian *n.* ધર્મશાસ્ત્ર dharmashaastra

theology *n.* ઈશ્વરના અસ્તિત્વને લગતું શાસ્ત્ર ishvaranaa astitvane lagatu shaastra

theorem *n.* પ્રમેય pramey

theoretical *adj.* સૈદ્ધાંતિક saidhaantik

theorist *n.* સિદ્ધાંત શોધનાર siddhant shodhanaar

theorize *v.t.* સિદ્ધાંત શોધવો siddhant shodhavo

theory *n.* માની લીધેલા સિદ્ધાંત maanee leedhelaa sidhdhaant

theosophy *n.* થિયોસોફી thiyosofee

therapeutic *adj.* રોગ મટાડનારું roga mataadanaarun

therapy *n.* ઉપચારશાસ્ત્ર upachaarashaastra

there *adv,* ત્યાં tyaan

thereby *adv.* એ રીતે ae rite

therefore *adv.* એના પરિણામ રૂપે aenaa parinaama roope

therein *adv.* એમાં Eman

thereupon *adv.* ના ફળ રૂપે naa fala roope

therm *n.* થર્મ એકમ tharm ekam

thermal *adj.* ઉષ્મીય ushmeeya

thermic *adj.* ઉષ્ણતા કે ગરમીનું ushnataa ke garameenu

thermometer *n.* ઉષ્ણતામાપક ushnataamaapak

thermos *n.* થર્મોસ tharmos

thesaurus *n.* માહિતીનો ભંડાર maahiteeno bhandaar

these *n.* વ્યક્ત અથવા વસ્તુ અંગે) આ, હાજર (vyakti ke vastu ange) aa, haajar

thesis *n.* મહાનિબંધ mahaanibandh

thew *n.* માણસનું સ્નાયુબળ maanasanu snaayubal

they *pro.* તેઓ teo

thick *adj.* જાડું jaadun

thicken *v.t.* જાડું કરવું jaadun karavun

thicket *n.* ગીચ ઝાડી geecha zaadee

thickness *n.* જાડાઈ jaadaai

thief *n.* ચોર. chor

thieve *v.i.* ચોરવું choravun

thievish *adj.* ચોર chor

thigh *n.* જાંઘ jaangh

thimble *n.* (દરજીની) અંગૂઠી. (darajeenee) angoothee

thin *adj.* પાતળું paatalu

thine *pro.* તારું taarun

thing *n.* કોઈ પણ ચીજ koi pana cheej

think *v.t.* વિચારવું vichaaravun

thinker *n.* વિચારક vichaarak

thinking *n.* અભિપ્રાય abhipraay

thinly *adv.* ઓછી રીતે ochhee reete

thinness *n.* પાતળાપણું paatalaapanun

third *adj.* ત્રીજું treejun

thirst *n.* તરસ taras

thirsty *adj.* તરસ્યું tarsyun

thirteen *n.* તેર tera

thirteenth *adj.* તેરમું teramun

thirtieth *adj.* ત્રીસમું treesamun

thirty *n.* ત્રીસ treesa

this *pro.* (વ્યક્ત અથવા વસ્તુ અંગે) આ, હાજર (vyakti ke vastu ange) aa, haajar

thither *adv.* તે જગ્યાએ te jagyaaae

thong *n.* વાધરી vaadharee

thorax *n.* વક્ષઃસ્થળ vakshahsthal

thorn *n.* કાંટો kaanto

thorny *adj.* કાંટાળું kaantaalun

thorough *adj.* સંપૂર્ણ sampurna

thoroughfare *n.* સાર્વજનિક માર્ગ saarvajanika maarg

thoroughly *adv.* સર્વથા sarvatha

those *pro.* those નું બહુવચન those nun bahoovachana

thou *pro.* બીજા પુરુષ એકવચન beejaa purusha aekavachan

though *conj.* છતાં chaataan

thought *n.* વિચાર કરવો તે vichaara karavo te

thoughtful *adj.* વિચારી vichaaree

thoughtless *adj.* અવિચારી avichaaree

thousand *adj.* સહસ્ત્ર sahastra

thraldom *n.* ગુલામી gulaamee

thrall *n.* ગુલામ gulaam

thrash *v.t.* મારવું maaravun

thread *n.* લાંબો ધાગો laambo dhaago

threadbare *adj.* જૂનું અને ઘસાઈ ગયેલું joonun ane ghasaai gayelun

threat *n.* ધમકી dhamakee

threaten *v.t.* ને ધમકાવવું ne dhamakaavavun

threatening *adj.* ડરાવતું daraavatun

three *adj.* ત્રણ trana

thresh *n.* ઝૂડવું zoodavun

threshold *n.* ઉંબરો umaro

threw *v.t.* ફેંકવુ fenkavu

thrice *adv.* ત્રણ વાર. trana vaara

thrift *n.* કરકસર karkasar

thrifty *adj.* ચિંતવ્યયી chintavyayee

thrill *v.t.* કમકમાટી kamakamaatee

thrive *v.i.* સમૃદ્ધ થવું samrudhdha thavun

thriving , સમૃદ્ધ samrudhdh

throat *n.* ગરદનનો આગળનો ભાગ garadanano aaganano bhaag

throb *v.i.* ધબકવું dhabakavun

throe *n.* તીવ્ર વેદના teevra vedanaa

thrombosis *n.* લોહી ગંઠાઈ જવું lohee ganthaai javun

throne *n.* આસન aasan

throng *v.t.* ટોળું tolun

throttle *v.t.* ગળું galun

through *adv.* માં થઈને maa thaine

throughout *adv.* દરેક ભાગમાં dareka bhaagamaa

throw *v.t.* ફેંકવુ fenkavu

thrum *n.* કંટાળાજનક વાદન kantaalaajanak vaadan

thrush *n.* મોં mon

thrust *v.t.* જોરથી ધક્કો મારવો jorathee dhakko maaravo

thrustings *n.* જોરથી ધક્કો મારવો jorathee dhakko maaravo

thud *n.* ધબ દઈને પડવું dhava daine padavun

thug *n.* ઠગ thag

thumb *n.* અંગૂઠો angootho

thump *v.t.* સખત ફટકો sakhata fatako

thunder *v.i.* વીજળીનો કડાકો veejaneeno kadaako

thunderbolt *n.* વીજળી પડવી veejanee padavee

thunderstorm *n.* કડાકા સાથેનું તોફાન kadaakaa saathenu tofaana

thursday *n.* ગુરુવાર guruvaara

thus *adv.* આ રીતે aa reete

thwart *adj.* નિષ્ફળ બનાવવું nishfala banaavavun

thy *pro.* તારું. taarun

thymol *n.* એક જંતુનાશક દવા. aeka jantunaashaka davaa

thyroid *adj.* થાયરોઇડ thaayaroid

thyself *pro.* તું પોતે tu pote

tibia *n.* ગના નળાનું હાડકું ganaa nalaanu haadakun

tic *n.* સ્નાયુનું સંકોચન snaayunu sankochana

tick *v.t.* બગાઈ bagaai

ticket *n.* ટિકિટ tikit

tickle *v.t.* ગલી galee

ticklish *adj.* નાજુક naajuk

tidal *adj.* ભરતીઓટ સંબંધી bharatee -ot sambandhee

tide *v.t.* દરિયાની ભરતીઓટ dariyaanee bharateeot

tidiness *n.* સફાઈ safaai

tidings *n.* સમાચાર samaachaar

tidy *adj.* સુઘડ sughad

tie *v.t.* દોરી doree

tiff *n.* નજીવો ઝઘડો najeevo zaghado

tiffin *n.* બપોરનું ખાણું. baporanu khaanun

tiger *n.* વાઘ vaagh

tight *adj.* સજ્જડ sajjad

tighten *v.t.* સજ્જડ કરવું sajjada karavun

tile *n.* નળિયું naliyun

till *v.t.* સુધી sudhee

tillage *n.* ખેડ khed

tiller *n.* સુકાન ફેરવવાનો દાંડો sukaana feravavaano daando

tilt *n.* એક બાજુએ નમવું aeka baajuae namavun

timber *n.* ઇમારતી લાકડું imaaratee laakadun

timbrel *n.* ઢોલકી tholakee

time *n.* સમય samay

time-bar *n.* વારંવાર vaaramvaar

timely *adj.* સમયસરનું samayasaranun

timepiece *n.* મેજ ઘડિયાળ mej ghadiyaal

time-table *n.* સમયપત્રક samayapatraka

timid *adj.* બીકણ beekan

timidity *n.* બીકણપણું bikanapanun

tin *n.* કલાઈ kalaai

tincal *n.* ટંકણખાર tankanakhaara

tincture *n.* માદક દ્રાવણ maadak draavan

tinder *n.* સૂકો પદાર્થ sooko padaarth

tine *n.* પંજેટી, કાંસકી, ઇ.નો દાંતો panjetee, kaansakee no daanto

tinge *v.t.* રંગની છટા કે છાયા ranganee chataa ke chaayaa

tingle *v.t.* માં કશુંક ભોંકાતું maa kashunka bhonkaatun

tinker *n.* ફેરિયો feriyo

tinkle *v.i.* ઘંટડીનો અવાજ થવો ghantadeeno avaaja thavo

tinsel *n.* તકલાદી વસ્તુ takalaadee vastu

tint *n.* જુદો રંગ judo rang

tiny *adj.* બહુ નાનું bahu naanun

tip *n.* અણી anee

tip-cat *n.* ટપિ કેટ રમત tip ket ramat

tipple *v.t.* દારૂનું વ્યસન daaroonu vyasan

tipsy *adj.* પીધેલ peedhel

tiptoe *n.* છુપાઈને જવું chhoopaaine javun

tiptop *v.t.* ઊંચી કક્ષાનું unchee kakshaanun

tirade *n.* નંદિત્મક ભાષણ nindaatmaka bhaashan

tire *v.t.* થાકવું thaakavun

tired *adj.* થાકેલા હોવું thaakelaa hovun

tiring *adj.* થકવી નાખતું thakavee naakhatun

tiro શિખાઉ shikhaaun

tiresome *adj.* ત્રાસદાયક. traasadaayak

tissue *n.* ઝીણું કાપડ zeenun kaapad

tit *n.* એક નાનું – ચપળ પક્ષી. eeka naanu - chapala pakshee

titan *n.* કદાવર માણસ kadaavar maanas

titbit *n.* સ્વાદિષ્ટ કોળિયો swaadishta koliyo

tithe *n.* દશાંશ કર dashaansh kar

titillate ગલીપચી કરવી galeepachee karavee

titilation સુખદ અને રોમાંચક sukhad ane romaanchak

title *n.* ચોપડી chopdee

titter *v.i.* ઠીઠી હસવું thitih hasavun

¶ittle *n.* રજ raj

tituler *adj.* ખિતાબ ધારણ કરવો khitaab dhaaran karvo

toad *n.* દેડકો dedako

toady *n.* ખુશામતિયો khushaamatiyo

toast *n.* દેવતા પર મૂકીને શેકવું devtaa par mookeene shekvun

tobacco *n.* તમાકુ tamaaku

tobacconist *n.* તમાકુનો વેપારી. tamaakuno vepaaree

tocsin *n.* ભયની સૂચના bhaynee soochnaa

today *n.* આજે aaje

toddle *v.i.* ભાંખોડીયે ચાલવું bhaankhodeeye chaalavun

toddy *n.* તાડી taadee

toe *n.* પગની આંગળી કે અંગૂઠો pagnee aanglee ke angootho

toffee *n.* ટોફી tofee

toft *n.* વિસ્તાર vistaar

toga *n.* રોમન ઝભ્ભો raman zabhbho

together *adv.* મંડળીમાં mandleema

toil *v.i.* સખત મહેનત કરવી sakhat mahenat karvee

toilet *n.* નહાવું nahaavun

toilsome *adj.* વૈતરું vaitarun

token *n.* નિશાની nishaanee

tola *n.* તોલા tolaa

tolerable *n.* સહ્ય sahya

tolerance *n.* સહનશક્તિ sahanashakti

tolerant *adj.* સહિષ્ણુ sahushnu

tolerate *v.t.* સહન કરવું sahana karavun

toleration સહિષ્ણુતા sahishnutaa

toll *n.* વેરો vero

tomato *n.* ટમાટો tamaato

tomb *n.* કબર kabar

tomboy *n.* ખેલાડી છોકરી khelaadee chhokaree

tom-cat *n.* બિલાડો bilaado

tome *n.* દળદાર ગ્રંથ daladaar granth

tomfool *n.* મૂરખવ્યક્તિ moorkhvyakti

tomfoolery *n.* મૂરખામીભર્યું વર્તન moorkhaameebharyu vartan

tomorrow *adv.* આવતી કાલ(નો દિવસ) aavatee kaala(no divas)

tomtom *n.* ઊંડા અવાજવાળું undaa avaajavaalun

ton *n.* એક વજન aeka vajan

tone *n.* ધ્વનિ dhvani

tonga *n.* બે પૈડાની ગાડી be paidaanee gaadee

tongs *n.pl.* ચીપિયો cheepiyo

tongue *n.* જીભ jeebh

tonguester *n.* વાર્તાઓ કહેનાર vaartaao kahenaar

tonic *adj.* પુષ્ટિકારક pushtikaarak

tonight *adv.* આજની રાત કે સાંજ. aajanee raata ke saanja

tonite *n.* એક વિસ્ફોટક aeka visfotaka

tonsil *n.* કાકડા kaakadaa

tonsure *n.* મુંડન કરવાની વિધિ mundana karavaanee vidhi

too *adv.* વધારામાં vadhaaraamaan

tool *n.* ઓજાર ojaar

tooth *n.* દાંત daant

top *n.* ટોચે toche

topaz *n.* પોખરાજ (મણિ). pokharaaj(mani)

toper *n.* દારૂડિયો daaroodiyo

topic *n.* વિષય vishay

topical *adj.* વિષયને લગતું vishayne lagatun

topknot *adj.* ચોટલી chotalee

topography *n.* સ્થાનિક ભૂગોળ sthaanika bhoogol

topsyturvy *adj.* નારાજ થવું naaraaja thavun

torch *n.* મશાલ mashaal

torment *n.* યાતના yaatanaa

tormina *n.* તીવ્ર teevra

tornado *n.* વંટોળ vantol

torpedo *n.* ટોરપીડો torpeedo

torpid *adj.* બધિરિતા badhirataa

torpidity *n.* બધિર bathir

torpor *n.* બધિરિત્વ badhiratva

torrent *n.* પ્રચંડ પૂરવાહ prachand pravaah

torrential *adj.* પૂરચંડી prachandee

torrid *adv.* અતિઉષ્ણ atiushna

torso *n.* માથું અને હાથપગ વિનાનુ ધડ maathun ane haathapaga vinaanu dhad

tortoise *n.* કાચબો. kaachabo

tortuous *adj.* આમળાવાળું aamlaavaalun

torture *n.* યાતના yaatanaa

tory *n.* રૂઢિચુસ્ત roodhichust

toss *v.t.* હળવેથી halavethee

total *adj.* સંપૂર્ણ sampoorna

totality *n.* સંપૂર્ણતા sampoornataa

totter *v.t.* અસ્થિર ઊભા રહેવું ashthira ubhaa rahevun

touch *v.t.* અડવું adavun

touching *adj.* હૃદયસ્પર્શી hridayasparshee

touchy *adj.* ચીડિયું cheediyun

tough *adj.* ભાંગવું મુશ્કેલ bhaangavun mushkel

tour *n.* મોજ માટે કરેલી મુસાફરી moja maate karelee musaafaree

tourist *n.* પ્રવાસી pravaasee

tournament *n.* ક્રીડાયુદ્ધ kreedaayudhdha

tourniquet *n.* ટુર્નિકિટ turniket

tout *n.* દલાલ dalaal

tow *v.t.* કાંતવાનું શણ kaantavaanun shan

toward *prep* દિશામાં dishaamaan

towel *n.* રૂમાલ roomaal

tower *n.* મિનારો minaaro

towering *adj.* ખૂબ ઊંચું ઉદાત્ત khooba unchun, udaatta

town *n.* નગર nagar

toxicology *n.* વિષવિદ્યા વિજ્ઞાન vishavidhyaa, vigyaana

toxin *n.* વિષ vish

toy *n.*

trace *n.* નિશાનની nishaanee

trachoma *n.* ટ્રાકોમા રોગ traakomaa rog

tracing *n.* અનુરેખણ anurekhan

track *n.* રસ્તો rasto

trackless *adj.* ગૂમ થઈ જવુ gooma thai javun

tract *n.* પ્રદેશ, મુલક, વિસ્તાર pradesha, mulaka, vistaar

tractability *n.* કહ્યાંગરું kahyaagarun

tractable *n.* કહ્યાંગરું kahyaagarun

tractile *adj.* લાંબુ થઈ શકે એવું laambu thai shake aevun

traction *n.* ખેંચવું khenchaun

tractive *adj.* ખેંચીને પાડી દેવું khencheene paadee devun

tractor *n.* ભારવાહક, બીજાં વાહનો bhaaravaahaka, beejaa vaahano

trade *n.* ધંધો; વિનિમિય વેપાર dhandho, vinimaya, vepaar

trader *n.* વેપારી vepaaree

tradesman *n.* દુકાનદાર dukaanadaar

trade mark *n.* ટ્રેડમાર્ક tredmaark

trade union *n.* મજૂર મહાજન majoor mahaajan

tradition *n.* પરંપરા paranparaa

traditional *adj.* પરંપરાગત paramparaagat

traduce *v.t.* નિંદા કરવી. nindaa karavee

traffic *v.i.* વેપાર vepaar

tragedian *n.* શોકાન્તિક નાટકનો અભિનેતા shokaantik naatakano abhinetaa

tragedy *n.* ઉદાત્ત શોકાન્તિક નાટક udaata shokaantika naatak

tragic *adj.* શોકાન્તિક નાટકનું – -ના જેવું shokaantika naatakanu, -naa jevun

trail *v.t.* ખેંચવું khenchavun

trailer *n.* વેલા જેવી વનસ્પતિ velaa jevee vanaspati

train *v.t.* તાલીમ આપવી laaleem aapvee

trainee *n.* તાલીમાર્થી taaleemaarthee

trainer *n.* તાલીમ આપનાર માણસ. taaleem aapnaar maanas

training *n.* તાલીમ taleem

trait *n.* વિશિષ્ટ ગુણ – લક્ષણ. vishishta gunn, laxan

traitor *n.* વિશ્વાસઘાત કરે તેવું vishvaatghaat kare tevun

traitorous *adj.* વિશ્વાસઘાત કરનાર vishvaatghaat karnaar

trajectory *n.* માર્ગ maarga

tram *n.* ટ્રામ traam

trammel *n.* માછલાં પકડવાની જાળ maachhlaa pakadvaane jaal

trample *v.t.* ચગદી નાંખવું chagadee naankhavun

trance *n.* નિદ્રા જેવી અવસ્થા nindraa jevee avasthaa

tranquil *adj.* ગંભીર gambheer

tranquillity *n.* સંપૂર્ણ સ્થિરતા sampoorn sthirtaa

tranquillize *v.t.* શાંત પાડવું દવા આપીને. shaant paadvu davaa aapine

trans *prep.* આરપાર aarpaar

transact *v.* કામ કે ધંધો કરવું kaam ke dhandho karvun

transaction *n.* સોદો sodo

transacend મર્યાદાઓ ઓળંગી maryaadaao olangee

transcendent *adj.* ચડિયાતું chadiyaatun

transcribe *v.t.* નકલ કરવી nakal karvee

transcription *n.* નકલ કરવી nakal karvee

transfer *v.t.* તબદીલ કરવું tabadeel karavun

transferable *adj.* તબદીલપાત્ર tabadeelpaatra

transfigure *v.t.* રૂપ rup

transfix *v.t.* ભાલા વતી આરપાર ભોંકવું bhaalaa vatee aarpaar bhonkvun

transform *v.t.* દેખાવ dekhaav

transformation *n.* કાયાપલટ kaayaapalat

transfuse *v.i.* તરબોળ કરવું tarabol karavun

transfusion *n.* તરબોળ કરવું tarbol karvun

transgress *v.t.* કાયદાનું ઉલ્લંઘન કે ભંગ કરવો kaaydaanu oolanghan ke bhanga karvo

transgression *n.* મર્યાદા વટાવવી તે maryaadaa vataavvee te

transgressor *n.* કાયદાનું ઉલ્લંઘન કરનાર kaaydaanu oolanghan karnaar

tranship *v.t.* ટ્રાન્સશિપ transship

transhipment *n.* ટરાન્સશપિમેન્ટ transsshipment

transient *adj.* ક્ષણિક xanik

transit *n.* અભિવહન abhivahan

transition *n.* એક અવસ્થા eek avasthaa

transitional *adj.* સંક્રાન્તિકાળ. sankraantikaal

transitive *adj.* સકર્મક. sakarmak

transitory *n.* ચંચલ chanchal

translate *v.t.* ભાષાંતર કરવું bhaashaantar karvun

translation *n.* ભાષાંતર bhaashaantar

translator *n.* ભાષાંતર કરવું bhaashaantar karvun

transliterate *v.t.* લવ્યિયંતર કરવું livyantar karavun

translucent *adj.* અર્ધપારદર્શક ardhapaardarshak

transmigrate *v.t.* બીજા દેહમાં જવું. beejaa deh ma javu

transmission *n.* રવાનગી ravaangee

transmit *v.t.* સંચારિત કરવું sanchaarit karvun

transmutable *adj.* કાયાપલટયોગ્ય kaayaapalatyogya

transmutation *n.* રૂપાંતર roopaantar

transmute *v.t.* રૂપાંતર કરવું roopaantar karvun

transom *n.* બારીમાં ચોઢેલું આડું લાકડું baareema chodhelu aadu laakdun

transparence *n.* પારદર્શકતા paardarshaktaa

transparent *n.* પારદર્શક paardarshak

transpire *v.t.* ઉત્સર્જન કરવું utsarjan karvun

transplant *v.t.* સ્થાપન કરવું staapan karvun

transport પરિવહન parivahan

transportation *n.* લઈ જવું કે લાવવું laee javu ke laavvun

transpose *v.t.* અરસપરસ જગ્યા બદલવી arasparas jagyaa badalvee

trans-ship ટરાન્સશપિ transsship

transverse *adj.* વાંકું vaankun

tranter *v.t.* વિક્રેતા vikkretaa

trap *n.* પાંજરું paanjrun

trapeze *n.* કસરતનો દાંડો kasaratano

daando

trapezium *n.* સમલંબક samalanbak

trappings *n.pl.* શોભાનો સાજશણગાર shobhaano saajanshangaar

trash *n.* કચરો kachchro

travail *v.i.* પ્રસવવેદના prasavavedanaa

travel *n.* પ્રવાસ pravaas

traveller *n.* મુસાફર musaafar

traverse *v.t.* આરપાર જવું aarapaara javun

travesty *n.* વિકૃત વિડંબન vikrut vidamban

trawl *n.* જાળ jaal

tray *n.* તાસક taasak

treachery *n.* વિશ્વાસઘાતી vishvaasaghaatee

treacle *n.* ગોળ gol

tread *v.t.* પગ મૂકવો paga mookavo

treadle *n.* પગ વતી ચલાવાતું યંત્ર paga vatee chalaavaatun yantra

treason *n.* રાજદ્રોહ rajadroha

treasure *n.* ખજાનો khajaano

treasurer *n.* ખજાનચી khajaanachee

treasury *n.* ખજાનો khajaano

treat *v.* આતિથ્ય aatithya

treatise *n.* મીમાંસા meemaansaa

treatment *n.* સારવાર saaravaar

treaty *n.* સંધિ sandhi

treble *adj.* ત્રેવડું trevadun

tree *n.* ઝાડ zaad

trek *n.* મુસાફરી કરવી musaafaree karavee

tremble *v.i.* ધ્રૂજવું dhroojavun

tremendous *adj.* ભયાનક bhayaanak

tremolo *n.* કંપમુક્ત સૂર kampayukta soora

tremor *n.* ધ્રૂજારી dhroojaaree

tremulous *n.* ધ્રૂજતું dhroojatun

trench *v.t.* ઊંડો ખાડો undo khaado

trenchant *adj.* તીક્ષ્ણ teekshana

trencher *n.* લાકડાનો મોટો થાળો laakadaano moto thaalo

trend *n.* વશિષ્ટ દિશા vishista dishaa

trepan હાડકું કાપવાની કરવત haadakun kaapavaanee karavat

trepidation *n.* ક્ષોભ kshobh

trespass *v.i.* અપપ્રવેશ apapravesh

trespasser *n.* અપપૂરવેશક apapraveshak

tress *n.* વાળની લટ vaalanee lat

tri *pre.* ત્રણ(ગણું) trana(ganun)

triad *n.* ત્રણનું જૂથ trananu jootha

trial *n.* અજમાયશ ajamaayash

triangle *n.* ત્રિભુજ tribhuj

triagular *adj.* ત્રિકોણીય trikoneeya

tribe *n.* આદિજાતી aadijaatee

tribulation *n.* ભારે કષ્ટ bhaare kashta

tribunal *n.* ન્યાયાલય nyaayaalay

tribune *n.* મંચ manch

tributary *adj.* ખંડણી આપવા પાત્ર khandanee aapavaa paatr

tribute *n.* અંજલિ anjali

trice *n.* ક્ષણવાર kshanavaar

trick *n.* છેતરવાની યુક્તિ chhetaravaanee yukti

trickery *n.* છેતરપિંડી chhetarapindee

trickle *v.t.* ટપકવું tapakavun

trickster *n.* ઠગ thag

tricolour *n.* તિરંગો tirango

trident *n.* ત્રિશૂળ trisool

triennial *adj.* ત્રણ વરસે થનારું trana varase thanaarun

trifle *n.* નજીવી વસ્તુ najeevee vastu

trifling નજીવું najeevun

trigger *n.* બંદૂકનો ઘોડો bandookano ghodo

trigon *n.* ત્રિકોણ trikona

trigonometry *n.* ત્રિકોણમિતિ trikonamiti

trill *n.* કંપયુક્ત સ્વર kampayukta svar

trillion *n.* પદ્મ padma

trilogy *n.* ત્રિમિતિ trimiti

trim સુવ્યવસ્થિત suvyavasthit

trimming *n.* ઝાલર zaalar

trine *adj.* ત્રણગણું tranaganun

trinket *n.* નકલી કે તકલાદી ઘરેનું nakalee ke takalaadee gharenu

trinketry *n.* ખોટા khotaa

trio *n.* ત્રણનું જૂથ trananu jooth

trip *n.* પ્રવાસ pravaas

tripartite *adj.* ત્રણ ભાગનું બનેલું trana bhaaganu banelu

triple *adj.* ત્રણગણું tranaganun

triplicate *adj.* સરખા ત્રણ ભાગવાળું sarakhaa trana bhaagavaalun

tripod *n.* ત્રિપિગું આસન tripagun aasan

tritet *adj.* રૂઢ roodh

triton *n.* નરમીન narameen

triumph *n.* વિજય vijay

triumphant *adj.* વિજયી vijayee

trivet *n.* તિરપાઈ tirapaayee

trivial *adj.* તુચ્છ tuchchha

triviality *n.* નજીવી કિંમત કે મહત્ત્વ najeevee kimmata ke mahatva

troll *v.t.* લહેરથી –નિરાંતે ગાવું laherathee – niraante gaavun

trolley *n.* નીચી ખુલ્લી ગાડી neechee khullee gaadee

trollop *n.* ગંદી ફૂવડ સ્ત્રી gandee koovada stree

trolly *n.* બે પૈડાની ગાડી be paidaanee gaadee

troop *n.* ભેગી થયેલી મંડળી bhegee thayelee mandalee

trooper *n.* ઘોડેસવાર સૈનિક ghodesavaar sainik

trophy *n.* વિજયચિહ્ન vijayachihna

tropic *n.* ઉષ્ણકટિબંધ ushnakatibandh

tropical *adj.* ઉષ્ણકટિબંધીય ushnakatibandheeya

trot *v.t.* દુડકી ચાલ dudakee chaal

troth *n.* વફાદારી vafaadaaree

trouble *n.* ત્રાસ traas

troublesome *adj.* ત્રાસ traas

trough *n.* પાણીનું પાત્ર paaneenun paatra

trounce *v.t.* સખત સજા કરવી sakhata sajaa karavee

troupe *n.* નટનટી natanatee

trousers *n.pl.* પાટલૂન paataloona

trousseau *n.* વધૂનો પોશાક vadhoono poshaak

trowel *n.* કડિયાનું લેલું kadiyaanu lelun

truant *n.* ગાપચી મારનાર વિદ્યાર્થી gaapachee maarnaar vidyaarthee

truce *n.* યુદ્ધવિરામ yudhdhviram

truck *n.* અદલાબદલી adalaabadalee

truckle *v.i.* ગુલામની જેમ વર્તવું gulaamnee jem vartavun

truculent *adj.* આક્રમક aakramak

trudge *v.i.* પગ ઘસડતાં ચાલવું paga ghasadatan chaalavun

TRUE હોય તેવું hoya tevun
truism દેખીતી રીતે સાચી વાત dekheetee reete saachee vaat
truly adv. સાચેસાચ saachesaach
trump card n. હુકમનું પાનું hukamanu paanun
trumpet n. તુરાઈ turaai
trumpeter n. સીંગું ફૂંકનાર singun foonkanaar
truncate v.t. બૂચું બનાવવું boochun banaavavun
truncheon n. પોલીસનો ડંડો poleesano dando
trundle v.t. ગબડવું gabadavun
trunk n. ઝાડનું થડ zaadanu thad
truss n. સૂકા ઘાસનો પૂળો sookaa ghaasano poolo
trust n. પાકો ભરોસો paako bharoso
trustee n. ટ્રસ્ટી trastee
trustful adj. ભરોસાપાત્ર bharosaapaatra
trustless adj. ભરોસાપાત્ર ન હોય એવું bharosaapaatra na hoya aevun
trustworthy adj. વિશ્વાસપાત્ર vishvaasapaatra
trusty n. વફાદાર vafaadaar
truth n. સત્ય satya
truthful adj. સાચું saachun
try v.t. પ્રયત્ન કરવો prayatna karavo
trying adj. કસોટી કરનારું kasotee karanaarun
tub n. ટબ tab
tube n. કાચ કે રબરની નળી kaacha ke rabaranee nalee
tuber n. મૂળમાં થતો ગઠ્ઠો – ગાંઠ moolamaa thato gaththo, gaanth
tuberculosis n. ફેફસાંનો ક્ષયરોગ. fefasaano kshayaroga
tuck કપડાની ગડી kapadaanee gadee
tuesday n. મંગળવાર. mangalavaara
tufa n. ખરબચડો ખડક. kharabachado khadaka
tuft n. ગુચ્છો guchchho
tug v.t. જોરથી ખેંચવું jorathee khenchavun
tuition n. ભણાવવું તે bhanaavavun te
tumble v.t. પડી જવું padee javun

tumbler n. બજાણિયો bajaaniyo
tumid adj. સૂજેલું soojelun
tumour n. સોજો sojo
tumult n. કોલાહલ kolaahal
tumultuous n. કોલાહલભર્યું kolaahalabharyu
tun n. દારૂનું મોટું પીપ daarunu motu peep
tune n. રાગ raag
tunic n. ટ્યુનિક tyunik
tunnel n. બોગદું bogadun
turban n. પાઘડી paaghadee
turbid adj. ડહોળાયેલું daholaayelun
turbine n. ટરબાઈન tarbain
turbulence n. તોફાન tofaan
turbulent adj. અશાંત બનેલું ashaanta banelu
turf n. જડિયાંવાળી જમીન jaadiyaanvaalee jameen
turgid adj. સૂજેલું soojelun
turkey n. તૂર્કી toorkee
turmeric n. હળદર. haladara
turmoil n. કોલાહલ kolaahal
turn v.t. ગોળ ફરવું gola faravu
turncoat n. પક્ષપલટું pakshapalatun
turner n. ખરાદી. kharaadee
turning n. ખરાદી કામનો છીલ kharaadee kaamano chhol
turnip n. સલગમ(નો છોડ). salagama(no chhoda)
turnout n. કાઢી મૂકવું kaadhee mookavun
turnover n. ઉપરથી પડવું uparathee padavun
turpentine n. ટર્પેન્ટાઈન tarpentaain
turpitude n. હલકટપણું halakatapanun
turret n. મિનારો minaaro
turtle n. એક જાતનું કબૂતર aeka jaatanu kabootar
tusk n. હાથી haathee
tussle n. ઝઘડો zaghado
tutelage n. વાલીપણું vaaleepanun
tutelary adj. સંરક્ષક sanrakshak
tutor n. ખાનગી શિક્ષક khaanagee shikshak
twaddle v.i. નિરસ લખાણ niras lakhaan
twain n. બે. be

twang *n.* ધનુષ્યનો ટંકાર dhanushyano tankaar

tweed *n.* ઊનનું કાપડ oonanun kaapad

twelfth *n.* બારમું baaramun

twelve *adj.* બાર baara

twenty *n.* વીસ veesa

twentieth *adj.* વીસમું, veesamu

twice *adv.* બેગણું begunun

twig *n.* ડાળખું daalakhun

twilight *n.* ઝાંખું અજવાળું zaankhu ajavaalun

twill *n.* પાંસળીદાર કાપડ paansaleedaar kaapad

twin *n.* પ્રતિરૂપ pratiroop

twine *n.* વીંટો veento

twinge *v.i.* સણકો sanako

twinkle *v.i.* ઝબૂકવું zabakavun

twinkling *n.* ઝગમગવું zagamagavun

twirl *v.t.* ચક્કર ચક્કર ફેરવવું chakkara chakkara feravavun

twist *v.t.* આમળવું aamalavun

twit *v.t.* ઠપકો આપવો thapako aapavo

twitch *v.t.* ધ્રૂજી ઊઠે તેવું dhroojee uthe tevun

twitter *v.i.* ચીંચી અવાજ cheencheen avaaj

two *adj.* બે(ની સંખ્યા). be(ne sankhyaa)

tympanum *n.* કાનનો પડદો kaanano padado

type *n.* પ્રકાર prakaar

type-writer *n.* ટાઇપ રાઇટર taip raiter

typhoid *n.* આંતરડાંનો તાવ aantaradaano taava

typhoon *n.* વંટોળિયો vantoliyo

typical *adj.* લાક્ષણિક laakshanik

typify *v.t.* નમૂનારૂપ namoonaaroop

typist *n.* ટાઇપિસ્ટ taaipist

typography *n.* મુદ્રણકલા mudranakalaa

tyrannical *adj.* જુલમગારના જેવું julamagaaranaa jevun

tyrannize *v.t.* જુલમ ગુજારવો julama gujaaravo

tyranny *n.* જુલમ julam

tyrant *n.* જુલમગાર julamaghar

tyre *n.* પૈડાં ઉપરની વાટ. paidaa uparanee vaata

tyro *n.* શિખાઉ shikaaun

ubiquitous *adj.* બધે હાજર badhe haajar

ubiquity *n.* બધે હાજર badhe haajar

udder *n.* ઢોરના આંચળ dhornaa aanchal

udometer *n.* વરષામાપક યંત્ર varshaamaapak yantra

ugliness *n.* અસુંદરતા asundartaa

ugly *adj.* કદરૂપું kadrupun

ulcer *n.* નાસૂર naasoor

ulcerate *v.i.* માં ચાંદી પડવી ma chaandee padvee

ulema *n.* ઉલેમા ulemaa

ulterior *adj.* અંતિમ antim

ultimate *adj.* છેવટનું chhevatnu

ultimatum *n.* શરતનું આખરી કહેણ sharatonu aakhree kahen

ultimo *n.* ગયા મહિનાનું gayaa mahinaanu

ultra *adj.* સમાસમાં પેલે પાર samaasamaa pelee paar

ultramarine *adj.* ચળકતો વાદળી રંગ chalakato vaadalee rang

ultr¡violet *n.* અદ્રશ્ય કિરણો adrashya kirano

umbel *n.* પુષ્પછત્ર pushachhatra

umbilicus *n.* નાભિ naabhi

umbra *n.* ગ્રહણ છાયા grahan chhaayaa

umbrage *n.* અપમાન apmaan

umbrella *n.* છત્રી chaatree

umpire *n.* મધ્યસ્થ madhyashtha

umpteen *prep.* ઘણા ghanaa

unabated *adj.* અતૂટ atoot

unable *adj.* અસમર્થ asamartha

unaccented *adj.* નિર્બળ nirbal

unacceptable *adj.* અસ્વિકાર્ય aswikaarya

unaccompanied *adj.* સાથી વિના sathee vinaa

unaccomplished *adj.* અધુરૂ adhuru

unacountable *adj.* બનિહિસાબી binhisaabee

unaccustomed *adj.* અસામાન્ય asamanyaa

unacqainted *adj.* અપરચિતિ aparichit

unaffected *adj.* અપ્રભાવચિ aprabhaavich

unaided *adj.* અસહાય asahaay

unalloyed *adj.* ભેજ વિનાનું bhej vinaanu

unanimity *n.* સર્વસંમતિ sarvasammati

unanimous સર્વસંમત sarvasammat

unappeasable *adj.* ખાઉધરો khaudharo

unapt *adj.* મંદબુદ્ધિ mandbudhhi

unarmed *n.* હથિયાર વગરનું hathiyaar vagarnu

unaspiring *adj.* આકસ્મિક aakasmik

unassailable *adj.* અભેધ્ય abhedhya

unassuming *adj.* નિરભિમાની nirabhimabnee

unattainable *adj.* અપ્રાપ્ય apraapya

unauthorized *adj.* અનધિકૃત anadhikruk

unavailing *adj.* ફાયદો થાય નહિ એવું faaydo thaay nahi evu

unavoidable *adj.* અનિવાર્ય anivaarya

unaware *adj.* અનપેક્ષિતપણે anapexitpane

unawares *adv.* એકાએક ekaaeka

unawed *adj.* કુંવારા હોવું kunwaaraa hovu

unbar *v.t.* ખોલવું kholvun

unbearable *adj.* અસહનીય asahneey

unbeaten અજેય ajey

unbelief *n.* નાસ્તિકતા naastiktaa

unbeliever *n.* નાસ્તિકત naastiktaa

unbend *n.* સીધું seedhu

unbending *adj.* સીધા ટટાર થવું seedhaa, tataar thavu

unblased નિરાધાર niraadhaar

unbidden *adj.* અનાહૂત anaahat

unblemished *adj.* નિષ્કલંક nishkalank

unblushing *adj.* બેશરમ besharam

unbolt *v.t.* ખોલી નાખવું kholee naakhvu

unbosom *v.i.* મનની વાત કહેવી mannee vaat kahevee

unbounded *adj.* અસીમ aseem

unbridled *adj.* નિરંકુશ nirankush

unbroken *n.* અભંગ abhang

unbuckle *v.t.* ખોલવું kholvu

uncalled *adj.* વણમાગી vanmaagee

uncase *v.t.* ખોલી દેવું kholee devu

unceasing *adj.* અક્ષીણ axeen

unceremonious *adj.* અનૌપચારિક anaupcharik

uncertain અનિશ્ચિત anishchit

uncertainty અનિશ્ચિતતા anishchittaa

unchain *v.t.* છૂટા કરી દેવું chhoota karee devu

unchancy *n.* યાદગાર yaadgaar

unchangeable *adj.* બદલી શકાય નહિ એવું badlee sakaay nahi evu

uncharitable *adj.* લોભી lobhee

unchaste *adj.* અશુદ્ધ ashauddhaa

uncircumspect *adj.* બેજવાબદાર bejavaabdaar

uncivil *adj.* અશિષ્ટ shishta

uncivilized *adj.* અસભ્ય ashabhy

unclaimed *adj.* લાવારિસ laavaaris

uncle *n.* કાકો kaako

unclean *adj.* અશુદ્ધ ashuddhaa

unclothe *v.t.* પોશાક ઉતારવા poshaak utaarvaa

unclouded *adj.* સાફ saaf

uncomfortable *adj.* અસુવિધાજનક ashuvidhaajanak

uncomely *adj.* અનિચ્છા anichhaa

uncommon *adj.* અસાધારણ asaadhaaran

unconcerned *adj.* ઉદાસીન udaaseen

uncoditional *adj.* બિનશરતી binshartee

uncongenial *adj.* જન્મજાત નહિ janmajaat nahee

unconnected *adj.* અસંબદ્ધ asambhadh

unconquerable *adj.* અજેય ajey

unconsitutional *adj.* ગેરબંધારણીય gerbandhaarneeya

uncontrolled *adj.* અનિયંત્રીત aniyantrita

uncork *v.t.* ખોલવું kholvu

uncouth *adj.* કઢંગું kadhangu

uncover ઢાંકણ કાઢવું dhaankan kaadhvun

unction *n.* હુંફાળું hufanlun

unctuous *adj.* જાડું jaadun

unculpable *adj.* સદોષ નહિ sadosh nahi

uncultivated *adj.* અસભ્ય asabhya

uncut *adj.* કાપ્યાવિનાનું kaapyaavinaanu

undaunted *adj.* નડિર nidar

undeceive *v.t.* સારા રસ્તા પર લાવવું saaraa rastaa par laavvu

undecided *n.* અસ્થિરચિત્તિત ashthirchitta

undefiled *adj.* નિર્મળ nirmal

undefined *adj.* અપરિભાષિત aparibhaashit

undeniable *adj.* નિર્વિવાદ nirvivaad

under *prep.* નીચે neeche

underage *n.* જરૂરી વયનો અભાવ jaruree vayno abhaav

underbid *v.t.* દામ ઓછો કરી દેવો daam oocho karee devo

undercharge *v.t.* અલ્પખર્ચ alpakharch

undergo *n.* માંથી પસાર થવું maanthee pasaar thavun

underground *adj.* ભૂમિગત bhoomigat

underlie *v.t.* કાયમ કરવું kaayam karvun

underline *v.t.* નીચે લીટી દોરવી neeche leetee dorvee

underling *n.* હાથ નીચેનો માણસ haath neecheno maanas

undermine *v.t.* નષ્ટ કરવું nashta karvun

undermost *adj.* સૌથી નીચે sauthee neeche

underneath *adv.* નીચે neeche

underrate *n.* હલકો અભિપ્રાય halako abhipraay

undersell *v.t.* અપવક્રિય apavikray

undersign *v.t.* નીચે કરેલી સહીવાળું neeche karelee saheevalu

understand *v.t.* અર્થ સમજવો aarth samajvo

understanding *n.* બુદ્ધિ buddhee

understood *n.* સમજણ samjan

undertake *n.* માથે લેવું maathe levun

undertaking *n.* ઉપાડેલું કામ upaadelu kaam

underwear *n.* આંતરવસ્ત્ર aantarvastra

underwood *n.* નાના છોડ naanaa chhod

underwriter *n.* વહાણનો વીમો ઉતારનાર vahaanano veemo utaaranaar

undeserving *adj.* અયોગ્ય ayogya

undigested *adj.* પચે નહી તેવું pache nahee tevu

undignified *adj.* નાલાયક naalaayak

undisputed *adj.* સાફ saaf

undivided *adj.* અવિભાજ્ય avibhajya

undo *v.t.* રદ કરવું rada karvun

undoing *n.* નાશ કરવો naasha karvo

undoubtedly *adv.* બેશક beshak

undress *v.t.* કપડાં ઉતારવાં kapdaa ootaarvaan

undue *adj.* વધારે પડતું vadhaare padtu

undulate *v.i.* લહેરાતું હોવું laheratun hovun

undulatory *adj.* લહેરીલું lahereelun

unduly *adv.* વધારે પડતું vadhaare padtun

undutiful *adj.* અકર્તવ્યનીષ્ઠ akartavyanishtha

unearth *v.t.* ખોદી કાઢવું khodee kaadhvun

uneasiness *n.* બેચેની bechenee

uneducated *adj.* અશિક્ષિત ashixit

unending અસીમ asheem

unemployed *adj.* વપરાશ વિનાનું vapraash vinaanun

unequal *adj.* અસમાન asamaan

uneven *adj.* ઊંચું-નીચું oonchoo-neechu

unexpected *adj.* અનપેક્ષિત anapexit

unfailing *adj.* અમોઘ amogh

unfair *adj.* અનૂચિત anoochit

unfamiliar *adj.* અજાણ્યું ajaanyu

unfasten વલિંબ કરવો vilamba karvo

unfavourable *adj.* પ્રતિકૂળ prateekul

unfeeling *adj.* નિર્મમ nirmam

unfit *adj.* લાયકાત વિનાનું laaykaat vinaanu

unfold *v.t.* ઉકેલવું ukelvun

unforeseen *adj.* અનપેક્ષિત anapekshit

unfortunate *adj.* કમનસીબ kamnasheeb

unfortunately *adv.* અભાગ્યું abhagyu

unfounded *adj.* નિરાધાર niraadhaar

unfrequented વારંવાર vaaramvaar

ungainly *adj.* કઢંગું kadhangun

ungenerous *adj.* કંજૂસ kanjoos

ungodly *adj.* અધાર્મિક adhaarmik

ungovernable બેકાબૂ bekaaboo

ungraceful *adj.* નમકહરામ namakharaam

ungrateful *adj.* અકૃતજ્ઞ akrutgna

unguarded *adj.* અરક્ષિત araxit

unhallowed *adj.* પવિત્ર ન કરેલું pavitra na karelu

unhappily *adv.* નાખુશીથી naakhusheethee

unhappy *adj.* અપ્રસન્ન aprasanaa

unhealthy માંદલું maandlu

unheard *adj.* ek sarakhun karavun akshut

unheeded *adj.* અસાવધાન asaavdhaan

unhinge *v.t.* અસ્થિર બનાવવું asthir banaavvun

unholy *adj.* અપવિત્ર apavitra

unhurt *adj.* અભેદ abhed

uniform *adj.* એકધારું aekadharun

uniformity *n.* એક સરખાપણું aeka sarakhaapanun

unify *v.t.* એક સરખું કરવું ek sarakhun karavun

unimpaired *n.* અછૂતું achutoon

unimproved *adj.* સુધારો sudharo

uninhabitable *adj.* નિર્જન nirjana

uninjured *adj.* જેને ઈજા ન થઈ હોય એવું jene ijaa n thai hoy aevu

unintelligible *adj.* અસ્પષ્ટ ashpasht

uninteresting શુષ્ક shushka

union *n.* સંઘ sangh

unique *adj.* અનન્ય ananya

unison *n.* સૂરનો મેળ soorano mela

unit *n.* એક aek

unite *v.t.* જોડાવું jodavun

unity *n.* એકતા aekataa

universal *adj.* બધાનું badhaanun

universallity *adv.* સર્વસામાન્યતા sarvasaamaanyataa

universe *n.* અખિલ સૃષ્ટિ akhila srushti

university *n.* વિશ્વવિદ્યાલય vishvavidhyaalay

unjust *adj.* અન્યાયપૂર્ણ anyaayapoorna

unkempt *adj.* અવ્યવસ્થિત avyavasthit

unkind *adj.* દુષ્ટ dushta

unknown *adj.* અજ્ઞાત agyaat

unknowingly *adj.* અજાણ્યે ajaanye

unlace *v.t.* બંધ વસ્તુ ખોલાવી bandha vastu kholaavee

unlawful *adj.* ગેરકાનૂની gerakaanoonee

unless *conj.* સિવાય sivaay

unlike *adj.* –ના જેવું નહિ naa jevun nahi

unlikely *adv.* અસંભવિત asambhavit

unlimited *adj.* અનિયંત્રિત aniyantrit

unload *v.t.* માલ ઉતારવો maal utaaravo

unlock *v.t.* તાળું– કળ ઉઘાડવી taalu - kala ughaadavee

unloose *v.t.* છોડવું chhodavun

unlucky *adj.* કમનસીબ kamanaseeb

unman *v.t.* નબળું બનાવવું nabalun banaavavun

unmanageable *adj.* અસહનીય asahaneeya

unmanly *adj.* ડરપોક darapoka, bhyayabheeta

unmannerly *adj.* રીતભાત વિનાનું reetabhaat vinaanun

unmask *v.t.* મુખવટો ઉતારવો mukhavato utaaravo

unmatched *adj.* બેજોડ bejod

unmixed *adj.* મિશ્રિત નહિ તેવું mishrita nahi tevun

unnatural *adj.* લાગણીઓ વિનાનું laaganio vinaanun

unnecessary *adj.* બિનજરૂરી binajaruree

unnerve *v.t.* મનોબળ તોડી નાખવું manobala todee naakhavun

unofficial *adj.* બિનસરકારી binasarkaaree

unpack *v.t.* ખોલવું kholavun

unpaid *adj.* વેતન ન ચૂકવેલું vetana n chookavelun

unparalleled *adj.* અજોડ ajoda

unpleasant અપ્રિય. apriya

unpolished *adj.* અસંસ્કારી asanskaaree

unpolite *adj.* અસભ્ય asabhya

unpopular અપ્રિય. apriya

unprepared *adj.* કાચ્ચું kaachchun

unpretending *adj.* સરળ saral

unproductive *adj.* ફળ વગરનું fal vagaranu

unprofitable *adj.* ગેરફાયદાવાળું gerafaayadaavaalu

unprotected *adj.* અરક્ષિત arakshita

unprovoked અકારણ akaarana

unpublished *adj.* અપ્રકાશિત aprakaashita

unquestionable *adj.* નિર્વિવાદ nirvivaad

unreal *adj.* અવાસ્તવિક avaastavik

unreasonable *adj.* ગેરવાજબી geravaajabee

unrelenting *adj.* નિર્દય nirdaya

unreliable *adj.* અવિશ્વાશનીય avishvaashaneeya

unreserved *adj.* સાફ દિલ saafa dil

unrest *n.* અશાંતિ ashaanti

unripe *adj.* અપરિપક્વ aparipakv

unrivalled *adj.* અજોડ ajod

unroll *v.t.* ઉકેલવું ukelavun

unruly *adj.* બેકાબૂ bekaaboo

unsafe *adj.* અસુરક્ષિત asurakshita

unsatisfactory *adj.* અસંતોષજનક asantoshajanaka

unsay *v.t.* પાછું લેવું paachun levun

unscrupulous *adj.* અનૈતિક anaitik

unseasonable કસમયનું kasamayanu

unseat *v.t.* આસનરહિત કરવું aasanarahit karavun

unseemly અઘટિત aghatit

unseen *adj.* અદ્રશ્ય adrashya

unserviceable *adj.* બેકાર bekaara

unsettled *adj.* અનિર્ણીત anirneet

unsheathe મ્યાનમાંથી નીકળેલું myaanamaathee neekalelun

unshod *adj.* જૂતા વિનાનું jootaa vinaanu

unsightly *adj.* કદરૂપું, ગંદું kadarupun

unsociable *adj.* એકાંતપ્રિય aekaantapriya

unsolicited *adj.* અપ્રાર્થીત apraartheeta

unsought જેની ખૂબ માંગ ન હોય એવું jenee khooba maanga n hoya aevun

unsound *adj.* અસ્વસ્થ asvasth

unsparing *adj.* ઉદાર udaar

unspeakable *adj.* શબ્દાતીત shabdaateet

unstable *adj.* અસ્થિર asthira

unsteady *adj.* અસ્થિર asthira

unsubstantial *adj.* ક્ષુદ્ર kshudra

unsuccesful *adj.* વિજયી vijayee

unsuitable નિષ્ફળ nishfala

unsullied *adj.* શુદ્ધ shuddh

unsurpassed નાયબ naayab

untaught *adj.* અશિક્ષિત ashikshit

untenable *adj.* અસ્થિર asthira

unthankful *adj.* અકૃતજ્ઞ akrutagyna

unthought *adj.* અવિચારી avichaaree

untidy *adj.* વ્યવસ્થિત નહિ એવું vyavasthita nahi aevun

until *prep.* ત્યાં સુધી tyaan sudhee

untimely *adv.* કવખતનું kvakhatanun

untiring *adj.* અથાક athaaka

unto *prep.* પર્યંત paryat

untold *adj.* અકથિત akathit

untolerable અસહ્ય asahya

untouchable *adj.* અસ્પૃશ્ય asprushya

untouched *adj.* અછૂત achhoota

untoward *adj.* આડું aadun

untrained *adj.* અશિક્ષિત ashikshit

untrue *adj.* જૂઠું juthoon

untruth *n.* અસત્ય asatya

unusual *n.* અસામાન્ય. asaamaanya

unvalued *adj.* અલ્પમુલ્ય alpamuly

unveil *v.t.* અનાવરણ વિધિ કરવો anaavarana vidhi karavee

unwarrantable *adj.* અનધિકૃત anadhikrut

unwarranted *adj.* અનધિકૃત anadhikrut

unwary *adj.* અચેત acheta

unwavering *adj.* સાબિત saabita

unwearying *adj.* અથાક athaak

unwelcome *adj.* અસત્કાર asatkaar

unwell *adj.* નાદુરસ્ત તબિયતવાળું naadurasta tabiyatavaalun

unwholesome *adj.* નાદુરસ્ત naadurast

unwieldy *adj.* અતિભારે. atibhaare

unwilling *adj.* અનિચ્છુક anichchhuk
unwise *adj.* મૂરખ moorkha
unwittingly *adv.* બદઇરાદો badairaado
unwonted *adj.* ક્યારેકનું kyaarekanu
unworthy *adj.* અયોગ્ય ayogy
unyielding *adv.* જીદ્દી jeeddee
up *adv.* ઉપર upar
upbraid *v.t.* ઠપકો આપવો thapako aapavo
upheaval *n.* ઊથલપાથલ uthalapaathal
upheave *v.t.* ઊથલપાથલ થવી uthalapaathala thavee
uphold *v.t.* સમર્થન કરવું samarthana karavun
upholster *v.t.* બેઠકમાં ગાદી bethaka maa gaadee
upkeep *n.* સારી હાલતમાં રાખવું saaree haalatamaa raakhavun
uplift *v.t.* ઊંચુ કરવું unchun karavun
upon *prep.* —ની ઉપર. nee upar
upper *adj.* ઉપરનું uparanu
uppish *adj.* સ્વમતાગ્રહી svamataagrahee
upright *adj.* ઊભું ubhun
uprising *n.* બળવો balavo
uproar *n.* હુલ્લડ hullad
upset *v.t.* ઊથલાવી દેવું uthalaavee devun
upshot *n.* પરિણામ parinaam
upstart *n.* લેભાગુ lebhaagu
up-to-date *adv.* પ્રવર્તમાન pravartamaan
upward *adj.* ઉપર upar
upwards *n.* —થી વધારે. thee vadhare
uranus *n.* યુરેનસ yurenasa
urban *adj.* શહેરી shaheree
urbane *adj.* વિવેકી vivekee
urchin *n.* તોફાની બાળક tofaanee balak
urge *v.t.* વિનંતી કરવી vinantee karavee
urgency *n.* તાકીદ taakeed
urgent *adj.* તાકીદનું taakeedanun
urinal *n.* મુતરડી mutaradee
urinary *adj.* પેશાબ કરવો. peshaaba karavo
urine *n.* પેશાબ peshaab
us *pro.* અમે ame
usage *n.* વાપરવાની રીત vaaparavaanee reet

use *v.t.* ઉપયોગિતા upayogitaa
used *v.t.* આદતી aadatee
useful *adj.* ઉપયોગી upayogee
useless *adj.* નકામું nakaamun
usher *n.* દરવાન daravaan
usual *adj.* સામાન્યપણે બનતું saamaanyapane banatun
usure *v.t.* વ્યાજે પૈસા ધીરનાર vyaaje paisaa dheeranaar
usurp *v.i.* પચાવી પાડવું pachaavee paadavun
usurpation *n.* પચાવી પાડવું pachaavee paadavun
usurper *n.* પચાવે પાડનાર pachaavee paadanaara
usury વ્યાજવટું vyaajavatun
utensil *n.* સાધન saadhan
uterus *n.* ગર્ભાશય. garbhaashay
utility *n.* ઉપયોગિતા upayogitaa
utmost *adj.* છેવટનું chhevatanun
utopia *n.* કાલ્પનિક રામરાજ્ય. kaalyanika ramaraajya
utopian *adj.* યૂટોપિયાનું. yootopiyaanu
utter *v.t.* તદ્દન taddan
utterance ઉચ્ચારણ uchchaaran
utterly *adv.* સર્વથા sarvathaa
uttermost *adj.* તદ્દન taddan
uvula *n.* જીભનો પાછલો ભાગ jeebhano paachalo bhag
uxorious *adj.* વહુઘેલો vahughelo

vacancy *n.* ખાલી જગ્યા Khaalee jagyaa
vacant *adj.* ખાલી khaalee
vacate *v.* ખાલી કરવું khaalee karavun
vacation *n.* લાંબી રજા laambee rajaa
vaccinate *v.t.* રોગ અવરોધક રસી મૂકવી rog avarodhak rasee mookavee
vaccination *n.* રસીકરણ raseekaran
vacillate *v.t.* ડગમગવું dagamagavun
vaciliation *n.* અસ્થિરિતા Asthirataa
vacuity *n.* સૂનકાર soonkaar

vacuum *n.* શૂન્યાવકાશ shoonyaavakaash

vagabond *n.* રખડુ rakhadu

vagary *n.* મનસ્વીપણું manasveepanoon

vagrancy *n.* રઝળપાટ razalpaat

vagrant *n.* રખડું માણસ rakhadun maanas

vague *adj.* અસ્પષ્ટ aspasht

vain *adj.* નિરર્થક nirarthak

vale *n.* વિદાય vidaay

valet *n.* અંગત નોકર Angat Nokar

valiant *adj.* બહાદુર bahaadur

valid *adj.* માન્ય Maany

validity *n.* માન્યતા Maanyataa

valise *n.* પ્રવાસની પેટી pravaasnee petee

valley *n.* ખીણ kheen

valorous *adj.* બહાદુરી bahaaduree

valour *n.* શૌર્ય shaurya

valuable *adj.* કીમતી keematee

valuation *n.* મુલવણી mulavanee

value *v.* કમિત આંકવી kimmat aankavee

valve *n.* પડદો padado

vampire *n.* લોહી ચૂસતું ભૂત lohee choonsatun bhoot

van *n.* મોટી ગાડી motee gaadee

vandal *n.* વિધ્વંસ vidhvans

vandalism *n.* જંગલીપણું jangaleepanun

vane *n.* ચકરડી chakaradee

vanguard *n.* આગેવાન

vanish *v.* લોપ પામવું lop paamavun

vanity *n.* મિથ્યાભિમાન mithyaabhimaan

vanquish *v.i.* જીતવું jeetavun

vanquisher *n.* વિજેતા vijetaa

vantage *n.* લાભ laabh

vapid *adj.* ફીકું feekun

vaporous *adj.* વરાળના રૂપ varaalanaa rupanu

vapour *n.* વરાળ varaal

variable *adj.* પરિવર્તનશીલ parivartansheel

variance *n.* અણબનાવ anabanaav

variation *n.* ભિન્નતા bhinnataa

variegated *n.* ભાતભાતનું bhaatbhaatnu

variety *n.* વિવિધિતા vividhataa

various *adj.* વિવિધિ પ્રકારનું vividh prakaaranu

vary *v.t.* બદલવું badalavu

vase *n.* પુષ્પપાત્ર pushpapaatra

vasectomy *n.* નસબંધી nasabandhee

vaseline *n.* વેસલિન vesalin

vassal *n.* નમ્ર સેવક namra sevak

vast *adj.* વિશાળ vishaal

vastation *n.* વિનાશ vinaash

vat *n.* મોટું પીપ motun peep

vault *n.* તિજોરી tijoree

vaunt *n.* બડાઈ હાંકવી badaai haankavee

veer *v.i.* દિશા બદલવી disha badalavee

vegetable *n.* વનસ્પતિ vanspati

vegetarian *n.* શાકાહારી shaakaahaaree

vegetate પરિવર્તનહીન parivartanheen

vegetation *n.* વનસ્પતિ સૃષ્ટિ vanaspti srushti

vehemence *n.* જોસવાળું joshavalun

vehement *adj.* પ્રચંડ prachanda

vehicle *n.* વાહન vaahan

veil *n.* પડદો padado

vein *n.* શિરા shira

velocity *n.* વેગ veg

velvet *n.* મખમલ malamala

venal *adj.* લાંચખાઉ laanchakhaau

vend વેચવું vechavun

vedetta *n.* વેર vera

vender *n.* વિક્રેતા vikreta

venerable *adj.* આદરણીય aadaraneeya

venerate *v.t.* પૂજ્યપાત્ર poojaapaatra

veneration *n.* પૂજ્યભાવ poojyabhaav

vengeance *n.* વેર ver

venial *adj.* ક્ષમ્ય kshamya

venison *n.* હરણનું માંસ harananun maans

venom *n.* ઝેર zer

venomous *adj.* ઝેરી zeree

ventage *n.* નાનું કાણું naanun kaanun

ventilate *v.t.* જાહેર કરવું jaaher karavun

ventilation *v.* સંવાતન samvaatan

ventilator *n.* વેન્ટિલેટર ventiletar

venture *v.t.* સાહસ saahas

venue *n.* સ્થળ sthal

venus *n.* શુક્રનોગ્રહ shukrano grah

veracious *adj.* સાચેસાચું saachesaachun

veracity *n.* સાચાપણું saachaapanun

verand *n.* ઓસરી osaree
verb *n.* ક્રિયાપદ kriyaapada
verbal *adj.* શાબ્દિક shaabdik
verbiage *n.* શબ્દાડંબર shabdaandabar
verbose *adj.* શબ્દાળુ shabdaalu
verdant *n.* વિપુલ લીલોતરીવાળું vipul leelotareevaalun
verdict *n.* પંચનો ચુકાદો panchano chukaado,
verdure હરિયાળી hariyaalee
verge *n.* કિનાર kinaar
verification ખરું છે કે નહિ તે જોવું kharun chhe ke nahi te jovun
verify *v.* સાબિત કરી આપવું saabit karee aapavun
verily *adv.* બેશક beshak
veritable *adj.* સાચું saachun
verity *n.* સત્યતા satyataa
vermilion *n.* ચળકતો રાતો રંગ chalakato raato rang
vermin *n.* સમૂહવાચક નામ samoohavaachak naam
vernacular *n.* ઘરગથ્થુ ભાષા gharagathhu bhaashaa
vernal *adj.* વાસંતિક vaasantik
versatile *adj.* બહુમુખી પ્રતિભાવાળું bahumukhee pratibhaavaalun
verse *n.* કવિતા kavitaa
versed *adj.* જાણકાર janakaar
versifier *n.* કવિ kavi
versify *v.t.* કવિતા રચવી kavitaa rachavee
version વૃત્તાન્ત vruttant
versus *prep.* વિરુદ્ધ virudhha
vertebra *n.* કરોડઅસ્થિનો કોઈ એક મણકો karod asthi no koi ek manako
vertex *n.* શિખર shikhar
vertical *adj.* લંબરૂપ lambaroop
vertigo *n.* તમ્મરનું દરદ tammarnu darad
very *adv.* અતિશય atishay
vesper *n.* સાંજની ઉપાસના saanjanee upaasanaa,
vessel *n.* વહાણ vahaan
vest *n.* અંદરથી પહેરવાનો કબજો andarathee paheravaano kabajo
vestal *adj.* કુંવારિકા kunvaarikaa
vested *adj.* કપડામાં સજ્જ kapadaamaan sajj

vestibule *n.* દેવડી devadee
vestige *n.* પગેરું pagerun
vestment *n.* વસ્ત્ર vastra
veteran *adj.* પીઢ peedh
veterinary *adj.* પશુરોગ સંબંધી pashurog sanbandhee
veto *n.* મનાઈ manaaee
vex *v.t.* ગુસ્સે કરવું gusse karavun
vexation *n.* ખીજવાટ kheejavata
vexatious *n.* ખીજવનારું kheejavanaarun
vexed *adj.* ખૂબ ચર્ચાયેલું khoob charchaayelun
viable *adj.* જીવી jeevee
viaduct *n.* માર્ગસેતુ maargasetu
vial *n.* નાનકડી શીશી naanakadee sheeshee
viamedia *n.* મધ્યમ માર્ગે mdh
viands *n.* ખોરાક khoraaka
vibrate *v.t.* કંપવું kampavun
vibration *n.* કંપન kanpan
vicar *n.* કોઈનો અવેજી કાર્યકર koino avejee karyakar
vice *n.* નાયબ naayab
vice-chancellor *n.* ઉપકુલપતિ upakulapati
vice-president *n.* ઉપ-પ્રમુખ upa-pramukha
viceregal *adj.* વાઈસરોયનું vaaisaroyanun
viceversa *adv.* ઊલટી રીતે oolatee reete
vicinity *n.* આડોશપાડોશ aadoshapadosh
vicious *adj.* દુર્ગુણી durgunee
vicissitude *n.* પરિસ્થિતિમાં પરિવર્તન pristhitimaa privartan
victim *n.* પીડિત peedit
victimize *v.t.* રંજાડવું ranjaadavun
victor *n.* હરીફાઈમાં જીતનાર hareephaaimaa jeetanaar
victorious *n.* વિજયી vijayee
victory *n.* વિજય vijay
vie *v.i.* સ્પર્ધામાં ઊતરવું spardhaamaa ootaravun
view *v.t.* અવલોકન avalokan

vigil *n.* સાવધાની saavadhaanee

vigilance *n.* તકેદારી takedaaree

vigilant *adj.* સાવધ saavadh

vigorous *adj.* જોશીલું josheelun

vilify *v.t.* બદનક્ષી કરવી badankshee karavee

villa *n.* અલાયદું નિવાસસ્થાન alaayadun nivaasasthaan

village *n.* ગામ gaam

villager *n.* ગામડાનો રહેવાસી gamadaano rahevaasee

villain *n.* દુષ્ટ માણસ dushta maanas

villainous *adj.* બદમાશીભર્યુ badamaasheebharyun

villainy *n.* દુષ્ટતા dushtataa

vindicate *v.t.* શંકાનું નિવારણ કરવું shankaanun nivaaran karavun

vindication *n.* દોષમુક્તિ doshamukti

vindicative *adj.* વેર લેવાની વૃત્તિવાળું ver levanee vruttivalun

vine *n.* દ્રાક્ષનો વેલો draakshano velo

vinegar *n.* કડવાશવાળો સ્વભાવ kadavaashavalo svabhaav

vinery *n.* દ્રાક્ષ ઉછેર કેન્દ્ર draksha uchher kendra

vineyard *n.* બગીચો દ્રાક્ષનો ddhraakshano bageecho

vintage *n.* ઊંચું જાતનું oonchun jaatanun

vintner *n.* દારૂ વેચનાર, કલાલ daaru vechanaar, kalaal

viola *n.* વાયોલાનો છીડ vaayolaano chood

violate *v.t.* અવગણના કરવી avagananaa karavee,

violation *n.* ઉલ્લંઘન ullanghan

violence *n.* હિંસા hinsaa

violent *n.* હિંસક hinsak

violet *n.* ભૂરો જાંબુડિયો રંગ bhooro jambudiyo rang

violin *n.* વાયોલિન vaayolin

violinist *n.* વાયોલિન વગાડનાર vaayolin vagaadanaar

viper એક નાનો ઝેરી સાપ ek naano zeree saap

virago *n.* કજિયાખોર સ્ત્રી, kajeeyakhor stree

virgin *n.* કુમારિકા kumaarika

virginity *n.* કૌમારત્વ kaumaaratva

virgo *n.* કન્યારાશિ kanyaaraashi

virile *adj.* પુરુષાતન purushaatan

virility *n.* પુરુષત્વ purushatva

virtual *adj.* વાસ્તવિક પણ હકીકતમાં નહિ vaastavik pan hakeekatamaa nhi

virtually *adv.* એ રીતે e reete

virtue *n.* સદાચાર sadaachaar

virtuoso *n.* કલાભિજ્ઞ kalaabhigna

virtuous *n.* શુદ્ધ ચારિત્ર્યવાળું shudhha chaaritryavaalu

virulence *n.* ઝેરીપણું zereepanun

virulent *n.* ઝેરી zeree

virus *n.* વિષાણુ vishaanu

visa *n.* પ્રવેશપત્ર પરવાનો praveshpatra paravaano

visage *n.* મુખમુદ્રા mukhamudra

visard *n.* બુરખો burakho

viscera *n.* આંતરડાં aantaradan

viscid *adj.* ચીકણું chinkanun

viscidity *n.* ચીકણાપણું chinkanapanun

visibility *n.* દૃષ્ટિમર્યાદા drashtimaryaadaa

visible *adj.* જોઈ શકાય એવું joi shakaay evun

visibly *adv.* જોઈ શકાય એવું joi shakaay evun

vision *adj.* દૃષ્ટિ drashti

visionary *adj.* સ્વપ્નદૃષ્ટા svapnadrashtaa

visitation *n.* વધિસિરની મુલાકાત vidhisarnee mulaakaat

visitor *n.* મુલાકાતી mulaakaatee

visor *n.* મુખવટો mukhavato

visual *adj.* દૃષ્ટિવિષયિક drashtivishayak

visualize *v.t.* કલ્પના કરવી kalpanaa karavee

vital *adj.* જીવનને લગતું jivanane lagatun

vitality *n.* જીવનશક્તિ jivanshakti

vitalize *v.t.* જીવનશક્તિનું પ્રદાન jivanshaktinun pradaan

vitals *n.* શરીરના મર્મ અવયવો shareerna marm avayavo

vitamin *n.* વિટામિન vitaamin

vitiate *v.t.* દૂષિત કરવું dushit karavun

vitreous *adj.* કાચના જેવું kaachna jevun

vitrify *v.t.* કાચ બનાવવો kaach banaavavo

vitriol *n.* ગંધકનો તેજાબ gandhak no tejaab

vituperate *v.t.* વખોડવું vakhodavun

vivacious *adj.* ઉત્સાહી utsaahi

vivacity *n.* ઉત્સાહ utsaah

vivid *adj.* ચળકતું chalakatun

vivify *v.t.* સજીવન કરવું sajeevan karavun

viz *adv.* અર્થાત arthaat

vizard *n.* બુરખો burakho

vocabulary *n.* શબ્દભંડોળ shabdabhandol

vocalist *n.* ગાયક gaayak

vocation *n.* વ્યવસાયને લગતું vyavsaayne lagatun

vocative *adj.* સંબોધન કારક sanbodhankaarak

vociferate *v.t.* રાડો પાડવી raado paadavee

vociferous *adj.* રાડારાડ કરતું raadaaraad karatun

vogue *n.* લોકપ્રિયિતા lokpriyataa

voice *n.* સાદ saad

void *adj.* રદબાતલ radbaatal

volatile *adj.* ચંચળ chanchal

volcano *n.* જ્વાળામુખી પર્વત jvaalaamukhee parvat

volition *n.* સંકલ્પશક્તિ sankalpashakti

volley *n.* શસ્ત્રોનો મારો shashtano maaro

volt *n.* વોલ્ટ vokt

voltage *n.* વીજળીના દબાણનું માપ veejaleena dabaananun maap

voluble *adj.* અવિરત બોલ્યા કરતું avirat bolya karatun

volume *n.* જથ્થો jaththo

voluminous *adj.* વિશાળ પ્રમાણનું vishaal pramaananun

voluntary *adj.* સ્વેચ્છિક svaichchhik

volunteer *n.* સ્વયંસેવક svayansevak

vomit *v.i.* ઊલટી કરવી oolatee karavee

voracious *adj.* ખાઉધરું khaaudharun

vortex *n.* વમળ vamal

votary *n.* ચુસ્ત અનુયાયી chust anuyaayee

vote *n.* મત, mat

voter *n.* મતદાર matadaar

vouch *v.t.* જવાબ આપવો javaab aapvo

voucher *n.* પૈસા આપ્યાનો દાખલો paisa aapyaano daakhalo

vouchsafe *v.t.* કૃપા કરવી krupa karavee

vow *n.* શપથ shapath

vowel *n.* સ્વર svar

voyage *n.* લાંબો પ્રવાસ laanbo pravaas

vulgar *adj.* અણઘડ anaghad

vulgarity *n.* અશિષ્ટતા ashishtata

vulnerable *adj.* અંશત: નિર્બળ anshatah nirbal

vulpine *adj.* લુચ્ચું luchchun

vulture *n.* ગીધ geedh

wad *n.* ડૂચો doocho

waddle *v.i.* ગજગતિ gajagati

wade *v.t.* પાણી ખૂંદતા ચાલવું paanee khoondata chaalavun

wafer *n.* વેફર vefar

wag *v.t.* આમતેમ હાલવું aamatem haalavun

wage *v.t.* રોજી rojee

wages *n.* મહેનતાણું mahenatanun

wager *n.* શરત sharat

waggery *n.* ટોળટીખળ tolateekhal

waggon *n.* ગાડું gaadun

wail *v.t.* વિલાપ vilaap

wailing *n.* વિલાપ vilaap

wain *n.* ગાડું gaadun

waist *n.* કમર kamar

waistband *n.* કમર પટ્ટો kamarapatto

wait *v.t.* પ્રતીક્ષા કરવી prateeksha karavee

waiter *n.* હજૂરિયો hajooriyo

waiting-room *n.* પ્રતિક્ષા ખંડ pratiksha khand

waitress *n.* હજૂરિયો hajooriyo

waive *v.t.* દાવો જતો કરવો daavo jato karavo

wake *v.t.* ઉઠવું uthavun

wakeful *adj.* જાગ્રત jaagrat

waken *v.t.* જાગવું jaagavun

wale *n.* મારનો સોળ maarano sol

walk *v.i.* ચાલવું chaalavun

wall *n.* ભીત bheent

wallet *n.* બટવો batavo

walnut *n.* અખરોટ akharot

waltz *n.* ત્રિતાલ નૃત્ય tritaal nruty

wan *adj.* નિસ્તેજ nistej

wand *n.* નાની પાતળી લાકડી naanee paatalee laakadee

wander *v.i.* રખડવું rakhadavun

wane *v.i.* ક્ષય kshay

want *v.t.* જરૂર હોવી jaroor hovee

wanting *adj.* વિહોનું vihonun

wanton *adj.* રમતિયાળ ramatiyaal

wantonness *n.* સ્વચ્છંદ svachchhand

war *n.* યુદ્ધ yuddh

warble *v.t.* લહેકો laheko

warbler *n.* વોરબ્લેર પક્ષી vorabler pakshee

ward *v.t.* સંભાળ sanbhaal

warden *adj.* ગૃહપતિ gruhapati

warder *n.* જેલનો અધિકારી jelano adhikaaree

wardrobe *n.* મોટું કબાટ motun kabaat

ware *n.* વેચાણ માટેનો માલ vechaan maateno maal

warehouse *n.* વખાર vakhaar

warfare *n.* યુદ્ધની પરિસ્થિતિ yuddhanee paristhiti

warlike *adj.* લડાયક, ladaayak

warm *adj.* હુંફાળું hunfaalun

warmly *adv.* હૂંફવાળું hoonfavaalun

warmth *n.* હૂંફ hoonf

warn *v.t.* ચેતવણી આપવી chetavanee aapavee

warning *n.* ચેતવણી chetavanee

warp *v.t.* ઊભો દોરો oobho doro

warrant *v.t.* હુકમ hukam

warranty *n.* ખાતરી khaataree

warren *n.* સસલાંની વસાહત sasalaannee vasaahat

warrior *n.* યોદ્ધો yoddho

wary *adj.* કાળજીવાળું kaalajeevaalun

was *p.p.* હતું hatun

wash *v.t.* શુદ્ધ કરવું shuddh karavun

washerman *n.* ધોબી dhobee

wasp *n.* ભમરી bhamaro

waspish *adj.* ચીઢિયું cheedhiyun

wastage *n.* બગાડ bagaad

waste *v.t.* બગાડ કરવો bagaad karavo

wasteful *adj.* ઉડાઉ udaau

watch *n.* સાવધાની saavadhaanee

watchful *adj.* જાગરૂક jaagarook

watchman *n.* ચોકીદાર chokeedaar

water *n.* પાણી paanee

waterfall *n.* ધોધ dhodh

watermelon *n.* તરબૂચ tarabuch

watery *adj.* પાણીનું paaneenun

wave *n.* મોજું mojun

waver *v.i.* અસ્થિર થવું asthir thavun

wax *n.* મીણ meen

waxen *adj.* મીણનું બનાવેલું meenanun banaavelun

way *n.* રસ્તો rasto

wayfarer *n.* (પગપાળો) વટેમાર્ગુ (pagapaalo) vatemaargu

waylay *v.t.* તાકમાં રહેવું taakman rahevun

we *pro* અમે ame

weak *adv.* દૂર્બળ durbal

weaken *v.t.* નબળું બનાવવું nabalun banaavavun

weakling *n.* નબળું માણસ nabalun maanas

weakly *adj.* નબળું nabalun

weak-hearted *adj.* નબળા હૃદયનું nabala radayvalu

weakness *n.* નબળાઈ nabalaaee

weal *n.* સોળ sol

wealth *n.* સંપત્તિ sanpatti

wealthy *adj.* શ્રીમંત shreemant

weapon *n.* હથિયાર hathiyaar

wear *v.t.* પહેરવું paheravun

weariness *n.* થાક thaak

wearisome *adj.* થકવી નાખનારું thakavee naakhanaarun

weary *adj.* થાકી ગયેલું, thaakee gayelun

weasel *n.* વીસેલ પ્રાણી veesel praanee

weather *n.* હવામાન havaamaan

weave *v.t.* વણવું vanavun

weaver *n.* વણકર vanakar

web *n.* કરોળિયાનું જાળું karoliyaanun jaalun

wed *v.i.* પરણવું paranavun

wedding *n.* લગ્ન lagn

wedge *n.* ફાચર faachar

wedlock *n.* લગ્નગ્રંથિ lagnagranthi

wednesday *n.* બુધવાર budhavaar

wee *adj.* બહુ નાનું bahun naanun

weed *n.* નીંદણ neendan

week *n.* સપ્તાહ saptaah

week-end *n.* સપ્તાહ અંત saptaah ant

weekly *adj.* સાપ્તાહિક saaptaahik

ween *v.i.* એમ માનવું કે... em maanavun ke

weep *v.i.* રડવું radavun

weft *n.* વાણો vaano

weigh *v.t.* વજન કરવું vajan karavun

weight *n.* વજન vajan

weighty *adj.* ભારે bhaare

weir *n.* બંધારો bandhaaro

weird *adj.* અલૌકિક alaukik

welcome *v.t.* સુસ્વાગતમ્ susvaagatam

weld *v.t.* ઝારવું jhaaravun

welfare *n.* કલ્યાણ kalyaan

well *n.* કૂવો koovo

well-bred *adj.* સારી રીતે saaree reete

well-known *adj.* સારી પેઠે જાણીતું saaree pethe jaaneetun

welter *v.i.* આળોટવું aalotavun

wench *n.* તરુણી tarunee

wend *v.t.* દિશામાં ચાલવું dishaaman chaalavun

went *p.p.* ગયું gayun

were *p.p.* હતા hata

west *n.* પશ્ચિમ pashchim

westerly *adj.* પશ્ચિમ તરફનું pashchim tarafanun

western *adj.* પાશ્ચાત્ય paashchaaty

westward *adv.* પશ્ચિમમાં આવેલું pashchimaman aavelun

wet *adj.* ભીનું beenun

whack *v.t.* લાકડીથી મારવું laakadeethee maaravun

whale *n.* વહેલ માછલી vahel maachhalee

wharfage *n.* ડક્કાભાડું dakkaabhaadun

what *pro.* શું shun

whatever *adj.* ગમે તે game te

wheat *n.* ઘઉં ghaun

wheedle ફોસલાવવું fosalaavavun

wheel *n.* પૈડું paidun

whelm *v.t.* ગરકાવ કરવું garakaav karavun

whelp *n.* કૂતરાનું બચ્ચું kootaraanun bachchun

whenever *adj.* જ્યારે પણ jyaare pan

whence *adv.* કઈ જગ્યાથી kaee jagyaathee

where *adv.* ક્યાં, kyan

whereabouts *n.* પત્તો patto

whereas વસ્તુસ્થિતિ જોતાં vastusthiti jotan

wherever *adv.* જ્યાં જ્યાં jyan jyan

whet *v.t.* ધાર ચડાવવી, dhaar chadaavavee

whether *conj.* અગર agar

which *pro.* કયું kayun

whiff *v.i.* ધુમાડાનો ગોટો dhumaadaano goto

while *adv.* સમયનો ગાળો samayano golo

whim *n.* લહેર laher

whimper *v.i.* કણસવું kanasavun

whimsical ઊટપટાંગ ootapataang

whip *v.t.* ચાબુક મારવી chaabuk maaravee

whirl *v.t.* ભ્રમણ bhraman

whirlpool *n.* વમળ vamal

whirlwind *n.* વાવંટોળ vaavantol

whisker *n.* કલ્લા kalla

whisky *n.* દારૂ daaroo

whisper *v.i.* ગુસપુસ બોલવું gusapus bolavun

whistle *n.* સિટી sitee

whit *n.* રજ raj

white *adj.* સફેદ safed

white-wash *v.t.* સંપૂરણ ધોવાણ sanpoorn dhovaan

whither *adv.* કયે ઠેકાણે kaye thekaane

whittle *n.* કમી કરવું kamee karavun

whiz *v.i.* સુસવાટો susavaato

who *pro.* કોણ kon

whoever *pro.* કોઈપણ માણસ koeepan maanas

whole *adj.* આખું aakhun

wholeheartedly *adv.* હૃદયપૂર્વકનું rhadayapoorvakanun

wholesale *n.* જથાબંધ વેપાર jathaabandh vepaar

wholesome *adj.* આરોગ્યવર્ધક aarogyavardhak

wholly *adv.* સંપૂર્ણપણે, sanpoornapane

whore *n.* વેશ્યા veshya

whose *pro.* કોનું konun

why *adv.* કેમ kem

wick *n.* દિવેટ divet

wicked *adj.* દુરાચારી duraachaaree

wickedness *n.* દુરાચારીપણું duraachaareepanun

wicker *adj.* નેતર netar

wicket *n.* નાનું બારણું naanun baaranun

wide *adj.* પહોળું paholun

widow *n.* વિધવા vidhava

widower *n.* વિધુર vidhur

widowhood *n.* વિધવાવસ્થા, vidhavaavastha

width *n.* પહોળાઈ paholaaee

wield *v.t.* કાબૂમાં રાખવું kaabooman raakhavun

wife *n.* પત્ની, patnee

wig *n.* કૃત્રિમ વાળની ટોપી kutrim vaalanee topee

wild *adj.* જંગલી jangalee

wile *n.* લુચ્ચાઈ luchchaaee

wilful *adj.* હેતુપૂર્વક કરેલું hetupoorvak karelun

will *n.* સંકલ્પ sankalp

willing *adj.* મરજીથી કરેલું marajeethee karelun

willingness *n.* ઇચ્છાશક્તિ eechchhaashakti

willow *n.* તાંતણા છૂટા પાડનારું એક જાતનું યંત્ર jaatanun yantr

wily *adj.* કપટી kapatee

win *v.t.* જીત મેળવવી jeet malavavee

wind *n.* પવન pavan

winding *adj.* વીંટવું veentavun

windmill *n.* પવનચક્કી pavanachakkee

window *n.* બારી baaree

window-dressing *n.* પ્રદર્શનકળા pradarshanakala

windy *adj.* વાવંટોળવાળું vaavantolavaalun

wine *n.* ફળનો દારૂ falano daaroo

wing *n.* પાંખ paankh

wink *v.t.* આંખ મટકાવવી aankh matakaavavee

winsome *adj.* આકર્ષક aakarshak

winter *n.* શિયાળો shiyaalo

wipe *v.t.* લૂછવું loochhavun

wire *n.* તાર taar

wire-gauze *n.* ઘટ્ટ તારજાળી ghatt taarajaalee

wireless *adj.* તાર વિનાનું taar vinaanun

wiry *adj.* તાર જેવું taar jevun

wisdom *n.* ડહાપણ dahaapan

wise *adj.* ડાહ્યું daahyun

wiseacre *n.* દોઢડાહ્યો dodhadaahyo

wisely *adj.* ડહાપણપૂર્વક dahaapanapoorvak

wish *v.t.* ઇચ્છા eechchha

wisp *n.* ઝૂડી jhoodee

wistful *adj.* આતુર aatur

wit બુદ્ધિ buddhi

witch *n.* ચૂડેલ choodel

witchcraft મેલી વિદ્યા melee vidya

witchery *n.* જાદુઈ વિદ્યા jaaduee vidya

with *prep.* સાથે saathe

withal *prep.* વધુમાં vadhuman

withdraw *v.t.* પાછું ખેંચવું paachhun khenchavun

wither *v.t.* કરમાવું karamaavun

withhold *v.t.* પાછું ખેંચવું paachhun khenchavun

within *adv.* અંદર andar

without *adv.* વગર vagar

withstand *v.t.* સામનો કરવો saamano karavo

witless *adj.* મૂર્ખ moorkh

witness *n.* સાક્ષી saakshee

witty *adj.* રમૂજી ramoojee

wizard *n.* આશ્ચર્યજનક aashcharyajanak

wizen *adj.* કૃશ krush

woe *n.* પીડા peeda

woebegone *adj.* શોકગ્રસ્ત shokagrast

woeful *adj.* દુઃખદાયક dukhadaayak

wolf *n.* વરુ varu

woman *n.* સ્ત્રી stree

womb *n.* ગર્ભાશય garbhaashay

wonder *n.* નવાઈ navaaee

wonderful *adj.* આશ્ચર્યકારક aashcharyakaarak

wont *n.* ટેવાયેલું tevaayelun

wonted *adj.* રોજનું rojanun

woo *v.t.* આકર્ષવું aakarshavun

wood *n.* જંગલ jangal

woodcutter *n.* કુહાડી kuhaadee

wooden *adj.* લાકડાનું laakadaanun

woodpecker *n.* લક્કડખોદ lakkadakhod

woodwork *n.* કાષ્ઠકામ kaashthakaam

woody *n.* જંગલવાળું jangalavaalun

wool *n.* ઊન oon

woollen *adj.* ઊની કાપડ oonee kaapad

word *n.* શબ્દ shabd

wording *n.* શબ્દરચના shabdarachana

work *n.* કામ kaamee

workable *adj.* ચલાવી શકાય એવું chalaavee shakaay evun

worker *n.* કામ કરનાર kaam karanaar

workhouse *n.* ગરીબો માટેનો આશ્રમ gareebo mateno aashram

workman *n.* કારીગર kaareegar

workmanship *n.* કારીગરનું કૌશલ્ય kaareegaranun kaushaly

world *n.* વિશ્વ vishv

worldly *adj.* દુન્યવી dunyavee

worl·wide *adj.* વિશ્વવ્યાપી vishvavyapee

worm *n.* કીડો keedo

worn પહેરવાથી જીર્ણ થયેલું paheravaathee jeern thayelun

worried *adj.* ચિંતાગ્રસ્ત chintagrasta

worry *v.t.* ચિંતા કરાવવી chinta karavee

worse વધુ ખરાબ vadhu kharaab

worship *n.* ભક્તિ bhakti

worst *adj.* સૌથી ખરાબ sauthee kharaab

worth *n.* લાયક laayak

worthless *adj.* નકામું nakaamun

worthy *adj.* સંમાનનીય sanmaananeey

would-be *adj.* હવે પછી થનારું have pachhee thanarun

wound *n.* જખમ jakham

wrangle *n.* ઝઘડો jhagado

wrangler *n.* ગોવાળિયો govaaliyo

wrap *v.t.* વીંટવું veentavun

wrapper *n.* છાપાનું વેષ્ટન chhaapaanun veshtan

wrath *n.* ક્રોધ krodh

wrathful *adj.* ક્રોધી krodhee

wreak *v.t.* ગુસ્સો સંતુષ્ટ કરવો gusso santusht karavo

wreath *n.* હાર haar

wreck *n.* અથડાઈને નાશ athadaaine naash

wreckage *n.* ભાંગી ગયેલી વસ્તુ bhaangee gayelee vastu

wrench *v.t.* જોરથી આમળવું jorathee aamalavun

wrest *v.t.* આમળવું aamalavun

wrestle *v.i.* કુસ્તી kustee

wrestler *n.* મલ્લ mall

wretch *n.* દુખી માણસ dukhee maanas

wretched *adj.* દુઃખી dukhee

wright *n.* ગાડાં બનાવનાર gaadan banaavanaar

wring *v.t.* દાબવું daabavun

wrinkle *n.* કરચલી karachalee

wrist *n.* હાથનું કાંડું haathanun kaandun

wristlet *n.* કંકણ kankan

writ *n.* ન્યાયાલય આદેશ nyaayaalay aadesh

write *v.t.* લખવું lakhavun

writer *n.* લેખક lekhak

writhe *v.i.* યાતના થવી yaatanaa thavee

writing *n.* લેખીત દસ્તાવેજ lekheet dastaavej

wrong *n.* ખોટું khotun

wroth *adj.* ગુસ્સે થયેલું gusse thayelun

wry *adj.* વક્રિત vikrut

wyvern *n.* સર્પાકાર ડ્રેગન sarpaakaar dregan

xanthine *n.* એક જાતનો પીળો રંગ ek jaatano peelo rang

xanthippe *n.* કર્કશા નારી karkasha naaree

xanthoma *n.* એક જાતનો ચામડીનો રોગ ek jaatano chaamadeeno rog

xebec *n.* ચાંચિયાઓનું વહાણ chaanchiyaaonun vahaan

xenomenia *n.* લોહીવા loheeva

xenon *n.* ઝેનોન વાયુ jhenon vaayu

xmas *n.* નાતાલ naataal

x-ray *n.* ક્ષ-કિરણો ksh - kirano

xylography *n.* કાષ્ઠનું કોતરકામ kaashthanun kotarakaam

xylol *n.* એક જાતનો અર્ક ek jaatano ark

xylonite *n.* કચકડું kachakadun

xylophagous *adj.* કાષ્ઠાહારી kaashthaahaaree

xyst *n.* મલ્લશાળા mallashaala

xystus *n.* મલ્લશાળા mallashaala

yacht *n.* ક્રીડાનૌકા kreedanauka

yachting *n.* નૌકાયન naukaayan

yak *n.* યાક yaak

yam *n.* રતાળુ rataalu

yap *v.t.* દરદથી પાડેલી ચીસ daradathee paadelee chees

yard *n.* વાર vaar

yarn *n.* કાંતેલું સૂતર kaantelun sootar

yawl *n.* સઢવાળી હોડી sadhavaalee hodee

yclept *adj.* નામે naame

ye *pro.* તમેનું જૂનું રૂપ tamenun joothanun roop

yea *adv.* હા haa

yean *v.t.* વિયાવું viyaavun

yeanling *n.* પ્રાણીનું બચ્ચું praaneenun bachchun

year *n.* વરૂષ varsh

yearly *adj.* વારૂષકિ vaarshik

yearn *v.i.* ઉત્કૃટ ઇચ્છા હોવી utkat eechchha hovee

yearning *n.* ઇચ્છા eechchha

yeast *n.* આથો aatho

yell *v.t.* ચીસ પાડવી chees paadavee

yellow *adj.* પીળું peelun

yellowish *adj.* પીળાશ પડતું peelaash padatun

yelp *v.i.* ભસવું bhasavun

yen *n.* જાપાની ચલણનો એકમ jaapaanee chalanano ekam

yeoman *n.* પાટીદાર paateedaar

yes *adv.* હા haa

yester *adj.* આનાથી આગલનું aanaathee aagalanun

yesterday *n.* ગઈકાલ gaeekaal

yet *adv.* તેમ છતાં tem chhatan

yew *n.* યૂનું ઝાડ yoonun zaad

yield *v.t.* ઊપજ oopaj

yoke *n.* ધુરા dhura

yolk *n.* જરદી jaradee

yon *adj.* પેલી બાજુનું pelee baajunun

yonder *adv.* પેલી પારનું pelee paaranun

yore *n.* ભૂતકાળ bhootakaal

you *pro.* તમે tame

young *adj.* જુવાન juvaan

youngster *n.* જુવાનિયો juvaaniyo

your *pro.* તમારું tamaarun

yours *pro.* આપનો aapano

yourself *pro.* તમે જાતે tame jaate

youth *n.* યૌવન yauvan

youthful *adj.* જુવાન juvaan

yule *n.* નાતાલનો તહેવાર taataalano tahevaar

zany *n.* મશ્કરો mashkaro

zeal *n.* ઉત્સાહ utsaah

zealot *n.* ઉત્સાહી utsaahee

zealous *adj.* ઉત્સાહી utsaahee

zealously *adv.* આતુરતાથી aaturataathee
zebra *n.* ઝીબ્રા jheebra
zebu *n.* મોટી ખૂંધવાળો બળદ motee khoondhavaalo balad
zenith *n.* ખસ્વસ્તિક khasvastik
zephyr *n.* પવનની આહ્લાદક મંદ લહેર pavananee aahlaadak mand laher
zero *n.* શૂન્ય soony
zest *n.* ઝાટકો jhaatako
zigzag *adj.* વાંકુંચૂકું vaankunchookun
zinc *n.* જસત ધાતુ jasat dhaatu
zionist *n.* ઝીયોવાદી zeeyovaadee
zodiac *n.* રાશચિક્ર raashichakr
zoic *adj.* પ્રાણીઓ સંબંધીત praaneeo sanbandheet
zoo *n.* પ્રાણી સંગ્રહાલય praanee sangrahaalay
zoochemistry *n.* પ્રાણી રસાયણશાસ્ત્ર praanee rasaayanshaastra

zoographer *n.* પશુનું વર્ણન કરનાર pashunun varnan karanaar
zoography *n.* પશુવર્ણન pashuvarnan
zoologist *n.* પ્રાણીવિદ્યાશાસ્ત્રી praaneevidyaashaastree
zoology *n.* પ્રાણીશાસ્ત્ર praaneeshaastr
zoomagnetism *n.* પ્રાણીવિષયક વદ્યિુદાકર્ષણ praaneevishayak vidyudaakarshan
zoonomy *n.* પ્રાણીજીવનનાં નિયમો praaneejeevananan niyamo
zoroastrian *adj.* જરથુપૂટરના ધર્મનું અનુયાયી jarathushtrana dharmanun anuyaayee
zymosis *n.* ઊભરો oobharo
zymotic *adj.* ઊભરાનું oobharaanun
zymurgy *n.* કણ્વિ રસાયણ kinva rasaayan

Gujarati-English

A

A-1 *adj.* એ-1 a-1

aa baajue aavelun *adv.* આ બાજુએ આવેલું hither

aa duniyaanun *adj.* આ દુનિયાનું mundane

aa reete *adv.* આ રીતે thus

aa saathe *adv.* આ સાથે herewith

aabaad thavun *v.t.* આબાદ થવું prosper

aabaroo *n.* આબરૂ repute

aabehoob *adj.* આબેહૂબ lifelike

aabehoob nakal *n.* આબેહૂબ નકલ replication

aabehoob nakal *n.* આબેહૂબ નકલ facsimile

aabehoob varnan *v.t.* આબેહૂબ વરણન portrait

aabhaaree *adj.* આભારી beholden

aabhaas *n.* આભાસ apparition

aabhaas *n.* આભાસ hallucination

Aabhlun *n.* આભળું spangle

aabohava *n.* આબોહવા climate

aabohavaaee *adj.* આબોહવાઈ climatic

aacharan *n.* આચરણ behaviour

aachchhaadan *n.* આચ્છાદન cloak

aachhaa chhinkanee rangnun *adj.* આછા છીંકણી રંગનું sorrel

aachhakalaapanun *n.* આછકલાપણું levity

aachho khyaal *n.* આછો ખ્યાલ inkling

aachho peelo rang *n.* આછો પીળો રંગ primrose

aad *n.* આડ bulwark

aadaanapradaan vrutti *v.t.* આદાનપ્રદાન વૃત્તિ reciprocity

aadaanpradaan *v.t.* આદાનપ્રદાન exchange

aadakataree soochana *n.* આડકતરી સૂચના hint

Aadambarvaalun *adj.* આડંબરવાળું stilted

aadanbar *n.* આડંબર ostentation

aadanbar *n.* આડંબર pretence

aadanbarayukt *adj.* આડંબરયુક્ત bombastic

aadanbaree *adj.* આડંબરી jaunty

aadanbaree *adj.* આડંબરી ostentatious

aadanbaree vaat *n.* આડંબરી વાત bombast

aadapedaash *n.* આડપેદાશ by-product

aadar *n.* આદર respect

aadaraneey *adj.* આદરણીય respectable

aadaraneeya *adj.* આદરણીય venerable

aadarapaatr *adj.* આદરપાત્ર reputable

aadarayukt *adj.* આદરયુક્ત reverent

aadarsh *adj.* આદર્શ ideal

aadarshavaadee *n.* આદર્શવાદી idealist

aadarshroop banaavavun *v.t.* આદર્શરૂપ બનાવવું idealize

aadatee *v.t.* આદતી used

aadateeyo *n.* આડતીયો middleman

Aadbhaade aapvun *v.t.* આડભાડે આપવું sublet

aadesh *n.* આદેશ mandate

aadesho *n.* આદેશો instruction

aadhaar *n.* આધાર crutch

aadhaar raakhavo *v.* આધાર રાખવો depend

aadhaarbhoot *n.* આધારભૂત dependable

aadhaarbhoot maahitee *n.* આધારભૂત માહિતી data

aadhaarit *adj.* આધારિત dependent

aadhaasheeshee *n.* આધાશીશી megrim

Aadhar aapvaa jog *adj.* આધાર આપવા જોગ supportable

aadhe *adv.* આધે off

aadhunik *adv.* આધુનિક alamode

aadhunik *adj.* આધુનિક modern

aadhyaaksharee mudra *n.* આદ્યાક્ષરી મુદ્રા. monogram

Aadhyaatmiktaa *n.* આધ્યાત્મિકતા spirituality

aadijaatee *n.* આદિજાતી tribe

aadiroop *n.* આદિરૂપ prototype

aadoshapadosh *n.* આડોશપાડોશ vicinity

aadu *n.* આદુ ginger

aadu fantaavun *v.t.* આડું ફંટાવું deflect

aaduaavalun moonkavun *v.t.* આડુંઅવળું મૂકવું mislay

aadun *adv.* આડું askance

aadun *adj.* આડું untoward

aadun nankhavun *v.t.* આડું નાંખવું interject

aadvaat *n.* આડવાટ by-path

aag *n.* આગ fire

aag holavanaar tukadee *n.* આગ હોલવનાર ટુકડી fire-brigade

aagaahee karavee *v.i.* આગાહી કરવી prognosticate

aagaamee *adj.* આગામી ensuing

aagadathee jovun *v.t.* આગળથી જોવુ foresee

aagahee karavee *v.t.* આગાહી કરવી bode

aagal *adj.* આગળ before

aagal chalaavavun *v.t.* આગળ ચલાવવું impel

aagal dekhaadavun *v.t.* આગળ દેખાડવું produce

aagal dhasee javun *v.t.* આગળ ધસી જવું. jut

aagal nikalee javun આગળ નકિળી જવું overtake

aagal padatun *adj.* આગળ પડતું outstanding

aagal padatun *adj.* આગળ પડતું prominent

Aagal Padtun *adj.* આગળ પડતું salient

aagal vadhavun આગળ વધવું advance

aagal vadhavun *v.i.* આગળ વધવું proceed

aagal, mokhare *adv.* આગળ, મોખરે along

aagal, saame, mokhare *adv.* આગળ, સામે, મોખરે ahead

aagalanu *adv.* આગળનું forward

aagalanun *adv.* આગળનું onward

aagaman *n.* આગમન advent

aagaman *n.* આગમન arrival

Aagbot *n.* આગબોટ steamer

aagevaan *n.* આગેવાન leader

aaghaat *n.* આઘાત percussion

Aaghaat pahochaadvo *v.t.* આઘાત પહોંચાડવો strike

aaghaat pahonchaadavo *v.t.* આઘાત પહોંચાડવો startle

aaghaatajanak *adj.* આઘાતજનક egregious

aaghaatajanak *adj.* આઘાતજનક horrible

Aaghaatjanak *adj.* આઘાતજનક shocking

aagiyo *n.* આગિયો glow-worm

aagna *n.* આજ્ઞા behest

aagnaa karavee *v.t.* આજ્ઞા કરવી enjoin

aagnaadhaarak *adj.* આજ્ઞાધારક biddable

aagnaankit *adj.* આજ્ઞાંકિત meek

aagnaanusaran *n.* આજ્ઞાનુસરણ obedience

Aagnaanuvartee *adj.* આજ્ઞાનુવર્તી sequacious

aagnaavaachak *adj.* આજ્ઞાવાચક imperative

Aagney dishaanun *adj.* આગ્નેય દિશાનું soutÆeast

Aagnyaakaaree *adj.* આજ્ઞાકારી subservient

aagrah *n.* આગ્રહ insistence

aagrahee *adj.* આગ્રહી assertive

aagrahee *n.* આગ્રહી importunity

aahaar *n.* આહાર livelihood

aahaar, pushtee aapavi *n.* આહાર, પુષ્ટિ આપવી aliment

aahavaan karavun *v.t.* આહવાન કરવું. convene

aahavaan karavun *v.t.* આહવાન કરવું invoke

aahuti *n.* આહુતિ offering

aajakaal *adv.* આજકાલ. nowadays

aajanee raata ke saanja *adv.* આજની રાત કે સાંજ. tonight

aaje *n.* આજે today

aajeejee *n.* આજીજી entreaty

aajeejee karavee *v.t.* આજીજી કરવી beseech

aajeejee karavee *v.t.* આજીજી કરવી conjure

aajeejee karavee *v.t.* આજીજી કરવી entreat

aajeejee karavee *v.t.* આજીજી કરવી implore

Aajeejee karvee te *n.* આજીજી કરવી તે solicitation

aajeevika *n.* આજીવિકા living

aajhaadee *n.* આઝાદી independence

Aajiji karnaar *adj.* આજીજી કરનાર suppliant

Aakaar *n.* આકાર shape

aakaaranee karavee *v.t.* આકારણી કરવી assess

aakaaraneekaar *n.* આકારણીકાર assessor

aakaarani *n.* આકારણી assessment

aakaash *n.* આકાશ ether

Aakaash *n.* આકાશ sky

aakaashaganga *n.* આકાશગંગા galaxy

aakaashaganga *n.* આકાશગંગા milky way

aakalan karavun *n.* આકલન કરવું fathom

aakarashavun *v.t.* આકર્ષવું fascinate

aakaro dhaal *n.* આકરો ઢાળ scarp

aakarshak *adj.* આકર્ષક attractive

aakarshak *adj.* આકર્ષક enticing

aakarshak *adj.* આકર્ષક winsome

aakarshak mahila *adj.* આકર્ષક મહિલા. blond,blonde

aakarshak saundary *n.* આકર્ષક સૌન્દર્ય glamour

aakarshak vastu *n.* આકર્ષક વસ્તુ loadstone

aakarshan આકર્ષણ attraction

aakarshavun *v.t.* આકર્ષવું attract

aakarshavun *v.t.* આકર્ષવું woo

aakarshavun te *n.* આકર્ષવું તે induction

aakarun *adj.* આકરું caustic

aakarun *adj.* આકરું rigorous

aakasmik *adj.* આકસ્મિક abrupt

aakasmik *adj.* આકસ્મિક casual

aakasmik *adj.* આકસ્મિક haphazard

aakasmik *adj.* આકસ્મિક unaspiring

aakasmik ghatana *n.* આકસ્મિક ઘટના hazard

aakhaabolun *v.t.* આખાબોલું bluff

aakhalo *n.* આખલો bull

aakharanu *adj.* આખરનું eventual

aakhlo *n.* આખલો taurus

aakhun *adj.* આખું whole

aakhun varas takanaarun *adj.* આખું વરસ ટકનારું perennial

aakramak *adj.* આક્રમક truculent

aakramak, svamataagrahee *adj.* આક્રમક, સ્વમતાગ્રહી aggressive

aakranaatmak *adj.* આક્રણાત્મક offensive

aakrshakata *n.* આકર્ષકતા grace

aakrutee *n.* આકૃતિ figure

aakruti *n.* આકૃતિ diagram

aakruti upasaavavee *v.t.* આકૃતિ ઉપસાવવી chase

aakrutidarshak આકૃતિદર્શક kaleidoscope

aakrutivaalu kagal *n.* આકૃતિવાળું કાગળ stencil

aakshep, aarop આક્ષેપ, આરોપ allegation

aaksmik vidhvans *n.* આકસ્મિક વિધ્વંસ crash

aalag karau *v.t.* અલગ કરવું detach

aalamb *n.* આલંબ fulcrum

aalas *n.* આળસ indolence

Aalas *n.* આળસ sloth

aalas raakhavee *v.i.* આળસ રાખવી dawdle

aalasee *n.* અળસી linseed

aalasu આળસુ dalliance

aalasu *adj.* આળસુ idle

aalasu *adj.* આળસુ lazy

aalasun *adj.* આળસું indolent

aalekh *n.* આલેખ graph

aalfaa *n.* આલ્ફા alpha

aalotavun *v.i.* આળોટવું welter

Aalsu *adj.* આળસુ slack

Aalsuno peer *n.* આળસુનો પીર sluggard

Aam *adj.* આમ so

aam janata *n.* આમ જનતા populace

aam tem fenkavun *v.t.* આમ તેમ ફેંકવું bandy

aamadavun *v.t.* આમળવું entwist

aamalavun *v.t.* આમળવું twist

aamalavun *v.t.* આમળવું wrest

aamantran *n.* આમંત્રણ invitation

aamantran aapavun *v.t.* આમંત્રણ આપવું invite

aamatem haalavun *v.t.* આમતેમ હાલવું wag

aamlaavaalun *adj.* આમણાવાળું tortuous

aamlee (nu jhaad) *n.* આમલી (નું ઝાડ). tamarind

Aamtem koodka maarvaa *v.i.* આમતેમ કૂદકા મારવા skip

aamukh *n.* આમુખ preamble

aanaathee aagalanun *adj.* આનાથી આગળનું yester

aanand *n.* આનંદ enjoyment

aanand *adv.* આનંદ gaily

aanand *n.* આનંદ glee

aanand aapavo *n.* આનંદ આપવો delight

aanand maanavo *v.t.* આનંદ માણવો enjoy

aanand maanavo *v.t.* આનંદ માણવો revel

aanand paryatan *v.t.* આનંદ પર્યટન excruciate

aanand parytan *n.* આનંદ પર્યટન jaunt

aanand pramod *n.* આનંદ પ્રમોદ rejoicing

aanand vinaanun haasy *v.t.* આનંદ વિનાનું હાસ્ય grin

aanandaashcharya *n.* આનંદાશ્ચર્ય admiration

aanandadaayak svabhaav *n.* આનંદદાયક સ્વભાવ felicity

aanandano prasang *n.* આનંદનો પ્રસંગ gala

aanandapoorvak gaavun *v.t.* આનંદપૂર્વક ગાવું carol

aanandee *adj.* આનંદી cheerful

aanandee *adj.* આનંદી cheery

aanandit karavun *v.t.* આનંદતિ કરવું exhilarate

aanandpoorn *adj.* આનંદપૂર્ણ delightful

aanchakavun *n.* આંચકવું snatch

aanchakee levun *v.t.* આંચકી લેવું grab

aanchako *n.* આંચકો brunt

aanchako *n.* આંચકો. flounce

aanchako *n.* આંચકો jerk

aanchako *n.* આંચકો shock

aanchako khaavo *v.i.* આંચકો ખાવો recoil

aanchako maaravo *v.t.* આંચકો મારવો. jolt

aanchal *n.* આંચળ dug

aanchal *n.* આંચળ teat

aandapramod *n.* આનંદ પ્રમોદ festivity

aandhalunkiyun *adv.* આંધળુંકિયું headlong

aandolan *n.* આંદોલન movement

aangalee *n.* આંગળી finger

aanjavun *v.t.* આંજવું dazzle

aankadaakeeya maahitee *n.* આકડાકીય માહિતી statistics

aankadaane lagatun *adj.* આંકડાને લગતું statistical

aankadee *n.* આંકડી barb

aankadeevalun gharenun *n.* આંકડીવાળું ઘરેણું brooch

aankado *n.* આંકડો digit

aankado *n.* આંકડો hook

aankado *n.* આંકડો loop

aankado *n.* આંકડો number

aankh *n.* આંખ eye

aankh matakaavavee *v.t.* આંખ મટકાવવી wink

aankh michelun *adj.* આંખ મીચેલું blindfold

aankh nee keekee *n.* આંખની કીકી eyeball

aankh ughaadavee *v.t.* આંખ ઉઘાડવી disabuse

aankhanee kanee *n.* આંખની કણી eyesore

aankhanee keekee *n.* આંખની કીકી iris

aankhanee paanpan *n.* આંખની પાંપણ lash

aankhano motiyo *n.* આંખનો મોતિયો. cataract

aankhanun popachun *n.* આંખનું પોપચું lid

aankhe joee shakaay evun *adj.* આંખે જોઈ શકાય એવું ocular

Aankhmaa aansu aavvaan te *n.* આંખમાં આંસુ આવવાં તે snivel

aantarada *n.pl.* આંતરડા bowels

aantaradaano taava *n.* આંતરડાંનો તાવ typhoid

aantaradan *n.* આંતરડાં viscera

aantaradun *n.pl.* આંતરડું intestines

aantaragnaateey vivaah *n.* આંતરજ્ઞાતીય વિવાહ intermarriage

aantararaashtriy *adj.* આન્તરરાષ્ટ્રીય international

aantaravigrh *n.* આંતરવિગ્રહ civil war

aantardaa *n.pl.* આંતરડાં entrails

aantaree levun *v.* આંતરી લેવું circumscribe

aantarik *adj.* આંતરિક interior

aantarvastra *n.* આંતરવસ્ત્ર underwear

aanteeghoontee *n.* આંટીઘૂંટી complexity

aantrapuchchha *n.* આંત્રપુચ્છ appendix

aantrapuchchhano sojo *n.* આંત્રપુચ્છનો સોજો appendicitis

aanushangik padaarth *n.* આનુષંગિક પદાર્થ appurtenance

aanuyaayee *n.* અનુયાયી devotee

aapacho *n.* અપચો indigestion

aapakhud *n.* આપખુદ autocrat

aapamaanajanak *adj.* અપમાનજનક derogatory

aapano *pro.* આપનો yours

aapanun *adj.* આપણું our

aapatti *n.* આપત્તિ calamity

aapattijanak *adj.* આપત્તિજનક. calamitous

aapattinun kaaran *n.* આપત્તિનું કારણ bane

aapavaanu kahevu *v.t.* આપવાનું કહેવું tender

aapavaanun kahevun *v.t.* આપવાનું કહેવું proffer

aapavadaai *n.* આપવડાઈ egotism

aapavadaaivaalo *adj.* આપવડાઈવાળો egotist

aapavitra banaavavun *v.t.* અપવિત્ર બનાવવું desecrate

aapavun *v.t.* આપવું confer

aapee shakaay evun *adj.* આપી શકાય એવું payable

aapel visheshahak *n.* આપેલ વિશિષહક indulgence

aapkhudshaahee *adj.* આપખુદશાહી autocratic

aapoorn *prep.* અપૂર્ણ demi

aapoorti karavee *v.t.* આપૂરતિ કરવી supply

aaraadhanaa, anjalee *n.* આરાધના, અંજલિ adoration

aaraam *n.* આરામ comfort

aaraam *n.* આરામ rest

aaraamadaayak khurashee *n.* આરામદાયક ખુરશી easychair

aaraamasheer *adj.* આરામશીર cushy

Aaraamthee chaalvun *n.* આરામથી ચાલવું saunter

Aarab *n.* આરબ saracen

aarakshan *n.* આરક્ષણ reservation

aaram *n.* આરામ ease

aaranbh *n.* આરંભ inception

aaranbh *n.* આરંભ opening

aarapaara javun *v.t.* આરપાર જવું traverse

aarasapahaan *n.* આરસપહાણ marble

aarogy shaastr *n.* આરોગ્ય શાસ્ત્ર hygiene

Aarogya ane Swachchhtaa *n.* આરોગ્ય અને સ્વચ્છતા sanitation

Aarogyadaayak *adj.* આરોગ્યદાયક salubrious

aarogyavardhak *adj.* આરોગ્યવર્ધક wholesome

aarop *n.* આરોપ charge

aarop mookavo *n.* આરોપ મૂકવો accusation

aarop mukavo *v.t.* આરોપ મુકવો arraign

aarop mukavo *v.t.* આરોપ મુકવો indict

aarop mukavon *v.* આરોપ મુકવો allege

aaropaman sandovaavun *v.t.* આરોપમાં સંડોવાવું incriminate

aarpaar *prep.* આરપાર trans

aarsh prayog *n.* આર્ષ પ્રયોગ. archaism

aarth samajvo *v.t.* અર્થ સમજવો understand

aarthik laabh maate karelun *adj.* આર્થિક લાભ માટે કરેલું commercial

Aarthik madad karvee *v.t.* આર્થિક મદદ કરવી subsidize

aarthik sahaay *n.* આર્થિક સહાય subsidy

aasan *n.* આસન throne

aasanarahit karavun *v.t.* આસનરહિત કરવું unseat

aasann આસન્નનું impending

aasapaasanun *n.* આસપાસનું peri

aaschhadan karavun *v.t.* આચ્છાદન કરવું enshrond

aasha *n.* આશા hope

aashaaspad *adj.* આશાસ્પદ promising

aashaavaalun *adj.* આશાવાળું rosy

aasharaathee kahevun *v.t.* આશરાથી કહેવું guess

aasharo *n.* આશરો lee

aasharo levo *v.i.* આશરો લેવો resort

Aashay *n.* આશય significance

aashay bataavavo *n.* આશય બતાવવો purpor

aashchary pamaadavun *v.t.* આશ્ચર્ય પમાડવું astonish

aashcharya *n.* આશ્ચર્ય surprise

aashcharyachakit karavun *v.t.* આશ્ચર્યચકિત કરવું amaze

aashcharyachakit karavun *n.* આશ્ચર્યચકિત કરવું amazement

aashcharyajanak *adj.* આશ્ચર્યજનક incredible

aashcharyajanak *n.* આશ્ચર્યજનક wizard

aashcharyakaarak *adj.* આશ્ચર્યકારક amazing

aashcharyakaarak *adj.* આશ્ચર્યકારક wonderful

aashcharyakaarak vastu *n.* આશ્ચર્યકારક વસ્તુ prodigy

aasheervaad *n.* આશીર્વાદ benediction

aasheervaad *n.* આશીર્વાદ blessing

aasheervaad aapava *v.t.* આશીર્વાદ આપવા bless

aasheervaad praapt *adj.* આશીર્વાદ પૂરાપ્ત. blessed

aashram *n.* આશ્રમ hermitage

aashray *n.* આશ્રય asylum

aashray *n.* આશ્રય recourse

aashray *n.* આશ્રય refuge

aashrayasthaan *n.* આશ્રયસ્થાન haven

aashrit *n.* આશ્રિત dependant

aashrit, aadhaarit *n.* આશ્રિત, આધારિત adjunct

aashvaasan *n.* આશ્વાસન consolation

aaspaas *adv.* આસપાસ about

Aaspaasnaa sanjogo *n.* આસપાસના સંજોગો situation

aastik *n.* આસ્તિક believer

aastik *n.* આસ્તિક theism

aatakaayat *n.* અટકાયત confinent

aatakaayat *v.* અટકાયત detain

aatakmaa raakhvun *n.* અટકમાં રાખવું detention

aatalun badhun nahi *adj.* આટલું બધું નહીં less

aatankavaad *n.* આતંકવાદ terrorism

aatashabaajee *n.* આતશબાજી fireworks

aath આઠ eight

aathamo *adj.* આઠમો eighth

aatho *n.* આથો ferment

aatho *n.* આથો yeast

aatho chadaavavo *n.* આથો ચડાવવો fermentation

aatisaar *n.* અતિસાર diarrhoea

aatisay paatalu *adj.* અતિશય પાતળું diaphanous

aatithy *n.* આતિથ્ય hospitality

aatithya *v.* આતિથ્ય treat

aatma *n.* આત્મા psyche

Aatma vishvaas *n.* આત્મ વિશ્વાસ self-confidence

aatma-, svat-, svayam- આત્મ–, સ્વત–, સ્વયં– auto

Aatmaa *n.* આત્મા soul

Aatmaa sambandhee *adj.* આત્મા સબંધી spiritual

aatmacharitra *n.* આત્મચરિત્ર autobiography

Aatmaghaatee આત્મઘાતી suicidal

aatmalakshee આત્મલક્ષી internal

Aatmalakshee *adj.* આત્મલક્ષી subjective

aatmanireekshan *n.* આત્મનિરિક્ષણ
introspection

aatmasaan karavun *v.t.* આત્મસાન
કરવું cherish

aatmasantosh *n.* આત્મસંતોષ
complacencency

aatmasantushta *adj.* આત્મસંતુષ્ટ
complacent

aatmasanyam *n.* આત્મસંયમ
continence

aatmavishvaas *n.* આત્મવિશ્વાસ
aplomb

aatmavishvaas no abhaav *n.*
આત્મવિશ્વાસનો અભાવ diffidence

aatmavishvaas no abhav *adj.*
આત્મવિશ્વાસ વિનાનું diffident

aatmavishvaasavaalun *adj.*
આત્મવિશ્વાસવાળું confident

Aatmhatyaa *n.* આત્મહત્યા suicide

Aatmodhdhaar *n.* આત્મોદ્ધાર
salvation

aato *n.* આટો flour

Aattrupti *n.* આતતૃપ્તિ satiety

aatur *adj.* આતુર eager

aatur *adj.* આતુર earnest

aatur *adj.* આતુર wistful

aaturataapoorvak *adv.* આતુરતાપૂર્વક
earnestly

aaurataathee *adv.* આતુરતાથી
zealously

aaturataathee pakadavun *v.t.*
આતુરતાથી પકડવું clutch

aaturtaa *n.* આતુરતા eagerness

aaturtaa *n.* આતુરતા earnestness

aaturtaapoorvak *adv.* આતુરતાપૂર્વક
eagerly

aatyantik *adj.* આત્યંતિક high

aauchitya *n.* ઔચિત્ય appropriateness

aaupachaarikataa *n.* ઔપચારિકતા
formality

aavaasee *adj.* આવાસી residential

aavajo આવજો goo·bye

aavak *n.* આવક income

aavakavero *n.* આવકવેરો income-tax

aavaran, *n.* આવરણ covering

aavardhak *n.* આવર્ધક magnifier

aavarodhak *n.* અવરોધક detriment

aavartak *adj.* આવર્તક recurrent

aavartak *adj.* આવર્તક rotative

aavashyak *adj.* આવશ્યક essential

aavashyak banaavavun *v.t.* આવશ્યક
બનાવવું entail

aavashyak hovun *v.t.* આવશ્યક હોવું
behove

aavashyak parinaam *n.* આવશ્યક
પરિણામ quantum

aavashyak saajasaamagree *n.*
આવશ્યક સાજસામગ્રી outfit

aavashyak saajasarnjaam *n.*
આવશ્યક સાજસરંજામ equipage

aavashyak vastu *n.* આવશ્યક વસ્તુ
desideratum

aavashyakta *n.* આવશ્યકતા
requirement

aavata mahinaanun *adj.* આવતા
મહિનાનું proximo

aavatee kaala(no divas) *adv.* આવતી
કાલ(નો દિવસ) tomorrow

aavavun *v.i.* આવવું arrive

aavavun *n.* આવવું come

aavavun *v.i.* આવવું come

aavdat *adj.* આવડત tact

aavesh *n.* આવેશ passion

aaveshayukta bhaasan *n.* આવેશયુક્ત
ભાષણ harangue

aavrutee *n.* આવૃત્તિ edition

aavyavasthaa *n.* અવ્યવસ્થા
derangement

aavyavasthit karavun *v.t.* અવ્યવસ્થિત
કરવું derange

aayaat karavun *v.t.* આયાત કરવું import

aayog *n.* આયોગ commission

abaadhit *n.* અબાધિત absolute

abaj *n.* અબજ billion

abarakh *n.* અબરખ mica

abhagyu *adv.* અભાગ્યું unfortunately

abhan, nirakshar *adj.* નિરિક્ષર
illiterate

abhang *n.* અભંગ unbroken

abhark *n.* અભ્રક talc

abhed *adj.* અભેદ unhurt

abhedhy *adj.* અભેદ્ય impervious

abhedhya *adj.* અભેધ્ય unassailable

abheeneta, nat *n.* અભિનિતા, નટ actor

abhilaashaa *adj.* અભિલાષા ambitious

abhimaanee *adj.* અભિમાની proud

abhinandan *n.* અભિનંદન compliment

abhinandan અભિનંદન congratulation

abhinandan aapava *v.t.* અભિનંદન આપવા congratulate

abhinandanaatmak *n.* અભિનંદનાત્મક complimentary

abhinna *adj.* અભિન્ન integral

abhipraay *n.* અભિપ્રાય opinion

abhipraay *n.* અભિપ્રાય thinking

abhipraay vyakt karavo *v.t.* અભિપ્રાય વ્યક્ત કરવો opine

abhipret *adj.* અભિપ્રેત implicit

abhipret hovun *v.t.* અભિપ્રેત હોવું connote

abhiruchi *n.* અભિરુચિ aptitude

abhiruchi *n.* અભિરુચિ liking

abhivaadan *n.* અભિવાદન applause

abhivaah, pravaah *n.* અભિવાહ, પ્રવાહ afflux

abhivahan *n.* અભિવહન transit

abhivyakt karavun *v.t.* અભિવ્યક્ત કરવું convey

abhivyakti *n.* અભિવ્યક્તિ expression

abhyaas *n.* અભ્યાસ practice

abhyaasakram *n.* અભ્યાસક્રમ curriculum

Abhyaasee *adj.* અભ્યાસી studious

Abhyaskram *n.* અભ્યાસક્રમ syllabus

achaanak aavelee aapatti *n.* અચાનક આવેલી આપત્તિ catastrophe

Achaanak athdaaman *n.* અચાનક અથડામણ skirmish

achaanak banavun *v.i.* અચાનક બનવું happen

achaanak vahevun *v.i.* અચાનક વહેવું spurt

achakaatun *n.* અચકાતું hesitation

achakaavavun *adj.* અચકાવવું hesitating

achal અચળ constant

achal *adj.* અચલ immobile

acheta *adj.* અચેત unwary

achhabada *n.* અછબડા chicken-pox

achhat *n.* અછત paucity

Achhat *n.* અછત scarcity

Achhat *n.* અછત shortage

achhoota *adj.* અછૂત untouched

achokkas *adj.* અચોક્કસ improper

achokkas *adj.* અચોક્કસ inaccurate

achook *adj.* અચૂક infallible

achutoon *n.* અછૂતું unimpaired

adaa karavun *v.t.* અદા કરવું redeem

adaakaaree, hangaamee *adj.* અદાકારી, હંગામી acting

adaalatee tapas *n.* અદાલતી તપાસ inquisition

Adaalatman daavo mandvo *v.t.* અદાલતમાં દાવો માંડવો sue

adabavaalun *adj.* અદબવાળું respectful

adachan *n.* અડચણ hindrance

adachan *n.* અડચણ hitch

adachan karanaaru *n.* અડચણ કરનારુ cumbrous

adachan karavee *v.i.* અડચણ કરવી encumber

adachan karavee *v.t.* અડચણ કરવી impede

adachanaroop *adj.* અડચણરૂપ cumbersome

adadho bhaag *n.* અડધો ભાગ half

adadiyo paththar *n.* અડદિયો પથ્થર granite

adag *adj.* અડગ resolute

adakatun *n.* અડકતું contiguity

adalaabadal *n.* અદલાબદલ permutation

adalaabadalee *n.* અદલાબદલી truck

adapalun અડપલું prank

Adaplaan karnaarun bhoot *n.* અડપલાં કરનારું ભૂત sprite

adavun *v.t.* અડવું touch

addabhut *adj.* અદ્ભુત marvellous

addabhut rasavaalun *adj.* અદ્ભુત રસવાળું romantic

addabhut vastu *n.* અદ્ભુત વસ્તુ marvel

adekhaaee *n.* અદેખાઈ malevolent

adekhaai aave evun *adj.* અદેખાઈ આવે એવું enviable

adhaar *adj.* અઢાર eighteen

adhaarmik *adj.* અધાર્મિક ungodly

adhaarmikata *n.* અધાર્મિકતા impiety

adhah patit *v.i.* અધઃપતતિ degenerate

adhahapatan thavun *v.i.* અધઃપતન થવું retrogress

adhahasvastik *n.* અધઃસ્વસ્તકિ nadir

adhahpaat karavo *v.t.* અધઃપાત કરવો degrade

adham *adj.* અધમ. misbegotten

Adham *adj.* અધમ slimy

adhamataa *n.* અધમતા baseness

adhavachche *adv.* અધવચ્ચે midway

adhelavun *v.t.* અઢેલવું recline

adheleene bethelun અઢેલીને બેઠેલું recumbent

adhik *n.* અધકિ plus

Adhikaadhik karvun *v.t.* અધકિાધકિ કરવું superadd

adhikaar *v.* અધકિાર accede

adhikaarakshetr *n.* અધકિારક્ષેત્ર. jurisdiction

adhikaaranee rooe karelun *adj.* અધકિારની રૂએ કરેલું official

adhikrut nondhaneedaar *n.* અધકૃિત નોંધણીદાર recorder

adhivaas *n.* અધવિાસ domicile

adhogati *n.* અધોગતિ perdition

adhomukh *adj.* અધોમુખ prone

Adhooriyun *adj.* અધૂરિયું stunted

adhoorun અધૂરું incomplete

adhuru *adj.* અધુરુ unaccomplished

adhyaksh *n.* અધ્યક્ષ president

adhyakshasthaan levun *v.t.* અધ્યક્ષસ્થાન લેવું preside

adhyatanashaileenun *adj.* અદ્યતનશૈલીનું chic

adhyayan *n.* અધ્યયન perusal

adhyetavrutti *n.* અધ્યેતાવૃત્તિ fellowship

adiyal *adj.* અડયિલ perverse

adiyal *adj.* અડયિલ pigheaded

Adlaabadal ke vinimay karvo *n.* અદલાબદલ કે વનિમિય કરવો swop

adraavya *adj.* અદ્રાવ્ય insoluble

adrashy *p.p.* અદૃશ્ય hidden

adrashy *adj.* અદૃશ્ય imperceptible

adrashya *adj.* અદૃશ્ય unseen

adrashya *n.* અદૃશ્ય disappearance

adrashya kirano *n.* અદૃશ્ય કરિણો ultr¡violet

adrashya thavun *v.i.* અદૃશ્ય થવું disappear

adrshy *adj.* અદૃશ્ય invisible

adviteey *adj.* અદ્વતીિય. inimitable

adviteey *adj.* અદ્વતીિય. matchless

adviteey *adj.* અદ્વતીિય peerless

adviteey vyakti *n.* અદ્વતીિય વ્યક્તિ phoenix

adyaahaar *n.* અધ્યાહાર ellipsis

ae rite *adv.* એ રીતે thereby

aek *n.* એક unit

aeka baajuae namavun *n.* એક બાજુએ નમવું tilt

aeka jaatanu kabootar *n.* એક જાતનું કબૂતર turtle

aeka jantunaashaka davaa *n.* એક જંતુનાશક દવા. thymol

aeka sarakhaapanun *n.* એક સરખાપણું uniformity

aeka vajan *n.* એક વજન ton

aeka visfotaka *n.* એક વસિ્ફોટક tonite

aekaantapriya *adj.* એકાંતપ્રયિ unsociable

aekaantariyo taava *adj.* એકાંતરયિો તાવ tertian

aekadharun *adj.* એકધારું uniform

aekar *n.* એકર acre

aekataa *n.* એકતા unity

aekatra karavun *v.t.* એકત્ર કરવું federate

aekdam *v.i.* એકદમ pop

aekko, sogathun *n.* એક્કો, સોગઠું, ace

aeliyo *n.* એળયિો aloe

aelyuminiyam *n.* એલ્યુમનિયિમ aluminium

aembyulans *n.* એમ્બ્યુલન્સ ambulance

aenaa parinaama roope *adv.* એના પરણિામ રૂપે therefore

aenshee *adj.* એંશી eighty

aergan *n.* એરગન airgun

aesheemu *adj.* એંશીમું eightieth

aesitilin *n.* એસટિલિન acetylene

afava *n.* અફવા bruit

afava *n.* અફવા canard

afava *n.* અફવા hearsay

afava *n.* અફવા rumour

afeen *n.* અફીણ opium

afeenano ark *n.* અફીણનો અરૂક laudanum

afeenano ark *n.* અફીણનો અરૂક morphia

agaaunun *adj.* અગાઉનું preceding

agaaunun *adj.* અગાઉનું prior

agaauthee *adv.* અગાઉથી beforehand

agaauthee aapavun *v.t.* અગાઉથી આપવું prepay

agaauthee jovun *v.t.* અગાઉથી જોવું presage

agaauthee kabajo *v.t.* અગાઉથી કબજો pre-occupy

agaauthee niradhaarit *adj.* અગાઉથી નિર્ધારિત destined

agaauthee niyat karavun *v.t.* અગાઉથી નિયત કરવું predestinate

agaauthee soochanaa *v.t.* અગાઉથી સૂચના forebode

agaauthee vichaaravun *n.* અગાઉથી વિચારવું premeditation

agaauthee, pahelan *adv.* અગાઉથી, પહેલાં already

agar *conj.* અગર whether

agatyata *n.* અગત્યતા importance

agaunu *adv.* અગાઉ formerly

aghaad *adj.* અગાધ fathomless

aghatit અઘટિત unseemly

agiyaar *adj.* અગિયાર eleven

agiyaaramu *adj.* અગિયારમું eleventh

agnaan *n.* અજ્ઞાન ignorance

agnaan *adj.* અજ્ઞાન ignorant

agneyvaadi *n.* અજ્ઞેયવાદી agnostic

agnidaah sanskaar karavo *v.t.* અગ્નિદાહ સંસ્કાર કરવો cremate

agnikrut *adj.* અગ્નિકૃત igneous

agochar *adj.* અગોચર impalpable

agochar *adj.* અગોચર intangible

agraadhikaar *adj.* અગ્રાધિકાર preferential

agraahy *adj.* અગ્રાહ્ય inadmissible

agradoot *n.* અગ્રદૂત harbinger

agradoot *n.* અગ્રદૂત herald

agrakrayaadhikaar *v.t.* અગ્રક્રયાધિકાર pre-emption

agrata *n.* અગ્રતા priority

agravartee, poorvakaalin *adj.*

અગ્રવર્તી, પૂર્વકાલીન anterior

agresar *n.* અગ્રેસર pioneer

agresar *adj.* અગ્રેસર premier

agresaratv અગ્રેસરત્વ precedence

agyaanagrast *adj.* અજ્ઞાનગ્રસ્ત benighted

agyaat *adj.* અજ્ઞાત unknown

aham *n.* અહં ego

ahamabhaav *n.* અહંભાવ egoism

ahamakendree *adj.* અહંકેન્દ્રી egocentric

ahankaar *n.* અહંકાર arrogance

ahankaar *n.* અહંકાર presumption

ahankaaree *adj.* અહંકારી arrogant

ahankaaree *adj.* અહંકારી conceited

ahanprem *n.* અહંપ્રેમ narcissism

aheen *adv.* અહીં here

Aheen taheen *adj.* અહીંતહીં sporadic

aheenthee *adv.* અહીંથી hence

ahesaan *n.* અહેસાન obligation

ahevaal aapavo *v.t.* અહેવાલ આપવો report

aikya *n.* ઐક્ય cartel

aikya *n.* ઐક્ય concordance

aitihaasik *adj.* ઐતિહાસિક historic

ajaan *adj.* અજાણ nescient

ajaanye *adj.* અજાણ્યે unknowingly

ajaanyu *adj.* અજાણ્યું unfamiliar

Ajab *adj.* અજબ stupendous

ajagar *n.* અજગર boa

ajagar *n.* અજગર python

ajamaayasee *adj.* અજમાયસી probationary

ajamaayash *n.* અજમાયશ trial

ajey *adj.* અજેય impregnable

ajey *adj.* અજેય invincible

ajey અજેય unbeaten

ajey *adj.* અજેય unconquerable

ajod *adj.* અજોડ incomparable

ajod *adj.* અજોડ unrivalled

ajoda *adj.* અજોડ unparalleled

akaaran aakraman *n.* અકારણ આક્રમણ aggression

akaarana અકારણ unprovoked

akal *adj.* અકળ incomprehensible

akalpy *adj.* અકલ્પ્ય inconceivable

akarmak *adj.* અકર્મક intransitive

akartavyanishtha *adj.* અકર્તવ્યનીષ્ઠ undutiful

akasmaat *n.* અકસ્માત accident

akathit *adj.* અકથિત untold

Akdaai, Magroori *n.* અકડાઈ કે મગરૂરી stiffness

akhaadhy *adj.* અખાદ્ય inedible

akhaado *n.* અખાડો arena

akhaado *n.* અખાડો gymnasium

akhaat *n.* અખાત gulf

akhanditata *n.* અખંડિતતા integrity

akharot *n.* અખરોટ walnut

akhila srushti *n.* અખિલ સૃષ્ટિ universe

akhoot અખૂટ inexhaustible

akkad *adj.* અક્કડ rigid

akkadavartanavaalun *adj.* અક્કડવર્તનવાળું prim

akrutagyna *adj.* અકૃતજ્ઞ unthankful

akrutgna *adj.* અકૃતજ્ઞ ungrateful

akseer eelaajagnaupaay *n.* અકસીર ઈલાજજ્ઞઉપાય panacea

akshaansh *n.* અક્ષાંશ latitude

aksham *v.t.* અક્ષમ disable

aksham *adj.* અક્ષમ incompetent

akshamata અક્ષમતા inability

akshamataa *n.* અક્ષમતા disability

akshamy *adj.* અક્ષમ્ય inexcusable

akshar *n.* અક્ષર character

akshar *n.* અક્ષર letter

akshar kotaravan *v.t.* અક્ષર કોતરવાં inscribe

akshare aksharanun *adj.* અક્ષરે અક્ષરનું literal

akshut *adj.* ek sarakhun karavun unheard

akushal *adj.* અકુશળ inapt

akushal અકુશળ inaptitude

alaayadun nivaasasthaan *n.* અલાયદું નિવાસસ્થાન villa

alabatt *adj.* અલબત્ત indeed

Alag alag *adj.* અલગ અલગ severally

alag karavun *v.t.* અલગ કરવું disunite

alag karavun te *v.t.* અલગ કરવું તે disconnect

alag paadavun *v.t.* અલગ પાડવું insulate

alag padavun *v.i.* અલગ પડવું differ

alag raakhelun *adj.* અલગ રાખેલું reserved

Alagthee *n.* અલગથી separately

alanakaaraprachur *adj.* અલંકારપ્રચુર florid

alankaar *n.* અલંકાર metaphor

alankaarashaastr *n.* અલંકારશાસ્ત્ર rhetoric

alaseeno chhod *n.* અળસીનો છોડ flax

alaukik *adj.* અલૌકિક weird

alaukik *adv.* અલૌકિક miraculous

allah *n.* અલ્લાહ allah

alp *adj.* અલ્પ low

alp *adj.* અલ્પ. meagre

alp *adj.* અલ્પ exigent

alp jaththo *n.* અલ્પ જથ્થો pittance

alpaahaar *n.* અલ્પાહાર refection

alpajanasattaak raajy *n.* અલ્પજનસત્તાક રાજ્ય oligarchy

alpakharch *v.t.* અલ્પખર્ચ undercharge

alpamaatra *n.* અલ્પમાત્રા modicum

alpamuly *adj.* અલ્પમુલ્ય unvalued

alpatam *n.* અલ્પતમ minimum

alpaviraam (,) *n.* અલ્પવિરામ (,) comma

amaap *adj.* અમાપ immeasurable

amal karanaar stree *n.* અમલ કરનાર સ્ત્રી executrix

amalaman chaalu *adj.* અમલમાં ચાલુ operative

amaldaar *n.* અમલદાર bureaucrat

amaryaad *adj.* અમર્યાદ illmitable

amaryaad *n.* અમર્યાદ infinite

amaryaad satta *n.* અમર્યાદા સત્તા freehold

amaryaada *n.* અમર્યાદા boundless

ame *pro* અમે we

ame *pro.* અમે us

ameerashaahee *n.* અમીરશાહી aristocracy

ameeree *adj.* અમીરી aristocratic

amerikanu ek chalan *n.* અમેરિકાનું ચલણ dollar

amogh *adj.* અમોઘ unfailing

amooly *adj.* અમૂલ્ય invaluable

amooly *adj.* અમૂલ્ય priceless
amoort *adj.* અમૂર્ત abstract
amoort *adj.* અમૂર્ત etherial
amoort *adj.* અમૂર્ત immaterial
amrut *n.* અમૃત ambrosia
amrut *n.* અમૃત elixir
amrut *n.* અમૃત nectar
amugrahasheel *adj.* અનુગ્રહશીલ indulgent
Amuk jagyaaye mookvun અમુક જગ્યાએ મૂકવું situate
Amuk ke chokkas sthal ke jagyaa *n.* અમુક કે ચોક્કસ સ્થળ કે જગ્યા spot
amuk tareeke varnan karavun *v.t.* અમુક તરીકે વર્ણન કરવું characterize
amuka dishaamaa javun *v.t.* અમુક દિશામાં જવું tend
amuka maryaadita samay *n.* અમુક મર્યાદતિ સમય term
Amukne Khaatar *n.* અમુકને ખાતર sake
anaadar *n.* અનાદર contempt
anaadar *n.* અનાદર disobedience
anaadar *v.t.* અનાદર disrespect
anaahat *adj.* અનાહત unbidden
anaajana daana *n.* અનાજના દાણા corn
anaajano daano *n.* અનાજનો દાણો grain
anaajano dalelo lot *n.* અનાજનો દળેલો લોટ. meal
anaajanun kothaar *n.* અનાજનું કોઠાર garner
anaajno locho *v.t.* અનાજનો લોચો mash
anaam raheene *adj.* અનામ રહીને anonymously
anaamat raakhanaar *n.* અનામત રાખનાર depositary
anaamat raakhavun *v.* અનામત રાખવું reserve
anaamik *adj.* અનામકિ nameless
anaath baalak *n.* અનાથ બાળક orphan
anaathaashram *n.* અનાથાશ્રમ orphanage
anaavarana vidhi karavee *v.t.* અનાવરણ વધિકિરવો unveil
anaavashyak અનાવશ્યક redundant

anabanaav *n.* અણબનાવ variance
anadhaaree aapatti *n.* અણધારી આપત્તતિ. havoc
anadhaaryun *adj.* અણધાર્યું accidental
anadhikruk *adj.* અનધકૃિત unauthorized
anadhikrut *adj.* અનધકૃિત unwarrantable
anadhikrut *adj.* અનધકૃિત unwarranted
anagamato maanas *n.* અણગમતો માણસ soda
anagamatun *adj.* અણગમતું repugnant
anagamo *n.* અણગમો disinclination
anagamo *n.* અણગમો disrelish
anagamo *n.* અરુચિ distaste
anagamo *n.* અણગમો repugnance
anagamo bataavavo *v.t.* અણગમો બતાવવો shrug
anagamo peda karanaarun *adj.* અણગમો પેદા કરનારું repulsive
anaghad *n.* અણઘડ oaf
anaghad *adj.* અણઘડ vulgar
anaitik *adj.* અનૈતકિ unscrupulous
anaitik aacharan *v.t.* અનૈતકિ આચરણ કરવું debauch
ananam *adj.* અણનમ immovable
ananam *adj.* અણનમ indomitable
anant *adj.* અનંત endless
ananya *adj.* અનન્ય unique
anapekshit *adj.* અનપેક્ષતિ unforeseen
anapexit *adj.* અનપેક્ષતિ unexpected
anapexitpane *adj.* અનપેક્ષતિપણે unaware
anasaar *n.* અણસાર resemblance
anasaara *adj.* અણસારા precursory
anaupachaarik *adj.* અનૌપચારકિ informal
anaupachaarik patr *n.* અનૌપચારકિ પત્ર memorandum
anaupcharik *adj.* અનૌપચારકિ unceremonious
anauras *n.* અનૌરસ bastard
anbaadee *n.* અંબાડી howdah
andaaj *n.* અંદાજ approximation
andaaj *n.* અંદાજ estimation
andaaj kaadavo *v.t.* અંદાજ કાઢવો estimate

andaajapatra *n.* અંદાજપત્ર budget
andaakaar *adj.* અંડાકાર oval
andaakrutee *n.* અંડાકૃતિ ellips
andaashay *n.* અંડાશય ovary
andakosh *n.* અંડકોષ testicle
andar *adv.* અંદર within
andar aavelun અંદર આવેલું inward
andar vahevun te *n.* અંદર વહેવું તે influx
andaranee baajunee jagya *n.* અંદરની બાજુની જગ્યા inside
andaranun *adj.* અંદરનું inner
andarathee paheravaano kabajo *n.* અંદરથી પહેરવાનો કબજો vest
andhaapo *n.* અંધાપો blindness
andhaar kotadee *n.* અંધારકોટડી dungeon
andhaaraavaalun *adj.* અંધારાવાળું gloomy
andhaaru *adj.* અંધારું dark
andhaaru karavun *v.t.* અંધારું કરવું darken
andhaarun *n.* અંધારું gloom
andhlipi *v.t.* અંધલિપિ braille
Andkosh *n.* અંડકોષ scrotum
anee *n.* અણી tip
aneedaar khoonto *n.* અણીદાર ખૂંટો picket
aneeyaalaapanu *n.* અણિયાળાપણું acuity
anek chijovaali rekard *n.* અનેક ચીજોવાળી રેકર્ડ album
anek ghatako vaalun *v.t.* અનેક ઘટકો વાળું multiply
Anek valaankovaalun *adj.* અનેક વળાંકોવાળું sinuous
anekaganu *n.* અનેકગણુ manifold
anekatv *n.* અનેકત્વ plurality
anenaas *n.* અનેનાસ pine-apple
ang kaapavun *n.v.* અંગ કાપવું amputate
angabhoot *adj.* અંતર્ભૂત intrinsic
angabhoot nahee tevun *adj.* અંગભૂત નહિ એવું extrinsic
angacheshta karavee *v.t.* અંગચેષ્ટા કરવી gesticulate
angachhedan *n.* અંગછેદન mutilation
angakaanti *n.* અંગકાંતિ complexion

angarakshak *n.* અંગરક્ષક body-guard
angasthiti *n.* અંગસ્થિતિ posture
angat *n.* અંગત private
angat maalamatta *n.pl.* અંગત માલમત્તા belonging
Angat Nokar *n.* અંગત નોકર valet
angat reete *adv.* અંગત રીતે privately
angootho *n.* અંગૂઠો thumb
angrejee bhaashaa *adj.* અંગ્રેજી ભાષા english
angrejiman bolavun *v.* અંગ્રેજીમાં બોલવું anglicize
anichchaavaalun *adj.* અનિચ્છાવાળું reluctant
anichchha *n.* અનિચ્છા reluctance
anichchhuk *adj.* અનિચ્છુક unwilling
anichhaa *adj.* અનિચ્છા uncomely
anidra (rogee) *n.* અનિદ્રા(રોગી) insomnia
Anine vakhte karelee madad *v.t.* અણીને વખતે કરેલી મદદ succour
anirnaayak *adj.* અનિર્ણાયક indecisive
anirneet *adj.* અનિર્ણીત unsettled
anirnit *adj.* અનિર્ણિત inconclusive
anirnit rahevun *v.i.* અનિર્ણીત રહેવું hover
Anischit sthiti *n.* અનિશ્ચિત સ્થિતિ suspense
anishchit *adj.* અનિશ્ચિત indefinite
anishchit *adj.* અનિશ્ચિત precarious
anishchit અનિશ્ચિત uncertain
anishchittaa અનિશ્ચિતતા uncertainty
anivaary *adj.* અનિવાર્ય indispensable
anivaary *adj.* અનિવાર્ય necessary
anivaary aavashyakata *n.* અનિવાર્ય આવશ્યકતા necessity
anivaarya *adj.* અનિવાર્ય unavoidable
aniyaalo thaanbhalo *n.* અણિયાળો થાંભલો stake
aniyaalun *adj.* અણિયાળું pointed
aniyamit *n.* અનિયમિત anomaly
aniyamit *adj.* અનિયમિત inconstant
aniyamit gati *n.* અનિયમિત ગતિ seesaw
aniyamit, vilakshan *adj.* અનિયમિત, વિલક્ષણ anomalous
aniyantrit *adj.* અનિયંત્રિત unlimited

aniyantrita *adj.* અનિયંત્રીત uncontrolled

anjali *n.* અંજલિ tribute

anjeer *n.* અંજીર fig

ankachinha *n.* અંકચિન્હ cipher

ankaganit *n.* અંકગણિત arithmetic

ankaganiteeya અંકગણિતીય arithmetical

ankit *adj.* અંકિત marked

ankur footavo *v.i.* અંકુર ફૂટવો germinate

ankush *n.* અંકુશ goad

annadar karanaar *v.t.* અનાદર કરનાર neglect

annajnu maap *n.* અનાજનું માપ bushel

anoochit *adj.* અનૂચિત unfair

ansh *n.* અંશ numerator

ansh *n.* અંશ segment

anshatah nirbal *adj.* અંશત: નિર્બળ vulnerable

Ansudhrelu *adj.* અણસુધરેલું savage

ant *v.t.* અંત finish

ant bhaag *n.* અંત ભાગ fag-end

anta laavavo *v.t.* અંત લાવવો terminate

anta laavee shakaaya aevun *n.* અંત લાવી શકાય એવું terminable

antakaal *adj.* અંતકાળ dying

antar *n.* અંતર distance

antar *n.* અંતર milage

antaraatmaano avaaj *n.* અંતરાત્માનો અવાજ. conscience

antaraay *n.* અંતરાય obstacle

antaraayarahit karavun *v.t.* અંતરાયરહિત કરવું obviate

antardashti *n.* અન્તરદૃષ્ટિ intuition

antargol *adj.* અન્તરગોળ concave

antastvacha *n.* અન્તસ્ત્વચા membrane

Antastvachaani kothalee *n.* અન્તસ્ત્વચાની કોથળી sac

Anthpur ke Janaankhaanun *n.* અન્તઃપુર કે જનાનખાનું seragilo

antim *adj.* અંતિમ ulterior

antimakriyaa *n.* અંતિમક્રિયા funeral

antimvidhi *n.* અંતિમવિધિ cremation

Antriksh *n.* અંતરિક્ષ space

antyavidhi *n.* અન્ત્યવિધિ obsequies

antyuktivaalu *adj.* અંત્યુક્તિવાળું tall

anu *n.* અણુ nucleus

anubhav *n.* અનુભવ experience

anubhavavun *v.t.* અનુભવવું feel

anubhooti *n.* અનુભૂતિ cognition

anuchit *adj.* અનુચિત inexpedient

anugaamee *n.* અનુગામી sequel

anugaamee *adj.* અનુગામી successive

anugrh karavo અનુગ્રહ કરવો condescend

anukanpa *n.* અનુકંપા ruth

anukaran *n.* અનુકરણ imitation

anukaran karanaar *n.* અનુકરણ કરનાર copyist

anukaran karavun *v.* અનુકરણ કરવું copy

anukaranaksham *adj.* અનુકરણક્ષમ imitable

anukaraneey namoono *n.* અનુકરણીય નમૂનો pattern

anukendreey *adj.* અણુકેન્દ્રીય nuclear

anukool *adj.* અનુકૂળ proper

anukool hovun *v.t.* અનુકૂળ હોવું assort

anukool karavun *v.t.* અનુકૂળ કરવું adapt

anukool thavun *v.i.* અનુકૂળ થવું temporize

anukoolan, anuroopataa *n.* અનુકૂલન, અનુરૂપતા adaptation

anukoolataa *n.* અનુકૂળતા convenience

Anukooltaa *n.* અનુકૂળતા suitability

Anukram *n.* અનુક્રમ sequence

anukramik *adj.* અનુક્રમિક consecutive

anukudataa *n.* અનુકૂળતા expediency

anullanghaneey *adj.* અનુલ્લંઘનીય insuperable

anumaan *n.* અનુમાન inference

Anumaan *v.t.* અનુમાન surmise

anumaan karavun *v.t.* અનુમાન કરવું forecast

anumaan karavun *v.t.* અનુમાન કરવું infer

anunaad karanaarun *adj.* અનુનાદ કરનારું resonant

Anunay karnaar *n.* અનુનય કરનાર suitor

anupayukt *adj.* અનુપયુક્ત inapplicable

Anupjaau *adj.* અણઉપજાઉ sterile

anuprasaar *n.* અનુપ્રાસ rhyme

anurekhan *n.* અનુરેખણ tracing

anuroop havun *v.i.* અનુરૂપ હોવું comport

anusaaravun *v.t.* અનુસરવું comply

anusaran *n.* અનુસરણ pursuance

anusaravun *v.t.* અનુસરવું follow

anusarmathan *n.* અનુસર્મથન ratification

anusarmathan karavun *v.t.* અનુસર્મથન કરવું ratify

anushangee *n.* અનુષંગી adherent

anushangee *n.* અનુષંગી corollary

anushthaan *n.* અનુષ્ઠાન observance

anuyaayee *n.* અનુયાયી retainer

anyaay *n.* અન્યાય injustice

anyaayapoorna *adj.* અન્યાયપૂરણ unjust

anyane karelee sonpanee *n.* અન્યને કરેલી સોંપણી relegation

anyathaa *adj.* અન્યથા else

anyatra hovaani dalil *adv.* અન્યત્ર હોવાની દલીલ alibi

anyavatee ladanaar *n.* અન્યવતી લડનાર champion

anyony *adj.* અન્યોન્ય mutual

aokanun fal *n.* ઓકનું ફળ acorn

aokee naakhavun *v.t.* ઓકી નાખવું disgorge

aot *n.* ઓટ ebb

apaaradarshak *adj.* અપારદર્શક opaque

apaaradarshakata *n.* અપારદર્શકતા opacity

apaarthiv *adj.* અપાર્થિવ astral

apacho *n.* અપચો dyspepsia

apaharan *n.* અપહરણ abduction

apaharan karavun te *v.t.* અપહરણ કરવું તે. kidnap

apaharan karvun *v.t.* અપહરણ કરવું abduct

apakeerti *n.* અપકીર્તિ infamy

apakeerti *n.* અપકીર્તિ opprobrium

apamaan *n.* અપમાન insult

apamaan karavun *n.* અપમાન કરવું affront

apamaanakaarakata *n.* અપમાનકારકતા insolence

apamrutyu tapaas *n.* અપમૃત્યુ તપાસ inquest

apapravesh *v.i.* અપપ્રવેશ trespass

apapraveshak *n.* અપપ્રવેશક trespasser

aparaadh *n.* અપરાધ delict

aparaadhee *n.* અપરાધી culprit

aparaadhee *n.* અપરાધી. malefactor

aparaneet yuvatee *n.* અપરણીત યુવતી damsel

aparibhaashit *adj.* અપરિભાષિત undefined

aparichit અપરચિતિ outlandish

Aparichit *n.* અપરચિતિ stranger

aparichit *adj.* અપરચિતિ unacqainted

aparimit *adj.* અપરમિતિ inordinate

aparineet *adj.* અપરણીત celibate

aparipakv *adj.* અપરિપક્વ unripe

aparipakv, apraudh *adj.* અપૂરૌઢ immature

aparyaaptata *adj.* અપર્યાપ્તતા insufficient

apavaad *n.* અપવાદ exception

apavikray *v.t.* અપવિક્રય undersell

apavitr *v.t.* અપવતિર્ profane

apavitra *adj.* અપવતિર્ unholy

apavitra karavun *n.* અપવતિર્ કરવું sacrilege

apayashakaarak *adj.* અપયશકારક discreditable

apeel karanaar *n.* અપીલ કરનાર appellant

apekshaa *conj.* અપેક્ષા than

apekshaa raakhee rahel *adj.* અપેક્ષા રાખી રહેલ expectant

apekshit *adj.* અપેક્ષિત prospective

apmaan *n.* અપમાન umbrage

apmrutyu pareekshak *n.* અપમૃત્યુ-પરીક્ષક coroner

apooratun *adj.* અપૂરતું inadequate

apoorn *adj.* અપૂરણ imperfect

apoornaak *n.* અપૂરણાંક fraction

Apoortu *adj.* અપૂરતું scarce

apraamaanik vyakti *adj.* અપ્રામાણિક વ્યક્તિ mendacious

apraamaanikata *n.* અપ્રામાણિકતા improbity

apraapya *adj.* અપ્રાપ્ય unattainable

apraartheeta *adj.* અપ્રરાર્થીત unsolicited

apraasangik *adj.* અપૂરાસંગકિ inopportune

aprabhaavich *adj.* અપૂરભાવચિ unaffected

aprabuddh - maanas અપૂરબુદ્ધ–માણ્સ heathen

aprakaashita *adj.* અપ્રકાશતિ unpublished

apramaansar *n.* અપ્રમાણસર disproportion

aprasanaa *adj.* અપ્રસન્ન unhappy

aprastut *n.* અપ્રસ્તુત dead letter

aprastut *adj.* અપ્રસ્તુત impertinent

aprastut *adj.* અપ્રસ્તુત irrelevant

apraudhatv અપરપિક્વતા, અપૂરૌઢત્વ immaturity

apraveshy અપૂરવેશ્ય impenetrable

apriy *adj.* અપૂરયિ horrid

apriya અપૂરયિ. unpleasant

apriya અપૂરયિ. unpopular

Apshabd uchchaarvvaa *n.* અપશબ્દ ઉચ્ચારવા slang

apushpa vanaspatee *n.* અપુષ્પ વનસ્પતિ fern

araajakataa, avyavastha *n.* અરાજકતા, અવ્યવસ્થા anarchy

araj *n.* અરજ petition

araj karavee *v.t.* અરજ કરવી supplicate

arajadaar *n.* અરજદાર applicant

arajee *n.* અરજી application

arajee karavee *v.i.* અરજી કરવી apply

arakshita *adj.* અરક્ષતિ unprotected

arasparas jagyaa badalvee *v.t.* અરસપરસ જગ્યા બદલવી transpose

araxit *adj.* અરક્ષતિ unguarded

Ardh paatloon *n.* અર્ધ પાટલૂન shorts

ardha *adj.* અર્ધ semi

ardhachandraakaar *n.* અર્ધચન્દ્રાકાર crescent

ardhamoorti *n.* અર્ધમૂર્તિ bust

ardhaogalelo baraf *n.* અર્ધઓગળેલો બરફ sleet

ardhapaardarshak *adj.* અર્ધપારદર્શક translucent

ardhdevee *n.* અર્ધદેવી demigod

Ardhnindrit *adj.* અર્ધનહ્દ્રિત somnolent

ardho bhaag *n.* અર્ધો ભાગ. moiety

areeso *n.* અરીસો looking-glass

arere ! *int.* અરેરે ! oh

ark kaadhavo *n.* અરૂક કાઢવો decoction

ark kaadhavo *n.* અરૂક કાઢવો extract

arochak *adj.* અરોચક invidious

arpan karavun *v.t.* અર્પણ કરવું. dedicate

artha karavo *v.t.* અર્થ કરવો decipher

artha karavo *v.t.* અર્થ કરવો interpret

arthaat *adv.* અર્થાત viz

arthaghatan અર્થઘટન interpretation

arthagrahan karavo *n.* અર્થગ્રહણ કરવો realization

arthapoorn soochak *n.* અર્થપૂર્ણ સૂચક meaning

arthashaastra *n.* અર્થશાસ્ત્ર economics

arthashaastree *n.* અર્થશાસ્ત્રી economist

arthatantra *n.* અર્થતંત્ર economy

arthhin bolavun *v.i.* અર્થહનિ બોલવું chatter

Arthpoorn reete *adj.* અર્થપૂર્ણ રીતે significantly

Arthvaalun *adj.* અર્થવાળું significant

asaadhaaran *adj.* અસાધારણ extraordinary

asaadhaaran *adj.* અસાધારણ fantastic

asaadhaaran *adj.* અસાધારણ odd

asaadhaaran *adj.* અસાધારણ preter–natural

asaadhaaran *adj.* અસાધારણ remarkable

asaadhaaran *adj.* અસાધારણ uncommon

asaadhaaran vyakti *n.* અસાધારણ વ્યક્તિ phenomenon

asaamaany અસામાન્ય rare

Asaamaanya *adj.* અસામાન્ય singular

asaamaanya *n.* અસામાન્ય. unusual

asaavdhaan *adj.* અસાવધાન unheeded

asabhy *adj.* અસભ્ય impolite

asabhya *adj.* અસભ્ય brusque
Asabhya *adj.* અસભ્ય surly
asabhya *adj.* અસભ્ય uncultivated
asabhya *adj.* અસભ્ય unpolite
asabhya banavun *v.t.* અસભ્ય બનવું coarsen
asabhyataa *n.* અસભ્યતા discourtesy
Asahaay *adj.* અસહાય stranded
asahaay *adj.* અસહાય unaided
asahaay, dayaapaatra *adv.* અસહાય, દયાપાત્ર adrift
asahaneeya *adj.* અસહનીય unmanageable
asahishnu *adj.* અસહિષ્ણુ impatient
asahishnuta *n.* અસહિષ્ણુતા impatience
asahishnuta *n.* અસહિષ્ણુતા intolerence
asahneey *adj.* અસહનીય unbearable
asahy *adj.* અસહ્ય intolerable
asahya અસહ્ય untolerable
asal *adj.* અસલ genuine
asal અસલ. primary
asalanun *adj.* અસલનું original
asamaan *adj.* અસમાન unequal
asamaanata *n.* અસમાનતા imparity
asamanyaa *adj.* અસામાન્ય unaccustomed
asamarth *adj.* અસમર્થ incapable
asamartha *adj.* અસમર્થ unable
asamata *n.* અસમતા irregularity
asambhadh *adj.* અસંબદ્ધ unconnected
asambhavit *adv.* અસંભવિત unlikely
asanbaddh vyaakhyaan *n.* અસંબદ્ધ વ્યાખ્યાન rhapsody
asangat *adj.* અસંગત absurd
asangat *adj.* અસંગત incompatible
asangat vaat *n.* અસંગત વાત paradox
asangatat *n.* અસંગતત absurdity
asankhy *adj.* અસંખ્ય countless
asankhy *adj.* અગણિત innumerable
asanmati darshaavavee *v.t.* અસંમતિ દર્શાવવી refuse
asanskaaree *adj.* અસંસ્કારી, જંગલી barbaric
asanskaaree *adj.* અસંસ્કારી ill-bred
asanskaaree *adj.* અસંસ્કારી unpolished

asanskaaree vartaav *adj.* અસંસ્કારી વર્તાવ boorish
asantosh *n.* અસંતોષ discontent
asantosh *n.* અસંતોષ dissatisfaction
asantoshajanaka *adj.* અસંતોષજનક unsatisfactory
asantusht અસંતુષ્ટ. discontented
asantusht *adj.* અસંતુષ્ટ disgruntled
asantusht karavun *v.t.* અસંતુષ્ટ કરવું dissatisfy
asantushth *adj.* અસંતુષ્ઠ disagreeble
asar *n.* અસર effect
asar *n.* અસર impact
asar karavee અસર કરવી affect
asatkaar *adj.* અસત્કાર unwelcome
asatya *n.* અસત્ય untruth
aseem *adj.* અસીમ unbounded
asekhaee *n.* અદેખાઈ envy
ashaanta banelu *adj.* અશાંત બનેલું turbulent
ashaanti *n.* અશાંતિ unrest
ashabhy *adj.* અસભ્ય uncivilized
ashakt *adj.* અશક્ત decrepit
ashaky banaavavun *n.* અશક્ય બનાવવું preclude
ashakya *adj.* અશક્ય impossible
ashauddhaa *adj.* અશુદ્ધ unchaste
asheem અસીમ unending
ashikshit *adj.* અશિક્ષિત untaught
ashikshit *adj.* અશિક્ષિત untrained
ashishtata *n.* અશિષ્ટતા vulgarity
ashixit *adj.* અશિક્ષિત uneducated
ashleel *adj.* અશ્લીલ indecent
ashleel *adj.* અશ્લીલ lewd
ashleel *adj.* અશ્લીલ obscene
ashleelata *n.* અશ્લીલતા obscenity
ashobhaneeyata *n.* અશોભનીયતા indecency
ashpasht *adj.* અસ્પષ્ટ unintelligible
ashraddhaalun *n.* અશ્રદ્ધાળું infidel
ashru *n.* અશ્રુ tear
ashtak *n.* અષ્ટક octave
ashtakon *n.* અષ્ટકોણ octagon
ashthira ubhaa rahevun *v.t.* અસ્થિર ઊભા રહેવું totter
ashthirchitta *n.* અસ્થિરચિત્ત undecided

ashubh *adj.* અશુભ ominous

Ashubh (nun soochak) *n.* અશુભ(નું સૂચક) sinister

ashuddh *adj.* અશુદ્ધ impure

ashuddhaa *adj.* અશુદ્ધ unclean

ashuvidhaajanak *adj.* અસુવિધાજનક uncomfortable

ashv *n.* અશ્વ horse

ashvaarohan *n.* અશ્વારોહણ equitation

askayaamat *n.* અસ્ક્યામત asset

askhalit *adj.* અસ્ખલિત fluent

askhalitatataa અસ્ખલિતતા fluency

Asooyaaprerit *adj.* અસૂયાપ્રેરિત spiteful

aspasht *adj.* અસ્પષ્ટ indistinct

aspasht *adj.* અસ્પષ્ટ obscure

aspasht *adj.* અસ્પષ્ટ vague

aspashta uchchaar *n.* અસ્પષ્ટ ઉચ્ચાર slur

aspashtapane bolavun *v.i.* અસ્પષ્ટપણે બોલવું mumble

asprusht *adj.* અસ્પૃષ્ટ intact

asprushya *adj.* અસ્પૃશ્ય untouchable

astavyast *adj.* અસ્તવ્યસ્ત pellmell

astavyast *adj.* અસ્તવ્યસ્ત dishevelled

astavyast *adj.* અસ્તવ્યસ્ત disorderly

astavyast karavun *v.t.* અસ્તવ્યસ્ત કરવું, desorganize

Asthi e avsheshonee petee *n.* અસ્થિ, ઈ. અવશેષોની પેટી shrine

Asthibandhan *n.* અસ્થિબંધન sinew

asthibandhan dharaavanaar *adj.* અસ્થિબંધન ધરાવનાર sinewy

asthibhang *n.* અસ્થિભંગ fracture

asthir *adj.* અસ્થિર infirm

asthir *adj.* અસ્થિર instable

asthir *adj.* અસ્થિર movable

asthir banaavvun *v.t.* અસ્થિર બનાવવું unhinge

asthir thavun *v.i.* અસ્થિર થવું waver

asthira *adj.* અસ્થિર unstable

asthira *adj.* અસ્થિર unsteady

asthira *adj.* અસ્થિર untenable

Asthirataa *n.* અસ્થિરતા vaciliation

Asthirpane zoolvun *v.t.* અસ્થિરપણે ઝૂલવું sway

astitva *n.* અસ્તિત્વ existence

Astitva dharaavvun *v.t.* અસ્તિત્વ ધરાવવું subsist

astitvaman rahevun *adj.* અસ્તિત્વમાં રહેવું lasting

astro *n.* અસ્તરો. razor

asundartaa *n.* અસુંદરતા ugliness

asurakshit *adj.* અસુરક્ષિત insecure

asurakshita *adj.* અસુરક્ષિત unsafe

asvaabhaavik *adj.* અસ્વાભાવિક abnormal

asvasth *v.t.* અસ્વસ્થ discompose

asvasth *adj.* અસ્વસ્થ unsound

asvasth karavun *v.t.* અસ્વસ્થ કરવું ruffle

asvastha karavun *v.t.* અસ્વસ્થ કરવું disturb

asvasthataa *n.* અસ્વસ્થતા discomfort

asvasthataa *v.t.* અસ્વસ્થતા disquiet

asveekaar *n.* અસ્વીકાર rejection

asveekaar karavo *v.t.* અસ્વીકાર કરવો repudiate

asvikrutee *n.* અસ્વીકૃતિઓ disallowance

Aswaabhaavik અસ્વાભાવિક strained

Aswabhaaviktaa *n.* અસ્વાભાવિકતા strangeness

aswikaarya *adj.* અસ્વીકાર્ય unacceptable

ataaree *n.* અટારી balcony

ataaro *n.* અટારો litter

atadaapanun, vaayadaapanun *n.* અતડાપણું, વાયડાપણું allergy

Atak *n.* અટક surname

atakaav *n.* અટકાવ restraint

atakaavavun *v.t.* અટકાવવું balk

atakaavavun *v.t.* અટકાવવું cumber

atakaavavun *v.t.* અટકાવવું hinder

atakaavavun *v.t.* અટકાવવું intercept

atakaavavun *v.t.* અટકાવવું let

atakaavavun *v.t.* અટકાવવું restrain

atakaayat *n.* અટકાયત confinement

atakaayatee *n.* અટકાયતી detenu

atakal karavee *n.* અટકળ કરવી conjecture

atakavun *v.i.* અટકવું desist

atakee padavun *n.* અટકી પડવું breakdown

atal *adj.* અટલ irrevocable

atee aanand thavo *n.* અતિઆનંદ થવો exultation

atee aanandit thayel *v.t.* અતિઆનંદિત થયેલ exult

atee saahasik *adj.* અતિસાહસિક foolhardy

ateeshay અતિશિય exorbitant

ateet *adj.* અતીત by-gone

athaak *adj.* અથાક indefatigable

athaak *adj.* અથાક unwearying

athaaka *adj.* અથાક untiring

Athaanaaman naakhvun *v.t.* અથાણામાં નાખવું souse

athadaaine naash *n.* અથડાઈને નાશ wreck

athadaaman *v.t.* અથડામણ clash

athadaaman *v.t.* અથડામણ encounter

athava *conj.* અથવા or

ati adheerun *adj.* અતિઅધીરું rash

ati chokkas *adj.* અતિચોક્કસ meticulous

ati dusht *n.* અતિદુષ્ટ malignity

ati sankshipta *adj.* અતિસંક્ષિપિત. curt

ati sooksm bhaag *n.* અતિસૂક્ષ્મ ભાગ jot

ati sooksm jantu *n.* અતિસૂક્ષ્મ જંતુ. mite

Ati uchcha prakaarnun *adj.* અતિ ઉચ્ચ પ્રકારનું superfine

Ati vidhvaan maanas *n.* અતિવિદ્વાન માણસ savant

atialankaaree *adj.* અતિઅલંકારી luxuriant

atialankrut *adj.* અતિઅલંકૃત. ornate

atibhaare *adj.* અતિભારે. unwieldy

atikraman *n.* અતિક્રમણ inroad

atikraman *n.* અતિક્રમણ invasion

atikraman karavun *v.t.* અતિક્રમણ કરવું encroach

atikraman karavun *v.t.* અતિક્રમણ કરવું invade

atilobhee *adj.* અતિલોભી greedy

Atimaanav *n.* અતિમાનવ superman

Atimaanushee *adj.* અતિમાનુષી superhuman

atipraacheen *adj.* અતિપિરાચીન immemorial

atirek karavo *v.t.* અતિરેક કરવો overdo

atireka taalnaaru *adj.* અતિરેક ટાળનારું temperate

atisaamaanya *n.* અતિસામાન્ય hackney

atishay *adj.* અતિશિય immoderate

atishay *adv.* અતિશિય very

atishay bhaar vade dabaavavun *v.t.* અતિશિય ભાર વડે દબાવવું. oppress

atishay dukh devun *v.* અતિશિય દુઃખ દેવું agonize

atishay harakhaayelun *v.t.* અતિશિય હરખાયેલું overjoy

atishay thandak *n.* અતિશિય ઠંડક frigidity

atishayataa *n.* અતિશિયતા plethora

atishayokti *n.* અતિશિયોક્તિ hyperbole

atishayokti *n.* અતિશિયોક્તિ exaggeration

atishayokti karavee *v.t.* અતિશિયોક્તિ કરવી exaggerate

atishayokti karavee *v.* અતિશિયોક્તિ કરવી heighten

atishayokti karavee *v.t.* અતિશિયોક્તિ કરવી magnify

atishayoktivaalun *adj.* અતિશિયોક્તિવાળું rhetorical

atishram *n.* અતિશ્રમ. overwork

atisookshm *adj.* અતિસૂક્ષ્મ infinitesimal

atisundar *adj.* અતિસુંદર exquisite

atithisatkaar karanaarun *adj.* અતિથિસત્કાર કરનારું hospitable

atiushna *adv.* અતિઉષ્ણ torrid

Atkaavvun *v.t.* અટકાવવું stop

atoot *adj.* અતૂટ unabated

attahaasya *n.* અટ્ટહાસ્ય convulsion

atyaachaar *n.* અત્યાચાર atrocity

atyaachaarabharyun અત્યાચારભર્યું outrageous

atyaachaaree *adj.* અત્યાચારી atrocious

atyaanand *n.* અત્યાનંદ rapture

atyaar sudhee *adv.* અત્યાર સુધી hitherto

atyant *n.* અત્યંત excess

atyant *adj.* અત્યંત extreme

atyant *adv.* અત્યંત extremely

atyant aananadit karavun અત્યંત આનંદતિ કરવું enrapt

atyant aananadit karavun *v.t.* અત્યંત આનંદતિ કરવું enrapture

auchity *n.* ઔચિત્ય pertinence

audaarya *n.* ઔદાર્ય bounty

audhyogik *adj.* ઔદ્યોગકિ industrial

aunsh *n.* ઔંશ ounce

aupachaarik vakhaan *n.* ઔપચારકિ વ્યાણ encomium

auras *adj.* ઔરસ legitimate

aushadh nirmaan *adj.* ઔષધ નરિમાણ pharmaceutical

aushadhaalay *n.* ઔષધાલય pharmacy

aushadhio *n.* ઔષધઓિ herbage

Avaaj *n.* અવાજ sound

Avaak *adj.* અવાક speechless

avaastavik *adj.* અવાસ્તવકિ unreal

avabhoomi *n.* અવભૂમિ subsoil

avadhi *n.* અવધિ period

avagananaa karavee, *v.t.* અવગણના કરવી violate

avaganavun *n.* અવગણવું pretermit

avagnaa karanaar *adj.* અવજ્ઞા કરનાર defiant

Avagnya ke upekshaapoorvak *adj.* અવજ્ઞા કે ઉપેક્ષાપૂર્વક slightingly

avakshep *n.* અવક્ષેપ precipitation

avalanban *v.i.* અવલંબન rely

avalanmban *v.i.* અવલંબન cadge

avale raste *adv.* અવળે રસ્તે astray

avalokan *n.* અવલોકન observation

avalokan *v.t.* અવલોકન view

avalokan karavun *v.t.* અવલોકન કરવું remark

avarajavar maarg *n.* અવરજવર માર્ગ passage

avarnaneey *adj.* અવર્ણનીય ineffable

avarodh *n.* અવરોધ barricade

avarodh *n.* અવરોધ barrier

avarodh *n.* અવરોધ constraint

avarodh *n.* અવરોધ hurdle

avarodh *n.* અવરોધ obstruction

avarodh karavo *v.t.* અવરોધ કરવો constrain

avashesh *n.* અવશેષ fossil

avashesho *n.* અવશેષો remains

avashesho *n.* અવશેષો ruins

avashisht *n.* અવશષ્ટિ relict

avashyanbaavee *adj.* અવશ્યંભાવી inevitable

avataran *n.* અવતરણ quotation

avataran karavun *n.* અવતરણ કરવું excerpt

avejee *n.* અવેજી proxy

Avejee *n.* અવેજી substitute

avejeemaa neemavun *v.t.* અવેજીમાં નીમવું depute

avibhajya *adj.* અવભિાજ્ય undivided

avichaaree *adj.* અવચિારી careless

avichaaree અવચિારી imprudent

avichaaree *adj.* અવચિારી indiscreet

avichaaree *adj.* અવચિારી reckless

avichaaree *adj.* અવચિારી thoughtless

avichaaree *adj.* અવચિારી unthought

avichaareepanaathee vartavun *adj.* અવચિારીપણાથી વર્તતું impetuous

avikaaree *adj.* અવકિારી immutable

avikaaree અવકિારી invariable

avinaashee અવનિાશી imperishable

avinaashee *n.* અવનિાશી indestructible

avinay *n.* અવનિય incivility

avinayee *adj.* અવનિયી discourteous

avinayee *adj.* અવનિયી pert

avirat *adj.* અવરિત ceaseless

avirat bolya karatun *adj.* અવરિત બોલ્યા કરતું voluble

avirat topamaaro *v.t.* અવરિત તોપમારો cannonade

avishvaas *v.t.* અવશ્વિાસ distrust

avishvaashaneeya *adj.* અવશ્વિાશનીય unreliable

avishvasaneey *adj.* અવશ્વિસનીય improbable

avismaraneey *adj.* અવસ્મિરણીય immortal

avivekee *n.* અવવિકી inconsiderate

avyakt *adj.* અવ્યક્ત latent

avyavahaary *adj.* અવ્યવહાર્ય impracticable

avyavasthit *adj.* અવ્યવસ્થતિ immethodical

avyavasthit *adj.* અવ્યવસ્થતિ random

avyavasthit *adj.* અવ્યવસ્થતિ unkempt

avyavasthit tolun *n.* અવ્યવસ્થતિ ટોળું mob

avyavasthit, vilakshan *adj.* અવ્યવસ્થતિ, વિલિક્ષણ amorphous

axeen *adj.* અક્ષીણ unceasing

ayaachaar karavo *v.t.* અત્યાચાર કરવો outrage

ayogy *adj.* અયોગ્ય ineligible

ayogy *adj.* અયોગ્ય unworthy

ayogy vartan *v.t.* અયોગ્ય વર્તવું misbehave

ayogya *adj.* અયોગ્ય undeserving

ayogya vartan *n.* અયોગ્ય વર્તન indignity

ayogyata *n.* અયોગ્યતા impropriety

B

baa *n.* બા ma

baabaagaadee *n.* બાબાગાડી perambulator

baabat *n.* બાબત item

baad karavun *v.t.* બાદ કરવું deduct

baad karavun *v.t.* બાદ કરવું detract

baad karelee rakam *n.* બાદ કરેલી રકમ deduction

Baad karvun *v.t.* બાદ કરવું subtract

baadaaeekhor *n.* બડાઈખોર braggart

baadabaakee karavee *n.* બાદબાકી કરવી detraction

baadashaahee *adj.* બાદશાહી imperial

baadashaahee *adj.* બાદશાહી regal

baadee najar thavee *v.i.* બાડી નજર થવી squint

baafavun *v.t.* બાફવું stew

baagakaam *n.* બાગકામ horticulture

baahooman bahoo parovava *v.t.* બાહુમાં બાહુ પરોવવા link

baahosh *adj.* બાહોશ astute

baahya *adj.* બાહ્ય external

baahya seemaa *n.* બાહ્ય સીમા fringe

baaj pakshee *n.* બાજ પક્ષી falcon

baaj pakshee *n.* બાજ પક્ષી hawk

baajaree *n.* બાજરી millet

baajhanbaajhee karavee *v.i.* બાઝંબાઝી કરવી grapple

Baaju *n.* બાજુ side

Baaju pramaane *adv.* બાજુ પ્રમાણે sidewise

baajue *prep.* બાજુએ beside

baajue khasavun *v.i.* બાજુએ ખસવું swerve

baajunun *adj.* બાજુનું lateral

Baajunun બાજુનું sidelong

baakaat raakhavun *v.t.* બાકાત રાખવું exclude

baakee rahelun *adj.* બાકી રહેલું residual

baakee rahevun *v.t.* બાકી રહેવું remain

baalahatya *n.* બાળહત્યા infanticide

baalak *n.* બાળક Babe

baalak *n.* બાળક baby

baalak *n.* બાળક child

baalak *n.* બાળક kiddy

baalak sanbandhee *adj.* બાળક સંબંધી infantile

baalako *n.* બાળકો children

baalakono sukataan rog *n.* બાળકોનો સુકતાન રોગ rickets

baalapan *n.* બાળપણ boyhood

baalapothee *n.* બાળપોથી primer

baalaveer *n.* બાલવીર scout

baalish *adj.* બાલિશ childish

baalish *adj.* બાલિશ puerile

baalishata *n.* બાલિશતા puerility

baalkanee *n.* બાલ્કની gallery

baalotiyu *n.* બાળોતિયું diaper

baalyaavastha *n.* બાલ્યાવસ્થા infancy

baamanu *adj.* બામનું balmy

baan *n.* બાણ arrow

baanano bhaatho બાણનો ભાથો. quiver

baandh *n.* બાંધ embankment

baandhakaam *n.* બાંધકામ construction

baandhavaano leero *n.* બાંધવાનો લીરો band

baandhavun *v.t.* બાંધવું attach

baandhavun *v.t.* બાંધવું bind

baandhavun *v.t.* બાંધવું build

baandhvaanun doradun *n.* બાંધવાનું દોરડું tether

baankado *n.* બાંકડો bench

baankado *n.* બાંકડો couch

baanu *n.* બાનુ dame

baany *n.* બાંય sleeve

baany vinaano tunko jhabhbho *n.* બાંય વિનાનો ટૂંકો ઝભ્ભો. cape

baanyadharee *n.* બાંયધરી gage

baanyadharee aapavee *v.t.* બાંયધરી આપવી avouch

baara *adj.* બાર twelve

baaradaan *n.* બારદાન receptacle

baaramun *n.* બારમું twelfth

baaranaanee kheentee *n.* બારણાની ખીંટી latch

baarano jumalo *n.* બારનો જુમલો dozen

baaranun *v.t.* બારણુ hatch

baaree *n.* બારી window

baareek *adj.* બારીક exiguous

baareekaaeethee jovun *v.t.* બારીકાઇથી જોવું inspect

baareekaaeethee jovun *v.t.* બારીકાઇથી જોવું regard

baareekaaeethee jovun te *n.* બારીકાઇથી જોવું તે inspection

baareema chodhelu aadu laakdun *n.* બારીમાં ચોઢેલું આડું લાકડું transom

baareeno kaach *n.* બારીનો કાચ pane

baashpeebhavan thavun *v.t.* બાષ્પીભવન થવું evaporate

baatalee *n.* બાટલી bottle

baatamidaar *n.* બાતમીદાર newsmonger

baath bheedvee *n.* બાથ ભીડવી tackle

baavaa aadam *n.* બાવા આદમ adam

baavalun *n.* બાવલું icon

baavaraapanu *v.t.* બાવરાપણું daze

baayalu *adj.* બાયલુ effeminate

baayalun *adj.* બાયલું recreant

babadavun te *v.i.* બબડવું તે grumble

bachaav karavo *v.* બચાવ કરવો defend

bachaavavun *v.t.* બચાવવું rescue

Bachaavnaar *n.* બચાવનાર saviour

Bachaavvu બચાવવું save

bachapan *n.* બચપણ childhood

bachchun *n.* બચ્ચું suckling

bachee javun *n.* બચી જવું survive

bachelo bhaag *n.* બચેલો ભાગ remnant

bachelo shesh bhaag *n.* બચેલો શેષ ભાગ residue

badaaee *n.* બડાઈ boast

badaaee *v.t.* બડાઈ brag

badaai haankavee *n.* બડાઈ હાંકવી vaunt

badaam *n.* બદામ almond

badaash *adj.* બડાશ rodomontade

badairaado *adv.* બદઈરાદો unwittingly

badalaamaan, mukaabale *prep.* બદલામાં, મુકાબલે against

badalaaman *adv.* બદલામાં instead

badalaaman aapavun *v.t.* બદલામાં આપવું render

badalaatun *adj.* બદલાતું irregular

badalavu *v.t.* બદલવું vary

badalavun *v.t.* બદલવું replace

badalee jaay tevun *adj.* બદલી જાય તેવું changeful

badalee naakhelun baalak *n.* બદલી નાખેલું બાળક changeling

badalee tukadee *n.* બદલી ટુકડી relay

badalo *n.* બદલો reprisal

badalo *v.t.* બદલો આપવો requite

badalo *n.* બદલો substitution

badalo vaalavo *v.t.* બદલો વાળવો retort

badamaash *n.* બદમાશ knave

badamaash *n.* બદમાશ rascal

badamaash *n.* બદમાશ rogue

badamaash *adj.* બદમાશ roguish

badamaash *n.* બદમાશ ruffian

badamaashee *n.* બદમાશી knavery

badamaashee *n.* બદમાશી rascality

badamaashee *n.* બદમાશી roguery

badamaasheebharyun *adj.* બદમાશીભર્યુ villainous

badanaam karavun *v.t.* બદનામ કરવું defame

badanaam karavun *v.t.* બદનામ કરવું dishonour

badanaamee karanaarun *adj.* બદનામી કરનારું opprobrious

badanakshee *n.* બદનક્ષી libel

badankshee karavee *v.t.* બદનક્ષી કરવી vilify

Badbaakee *n.* બાદબાકી subtraction

Badgoi *n.* બદગોઈ slander

badhaa, samagra *adj.* બધા, સમગ્ર all

badhaanun *adj.* બધાનું universal

badhe haajar *adj.* બધે હાજર ubiquitous

badhe haajar *n.* બધે હાજર ubiquity

badhir karavun *v.t.* બધિર કરવું deafen

badhirataa *adj.* બધિરતા torpid

badhiratva *n.* બધિરિત્વ torpor

badlee sakaay nahi evu *adj.* બદલી શકાય નહિ એવું unchangeable

badmaash *n.* બદમાશ dastard

bagaad *n.* બગાડ wastage

bagaad karavo *v.t.* બગાડ કરવો waste

bagaaee *n.* બગાઈ gadfly

bagaai *v.t.* બગાઈ tick

bagaasu khaavun બગાસું ખાવું gape

bagaayat pravruti *n.* બગાયત પ્રવૃત્તિ gardening

bagadelun, anuchit *adj.* બગડેલું, અનુચિત amiss

bagalaanee ek jaat *n.* બગલાની એક જાત. heron

bagalo *n.* બગલો stork

bagalun *n.* બગલું crane

bagee *n.* બગી chaise

bageechaakaam *n.* બગીચાકામ landscape

bageecho *n.* બગીચો garden

bagichaaman ekant bethak *n.* બગીચામાં એકાંત બેઠક alcove

bahaadoor *adj.* બહાદૂર doughty

bahaadur *adj.* બહાદૂર gallant

bahaadur *adj.* બહાદૂર intrepid

Bahaadur *adj.* બહાદૂર stout

bahaadur *adj.* બહાદૂર valiant

bahaaduree *adj.* બહાદૂરી valorous

bahaadureeno dekhaav *n.* બહાદૂરીનો દેખાવ bravado

bahaanun *n.* બહાનું pretext

bahaanun બહાનું subterfuge

bahaar dhakelavun *v.t.* બહાર ધકેલવું extrude

bahaar fenkavun *v.t.* બહાર ફેંકવું eject

bahaar javun *n.* બહાર જવું egress

bahaar kaadhavun *v.t.* બહાર કાઢવું emit

bahaar kaadhavun *v.t.* બહાર કાઢવું expel

bahaar kadhavun *v.t.* બહાર કાઢવું educe

bahaar karavaanun *adj.* બહાર કરવાનું outdoor

bahaar neekadavun te *n.* બહાર નીકળવું તે emanation

bahaar neekalavun *v.t.* બહાર નીકળવું protrude

bahaar vahee jatu *adj.* બહાર વહી જતું effluent

bahaaranee baaju *n.* બહારની બાજુ outside

bahaarano vaibhav *n.* બહારનો વૈભવ appearance

bahaaranu *adj.* બહારનું exterior

bahaaranu *adj.* બહારનું extraneous

bahaaranun *adv.* બહારનું outward

bahaaravatiyo *n.* બહારવટિયો bandit

bahaaravatiyo *n.* બહારવટિયો outlaw

bahalee aapavee *v.t.* બહાલી આપવી approve

baheru *adj.* બહેરું deaf

bahetar *adj.* બહેતર better

bahigol *adj.* બહિર્ગોળ convex

bahirvastra *n.* બહિર્વસ્ત્ર apron

bahishkaar *v.t.* બહિષ્કાર boycott

bahishkaar karavo *v.t.* બહિષ્કાર કરવો excommunicate

bahishkrut *adj.* બહિષ્કૃત outcast

bahu dheeme javun *n.* બહુ ધીમે જવું lag

Bahu jorthee ghasvun *v.t.* બહુ જોરથી ઘસવું scrub

bahu naanun *adj.* બહુ નાનું tiny

bahubhooj aakruti *n.* બહુભૂજ આકૃતિ polygon

bahumatee *n.* બહુમતી majority

bahumukhee pratibhaavaalun *adj.* બહુમુખી પ્રતિભાવાળું versatile

bahun naanun *adj.* બહું નાનું wee

bahupatneeprathaavaalun *n.* બહુપત્નીપ્રથાવાળું polyandry

bahupatneetva *n.* બહુપત્નીત્વ polygamy

bahuroopee *adj.* બહુરૂપી multiform

bahuvachan *adj.* બહુવચન plural

bahuvidh bahul *n.* બહુવિધિ બહુલ. multiple

bahuvidhata *n.* બહુવિધિતા multiplicity

bairaano orado *n.* બૈરાનો ઓરડો harem

bajaaniyo *n.* બજાણિયો acrobat

bajaaniyo *n.* બજાણિયો tumbler

bajaar *n.* બજાર bazaar

bajaar *n.* બજાર emporium

bajaar *n.* બજાર market

bajaar *n.* બજાર mart

Bajaar karvun te *n.* બજાર કરવું તે shopping

Bajaaru meethainu chaktu *n.* બજારુ મીઠાઈનું ચક્તું sweetmeat

bajaavaneedaar *n.* બજાવણીદાર bailiff

bakabak karavee *v.t.* બકબક કરવી bleat

bakabak karavee *v.t.* બકબક કરવી clack

bakabak ke lavaaro *n.* બકબક કે લવારો gabble

bakaro *n.* બકરો goat

bakavaat *n.* બકવાટ prattle

bakhatar *n.* બખ્તર armour

bakhatar banaavanaar *n.* બખ્તર બનાવનાર armourer

bakshees *n.* બક્ષિસ premium

bakshis *n.* બક્ષિસ bonus

bakshis *n.* બક્ષિસ largese

bakshis *n.* બક્ષિસ reward

bakshis aapavee *v.t.* બક્ષિસ આપવી bestow

bal *n.* બળ force

balaachaalee *n.* બોલાચાલી fracas

balaatkaar karavo *v.t.* બળાત્કાર કરવો ravish

balaatkaare streesanbhog *n.* બળાત્કારે સ્ત્રીસંભોગ rape

balad *n.* બળદ bullock

balad *n.* બળદ ox

balatan, *n.* બળતણ fuel

balatananaa laakadaa *n.* બળતણના લાકડા firewood

balatananun laakadun *n.* બળતણનું લાકડું billet

balatara *n.* બળતરા inflammation

balatun, pradeept *v.t.* બળતું, પ્રદીપ્ત alight

balatun, salagatun *adv.* બળતું, સળગતું afire

balavaakhor *adj.* બળવાખોર disobedient

balavaakhor *n.* બળવાખોર rebel

balavaakhor, bandakhor *adj.* બંડખોર mutinous

balavaan *adj.* બળવાન irresistible

balavaan *adj.* બળવાન potent

balavaan *adj.* બળવાન redoubtable

balavaan athava mall jevi stree *n.* બળવાન અથવા મલ્લ જેવી સ્ત્રી amazon

balavaanee kshamataavaalun *adj.* બળવાની ક્ષમતાવાળું combustible

balavattar karavun *v.t.* બળવત્તર કરવું reinforce

balavo *n.* બળવો insurrection

balavo *n.* બળવો rebellion

balavo *n.* બળવો. rising

balavo *adj.* બળવો seditious

balavo *n.* બળવો uprising

balavo karanaar *n.* બળવો કરનાર insurgent

balavo karavo *v.t.* બળવો કરવો revolt

baleekrut બલીકૃત reinforced

bali *n.* બલિ oblation

balidaan aapanaar *n.* બલિદાન આપનાર sacrificer

balidaan aapavun *v.t.* બલિદાન આપવું immolate

balidaan aapavun *v.t.* બલિદાન આપવું sacrifice

balidaan ne lagatun *adj.* બલિદાનને લગતું sacrificial

balloonman udanaar *n.* બલૂનમાં ઉડનાર balloonist

Balvaan *adj.* બળવાન strong

bamanu *n.* બમણું double

banaatnu kaapad *n.* બનાતનું કાપડ felt

banaav *n.* બનાવ event

banaavat *n.* બનાવટ fabrication

banaavatee *adj.* બનાવટી bogus

Banaavatee *adj.* બનાવટી spurious

banaavatee dastavej *n.* બનાવટી દસ્તાવેજ forge

banaavatee karavun *v.t.* બનાવટી કરવું counterfeit

banaavavun *v.t.* બનાવવું make

band *n.* બંડ mutiny

band karanaar *n.* બંડ કરનાર mutineer

bandar *n.* બંદર harbour

bandar *n.* બંદર port

bandee *n.* બાંડી blouse

bandee *n.* બંદી hostage

bandee karanaar *n.* બંદી કરનાર captor

bandh *n.* બંધ barrage

bandh બંધ break-water

bandh karavun *v.t.* બંધ કરવું cease

bandh karavun *v.t.* બંધ કરવું close

bandh karavun *v.t.* બંધ કરવું discontinue

bandh karavun *n.* બંધ કરવું seal

bandh karavun *n.* બંધ કરવું stoppage

Bandh karvun ke thavun *v.t.* બંધ કરવું કે થવું shut

bandha vastu kholaavee *v.t.* બંધ વસ્તુ ખોલાવી unlace

bandhaaro *n.* બંધારો weir

bandhabesatun *adv.* બંધબેસતું appropriately

bandhabestun *adj.* બંધબેસતું apposite

bandhak *adj.* બંધક astringent

bandhan mukti *n.* બંધનમુક્તિ emancipation

bandhanaavastha *n.* બંધનાવસ્થા captivity

bandhanakaarak *adj.* બંધનકારક binding

bandhanakaarak *adj.* બંધનકારક obligatory

bandhanmukta karavun *v.t.* બંધનમુક્ત કરવું emancipate

bandhbesatun *n.* બંધબેસતું appropriation

Bandhbeshtun *adj.* બંધબેસતું suitable

bandhutva *n.* બંધુત્વ brotherhood

bandook *n.* બંદૂક gun

bandook *n.* બંદૂક musket

bandookanee golee *n.* બંદૂકની ગોળી bullet

bandookano ghodo *n.* બંદૂકનો ઘોડો trigger

bandookano kundo *n.* બંદૂકનો કુંદો butt

bandookavaalo sipaaee *n.* બંદૂકવાળો સિપાઈ musketeer

bandooknee naal બંદૂકની નાળ calibre

bangadee *n.* બંગડી bangle

bangalee *n.* બંગલી lodge

banglo *n.* બંગલો bunglow

bank vyavasaay *n.* બેંક વ્યવસાય banking

bankano vyavasthapak *n.* બેંકનો વ્યવસ્થાપક banker

banne *prep.* બન્ને both

bapor *n.* બપોર afternoon

bapor *n.* બપોર midday

bapor *n.* બપોર noon

baporanu khaanun *n.* બપોરનું ખાણું. tiffin

baraabar palaalavun *v.t.* બરાબર પલાળવું soak

baraar paadanaaru *adj.* બહાર પાડનારું emergent

barachhat *adj.* બરછટ brushy

barachhat *n.* બરછટ coarse

barad *adj.* બરડ brittle

barad *adj.* બરડ crisp

baraf *n.* બરફ ice

Baraf *n.* બરફ snow

Baraf aachchhaadit *n.* બરફ આચ્છાદિત snowy

barafagaadee *n.* બરફગાડી sleigh

barafanee paat *n.* બરફની પાટ icicle

barafano pahaad *n.* બરફનો પહાડ berg

barataraf karavun *v.t.* બરતરફ કરવું discharge

baratarafee *n.* બરતરફી recall

Barchhat vaalno jaththo *n.* બરછટ વાળનો જથ્થો shag

Bardaano uparno bhaag *n.* બરડાનો ઉપરનો ભાગ shoulder

barobariyo *n.* બરોબરિયો compeer

barobariyun *adj.* બરોબરિયું coequal

Barol *n.* બરોળ spleen

bas *n.* બસ bus

bastikriya *n.* બસ્તક્રિયા enema

bataako *n.* બટાકો. potato

batak *n.* બતક duck

batakano avaaj *v.i.* બતકનો અવાજ quack

batakanu bacchu *n.* બતકનું બચ્ચું duckling

batan *n.* બટન button

batavo *n.* બટવો purse

batavo *n.* બટવો wallet

bathir *n.* બધર torpidity

bauddhik *n.* બૌદ્ધિક intellectual

bayaan karavun *v.t.* બયાન કરવું relate

be *n.* બે. twain

be dhankananvaalun *adj.* બે ઢાંકણાંવાળું bivalve

be grahovaalun *adj.* બે ગૃહોવાળું bicameral

be maalvaalu *adj.* બે માળવાળું. duplex

be paidaanee gaadee *n.* બે પૈડાની ગાડી tonga

be paidaanee gaadee *n.* બે પૈડાની ગાડી trolly

be(ne sankhyaa) *adj.* બે(ની સંખ્યા). two

beaabaroo *n.* બેઆબરૂ disrepute

beadab *adj.* બેઅદબ presumptuous

bebhaan *adj.* બેભાન faint

Bebhaan avasthaamaan *adj.* બેભાન અવસ્થામાં stupid

bebhaan karavun *v.t.* બેભાન કરવું stun

bechenee *v.i.* બેચેની fidget

bechenee *n.* બેચેની uneasiness

bedamintannun fool *n.* બેડમિન્ટનનું ફૂલ shuttlecock

bedarakaar *adj.* બેદરકાર negligent

bedarakaar *adj.* બેદરકાર regardless

bedarakaaree *n.* બેદરકારી negligence

bedarakaareethee karelun *adj.* બેદરકારીથી કરેલું perfunctory

bedee *v.t.* બેડી shackle

bedol *n.* બેડોળ clumsy

Bedol *adj.* બેડોળ shapeless

bee *n.* બી seed

Bee ropvun *n.* બી રોપવું sow

beeban gothavanaar *n.* બીબાં ગોઠવનાર compositor

beebhats *adj.* બીભત્સ nasty

beebhats vaanee *n.* બીભત્સ વાણી ribaldry

beech naamanun vruksh *n.* બીચ નામનું વૃક્ષ beech

Beedee, pensil e nu thoonthoo *n.* બીડી, પેનસલિ ઇ.નું ઠૂંઠું stub

beejaa deh ma javu *v.t.* બીજા દેહમાં જવું. transmigrate

beejaa purusha aekavachan *pro.* બીજા પુરુષ એકવચન thou

beejaaman vileen karavun *v.t.* બીજામાં વિલીન કરવું merge

beejaashayo kaadhavaa *v.t.* બીજાશયો કાઢવા spay

beejee reete *adv.* બીજી રીતે otherwise

Beejnun kochlun *n.* બીજનું કોચલું shell

Beeju *adj.* બીજું second

beejun *adj.* બીજું other

beek *n.* બીક cowardice

beekan *n.* બીકણ coward

beekan *adj.* બકિણ ferful

beekan *adj.* બીકણ pusillanimous

beekan *adj.* બીકણ timid

Beemathi uchhrelo chhod *n.* બીમાંથી ઉછરેલો છોડ seedling

beentaari sandesho *n.* બનિતારી સંદેશો aerogram

beenun *adj.* ભીનું wet

beetano kand *n.* બીટનો કંદ beet

beganun *adv.* બેગણું twice

begapaaip *n.* બેગપાઈપ bagpipe

Behoshee *n.* બેહોશી stupor

beja karata pahela karavun *v.t.* બીજા કરતા પહેલા કરવું forestall

bejavaabadaar *adj.* બેજવાબદાર irresponsible

bejavaabdaar *adj.* બેજવાબદાર uncircumspect

bejavaalee neechaanavaalee jameen *n.* ભેજવાળી નીચાણવાળી જમીન fen

bejod *adj.* બેજોડ unmatched

bekaaboo બેકાબૂ ungovernable

bekaaboo *adj.* બેકાબૂ unruly

bekaara *adj.* બેકાર unserviceable

bekaboo thaeene *adv.* બેકાબૂ થઈને amuck

bekteriyaana jantun *n.* બેક્ટેરિયાનાં જંતું bacillus

belagaam *adj.* બેલગામ rabid

bemaanthee eke nahi *adv.* બેમાંથી એકે નહ neither

bemaathee koye ek *adj.* બેમાંથી કોઈ એક either

benk *n.* બેન્ક bank

bepagun praanee *n.* બેપગું પૂરાણી biped

beparava *adj.* બેપરવા remiss

beri *n.* બેરી berry

beriyam *n.* બેરયિમ barium

beromeetar *n.* બેરોમીટર barometer

beronet *n.* બેરોનેટ baronet

besaadavun *v.t.* બેસાડવું fix

besavun *v.i.* બેસવું sit

beshak *adv.* બેશક undoubtedly

beshak *adv.* બેશક verily

besharam *adj.* બેશરમ impudent

Bcsharam *adj.* બેશરમ shameless

besharam *adj.* બેશરમ unblushing

besooraapanu બેસૂરાપણું dissonance

Bestu *adj.* બેસતું sedentary

beswaad *adj.* બેસ્વાદ distasteful

bethaakhaau nokaree *n.* બેઠાખાઉ નોકરી sinecure

Bethak *n.* બેઠક session

bethak *n.* બેઠક sitting

bethaka maa gaadee *v.t.* બેઠકમાં ગાડી upholster

bethelo avaaj *adj.* બેઠેલો અવાજ hoarse

bevadu *adj.* બેવડું dual

bevadun *adj.* બેવડું binary

bevafaa *adj.* બેવફા disloyal

bevakoof banaavavun *v.t.* બેવકૂફ બનાવવું stupefy

bevakoofeebharelu *adj.* બેવકૂફીભરેલુ foolish

bhaadaanee motaragaadee *n.* ભાડાની મોટરગાડી cab

bhaadaanee oradee *n.* ભાડાની ઓરડી lodging

bhaade fartee motor gaadee *n.* ભાડે ફરતી મોટર ગાડી taxi

bhaade raakhavun *v.t.* ભાડે રાખવું hire

bhaadootee *adj.* ભાડૂતી mercenary

bhaadootee maanas *n.* ભાડૂતી માણસ hireling

bhaadu *n.* ભાડું fare

bhaadun *n.* ભાડું rental

bhaaeebandh *n.* ભાઈબંધ brethren

bhaag *n.* ભાગ portion

Bhaag *n.* ભાગ slice

bhaag kaadhee aapavo *v.t.* ભાગ કાઢી આપવો apportion

bhaag karavaa *v.t.* ભાગ કરવા dismember

bhaag paadanaar *n.* ભાગ પાડનાર divider

bhaag paadava *v.t.* ભાગ પાડવા bisect

Bhaag paadvaa ke padvaa *v.t.* ભાગ પાડવા કે પડવા sever

bhaagaakaaranun fal *n.* ભાગાકારનું ફળ quotient

bhaagedu *adj.* ભાગેડુ fugitive

bhaagedun maanas *n.* ભાગેડું માણસ runaway

bhaagee janaar sainik *n.* ભાગી જનાર સૈનકિ deserter

bhaageedaar *n.* ભાગીદાર copartner

Bhaageedaar *n.* ભાગીદાર shareholder

bhaagi shakaay tevun *adj.* ભાગી શકાય એવું divisible

Bhaagye j *adv.* ભાગ્યે જ scarcely

Bhaagye j *adj.* ભાગ્યે જ seldom

bhaagye ja pooratun *adj.* ભાગ્યે જ પૂરતું marginal

bhaaichaaro *adj.* ભાઈચારો brotherly

bhaajak *n.* ભાજક denominator

bhaajak *n.* ભાજક divisor

bhaalaa vatee aarpaar bhonkvun *v.t.* ભાલા વતી આરપાર ભોંકવું transfix

bhaalakane ramaadavun *v.t.* બાળકને રમાડવું dandle

bhaalo *n.* ભાલો bill

bhaalo *n.* ભાલો harpoon

bhaalo *n.* ભાલો javelin

bhaalo *n.* ભાલો pike

bhaamak daleel *n.* ભ્રામક દલીલ sophistry

bhaangavun mushkel *adj.* ભાંગવું મુશ્કેલ tough

bhaangee gayelee vastu *n.* ભાંગી ગયેલી વસ્તુ wreckage

bhaankhodeeye chaalavun *v.i.* ભાંખોડીયે ચાલવું toddle

bhaar *n.* ભાર encumbrance

bhaar devo *n.* ભાર દેવો accent

bhaar mookavo *v.t.* ભાર મૂકવો. emphasize

bhaarapoorvakanu *adj.* ભારપૂરવકનું emphatic

bhaararoop *adj.* ભારરૂપ onerous

bhaarateey khedoot "raiyat" *n.* ભારતીય ખેડૂત "રૈયત" ryot

bhaaravaahak ghodo *n.* ભારવાહક ઘોડો sumpter

bhaaravaahaka, beejaa vaahano *n.* ભારવાહક, બીજાં વાહનો tractor

bhaare *adj.* ભારે weighty

bhaare kaapad *n.* ભારે કાપડ tapis

bhaare kashta *n.* ભારે કષ્ટ tribulation

Bhaare kimti *adj.* ભારે કીમતી sumptuous

bhaare tofan *n.* ભારે તોફાન blizzard

bhaare upadrav *n.* ભારે ઉપદ્રવ plague

bhaarpoorvak *v.t.* ભારપૂરવક adjure

bhaarpurvak bolavun *v.t.* ભારપૂરવક બોલવું declaim

bhaashaa *n.* ભાષ language

bhaashaana moolaksharo *n.* ભાષાના મૂળાક્ષરો alphabet

bhaashaana moolaksharo *adj.* ભાષાના મૂળાક્ષરો alphabetical

bhaashaantar *n.* ભાષાંતર rendering

bhaashaantar *n.* ભાષાંતર translation

bhaashaantar karavun *v.* ભાષાંતર કરવું construe

bhaashaantar karvun *v.t.* ભાષાંતર કરવું translate

bhaashaantar karvun *n.* ભાષાંતર કરવું translator

bhaashaashaastree *n.* ભાષાશાસ્ત્રી linguist

bhaashaavidd *n.* ભાષાવિદ્દ philogist

bhaashaavignaan *n.* ભાષાવિજ્ઞાન philology

bhaashan *n.* ભાષણ lecture

bhaashan *n.* ભાષણ oration

bhaashya *n.* ભાષ્ય commentary

bhaat *n.* ભાટ bard

bhaatbhaatnu *n.* ભાતભાતનું variegated

bhaatrubhaav *adj.* ભ્રાતૃભાવ fraternal

bhaatrubhagineeno hatyaaro *n.* ભ્રાતૃભગિનીનો હત્યારો fratricide

bhaatrutva, bhaaichaaro *n.* ભાઇચારો fraternity

bhaav ભાવ rate

bhaav jagaadavo *v.t.* ભાવ જગાડવો. evoke

bhaav vishe rakajhak karavee *v.i.* ભાવ વિષે રકઝક કરવી higgle

bhaavana vinaanun *adj.* ભાવના વિનાનું impassive

bhaavanaano udrek *n.* ભાવનાનો ઉદ્રેક outburst

bhaavanaasheel *adj.* ભાવનાશીલ emotional

bhaavanaasheel *adj.* ભાવનાશીલ fond

bhaavashoony *adj.* ભાવશૂન્ય null

bhaavashoony reete *adv.* ભાવશૂન્ય રીતે coldly

bhaavee *n.* ભાવિ fortune

bhaaveenee aagaahee *n.* ભાવીની આગાહી prophecy

bhaavi *n.* ભાવિ future

bhaavi choochak *v.t.* ભાવિ સૂચક portend

bhabhakaadaar *n.* ભભકાદાર flamboyant

bhabhakaadaar *adj.* ભભકાદાર majestic

bhabhakaadaar poshaak *n.* ભભકાદાર પોશાક finery

bhadakaavavun *v.t.* ભડકાવવું appal

bhadavo *n.* ભડવો pimp

bhadhatee *n.* બઢતી turtherance

Bhadkaavee maarvu *n.* ભડકાવી મારવું scare

bhadooti khoonee *n.* ભાડૂતી ખૂની assassin

bhagandar *n.* ભગંદર fistula

bhagavilaas *n.* ભોગવિલાસ dissipation

Bhagavu *n.* ભગવું saffron

bhaginitva *n.* ભગીનીત્વ sisterhood

bhagye ja *adv.* ભાગ્યે જ barely

bhagye ja *n.* ભાગ્યે જ barely

bhajan *n.* ભજન hymn

bhakti *n.* ભક્તિ devotion

bhakti *n.* ભક્ત worship

bhaktimay ભક્તમિય devotional

bhalaaman *n.* ભલામણ recommendation

bhalaaman karavaa jevun *adj.* ભલામણ કરવા જેવું advisable

bhalaaman karavee *n.* ભલામણ કરવી recommend

bhalaaman patra *n.pl.* ભલામણ પત્ર credentials

bhalamanasaaee *n.* ભલમનસાઇ goodwill

bhamaavavun *v.t.* ભમાવવું. mislead

bhamaro *n.* ભમરો hornet

bhamaro *n.* ભમરી wasp

bhammar *n.* ભમ્મર eyebrow

bhanaavavun te *n.* ભણાવવું તે tuition

bhanatar *n.* ભણતર learning

bhanavun *v.t.* ભણવું learn

bhandol *n.* ભંડોળ fund

bhang karavo *v.t.* ભંગ કરવો infringe

bhankhodiye chaalavun *v.i.* ભાંખોડિયે ચાલવું creep

Bhanvarkadee *n.* ભંવરકડી swivel

bhapakaadaar *adj.* ભપકાદાર gorgeous

bhapakaadaar ભપકાદાર pompous

bhapakaavaalu *adj.* ભપકાવાળું dashing

bhapakaavaalun *adj.* ભપકાવાળું gaudy

Bharaai rahevun ભરાઈ રહેવું skulk

bharaavadaar *adj.* ભરાવદાર rotund

bharaavo ભરાવો congestion

bharaavo karavo *v.t.* ભરાવો કરવો congest

bharakhee javun *v.t.* ભરખી જવું devour

bharanaposhan *n.* ભરણપોષણ maintenance

bharapaaee karavun *v.t.* ભરપાઈ કરવું reimburse

bharapaai karavun *v.t.* ભરપાઈ કરવું recoup

bharapoor *adj.* ભરપૂર lavish

bharapoor *adj.* ભરપૂર plentiful

bharatakaam *n.* ભરતકામ embroidery

bharatakaamavaalun kaapad *n.* ભરતકામવાળું કાપડ brocade

bharatee ભરતી flux

bharatee karavee *v.t.* ભરતી કરવી recruit

bharatee -ot sambandhee *adj.* ભરતીઓટ સંબંધી tidal

bharatiyun *n.* ભરતિયું invoice

bharavadaar angavaalee *adj.* ભરાવદાર અંગવાળી buxom

bharavun *v.t.* ભરવું fill

Bhare saymee *n.* ભારે સંયમી stoic

bharehaathvalun *adj.* ભારેહાથવાળું butterfingered

bharosaapaatra *adj.* ભરોસાપાત્ર trustful

bharosaapaatra na hoya aevun *adj.* ભરોસાપાત્ર ન હોય એવું trustless

bharose mookavun *v.t.* ભરોસે મૂકવું entrust

bharoso *n.* ભરોસો credence

bharti *n.* ભરતી stuffing

Bharvaad *n.* ભરવાડ shepherd

bhasavun *v.i.* ભસવું yelp

bhatakavun *n.* ભટકવું gad

bhathiyaarakhaanun *n.* ભઠિયારખાનું bakery

bhathiyaaro *n.* ભઠિયારો baker

bhaththee *n.* ભઠ્ઠી furnace

bhaththee *n.* ભઠ્ઠી kiln

bhaththee *n.* ભઠ્ઠી oven

bhaththee chaalak *n.* ભઠ્ઠી ચાલક stoker

bhatreejee *n.* ભત્રીજી niece

bhautik *n.* ભૌતિક material

bhautik *adj.* ભૌતિક physical

bhautik padaart dravy *n.* ભૌતિક પદાર્થ દ્રવ્ય matter

bhautik vignaan *n.* ભૌતિક વિજ્ઞાન physics

bhavaa chadaavavaa *v.t.* ભવાં ચડાવવાં frown

bhavishy *n.* ભવિષ્ય prediction

bhavishy bhaakhavun *v.t.* ભવિષ્ય ભાખવું predict

bhavishy kahevun *n.* ભવિષ્ય કહેવું prophesy

bhavishya bhaakavun ભવિષ્ય ભાખવું foretell

bhavishya bhaakhavun *n.* ભવિષ્ય ભાખવું augur

bhavishya jaanavun ભવિષ્ય જાણવું divination

bhavishya kahenaar *n.* ભવિષ્ય કહેનાર fortune-teller

Bhavishyaa bhaakhvun *v.t.* ભવિષ્ય ભાખવું soothsay

Bhavishyaa kahenaar *n.* ભવિષ્ય કહેનાર soothsayer

bhavishyaman kadee nahi *adv.* ભવિષ્યમાં કદી નહિ. nevermore

bhavishyavaanee vidyaa *n.* ભવિષ્યવાણી વિદ્યા necromancy

bhavishyavettaane lagatun *adj.* ભવિષ્યવેત્તાને લગતું prophetic

bhavy *adj.* ભવ્ય glorious

bhavy *adj.* ભવ્ય magnificent

bhavy *adj.* ભવ્ય palatial

bhavya *adj.* ભવ્ય elegant

bhavya *adj.* ભવ્ય grandiose

Bhavya *adj.* ભવ્ય stately

Bhavya *adj.* ભવ્ય superb

bhavyata *n.* ભવ્યતા majesty

bhay *n.* ભય fear

bhayaanak *adj.* ભયાનક awesome

bhayaanak *n.* ભયાનક dread

bhayaanak *n.* ભયાનક dreadful

bhayaanak *adj.* ભયાનક ghastly

bhayaanak *adj.* ભયાનક heinous

bhayaanak *adj.* ભયાનક tremendous

bhayaanak, jabaru *adj.* ભયાનક formidable

bhayabeeta karee naakhavun *v.t.* ભયભીત કરી નાખવું terrorize

bhayabheet *adj.* ભયભીત aghast

bhayabheet karavun *v.t.* ભયભીત કરવું terrify

bhayabheet, dvidhaamaan *adj.* ભયભીત, દ્વિધામાં afraid

bhayajanak *adj.* ભયજનક alarming

bhayajanak *n.* ભયજનક terrible

bhayankar *adj.* ભયંકર dire

bhayankar *adj.* ભયંકર terrific

bhayankar kantaalaajanak *adj.* ભયંકર કંટાળાજનક gruesome

Bhayankar mohak stree *n.* ભયંકર મોહક સ્ત્રી siren

bhayaroop *adj.* ભયરૂપ breakneck

bhaynee soochnaa *n.* ભયની સૂચના tocsin

bhed hovo *v.t.* ભેદ હોવો differentiate

bhed karavo *v.t.* ભેદ કરવો distinguish

bhed paadavo *v.t.* ભેદ પાડવો discriminate

bhedabhaav *n.* ભેદભાવ discrimination

bheed *n.* ભીડ concourse

bheeda karavee *v.t.* ભીડ કરવી huddle

bheekshuk *n.* ભિક્ષુક friar

bheenaash *n.* ભીનાશ humidity

bheenaashavaalun *adj.* ભીનાશવાળું humid

Bheengdaa *n.* ભીંગડા scale

bheent *n.* ભીંત wall

bheent patr *n.* ભીંત પત્ર placard

bheentachitra *n.* ભીંતચિત્ર fresco

bheenu *adj.* ભીનું dank

Bheenun thayelun *adj.* ભીનું થયેલું sloppy

bheeshan aakraman *n.* ભીષણ આક્રમણ. onslaught

bhegee thayelee mandalee *n.* ભેગી થયેલી મંડળી troop

bhego karelo jaththo *n.* ભેગો કરેલો જથ્થો hoard

bhegu karavun *v.t.* ભેગું કરવું embed

bhegu karavun *v.t.* ભેગુ કરવું gather

bhegu thavun *v.t.* ભેગુ થવુ congregate

bhegun karanaaro *n.* ભેગું કરનારો collector

Bhej *n.* ભેજ damp

bhej *n.* ભેજ moisture

bhej vinaanu *adj.* ભેજ વિનાનું unalloyed

bhejavaalun *adj.* ભેજવાળું moist

Bhejvaalee pochee jameen *n.* ભેજવાળી પોચી જમીન swamp

bhekhad *n.* ભેખડ precipice

bhelavavaanee kriya *v.t.* ભેળવવાની ક્રિયા admixiture

bhelavavun *v.t.* ભેળવવું admix

bhelavavun *v.t.* ભેળવવું blend

bhelavavun *v.t.* ભેળવવું commingle

bhelsel karavee *v.t.* ભેળસેળ કરવી adulterate

bhens *n.* ભેંસ buffalo

bhet *n.* ભેટ present

bhetavun *v.t.* ભેટવું clasp

bhetavun *v.t.* ભેટવું embrace

bhgnanaukaano yatree *n.* ભગ્નનૌકાનો યાત્રી castaway

bhikhaaree *n.* ભિખારી beggar

bhikshaa, daan *n.* ભિક્ષા, દાન alms

bhikshaavrutee *n.* ભિક્ષાવૃત્તિ begging

bhikshuk *n.* ભિક્ષુક mendicant

bhinn *adj.* ભિન્ન dissimilar

bhinn lakshanavaalun ભિન્ન લક્ષણવાળું heterogeneous

bhinnataa *n.* ભિન્નતા variation

bhogavaadee *n.* ભોગવાદી epicurean

bhogavato *n.* ભોગવટો tenancy

bhogavilaas *n.* ભોગવિલાસ debauchery

bhojan *n.* ભોજન repast

bhojan baad misthaan *n.* ભોજન બાદ મિષ્ઠાન્ન dessert

bhojan pachheenun *adj.* ભોજન પછીનું postprandial

bhojanaalay *n.* ભોજનાલય restaurant

bhojanapatr *n.* ભોજનપત્રક menu

bhojanashaala *n.* ભોજનશાળા refectory

bholapan ભોળપણ credulity

bholun *adj.* ભોળું credulous

bhonkavun *v.t.* ભોંકવું jab

bhonkavun *v.t.* ભોંકવું prick

bhonkavun *n.* ભોંકવું spear

bhonyarun *n.* ભોંયરું basement

bhonyarun *n.* ભોંયરું bunker

bhonyarun *n.* ભોંયરું cellar

bhonyarun *n.* ભોંયરું crypt

bhonyataliyaano majalo *n.* ભોંયતળિયાનો મજલો ground floor

bhoogarbh maarg *n.* ભૂગર્ભ માર્ગ subway

Bhoogarbhsurang *n.* ભૂગર્ભસુરંગ sap

bhoogol *n.* ભૂગોળ geography

bhookee *n.* ભૂકી powder

bhookh *n.* ભૂખ appetite

bhookh *n.* ભૂખ hunger

Bhookh maro *v.i.* ભૂખ મરો starve

bhookhamaro ભૂખમરો hardship

bhookhamaro *n.* ભૂખમરો starvation

bhookhand *n.* ભૂખંડ mainland

bhookhyaan thavun *v.t.* ભૂખ્યાં થવું famish

bhookhyun *adj.* ભૂખ્યું hungry

bhookhyun *adj.* ભૂખ્યું peckish

bhooko karavo *v.t.* ભૂકો કરવો smash

bhool *n.* ભૂલ error

bhool karavee *v.i.* ભૂલ કરવી err

bhool karavee *v.t.* ભૂલ કરવી mistake

bhool sudhaaravee *v.* ભૂલ સુધારવી amend

bhoolabharelu *adj.* ભૂલભરેલું erroneous

bhoolabharelu *adj.* ભૂલભરેલું FALSE

bhoolabharelu *n.* ભૂલભરેલું falsity

Bhoomi neechenun *adj.* ભૂમિ નીચેનું subterranean

bhoomigat *adj.* ભૂમિગત underground

bhoomiti *n.* ભૂમિતિ geometry

bhoondano vaado *n.* ભૂંડનો વાડો sty

bhoonsee naakhavun *v.t.* ભૂસી નાખવું efface

bhoonsee naakhavun *v.t.* ભૂસી નાખવું erase

bhoonsee naakhavun te *n.* ભૂસી નાખવું તે erasure

bhooprushtha *n.* ભૂપૃષ્ઠ crust

bhoora rangnu chopagun praanee *n.* ભૂરા રંગનું ચોપગું પૂરાણી badger

bhooro jambudiyo rang *n.* ભૂરો જાંબુડિયો રંગ violet

bhoorun *adj.* ભૂરું russet

bhooshir *n.* ભૂશિર headland

bhoostarashaastra *n.* ભૂસ્તરશાસ્ત્ર geology

bhoosun *n.* ભૂસું bran

bhoot *n.* ભૂત phantom

Bhoot *n.* ભૂત spectre
Bhoot *n.* ભૂત spook
Bhoot jevun *adj.* ભૂત જેવું spectral
bhootakaal *n.* ભૂતકાળ yore
bhootanaa jevun *adj.* ભૂતના જેવું ghostly
bhootapoorv *adj.* ભૂતપૂર્વ former
bhootapoorv *adj.* ભૂતપૂર્વ quondam
bhootapoorva vidyaarthee *n.* ભૂતપૂર્વ વદ્યિાર્થી alumnus
bhraamak *adj.* ભ્રામક deceptive
bhraamak *n.* ભ્રામક gloss
bhraamak maahitee *n.* ભ્રામક માહતી propaganda
bhram *n.* ભ્રમ illusion
bhram *n.* ભ્રમ phantasm
bhram door karavo *v.t.* ભ્રમ દૂર કરવો disillusion
bhraman *v.t.* ભ્રમણ whirl
bhramanaa *n.* ભ્રમણા delusion
bhramit karavun *adj.* ભ્રમતિ કરવું dissoute
bhrasht thavun te *n.* ભ્રષ્ટ થવું તે degeneration
bhrashtaachaar *n.* ભ્રષ્ટાચાર corruption
Bhrast karvun ke thavun te *n.* ભ્રષ્ટ કરવું કે થવું તે seduction
bhrsht na karaay evun ભ્રષ્ટ ન કરાય એવું inviolable
bhulaavanaarun ભુલાવનારું oblivious
bhulabhulaamanee *n.* ભુલભુલામણી labyrinth
bhulabhulaamanee *n.* ભુલભુલામણી maze
bhulakanu *adj.* ભુલકણું forgetful
bhulane paatra *adj.* ભૂલને પાત્ર fallible
bhurjvruksha *n.* ભૂરજવૃક્ષ birch
bidaan *n.* બડાિણ inclosure
bihaamanun *adj.* બહાિમણું hideous
bihaamanun બહાિમણું monstrous
bijaganit *n.* બીજગણતિ algebra
bijaganitvishayak *adj.* બીજગણતિવષિયક algebrical
bijee koi thekaade *adv.* બીજે કોઇ ઠેકાણે elsewhere

biju ghero ghaalavo *v..t* બીજું ઘેરો ઘાલવો besiege
biju, vadhaaranun, judun *adj.* બીજું, વધારાનું, જુદું another
bikanapanun *n.* બીકણપણું timidity
bil *n.* બલિ burrow
bilaadee *n.* બલાિડી cat
bilaadee *n.* બલાિડી tabby
bilaadeeno top *n.* બલાિડીનો ટોપ mushroom
bilaadeenun bachchun *n.* બલાિડીનું બચ્ચું kitten
bilaado *n.* બલાિડો tom-cat
biladeena kulanu praanee *adj.* બલાિડાના કુળનું પુરાણી feline
biliyards *n.* બલિયિર્ડ્સ billiards
binaasarakaarak *adj.* બનિઅસરકારક ineffective
binaasarakaarak banaavavun *v.t.* બનિઅસરકારક બનાવવું nullify
binaganbheerataa *adj.* બનિગંભીરતા flippant
binajaruree *adj.* બનિજરૂરી dispensable
binajaruree *adj.* બનિજરૂરી unnecessary
binalashkaree maanas *n.* બનિલશ્કરી માણસ civilian
binamahattvanun *adj.* બનિમહત્ત્વનું insignificant
binanubhavee *adj.* બનિઅનુભવી callow
binasarkaaree *adj.* બનિસરકારી unofficial
bindu *n.* બંદિુ point
binhisaabee *adj.* બનિહસિાબી unacountable
bin-kushal *adj.* બનિ–કુશળ inept
Binsaampradaayik *adj.* બનિસાંપ્રદાયકિ secular
binshartee *adj.* બનિશરતી uncoditional
binvasiyatee *adj.* બનિવસયિતી intestate
biskit *n.* બસ્કિટિ biscuit
bivadaavavun *v.t.* બવિડાવવું frighten
bivadaavavun *v.t.* બવિડાવવું intimidate
bivadaavavun, chonkavavun *v.* બવિડાવવું, ચૉકાવવું affright

bivadaavee naakhavun *v.t.* બવિડાવી નાખવું overawe

bod *n.* બૉડ lair

bodh aapavo *v.t.* બોધ આપવો enlighten

bodh aapavo *n.* બોધ આપવો enlightenment

bodhapaath *v.i.* બોધપાઠ lesson

bodhavaalee praaneekathaa *n.* બોધવાળી પૂરાણીકથા fable

bodhavaarta *n.* બોધવાર્તા parable

bogadun *n.* બોગદું tunnel

bogee *n.* બોગી bogie

bojaaroop *adj.* બોજારૂપ burdensome

bojo *n.* બોજો burden

bojo *n.* બોજો load

bojo utaaravo *v.t.* બોજો ઉતારવો disburden

bolaachaali *n.* બોલાચાલી fray

bolaavavun *v.t.* બોલાવવું call

bolakno maanas *n.* બોલકણો માણસ talker

bolatee filmo *n.* બોલતી ફિલ્મો talkies

bolavaanee shailee *n.* બોલવાની શૈલી diction

bolavu *v.i.* બોલવું talk

bolavun *v.t.* બોળવું immerse

bolavun *v.i.* બોળવું plunge

Bolavun *v.i.* બોલવું speak

bolee bolanaar *n.* બોલી બોલનાર bidder

bolee bolavee *v.t.* બોલી બોલવી bid

Bolee ke sharat karnaar *n.* બોલી કે શરત કરનાર stipulator

bolee uthavun *v.i.* બોલી ઉઠવું exclaim

Bolnaar *n.* બોલનાર speaker

Bolvaanee kriyaa *n.* બોલવાની ક્રિયા speech

bomb *n.* બૉંબ bomb

boochanaa jhaad *n.* બૂચના ઝાડ cork

boochthee bandh karavun બૂચથી બંધ કરવું stopple

boochun banaavavun *v.t.* બૂચું બનાવવું truncate

boom maaranaar *n.* બૂમ મારનાર crier

boothun *adj.* બૂઠું obtuse

boyun *v.t.* બોયું buoy

brahmaand *n.* બ્રહ્માંડ cosmos

brahmcharya *n.* બ્રહ્મચર્ય celibacy

branmaad *n.* બ્રહ્માંડ macrocosm

brigedno vado *n.* બ્રિગેડનો વડો brigadier

british janata *adj.* બ્રિટિશ જનતા british

British naanaanun ke naanaaman *n.* બ્રિટિશ નાણાંનું કે નાણામાં sterling

bruhadantra *n.* બૃહદ અંત્ર colon

buddhee *n.* બુદ્ધિ understanding

buddheemaan *dj.* બુદ્ધિમાન acute

buddhi *n.* બુદ્ધિ intellect

buddhi *n.* બુદ્ધિ intelligence

buddhi બુદ્ધિ wit

buddhigraahy *adj.* બુદ્ધિગ્રાહ્ય intelligible

buddhigraahya *adj.* બુદ્ધિગ્રાહ્ય comprehensible

buddhiheen *adj.* બુદ્ધિહીન brainless

buddhiheen *adj.* બુદ્ધિહીન irrational

buddhiman chadiyaatun *v.t.* બુદ્ધિમાં ચડિયાતું outwit

buddhishaalee *n.* બુદ્ધિશાળી ingenuity

buddhithee viruddh *adj.* બુદ્ધિથી વિરુદ્ધ preposterous

budhavaar *n.* બુધવાર wednesday

buking kacheree *n.* બુકિંગ કચેરી booking-office

buland *adj.* બુલંદ loud

buldog *n.* બુલડોગ bull-dog

bumaraan *n.* બુમરાણ outcry

buraj બુરજ bastion

burakhaadhaaree vyakti *n.* બુરખાધારી વ્યક્તિ mask/masque

burakho *n.* બુરખો visard

burakho *n.* બુરખો vizard

C

Chaabuk *n.* ચાબુક scourge

chaabuk maaravee *v.t.* ચાબુક મારવી whip

chaabukthee maravun *n.* ચાબુકથી મારવું flogging

chaadar *n.* ચાદર bed-spread

chaadar *n.* ચાદર counterpane

chaadar *n.* ચાદર coverlet

Chaadar *n.* ચાદર sheet

chaadiyo *n.* ચાડિયો backbiter

chaadiyo *n.* ચાડિયો scarecrow

chaahanaa *n.* ચાહના esteem

chaahanaa *n.* ચાહના favour

Chaakar *n.* ચાકર servitor

chaala paadanaar *n.* ચાળા પાડનાર mimic

chaalaakee *n.* ચાલાકી quickness

chaalaakee karavee *v.t.* ચાલાકી કરવી rig

chaalabaajee *n.* ચાલબાજી. machination

chaalakayantr *n.* ચાલકયંત્ર motor

chaalatun *adv.* ચાલતું afoot

chaalavaanee dhab *n.* ચાલવાની ઢબ gait

chaalavun *v.i.* ચાલવું walk

chaalee *n.* ચાલી chawl

chaalis *adj.* ચાળીસ forty

chaalisamo *adj.* ચાળીસમો fortieth

chaalnaar *n.* ચાલનાર mover

Chaalnee *n.* ચાળણી sieve

Chaalnee vatee chaalvun *v.t.* ચાળણી વતી ચાળવું sift

chaalu raakhavun *v.t.* ચાલુ રાખવું continue

chaalyo jaa *int.* ચાલ્યો જા begone

chaamaacheediyun *n.* ચામાચીડિયું bat

chaamadiyo *n.* ચામડિયો tanner

chaamadun *n.* ચામડું leather

chaamadun kamaavavun *n.* ચામડું કમાવવું tan

Chaamda e no bakalvaalo pato *n.* ચામડા ઇ.નો બકલવાળો પટો strap

Chaamdee *n.* ચામડી skin

chaanch *n.* ચાંચ beak

chaanchal *n.* ચાંચડ flea

chaanchiyaageeree *n.* ચાંચિયાગીરી piracy

chaanchiyaagiri *adj.* ચાંચિયાગીરી piratical

chaanchiyaaonun vahaan *n.* ચાંચિયાઓનું વહાણ xebec

chaanchiyo *n.* ચાંચિયો. freebooter

Chaanchiyo *n.* ચાંચિયો searover

Chaandee *n.* ચાંદી silver

chaandun *n.* ચાંદું canker

chaanee jaat *n.* ચાની જાત pekoe

chaano chhod *n.* ચાનો છોડ tea

chaapado *n.* ચાપડો clamp

chaaparaa maatenaa chhaaj *v.t.* છાપરા માટેનાં છાજ thatch

chaapavun *v.t.* છાપવું print

chaapnee saame hovun *v.t.* ચાપની સામે હોવું subtend

chaar *n.* ચાર four

chaar bhaagavaalun *n.* ચાર ભાગવાળું quadruple

chaar sapaatee *n.* ચાર સપાટી tetrahedron

chaaraasangrahasthaan *n.* ચારા સંગ્રહસ્થાન silo

chaararasta *n.* ચારરસ્તા cross-road

Chaaritrya *n.* ચારિત્ર્ય stripe

chaaritryabal *n.* ચારિત્ર્યબળ morale

chaaritryasheel *adj.* ચારિત્ર્યશીલ chaste

chaas *n.* ચાસ furrow

chaat *n.* છત ceiling

chaataan *conj.* છતાં though

chaatee naakhavun *v.t.* ચાટી નાખવું lick

chaateenu bakhatar *n.* છાતીનું બખતર breastplate

chaatraalay *n.* છાત્રાલય boarding

chaatree *n.* છત્રી umbrella

chaavanee *n.* છાવણી encampment

chaavavun *v.t.* ચાવવું chew

chaavavun ચાવવું masticate

chaavee *n.* ચાવી key

chaaveeroop shabdo *n.* ચાવીરૂપ શબ્દો clue

chadaan *n.* ચડાણ ascent

chadaan *adj.* ચડાણ ascendant

chadautar *n.* ચઢઊતર fluctuation

chadautar karavee *v.t.* ચઢઊતર કરવી fluctuate

chadee javun *v.t.* ચડી જવું excel

chadelun kaam *n.pl.* ચડેલું કામ arrears

Chadhiyaataapanun *n.* ચઢિયાતાપણું superiority

chadiyaatun *adj.* ચડિયાતું surpassing

chadiyaatun *adj.* ચડિયાતું transcendent

chadiyaatun banavun *v.t.* ચડિયાતું બનવું surpass

chagadavun *v.* ચગદવું crush

chagadavun *n.* ચગદવું jam

chagadee naankhavun *v.t.* ચગદી નાંખવું trample

chaheraa parnaa bhaav *n.* ચહેરા પરના ભાવ countenance

chaheraanu *adj.* ચહેરાનું facial

chahero *n.* ચહેરો face

chakachakit *adj.* ચકચકિત polished

chakamakano paththar *n.* ચકમકનો પથ્થર flint

chakaradee *n.* ચકરડી vane

chakaravo levo *v.i.* ચકરવો લેવો gyrate

chakkara chakkara feravavun *v.t.* ચક્કર ચક્કર ફેરવવું twirl

Chaklee *n.* ચકલી sparrow

chakor *n.* ચકોર spruce

chakra *n.* ચક્ર cycle

chakravaat *n.* ચક્રવાત cyclone

chalaavavun *v.t.* ચલાવવું operate

chalaavee shakaay evun *adj.* ચલાવી શકાય એવું workable

chalachitragrah *n.* ચલચિત્રગૃહ cinema

chalakaat *n.* ચળકાટ fervency

chalakato raato rang *n.* ચળકતો રાતો રંગ vermilion

chalakato vaadalee rang *adj.* ચળકતો વાદળી રંગ ultramarine

chalakatu ચળકતું fervid

chalakatun *adj.* ચળકતું bright

chalakatun ચળકતું silvery

chalakatun *adj.* ચળકતું vivid

chalakatun karavun *v.t.* ચળકતું કરવું polish

chalakavun *v.* ચળકવું glitter

chalanee not *n.* ચલણી નોટ note

chalaval chalaavavi *v.* ચળવળ ચલાવવી agitate

Chalkaat *n.* ચળકાટ sheen

Chalkvun *v.i.* ચળકવું scintillate

chalval, virodh *n.* ચળવળ, વિરોધ agitation

chamakaavavun *v.t.* ચમકાવવું brighten

chamakatun *adj.* ચમકતું lustrous

chamatkaar *n.* ચમત્કાર miracle

chamatkaar *n.* ચમત્કાર thaumatge

chamboo *n.* ચંબૂ ewer

Chamcho *n.* ચમચો spoon

chamelee *n.* ચમેલી jasmine

Champal *n.* ચંપલ sandal

chanch maaravee *v.t.* ચાંચ મારવી peck

chanchal *adj.* ચંચળ erratic

chanchal *adj.* ચંચળ fickle

chanchal *adj.* ચંચળ giddy

chanchal *n.* ચંચલ transitory

chanchal *adj.* ચંચળ volatile

chandaal chokadee *n.* ચંડાળચોકડી cabal

Chandannu Laakdun *n.* ચંદનનું લાકડું sandal-wood

chandaravo *n.* ચંદરવો awning

chandol *n.* ચંડોળ lark

Chandol pakshee *n.* ચંડોળ પક્ષી skylark

chandr *n.* ચન્દ્ર moon

chandrak vijeta *n.* ચન્દ્રક વજિતા medallist

chandrane lagatun *adj.* ચંદ્રને લગતું lunar

Chandranee neechenun *adj.* ચંદ્રની નીચેનું sublunary

chaniyo *n.* ચણિયો petticoat

chaniyo *n.* ચણિયો skirt

chano *n.* ચણો gram

chapal *v.t.* ચપળ brisk

chapal *adj.* ચપળ dexterous

chapal *adj.* ચપળ nimble

Chapal *adj.* ચપળ spry

chapatee pattee *n.* ચપટી પટ્ટી slat

charabee *adj.* ચરબી fat

charabee jevun *adj.* ચરબી જેવું fatty

charavun *v.t.* ચરવું graze

charch saathe jodaayelu *adj.* ચર્ચ સાથે જોડાયેલું ecciesiastical

charcha *n.* ચર્ચા debate

charchaa *n.* ચર્ચા discussion

charchaa karavee *v.t.* ચર્ચા કરવી discuss

Charchaa parishad *n.* ચર્ચા પરિષદ symposium

Charchaamandal *n.* ચર્ચામંડળ seminar

charchaano melaavado *n.* ચર્ચાનો મેળાવડો meeting

charchaapaatra *adj.* ચર્ચાપાત્ર debatable

charchaasthaan *n.* ચર્ચા સ્થાન forum

charchaavichaaranaa *n.* ચર્ચાવિચારણા deliberation

charo *n.* ચરો pasture

charu *n.* ચરુ boiler

charu *n.* ચરુ caldron

chasak *n.* ચસક crick

chashma *n.* ચશ્મા lens

chashma banaavanaar *n.* ચશ્મા બનાવનાર optician

chashmaposhee *n.* ચશ્મપોશી connivance

chashmaposhee karavee *v.t.* ચશ્મપોશી કરવી connive

chasmaa *n.* ચશ્મા eye-glasses

Chasmaa *n.pl.* ચશ્મા specs

chataaee *n.* ચટાઈ mat

Chatnee *n.* ચટણી sauce

chaturbhuj *adj.* ચતુર્ભુજ quadrilateral

chaturbhuj aakruti *n.* ચતુર્ભુજ આકૃતિ quadrangle

chatushbhaag *n.* ચતુષ્ભાગ quadrant

chatuvaarshik *adj.* ચતુવાર્ષિક quadrennial

chaud *n.* ચૌદ fourteen

chaukachaal *n.* ચૌકચાલ canter

chedaan karavaa *v.t.* ચેદાં કરવા manipulate

chedan karavaan *v.t.* ચેદાં કરવાં falsify

cheed *adj.* ચીડ petulant

cheedavavun *v.t.* ચીડવવું chafe

cheedavavun ચીડવવું, exasperate

cheedavavun *v.t.* ચીડવવું irritate

cheedhiyun *adj.* ચીઢિયું pettish

Cheedhiyun *adj.* ચીઢિયું snappish

cheedhiyun *adj.* ચીઢિયું waspish

cheediyun *adj.* ચીડિયું choleric

cheediyun *n.* ચીડિયું testy

cheediyun *adj.* ચીડિયું touchy

cheednu vruksh *n.* ચીડનું વૃક્ષ fir

cheejh *n.* ચીઝ cheese

cheekano padaarth *n.* ચીકણો પદાર્થ slime

cheekanun *adj.* ચીકણું oily

cheelo *n.* ચીલો rut

cheematee khanavee *v.t.* ચીમટી ખણવી, pinch

cheencheen avaaj *v.i.* ચીંચી અવાજ twitter

cheencheen karavun *v.t.* ચીંચી કરવું chirp

cheenee *adj.* ચીની chinese

cheenkanee maatee *n.* ચીકણી માટી clay

cheentharehaal *adj.* ચીંથરેહાલ ragged

cheentharun *n.* ચીંથરું tatter

cheepiyo *n.pl.* ચીપિયો tongs

cheeraabandhee karavee *v.t.* ચીરાબંધી કરવી pave

cheeravun *v.t.* ચીરવું lacerate

cheeravun *v.t.* ચીરવું rend

cheero *n.* ચીરો rent

Chees *n.* ચીસ shrick

chees paadavee *n.* ચીસ પાડવી scream

chees paadavee *v.t.* ચીસ પાડવી yell

cheetharun *n.* ચીંથરું rag

chek *n.* ચેક cheque

chep *n.* ચેપ infection

chep lagaadavo *v.t.* ચેપ લગાડવો infect

cheparahit karavun *v.t.* ચેપરહિત કરવું disinfect

chepee *adj.* ચેપી contagious

chepee *adj.* ચેપી infectious

chepee rog *n.* ચેપી રોગ contagion

cheprodhak, jantunaashak *adj.* ચેપરોધક, જંતુનાશક antiseptic

cheree *n.* ચેરી cherry

chetanaa *n.* ચેતના sense

chetanaahin ચેતનાહિન insensible

chetanavantun *adj.* ચેતનવંતું lively

chetanaviheen *adj.* ચેતનવિહીન inert

chetavanee *n.* ચેતવણી warning

chetavanee aapavee *v.t.* ચેતવણી આપવી warn

chetavanee, soochana ચેતવણી, સૂચના alarm

chetavaneesoochak *n.* ચેતવણીસૂચક beacon

chetavani, soochana *n.* ચેતવણી, સૂચના alarm

chh (ni sankhyaa, 6) *adj.* છ (ની સંખ્યા, ૬) six

Chh ganun *adj.* છગણું sixfold

chhaajaleeo છાજલીઓ shelve

chhaal *n.* છાલ rind

chhaal ukhedavee *v.t.* છાલ ઉખેડવી excoriate

chhaalan *n.* છાલાં husk

chhaan *n.* છાણ dung

chhaan *n.* છાણ manure

chhaan *n.* છાણ muck

chhaanamaana saanbhalavun *v.t.* છાનમાના સાંભળવું overhear

chhaano khoono *n.* છાનો ખૂણો by-corner

Chhaantaa Undaadavaa *v.t.* છાંટા ઉડાડવા dabble

chhaapaamaar yuddh *n.* છાપામાર યુદ્ધ guerrila

chhaapaano khabarapatree *n.* છાપાનો ખબરપત્રી correspondent

chhaapaanun veshtan *n.* છાપાનું વેષ્ટન wrapper

chhaapakaam *n.* છાપકામ printing

chhaapakhaanaavaalo *n.* છાપખાનાવાળો. printer

chhaaparaanee valee *n.* છાપરાની વળી rafter

chhaaparee *n.* છાપરી cot

chhaaparun *n.* છાપરું hovel

chhaapavaanun yantr *n.* છાપવાનું યંત્ર printing press

chhaapbhool *n.* છાપભૂલ erratum

chhaapel hastapatrak *n.* છાપેલ હસ્તપત્રક handbill

chhaapelee aakrute *n.* છાપેલી આકૃતિ engraving

chhaapo *n.* છાપો raid

chhaaree *n.* છારી tartar

chhaash *n.* છાશ buttermilk

chhaatakun karavun *v.t.* છાકટું કરવું intoxicate

chhaatee *n.* છાતી bosom

chhaatraalay *n.* છાત્રાલય hostel

chhaavanee naakhavee *v.t.* છાવણી કરવી encamp

Chhaayaa *n.* છાયા shade

Chhaayaavaalun *adj.* છાયાવાળું shady

chhaayaayantra *n.* છાયાયંત્ર sun-dial

Chhachhundar *n.* છછુંદર shrew

chhadeedaar *n.* છડીદાર beadle

chhadmanaam dhaaran *v.t.* છદ્મનામ ધારણ personate

chhajalee *n.* છાજલી shelf

Chhajtu *adj.* છાજતું seemly

chhalakun *n.* છાલકું pannier

chhalango maarata dodavun *v.i.* છલંગો મારતા દોડવું gallop

chhalochhal bharavun *v.t.* છલોછલ ભરવું cram

chhalochhal bharelun *adj.* છલોછલ ભરેલું replete

chhantaa udaadavaa *v.t.* છાંટા ઉડાડવા spatter

chhantaa udaadavaa *v.t.* છાંટા ઉડાવવા splash

chhantakaaravun *v.* છંટકારવું bedew

chhantakaav *n.* છંટકાવ sprinkling

chhap *n.* છાપ impression

chhapaanee naanee avrutti *n.* છાપાની નાની આવૃત્તિ tabloid

chhapo, chhupaayelun lashkar *n.* છાપો, છુપાયેલું લશ્કર ambush

chharee *n.* છરી blade

chharee *n.* છરી knife

chharee *n.* છરી tang

chhareechappan banaavanaar *n.* છરીચપ્પાં બનાવનાર cutler

chhataadaar *adj.* છટાદાર. modish

chhatakabaaree *n.* છટકબારી loop-hole

chhatakun gothavavun *n.* છટકું ગોઠવવું bait

chhatanee *n.* છટણી retrenchment

chhatanee karavee *v.t.* છટણી કરવી retrench

chhaththee vibhakti *n.* છઠ્ઠી વિભક્તિ genitive

Chhaththun *adj.* છઠ્ઠું sixth

chhatoochhatoo *int.* છટૂછટૂ pshaw

chhatu karavun *v.t.* છતું કરવું expose

chhe *v.i.* છે is

chhedeene javun *v.t.* છેદીને જવું intersect

chhedo *n.* છેડો end

chhedo, chhedaanu છેડો, છેડાનું extremity

chheechharun *adj.* છીછરૂં superficial

chheenavee levee *v.t.* છીનવી લેવી deplume

chheenavee levun *v.t.* છીનવી લેવું bereave

chheenee *n.* છીણી chisel

chheenkanee *adj.* છીકણી brown

chheenkanee *n.* છીકણી snuff

chheent *n.* છીટ chintz

chhekavun *v.t.* છેકવું delete

chhekee naakhavun *v.t.* છેકી નાખવું expunge

Chheko *n.* છેકો score

chhelachhabeelo *n.* છેલછબીલો fop

chhellu *adj.* છેલ્લુ last

chhetaranaaru *adj.* છેતરનારૂ deceitful

chhetarapindee *n.* છેતરપીંડી deceit

chhetarapindee *n.* છેતરપીંડી eye-wash

chhetarapindee *n.* છેતરપીંડી forgery

chhetarapindee *n.* છેતરપીંડી trickery

chhetaravaanee yukti *n.* છેતરવાની યુક્તિ trick

chhetaravun *v.* છેતરવું cheat

chhetaravun *v.t.* છેતરવું circumvent

chhetaravun *v.i.* છેતરવું con

chhetaravun *v.t.* છેતરવું cozen

chhetaravun *v.t.* છેતરવું deceive

chhetaravun *v.t.* છેતરવું defraud

chhetaravun *v.t.* છેતરવું delude

chhetaravun *n.* છેતરવું dupe

chhetareene levadaavavun *v.t.* છેતરીને લેવડાવવું impose

chhetarnaarun *adj.* છેતરનારૂ elusive

Chhetrvun *v.t.* છેતરવું swindle

chhevatanun *adj.* છેવટનું utmost

chhevate, ante *adv.* છેવટે, અંતે after all

chhevatnu *adj.* છેવટનું ultimate

Chhichhrun *asj.* છીછરૂ shallow

chhidr *n.* છિદ્ર pore

chhidra *n.* છિદ્ર aperture

chhidraanveshee છિદ્રાન્વેષી captious

chhidrovaalun *adj.* છિદ્રોવાળું porous

Chhink khaavee te *v.i.* છીંક ખાવી તે sneeze

Chhipaavvee *v.t.* છપાવવી slake

chhod ropava *n.* છોડ રોપવા dibble

chhodavun *v.t.* છોડવું unloose

chhodee deedhelee baabat *v.t.* છોડી દીધેલી બાબત omit

chhodee devun *v.t.* છોડી દેવું cede

chhodee devun છોડી દેવું omission

chhodi devun *v.* છોડી દેવું abandon

chhodiya kaadhavan *n.* છોડિયાં કાઢવાં chip

Chhodnee daandee *n.* છોડની દાંડી stalk

chhokaree *n.* છોકરી girl

chhokaree *n.* છોકરી. lass

chhokaro *n.* છોકરો boy

chhokarvaad *n.* છોકરવાદી flippancy

chholavun *v.t.* છોલવું peel

Chholee kaadhvu *v.t.* છોલી કાઢવું scrape

chhoondnun *n.* છુંદણું tattoo

Chhoondvun *v.t.* છુંદવું squash

chhoontun taalun *n.* છૂંટું તાળું padlock

chhoopaaine javun *n.* છુપાઈને જવું tiptoe

chhoota karee devu *v.t.* છૂટા કરી દેવું unchain

chhoote haathe veravun છૂટે હાથે વેરવું squander

chhootu karavun *v.t.* છૂટું કરવું disengage

chhootu paadavun *v.t.* છૂટું પાડવું disjoin

chhootunchhavaayelun *adj.* છૂટુંછવાયેલું sparse

chhotak vechaan karavun *v.i.* છૂટક વેચાણ કરવું retail

chhun *v.t.* છું am

chhundo karavo *v.t.* છુંદો કરવો mince

chhupaavavun *v.t.* છુપાવવું conceal

chhupaavavun *v.* છુપાવવું dissemble

chhupaavavun *v.t.* છુપાવવું hide

chhupaavun *v.i.* છુપાવું lurk
Chhupaavvun છુપાવવું secrete
chhutak kaam karanaar *n.* છૂટક કામ કરનાર jobber
chhutakaaro *n.* છૂટકારો. riddance
Chidanyelun *adj.* ચડિયેલું shirty
chidavavun *v.* ચીડવવું acerbate
Chikaash *n.* ચીકાશ stickiness
chinaaee maatee *n.* ચિનાઈ માટી china
chingaaree *n.* ચિનગારી. ember
chinha *n.* ચિહ્ન mark
chinkalun *adj.* ચકિણું clammy
chinkanapanun *n.* ચીકણાપણું viscidity
chinkanun *adj.* ચીકણું viscid
chinpaanjhee *n.* ચપાંજી chimpanzee
chinta karavee *v.t.* ચિંતા કરાવવી worry
chinta, kaalajee *n.* ચિંતા, કાળજી anxiety
Chintaa *n.* ચિંતા solicitude
chintaagrast *n.* ચિંતાગ્રસ્ત careworn
chintaagrast *adj.* ચિન્તાગ્રસ્ત pensive
chintaajanak *adj.* ચિંતાજનક distressful
chintagrasta *adj.* ચિંતાગ્રસ્ત worried
chintan karavun *v.t.* ચિંતન કરવું cogitate
chintan karavun *v.t.* ચિંતન કરવું meditate
chintatur, utsuk *adj.* ચિંતાતુર, ઉત્સુક anxious
chintvyayee *adj.* ચિંતવ્યયી thrifty
chiraad *n.* ચરાડ fissure
chiranjeev karavun *v.t.* ચિરંજીવ કરવું immortalize
Chirantaran narakavaas *n.* ચિરંતન નરકવાસ damnation
chirasthaayeepanun *n.* ચરિસ્થાયીપણું perpetuity
chiroot *n.* ચરૂટ cheroot
chirsthaayee *prep.* ચરિસ્થાયી abiding
chita *n.* ચિતા pyre
chiththee *n.* ચિઠ્ઠી chit
chiththee *n.* ચિઠ્ઠી coupon
chitr *n.* ચિત્ર picture
chitrakaar *n.* ચિત્રકાર painter
chitrapat *n.* ચિત્રપટ film
chitrapat *n.* ચિત્રપટ movie

chitrapatnu bhaashaantar *v.t.* ચિત્રપટનુ ભાષાંતર dub
chitraroom *n.* ચિત્રરૂમ drawing room
chitrashalaakaa *n.* ચિત્રશલાકા crayon
chitt haree levun *v.* ચિત્ત હરી લેવું captivate
chittabhramanaa *n.* ચિત્તભ્રમણા delirium
chittakshobhakaarak *n.* ચિત્તક્ષોભકારક distraction
chivatvaalu *adj.* ચીવટવાળું dogged
Chodaayelun *adj.* ચડિયેલું sullen
chodavun, besaadavun *v.* ચોડવું, બેસાડવું affix
chok *n.* ચોક chalk
chok *n.* ચોક crossing
chokalet *n.* ચોકલેટ chocolate
chokaramat *adj.* છોકરમત boyish
chokaro *n.* છોકરો chap
chokasaaee *n.* ચોકસાઈ precision
chokasaaee, baarikee *n.* ચોકસાઈ, બારીકી accuracy
chokee *v.t.* ચોકી guard
chokee *n.* ચોકી look-out
chokee pahero *adj.* ચોકી પહેરો patrol
Chokeedaar *n.* ચોકીદાર sentry
chokeedaar *n.* ચોકીદાર watchman
chokha *n.* ચોખા rice
chokhaliyun *adj.* ચોખલિયું fastidious
chokhkhun karavun *v.t.* ચોખ્ખું કરવું refine
chokkas *adv.* ચોક્કસ certainly
chokkas *adj.* ચોક્કસ exact
Chokkas *adj.* ચોક્કસ strict
Chokkas arth ke aashay ચોક્કસ અર્થ કે આશય signification
chokkas shabdovaalun *n.* ચોક્કસ શબ્દોવાળું precise
chokkas swaroopavaalu *n.* ચોક્કસ સ્વરૂપવાળું determinate
chokkas, baraabar *adj.* ચોક્કસ, બરાબર accurate
chokkasaaee *n.* ચોકસાઈ nicety
Chokksaai *n.* ચોકસાઈ stickler
cholee *n.* ચોળી bodice
chomaasaanun *adj.* ચોમાસાનું rainy
chomaasun *n.* ચોમાસું monsoon

chomer veravun *v.t.* ચોમેર વેરવું scatter

chomer vikheravun *v.t.* ચોમેર વિખેરવું disseminate

Chonte evun *adj.* ચોંટે એવું sticky

chontee rahevun *v.i.* ચોંટી રહેવું cleave

choodel *n.* ચૂડેલ witch

chookavanu karavun *v.t.* ચૂકવણું કરવું. disburse

chookavun *n.* ચૂકવું miss

choolo *n.* ચૂલો. fire-place

choolo *n.* ચૂલો. hearth

choolo *n.* ચૂલો stove

choonee *n.* ચૂંઇ gill

choono *n.* ચૂનો lime

choontanee *n.* ચૂંટણી elction

choontanee niyukt *n.* ચૂંટણી નિયુક્ત elective

choontavun *v.t.* ચૂંટવું elect

choop *adj.* ચૂપ mute

choop besaadavun *v.t.* ચૂપ બેસાડવું gag

choop raakhavun *v.t.* ચૂપ રાખવું hush

choorechooraa karavaa *v.t.* ચૂરેચૂરા કરવા disrupt

choosee - shoshee levun *v.t.* ચૂસી – શોષી લેવું imbibe

Choosvun *n.* ચૂસવું suck

chootaachhedaa *v.t.* છૂટાછેડા divorce

chootak vechaankaar *n.* છૂટક વેચાણકાર retailer

chootun karanaar *n.* છૂટું કરનાર reliever

chootun karavun *v.t.* છૂટું કરવું release

choovo *n.* ચૂવો leak

choovo te *n.* ચૂવું તે leakage

chopaaniyun *n.* ચોપાનિયું leaflet

chopadavaanun osad *n.* ચોપડવાનું ઓસડ liniment

chopadeeo baandhanaar *n.* ચોપડીઓ બાંધનાર binder

chopadeeono prakaashak *n.* ચોપડીઓનો પ્રકાશક publisher

chopado *n.* ચોપડો tach

chopagun pashu *n.* ચોપગું પશુ quadruped

chopdee *n.* ચોપડી title

chor *n.* ચોર. thief

chor *adj.* ચોર thievish

chorano *n.* ચોરણો breeches

choravaano rog *n.* ચોરવાનો રોગ kleptomania

choravun *v.i.* ચોરવું thieve

choree *n.* ચોરી larceny

choree *n.* ચોરી. theft

Choree karvee *v.t.* ચોરી કરવી steal

choreechhoopeethee karelu *adj.* ચોરીછૂપીથી કરેલું furtive

Choreechoopkee *n.* ચોરીચૂપકી stealth

Choreeno maal *n.* ચોરીનો માલ swag

choreethee karelun *adj.* ચોરીથી કરેલું stealthy

Choreethee karelun *adj.* ચોરીથી કરેલું surreptitious

chotalee *adj.* ચોટલી topknot

chotaraf chhantavun *v.t.* ચોતરફ છાંટવું besprinkle

chotaraf faree valavun *v.t.* ચોતરફ ફરી વળવું surround

chotho bhaag *adj.* ચોથો ભાગ fourth

chotho bhaag *n.* ચોથો ભાગ quarter

chukaado *n.* ચુકાદો adjudication

chukaado *n.* ચુકાદો conviction

chukaado *n.* ચુકાદો judgement

chukaado aapavo *v.t.* ચુકાદો આપવો adjudicate

chukavanee *n.* ચુકવણી payment

chun chun avaaj karavo *v.i.* ચૂંચૂં અવાજ કરવો creak

chunando varg *n.* ચુનંદો વર્ગ elite

chunban *v.t.* ચુંબન caress

chunban *n.* ચુંબન kiss

chundavun *n.* છૂંદવું, bruise

chupchaap ચુપચાપ silently

Chust aavran *n.* ચુસ્ત આવરણ sheath

chust anuyaayee *n.* ચુસ્ત અનુયાયી votary

ciment *n.* સિમિન્ટ cement

D

daab *n.* દાબ repression

daabala *v.t.* ડાબલા blinker

daabavun *v.t.* દાબવું compress
daabavun *v.t.* દાબવું press
daabavun *v.t.* દાબવું wring
daabee baajunun *adj.* ડાબી બાજુનું left
Daabee devun ડાબી દેવું suppress
daadaa *n.* દાદા grandfather
daadaageeree karavee *v.t.* દાદાગીરી કરવી bully
daadam *n.* દાડમ pomegranate
daadar *n.* દાદર ringworm
daadhee *n.* દાઢી beard
Daadro *n.* દાદરો staircase
daaee *n.* દાઈ midwife
Daagh vinaanun *adj.* ડાઘ વિનાનું stainless
daagho *n.* ડાઘો fleck
Daagho *n.* ડાઘો smudge
daagho *n.* ડાઘો taint
daaghvaalu *n.* ડાઘવાળુ double-dealer
daahyu *adj.* ડાહ્યું sapient
Daahyu, Chatur *adj.* ડાહ્યું, ચતુર sagacious
daahyun *adj.* ડાહ્યું wise
daakhal karavun *n.* દાખલ કરવું admission
daakhal karavun *v.* દાખલ કરવું admit
daakhal karavun *v.t.* દાખલ કરવું inject
daakhal thavun *v.t.* દાખલ થવું enter
daalakhun *n.* ડાળખું twig
daam oocho karee devo *v.t.* દામ ઓછો કરી દેવો underbid
daamar *n.* ડામર bitumen
daamar *n.* ડામર coal-tar
daamar *n.* ડામર pitch
daamar *n.* ડામર tar
daamar chopdelu *adj.* ડામર ચોપડેલું. tarry
Daamf *v.t.* ડંફ stride
daan *n.* દાન charity
daan *n.* દાન donation
daan karavun *v.t.* દાન કરવું donate
daan par nabhatun *n.* દાન પર નભતું charitable
daan sweekarnaar *n.* દાન સ્વીકારનાર donee
daana *v.t.* દાવા claim

daanavrutee *n.* દાનવૃતિ beneficence
Daanchoree *n.* દાણચોરી smuggling
daanchoree karavee *v.t.* દાણચોરી કરવી smuggle
daando દાંડો bar
Daando *n.* દાંડો shaft
daanpatyaavastha *n.* દાંપત્યાવસ્થા matrimony
daant *n.* દાંત tooth
daant nu chokathu *n.* દાંતનું ચોકઠું denture
daant vinaanu *n.* દાંત વિનાનું eden
daanta *n.pl.* દાંત teeth
daanta aavavaa, doodhiyaa daanta *v.t.* દાંત આવવા, દૂધિયા દાંત teethe
daantaa paadavaa *v.t.* દાંતા પાડવા cog
daantaavaalu aojaar *n.* દાંતાવાળું ઓજાર fork
daantano paruno rog *n.* દાંતનો પરુનો રોગ pyorrhoea
daaroo *n.* દારૂ ale
daaroo *n.* દારૂ liquor
daaroo *n.* દારૂ whisky
daaroo banaavavo *v.t.* દારૂ બનાવવો brew
daaroo bharavaanu paatra *n.* દારૂ ભરવાનું પાત્ર flagon
daaroo dheenchavo *v.t.* દારૂ ઢીચવો bib
daaroo dhinchavo *v.i.* દારૂ ઢીચવો carouse
daaroo gaalavaanun saadhan *adj.* દારૂ ગાળવાનું સાધન still
daaroodiyo *n.* દારૂડિયો toper
daaroogolo *n.* દારૂગોળો munition
daarookhaana jevun *adj.* દારૂખાના જેવું pyrotechnic
daaroono ghoont *n.* દારૂનો ઘૂંટ dram
daaroono ghoontado *n.* દારૂનો ઘૂંટડો nip
daaroonu vyasan *v.t.* દારૂનું વ્યસન tipple
daaroonun karakhanun *n.* દારૂનું કારખાનું brevery
daaroonun peep *n.* દારૂનું પીપ cask
daaru gaalanaar *n.* દારૂ ગાળનાર distiller
daaru peedhel *adj.* દારૂ પીધેલ drunken

daaru vechanaar, kalaal *n.* દારૂ વેચનાર, કલાલ vintner

daarudiyo *n.* દારૂડિયો. drunkard

daarugolo *n.* દારુગોળો gunpowder

daarunee aadat *n.* દારુની આદત drunkenness

daarunu motu peep *n.* દારૂનું મોટું પીપ tun

daarunun paatra *n.* દારૂનું પાત્ર tankard

daasee *n.* દાસી chambermaid

daataa *n.* દાતા benefactor

daataa *n.* દાતા donor

daatavun *v.t.* દાટવું overwhelm

daatelun kaadhavun *v.t.* દાટેલું કાઢવું disinter

Daato *n.* દાટો stopper

Daatrdun *n.* દાતરડું sickle

daavaanal *n.* દાવાનળ conflagration

daavapech, vyooh *n.* દાવપેચ, વ્યૂહ manoeuvre

daavo *n.* દાવો litigation

daavo jato karavo *v.t.* દાવો જતો કરવો disclaim

daavo jato karavo *v.t.* દાવો જતો કરવો waive

daavo maandavo *v.t.* દાવો માંડવો litigate

daavo rajoo karavo te *n.* દાવો રજૂ કરવો તે. assertion

daavpech *v.t.* દાવપેચ dodge

daayako *n.* દાયકો decade

dabaan *n.* દબાણ pressure

Dabaan *n.* દબાણ stress

dabaavee raakhavun *v.t.* દબાવી રાખવું repress

dabaavee shakaay tevun *adj.* દબાવી શકાય તેવું compressible

dabo *n.* ડબો bin

dado *n.* દડો ball

dafan *n.* દફન burial

Dafan *n.* દફન sepulture

dafan karavun *v.t.* દફન કરવું bury

dafatarkhaanun *n.* દફતરખાનું archives

dafol *n.* ડફોળ duffer

dagaabaaj *n.* દગાબાજી craftiness

dagadago *n.* દગદગો compunction

dagalun *n.* ડગલું pace

dagamagavun *v.t.* ડગમગવું vacillate

dago *n.* દગો betrayal

dago *n.* દગો deception

dago *n.* દગો double-cross

dago devo *v.t.* દગો દેવો. betray

dahaapan *n.* ડહાપણ prudence

Dahaapan *n.* ડહાપણ sagacity

dahaapan *n.* ડહાપણ wisdom

dahaapanapoorvak *adj.* ડહાપણપૂર્વક wisely

dahej *n.* દહેજ dowry

daheshat *n.* દહેશત awe

daheshat દહેશત. misgiving

daholaayelun *adj.* ડહોળાયેલું milky

daholaayelun *adj.* ડહોળાયેલું turbid

Dahyu *n.* ડાહ્યું sage

Dainik *adj.* દૈનિક daily

daitya *n.* દૈત્ય belial

daivee aadesh *n.* દૈવી આદેશ commandment

daivee saakshaatkaar *n.* દૈવી સાક્ષાત્કાર revelation

daivee svaroop *n.* દૈવી સ્વરૂપ deity

daiveesajaa *n.* દૈવીસજા commination

daivik *adj.* દૈવિક divine

dakhal *n.* દખલ interference

dakkaabhaadun *n.* ડક્કાભાડું wharfage

dakkaavero *n.* ડક્કાવેરો quayage

daksheen dhruvapradeshanun *adj.* દક્ષિણ ધ્રુવપ્રદેશનું antarctic

Dakshin dishaa *n.* દક્ષિણ દિશા south

Dakshin dishaa taraf દક્ષિણ દિશા તરફ southward

dakshinaavart *adj.* દક્ષિણાવર્ત clockwise

Dakshinmaan *adj.* દક્ષિણમાં southern

dalaal *n.* દલાલ broker

dalaal *n.* દલાલ tout

dalaalee *n.* દલાલી brokerage

daladaar granth *n.* દળદાર ગ્રંથ tome

dalavaanee ghantee *n.* દળવાની ઘંટી mill

dalavun *v.t.* દળવું grind

daleel *n.* દલીલ argument

daleel *n.* દલીલ plea

daleel *n.* દલીલ reasoning

daleel karavee *v.i.* દલીલ કરવી argue

daleel karavee *v.t.* દલીલ કરવી contend

daleelayukt charchaa *n.* દલીલયુક્ત ચર્ચા disputation

daleelvaalun *adj.* દલીલવાળું argumentive

dam *n.* દમ asthma

dam vagar nu paamar *adj.* દમ વગરનું, પામર tame

Dam vinaanu lakhaan *v.t.* દમ વિનાનુ લખાણ scribble

daman karavun *v.t.* દમન કરવું persecute

Dambh *n.* દંભ snobbery

Dambhee *n.* દંભી snob

damee *n.* ડમી dummy

danbhee *n.* દંભી pedant

dand *adj.* દંડ fine

dand ke beejee koee saja *n.* દંડ કે બીજી કોઈ સજા penalty

dandanaayak *n.* દંડનાયક magistrate

dandhorojagaar *n.* ધંધોરોજગાર profession

dandooko *n.* દંડૂકો cudgel

danduko *n.* દંડૂકો bludgeon

danfaash *n.* દંફાશ gasconade

danfaashiyun maanas *n.* દંફાશિયું માણસ gascon

Dankhrahit *n.* ડંખરહતિ stingless

dantya *adj.* દન્ત્ય dental

dantyavaidya *n.* દન્તવૈદ્ય dentist

dantyavidyaa *n.* દન્તયવદિયા dentistry

dar kalaake banatun *adj.* દર કલાકે બનતું hourly

dar koshtak *n.* દર કોષ્ટક tariff

dar laayak *adj.* દર લાયક ratable

dar varse *adv.* દર વરસે annually

daraavatun *adj.* ડરાવતું threatening

darabaaree *n.* દરબારી courtier

darabaaree gaadee *n.* દરબારી ગાડી coach

Darad *v.t.* દરદ suffer

daradathee paadelee chees *v.t.* દરદથી પાડેલી ચીસ yap

daragujar karavun *v.t.* દરગુજર કરવું condone

darajjaaman ootaratun *adj.* દરજ્જામાં

ઊતરતું puisne

darajjo *n.* દરજ્જો grade

darakhaast *n.* દરખાસ્ત proposition

darakhaast mukavee *v.t.* દરખાસ્ત મુકવી propose

daramiyaan *prep.* દરમિયાન during

daramyaanageeree *n.* દરમ્યાનગીરી intervention

daramyaanageeree karavee દરમ્યાનગીરી કરવી intervene

darapok *adj.* ડરપોક cowardly

darapok maanas *n.* ડરપોક માણસ craven

darapoka, bhyayabheeta *adj.* ડરપોક unmanly

dararoj raate thatun *adj.* દરરોજ રાતે થતું nightly

daravaajaavaalo praveshamaarg *n.* દરવાજાવાળો પ્રવેશમાર્ગ gateway

daravaajo *n.* દરવાજો gate

daravaajo *n.* દરવાજો portal

daravaan *n.* દરવાન janitor

daravaan *n.* દરવાન porter

daravaan *n.* દરવાન usher

Dard *n.* દર્દ soreness

dareeyaaee *adj.* દરિયાઈ nautical

dareeyayee safar દરિયાઈ સફર cruise

darek *adj.* દરેક each

dareka bhaagamaa *adv.* દરેક ભાગમાં throughout

daridr *n.* દરિદ્ર pauper

daridrata *n.* દરિદ્રતા pauperism

dariya par *adv.* દરિયા પર afloat

dariyaaee lootaaro *n.* દરિયાઈ લૂટારો pirate

dariyaaee luntero *n.* દરિયાઈ લુંટેરો rover

dariyaaee maachhalee *n.* દરિયાઈ માછલી dolphin

dariyaai *adj.* દરિયાઈ maritime

dariyaai abaabeel *adj.* દરિયાઈ અબાબીલ tern

dariyaakaantho *n.* દરિયાકાંઠો coast

Dariyaakathaano pradesh *n.* દરિયાકાંઠાનો પ્રદેશ seaboard

dariyaakinaaro *adv.* દરિયાકિનારો ashore

dariyaanee bharateeot *v.t.* દરિયાની ભરતીઓટ tide

dariyaanun *adj.* દરિયાનું marine

dariyaanun paanee *n.* દરિયાનું પાણી brine

dariyaee pakshee *n.* દરિયાઈ પક્ષી albatross

Dariyo *n.* દરિયો sea

dariyo khedavo *v.t.* દરિયો ખેડવો navigate

Darjan *n.* દરજણ seamstress

darjee *n.* દરજી; tailor

darjee kaam kartee mahilaa *n.* દરજી કામ કરતી મહિલા tailoress

daroogolo *n.* દારૂગોળો ammunition

darpan *n.* દર્પણ mirror

darvaajo *n.* દરવાજો door

das *adj.* દસ ten

das laakh *n.* દસ લાખ million

dasadavun *adj.* દસડવું tenfold

dasamu *adj.* દસમું tenth

dasavarsheey *adj.* દસવર્ષીય decennial

dasha *n.* દશા plight

dashaansh kar *n.* દશાંશ કર tithe

dashaanshamaapan *n.* દશાંશમાપન metre

dashabhuj *n.* દશભુજ decagon

dashansh *adj.* દશાંશ decimal

dastaavej *n.* દસ્તાવેજ document

Dastaavej *n.* દસ્તાવેજ signatory

dastaavejne lagatu *aj.* દસ્તાવેજને લગતું documentary

dattak levun *v.t.* દત્તક લેવું adopt

dava *n.* દવા medicine

davaa *n.* દવા drug

davaa *n.* દવા lotion

davaakhaanu *n.* દવાખાનું dispensary

davaakhaanun *n.* દવાખાનું clinic

davaanee maatraa *n.* દવાની માત્રા dose

davaanee teekadee *n.* દવાની ટીકડી pill

davaano ghoontado *n.* દવાનો ઘૂંટડો potion

davaanun *adj.* દવાનું medicinal

davaao vechanaar *n.* દવાઓ વેચનાર chemist

davaavaalo *n.* દવાવાળો. druggist

daya *n.* દયા pity

dayaaheen *adj.* દયાહીન pitiless

dayaajanak *adj.* દયાજનક pitiful

dayaalu *adj.* દયાળુ beneficent

dayaalu *adj.* દયાળુ clement

dayaalu *n.* દયાળુ compassionate

dayaapaatr *adj.* દયાપાત્ર poor

dayaapaatrajanak *adj.* દયાપાત્રજનક pitiable

dayaasheel *adj.* દયાશીલ merciful

dayanemo *n.* ડાયનેમો dynamo

ddhraakshano bageecho *n.* બગીચો vineyard

december *n.* ડિસેમ્બર december

dedakaanun bachchun *n.* દેડકાનું બચ્ચું tadpole

dedako *n.* દેડકો. frog

dedako *n.* દેડકો toad

deekaree *n.* દીકરી daughter

deenata *n.* દીનતા humility

deeptimaan *adj.* દીપ્તિમાન radiant

deergh *adj.* દીર્ઘ long

deerghaayushy *n.* દીર્ઘાયુષ્ય longevity

deerghadrashti *n.* દીર્ઘદ્રષ્ટિ clairvoynce

deesa *n.* દિશા direction

deevaadaandee *n.* દીવાદાંડી pharos

Deevaankhaanu *n.* દીવાનખાનું saloon

deevaanun *adj.* દીવાનું crazy

deevaanun *adj.* દીવાનું lunatic

deevaanun banaavavun *v.t.* દીવાનું બનાવવું craze

deevaasalee *n.* દીવાસળી lucifer

deevaasalee *n.* દીવાસળી. match

deevo *n.* દીવો lamp

deevo karavo દીવો કરવો illumine

defodil *n.* ડેફોડિલ daffodil

dehaantdand *n.* દેહાંતદંડ execution

dekhaadavun *adj.* દેખાવડું showy

dekhaav *v.t.* દેખાવ transform

dekhaavadun *adj.* દેખાવડું comely

dekharekh raakhanaar *n.* દેખરેખ રાખનાર overseer

dekharekha raakhavee *v.t.* દેખરેખ રાખવી monitor

dekharekha raakhavee *v.t.* દેખરેખ રાખવી oversee

dekharekha raakhavee દેખરેખ રાખવી superintend

dekheetee reete *adv.* દેખીતી રીતે apparently

dekheetee reete saachee vaat દેખીતી રીતે સાચી વાત truism

dekheetun *adj.* દેખીતું apparent

dekheetun *v.t.* દેખીતું manifest

dekheetun *adj.* દેખીતું obvious

dekheetun *adj.* દેખીતું seeming

Dekhrekh *n.* દેખરેખ surveillance

Dekhrekh raakhnaar *n.* દેખરેખ રાખનાર superintendent

delaaso *n.* દિલાસો solace

denagee *n.* દેણગી gift

Deree *n.* ડેરી dairy

derik *n.* ડેરિક derrick

desh *n.* દેશ country

deshaabhimaanavaalun *adj.* દેશાભિમાનવાળું patriotic

deshaagaman karavun *v.t.* દેશાગમન કરવું immigrate

deshaagat *n.* દેશાગત immigrant

deshabandhu *n.* દેશબંધુ compatriot

deshabhakt *n.* દેશભક્ત patriot

deshadaajh *n.* દેશદાઝ patriotism

deshanikaal *n.* દેશનિકાલ deportation

deshanikaal karavun *v.t.* દેશનિકાલ કરવું proscribe

deshapaar karavun *v.t.* દેશપાર કરવું deport

deshavato *v.t.* દેશવટો exile

deshnikaal karavun *v.t.* દેશનિકાલ કરવું banish

deshnikaal karavun, *v.t.* દેશનિકાલ કરવું expatriate

devaa mokoofee *n.* દેવા મોકૂફી moratorium

devaadaar *n.* દેવાદાર debtor

devaalay *n.* દેવાલય fane

devadaar *n.* દેવદાર mast

devadee *n.* દેવડી vestibule

devadoot *n.* દેવદૂત cherub

devadoot *n.* દેવદૂત seraph

devadoot, faristo *n.* દેવદૂત, ફરિસ્તો angel

Deval *n.* દેવળ sanctuary

devalanee bethak *n.* દેવળની બેઠક pew

devalanun chogaan *n.* દેવળનું ચોગાન church-yard

devalno dharmaguru *n.* દેવળનો ધર્મગુરુ chaplain

devanu sthaan aapavun *v.t.* દેવનું સ્થાન આપવું deify

devata par shekavun *v.t.* દેવતા પર શેકવું roast

devatva દેવત્વ divinity

devavaanee *n.* દેવવાણી oracle

devee *n.* દેવી goddess

deveekaran *n.* દેવીકરણ apotheosis

devnindaa *v.t.* દેવનિંદા blaspheme

devtaa par mookeene shekvun *n.* દેવતા પર મૂકીને શેકવું toast

devun *n.* દેવું debt

dhaaar *n.* ધાર edge

Dhaad *n.* ધાડ dacoity

dhaad paadavee *v.t.* ધાડ પાડવી maraud

Dhaadpaadu *n.* ધાડપાડુ dacoit

Dhaal ઢાલ shield

Dhaal ke dholaavvaalee jameen *n.* ઢાળ કે ઢોળાવ વાળી જમીન slope

dhaalavaalee sapaatee *n.* ઢાળવાળી સપાટી cant

dhaalavaalo maarg *v.i.* ઢાળવાળો માર્ગ ramp

dhaandhal *n.* ધાંધલ fuss

dhaandhal, khatapat *n.* ધાંધલ, ખટપટ ado

dhaandhaliyun *adj.* ધાંધલિયું clamorous

dhaandhaliyun *adj.* ધાંધલિયું rowdy

dhaankan kaadhvun ઢાંકણ કાઢવું uncover

dhaankanun *n.* ઢાંકણું cover

dhaankanun *n.* ઢાંકણું mantle

dhaankpichhedo *n.* ઢાંકપિછેડો camouflage

dhaanya bhandaar *n.* ધાન્ય ભંડાર granary

dhaanyano paak *n.* ધાન્યનો પાક crop

dhaar chadaavavee *v.t.* ધાર ચડાવવી, whet

dhaaraasabhaa *n.* ધારાસભા senate

dhaaradaar karavun *v.t.* ધારદાર કરવું sharpen

dhaaran karavun *v.t.* ધારણ કરવું assume

dhaaranaa *n.* ધારણા expectation

dhaaravun *v.t.* ધારવું expect

dhaaravun *v.t.* ધારવું intend

dhaarmik *adj.* ધાર્મિક godly

dhaarmik *adj.* ધાર્મિક pious

dhaarmik *n.* ધાર્મિક puritan

dhaarmik *adj.* ધાર્મિક religious

dhaarmik pravachan *n.* ધાર્મિક પ્રવચન sermon

dhaarmik sanpradaay *n.* ધાર્મિક સંપ્રદાય cult

dhaarmik siddhaant *n.* ધાર્મિક સદ્ધિધાંત dogma

dhaarmik vidhi *n.* ધાર્મિક વિધિ celebration

dhaarmikata *n.* ધાર્મિકતા piety

Dhaatu kaam karnaar *n.* ધાતુ કામ કરનાર smith

dhaatukaamanu kaarakhanu *n.* ધાતુકામનું કારખાનું foundry

dhaatuno dhaaliyo *n.* ધાતુનો ઢાળિયો ingot

dhaatuno samaan *n.* ધાતુનો સામાન hardware

dhaatunun *adj.* ધાતુનું metallic

dhab *n.* ઢબ deportment

dhabakaaro *n.* ધબકારો palpitation

dhabakavun *v.i.* ધબકવું palpitate

dhabakavun *v.i.* ધબકવું throb

dhabbo lagaadavo *v.t.* ધબ્બો લગાડવો smear

dhadaako *n.* ધડાકો blast

dhadako *v.t.* ધડાકો bang

dhagadhagatun *adv.* ધગધગતું ablaze

dhagalo *n.* ઢગલો heap

dhagalo *n.* ઢગલો pile

dhagalo karavo *n.* ઢગલો કરવો dump

dhairyayukt stree *adj.* ધૈર્યયુક્ત સ્ત્રી chivalrous

dhairyayuktdaakshiny *n.* ધૈર્યયુક્ત સ્ત્રીદાક્ષણિય chivalry

Dhairyvaalo *n.* ધૈર્યવાળો stoicism

dhakelavun *v.t.* ધકેલવું push

dhakhadhakhavun *v.i.* ધખધખવું glow

dhakkamukki *n.* ધક્કામુક્કી scuffle

dhamaachakadee *n.* ધમાચકડી revelry

dhamaaliyo bakavaas *n.* ધમાલિયો બકવાસ rant

dhamakaavavun *v.* ધમકાવવું browbeat

dhamakee *n.* ધમકી threat

dhaman *n.* ધમણ bellows

dhamanee *n.* ધમની artery

dhan *n.* ધણ herd

dhanaadhy, saadhansampan *adj.* ધનાઢ્ય, સાધનસંપન્ન affluent

dhanavargit *adj.* ધનગર્વિત purse-proud

Dhandhaadaaree khaarvo *n.* ધંધાદારી ખારવો sailor

dhandhaanee taalim *n.* ધંધાની તાલીમ apprentice

dhandhero *n.* ઢંઢેરો promulgation

dhandho *n.* ધંધો avocation

dhandho *n.* ધંધો calling

dhandho, vinimaya, vepaar *n.* ધંધો; વિનિમય વેપાર trade

dhandun *adj.* ઠંડું icy

dhanikata ધનિકતા opulence

dhanikavarg *n.* ધનિકવર્ગ plutocracy

dhanurvaa *n.* ધનુર્વા tetanus

dhanushy *n.* ધનુષ્ય cross-bow

dhanushya *n.* ધનુષ્ય bow

dhanushyano tankaar *n.* ધનુષ્યનો ટંકાર twang

dharapakad *n.* ધરપકડ apprehension

dharapakad karavee *v.t.* ધરપકડ કરવી apprehend

dharapakad karavee *v.t.* ધરપકડ કરવી arrest

dharatee ke pruthaveenun *adj.* ધરતી કે પૃથ્વીનું terrestrial

dharateekamp *n.* ધરતીકંપ earthquake

dharateekanpnun *adj.* ધરતીકંપનું seismal

dharee *n.* ધરી axle

dharm *n.* ધર્મ religion

dharmaadhyksh *n.* ધર્માધ્યક્ષ bishop

dharmaandh *adj.* ધર્માંધ fanatic

dharmaandhataa *n.* ધર્માંધતા fanaticism

dharmaghelun *adj.* ધર્મઘેલું religiose

dharmaguruonun raajy ધર્મગુરુઓનું રાજ્ય hierogtyph

dharmaprasaarakamandal sanbandhee *n.* ધર્મપ્રસારકમંડળ સંબંધી missionary

dharmasabhaa *n.* ધર્મસભા synod

dharmashaasan *n.* ધર્મશાસન theocracy

dharmashaastra *n.* ધર્મશાસ્ત્ર theologian

dharmayuddh ધર્મયુદ્ધ crusade

dharmopadesh *n.* ધર્મોપદેશક ecclesiastic

dharmopadesh aapavo *v.t.* ધર્મોપદેશ આપવો preach

Dharmpitaa *n.* ધર્મપતા sponsor

dharmsankat *n.* ધર્મસંકટ dilemma

dharobo *n.* ધરોબો intimacy

dharshan *n.* ધર્ષણ friction

dhartee *n.* ધરતી terra

dharuvaadee *n.* ધરુવાડી nursery

dhasaavavun *v.t.* ઠસાવવું dogmatize

dhasaavavun *v.t.* ઠસાવવું inculcate

dhasavun *v.t.* ધસવું fling

Dhasdaataa chaalvun *v.t.* ઠસડાતાં ચાલવું shuffle

dhating *n.* ધતગિ humbug

dhava daine padavun *n.* ધબ દઈને પડવું thud

Dhavdaavvun *v.t.* ધવડાવવું suckle

dheel karya karavee *v.t.* ઢીલ કર્યા કરવી linger

dheel karya karavee *v.t.* ઢીલ કર્યા કરવી procrastinate

Dheelun *v.t.* ઢીલું slacken

dheelun karavun *v.t.* ઢીલું કરવું loosen

dheelun karavun *v.t.* ઢીલું કરવું loose

Dheeme Dheeme *adv.* ધીમે ધીમે slowly

dheeme dheeme aagal vadhavun *v.t.* ધીમે ધીમે આગળ વધવું forge

Dheeme dheeme padvun *v.i.* ધીમે ધીમે પડવું sink

dheeme kaam karavun *v.i.* ધીમે કામ કરવું plod

dheemedheeme ધીમેધીમે by and by

dheemu *adj.* ધીમું tardy

Dheemun *adj.* ધીમું slow

dheenchan *n.* ઢીંચણ knee

dheengalee *n.* ઢીંગલી doll

dheeraj *n.* ધીરજ forbear

dheeraj raakhavee ધીરજ રાખવી forbearance

dheerajavaalun *adj.* ધીરજવાળું patient

dhekada maravan *v.i.* ઠેકડા મારવા hop

dhel *n.* ઢેલ peahen

dheravun *v.t.* ઘેરવું encompass

dheree levun *v.t.* ઘેરી લેવું engulf

dheree levun *v.t.* ઘેરી લેવું enlace

dhigaamastee ધિંગામસ્તી romp

dhikkaar *n.* ધિક્કાર reprobation

dhikkaaravun *v.t.* ધિક્કારવું abominate

dhikkaaravun *v.t.* ધિક્કારવું execrate

dhikkaaravun *adj.* ધિક્કારવું reprobate

Dhikkar *v.t.* ધિક્કાર scorn

dhikkaravaachak udagaar ધિક્કારવાચક ઉદ્ગાર fie

dhime dhime radavun *v.i.* ધીમે ધીમે રડવું mewl

dhobee *n.* ધોબી washerman

dhodaav *n.* ઢોળાવ declivity

dhodh *n.* ધોધ waterfall

Dhodhamaar varasaad *n.* ધોધમાર વરસાદ downpour

dhodhamaar varsaad ધોધમાર વરસાદ downfall

dhol *n.* ઢોલ tambour

dholaaighar *n.* ધોલાઇઘર laundry

dholaavavaalu *n.* ઢોળાવવાળું downhill

dholachee *n.* ઢોલચી drummer

Dholvun *n.pl.* ઢોળવું slop

Dholvun *v.i.* ઢોળવું spill

dhong *n.* ઢોંગ dissimulation

Dhong *n.* ઢોંગ sham

dhong *adj.* ઢોંગ simulation

dhong karavo *n.* ઢોંગ કરવો feint

dhong karavo *v.t.* ઢોંગ કરવો simulate

dhongee ઢોંગી impostor

dhool *n.* ધૂળ dust

dhoolvaalu *adj.* ધૂળવાળું dusty

dhoomaketu *n.* ધૂમકેતુ comet

Dhoomrapaan karnaar *n.* ધૂમ્રપાન કરનાર smoker

dhoon *n.* ધૂન crank

Dhoondhvaatun *adj.* ધૂંધવાતું smouldering

dhoop *n.* ધૂપ incense

Dhoopchhanv *n.* ધૂપછાંવ shot

dhootaaraageeree *n.* ધૂતારાગીરી racketeering

dhoovo *n.* ઢૂવો. dune

dhor *n.* ઢોર cattle

dhor aparaadh *n.* ઘોર અપરાધ enormity

dhoranu tolu *v.t.* ઢોરનું ટોળું drove

dhoree maarg *n.* ધોરી માર્ગ highway

dhornaa aaanchal *n.* ઢોરના આંચળ udder

dhovaan *n.* ધોવાણ erosion

dhovun, nahaavun *v.t.* ધોવું, નહાવું lave

dhraasko *n.* ધ્રાસ્કો fright

dhrmaandh maanas *n.* ધર્માંધ માણસ bigot

dhroojaaree *n.* ધ્રૂજારી tremor

dhroojatun *n.* ધ્રૂજતું tremulous

dhroojavun *v.i.* ધ્રૂજવું tremble

dhroojee uthe tevun *v.t.* ધ્રૂજી ઊઠે તેવું twitch

Dhroojvun *v.t.* ધ્રૂજવું shiver

Dhroojvun *v.i.* ધ્રૂજવું shudder

dhruna - soog peda karavee *v.t.* ધૃણા–સૂગ પેદા કરવી nauseate

dhrunaaspad *adj.* ધૃણાસ્પદ beastly

dhrunaaspad *adj.* ધૃણાસ્પદ grisly

dhrunaaspad *adj.* ધૃણાસ્પદ loathsome

dhrunaspad *adj.* ધૃણાસ્પદ abominable

dhrurnaakshasthaapee *n.* ધૃરણાક્ષસ્થાપી gyroscope

dhrushtataa *n.* ધૃષ્ટતા temerity

dhruvanun paasenun *n.* ધ્રુવનું પાસેનું polar

dhruvapad *v.i.* ધ્રુવપદ refrain

dhumaadaano goto *v.i.* ધુમાડાનો ગોટો whiff

Dhumaadaavaalun *adj.* ધુમાડાવાળું smoky

dhumaadiyun *n.* ધુમાડિયું chimney

Dhumaado *n.* ધુમાડો smoke

dhumaado, gusso *n.* ધુમાડો, ગુસ્સો fume

dhummas *n.* ધુમ્મસ fog

dhummas *n.* ધુમ્મસ haze

dhummas *n.* ધુમ્મસ mist

dhummasavaadu *n.* ધુમ્મસવાળું fogy

dhura *n.* ધુરા yoke

dhurandhar *n.* ધુરંધર magnate

dhut ke jugaar ramavo *v.i.* દ્યૂત કે જુગાર રમવો gamble

dhutakaaravun *n.* ધુતકારવું rebuff

dhvaj *n.* ધ્વજ flag

dhvaneenun kanpan *n.* ધ્વનિનું કંપન quaver

dhvani *n.* ધ્વનિ tone

dhvanishaastr *n.* ધ્વનિશાસ્ત્ર. phonology

dhvanivardhak yantr *n.* ધ્વનિવર્ધક યંત્ર microphone

dhvanivardhak yantr *n.* ધ્વનિવર્ધક યંત્ર mike

dhvansh karavo *v.t.* ધ્વંશ કરવો rase

dhyaan aapavun *v.t.* ધ્યાન આપવું attend

dhyaan dharavun *n.* ધ્યાન ધરવું meditation

dhyaan dharavun *v.i.* ધ્યાન ધરવું muse

dhyaanabhang karavo *v.t.* ધ્યાનભંગ કરવો distract

dhyaanaman levun *v.t.* ધ્યાનમાં લેવું heed

dhyaanapoorvak saanbhalavun *v.i.* ધ્યાનપૂર્વક સાંભળવું. hearken

dhyaanapoorvak saanbhalavun *v.i.* ધ્યાનપૂર્વક સાંભળવું listen

dhyaanapoorvak vaanchavun *v.t.* ધ્યાનપૂર્વક વાંચવું peruse

dhyaanman levun *v.t.* ધ્યાનમાં લેવું envisage

dikhaaoo ane bhabhakaadaar *adj.* દિખાઉ અને ભભકાદાર tawdry

dilaaso aapavo *v.t.* દિલાસો આપવો console

dilaaso aapavo te *n.* દિલાસો આપવો તે condolence

Dilne Sahaaro Aapvo *n.* દિલને સહારો આપવો salve

dipado *n.* દિપડો leopard

dipado *n.* દિપડો panther

dipthereeyaa *n.* ડિપ્થેરીયા diphtheria
disha badalavee *v.i.* દિશા બદલવી veer
dishaamaan *prep* દિશામાં toward
dishaaman chaalavun *v.t.* દિશામાં ચાલવું wend
distempar *n.* ડિસ્ટેમ્પર distemper
divaadaandee *n.* દિવાદાંડી lighthouse
divaaswapna *n.* દિવાસ્વપ્ન fantasy
divas *n.* દિવસ day
divas nu mukhya bhojan *n.* દિવસનું મુખ્ય ભોજન dinner
Divasnu Chhellu bhojan *n.* દિવસનું છેલ્લું ભોજન supper
divet *n.* દિવેટ wick
Divya *adj.* દિવ્ય supernal
divyaanand *n.* દિવ્યાનંદ beatitude
dod *adj.* દોડ running
dodavun *v.t.* દોડવું run
dodhadaahyo *n.* દોઢડાહ્યો wiseacre
Dohvun *n.* દોહવું stroke
dokeeyun karavun *v.i.* ડોકીયું કરવું peep
dokiyan karava *n.* ડોકિયાં કરવા peer
dol *n.* ડોલ bucket
dol *n.* ડોલ pail
Dol *v.i.* ડોલ swagger
Dol je dekhaav karvo *n.* ડોળ કે દેખાવ કરવો swank
dol karavo *v.t.* ડોળ કરવો pose
dol karavo *v.t.* ડોળ કરવો pretend
dolan *v.i.* દોલન oscillate
dolan *n.* દોલન oscillation
dolarano somo bhaag *n.* ડોલરનો સોમો ભાગ cent
Dolghaalun *n.* ડોળઘાલુ stilt
dominik sampradaayanu *n.* ડૉમનિકિ સંપ્રદાયનું dominic
doob *n.* ડૂબ submersion
doobalun *adj.* દૂબળું puny
doobalun ghodun *n.* દૂબળું ઘોડું jade
doobavun *v.t.* ડૂબવું drown
Doobelun *adj.* ડૂબેલું sunken
doocho *n.* ડૂચો plug
doocho *n.* ડૂચો wad
doodh *n.* દૂધ milk
doodhavaalo *adj.* દૂધવાળો. milkman
doondaalun *adj.* દૂંદાળું pot-belly
doondhalun *adj.* ધૂંધળું nabulous

door *adv.* દૂર away
door *prep.* દૂર tele
door karavun *v.t.* દૂર કરવું eliminate
door karavun *v.t.* દૂર કરવું remove
Door karvun *v.t.* દૂર કરવું shun
door rahevun *n.* દૂર રહેવું avoidance
door, laanbaa antare *adj.* દૂર, લાંબા અંતરે afar
doorabeen *n.* દૂરબીન binocular
dooradarshanno set *n.* દૂરદર્શનનો સટ television
doorana sanbandhavaalun *adj.* દૂરના સંબંધવાળું remote
doorandeshee *n.* દૂરંદેશી foresight
dooranee vasaahat *n.* દૂરની વસાહત. outpost
dooranu *adj.* દૂરનું distant
dooranu *adj.* દૂરનું far
doorasth *adj.* દૂરસ્થ outlying
doorathee jonaar *adj.* દૂરથી જોનાર bystander
doorathee jovun *v.t.* દૂરથી જોવું descry
doorbeena *n.* દૂરબીન telescope
dooshit karavun *v.t.* દૂષિત કરવું contaminate
dooshit karavun *v.t.* દૂષિત કરવું pollute
Dooskun *v.i.* ડૂસકું sob
doraano dado *n.* દોરાનો દડો clew
doradaanaa koochaa *n.* દોરડાના કૂચા oakum
doradun *n.* દોરડું rope
doravun *v.t.* દોરવું lead
doree *n.* દોરી tag
doree *v.t.* દોરી tie
Doree jevun *adj.* દોરી જેવું stringy
Doreeo *n.* દોરીઓ string
dosh *n.* દોષ demerit
dosh *n.* દોષ fault
dosh *n.* દોષ flaw
dosh *n.* દોષ foible
dosh *n.* દોષ guilt
dosh *n.* દોષ reprehension
doshaaropan *v.t.* દોષારોપણ blame
doshaaropan karvun *v.* દોષારોપણ કરવું accuse
doshaik drashtee *n.* દોષૈક દૃષ્ટિ carping

doshamukt karavun *v.t.* દોષમુક્ત કરવું acquit

doshamukt karvun *v.t.* દોષમુક્ત કરવું exculpate

doshamukti *n.* દોષમુક્તિ vindication

doshapaatr *adj.* દોષપાત્ર reprehensible

doshapaatra *adj.* દોષપાત્ર culpable

dosharahit *adj.* દોષ રહિત faultless

doshayukt *adj.* દોષયુક્ત faulty

draaksh *n.* દ્રાક્ષ grape

draakshano ras *v.* દ્રાક્ષનો રસ must

draakshano velo *n.* દ્રાક્ષનો વેલો vine

draavya *adj.* દ્રાવ્ય soluble

dradh nishchay vinaanun *adj.* દૃઢ નિશ્ચય વિનાનું irresolute

dradh vishvaas *n.* દૃઢ વિશ્વાસ confidence

dradhataa *n.* દૃઢતા assertiveness

dradhataa *n.* દૃઢતા fastness

dradhikaran *n.* દૃઢીકરણ affirmation

draksha uchher kendra *n.* દ્રાક્ષ ઉછેર કેન્દ્ર vinery

drashtaantaroop *n.* દ્રષ્ટાંતરૂપ representative

drashti *adj.* દૃષ્ટિ vision

drashti maryaada *n.* દૃષ્ટિ મર્યાદા purview

drashtibhram *n.* દૃષ્ટિભ્રમ mirage

drashtibindu *n.* દૃષ્ટિબિંદુ outlook

drashtiheen *adj.* દૃષ્ટિહીન blind

drashtimaryaadaa *n.* દૃષ્ટિમર્યાદા visibility

drashtinun *n.* દૃષ્ટિનું optic

drashtinun sanbandhee *adj.* દૃષ્ટિનું સંબંધી optical

drashtivishayak *adj.* દૃષ્ટિવિષયક visual

Dravak *adj.* દ્રાવક solvent

Dravya *n.* દ્રાવ્ય solubility

dravyalobh *n.* દ્રવ્યલોભ greed

drimukhee raajpaddhati *n.* દ્વિમુખી રાજપદ્ધતિ diarchy

Drudh *v.* દૃઢ steady

Drusti *n.* દૃષ્ટિ sight

dubaadavun *v.t.* ડુબાડવું dip

Dubaadvun *v.t.* ડુબાડવું submerse

dubavun *v.t.* ડુબવું submerge

dubhaashiyo *n.* દુભાષિયો interpreter

dubhaavavun *v.t.* દુભાવવું grieve

dubhaavavun *v.t.* દુભાવવું scandalize

dudakee chaal *v.t.* દુડકી ચાલ trot

dugdhamaan *n.* દુગ્ધમાન lactometer

dukaal *n.* દુકાળ drought

dukaal *n.* દુકાળ famine

Dukaan *n.* દુકાન shop

Dukaan *n.* દુકાન stall

dukaanadaar *n.* દુકાનદાર tradesman

dukaanadaar nu paatiyu *n.* દુકાનદારનું પાટિયું facia

dukh *n.* દુઃખ dolour

Dukh *n.* દુઃખ sadness

dukh *n.* દુઃખ suffering

dukh vyakt karavun *v.t.* દુઃખ વ્યકત કરવું lament

dukhad *adj.* દુઃખદ dolorous

Dukhad *adv.* દુઃખદ sadly

dukhadaayak *adj.* દુઃખદાયક grievous

dukhadaayak *adj.* દુઃખદાયક woeful

dukhakaaree *adj.* દુઃખકારી biting

dukhanun kaaran, vedanaa *n.* દુઃખનું કારણ, વેદના affliction

dukhavun, vedanaa *v.t.* દુખવું, વેદના ache

Dukhee *adj.* દુઃખી sad

dukhee *adj.* દુઃખી wretched

dukhee maanas *n.* દુઃખી માણસ wretch

Dukhee Thavu - Karvu *v.t.* દુઃખી થવું – કરવું. sadden

dukhee thavun *v.i.* દુઃખી થવું repine

dukhotpaadak, pidaakaaree *adj.* દુઃખોત્પાદક, પીડાકારી afflictive

dukkar *n.* ડુક્કર pig

Dukkar *n.* ડુક્કર swine

dukkaranee charabee *n.* ડુક્કરની ચરબી lard

dukkaranu maans *n.* ડુક્કરનું માંસ bacon

dukkaranun maans *n.* ડુક્કરનું માંસ pork

Dukkarnee maadaa *v.t.* ડુક્કરની માદા sow

dunavayee *adj.* દુન્યવી earthly

dungalee *n.* ડુંગળી onion

Duniyaadaareeman kushal *v.t.* દુનિયાદારીમાં કુશળ sophisticate

dunvayee *adj.* દુન્યવી earthy

dunyavee *adj.* દુન્યવી worldly

duraachaar *n.* દુરાચાર meanness

duraachaaree *adj.* દુરાચારી profigate

duraachaaree *adj.* દુરાચારી wicked

duraachaaree vyakti *n.* દુરાચારી વ્યક્તિ blackguard

duraachaareepanun *n.* દુરાચારીપણું wickedness

duraagrah દુરાગ્રહ pertinacity

duraagrahee *adj.* દુરાગ્રહી headstrong

duraagrahee *adj.* દુરાગ્રહી obdurate

duraagrahee *adj.* દુરાગ્રહી pertinacious

duraaraadhy *adj.* દુરારાધ્ય implacable

Duragrah *n.* દુરાગ્રહ stubbornness

durast raakhavun *v.t.* દુરસ્ત રાખવું maintain

durbal *adv.* દુર્બળ weak

durdasha *n.* દુર્દશા predicament

durdevee ghatana *n.* દુર્દૈવી ઘટના mischance

durdevee ghatana *n.* દુર્દૈવી ઘટના misfortune

durgandh *n.* દુર્ગંધ reek

Durgandh *n.* દુર્ગંધ stench

Durgandhvalun *adj.* દુર્ગંધવાળું smelly

durghatana *n.* દુર્ઘટના mishap

durgunee *adj.* દુર્ગુણી vicious

durjan *n.* દુર્જન. miscreant

durlaksh *adj.* દુર્લક્ષ inattentive

durlaksh *n.* દુર્લક્ષ oversight

durupayog karavo *v.t.* દુરૂપયોગ કરવો misapply

durupayog karavo *v.t.* દુરૂપયોગ કરવો misuse

durvyavhaar karavo *v.t.* દુર્વ્યવહાર કરવો maltreat

dusaahas *n.* દુસાહસ misadventure

dushit karavun *v.t.* દૂષિત કરવું vitiate

dushkaal *v.t.* દુષ્કાળ draught

dushkarm *n.* દુષ્કર્મ. misdeed

dushman *n.* દુશ્મન enemy

dushman *n.* દુશ્મન foe

dusht *adj.* દુષ્ટ evil

dusht *adj.* દુષ્ટ iniquitous

dusht *adj.* દુષ્ટ nefarious

dushta *adj.* દુષ્ટ unkind

dushta maanas *n.* દુષ્ટ માણસ villain

dushtataa *n.* દુષ્ટતા villainy

dustar *adj.* દુસ્તર insurmountable

dvaaramandap *n.* દ્વારમંડપ porch

dvaarmandap *n.* દ્વારમંડપ portico

dvaarpaal *n.* દ્વારપાળ doorkeeper

dveepakalp *n.* દ્વીપકલ્પ peninsula

dvesh *n.* દ્વેષ rancour

dveshabhaav *n.* દ્વેષભાવ malice

dvesheelun *adj.* દ્વેષીલું rancorous

dviarthee *adj.* દ્વિઅર્થી equivocal

dviarthee bolavun દ્વિઅર્થી બોલવું equivocate

dviarthee, anishchitaarth *adj.* દ્વિઅર્થી, અનિશ્ચિતાર્થ ambiguous

dviarthee, sandigdh *n.* દ્વિઅર્થી, સંદિગ્ધ ambiguity

dvibhaajak *n.* દ્વિભાજક bisector

dvibhaajan karavun *v.t.* દ્વિભાજન કરવું bifurcate

dvibhaashee *adj.* દ્વિભાષી bilingual

dvimaasik દ્વિમાસિક bimonthly

dvipadee *adj.* દ્વિપદી binomial

dvipakshee *adj.* દ્વિપક્ષી bilateral

dvivaarshik *adj.* દ્વિવાર્ષિક biennial

Dwesh *n.* દ્વેષ spite

dyaan aapavun *v.i.* ધ્યાન આપવું beware

E

E J *n.* એ જ selfsame

E j reete ke prakaare *adv.* એ જ રીતે કે પ્રકારે similarly

e ja pramaane *adv.* એ જ પ્રમાણે likewise

e reete *adv.* એ રીતે virtually

echhchaneey *adj.* ઇચ્છનીય desirable

echhsha *v.t.* ઇચ્છા desire

echhshaarthark *adj.* ઇચ્છાર્થક desiderative

echsavaalu *adj.* ઇચ્છાવાળું desirous
Edee *adj.* એદી slovenly
eechchha *v.t.* ઇચ્છા wish
eechchha *n.* ઇચ્છા yearning
eechchhaashakti *n.* ઇચ્છાશક્તિ willingness
eeja pahonchaadavee *v.t.* ઇજા પહોંચાડવી mutilate
eek avasthaa *n.* એક અવસ્થા transition
eeka naanu - chapala pakshee *n.* એક નાનું – ચપળ પક્ષી. tit
eelaaj *n.* ઇલાજ remedy
eelaayachee *n.* ઇલાયચી cardamom
eemaarat *n.* ઇમારત building
eenaam *n.* ઇનામ booty
eenaam *n.* ઇનામ prize
eenaam *n.* ઇનામ requital
eenakaar *n.* ઇનકાર refusal
eenakaar karavo *v.t.* ઇનકાર કરવો gainsay
eenda sevavan *v.t* ઇંડા સેવવાં brood
eendriy dvaara jaanavun ઇન્દ્રિય દ્વારા જાણવું perceive
eendriyadaman karavun *v.t.* ઇંદ્રિયદમન કરવું mortify
eendriyadaman karavun te *n.* ઇન્દ્રિયદમન કરવું તે mortification
eendriyagamy ઇન્દ્રિયગમ્ય perceptible
eent *n.* ઇંટ brick
eentono bhaththo *n.* ઇંટોનો ભઠ્ઠો brick-kiln
eeraadaapoorvak karelun ઇરાદાપૂર્વક કરેલું intentional
eersha *n.* ઇર્ષા jealousy
eershaalun *adj.* ઇર્ષાળું jealous
eeshaaro *n.* ઇશારો beck
eeshaaro *n.* ઇશારો cue
eeshaaro karavo *v.t.* ઇશારો કરવો beckon
eeshaaro karavo *v.t.* ઇશારો કરવો imply
eeshu khrist *n.* ઇશુ ખ્રિસ્ત christ
eeshu khrist *n.* ઇશુ ખ્રિસ્ત redeemer
eeshuno kroos *n.* ઇશુનો ક્રૂસ rood
eeshvar ninda *n.* ઇશ્વર નિંદા blasphemy
eetihaas *n.* ઇતિહાસ history

eeyal *n.* ઇયળ caterpillar
eeyal *n.* ઇયળ larva
ejaner *n.* ઇજનેર engineer
ek એક a
ek aankhavaalun *adj.* એક આંખવાળું monocular
ek abaj *n.* એક અબજ milliard
ek baajue *adv.* એક બાજુએ aside
Ek baajue vaalvuun *v.t.* એક બાજુએ વાળવું shunt
ek baajue, judee rite *adv.* એક બાજુએ, જુદી રીતે apart
ek dashaansh meetar *n.* એક દશાંશ મીટર decimetre
ek jaat nee lambee kataar *n.* એક જાતની લાંબી કટાર dirk
ek jaatanee kobee *n.* એક જાતની કોબી kale
ek jaatano ark *n.* એક જાતનો અરૂ xylol
ek jaatano chaamadeeno rog *n.* એક જાતનો ચામડીનો રોગ xanthoma
ek jaatano keedo *n.* એક જાતનો કીડો maggot
ek jaatano peelo rang *n.* એક જાતનો પીળો રંગ xanthine
ek jaatano saap *n.* એક જાતનો સાપ cobra
ek jaatanun anaaj *n.* એક જાતનું અનાજ rye
ek jaatnun plastik *n.* એક જાતનું પ્લાસ્ટિક celluloid
ek jheree vanaspati *n.* એક ઝેરી વનસ્પતિ hemlock
ek karavun *n.* એક કરવું combine
ek karod paraardh *n.* એક કરોડ પરાર્ધ quadrillion
ek meethaaee *n.* એક મીઠાઈ candy
ek naanee top *n.* એક નાની તોપ mortar
ek naano zeree saap એક નાનો ઝેરી સાપ viper
ek naanun pakshee *n.* એક નાનું પક્ષી bunting
ek netrarog *n.* એક નેત્રરોગ glaucoma
Ek pachhee ek *adv.* એક પછી એક singly
ek pakshi *adj.* એક પક્ષી exparte

ek patneetva *n.* એક પત્નીત્વ monogamy

ek pauraanik devata *n.* એક પૌરાણિક દેવતા nymph

ek saathe *adj.* એક સાથે simultaneous

Ek Sarakhun *adj.* એક સરખું same

ek sarakhun karavun *v.t.* એક સરખું કરવું unify

ek satra *n.* એક સત્ર semester

ek tantuvaadh *n.* એક તંતુવાદ્ય mandoline

ekaad koee *pron.* એકાદ કોઈ anything

ekaadikaar *n.* એકાધિકાર. monopoly

ekaadikaar melavavo *v.t.* એકાધિકાર મેળવવો. monopolize

ekaadikaarano samarthak *n.* એકાધિકારનો સમર્થક monopolist

Ekaaek *adv.* એકાએક suddenly

ekaaeka *adv.* એકાએક unawares

ekaagra karavun *v.* એકાગ્ર કરવું concentrate

ekaagrataa *n.* એકાગ્રતા concentration

ekaakee *n.* એકાકી solo

ekaakee, ekaladokal *adj.* એકાકી, એકલદોકલ alone

Ekaant Jagyaa *n.* એકાન્ત જગ્યા seclusion

ekaant khoono *n.* એકાન્ત ખૂણો nook

ekaantavaasee *n.* એકાંતવાસી recluse

Ekaantvaalee jagyaa *n.* એકાન્તવાળી જગ્યા solitude

ekabijaa par aadun *adv.* એકબીજા પર આડું across

ekadam *adv.* એકદમ. instantly

ekadam sfurelo vichaar *n.* એકદમ સ્ફુરેલો વિચાર inspiration

ekadhaarun *adj.* એકધારું monotonous

ekakendree *adj.* એકકેન્દ્રી concentric

ekalavaayun *adj.* એકલવાયું lorn

ekalun *adj.* એકલું lone

ekalun *adj.* એકલું one

ekalun padelun *adj.* એકલું પડેલું lonely

ekam *n.* એકમ entity

ekamaatra, ananya *adj.* એકમાત્ર, અનન્ય exclusive

ekamat *n.* એકમત concert

ekamat thavun *v.i.* એકમત થવું concur

Ekantman mookvu *v.t.* એકાંતમાં મૂકવું seclude

ekanun ek *adj.* એકનું એક only

ekaraag *n.* એકરાગ consonance

ekaraag *n.* એકરાગ rapport

ekaraag, sumel *n.* એકરાગ સુમેળ congruence

ekaraar *n.* એકરાર avowal

ekathun karavun *v.t.* એકઠું કરવું amass

ekatr karavun *v.t.* એકત્ર કરવું mingle

ekatra karavun *v.t.* એકત્ર કરવું assemble

ekatra karavun *v.t.* એકત્ર કરવું muster

ekatreekaran *n.* એકત્રીકરણ integration

ekatrit, ekandar *v.* એકત્રતિ, એકંદર aggregate

ekatv *n.* એકત્વ identity

ekavaakyata *n.* એકવાક્યતા harmony

ekavaar *adv.* એકવાર once

Ekdam uthelun vantol *n.* એકદમ ઉઠેલું વંટોળ squall

ekee vakhate thavun *v.i.* એકી વખતે થવું coincide

ekeetase jovun *v.i.* એકીટસે જોવું stare

ekeshvaravaad *n.* એકેશ્વરવાદ monotheism

Ekltaa *n.* એકલતા solitariness

Eklun (rahetun) *adj.* એકલું (રહેતું) solitary

Eklun hovaapanun *n.* એકલું હોવાપણું singularity

Ektaa *n.* એકતા solidarity

Ektra bolaavvun *v.t.* એકત્ર બોલાવવું summon

elachee ane tena maanaso *n.* એલચી અને તેના માણસો legation

em maanavun ke *v.i.* એમ માનવું કે... ween

emaarat *n.* ઈમારત edifice

Eman *adv.* એમાં therein

emoneeya, navasa *n.* એમોનિયા, નવસા ammonia

enaa jevuj j *adj.* એના જેવું જ tantamount

enakaar *n.* ઈનકાર denial

enakaar karavo *v.i.* ઇનકાર કરવો decline

enakaar karavo *v.t.* ઇનકાર કરવો deny

enjin vina udavun *v.i.* એંજિન વિના ઉડવું glide

Ep ke mankee (Vaandro) *n.* એપ કે મંકી (વાંદરો) simian

eraadaapurvakanu *v.t.* ઇરાદાપૂર્વકનું deliberate

Eran *n.* એરણ stithy

erandiyun *n.* એરંડિયું castor oil

ershaadu *adj.* ઇર્ષાળુ envious

eshaaraamanee vastu *n.* એશઆરામની વસ્તુ luxury

etalun ja nahi *adj.* એટલું જ નહિ nay

etarnee *n.* એટર્ની attorney

ethens, etikaanun *n.* એથેન્સ, એટિકાનું attic

evee sharate ke *conj.* એવી શરતે કે provided

$$\boxed{\textbf{F}}$$

faachar *n.* ફાચર wedge

faad ફાટ interstice

faadavun *v.t.* ફાડવું rive

faadee naakhavun *v.t.* ફાડી નાખવું rip

faafaa maaravaa *v.i.* ફાંફાં મારવાં fumble

faajal *n.* ફાજલ surplus

faajal paadavun *v.t.* ફાજલ પાડવું spare

faalavaayeli vyakati *n.* ફાળવાયેલી વ્યક્તિ allottee

faalavanee *n.* ફાળવણી allocation

faalavanee *n.* ફાળવણી allotment

faalavavun *v.* ફાળવવું allocate

faalavavun *v.* ફાળવવું allot

faalavun ફાળવું flourish

faalo aapanaar *n.* ફાળો આપનાર contributor

faalo aapavo *v.t.* ફાળો આપવો contribute

faanas *n.* ફાનસ lantern

faankado *n.* ફાંકડો beau

faankado maanas *n.* ફાંકડો માણસ popinjay

faanseeno maanchado *n.* ફાંસીનો માંચડો gallows

faanso *v.t.* ફાંસો gin

faanso *n.* ફાંસો noose

faanto *n.* ફાંટો offset

faaseevaad *n.* ફાસીવાદ fascism

faat *n.* ફાટ cleft

faat *n.* ફાટ crevice

Faat *v.t.* ફાટ slit

faat paadavee *v.t.* ફાટ પાડવી split

faatavun *n.* ફાટવું eruption

faatavun *v.t.* ફાટવું rupture

faatee nikalavun *v.t.* ફાટી નીકળવું erupt

faayado *n.* ફાયદો benefit

faaydo thaay nahi evu *adj.* ફાયદો થાય નહિ એવું unavailing

fakeer *n.* ફકીર dervish

Fakt *adv.* ફક્ત solely

Fakta ek j *adj.* ફક્ત એક જ single

fal *n.* ફળ fruit

fal athava maansano ras *n.* ફળ અથવા માંસનો રસ. juice

fal vagaranu *adj.* ફળ વગરનું unproductive

faladrup *adj.* ફળદ્રુપ fertile

faladrup banaavavun *v.t.* ફળદ્રુપ બનાવવું fertilize

faladrupataa *n.* ફળદ્રુપતા fecundity

faladrupataa *n.* ફળદ્રુપતા fertility

falajhaadanee vaadee *n.* ફળઝાડની વાડી orchard

falajyotish *n.* ફળજ્યોતિષ astrology

falajyotishee *n.* ફળજ્યોતિષી astrologer

falano daaroo *n.* ફળનો દારૂ wine

falano murabbo *n.* ફળનો મુરબ્બો jelly

falano thaliyo *n.* ફળનો ઠળિયો pit

falanun beej *n.* ફળનું બીજ pip

falapraapapti *n.* ફળપ્રાપ્તિ fruition

falaprad *adj.* ફળપ્રદ prolific

falashruti *n.* ફળશ્રુતિ progeny

faleebhoot thavun *v.i.* ફળીભૂત થવું fructify

faleet karavun *v.t.* ફલિત કરવું fecundate

falono vepaaree *n.* ફળોનો વેપારી fruiterer

fanfosavavun *v.i.* ફંફોસવવું grope

Fanseeno Manchdo *n.* ફાંસીનો માંચડો scaffold

fantaayukt sheengadaao *n.pl.* ફાંટાયુક્ત શિંગડાઓ antlers

faraak *n.* ફરાક frock

faraar *v.* ફરાર abscond

faraj *n.* ફરજ duty

faraj paadavee *v.* ફરજ પાડવી compel

faraj paadavee *v.t.* ફરજ પાડવી obligate

faraja bajaavavee *v.t.* ફરજ બજાવવી officiate

farajiyaat *adj.* ફરજિયાત compulsory

farajiyaat bharatee *n.* ફરજિયાત ભરતી conscription

farajiyaat bharatee karaayelu *adj.* ફરજિયાત ભરતી કરેલું conscript

farajiyaat ugharaanun *v.t.* ફરજિયાત ઉઘરાણું levy

farakadee *n.* ફરકડી spool

farasabandhee *n.* ફરસબંધી pavement

farasee *n.* ફરસી gouge

faree bhareedevun *v.t.* ફરી ભરીદેવું replenish

faree bolanun *v.t.* ફરી બોલવું repeat

faree chaalu thavun te *n.* ફરી ચાલુ થવું તે continuation

faree ekatr aanavun *v.t.* ફરી એકત્ર આણવું reunite

faree ekavaar, valee *adv.* ફરી એકવાર, વળી again

faree ekha devee *v.i.* ફરી દેખા દેવી reappear

Faree faree maagvun *v.t.* ફરી ફરી માગવું solicit

faree joee javun *n.* ફરી જોઇ જવું revise

faree savaar thavun *v.t.* ફરી સવાર થવું remount

faree sharoo karavun *v.i.* ફરી શરૂ કરવું resume

faree tandurast thavun *v.t.* ફરી તંદુરસ્ત થવું recuperate

faree veemo utaraavavo *v.t.* ફરી વીમો ઉતરાવવો reinsure

fareethee gothavavun *v.t.* ફરીથી ગોઠવવું readjust

fareethee naanun rokavun *v.t.* ફરીથી નાણું રોકવું reinvest

fareethee pakadavun *v.t.* ફરીથી પકડવું recapture

fareethee yaad aavavun *v.i.* ફરીથી યાદ આવવું recur

fareethi, navesar *adv.* ફરીથી, નવેસર afresh

farithee, navesarathee *adv.* ફરીથી, નવેસરથી anew

fariyaad *n.* ફરિયાદ complaint

fariyaad *adj.* ફરિયાદ complaint

fariyaad *n.* ફરિયાદ plaint

fariyaad karavee *v.t.* ફરિયાદ કરવી complain

fariyaadapaksh *n.* ફરિયાદપક્ષ prosecution

fariyaadee *n.* ફરિયાદી claimant

fariyaadee *n.* ફરિયાદી plaintiff

fasaavavun *v.t.* ફસાવવું beguile

fataakado *n.* ફટાકડો cracker

fatakaaravun *v.* ફટકારવું baste

fatakaaravun *v.t.* ફટકારવું flog

fatakadee *n.* ફટકડી alum

fatako *n.* ફટકો dint

fatako maaravo *v.t.* ફટકો મારવો crump

fatavo *n.* ફતવો prescript

fateh *n.* ફતેહ eclat

february maheeno *n.* ફેબ્રુઆરી મહિનો february

feekaash *n.* ફીકાશ pallor

feekun *adj.* ફીકું vapid

feen *n.* ફીણ foam

Feen aavvun *n.* ફીણ આવવું spume

feen bahaar kaadhvun *n.* ફીણ બહાર કાઢવું froth

Feenvaalun aavvun *adj.* ફીણવાળું આવવું spumy

feerakee *n.* ફીરકી reel

feet *n.* ફીત riband

fefasaanne lagatun *adj.* ફેફસાંને લગતું pulmonary

fefasaanno sojo *n.* ફેફસાંનો સોજો pneumonia

fefasaano kshayarog *n.* ફેફસાનો ક્ષયરોગ phthisis

fefasaano kshayaroga *n.* ફેફસાંનો ક્ષયરોગ. tuberculosis

fefasaano rogee *adj.* ફેફસાનો રોગી epileptic

fefasun *n.* ફેફસું. lung

fefiyo *n.* ફેરિયો. hawker

felaavavun *v.t.* ફેલાવવું expand

felaavavun *v.t.* ફેલાવવું extend

felaavun ફેલાવું suffuse

Felaavvun *v.t.* ફેલાવવું spread

fenkavu *v.t.* ફેંકવુ threw

fenkavu *v.t.* ફેંકવુ throw

fenkavun *v.t.* ફેંકવું dart

fenkavun *v.t.* ફેંકવું launch

fenkee devun *v.t.* ફેંકી દેવું discard

ferafaar *n.* ફેરફાર modification

ferafaar karava *v.t.* ફેરફાર કરવો innovate

ferafaar karava *v.t.* ફેરફાર કરવા. modify

ferafaar karavo *v.t.* ફેરફાર કરવો change

ferakhaataree aapavee *v.t.* ફેરખાતરી આપવી reassure

ferashastreekaran *v.t.* ફેરશસ્ત્રીકરણ rearm

feratapaasanee *n.* ફેરતપાસણી review

feravavun *v.t.* ફેરવવું circulate

feravavun *v.t.* ફેરવવું convert

feravavun, badalavun *v.* ફેરવવું, બદલવું alter

feriyaano dhandho karavo *v.t.* ફેરિયાનો ધંધો કરવો peddle

feriyo *n.* ફેરિયો. pedlar

feriyo *n.* ફેરિયો tinker

Feshanebal *adj.* ફેશનબલ stylish

fikkaash *n.* ફિક્કાશ paleness

fikkun *adj.* ફિક્કું pale

file *n.* ફાઈલ file

firakee *n.* ફિરકી bobbin

fitakaar *n.* ફિટકાર odium

flat prakaaranaa aavaas *adj.* ફ્લેટ પ્રકારના આવાસ flat

foee *n.* ફોઇ aunt

folleeo, kheel *n.* ફોલ્લીઓ, ખીલ acne

follo *n.* ફોલ્લો blister

follo *n.* ફોલ્લો. pock

fonograaf *n.* ફોનોગ્રાફ phonograph

foodeeno *n.* ફૂદીનો mint

foog *n.* ફૂગ fungus

foog *n.* ફૂગ mildew

fool *n.* ફૂલ flower

fool kheelava *n.* ફૂલ ખીલવાં blossom

foolaavavun *v.t.* ફૂલાવવું bloat

foolagobee *n.* ફૂલગોબી cauliflower

foolamaanno paraag *n.* ફૂલમાંનો પરાગ pollen

Foolmaano narkesar *n.* ફૂલમાંનો નરકેસર stamen

foolo aavavaano samay *n.* ફૂલો આવવાનો સમય florescence

foolonee kalagee *n.* ફૂલોની કલગી bouquet

foolonee kyaaree *n.* ફૂલોની ક્યારી flowerpot

foomatun *n.* ફૂમતું cockade

foomatun *n.* ફૂમતું tassel

foonk *n.* ફૂંક puff

foonkaavun *v.t.* ફૂંકાવું blow

foorcha *n.* ફૂર્ચા cartilage

footano baaramo bhaag *n.* ફૂટનો બારમો ભાગ inch

footato fanago *n.* ફૂટતો ફણગો offshoot

footbol *n.* ફૂટબોલ football

foovaaro *n.* ફૂવારો fountain

foovaaro *n.* ફૂવારો jet

fosalaavavun ફોસલાવવું wheedle

fosfaras *n.* ફોસ્ફરસ phosphorus

fosfaric *adj.* ફોસ્ફરિક phosphoric

fotarun *n.* ફોતરું hull

fotograafee *n.* ફોટોગ્રાફી. photography

french havelee *n,.* ફ્રેંચ હવેલી chateau

fugavo *n.* ફુગાવો inflation

fulaavavun *v.t.* ફુલાવવું distend

fulanee kalee *n.* ફૂલની કળી bud

Fuvaaro *n.* ફુવારો spray

Fuvad naar *n.* ફૂવડ નાર slut

G

gaabadun *n.* ગાબડુ, દર, રાફડો hole
gaadaabhaadun *n.* ગાડાભાડું carriage
gaadaabhaadun *n.* ગાડાભાડું cartage
gaadalun *n.* ગાદલું mattress
gaadalun *n.* ગાદલું rug
gaadan banaavanaar *n.* ગાડાં બનાવનાર wright
gaadee *n.* ગાડી car
gaadee *n.* ગાદી pad
gaadee par besaadavun *v.t.* ગાદી પર બેસાડવું enthrone
gaadeenasheen raanee *n.* ગાદીનશીન રાણી regina
gaadeenee satee *n.* ગાડીની સાટી chassis
gaadun *n.* ગાડું waggon
gaadun *n.* ગાડું wain
gaafelapanun *n.* ગાફેલપણું lethargy
gaajar *n.* ગાજર carrot
gaal denaarun *adj.* ગાળ દેનારું abusive
gaal devee *v.* ગાળ દેવી abuse
gaalapacholiyan *n.* ગાલપચોળિયાં mumps
gaaleeyo *n.* ગાળીયો lasso
Gaalo bhaandnaaru *adj.* ગાળો ભાંડનારું scurrilous
gaalo devee *v.t.* ગાળો દેવી becall
gaalo devee *v.t.* ગાળો દેવી bespatter
gaam *n.* ગામ village
gaamadaaman rahevun *v.t.* ગામડામાં રહેવું rusticate
gaamadaanun *adj.* ગામડાનું rural
gaamadiyo *n.* ગામડિયો bumpkin
gaamathee *adj.* ગામઠી rustic
gaandapan *n.* ગાંડપણ lunacy
gaandapan *n.* ગાંડપણ mania
gaandu *adj.* ગાંડુ insane
gaandu banaavavun *v.t.* ગાંડુ બનાવવું madden
gaandun *adj.* ગાંડું maniac
gaaniyun *n.* ગાંડિયું madcap
gaansadee ગાંસડી bale

gaanth *n.* ગાંઠ knot
gaanthogaanthovaalun *adj.* ગાંઠોગાંઠોવાળું knotty
gaapachee maarnaar vidyaarthee *n.* ગાપચી મારનાર વિદ્યાર્થી truant
Gaavun *v.i.* ગાવું sing
gaay *n.* ગાય cow
Gaayak *n.* ગાયક singer
Gaayak *n.* ગાયક songster
gaayak *n.* ગાયક vocalist
gaayakvrund *n.* ગાયકવૃંદ chorus
gaayakvrundno sabhya *n.* ગાયકવૃંદનો સભ્ય chorister
gaayan ગાયન recitation
gaayan kaaryakram *n.* ગાયન કાર્યક્રમ recital
Gaayikaa *n.* ગાયિકા songatress
gaaynun bachchun *n.* ગાયનું બચ્ચુ calf
gaayo *n.* ગાયો kine
gabadaavee devun *v.t.* ગબડાવી દેવું overthrow
gabadatan javun te *v.t.* ગબડતાં જવું તે roll
gabadavun *v.t.* ગબડવું trundle
gabharaat *n.* ગભરાટ bewilderment
gabharaat ગભરાટ funk
gabharaat *n.* ગભરાટ panic
gabharaatiyun *adj.* ગભરાટિયું nervous
gabharaavavun *v.t.* ગભરાવવું horrify
gabharaayelun *adj.* ગભરાયેલું awestruck
gabharavun *v.t.* ગભરાવું blench
gada *n.* ગદા mace
gadagadaat karavo *v.t.* ગડગડાટ કરવો rumble
gaddhaavaitaru *n.* ગધ્ધાવૈતરું drudgery
gadee *v.t.* ગડી ply
gadh *n.* ગઢ fortress
Gadh *n.* ગઢ stronghold
gadhedaanun bhoonkavun *v.t.* ગધેડાનું ભૂંકવું bray
gadhedu *n.* ગધેડુ donkey
gadhedun *n.* ગધેડું ass
gady *n.* ગદ્ય prose
gaeekaal *n.* ગઈકાલ yesterday
gafalat karanaar *n.* ગફલત કરનાર mutt

Gaganchumbee imaarat n. ગગનચુંબી ઇમારત sky-scraper

gahan adj. ગહન profound

gajagati v.i. ગજગતિ waddle

galaapattee n. ગળાપટ્ટી collar

galagoto n. ગલગોટો. marigold

galanee n. ગળણી colander

galanee v.t. ગળણી filter

galanee n. ગળણી funnel

galapatto n. ગલપટ્ટો. muffler

galapatto n. ગલપટ્ટો scarf

galavun v.i. ગળવું ooze

galee v.t. ગલી tickle

galee rotee n. ગલી રોટી bun

galeepachee karavee ગલીપચ્ચી કરવી titillate

galu dabaavavun v.t. ગળુ દબાવવું strangle

galun n. ગળું gullet

galun v.t. ગળું throttle

Galyun adj. ગળ્યું sweet

galyun karavun v.t. ગળ્યું કરવું sweeten

gamaan n. ગમાણ. manger

gamaar n. ગમાર. lout

gamadaano rahevaasee n. ગામડાનો રહેવાસી villager

gamageen adj. ગમગીન glum

Gamageen adj. ગમગીન. sable

gamageen banaavavun v.t. ગમગીન બનાવવું deject

gamananee disha n. ગમનની દિશા course

gambheer adj. ગંભીર tranquil

Gambheerta n. ગંભીરતા seriousness

game te pron. ગમે તે anyone

game te adj. ગમે તે whatever

game te reete adv. ગમે તે રીતે however

game te rite adv. ગમે તે રીતે anyhow

game tem adv. ગમે તેમ anyway

game tyan adv. ગમે ત્યાં anywhere

ganaa nalaanu haadakun n. ગના નળાનું હાડકું tibia

ganaay nahi evun adj. ગણાય નહિ એવું incalculable

ganaganaat v.i. ગણગણાટ hum

ganaganaat n. ગણગણાટ murmur

ganaganaat v.i. ગણગણાટ sizzle

ganaganaat karavo v.t. ગણગણાટ કરવો, buzz

ganaganavun v.t. ગણગણવું mutter

ganataree n. ગણતરી calculation

ganataree n. ગણતરી computation

ganataree n. ગણતરી enumeration

ganataree n. ગણતરી numeration

ganataree n. ગણતરી reckoning

ganataree kaadhavee v.t. ગણતરી કાઢવી reckon

ganataree karavaanee v. ગણતરી કરવી calculate

ganataree karavee v.t. ગણતરી કરવી count

ganataree karavee v.t. ગણતરી કરવી enumerate

ganatareekaar n. ગણતરીકાર scorer

ganatavya n. ગંતવ્ય destination

ganavesh n. ગણવેશ livery

ganaveshadhaaree nokar n. ગણવેશધારી નોકર footman

ganavun v. ગણવું compute

ganavun v.t. ગણવું deem

gandakee n. ગંદકી dirt

gandakee, gandu saahity n. ગંદકી, ગંદુ સાહિત્ય garbage

gandavaad n. ગંદવાડ filth

gandavaad n. ગંદવાડ mess

gandee koovada stree n. ગંદી કૂવડ સ્ત્રી trollop

gandhaatee stree n. ગંધાતી સ્ત્રી slattern

Gandhaavun n. ગંધાવું stink

gandhak n. ગંધક brimstone

Gandhak n. ગંધક sulphur

gandhak no tejaab n. ગંધકનો તેજાબ vitriol

Gandhaknaa jevun adj. ગંધકના જેવું sulphurous

Gandhaknaa jevun adj. ગંધકના જેવું sulphury

gandhataru n. ગંધતરુ cedar

gandhayelun pravaahee n. ગંધાયેલું પૂરવાહી gore

Gandhkaamlnaa ksharvaalun n. ગંધકામ્લના ક્ષારવાળું sulphate

gandu *adj.* ગંદું dirty

gandu banaavavun *v.t.* ગંદુ બનાવવું defile

gandu karavun *v.t.* ગંદુ કરવું befoul

gandu karavun *v.t.* ગંદુ કરવું besmirch

gandu maanas *n.* ગંદું માણસ ragamuffin

Gandun *adj.* ગંદું squalid

ganika *n.* ગણિકા courtesan

ganitashaastr *n.* ગણિતશાસ્ત્ર. mathematics

ganitashaastree *n.* ગણિતશાસ્ત્રી arithmetician

ganotapato *n.* ગણોતપટો lease

ganotiyaao *n.* ગણોતિયાઓ tenantry

ganthaaee javun *v.t.* ગંઠાઈ જવું clot

gappan *n.* ગપ્પાં gossip

gappan maaravn *v.t.* ગપ્પાં મારવાં confabulate

gappan maravan *v.i.* ગપ્પાં મારવાં chat

gappu *n.* ગપ્પું fib

gar *n.* ગર pith

gar *n.* ગર pulp

garabad *n.* ગરબડ flurry

garadan *n.* ગરદન. nape

garadan *n.* ગરદન neck

garadanano aaganano bhaag *n.* ગરદનનો આગળનો ભાગ throat

garagadee *n.* ગરગડી pulley

garajavaalun *adj.* ગરજવાળું. necessitous

garajavaalun *adj.* ગરજવાળું needy

garajavun *v.t.* ગરજવું bellow

garakaav karavun *v.t.* ગરકાવ કરવું whelm

garam *adj.* ગરમ fervent

garam kanjee *n.* ગરમ કાંજી caudle

garam paaneeno jharo *n.* ગરમ પાણીનો ઝરો geyser

garama mijaajavaalun *adj.* ગરમ મજિાજવાળું irascible

garamapaaneeno shek *n.* ગરમપાણીનો શેક stupe

garamee aapee aogaalavun *v.t.* ગરમી આપી ઓગાળવું fuse

garamee thee balavun *n.* ગરમીથી બળવું deflagration

garayukt *v.t.* ગરયુક્ત pulpy

garbh *n.* ગર્ભ core

garbh *n.* ગર્ભ foetus

garbh dhaaran karavo *v.t.* ગર્ભ ધારણ કરવો conceive

garbha *n.* ગર્ભ embryo

garbha *adj.* ગર્ભ embryonic

garbhaashay *n.* ગર્ભાશય matrix

garbhaashay *n.* ગર્ભાશય. uterus

garbhaashay *n.* ગર્ભાશય womb

garbhadhaaran *n.* ગર્ભધારણ gestation

garbhadhaarana *n.* ગર્ભધારણા conception

garbhagruh, gabhaaro *n.* ગર્ભગૃહ, ગભારો adytum

garbhanirodhak *adj* ગર્ભનિરોધક contraceptive

garbhapaat karvo *v.* ગર્ભપાત કરવો abort

garbhpaat karaavnarun *adj.* ગર્ભપાત કરાવનારું abortive

gareeb banaavavun *v.t.* ગરીબ બનાવવું impoverish

gareebaaee *n.* ગરીબાઈ poverty

gareebo mateno aashram *n.* ગરીબો માટેનો આશ્રમ workhouse

garjana *n.* ગર્જના roar

garjanaarun *adj.* ગર્જનારું roaring

garjavun *n.* ગર્જવું bluster

garud *n.* ગરુડ eagle

garud jevun *adj.* ગરુડ જેવું aquiline

garudanu bachchu *n.* ગરુડનું બચ્ચુ eaglet

garv *n.* ગર્વ pride

gatagataavavun *v.t.* ગટગટાવવું gulp

gatagataavavun *v.i.* ગટગટાવવું quaff

gataravyavasthaa *n.* ગટરવ્યવસ્થા drainage

gatee vadhaaravee *v.* ગતિ વધારવી accelerate

gateevardhan *n.* ગતિવર્ધન acceleration

gati aapanaarun jor *n.* ગતિ આપનારું જોર impetus

gati avarodhavee *v.t.* ગતિ અવરોધવી retard

gatimaan *adv.* ગતિમાન astir

gatiprerak yanta *n.* ગતિપ્રેરક યંત્ર engine

gatisheel banaavavun *v.t.* ગતિશીલ બનાવવું mobilize

gauan *adj.* ગૌણ ancilliary

gaukhaniyo vidhyaarthee *n.* ગૌખણિયો વદ્દિયાર્થી mug

gaumaans *n.* ગૌમાંસ beef

gaun *adj.* ગૌણ inferior

gaun paadaree *n.* ગૌણ પાદરી deacon

gaurav apaavavun *v.t.* ગૌરવ આપવું dignify

gayaa mahinaanu *n.* ગયા મહિનાનું ultimo

gayun *p.p.* ગયું went

geech *adj.* ગીચ dense

geech jhaadee *n.* ગીચ ઝાડી brake

geech oogelun *adj.* ગીચ ઊગેલું bushy

geecha zaadee *n.* ગીચ ઝાડી thicket

geechataa *n.* ગીચતા density

geechavasteevaalun *n.* ગીચવસ્તીવાળું populous

geedh *n.* ગીધ vulture

geere mukelee vastu ગિરિ મુકેલી વસ્તુ pawn

geero *n.* ગીરો mortgage

geero lenaar *n.* ગીરો લેનાર mortgagee

geero mukelee vastu *n.* ગીરો મુકેલી વસ્તુ pledge

geerodaar *n.* ગીરોદાર pawnee

gendeedado *n.* ગેંડીદડો hockey

gendo *n.* ગેંડો. rhinoceros

geraaabaroon *n.* ગેરઆબરૂ ignominy

gerafaayadaavaalu *adj.* ગેરફાયદાવાળું unprofitable

gerakaanoonee *adj.* ગેરકાનૂની unlawful

gerakaayade *adj.* ગેરકાયદે, illegitimate

gerakaayade *adj.* ગેરકાયદે, નષિદ્દિષ illicit

gerakaayadesar *adj.* ગેરકાયદેસર illegal

geralaabh *n.* ગેરલાભ disadvantage

geralaabh karanaaru *adj.* ગેરલાભ કરનારું disadvantageous

geralaayak ગેરલાયક disqualify

geramaarge doravun *v.t.* ગેરમાર્ગે દોરવું misdirect

gerasamaj *n.* ગેરસમજ misapprehension

gerasamaj *n.* ગેરસમજ misunderstanding

gerasamaj karavee *v.t.* ગેરસમજ કરવી misapprehend

geravaajabee *adj.* ગેરવાજબી indefensible

geravaajabee *adj.* ગેરવાજબી unreasonable

geravalle javun ગેરવલ્લે જવું miscarry

geravyavasthaapan *v.t.* ગેરવ્યવસ્થાપન. mismanage

geravyavsthaa *n.* ગેરવ્યવસ્થા disorder

gerbandhaarneeya *adj.* ગેરબંધારણીય unconsitutional

gerej *n.* ગેરેજ garage

gerhaajar *adj.* ગેરહાજર absent

gerhaajaree *n.* ગેરહાજરી absence

germaarge doravun *v.t.* ગેરમાર્ગે દોરવું misguide

gesomeetar *n.* ગેસોમીટર gasometer

ghaananun fotarun *n.* ધાનનું ફોતરું chaff

ghaas *n.* ઘાસ sedge

ghaas vaadhavun *v.t.* ઘાસ વાઢવું mow

ghaasachaaro *n.* ઘાસચારો grass

ghaasachaaro *n.* ઘાસચારો provender

ghaasalet *n.* ઘાસલેટ kerosene

ghaasanee ganjee *n.* ઘાસની ગંજી hay

ghaasanee ganjee *n.* ઘાસની ગંજી rick

ghaasanee ganjee *n.* ઘાસની ગંજી stack

ghaasanu jangal *n.* ઘાસનું જંગલ savanna

ghaasavaalee jameen *n.* ઘાસવાળી જમીન meadow

ghaasno pato *n.* ઘાસનો પટો swath

ghaat aapavo *v.t.* ઘાટ આપવો mould

ghaat aapavo *v.t.* ઘાટ આપવો prune

ghaataank *n.* ઘાતાંક log

ghaatakee *adj.* ઘાતકી inhuman

ghaatanaukaa *n.* ઘાટનૌકા ferry

Ghaatdaar *adj.* ઘાટદાર shapely

ghadapanni nabalaayee *n.* ઘડપણની નબળાઈ dotage

ghadavun *v.t.* ઘડવું formulate

ghadiyaal *n.* ઘડિયાળ clock
ghadiyaalanun lolak *n.* ઘડિયાળનું લોલક pendulum
Ghadpannee nablaai *n.* ઘડપણની નબળાઈ senility
ghamandee *adj.* ઘમંડી dogmatic
ghamandee *adj.* ઘમંડી haughty
ghamandee *adj.* ઘમંડી overweening
ghan *n.* ઘન cube
ghan vartul *n.* ઘન વર્તુલ globe
ghanaa *prep.* ઘણા umpteen
Ghanee mahenat karnaarun *adj.* ઘણી મહેનત કરનારું strenuous
ghanee motee sankhya *n.* ઘણી મોટી સંખ્યા myriad
ghant *n.* ઘંટ bell
ghantadeeno avaaja thavo *v.i.* ઘંટડીનો અવાજ થવો tinkle
ghantano avaaj karavo *v.t.* ઘંટનો અવાજ કરવો clink
ghantavaalo minaaro *n.* ઘંટવાળો મિનારો belfry
ghanteevaalo *n.* ઘંટીવાળો miller
ghanun *adj.* ઘણું much
ghanun kareene *adv.* ઘણું કરીને mostly
ghanun kareene *adj.* ઘણું કરીને probably
ghanun mahattvanun *adj.* ઘણું મહત્ત્વનું momentous
ghar *n.* ઘર dwelling
ghar *n.* ઘર house
gharaak *n.* ઘરાક client
gharaako *n.* ઘરાકો clientele
gharafodun *n.* ઘરફોડું burglar
gharagathhu bhaashaa *n.* ઘરગથ્થુ ભાષા vernacular
gharano bhaadoot *n.* ઘરનો ભાડૂત tenant
gharbhapaat *n.* ગર્ભપાત abortion
Ghardun thayelun *adj.* ઘરડું થયેલું senescent
gharelu *adj.* ઘરેલુ domestic
gharghatthun *n.* ઘરગથ્થું household
ghasaaro *n.* ઘસારો depreciation
ghasadaatun sarakavun *v.t.* ઘસડાતું સરકવું crawl
ghasadaavun *v.i.* ઘસડાવું drift

ghasadavun *v.t.* ઘસડવું drag
ghasadavun *v.t.* ઘસડવું haul
ghasavun *v.t.* ઘસવું dash
ghasavun *v.t.* ઘસવું rub
ghasavun *v.i.* ઘસવું rush
Ghasdavun *v.t.* ઘસડવું scrawl
ghasee kaadhavun *v.t.* ઘસી કાઢવું erode
ghaseene chalakatun *v.t.* ઘસીને ચળકતું કરવું burnish
ghaseene saaf karavun *n.* ઘસીને સાફ કરવું scour
ghat pooravee *v.t.* ઘટ પૂરવી eke
ghataadavun *v.t.* ઘટાડવું bate
ghataadavun *v.t.* ઘટાડવું minimize
ghataadavun *v.t.* ઘટાડવું reduce
ghataado *n.* ઘટાડો curtailment
ghataado *n.* ઘટાડો diminution
ghatak *n.* ઘટક component
ghatak *adj.* ઘટક constituent
ghatak dravy *n.* ઘટક દ્રવ્ય ingredient
ghatana *n.* ઘટના affair
ghatana *n.* ઘટના incident
ghatavun *n.* ઘટવું decrease
ghatavun *v.i.* ઘટવું dwindle
Ghatnaa sthal *n.* ઘટના સ્થળ scene
ghatt banaavavun *v.t.* ઘટ્ટ બનાવવું condense
ghatt taarajaalee *n.* ઘટ્ટ તારજાળી wire-gauze
ghaun *n.* ઘઉ wheat
ghenamaa *adj.* ઘેનમાં drowsy
ghenamaa hovun *v.t.* ઘેનમાં હોવું doze
ghenanee davaa *n.* ઘેનની દવા heroin
ghenanee davaa *adj.* ઘેનની દવા narcotic
gher ravaana karavun *adj.* ઘેર રવાના કરવું invalid
gheravun *v.t.* ઘેરવું gird
gheree levun *v.t.* ઘેરી લેવું beset
ghero *n.* ઘેરો siege
ghero ghaalavo *v.t.* ઘેરો ઘાલવો beleaguer
ghero vaadalee rang *n.* ઘેરો વાદળી રંગ indigo
ghetaano vaado *n.* ઘેટાંનો વાડો fold

ghetaanun bachchun *n.* ઘેટાનું બચ્ચું lamb

ghetanbakaraannun maans *n.* ઘેટાંબકરાનું માંસ. mutton

Ghetanno vaado *n.* ઘેટાંનો વાડો sheep-cote

ghetee *n.* ઘેટી ewe

gheto *n.* ઘેટો ram

Ghetun *n.* ઘેટું sheep

ghoda par besanaar *n.* ઘોડા પર બેસનાર rider

ghoda par besavun *v.t.* ઘોડા પર બેસવું ride

ghodaadalano sipaai *n.* ઘોડાદળનો સિપાઈ lancer

ghodaagaadee *n.* ઘોડાગાડી buggy

ghodaagaadee haankanaaro *n.* ઘોડાગાડી હાંકનારો coachman

ghodaana jeetano pato *n.* ઘોડાના જીતનો પટો girth

ghodaane saaj *n.* ઘોડાને સાજ harness

ghodaanee chaal *v.* ઘોડાનીચાલ amble

ghodaapoor *n.* ઘોડાપૂર deluge

ghodaapoor sambandhit *adj.* ઘોડાપૂર સંબંધિત diluvial

ghodadalano sainik *n.* ઘોડદળનો સૈનિક dragoon

ghodadoa *n.* ઘોડદોડ race-course

ghodanu vachheru, *n.* ઘોડાનું વછેરું foal

ghodee *n.* ઘોડી rack

ghodesavaar sainik *n.* ઘોડેસવાર સૈનિક trooper

ghodesavaar senaa *n.* ઘોડેસવાર સેના cavalry

ghodesavaarano bhaalo *n.* ઘોડેસવારનો ભાલો lance

ghodesavaaree *n.* ઘોડેસવારી riding

ghodesavaareeman kabel *n.* ઘોડેસવારીમાં કાબેલ horseman

ghodesavaaronun saraghas *n.* ઘોડેસવારોનું સરઘસ cavalcade

ghodiyaaghar *n.* ઘોડિયાઘર creche

ghodo *n.* ઘોડો ambler

ghogharo avaaj *v.t.* ઘોઘરો અવાજ croak

ghogharo saad *v.t.* ઘોઘરો સાદ burr

ghonchavun *v.t.* ઘોંચવું prod

ghonghaat *n.* ઘોંઘાટ clamour

ghoodee *n.* ઘોડી mare

ghoommat *n.* ઘુમ્મટ dome

ghoontado bharavo *v.t.* ઘૂંટડો ભરવો sip

ghoontaniye padavun *v.i.* ઘૂંટણિયે પડવું kneel

ghor andhaaraavaalun *adj.* ઘોર અંધારાવાળું murky

Ghorvun te *v.i.* ઘોરવું તે snore

Ghranendriya *n.* ઘ્રાણેન્દ્રિય smell

ghurakavun *n.* ઘુરકવું growl

ghuvad *n.* ઘુવડ owl

gitaarana jevun ek vaadhya *n.* ગિટારના જેવું એક વાદ્ય banjo

giyar *n.* ગીયર gear

glaani *n.* ગ્લાનિ dejection

glisareen *n.* ગ્લિસરીન glycerine

glukoz *n.* ગ્લુકોઝ glucose

gnaan *n.* જ્ઞાન knowledge

gnaanatantu *n.* જ્ઞાનતંતુ nerve

gnaankosh *n.* જ્ઞાનકોશ encyclopedia

gnaati *n.* જ્ઞાતિ caste

gochar ગોચર pasturage

godadun *n.* ગોદડું quilt

godee *n.* ગોદી dock

godo maaravo *n.* ગોદો મારવો poke

gokalagaay *n.* ગોકળગાય snail

gokhalo *n.* ગોખલો niche

gokhanapattee *n.* ગોખણપટ્ટી rote

gokhanapattee karanaarun *n.* ગોખણપટ્ટી કરનારું crammer

gol *adj.* ગોળ round

gol *n.* ગોળ treacle

gol gol bolavuu te *n.* ગોળ ગોળ બોલવું તે circumlocution

gol kaankaree *v.t.* ગોળ કાંકરી cobble

gol khadak *n.* ગોળ ખડક boulder

gol leeso kaankaro *n.* ગોળ લીસો કાંકરો pebble

gol orado *n.* ગોળ ઓરડો rotunda

gol topee *n.* ગોળ ટોપી bonnet

gola faravu *v.t.* ગોળ ફરવું turn

golaakaar *n.* ગોળાકાર circular

Golaakaar *adj.* ગોળાકાર spherical

golaardh *n.* ગોળાર્ધ hemisphere

golamatol *adj.* ગોળમટોળ plump

golandaaj *n.* ગોલંદાજ bowler

golandaajee *n.* ગોલંદાજી bowling

golanee rasee *n.* ગોળની રસી molasses

golee *n.* ગોળી pellet

golee maaravee *n.* ગોળી મારવી shoot

goleebaar *n.* ગોળીબાર shooting

goleeya padaarth *n.* ગોળીય પદાર્થ spheroid

golfanee ramat *n.* ગોલ્ફની રમત golf

golo *n.* ગોળો bulb

Golo *n.* ગોળો sphere

gomed *n.* ગોમેદ agate

goodh *adj.* ગૂઢ abstruse

goodh *adj.* ગૂઢ inscrutable

goodh baabat *n.* ગૂઢ બાબત mystery

goodhaarthavaalun *adj.* ગૂઢાર્થવાળું cryptic

googlee *n.* ગૂગલી googly

gooma thai javun *adj.* ગૂમ થઈ જવું trackless

goomadun *n.* ગૂમડું blain

goonapaat *n.* ગૂણપાટ hessian

goonapaat *n.* ગૂણપાટ sackcloth

Goonch *v.i.* ગૂંચ snarl

goonch ukelavee *adj.* ગૂંચ ઉકેલવી extricable

goonch ukelavee *v.t.* ગૂંચ ઉકેલવી extricate

goonchalun *n.* ગૂંચળું gyrus

goonchavaado *n.* ગૂંચવાડો confusion

goonchavan bharelun *adj.* ગૂંચવણ ભરેલું intricate

goonchavanaman naakhavun *v.t.* ગૂંચવણમાં નાખવું muddle

goonchavanmaan naakhavun *v.t.* ગૂંચવણમાં નાખવું baffle

goonchavavu *v.t.* ગૂંચવવું tangle

goonchavavun *v.t.* ગૂંચવવું ravel

goonchavee naakhavun *v.t.* ગૂંચવી નાખવું confuse

goondelee kanak *n.* ગૂંદેલી કણક dough

goongalaavavaun *v.t.* ગૂંગળાવવું asphyxlate

goongalaavavun *v.t.* ગૂંગળાવવું choke

goongalaavavun *v.t.* ગૂંગળાવવું stifle

Goonglaaman *n.* ગૂંગળામણ suffocation

Goonglaavvun *v.t.* ગૂંગળાવવું suffocate

Goonglaavvvun ગૂંગળાવવું smother

goonthavun *v.t.* ગૂંથવું knit

goonthela vaal *n.* ગૂંથેલા વાળ braid

goonthelee cheejo *n.* ગૂંથેલી ચીજો hosiery

gopakaavy *n.* ગોપકાવ્ય idyll

gopaneey *adj.* ગોપનીય secretive

gotaalo karavo *v.t.* ગોટાળો કરવો jumble

gothavan *v.t.* ગોઠવણ adjustment

gothavavun *v.t.* ગોઠવવું adjust

gothiyo *n.* ગોઠિયો playmate

Gothun khaavu *v.i.* ગોથું ખાવું stumble

govaalan *n.* ગોવાલણ milkmaid

govaaliyo *n.* ગોવાળિયો wrangler

graahak *n.* ગ્રાહક customer

graahakoni yaadee *n.* ગ્રાહકોની યાદી directory

graahya, sveekaary *adj.* ગ્રાહ્ય, સ્વીકાર્ય admissible

graamin, anaghad *adj.* ગ્રામીણ, અણઘડ agrestic

grah *n.* ગ્રહ asteroid

grah *n.* ગ્રહ planet

grahan *n.* ગ્રહણ eclipse

grahan *adj.* ગહન recondite

grahan chhaayaa *n.* ગ્રહણ છાયા umbra

grahan karanaar *n.* ગ્રહણ કરનાર recipient

grahanashakti *n.* ગ્રહણશક્તિ perception

grahanasheel *adj.* ગ્રહણશીલ receptive

grahanee bhramanakaksha *n.* ગ્રહની ભ્રમણકક્ષા orbit

grahanee kaksha *n.* ગ્રહની કક્ષા node

Grahanksham *adj.* ગ્રહણક્ષમ susceptible

gram *n.* ગ્રામ gramme

gramophon *n.* ગ્રામોફોન gramophone

granth *n.* ગ્રંથ scripture

granthaalay *n.* ગ્રંથાલય library

granthasoochi *n.* ગ્રંથસૂચિ bibliography

granthee *n.* ગ્રંથી gland
granthkeet *n.* ગ્રંથકીટ bookworm
gruhamaataa *n.* ગૃહમાતા matron
gruhapati *adj.* ગૃહપતિ warden
gruheet dharavun *v.t.* ગૃહીત ધરવું presume
gruheet siddhaant *n.* ગૃહીત સદ્ધિાન્ત postulate
gruhinee *n.* ગૃહણિી housewife
gsarvavidhyaasangrah *n.* સર્વવદ્યિાસંગ્રહ cyclopaedia
gubbaaro *n.* ગુબ્બારો, balloon
guchchho *n.* ગુચ્છો tuft
gudaamaan naakhavaanee sogati *n.* ગુદામાં નાંખવાની સોગટી suppository
gufa *n.* ગુફા cave
gufaa *n.* ગુફા den
gufaana jevee rachana *n.* ગુફાના જેવી રચના grotto
Gujaran *n.* ગુજરાન sustenance
gulaabano chhod *n.* ગુલાબનો છોડ rose
gulaabavaadee *n.* ગુલાબવાડી rosary
gulaabee *n.* ગુલાબી pink
gulaabee ranganun *adj.* ગુલાબી રંગનું roseate
gulaam *adj.* ગુલામ dormant
Gulaam *n.* ગુલામ slave
gulaam *n.* ગુલામ thrall
gulaamee *n.* ગુલામી bondage
Gulaamee *n.* ગુલામી servitude
gulaamee *n.* ગુલામી thraldom
Gulaamee dashaa *n.* ગુલામી દશા servility
Gulaamee vrutinun *adj.* ગુલામી વૃત્તનિું servile
Gulaamee(nee dashaa) *n.* ગુલામી(ની દશા) slavery
Gulaameenee vrutivaalun *adj.* ગુલામીની વૃત્તવિાળું slavish
gulaamnee jem vartavun *v.i.* ગુલામની જેમ વર્તવું truckle
gulaamono vepaaree *n.* ગુલામોનો વેપારી slaver
gumaavelun *adj.* ગુમાવેલું lost
gun gaava *v.t.* ગુણ ગાવા extol
gunaahit *adj.* ગુનાહતિ guilty

gunaakaar *n.* ગુણાકાર multiplication
gunaashodhak *n.* ગુનાશોધક detective
gunaavignan *n.* ગુનાવજ્ઞિાન criminology
gunadharm *n.* ગુણધર્મ quality
gunadharmanee drashtee *adj.* ગુણધર્મની દ્રષ્ટીએ qualitative
gunadoshavivechan *n.* ગુણદોષવિચન criticism
gunapaat *n.* ગુણપાટ gunny
gunavaachak visheshan *n.* ગુણવાચક વશિેષણ epithet
gunavatta *n.* ગુણવત્તા gradation
gunavattaa *n.* ગુણવત્તા endowment
gunavattaa ghataadavee *n.* ગુણવત્તા ઘટાડવી debasement
gunchavaayelu *n.* ગૂંચવાયેલું disarry
gunchavavun *v.t.* ગૂંચવવું bewilder
gunchavavun *v.t.* ગૂંચવવું puzzle
gundar *n.* ગુંદર glue
gundar *n.* ગુંદર gum
gundharma ferfaar *n.* ગુણધર્મ ફેરફાર denature
gunegaar *adj.* ગુનેગાર criminal
gunegaar jaaher karavun *v.t.* ગુનેગાર જાહેર કરવું convict
gunjaash *n.* ગુંજાશ scope
gunjaash hovee *v.* ગુંજાશ હોવી afford
gunkaarak *adj.* ગુણકારક efficacious
guno *n.* ગુનો crime
gunottar *n.* ગુણોત્તર ratio
gunthelun jaakit *n.* ગૂંથેલું જાકિટ jersey
gupt *n.* ગુપ્ત covert
gupt *adj.* ગુપ્ત privy
Gupta *n.* ગુપ્ત secret
Gupta raakhvun te *n.* ગુપ્ત રાખવું તે secrecy
guptataa *n.* ગુપ્તતા concealment
guru grah *n.* ગુરુ ગ્રહ jupiter
gurutvaakarshan *n.* ગુરુત્વાકર્ષણ gravitation
gurutvaakarshan *n.* ગુરુત્વાકર્ષણ gravity
guruvaara *n.* ગુરુવાર thursday
gusapus bolavun *v.i.* ગુસપુસ બોલવું whisper

gussaanun kaaran *n.* ગુસ્સાનું કારણ provocation

gusse karavun *v.t.* ગુસ્સે કરવું enrage

gusse karavun ગુસ્સે કરવું infuriate

gusse karavun *v.t.* ગુસ્સે કરવું vex

Gusse thavun *v.i.* ગુસ્સે થવું sulk

gusse thayelun *adj.* ગુસ્સે થયેલું wroth

gusso santusht karavo *v.t.* ગુસ્સો સંતુષ્ટ કરવો wreak

gusso, krodh *n.* ગુસ્સો, ક્રોધ anger

gyaan kautukee *n.* જ્ઞાન કૌતુકી amateur

gyaan maryaada *v.t.* જ્ઞાન મર્યાદા ken

H

ha *adv.* હા ay

haa *adv.* હા yea

haa *adv.* હા yes

haadakaavaalun *adj.* હાડકાવાળું osseous

haadakun *n.* હાડકું bone

haadakun kaapavaanee karavat હાડકું કાપવાની કરવત trepan

haadavaid *n.* હાડવૈદ bone-setter

Haadpinjar *n.* હાડપિંજર skeleton

haajar *adj.* હાજર present

haajar javaab *n.* હાજર જવાબ repartee

haajaree *n.* હાજરી attendance

haajaree *n.* હાજરી presence

haajaree *n.* હાજરી roll-call

haajaree patrak *n.* હાજરી પત્રક musterroll

haal *adv.* હાલ now

haalaakee *n.* હાલાકી privation

haalachaal *n.* હાલચાલ locomotion

haalaradun *n.* હાલરડું lullaby

Haale nahee evun *n.* હાલે નહિ એવું stable

haanfatun *adj.* હાંફતું breathless

haanfavun *v.t.* હાંફવું gasp

haanfavun *v.t.* હાંફવું pant

Haani *n.* હાનિ damage

haanikaarak *adj.* હાનિકારક baleful

haanikaarak *adj.* હાનિકારક malign

haanikaarak *adj.* હાનિકારક noxious

haankavun *n.* હાંકવું drive

haankavun *v.t.* હાંકવું propel

haankee kaadhavun *n.* હાંકી કાઢવું sack

haansadee *n.* હાંસડી collarbone

haansiyo *n.* હાંસિયો margin

haar *n.* હાર wreath

haar, toran *n.* હાર, તોરણ garland

haarabandh gothavavun *v.t.* હારબંધ ગોઠવવું range

haarabandh sainiko *n.* હારબંધ સૈનિકો rank

haasy *n.* હાસ્ય laughter

haasyaaspad *adj.* હાસ્યાસ્પદ ludicrous

haasyaaspad *adj* હાસ્યાસ્પદ ridiculous

haasyaaspad vidhi *n.* હાસ્યાસ્પદ વિધિ mummery

haasyajanak nakal *n.* હાસ્યજનક નકલ burlesque

haasyajanakata *n.* હાસ્યજનકતા humour

haasyavinod *n.* હાસ્યવિનોદ mirth

haath *n.* હાથ arm

haath *n.* હાથ hand

haath neecheno maanas *n.* હાથ નીચેનો માણસ underling

Haath nichenun *n.* હાથ નીચેનું subordinate

haath vatee karelun *adj.* હાથ વતી કરેલું manual

haathaa vagaranee bethak *n.* હાથા વગરની બેઠક stool

haathaavaalee khurashee *n.* હાથાવાળી ખુરશી arm-chair

haathagaadee *n.* હાથગાડી barrow

haathakadee *n.* હાથકડી fetters

haathakadee *n.* હાથકડી handcuffs

haathakadee *n.* હાથકડી manacle

haathanun kaandun *n.* હાથનું કાંડું wrist

haathapag khenchaava *n.* હાથપગ ખેંચાવા cramp

haatharoomaal *n.* હાથરૂમાલ handkerchief

haatharoomaal *n.* હાથરૂમાલ kerchief

haathee *n.* હાથી elephant

haathee *n.* હાથી tusk

haatheedaant *n.* હાથીદાંત ivory

haatho *n.* હાથો handle

haau *n.* હાઉ chimera

habasee *n.* હબસી. negro

habasee *n.* હબસી nigger

had *v.t.* હદ march

had, gheraavo *n.* હદ, ઘેરાવો ambit

hadahadatun *adj.* હડહડતું arrant

hadahadatun *adj.* હડહડતું blatant

hadakava *n.* હડકવા hydrophobia

hadapaaree *n.* હદપારી banishment

hadapachee *n.* હડપચી chin

hadapinjar *n.* હાડપિંજર carcass

Hadselo *v.t.* હડસેલો shove

hadtaal todnaar *n.* હડતાલ તોડનાર blackleg

haidrojan *n.* હાઇડ્રોજન hydrogen

hajaam *n.* હજામ barber

hajee vihyamaan *adj.* હજી વિધ્યમાન extant

hajooriyo *n.* હજૂરિયો waiter

hajooriyo *n.* હજૂરિયો waitress

hakaalapattee *n.* હકાલપટ્ટી expulsion

hakaaraatmak, bhaavdarshak હકારાત્મક, ભાવદર્શક affirmative

hakadaar *adj.* હકદાર eligible

hakanun *adj.* હકનું rightful

hakasaaee *n.* હકસાઈ perquisite

hakeekat *n.* હકીકત fact

hakkapatrak *n.* હક્કપત્રક chart

hal *v.i.* હળ plough

halaavavun *v.t.* હલાવવું move

Halaavvun ke haalvun *v.t.* હલાવવું કે હાલવું shake

haladara *n.* હળદર. turmeric

halakaaee *n.* હલકાઈ abjectness

halakat *n.* હલકટ ribald

halakat maanas *n.* હલકટ માણસ. louse

halakatapanun *n.* હલકટપણું turpitude

halako abhipraay *n.* હલકો અભિપ્રાય underrate

halaku paadavun *v.t.* હલકું પાડવું demean

halakun *adj.* હલકું abject

halakun *adj.* હલકું, base

halakun *v.t.* હલકું belittle

halakun *adj.* હલકું menial

halakun paadavun *v.* હલકું પાડવું humiliate

halakun paadavun *v.t.* હલકું પાડવું lower

halavee taapalee *n.* હળવી ટાપલી rap

Halavee Thaapad *v.t.* હળવી થાપડ dab

halavethee *v.t.* હળવેથી toss

halavo badaamee rang *adj.* હળવો બદામી રંગ hazel

halavo ganagan avaaj *n.* હળવો ગણગણ અવાજ coo

halavo zapaato *n.* હળવો ઝપાટો flick

halavun karavun *v.t.* હળવું કરવું lighten

Halensanee jodmaanu ek *n.* હલેસાંની જોડમાંનું એક scull

halesan maaranaar *n.* હલેસાં મારનાર oarsman

halesan maaravan *v.t.* હલેસાં મારવા paddle

halesun *n.* હલેસું oar

halkat *n.* હલકટ scurvy

Halkat *v.i.* હલકટ sneak

hamanan *adv.* હમણાં presently

hamanan hamanan *adv.* હમણાં હમણાં recently

hammesha, satat *adv.* હંમેશાં, સતત forever

hanahanavun *v.t.* હણહણવું neigh

hankaaravun *n.* હંકારવું steerage

hanmesha, sarvada *adv.* હંમેશાં, સર્વદા always

hanmeshaan હંમેશાં aye

hanmeshanun *adj.* હંમેશનું quotidian

hans હંસ gander

hans *n.* હંસ goose

hapato *n.* હપતો instalment

haraajeeman bolee *n.* હરાજીમાં બોલી bidding

Haraamkhor *n.* હરામખોર scamp

Haraamkhor *n.* હરામખોર scapegrace

Haraamkhor *n.* હરામખોર scoundrel

haraavavun *v.t.* હરાવવું checkmate

haraavavun *v.t.* હરાવવું discomfit

haraavavun *v.t.* હરાવવું overpower

harakh *n.* હરખ joy

haran *n.* હરણ deer

haran *n.* હરણ reindeer

harananee maadaa *n.* હરણની માદા. doe

harananor nar *n.* હરણનો નર hart

harananu bachchu *n.* હરણનું બચ્ચું fawn

harananun maans *n.* હરણનું માંસ venison

harasanun darad *n.* હરસનું દરદ piles

harataal *n.* હરતાલ orpiment

Haree javun હારી જવું succumb

hareef *n.* હરીફ competitor

hareef *n.* હરીફ rival

hareefaaee *n.* હરીફાઈ competition

hareefaaee *n.* હરીફાઈ rivalry

hareefaaee karavee *v.i.* હરીફાઈ કરવી compete

hareephaaimaa jeetanaar *n.* હરીફાઈમાં જીતનાર victor

hariyaalee *n.* હરિયાળી greenery

hariyaalee હરિયાળી verdure

Hariyaalee(no tukdo) *n.* હરિયાળી(નો ટુકડો) sod

harshghelun *adj.* હરષઘેલું. jubilant

hasaavanaar vyakti *n.* હસાવનાર વ્યક્તિ comedian

hasanaarun *adj.* હસનારું risible

hasatun *adj.* હસતું merry

hasavun *v.t.* હસવું laugh

hashe *adv.* હશે shall

hastaakshar *n.* હસ્તાક્ષર handwriting

Hastaakshar *n.* હસ્તાક્ષર script

hastaantar karavun *n.* હસ્તાંતર કરવું cession

hastalikhit *n.* હસ્તલિખિત manuscript

hastarekhaashaastr *n.* હસ્તરેખાશાસ્ત્ર palmistry

hastarekhaashaastree *n.* હસ્તરેખાશાસ્ત્રી palmist

hastaudhyog *n.* હસ્તઉદ્યોગ handicraft

hastkshep karavo *v.i.* હસ્તક્ષેપ કરવો meddle

hastkshepee *adj.* હસ્તક્ષેપી meddlesome

Hasvun *v.i.* હસવું smile

hasyotpaak *n.* હાસ્યોત્પાદ humorous

hata *p.p.* હતા were

hataash *adj.* હતાશ downcast

hataashaa *n.* હતાશા despondency

hataashaa *n.* હતાશા frustration

Hath neechenu *adj.* હાથ નીચેનું subaltern

hathaagrahee *n.* હઠાગ્રહી doctrinaire

hatheelaapanun *n.* હઠીલાપણું obstinacy

hatheelun *adj.* હઠીલું intractable

hatheelun *adj.* હઠીલું obstinate

hatheelun *adj.* હઠીલું recalcitrant

hatheelun *adj.* હઠીલું refractory

Hatheelun *adj.* હઠીલું stubborn

hathelee *n.* હથેલી palm

Hathiyaar *n.* હથિયાર staff

hathiyaar *n.* હથિયાર, weapon

hathiyaar vagarnu *n.* હથિયાર વગરનું unarmed

hathodee *n.* હથોડી hammer

hathodo *n.* હથોડો mallet

hatosaahit karavun *adj.* હતોત્સાહિત dejected

hatun *p.p.* હતું was

hatyaa *n.* હત્યા assassination

hatyaakaand *n.* હત્યાકાંડ massacre

havaa *n.* હવા air

havaa kaadhavee *v.t.* હવા કાઢવી deflate

havaa pamp *n.* હવા પંપ air-pump

havaa ujaasvaalun *adj.* હવા ઉજાસવાળું airy

havaadaar *adj.* હવાદાર breezy

havaaee chhatree *n.* હવાઈ છત્રી parachute

havaaee mathak *n.* હવાઈ મથક aerodrome

havaaee tapaal *n.* હવાઈ ટપાલ airmail

havaaee vahaan *n.* હવાઈ વહાણ airship

havaamaan *n.* હવામાન weather

havaamaanashaastr *n.* હવામાનશાસ્ત્ર meteorology

havaanu dabaan *n.* હવાનું દબાણ depression

Havaanun tofaan *n.* હવાનું તોફાન storm

Havaaujaas vinaanun *adj.* હવાઉજાસ વિનાનું stuffy

havaavaalun *adj.* હવાવાળું pneumatic

havaee jahaaj *n.* હવાઈ જહાજ aircraft

havasakhor maanas *n.* હવસખોર માણસ satyr

have pachhee *adv.* હવે પછી forth

have pachhee thanarun *adj.* હવે પછી થનારું would-be

havethee *adv.* હવેથી henceforth

hayadrolic *adj.* હાયડ્રોલિક hydraulic

hedakee *n.* હેડકી hiccup

heejarat *n.* હિજરત exodus

heenata *n.* હીનતા inferiority

heero *n.* હીરો diamond

helicoptar *n.* હેલિકોપ્ટર helicopter

helo હેલો hallo

heraan karavun *v.t.* હેરાન કરવું bother

heraan karavun *v.t.* હેરાન કરવું drat

herata pamaadavun *v.t.* હેરત પમાડવું astound

hetu *adj.* હેતુ intent

hetu *n.* હેતુ intention

hetupoorvak *adj.* હેતુપૂર્વક purposely

hetupoorvak karelun *adj.* હેતુપૂર્વક કરેલું wilful

hevaan jevun vartan *n.* હેવાન જેવું વર્તન beastliness

hevaaniyat *n.* હેવાનિયત barbarity

hileeyam *n.* હલીયમ helium

himaayat, tarafadaaree *n.* હિમાયત, તરફદારી advocacy

himanadee *n.* હિમનદી glacier

himmat khovee *v.t.* હિમત ખોવી dismay

himshilaa *n.* હિમશિલા avalanche

hin maanas, dhor હીન માણસ, ઢોર albino

hindano vatanee *n.* હિન્દનો વતની indian

Hindi lashkree sipaai *n.* હિન્દી લશ્કરી સિપાઈ sepoy

hinmat *n.* હિમત. boldness

hinmat *n.* હિમત courage

hinmat *n.* હિમત mettle

hinmat aapavee *v.t.* હિમત આપવી hearten

hinmatavaan *adj.* હિમતવાન courageous

hinsaa *n.* હિંસા violence

hinsak *adj.* હિંસક fiercely

hinsak *n.* હિંસક violent

hisaab *n.* હિસાબ aud'it

hisaab *v.t.* હિસાબ tally

hisaab tapaasanee *n.* હિસાબ તપાસણી audition

hisaab tapaasanees *n.* હિસાબ તપાસનીસ auditor

hisaabanee khaataavahee *n.* હિસાબની ખાતાવહી ledger

hisaabanees *n.* હિસાબનીસ book-keeper

hisabanis, muneem *n.* હિસાબનીસ, મુનીમ accountant

hisso *n.* હિસ્સો lot

Hisso *n.* હિસ્સો share

histereeyaagrasta *adj.* હિસ્ટેરીયાગ્રસ્ત hysteric

hitakaaree *adj.* હિતકારી benevolent

hitakaareevruti *n.* હિતકારીવૃત્તિ benevolence

hodakun *n.* હોડકું canoe

hoddedaar *n.* હોદ્દેદાર dignitary

hoddedaar *n.* હોદ્દેદાર functionary

hoddo *n.* હોદ્દો designation

hodee *n.* હોડી bark

hodee *n.* હોડી barque

hodee *n.* હોડી boat

hodee *v.i.* હોડી punt

hodee nu tootak *n.* હોડીનું તૂતક deck

hokaayantra *v.t.* હોકાયંત્ર compass

holavaai gayelu *adj.* હોલવાઈ ગયેલું extinct

holavaavun *n.* હોલવાવું extinction

Holeenu naaliyer *n.* હોળીનું નાળિયેર scapegoat

honaarat *n.* હોનારત disaster

honshiyaar *adj.* હોશિયાર clever

honshiyaaree *n.* હોશિયારી cleverness

hoonf *n.* હૂંફ warmth

hoonfaalun *adj.* હૂંફાળું cosy
hoonfavaalun *adv.* હૂંફવાળું warmly
hoshiyaar *adj.* હોશિયાર intelligent
Hoshiyaar *adj.* હોશિયાર smart
Hoshiyaaree *n.* હોશિયારી sleight
hoshiyaareethee taalavun *v.t.* હોશિયારીથી ટાળવું elude
hotalano baal nokar *n.* હોટલનો બાળ નોકર page
hoth *n.* હોઠ lip
hothorn'no teto *n.* હોથોર્ન'નો ટેટો haw
hovaano dhong karavo *v.t.* હોવાનો ઢોંગ કરવો impersonate
hovun *v.i.* હોવું be
hovun *n.* હોવું being
hovun *v.i.* હોવું exist
hoya tevun હોય તેવું TRUE
hridayasparshee *adj.* હૃદયસ્પર્શી touching
hrushtapushta *adj.* હૃષ્ટપુષ્ટ strapping
hufanlun *n.* હુંફાળું unction
hukam *v.t.* હુકમ warrant
hukam karavo *v.t.* હુકમ કરવો dictate
hukam naa maanavo *v.i.* હુકમ ન માનવો disobey
hukamanaamu *n.* હુકમનામું decree
hukamanu paanun *n.* હુકમનું પાનું trump card
hulaamanun naam *n.* હુલામણું નામ by-name
hullad *n.* હુલ્લડ riot
hullad *n.* હુલ્લડ uproar
humalaakhor *n.* હુમલાખોર assailant
humalo *n.* હુમલો foray
humalo *n.* હુમલો attack
humalo karavo *v.t.* હુમલો કરવો pounce
humalo karavon *v.t.* હુમલો કરવો assault
hun - he - henee - bolyun *n.* હું - તે - તેણી - બોલ્યું quoth
hun padun darshaavavun *v.t.* હું પદં દર્શાવવું domineer
hunfaalun *adj.* હુંફાળું warm
huryo bolaavavo *v.i.* હુર્યો બોલાવવો hoot
hystpust *adj.* હૃષ્ટપુષ્ટ chubby

I

Imaarat ke vahaan uplo bhaag *n.* ઈમારત કે વહાણનો ઉપલો ભાગ superstructure
imaaratee laakadun *n.* ઈમારતી લાકડું timber
indaani safedi *n.* ઈંડાની સફેદી albumen
Indraneel Mani *n.* ઈન્દ્રનીલ મણિ sapphire
indu *n.* ઈંડું egg
Iraadaapurvak bhaangfod *n.* ઈરાદાપૂર્વકની ભાંગફોડ sabotage
ishvara athavaa deva *pref.* ઈશ્વર અથવા દેવ theo
ishvaranaa astitvane lagatu shaastra *n.* ઈશ્વરના અસ્તિત્વને લગતું શાસ્ત્ર theology
ishvaravaadee *n.* ઈશ્વરવાદી theist
istar *n.* ઈસ્ટર easter
itaalik aksharo *n.pl.* ઈટાલિક અક્ષરો italics

J

Jaadaa Barchhat vaalvaalun *adj.* જાડા બરછટ વાળવાળું shaggy
jaadaai *n.* જાડાઈ thickness
jaadiyaanvaalee jameen *n.* જડિયાંવાળી જમીન turf
jaadoogar *n.* જાદૂગર juggler
jaadu *n.* જાદૂ magic
jaadu karavun *v.t.* જાદૂ કરવું enchant
jaaduee vidya *n.* જાદુઈ વિદ્યા witchery
jaadugar *n.* જાદૂગર charmer
jaadugar *n.* જાદૂગર conjurer
jaadugar *n.* જાદૂગર magician
jaadun *adj.* જાડું portly
jaadun *adj.* જાડું thick
jaadun *adj.* જાડું unctuous
jaadun karavun *v.t.* જાડું કરવું thicken

Jaaduno mantra *v.i.* જાદુનો મંત્ર spell

Jaadutonaanee kriyaa *n.* જાદુટોણાની ક્રિયા sorcery

jaadutono જાદુટોણો incantation

Jaadutono karnaar bhoovo *n.* જાદુટોણો કરનાર ભૂવો sorcerer

jaafaree *n.* જાફરી lattice

jaagarook *adj.* જાગરૂક watchful

jaagavun *v.t.* જાગવું awake

jaagavun *v.t.* જાગવું waken

jaageer *n.* જાગીર manor

jaageerne lagatun *adj.* જાગીરને લગતું feudal

jaagrat *adj.* જાગ્રત wakeful

jaagrat karanaar avaaj *n.* જાગ્રત કરનાર અવાજ clarion

jaagrut *v.t.* જાગ્રત bestir

jaaher asveekrutee *n.* જાહેર અસ્વીકૃતિ disclaimer

jaaher karavun *v.t.* જાહેર કરવું announce

jaaher karavun *v.t.* જાહેર કરવું declare

jaaher karavun *v.t.* જાહેર કરવું enunciate

jaaher karavun *v.t.* જાહેર કરવું proclaim

jaaher karavun *v.t.* જાહેર કરવું ventilate

jaaher khabar *n.* જાહેરખબર advertisement

Jaaher na thavaa devun *n.* જાહેર ન થવા દેવું suppression

jaaher nivedan, sandesho *n.* જાહેર નિવેદન, સંદેશો announcement

jaaher smaranotsav *v.t.* જાહેર સ્મરણોત્સવ commemoration

Jaaher tamaasho *n.* જાહેર તમાશો spectacle

jaaher utsav *n.* જાહેર ઉત્સવ pageant

jaaher vyaakhyaan *n.* જાહેર વ્યાખ્યાન prelate

jaaheraat *n.* જાહેરાત declaration

jaaheraat *n.* જાહેરાત enunciation

jaaheraat *n.* જાહેરાત proclamation

jaaheraat karavee *v.* જાહેરાત કરવી advertise

jaaheraman vihaar *n.* જાહેરમાં વિહાર promenade

jaahernaamu *n.* જાહેરનામુ manifesto

jaakeet *n.* જાકીટ jacket

jaal *n.* જાળ net

jaal *n.* જાળ trawl

jaalamaa fasaavavun જાળમાં ફસાવવું entangle

jaalaman pakadavun *v.t.* જાળમાં પકડવું mesh

jaalee *n.* જાળી grid

jaaleenee sagadee *n.* જાળીની સગડી grill

jaaleeno kathero *n.* જાળીનો કઠેરો grating

jaamafal *n.* જામફળ guava

jaameen *n.* જામીન bail

jaameenakhat *n.* જામીનખત guarantee

jaan *n.* જાણ intimation

jaanakaaree *n.* જાણકારી information

jaanbudiyo rang *adj.* જાંબુડિયો રંગ purple

jaanee dost *n.* જાની દોસ્ત crony

jaaneejoeene *adv.* જાણીજોઈને knowingly

jaangh *n.* જાંઘ thigh

jaanhaani *n.* જાનહાનિ casualty

jaansachidhdhee *n.* જાંસાચઢિઢી blackmail

jaanyuaaree mahino *n.* જાન્યુઆરી મહિનો. january

jaapaanano baadashaah *n.* જાપાનનો બાદશાહ mikado

jaapaanee chalanano ekam *n.* જાપાની ચલણનો એકમ yen

jaasoos *n.* જાસૂસ emissary

jaasoosee *adj.* જાસૂસી eminet

jaasoosee *n.* જાસૂસી espial

jaasoosee *n.* જાસૂસી espionage

jaasusee kutaro *n.* જાસૂસી કૂતરો bloodhound

Jaat *n.* જાત sort

jaatanun yantr *n.* તાંતણા છૂટા પાડનારું એક જાતનું યંત્ર willow

jaati *n.* જાતિ kind

jaati *n.* જાતિ species

Jaatjaatnun parchooran *adj.* જાતજાતનું પરચૂરણ sundry

jaatraalun *n.* જાત્રાળું pilgrim

jaatraauono sangh *n.* જાત્રાળુઓનો સંઘ caravan

jabaradastee *n.* જબરદસ્તી coercion

jabaradastee *n.* જબરદસ્તી compulsion

jabaradastee karavee *v.t.* જબરદસ્તી કરવી coerce

jabaradastee karavee *v.t.* જબરદસ્તી કરવી foist

jabaradasteepoorvak *adj.* જબરદસ્તીપૂર્વક coercive

jabaradasteethee જબરદસ્તીથી perforce

jabaradasteevaalu *adj.* જબરદસ્તીવાળું forcible

Jabrun *adj.* જબરું stalwart

jad *adj.* જડ blunt

jad *adj.* જડ fatuous

jad *n.* જડ humdrum

jad banaavavun *v.t.* જડ બનાવવું benumb

jadabaanun haadakun *n.* જડબાનું હાડકું mandible

jadabuddhi maanas *n.* જડબુદ્ધિમાણસ idiot

jadapooja *n.* જડપૂજા fetish

jadavaad *n.* જડવાદ materialism

jadavun *v.t.* જડવું inlay

jadavun *v.t.* જડવું mount

jadit vastu *n.* જડિત વસ્તુ fixture

jadoogar *n.* જાદૂગર enchanter

Jagyaa *n.* જગ્યા stead

Jagyaanee chootvaalun *adj.* જગ્યાની છૂટવાળું spacious

jahaaj *n.* જહાજ brig

Jahaaj rokaay te jagyaan *n.* જહાજ રોકાય તે જગ્યા ship-yard

jahaajavaado *n.* જહાજવાળો dockyard

jahaajno naash *n.* જહાજનો નાશ shipwreck

jajiyaavero *n.* જજિયાવેરો poll-tax

jakaat *n.* જકાત excise

jakaat *n.* જકાત octroi

jakaat veraane paatra *adj.* જકાત વેરાનેપાત્ર dutiable

jakham *n.* જખમ wound

jakhamee karavun *v.t.* જખમી કરવું stab

Jakhamnee nishaani *n.* જખમની નિશાની scar

jalabanbol *adj.* જળબંબોળ swampy

jalabilaadee *n.* જળબિલાડી otter

jaladee bagade evun જલદી બગડે એવું perishable

jaladee, taakide *adv.* જલદી, તાકીદે apace

jalaghodo *n.* જળઘોડો. hippopotamus

jalakookadee *v.i.* જળકૂકડી mew

jalakukadee *n.* જળકૂકડી pelican

jalamaarg naalun *n.* જળમાર્ગ નાળું aqueduct

jalapaatra *n.* જલપાત્ર font

jaleeya *adj.* જલીય aquatic

jallaad *n.* જલ્લાદ hanger

jalllaad *n.* જલ્લાદ executioner

jalo *n.* જળો leech

jalodar *n.* જલોદર dropsy

jamaa karavun *v.t.* જમા કરવું deposit

jamaa karavun જમા કરવાની જગ્યા depository

Jamaai *n.* જમાઈ son-in-law

jamaiyo *n.* જમૈયો rapier

jamanun *n.* જમણું starboard

jamavun *v.i.* જમવું dine

jameen *v.t.* જમીન land

jameenadost karavun *v.t.* જમીનદોસ્ત કરવું raze

jameenano tukado *n.* જમીનનો ટુકડો plot

Jameendaar *n.* જમીનદાર squire

janaavavun *v.t.* જણાવવું inform

janakaar *adj.* જાણકાર versed

jananedriyo sanbandhee *adj.* જનનેન્દ્રિયો સંબંધી genital

Janeeboojeene karelun *adj.* જાણીબૂજીને કરેલું studied

jangal *adj.* જંગલ desert

jangal *n.* જંગલ forest

jangal *n.* જંગલ wood

jangalano rakshak *n.* જંગલનો રક્ષક ranger

jangalavaalun *n.* જંગલવાળું woody

jangalee *n.* જંગલી barbarian

jangalee *adj.* જંગલી diabolical

jangalee *adj.* જંગલી feral

jangalee *adj.* જંગલી wild

jangalee dekhaatun *adj.* જંગલી દેખાતું haggard

jangalee dukkar *n.* જંગલી ડુક્કર boar

jangalee gaay *n.* જંગલી ગાય bison

jangalee kaagado *n.* જંગલી કાગડો jackdaw

jangalee kaagado *n.* જંગલી કાગડો raven

jangaleepanun *n.* જંગલીપણું vandalism

jangaliyat *n.* જંગલિયત barbarism

jangam milakat *n.* જંગમ મિલકત chattel

janma *n.* જન્મ birth

janma adhikaar *n.* જન્મ અધિકાર birth-right

janma sthal *n.* જન્મ સ્થળ birth-place

janma taareekh *n.* જન્મ તારીખ birthday

janmaakshar *n.* જન્માક્ષર horoscope

janmajaat *p.p.* જન્મજાત born

janmajaat *adj.* જન્મજાત congenital

janmajaat *adj.* જન્મજાત inborn

janmajaat nahee *adj.* જન્મજાત નહિ uncongenial

janmapatrika *n.* જન્મપત્રિકા. nativity

janmathee *adj.* જન્મથી. natal

jantu *n.* જંતુ insect

jantunaashak *n.* જંતુનાશક germicide

Janturahit je vyandhy banaavuun જંતુરહિત કે વંધ્ય બનાવવું sterilize

jantushastra જંતુશાસ્ત્ર entomology

japat karavun *v.t.* જપત કરવું confiscate

japat karavun te *n.* જપત કરવું તે confiscation

japt karavun *v.t.* જપ્ત કરવું seize

jara thobhavun *v.t.* જરા થોભવું pause

Jaraa khasvun ke khasedvun *v.i.* જરા ખસવું કે ખસેડવું stir

jaraak khaarun *adj.* જરાક ખારું brackish

Jaraamaa kantaale evun *n.* જરામાં કંટાળે એવું squeamish

jaradaalu *n.* જરદાળુ apricot

jaradee *n.* જરદી yolk

jarathushtrana dharmanun anuyaayee *adj.* જરથુષ્ટ્રના ધર્મનું અનુયાયી zoroastrian

jaroor *n.* જરૂર need

jaroor hovee *v.t.* જરૂર હોવી want

Jaroor kartaan vadhaare *adj.* જરૂર કરતાં વધારે superfluous

jarooree *adj.* જરૂરી needful

jarooree *adj.* જરૂરી requisite

jarooreeyaatavaalun *adj.* જરૂરીયાતવાળું indigent

jarooriyato *n.pl.* જરૂરીયાતો needs

jaruree vayno abhaav *n.* જરૂરી વયનો અભાવ underage

Jasat *n.* જસત spelter

jasat dhaatu *n.* જસત ધાતુ zinc

Jasoosee karnaar *n.* જાસૂસી કરનાર spy

jasoosee purvekshan જાસૂસી પૂરવેક્ષણ reconnaissance

jasoosee purvekshan karavun *v.t.* જાસૂસી પૂરવેક્ષણ કરવું reconnoitre

jateel *adj.* જટિલ complex

jateelataa *n.* જટીલતા intricacy

jathaabandh vepaar *n.* જથાબંધ વેપાર wholesale

jathar *n.* જઠર gut

jatho *n.* જથો quantity

jaththamay *adj.* જથ્થામય bulky

jaththo *n.* જથ્થો volume

jatil banaavavun *v.t.* જટિલ બનાવવું complicate

jatpee *n.* જપ્તી seizure

jatu karavun *n.* જંતુ કરવું forefeiture

jatu karavun જંતુ કરવું renounce

jav *n.* જવ malt

Javaa devun *n.* જવા દેવું show

javaab aapavo *v.t.* જવાબ આપવો account

javaab aapavo *n.* જવાબ આપવો reply

javaab aapavo *v.t.* જવાબ આપવો respond

javaab aapavo *v.t.* જવાબ આપવો vouch

javaabadaar *adj.* જવાબદાર liable

javaabadaar *adj.* જવાબદાર responsible

javaabadaar hovun te *n.* જવાબદાર હોવું તે liability

javaabadaar, uttaradaayee *adj.* જવાબદાર, ઉત્તરદાયી answerable

javaabadaaree *n.* જવાબદારી onus

javaabadaaree *n.* જવાબદારી responsibility

javaabdaar *adj.* જવાબદાર accountable

javalle ja *adv.* જવલ્લે જ rarely

javano sharaab *n.* જવનો શરાબ beer

javun *v.i.* જવું go

jayajayakaar *int.* જયજયકાર hurrah

jayantee *n.* જયંતી jubilee

jayantee, varshagaanth *n.* જયંતી, વર્ષગાંઠ anniversary

jayeshtha *adj.* જ્યેષ્ઠ eldest

Jayeshthtaa *n.* જ્યેષ્ઠતા seniority

jeebh *n.* જીભ tongue

jeebhaajodee *n.* જીભાજોડી bickering

jeebhano paachalo bhag *n.* જીભનો પાછલો ભાગ uvula

jeeddee *adv.* જીદ્દી unyielding

Jeen *n.* જીન saddle

Jeengar *n.* જીનગર saddler

jeeraaf *n.* જીરાફ camelopard

jeernoddhaar karavo *v.t.* જીર્ણોદ્ધાર કરવો renovate

jeerun *n.* જીરું cumin

jeet malavavee *v.t.* જીત મેળવવી win

jeeta *n.* જીત conquest

jeetavun *v.i.* જીતવું vanquish

Jeetvun જીતવું surmount

jeev khaavo *v.t.* જીવ ખાવો pester

jeevaanu sambandhee *adj.* જીવાણુ સંબંધી bacterial

jeevaanu vigyaan *n.* જીવાણુ વજ્ઞિઆન bacteriology

jeevaanun *n.* જીવાણું microbe

jeevadhaaree, praani *n.* જીવધારી, પૂરાણી animal

jeevalen *adj.* જીવલેણ deadly

jeevalen *adj.* જીવલેણ fatal

jeevalen *adj.* જીવલેણ lethal

jeevan *n.* જીવન life

jeevanacharitra જીવનચરિત્ર biography

jeevanacharitrakaar *n.* જીવનચરિત્રકાર biographer

jeevanalakshy *n.* જીવનલક્ષ્ય. mission

Jeevanrasvaalu *adj.* જીવનરસવાળું sappy

jeevaras *n.* જીવરસ protoplasm

jeevatun *adj.* જીવતું live

jeevatun, chetanvantun *v.* જીવતું, ચેતનવંતું animate

jeevavigyaan *n.* જીવવજ્ઞિઆન biology

jeevavigyaanee જીવવજ્ઞિઆની biologist

jeevee *adj.* જીવી viable

Jeevtaa rahevun te *n.* જીવતા રહેવું તે subsistence

jelano adhikaaree *n.* જેલનો અધિકારી warder

jelar *n.* જેલર gaoler

jene ijaa n thai hoy aevu *adj.* જેને ઈજા ન થઈ હોય એવું uninjured

jenee khooba maanga n hoya aevun જેની ખૂબ માંગ ન હોય એવું unsought

jhaad *n.* ઝાડ bush

jhaadanee daalee daalakhan kaapavan *v.t.* ઝાડનાં ડાળી ડાળખાં કાપવાં lop

jhaadanee dalee *n.* ઝાડની ડાળી bough

jhaadavaanee khetee *n.* ઝાડવાની ખેતી arboriculture

jhaadavaanee vaad *n.* ઝાડવાની વાડ hedge

jhaadee *n.* ઝાડી coppice

jhaakal *n.* ઝાકળ rime

jhaakalavaalun *adj* ઝાકળવાળું rimy

jhaalar *n.* ઝાલર gong

jhaalar lagaadavee *v.t.* ઝાલર લગાડવી crimp

jhaalvu *v.t.* ઝાલવું take

jhaankalavaalun *adj.* ઝાંકળવાળું misty

jhaankhap *n.* ઝાંખપ obscurity

jhaankhee drashtivaalun *adj.* ઝાંખી દ્રષ્ટિવાળું purblind

jhaankhee karavee *n.* ઝાંખી કરવી glimpse

jhaankhee, drashtivaalun *adj.* ઝાંખી દ્રષ્ટિવાળું blear

jhaaravun *v.t.* ઝારવું weld

jhaatako *n.* ઝાટકો zest

jhabhbho *n.* ઝભ્ભો gown

jhabhbho *n.* ઝભ્ભો robe

jhadap *n.* ઝડપ celerity

jhadap *n.* ઝડપ rapidity

jhadapee vahaan *n.* ઝડપી વહાણ clipper

jhadapi, chapal *adj.* ઝડપી, ચપળ agile

jhagadaakhor vrudhdha ઝઘડાખોર વૃધ્ધા. battle-axe

jhagadaani pataavat *n.* ઝઘડાની પતાવટ arbitration

jhagadavun *v.i.* ઝઘડવું bicker

jhagado *n.* ઝઘડો wrangle

jhagado patavavo *v.t.* ઝઘડો પતાવવો arbitrate

jhagamagavun *n.* ઝગમગવું glare

jhalahalatun *adj.* ઝળહળતું resplendent

jhanakaar *n.* ઝણકાર jingle

jhankhana *n.* ઝંખના. craving

jhankhap *n.* ઝાંખપ blur

jhankho prakaash *v.i* ઝાંખો પ્રકાશ glimmer

jhankhu *v.t.* ઝાખું tarnish

jharadanjhaankhara *n.* ઝરડાંઝાંખરા brushwood

jharamar jharamar varasavun *v.t.* ઝરમર ઝરમર વરસવું mizzle

jhaveraat *n.* ઝવેરાત. jewellery

jhaveraatnee petee *n.* ઝવેરાતની પેટી casket

jhaveree *n.* ઝવેરી. jeweller

jheebra *n.* ઝીબ્રા zebra

jheenun kaapad *n.* ઝીણું કપડું cambric

jhenon vaayu *n.* ઝેનોન વાયુ xenon

jher *n.* ઝેર poison

jheree *adj.* ઝેરી poisonous

jheree goomadun *n.* ઝેરી ગૂમડું carbuncle

jheree saap *n.* ઝેરી સાપ adder

jhok *n.* ઝોક tendency

jhokun *n.* ઝોકું nap

jholee *n.* ઝોળી hammock

jhoodavun *v.t.* ઝૂડવું belabour

jhoodee *n.* ઝૂડી wisp

jhoolaakhurashee *n.* ઝૂલાખુરશી rocking-chair

jhoolathee sajaavavun *n.* ઝૂલથી સજાવવું caparison

jhoomakhun *n.* ઝૂમખું bunch

jhoonpadee *n.* ઝૂંપડી hut

jhooravun *n.* ઝૂરવું pine

jhumakhun *n.* ઝૂમખું cluster

jhunbesh *n.* ઝૂંબેશ campaign

jiddee *adj.* જદ્દી inflexible

jiletin *n.* જીલેટિન gelatine

jillo *n.* જિલ્લો. district

jiraaf *n.* જિરાફ giraffe

Jirnasheerna *adj.* જીર્ણશીર્ણ shabby

jivanane lagatun *adj.* જીવનને લગતું vital

jivanshakti *n.* જીવનશક્તિ, vitality

jivanshaktinun pradaan *v.t.* જીવનશક્તિનું પ્રદાન vitalize

jivatun, sakriy *adj.* જીવતું, સક્રિય alive

jivavaad, sarvchetanvaad *n.* જીવવાદ, સર્વચેતનવાદ animism

jo *conj.* જો if

jodaan *n.* જોડાણ attachment

jodaan *n.* જોડાણ coalition

jodaan *n.* જોડાણ connection

jodaan *n.* જોડાણ joint

jodaanee doree *n.* જોડાની દોરી lace

jodaayelun *adj.* જોડાયેલું confederate

jodaayelun hovun *v.t.* જોડાયેલું હોવું adjoin

jodaayelun, malatun *adj.* જોડાયેલું, મળતું allied

jodakanaanjodun *n.* જોડકણાંજોડું poetaster

jodavun *v.* જોડવું append

jodavun *n.* જોડવું associate

jodavun *v.t.* જોડવું conjoin

jodavun *v.t.* જોડવું connect

jodavun *v.t.* જોડવું join

jodavun *v.t.* જોડવું unite

jodavun, jodavun *v.* જોડવું, જોડાવું agglutinate

jodee *n.* જોડી pair

jodelee saankal *n.* જોડેલી સાંકળ concatenation

jodine ek karavun *v.* જોડીને એક કરવું alligate

Jodnee spardhaanee ramat *n.* જોડણી સ્પર્ધાની રમત spelling

jodo *n.* જોડો boot

jogavaaee *n.* જોગવાઈ clause

Joi shakaay evun *adj.* જોઈ શકાય એવું striking

joi shakaay evun *adj.* જોઈ શકાય એવું visible

joi shakaay evun *adv.* જોઈ શકાય એવું visibly

Joie tetlun *adj.* જોઈએ તેટલું sufficient

joke, yadhyapee *conj.* જોકે, યદ્યપિ albeit

joke, yadhyapee *conj.* જોકે, યદ્યપિ although

jokee *n.* જોકી jockey

jokham *n.* જોખમ danger

jokham *n.* જોખમ jeopardy

jokham *n.* જોખમ peril

jokham *n.* જોખમ risk

jokham bharelun *adj.* જોખમ ભરેલું risky

jokhamakaarak *adj.* જોખમમકારક dangerous

jokhamama naakhavun જોખમમાં નાખવું endanger

jokhamaman naakhavun *v.t.* જોખમમાં નાખવું imperil

jokhamaman naakhavun *v.t.* જોખમમાં નાખવું. jeopardize

jokhamee *adj.* જોખમી perilous

Jom *n.* જોમ stamina

jomavaalu *adj.* જોમવાળું, dynamic

Jonaaro *n.* જોનારો seer

joojun puraanun *adj.* જૂનું પુરાણું hoary

Joonee kahevat *n.* જૂની કહેવત saw

joonun ane ghasaai gayelun *adj.* જૂનું અને ઘસાઈ ગયેલું threadbare

joonun thai javun *v.t.* જૂનું થઇ જવું superannuate

jooreeno sadasy *n.* જૂરીનો સદસ્ય jury

jootaa vinaanu *adj.* જૂતા વિનાનું unshod

jooth *n.* જૂથ batch

jooth *n.* જૂથ group

joothadhaaree *adj.* જૂથચારી gregarious

joothano pakshapaat *n.* જૂથનો પક્ષપાત favouritism

joothun *n.* જૂઠું lie

joothun bolanaaro *n.* જૂઠું બોલનારો liar

joraavar *adj.* જોરાવર mighty

joradaar athadaaman *n.* જોરદાર અથડામણ collision

joradaar pavan *n.* જોરદાર પવન gale

jorathee aamalavun *v.t.* જોરથી આમળવું wrench

jorathee dhakko maaravo *v.t.* જોરથી ધક્કો મારવો thrust

jorathee dhakko maaravo *n.* જોરથી ધક્કો મારવો thrustings

jorathee fenkavun *v.t.* જોરથી ફેંકવું hurl

jorathee khenchavun *v.t.* જોરથી ખેંચવું tug

josadaan *n.* જોસદાન portfolio

joseelun, chetanvantun *adj.* જોસીલું, ચેતનવંતું animated

joshavalun *n.* જોસવાળું vehemence

josheelun *adj.* જોશીલું intense

josheelun *adj.* જોશીલું vigorous

jovun *v.t.* જોવું look

jovun જોવું see

jubaanee *n.* જુબાની depostion

jubaanee aapavee *v.* જુબાની આપવી. depose

judaa paadavun *n.* જુદા પડવું disunion

judaaee, chittabhram *n.* જુદાઈ, ચિત્તભ્રમ alienation

judo rang *n.* જુદો રંગ tint

Judu padvu te *n.* જુદું પડવું તે secession

Judun kaadhvun ke karvun *v.i.* જુદું કાઢવું કે કરવું sequester

jugaaree *n.* જુગારી gamester

jugaarno addo *n.* જુગારનો અડ્ડો casino

julam *n.* જુલમ oppression

julam *n.* જુલમ tyranny

julam karanaar *n.* જુલમ કરનાર oppressor

julama gujaaravo *v.t.* જુલમ ગુજારવો tyrannize

julamagaaranaa jevun *adj.* જુલમગારના જેવું tyrannical

julamaghar *n.* જુલમગાર tyrant

julmee *adj.* જુલ્મી oppressive

junavaanee *adj.* જુનવાણી antique

junavaani, kaalagrast *adj.* જુનવાણી, કાલગ્રસ્ત antiquated

jupitaranun mandir *n.* જુપટિરનું મંદિર capitol

jussaavaalu *adj.* જુસ્સાવાળું energetic

jusso *n.* જુસ્સો energy

jusso *n.* જુસ્સો fervour

jusso *n.* જુસ્સો spirit

juthoon *adj.* જુઠું untrue

juvaan *adj.* જુવાન young

juvaan *adj.* જુવાન youthful

Juvaan gaamdiyo જુવાન ગામડિયો swain

juvaaniyo *n.* જુવાનિયો. lad

juvaaniyo *n.* જુવાનિયો youngster

jvaalaa vagar salagavun *v.i.* જ્વાળાવગર સળગવું smoulder

jvaalaamukhee parvat *n.* જ્વાળામુખી પર્વત volcano

jvaalaamukheenun modhun *n.* જ્વાળામુખીનું મોઢું crater

jvalan *n.* જ્વલન combustion

jvalanasheel *adj.* જ્વલનશીલ flameable

jvalanasheel *adj.* જ્વલનશીલ inflammable

Jya (Bhoomiti- Trikonmiti) *n.* જ્યા (ભૂમતિ-ત્રિકોણમતિ) sine

jyaare pan *adj.* જ્યારે પણ whenever

jyan jyan *adv.* જ્યાં જ્યાં wherever

jyot *n.* જ્યોત flame

K

kaaapadnee kinaar *n.* કાપડની કનિાર hem

kaabaracheetarun *n.* કાબરચીતરું roan

kaabarcheetaru *n.* કાબરચીતરું dapple

kaaboo *n.* લશ્કરનો ઉપરી – સરદાર commandant

kaabooman raakhavun *v.t.* કાબૂમાં રાખવું wield

kaach *n.* કાચ glass

kaach *n.pl.* કાચ glasses

kaach banaavavo *v.t.* કાચ બનાવવો vitrify

kaacha ke rabaranee nalee *n.* કાચ કે રબરની નળી tube

kaachabo *n.* કાચબો. tortoise

kaachalee *n.* કાચલી nutshell

kaachamani *n.* કાચમણિ quartz

kaachanaa jevo ek padaarth *n.* કાચના જેવો એક પદાર્થ enamel

kaachchun *adj.* કાચ્યું unprepared

kaachee dhaatu *n.* કાચી ધાતુ ore

kaachindo *n.* કાચિંડો lizard

kaachna jevun *adj.* કાચના જેવું vitreous

kaachun kedakhaanun *n.* કાચું કેદખાનું lock-up

kaachun sonun *n.* કાચું સોનું nugget

kaadav *n.* કાદવ dregs

kaadav *n.* કાદવ mire

kaadav *n.* કાદવ mud

kaadavavaalun *adj.* કાદવવાળું. muddy

kaadhee mookavun *n.* કાઢી મૂકવું turnout

kaafalo *v.i.* કાફલો fleet

kaagadaano "ka" "ka" avaaj *n.* કાગડાનો 'કા' 'કા' અવાજ caw

kaagal *n.* કાગળ paper

kaagalana 2) ghaa *n.* કાગળના ૨) ધા ream

kaagalano ghaa *n.* કાગળનો ધા quire

kaagalno kad *n.* કાગળનો કદ demy

kaajal *n.* કાજળ collyrium

Kaajal ke meshno popdo *n.* કાજળ કે મેશનો પોપડો smut

kaakaakauva *n.* કાકાકૌવા cockatoo

kaakadaa *n.* કાકડા tonsil

kaakadaano sojo *n.* કાકડાનો સોજો quinsy

kaakadee *n.* કાકડી. cucumber

kaakee *n.* કાકી aunty

kaako *n.* કાકો uncle

kaal maapavaanun yantra *n.* કાળ માપવાનું યંત્ર chronometer

kaalaa rangnun *adj.* કાળા રંગનું blackish

kaalaamaree *n.* કાળામરી pepper

kaalagrast *adj.* કાલગ્રસ્ત obsolete

kaalajee *adj.* કાળજી heedful

kaalajee raakhavee *v.t.* કાળજી રાખવી look after

kaalajeepoorvak tapaasavun *n.* કાળજીપૂર્વક તપાસવું investigate

kaalajeevaalun *adj.* કાળજીવાળું careful

kaalajeevaalun *adj.* કાળજીવાળું wary

kaalakramaanusaaree *adj.* કાલક્રમાનુસારી chronological

kaalavyutkram, kaladosh *n.* કાલવ્યુતક્રમ, કાલદોષ anachronism

kaaleesukee draaksh *n.* કાળીસુકી દ્રાક્ષ plum

kaaleeyaar, haran *n.* કાળિયાર, હરણ antelope

kaalgrast *adj.* કાલગ્રસ્ત defunct

kaalo jhabhbho *n.* કાળો ઝભ્ભો cassock

kaalpanik *adj.* કાલ્પનિક fictious

kaalpanik *n.* કાલ્પનિક imaginary

kaalpanik *adj.* કાલ્પનિક speculative

kaalu *adj.* કાળુ black

Kaalu padelun *adj.* કાળું પડેલું swarthy

kaalun *n.* કાળું rook

kaalun kaalun bolavun *v.t.* કાળું કાળું બોલવું babble

kaalun karavun *v.t.* કાળું કરવું blacken

kaalun polish *n.* કાળું પૉલિશ blacking

kaalyanika ramaraajya *n.* કાલ્પનિક રામરાજ્ય. utopia

kaam karanaar *n.* કામ કરનાર worker

kaam karavun *v.t.* કામ કરવું do

kaam ke dhandho karvun *v.* કામ કે ધંધો કરવું transact

Kaam maa dheel karavee *v.t.* કામમાં ઢીલ કરવી dally

kaamaatur *adj.* કામાતુર prurient

kaamaatur *adj.* કામાતુર randy

kaamachalaau *n.* કામચલાઉ interim

kaamachalaau dukaan *v.t.* કામચલાઉ દુકાન booth

kaamageeree bajaavanee *n.* કામગીરી બજાવણી performance

kaamalo *n.* કામળો blanket

kaamamaa levun *v.t.* કામમાં લેવું employ

kaamaman daakhal *n.* કામમાં દાખલ interpellation

kaaman karavun *n.* કામણ કરવું enchantment

kaamano samay *n.* કામનો સમય bout

kaamchalaau *adj.* કામચલાઉ temporary

Kaamchor thavun *v.t.* કામચોર થવું shirk

kaamee *n.* કામી leer

kaamee *adj.* કામી passionate

kaamee *n.* કામ work

kaamottejak *adj.* કામોત્તેજક luscious

kaan *n.* કાન ear

kaan ughaadavaa *v.i.* કાન ઉઘાડવા expostulate

kaanaavaalee sheeshee *n.* કાણાવાળી શીશી cruet

kaanakhajooro *n.* કાનખજૂરો centipede

kaanan paadavun *v.t.* કાણાં પાડવાં perforate

kaanane lagatun *adj.* કાનને લગતું aural

kaananee boot *n.* કાનની બૂટ lobe

kaanano padado *n.* કાનનો પડદો tympanum

kaanasano avaaj *n.* કાનસનો અવાજ rasp

kaanbalo *n.* કાંબળો plaid

kaanchalee *n.* કાંચળી slough

kaangaaroo *n.* કાંગારૂ kangaroo

kaanjee *n.* કાંજી gruel

kaankaree *n.* કાંકરી grit

kaanoon *n.* કાનૂન law

kaanoon *n.* કાનૂન regulation

kaanoonee sthite *n.* કાનૂની સ્થતિ status

kaanp *adj.* કાંપ alluvium

kaanp *n.* કાંપ silt

kaanpavaalun *adj.* કાંપવાળું alluvial

kaansakee *v.t.* કાંસકી comb

kaantaabodh *n.* કાન્તાબોધ curtain-lecture

kaantaadaar *heat* કાંટાદાર prickly

kaantaalo chhod *n.* કાંટાળો છોડ bramble

kaantaalun *adj.* કાંટાળું prickly

kaantaalun *adj.* કાંટાળું thorny

kaantavaanun shan *v.t.* કાંતવાનું શાણ tow

kaantelun sootar *n.* કાંતેલું સૂતર yarn

kaanto *n.* કાંટો thorn

Kaantvaanee traak *n.* કાંતવાની ત્રાક spindle

Kaanun *n.* કાણું slot

kaanun paadavun *v.t.* કાણું પાડવું broach

kaapad *n.* કાપડ cloth

kaapad *n.* કાપડ fabric

kaapadiyo *n.* કાપડિયો. draper

kaapalee *n.* કાપલી clipping

kaapalee *n.* કાપલી label

kaapanee lananeenee mausam *n.* કાપણી લણણીની મૌસમ harvest

kaapavun *v.t.* કાપવું chop

kaapavun *v.t.* કાપવું cut

Kaapee kaadhelo bhaag *n.* કાપી કાઢેલો ભાગ section

kaapee naakhavun te *n.* કાપી નાખવું તે amputation

kaapyaavinaanu *adj.* કાપ્યાવિનાનું uncut

kaaraagrah *n.* કારાગૃહ prison

kaarabhaaree *n.* કારભારી regent

kaarakaanu *n.* કારખાનું factory

kaarakun *n* કારકુન clerk

kaaramee chees *v.t.* કારમી ચીસ howl

kaaran *v.t.* કારણ cause

kaaran *n.* કારણ reason

kaaran bataavavun *v.i.* કારણ બતાવવું plead

kaaranadarshak *adj.* કારણદર્શક causal

kaaranbhoot *n.* કારણભૂત ascription

kaaranbhoot *n.* કારણભૂત attribute

kaaranke *conj.* કારણકે because

kaaratoos *n.* કારતૂસ cartridge

kaaratoosno pato *n.* કારતૂસનો પટો bandolier

kaarban *n.* કારબન carbon

Kaarbhaaree *n.* કારભારી steward

kaarbhaaree, aadatiyo *n.* કારભારી,આડતિયો agent

kaareegar *n.* કારીગર artisan

kaareegar *n.* કારીગર fitter

kaareegar *n.* કારીગર workman

kaareegaranun kaushaly *n.* કારીગરનું કૌશલ્ય workmanship

kaareegaree *n.* કારીગરી artistry

kaarkeerdi *n.* કારકીર્દિ career

kaarkoonee *adj.* કારકૂની clerical

kaarobaar *n.* કારોબાર business

kaarya karavun *v.i.* કાર્ય કરવું function

kaaryaalay *n.* કાર્યાલય bureau

kaaryaalay *n.* કાર્યાલય office

kaaryakram *n.* કાર્યક્રમ programme

kaaryaksham *n.* કાર્યક્ષમ efficient

kaaryaksham banaavavun *v.t.* કાર્યક્ષમ બનાવવું capacitate

kaaryakshamataa *n.* કાર્યક્ષમતા efficacy

kaaryakushal *adj.* કાર્યકુશળ able

kaaryapranaalee *n.* કાર્યપ્રણાલી. procedure

kaaryasoochi *n.* કાર્યસૂચિ agenda

kaashthaahaaree *adj.* કાષ્ઠાહારી xylophagous

kaashthakaam *n.* કાષ્ઠકામ woodwork

kaashthanun kotarakaam *n.* કાષ્ઠનું કોતરકામ xylography

kaashthaushadhee *n.* કાષ્ઠૌષધિ herb

kaat *n.* કાટ corrosion

kaat *n.* કાટ rust

kaatakhoone chhedatun *adj.* કાટખૂણે છેદતું cross-wise

kaatakhoono *n.* કાટખૂણો right angle

kaatamaal *n.* કાટમાળ debris

Kaatar *n.* કાતર scissors

kaatar *n.pl.* કાતર shears

kaatarelu *n.* કાતરેલું fleece

kaatarelu *adj.* કાતરેલું fleecy

kaatariyun *n.* કાતરિયું garret

kaathee *n.* કાથી coir

kaatho *n.* કાથો catechu

Kaatrvun *v.t.* કાતરવું snip

kaavataraabaaj *adj.* કાવતરાખોર designing

kaavatarun *n.* કાવતરું conspiracy

kaavatarun *n.* કાવતરું intrigue

kaavatarun karavun *v.t.* કાવતરું કરવું conspire

Kaavtraabaaj *adj.* કાવતરાબાજ sly

kaavy *n.* કાવ્ય poem

kaavyaanubhoote *n.* કાવ્યાનુભૂતિ afflatus

kaavyaatmak *adj.* કાવ્યાત્મક poetic

kaavyakanika *n.* કાવ્યકણિકા couplet

kaavyaman rachelun *adj.* કાવ્યમાં રચેલું poetical

kaavyano khand *n.* કાવ્યનો ખંડ canto

Kaavyano shlok *n.* કાવ્યનો શ્લોક stanza

kaavyasaundary *n.* કાવ્યસૌન્દર્ય poetry

kaayaakalp *n.* કાયાકલ્પ rejuvenation|દ|ૐ

kaayaakalp karavo *v.i.* કાયાકલ્પ કરવો. rejuvenate

kaayaapalat *n.* કાયાપલટ transformation

kaayaapalatyogya *adj.* કાયાપલટયોગ્ય transmutable

kaayada ghadanaar *n.* કાયદા ઘડનાર legislator

kaayada ghadava te કાયદા ઘડવા તે legislation

kaayadaanee sanhita *n.* કાયદાની સંહિતા code

kaayadaaonee petee *n.* કાયદાઓની પેટી ark

kaayadaashaastr *n.* કાયદાશાસ્ત્ર jurisprudence

kaayadaashaastree *n.* કાયદાશાસ્ત્રી. jurist

kaayadesar *adj.* કાયદેસર lawful

kaayadesar *adj.* કાયદેસર statutory

kaayadesar karavun *v.t.* કાયદેસર કરવું, legalize

kaayadesar kinmat *n.* કાયદેસર કિમત assize

kaayadesaranun *adj.* કાયદેસરનું legal

kaayado *n.* કાયદો act

kaayado *n.* કાયદો statute

kaayado ghadavo *v.t.* કાયદો ઘડવો enact

kaayado ghadavon *v.t.* કોયદો ઘડવો legislate

kaayam karvun *v.t.* કાયમ કરવું underlie

kaayamanun કાયમનું indelible

kaayamanun *n.* કાયમનું perpetual

kaayamanun gumaavelun *adj.* કાયમનું ગુમાવેલું irretrievable

kaayamee *adj.* કાયમી even

kaayamee *n.* કાયમી permanent

kaayamee banaavavun કાયમી બનાવવું perpetuate

Kaayano thasso *n.* કાયમનો ઠસ્સો stereotype

kaayar *n.* કાયર poltroon

kaaydaanu oolanghan karnaar *n.* કાયદાનું ઉલ્લંઘન કરનાર transgressor

kaaydaanu oolanghan ke bhanga karvo *v.t.* કાયદાનું ઉલ્લંઘન કે ભંગ કરવો transgress

kabaat *n.* કબાટ closet

kabaat *n.* કબાટ cupboard

kabajaamaa levun *v.t.* કબજામાંથી લેવું dispossess

kabajaaman raakhavun *v.t.* કબજામાં રાખવું retain

kabajedaar કબ્જેદાર occupant

kabajiyaat *n.* કબ્જિયાત constipation

kabajiyaat thavee *v.t.* કબ્જિયાત થવી constipate

kabajo *n.* કબ્જો keeping

kabajo *n.* કબ્જો occupancy

kabajo *n.* કબ્જો possession

kabajo karavaanee prakriya *n.* કબ્જો કરવાની પ્રક્રિયા occupation

kabar *n.* કબર grave

Kabar *n.* કબર sepulchre
kabar *n.* કબર tomb
kabaramaa daatavun *v.t.* કબરમાં દાટવું entomb
kabeelo *n.* કબીલો clansman
kabool karavun *v.t.* કબૂલ કરવું avow
kabool karavun *n.* કબૂલ કરવું compliance
kabool karavun *v.t.* કબૂલ કરવું confess
kaboolaat *n.* કબૂલાત confession
kaboolamin aanavun *v.t.* કાબૂમાં આણવું chasten
kabootar *n.* કબૂતર pigeon
kabootar *n.* કબૂતર dove
kabootarakhaanun *n.* કબૂતરખાનું pigeon-hole
kabrastaan *n.* કબરસ્તાન cemetery
kachadaayelu *adj.* કચડાયેલું downtrodden
kachadee naakhavun *v.t.* કચડી નાખવું quell
kachakachaat *n.* કચકચાટ chatterbox
kachakachiyun કચકચિયું petulance
kachakadun *n.* કચકડું xylonite
kacharo *n.* કચરો dross
kacharo *n.* કચરો offal
kacharo *n.* કચરો trash
Kachdvun *v.t.* કચડવું squeeze
kacheree *n.* કચેરી agency
kachoree *n.* કચોરી pie
kachunbar *v.i.* કચુંબર has
kadaach *adv.* કદાચ perchance
kadaach *adv.* કદાચ perhaps
kadaachane *conj.* કદાચને lest
kadaakaa saathenu tofaana *n.* કડાકા સાથેનું તોફાન thunderstorm
kadaako karavo *v.t.* કડાકો કરવો crack
kadaavar *adj.* કદાવર elephantine
kadaavar *adj.* કદાવર hefty
kadaavar maanas *n.* કદાવર માણસ titan
kadachhee *n.* કડછી ladle
Kadak *adj.* કડક severe
Kadak *adj.* કડક stringent
kadak daaroo *n.* કડક દારૂ brandy
kadakaaee *n.* કડકાઈ rigidity
Kadam ke daglun bharvun *v.i.* કદમ કે

ડગલું ભરવું step
kadar *n.* કદર appreciation
kadar karanaarun *adj.* કદર કરનારું aesthetic
kadar karavee *v.t.* કદર કરવી appreciate
kadardaaneevaalun *adj.* કદરદાનીવાળું appreciative
kadaroopun *adj.* કદરૂપું homely
kadarupun *adj.* કદરૂપું, ગંદું unsightly
kadavaash, katutaa *n.* કડવાશ, કટુતા acerbity
kadavaash, vafataaee *n.* કડવાશ, નફ્ફટાઈ gall
kadavaashavalo svabhaav *n.* કડવાશવાળો સ્વભાવ vinegar
kadavee teekaa *n.* કડવી ટીકા diatribe
kadavun *adj.* કડવું bitter
kadavun banaavavun *v.t.* કડવું બનાવવું embitter
kadee *n.* કડી buckle
kadhangaapanun *n.* કઢંગાપણું awkwardness
kadhangee reete *n.* કઢંગી રીતે awkwardly
kadhango, bedol *n.* કઢંગો, બેડોળ antic
kadhangu *adj.* કઢંગુ awkward
kadhangu *adj.* કઢંગું uncouth
kadhangun *adj.* કઢંગું ungainly
kadhedo *n.* કઠેડો banister
kadhee banaavavee *v.t.* કઢી બનાવવી curry
kadiyaano olanbo *n.* કડિયાનો ઓળંબો plumb
kadiyaanu lelun *n.* કડિયાનું લેલું trowel
kadiyo *n.* કડિયો bricklayer
kadiyo *n.* કડિયો. mason
Kadkaai *n.* કડકાઈ severity
kadrupun *adj.* કદરૂપું ugly
Kadvee mashkareevaalu *adj.* કડવી મશ્કરીવાળું sardonic
kaee jagyaathee *adv.* કઈ જગ્યાથી whence
kafan *n.* કફન pall
kahee mookavun *v.t.* કહી મૂકવું bespeak
kaheevat *n.* કહેવત by-word
kahen *v.t.* કહેણ offer

kahevat *n.* કહેવત proverb

kahevat, sutra *n.* કહેવત, સૂત્ર adage

kahevataroop banelun *adj.* કહેવતરૂપ બનેલું proverbial

Kahevun *v.t.* કહેવું say

kahevun કહેવું tell

Kahovaan kare evun *adj.* કહોવાણ કરે એવું septic

kahovadaavavun *v.i.* કહોવડાવવું rot

kahyaa ke bolyaa vinaa soochit *adj.* કહ્યા કે બોલ્યા વિના સૂચિત tacit

kahyaagaru *adj.* કહ્યાગરું docile

kahyaagaru *adj.* કહ્યાગરું ductile

kahyaagarun *n.* કહ્યાંગરું tractability

kahyaagarun *n.* કહ્યાંગરું tractable

kaink *n.* કંઈક aught

kajeeyakhor stree *n.* કજિયાખોર સ્ત્રી, virago

kajiyaakhor *adj.* કજિયાખોર pugnacious

kajiyaakhor *adj.* કજિયાખોર quarrelsome

kajiyaakhor svabhaav કજિયાખોર સ્વભાવ pugnacity

kajiyo *n.* કજિયો brawl

kajiyo *n.* કજિયો broil

kajiyo karavo *v.i.* કજિયો કરવો quarrel

kakadaavava *v.t.* કકડાવવા gnash

kakkaavaar soochee *n.* કક્કાવાર સૂચિ index

kaksh *n.* કક્ષા locus

kakshaaman faravun *v.i.* કક્ષામાં ફરવું rotate

kalaa *n.* કલા art

kalaabhavan *n.* કલાભવન polytechnic

kalaabhigna *n.* કલાભિજ્ઞ virtuoso

kalaai *n.* કલાઈ nickel

kalaai *n.* કલાઈ tin

Kalaainee khaan *n.* કલાઈની ખાણ stannary

Kalaainun ke tene lagtun *adj.* કલાઈનું કે તેને લગતું stannic

kalaak *n.* કલાક hour

kalaatmak *adj.* કલાત્મક artistic

kalagee *n.* કલગી crest

kalam *n.* કલમ graft

kalam *n.* કલમ pen

kalam aaropan *v.t.* કલમ આરોપણ ingraft

kalamanee taank *n.* કલમની ટાંક nib

kalan *n.* કળણ marsh

kalan *n.* કળણ morass

kalan *n.* કળણ quagmire

Kalank *n.* કલંક stigma

kalank lagaadavun *v.t.* કલંક લગાડવું blemish

kalank lagaadavun *v.t.* કલંક લગાડવું blot

kalankit karavun *v.t.* કલંકિત કરવું imbrue

kalankit karavun *v.t.* કલંકિત કરવું sully

kalaso *n.* કોલસો coke

kalavun *n.* કળવું discernment

kaleechoono *n.* કળીચૂનો quicklime

kalla *n.* કલ્લા whisker

kalpak *adj.* કલ્પક imaginative

kalpana *n.* કલ્પના notion

kalpana *n.* કલ્પના phantasy

kalpanaa *adj.* કલ્પના fancy

kalpanaa karanaar *n.* કલ્પના કરનાર speculator

kalpanaa karavee કલ્પના કરવી speculate

kalpanaa karavee *v.t.* કલ્પના કરવી visualize

kalpanaano tukko *n.* કલ્પનાનો તુક્કો. figment

kalpanaashakti *n.* કલ્પનાશક્તિ imagination

kalpanaatarang *n.* કલ્પનાતરંગ reverie

kalpaneey *adj.* કલ્પનીય imaginable

kalpaneeya *adj.* કલ્પનીય conceivable

kalpit dharee *n.* કલ્પિત ધરી axis

kalpit vaat *n.* કલ્પિત વાત fiction

Kalun *adj.* કાળું sombre

kalyaan *n.* કલ્યાણ welfare

kamaad *n.* કમાડ shutter

kamaan *n.* કમાન. arc

kamaanee *n.* કમાણી earnings

kamaavun *v.t.* કમાવું earn

kamajor banaavavun *v.t.* કમજોર બનાવવું debilitate

kamajor banaavavun *v.t.* કમજોર બનાવવું enfeeble

kamajoree n. કમજોરી debility

kamakamaatee n. કમકમાટી horror

kamakamaatee v.t. કમકમાટી thrill

kamakho n. કમખો brassier

kamal n. કમળ. lotus

kamalanu fool n. કમળનું ફૂલ lily

kamalo n. કમળો. jaundice

kamanaseeb adj. કમનસીબ unlucky

kamar n. કમર loin

kamar n. કમર waist

kamarapato baandhavo v. કમરપટો બાંધવો girdle

kamarapatto n. કમર પટ્ટો waistband

kamarnun hadakun n. કમરનું હાડકું backbone

kamee karavun n. કમી કરવું whittle

kamnasheeb adj. કમનસીબ unfortunate

kamod n. કમોડ lavatory

kampaaoondar n. કમ્પાઉન્ડર compounder

kampavun v.t. કાંપવું vibrate

kampayukta soora n. કંપયુક્ત સૂર tremolo

kampayukta svar n. કંપયુક્ત સ્વર trill

kanasavun v.i. કણસવું groan

kanasavun v.i. કણસવું whimper

kandaraa n. કંદરા tendon

kanee nahi n. કંઈ નહઈ naught

kangaal adj. કંગાળ beggarly

kangaal adj. કંગાળ miserable

kangaaliyat n. કંગાલયિત beggary

kangaaliyat n. કંગાલયિત misery

kangaaliyat n. કંગાલયિત penury

kanjoos adj. કંજૂસ illiberal

kanjoos n. કંજૂસ. miser

kanjoos n. કંજૂસ niggard

Kanjoos adj. કંજૂસ stingy

kanjoos adj. કંજૂસ ungenerous

kankan n. કંકણ bracelet

kankan n. કંકણ wristlet

kanp vistaar n. કંપ વિસ્તાર amplitude

kanpan n. કંપન vibration

kanpanee adj. કંપની corporate

kanpavun v.i. કંપવું quake

kanpbhoomi n. કંપભૂમિ bog

kansun n. કાંસું bronze

kantaalaabharelun adj. કંટાળાભરેલું tedious

kantaalaajanak કંટાળાજનક irksome

kantaalaajanak vaadan n. કંટાળાજનક વાદન thrum

kantaalo n. કંટાળો boredom

kantaalo n. કંટાળો tedium

kantaan n. કંતાન canvas

kantaanajanak adj. કંટાળાજનક fulsome

kantak n. કંટક prickle

kanthasthaaneey n. કંઠસ્થાનીય guttural

kantho n. કાંઠો brink

Kanthsangeet n. કંઠસંગીત song

kanyaano var n. કન્યાનો વર bridgeroom

kanyaaraashi n. કન્યારાશિ virgo

kaolaso n. કોલસો coal

kaolejano vidhyaarthee n. કૉલેજનો વદ્યિાર્થી collegian

kaoshalya n. કૌશલ્ય dexterity

kapaal n. કપાળ brow

kapaal n. કપાળ forehead

kapaas n. કપાસ cotton

kapachee n. કપચી metal

kapadaa kaadhavaa v.t. કાપડા કાઢવા strip

kapadaa paheravaa v.t. કપડા પહેરવા don

kapadaa paheravaa v.t. કપડાં પહેરવા dress

kapadaa utaaravaa v.t. કપડાં ઉતારવાં disrobe

kapadaamaan sajj adj. કપડામાં સજ્જ vested

kapadaanee gadee કપડાની ગડી tuck

kapadan n. કપડાં clothes

kapata karavun v.t. કપટ કરવું hoodwink

kapatabhaav n. કપટભાવ duplicity

kapatapoorvak adj. કપટપૂર્વક disingenuous

kapatee adj. કપટી devious

kapatee adj. કપટી wily

kapatjaal n. કપટજાળ collusion

kapatjaal rachavee *v.t.* કપટજાળ રચવી collude

kapdaa ootaarvaan *v.t.* કપડાં ઉતારવાં undress

kapoor *n.* કપૂર camphor

Kaptaan *n.* કપ્તાન skipper

kar *n.* કર tax

kar besaadvo ke bharvo te *n.* કર બેસાડવા કે ભરવા તે. taxation

karaabaddha umedavaari *n.* કરારબદ્ધ ઉમેદવારી apprenticeship

karaamat *n.* કરામત knack

karaar *n.* કરાર bond

karaar *n.* કરાર compact

karaar *n.* કરાર contract

karaar *n.* કરાર covenant

karachalee *n.* કરચલી crease

karachalee *n.* કરચલી wrinkle

karachalee paadavee *v.t.* કરચલી પડવી ruck

karachaleeo paadavee *v.t.* કરચલીઓ પાડવી crumple

karachalo *n.* કરચલો crab

karadavun *v.t.* કરડવું bite

karadee khaavun te *v.t.* કરડી ખાવું તે nibble

karaj bharapaaee *n.* કરજ ભરપાઈ liquidate

karajano fadacho *n.* કરજનો ફડચો liquidation

karakasar karanaaru *adj.* કરકસર કરનારું economical

karakasar karavee *v.t.* કરકસર કરવી economize

karakasariyu *adj.* કરકસરિયું frugal

karakasariyun *adj.* કરકસરિયું canny

karakasariyun *adj.* કરકસરિયું chary

karakasariyun *adj.* કરકસરિયું provident

karamaav *v.i.* કરમાવ fade

karamaavun *adj.* કરમાવું faded

karamaavun *v.t.* કરમાવું wither

karamada *n.* કરમદા raspberry

karanaaee *n.* કરનાઈ cornet

karandiyo *n.* કરંડિયો hamper

karataal *n.* કરતાલ cymbal

karavaanee reet *n.* કરવાની રીત process

karelun *n.* કરેલું done

kark (raashi) *n.* કર્ક (રાશિ) cancer

karkasar *n.* કરકસર thrift

karkash *adj.* કર્કશ harsh

karkash avaaj karavo *n.* કર્કશ અવાજ કરવો jar

karkasha naaree *n.* કર્કશા નારી xanthippe

Karkasriyun *adj.* કરકસરિયું sparing

karm *n.* કર્મ object

Karmaayelun *adj.* કરમાયેલું sere

karmachaaree *n.* કર્મચારી employee

karmachaaree varg *n.* કર્મચારી વર્ગ personnel

karmanee vibhakti *pro.* કર્મની વિભક્તિ thee

karn *n.* કર્ણ hypotenuse

karod *n.* કરોડ crore

Karod *n.* કરોડ spine

karod asthi no koi ek manako *n.* કરોડઅસ્થિનો કોઇ એક મણકો vertebra

karod ke prushtvanshnun *adj.* કરોડ કે પૃષ્ઠવંશનું spinal

karoliyaanee jaal *n.* કરોળિયાની જાળ cobweb

karoliyaanun jaalun *n.* કરોળિયાનું જાળું web

karpaatra *adj.* કરપાત્ર taxable

kartavyanisht *adj.* કર્તવ્યનિષ્ટ dutiful

kartavyatatpar *adj.* કર્તવ્યતત્પર obedient

kartooto *n.* કરતૂતો doings

karun *adj.* કોરું blank

karunaa *n.* કરુણા compassion

karunaajanak *adj.* કરુણાજનક pathetic

karunaras *n.* કરુણરસ pathos

Karveraamaathee mukt *adj.* કરવેરામાંથી મુક્ત scotfree

Karvero *n.* કરવેરો scot

karyakshetra *n.* કાર્યક્ષેત્ર domain

karyun *p.p.* કર્યું made

kasaaee *n.* કસાઈ butcher

kasamayanu કસમયનું unseasonable

kasarat *n.* કસરત exercise

kasaratano daando *n.* કસરતનો દાંડો trapeze

kaseene baandhavun *v.t.* કસીને બાંધવું belay

kashaa swaadvinany *adj.* કશા સ્વાદ વિનાનું tasteless

Kashaak maate dilgeer *adj.* કશાક માટે દિલગીર sorry

kashaakano naano bhaag *n.* કશાકનો નાનો ભાગ speckle

kashaakano ullekh karavo *v.t.* કશાકનો ઉલ્લેખ કરવો mention

kashun nahi *n.* કશું નહિ nothing

kasoor *n.* કસૂર default

kasooravaar *n.* કસૂરવાર defaulter

kasotee *n.* કસોટી ordeal

kasotee *n.* કસોટી test

kasotee karanaarun *adj.* કસોટી કરનારું trying

kastooree *n.* કસ્તૂરી musk

kasuvaavad *n.* કસુવાવડ miscarriage

kataaksh *v.i.* કટાક્ષ gibe

kataaksh કટાક્ષ jibe

kataakshavaalun - lakhaan *n.* કટાક્ષવાળું - લખાણ lampoon

Kataar *n.* કટાર dagger

kataar *n.* કટાર kukri

kataar *n.* કતાર queue

Kataar *n.* કટાર scimitar

kataayelun *adj.* કટાયેલું rusty

katal *n.* કતલ slaughter

Katalkhaanu *n.* કતલખાનું slaughter-house

katalkhaanun *n.* કતલખાનું abattoir

kathaanaayak *n.* કથાનાયક protagonist

kathalavun *v.i.* કથળવું deteriorate

Kathan *v.t.* કઠણ stiffen

kathan ane bhaare *n.* કઠણ અને ભારે ebony

Kathan banaavvun *v.t.* કઠણ બનાવવું solidify

kathan charabee *n.* કઠણ ચરબી tallow

kathapootalee *n.* કઠપૂતળી puppet

kathero *n.* કઠેરો rail

Kathin parishram *v.t.* કઠિન પરિશ્રમ struggle

katholano daano *n.* કઠોળનો દાણો bean

kathor *adj.* નિષ્ઠુર inexorable

kathorapane *adv.* કઠોરપણે hardly

kathorata *n.* કઠોરતા obduracy

kathorataa *n.* કઠોરતા asperity

Kathortaa *n.* કઠોરતા strictness

kativa *n.* કટિવા lumbago

katleaam *n.* કત્લેઆમ carnage

katokatee *n.* કટોકટી crisis

katokatee *n.* કટોકટી emergency

katoro *n.* કટોરો beaker

Katraatun *adj.* કતરાતું slant

kattar *n.* કટ્ટર diehard

kattaravaadee *n.* કટ્ટરવાદી extremist

Katun ke Kadvun *adj.* કટું કે કડવું sarcastic

katuta *n.* કટુતા bitterness

Katutaa *n.* કટુતા sting

kaubhaand *n.* કૌભાંડ fraud

kaumaaratva *n.* કૌમારત્વ virginity

kaumayabhang karavo *v.t.* કૌમાર્યભંગ કરવો deflower

kaushaly *n.* કૌશલ્ય proficiency

kauvat aapanaar *adj.* કૌવત આપનાર nutritious

kavi *n.* કવિ poet

kavi *n.* કવિ versifier

kavita *n.* કવિતા poesy

kavitaa *n.* કવિતા verse

kavitaa rachavee *v.t.* કવિતા રચવી versify

kayaamat no divas *n.* કયામતનો દિવસ doomsday

kaye thekaane *adv.* ક્યે ઠેકાણે whither

kayun *pro.* કયું which

ked *n.* કેદ durance

kedakhaanun *n.* કેદખાનું gaol

kedakhaanun *n.* કેદખાનું jail

kedaman naakhavun *v.t.* કેદમાં નાખવું imprison

kedaman puravun *v.t.* કેદમાં પૂરવું incarcerate

kedee *n.* કેદી captive

kedee *n.* કેદી prisoner

kedeeonee tolee *n.* કેદીઓની ટોળી gang

kedethee valee gayelee doshee *n.* કેદેથી વળી ગયેલી ડોશી crone

keedee *n.* કીડી emmet

keedo *n.* કીડો worm

keematee *adj.* કીમતી valuable

keemiyaagar *n.* કીમિયાગર alchemist

keemiyo *n.* કીમિયો alchemy

keenaakhor *adj.* કીનાખોર revengeful

keeranasampaat bindu *n.* કરિણસંપાત બિંદુ focus

keerti *n.* કીર્તિ fame

keerti *n.* કીર્તિ glory

keeshor *adj.* કિશોર adolescent

keetak *n.* કીટક moth

kek *n.* કેક cake

kel *n.* કેળ plantain

kelareemaapak yantr *n.* કેલરીમાપક યંત્ર calorimeter

kelavaay evun *adj.* કેળવાય એવું malleable

kelavaneekaar *n.* કેળવણીકાર educationist

keleedoskop *adj.* કેલીડોસ્કોપ kaleidoscopic

kelipar *n.* કેલિપર calliper

kelsium *n.* કેલ્શિયમ calcium

kelun *n.* કેળું banana

kem *adv.* કેમ why

kem jaane *adv.* કેમ જાણે quasi

kemeraa *n.* કેમેરા camera

kendra *n.* કેન્દ્ર centre

kendraapagaamee *adj.* કેન્દ્રાપગામી centrifugal

kendragaamee *adj.* કેન્દ્રગામી centripetal

kendragaamee *v.t.* કેન્દ્રગામી converge

kendranu *adj.* કેન્દ્રનું focal

kendreekaran karavun *v.t.* કેન્દ્રીકરણ કરવું centralize

kendreeya *v.t.* કેન્દ્રીય central

keree *n.* કેરી mango

keret *n.* કેરેટ carat

keshavaalee *n.* કેશવાળી mane

Ketlaak *adj.* કેટલાક several

Ketlunk *adj.* કેટલુંક some

keval naamaman rahelun *adj.* કેવળ નામમાં રહેલું nominal

kevee reete *adv.* કેવી રીતે how

khaabochiyun *n.* ખાબોચિયું puddle

khaadavun *v.t.* ખાળવું fend

khaadee *adj.* ખાડી bay

khaadelu ખાધેલું eaten

khaadh *n.* ખાધ deficit

khaadhaakhorakee *n.* ખાધાખોરાકી alimony

Khaado *n.* ખાડો socket

khaady padaarth *n.* ખાદ્ય પદાર્થ cereal

khaadya *adj.* ખાદ્ય edible

khaadya vastu *adj.* ખાદ્ય વસ્તુ eatable

khaaee *n.* ખાઈ abyss

khaaee *n.* ખાઈ chasm

khaal *n.* ખાલ pelt

khaalakoovo *n.* ખાળકૂવો cesspool

khaalasaa karavun *v.* ખાલસા કરવું annex

khaalee *adj.* ખાલી empty

khaalee *adj.* ખાલી inane

khaalee *adj.* ખાલી vacant

Khaalee jagyaa *n.* ખાલી જગ્યા vacancy

khaalee karavun *v.t.* ખાલી કરવુ deplete

khaalee karavun *v.t.* ખાલી કરવું evacuate

khaalee karavun *n.* ખાલી કરવું siphon

khaalee karavun *v.* ખાલી કરવું vacate

khaaleepanu ખાલીપણુ emptiness

khaamee *n.* ખામી defect

khaamee *n.* ખામી drawback

khaamee vinaanun *adj.* ખામી વિનાનું perfect

khaameeyukta *adj.* ખામીયુક્ત defective

khaanadaanee *n.* ખાનદાની nobility

khaanagee *adj.* ખાનગી esoteric

khaanagee *n.* ખાનગી privacy

khaanagee deval *n.* ખાનગી દેવળ chapel

khaanagee ispitaal *n.* ખાનગી ઇસ્પિતાલ nursinghome

khaanagee raakhavaa jevun *adj.* ખાનગી રાખવા જેવું confidential

khaanagee shikshak *n.* ખાનગી શિક્ષક tutor

khaanasaamo *n.* ખાનસામો butler

khaanch *n.* ખાંચ nick

khaancho *n.* ખાંચો notch

Khaand *n.* ખાંડ sugar

khaaniyo *n.* ખાણિયો miner

khaanpaannee vyavastha *v.t.* ખાનપાનની વ્યવસ્થા cater

khaara paaneenun *adj.* ખારા પાણીનું briny

khaaraapaaneenu sarovar *n.* ખારાપાણીનું સરોવર lagoon

khaareelun *adj.* ખારીલું malignant

Khaarvo *n.* ખારવો seaman

Khaas kareene ખાસ કરીને specially

khaataree *n.* ખાતરી assurance

khaataree *n.* ખાતરી warranty

khaataree aapavee *v.t.* ખાતરી આપવી assure

khaataree karaavavee *v.* ખાતરી કરાવવી persuade

khaataree karavee *v.t.* ખાતરી કરવી ensure

khaataree karavi *v.t.* ખાતરી કરવી ascertain

khaatareepoorvak *adj.* ખાતરીપૂર્વક assured

khaatareepoorvak *adj.* ખાતરીપૂર્વક assuredly

khaate *prep.* ખાતે at

Khaatreepoorvak *adv.* ખાતરીપૂર્વક surely

khaatu *adj.* ખાટું tart

khaaudharo *n.* ખાઉધરો glutton

khaaudharun *adj.* ખાઉધરું voracious

Khaavaa peevaamaan atirek *n.* ખાવા પીવામાં અતિરિક surfeit

Khaavaanun e poortun na aapvun *v.t.* ખાવાનું ઇ. પૂરતું ન આપવું stint

khabar aapavee *v.t.* ખબર આપવી apprise

khabarapatree *n.* ખબરપત્રી reporter

khacharo *n.* કચરો rubbish

khadak *n.* ખડક rock

khadakaal *adj.* ખડકાળ reefy

khadakaal *adj.* ખડકાળ rocky

khadakhadaat *v.i.* ખડખડાટ rustle

khadakhadaat karavo *v.i.* ખડખડાટ કરવો rattle

khadaknee karaad *n.* ખડકની કરાડ reef

khadatal *adj.* ખડતલ robust

khadatal baandhaanun *adj.* ખડતલ બાંધાનું burly

khadee padavun *v.t.* ખડી પડવું derail

khagolashaastra *n.* ખગોળશાસ્ત્ર astronomy

khagolashaastree *n.* ખગોળશાસ્ત્રી astronomer

khajaanachee *n.* ખજાનચી treasurer

khajaano *n.* ખજાનો treasure

khajaano *n.* ખજાનો treasury

khajavaal *n.* ખજવાળ itch

khakhadee gayelun *adj.* ખખડી ગયેલું rickety

khalaas karavun *v.t.* ખલાસ કરવું exhaust

khalaaseeono bedo *n.* ખલાસીઓનો બેડો crew

khalabhalaat *n.* ખળભળાટ commotion

khalakhal vahevun *v.i.* ખળખળ વહેવું purl

khalel *n.* ખલેલ distrubance

Khalkoovo *n.* ખાળકૂવો sesspool

khameer *n.* ખમીર barm

khameeraheet *adj.* ખામીરહતિ fire-proof

Khamees *n.* ખમીસ shirt

khanakhanaat *n.* ખણખણાટ clatter

khand *n.* ખંડ compartment

khandalee ugharaavavee *v.t.* ખંડણી ઉઘરાવવી extort

khandan karavun *v.t.* ખંડન કરવું confute

khandan karavun *v.t.* ખંડન કરવું rebut

khandanee *n.* ખંડણી ransom

khandanee aapavaa paatr *adj.* ખંડણી આપવા પાત્ર tributary

khandiyer haalat *v.t.* ખંડયિર હાલત dilapidate

khandiyu *n.* ખંડયું feudatory

khanij *n.* ખનિજ mineral

khanij (dhaatu) vidhya *n.* ખનિજ (ધાતુ) વદિ્યા mineralogy

khanij tel *n.* ખનિજ તેલ diesel

khanij tel *n.* ખનિજ તેલ rock-oil

khanjan *n.* ખંજન dimple

khankhanvun *v.t.* ખણખણવું clang

khant *n.* ખંત diligence

khanteelu *n.* ખંતીલું diligent

khanteelun *adj.* ખંતીલું painstaking

khanteelun *adj.* ખંતીલું persistent

Khanteelun *adj.* ખંતીલું sedulous

khantpoorvak *adv.* ખંતપૂર્વક actively

Khap kartaa vadhaaraanun *n.* ખપ કરતા વધારાનું superfluity

kharaa dilanun *adj.* ખારા દિલનું heartfelt

Kharaa dilthee *adv.* ખરા દિલથી sincerely

kharaab *adj.* ખરાબ bad

kharaabaano pat *n.* ખરાબાનો પટ moor

Kharaabe chadvun *n.* ખરાબે ચડવું strand

kharaad *n.* ખરાદ lathe

kharaadee *n.* ખરાદી. turner

kharaadee kaamano chhol *n.* ખરાદી કામનો છોલ turning

kharabachado khadaka *n.* ખરબચડો ખડક. tufa

kharabachadun *n.* ખરબચડું rough

kharabachadun *adj.* ખરબચડું rugged

kharach upar kaaboo ખરચ ઉપર કાબૂ purse-strings

Kharachne lagtun *adj.* ખરચને લગતું sumptuary

kharadavun *v.t.* ખરડવું basmear

kharajavun *n.* ખરજવું eczema

Kharatal ખડતલ sturdy

kharch *n.* ખર્ચ cost

kharch ખર્ચ expenditure

kharch upaadavo *v.* ખર્ચ ઉપાડવો defray

kharcha karavo *v.t.* ખર્ચ કરવો incur

kharchvun *v.t.* ખર્ચવું expend

Kharchvun *v.t.* ખર્ચવું spend

Khardo *n.* ખરડો sketch

khareedanaar *n.* ખરીદનાર buyer

khareedee *v.t.* ખરીદી purchase

khareedee karavee *v.t.* ખરીદી કરવી buy

kharekhar *adv.* ખરેખર forsooth

kharekhar *adv.* ખરેખર really

kharun *n.* ખરું kosher

kharun chhe ke nahi te jovun ખરું છે

કે નહિ તે જોવું verification

kharun, chaalun *adj.* ખરું, ચાલુ actual

khasakhasano chhod *n.* ખસખસનો છોડ poppy

khasavun *v.t.* ખસવું budge

khasedavun *n.* ખસેડવું displacement

khasedee shakaay evun *v.t.* ખસેડી શકાય એવું mobile

khasee karavun *v.t.* ખસી કરવું emasculate

khasee karelo kookado *n.* ખસી કરેલો કૂકડો capon

Khasee karyaa vinaano ghodo *n.* ખસી કર્યા વિનાનો ઘોડો stallion

khasee kravun *n.* ખસી કરવું geld

khasi karavee *v.t.* ખસી કરવી castrate

khasvastik *n.* ખસ્વસ્તિક zenith

Khasvun *v.i.* ખસવું shift

khataaro *n.* ખટારો cart

khataaro *n.* ખટારો. lorry

Khataash *n.* ખટાશ sourness

khataash, tejabitaa *n.* ખટાશ, તેજાબિતા acidity

Khataashvaalun *adj.* ખટાશવાળું sour

khaudharo *adj.* ખાઉધરો unappeasable

khaudharu *adj.* ખાઉધરું edacious

khavaaee javun *v.t.* ખવાઈ જવું corrode

khavadaavavun *v.t.* ખવડાવવું feed

khed *n.* ખેડ cultivation

khed *n.* ખેડ tillage

khed karavo *v.t.* ખેડ કરવો regret

khedaau *adj.* ખેડાઉ arable

khedavaalaayak jameen *n.* ખેડવાલાયક જમીન lea

khedoot *n.* ખેડૂત farmer

khedoot *n.* ખેડૂત peasant

khedootavarg *n.* ખેડૂતવર્ગ peasantry

kheejanun naam *n.* ખીજનું નામ nickname

kheejavanaarun *n.* ખીજવનારું vexatious

kheejavata *n.* ખીજવાટ vexation

kheel *n.* ખીલ. pimple

kheelee *n.* ખીલી tack

kheelelee sthitiman *adv.* ખીલેલી સ્થિતિમાં abloom

kheelo *n.* ખીલો peg

kheelo *n.* ખીલો pivot

Kheen *n.* ખીણ dale

kheen *n.* ખીણ valley

kheerun *n.* ખીરું leaven

kheesun *n.* ખીસું pocket

khelaadee *n.* ખેલાડી player

khelaadee chhokaree *n.* ખેલાડી છોકરી tomboy

Kheldilee *n.* ખેલદિલી sportsmanship

khenchanaar *n.* ખેંચનાર drawer

khenchaun *n.* ખેંચવું traction

khenchavun *v.t.* ખેંચવું draw

khenchavun ખેંચવું drew

khenchavun *v.t.* ખેંચવું trail

khenchee kaadhavun *v.t.* ખેંચી કાઢવું pluck

khencheene paadee devun *adj.* ખેંચીને પાડી દેવું tractive

khenchelu *adj.* ખેંચેલું taut

khepiyo *n.* ખેપિયો courier

khepiyo *n.* ખેપિયો runner

kheraat *n.* ખેરાત dole

khes *jn.* ખેસ sash

khetar *n.* ખેતર farm

khetar *n.* ખેતર field

khetaraman *adv.* ખેતરમાં afield

khetee *n.* ખેતી farming

kheteenun ojaar *n.* ખેતીનું ઓજાર cultivator

Khetgulaamee *n.* ખેતગુલામી serfdom

khetivaadi ખેતીવાડી agricultural

khetivaadi, krushi vignaan *n.* ખેતીવાડી, કૃષિવિજ્ઞાન agriculture

khijaayelu *adj.* ખજિયેલું furious

khirun *n.* ખીરું beestings

khisakolee *adj.* ખસિકોલી rodent

khisakolee *n.* ખસિકોલી squirrel

khissaakaataru maanas *n.* ખસિસાકાતરુ માણસ pickpocket

khitaab dhaaran karvo *adj.* ખતિાબ ધારાણ કરવો tituler

khobochiyun *n.* ખોબોચયિું plash

khodanee karavee *v.t.* ખોદણી કરવી pry

khodavun *v.* ખોદવું delve

khodavun *v.t.* ખોદવું dig

khodavun ખોદવું excavate

khodee kaadhanaaru *n.* ખોળી કાઢનારું ferret

khodee kaadhavun *v.t.* ખોદી કાઢવું exhume

khodee kaadhvun *v.t.* ખોદી કાઢવું unearth

Khodo *n.* ખોડો scurf

Khodvaanun ojaar *n.* ખોદવાનું ઓજાર spade

khokhaamaa mukavun ખોખામાં મૂકવું encase

khol *n.* ખોળ oil-cake

kholaakhol karavee *v.t.* ખોળાખોળ કરવી rummage

kholavun *v.t.* ખોલવું unpack

kholee devu *v.t.* ખોલી દેવું uncase

kholee naakhvu *v.t.* ખોલી નાખવું unbolt

kholo *n.* ખોળો lap

kholvu *v.t.* ખોલવું unbuckle

kholvu *v.t.* ખોલવું uncork

kholvun *v.t.* ખોલવું unbar

khoob balavaan *adj.* ખૂબ બળવાન powerful

khoob charchaayelun *adj.* ખૂબ ચર્ચાયેલું vexed

khoob j achokkas samay *n.* ખૂબ જ અચોક્કસ સમય eon

Khoob moto *adj.* ખૂબ મોટો stentorian

khoob utsaahee ખૂબ ઉત્સાહી impassioned

khoob vajanadaar *n.* ખૂબ વજનદાર heavy

khoob vegavaalu *v.t.* ખૂબ વેગવાળું express

Khoob vyaapak *n.* ખૂબ વ્યાપક sweeping

khooba unchun, udaatta *adj.* ખૂબ ઊંચું ઉદાત્ત towering

khoon karavun *v.t.* ખૂન કરવું assassinate

khoonaamaapak *n.* ખૂણામાપક sextant

khoonakhaar jang *adj.* ખૂનખાર જંગ bloody

khoonamaapak *n.* ખૂણા માપક theodolite

khoonarejeevaalun *adj.* ખૂનરેજીવાળું gory

khoonche tevun *adj.* ખૂંચે તેવું mordant

khoonee *adj.* ખૂની murderous

khoono *n.* ખૂણો corner

khoontaanee vaad *n.* ખૂંટાની વાડ paling

Khooto yuktivaad karnaar *n.* ખોટો યુકતિવાદ કરનાર sophist

khopadeenee chaamadee *n.* ખોપડીની ચામડી scalp

khoparee *n.* ખોપરી cranium

Khopree *n.* ખોપરી skull

khoraak *n.* ખોરાક food

khoraak aapurti *v.t.* ખોરાક આપૂર્તિ purvey

khoraak pachaavavo *v.t.* ખોરાક પચાવવો digest

khoraaka *n.* ખોરાક viands

khoraakano puravatho *n.* ખોરાકનો પુરવઠો commissariat

khoravee naakhavun *n.* ખોરવી નાંખવું disruption

khorun *adj.* ખોરું rancid

khot *n.* ખોટ loss

khota sogan leva *v.t.* ખોટા સોગન લેવા perjure

khotaa *n.* ખોટા trinketry

Khote raste lai janaarun *adj.* ખોટે રસ્તે લઈ જનારું seductive

Khotee daleel *n.* ખોટી દલીલ sophism

khotee jagyaae mookavun *v.t.* ખોટી જગ્યાએ મૂકવું misplace

khotee jubaanee ખોટી જુબાની perjury

Khotee maanyataa *n.* ખોટી માન્યતા superstition

khotee rajooaat karavee *v.t.* ખોટી રજૂઆત કરવી misrepresent

khoto khyal aapavo *v.t.* ખોટો ખ્યાલ આપવો belie

khoto nyaay karavo *v.t.* ખોટો ન્યાય કરવો misjudge

khotu puravaar karavun *v.* ખોટું પુરવાર કરવું disprove

khotun *n.* ખોટું wrong

khotun *adj.* ખોટું incorrect

khotun chhaapavun *n.* ખોટું છાપવું. misprint

khotun kaam karavun *v.t.* ખોટું કામ કરવું perpetrate

khotun mantavy *n.* ખોટું મંતવ્ય misbelief

khotun naam *n.* ખોટું નામ misnomer

khristee *n.* ખૂરસ્તી. christian

khristee deval *n.* ખૂરસ્તી દેવળ church

khristee dharm *n.* ખૂરસ્તી ધર્મ christianity

khristee dharmopadeshako *n.* ખૂરસ્તી ધર્મોપદેશકો clergy

khristee vidhi *n.* ખૂરસ્તી વિધિ sacrament

khristi dharmagranth *n.* ખૂરસ્તિ ધર્મગ્રંથ bible

Khub galyun *n.* ખૂબ ગળ્યું saccharin

khulaasaa laayak *adj.* ખુલાસા લાયક explicable

khulaaso *n.* ખુલાસો clarification

khulaaso *n.* ખુલાસો explanation

Khulaaso ke ukel karvo *v.t.* ખુલાસો કે ઉકેલ કરવો solve

khullaaman naakhelo padaav *n.* ખુલ્લામાં નાખેલો પડાવ bivouac

khullo chok *n.* ખુલ્લો ચોક courtyard

khullun *adj.* ખુલ્લું overt

khullun karavun *n.* ખુલ્લું કરવું exposure

khurashee *n.* ખૂરશી chair

khush *adv.* ખુશ fain

khush *adj.* ખુશ. joyful

khush mijaaj *adj.* ખુશ મિજાજ jolly

khushaamat *v.* ખુશામત flatter

Khushaamat *n.* ખુશામત sycophancy

khushaamat karavee *v.t.* ખુશામત કરવી adulate

khushaamat karavee *v.t.* ખુશામત કરવી blandish

khushaamat karavee *n.* ખુશામત કરવી flattery

khushaamatiyo *n.* ખુશામતિયો flatterer

khushaamatiyo *n.* ખુશામતિયો. lackey

khushaamatiyo *n.* ખુશામતિયો toady

Khushaamatiyo *n.* ખુશામતિયો sycophant

khushamijaaj *adj.* ખુશમજિાજ debonair

khushamijaaj *adj.* ખુશમજિાજ hearty

khushamijaajee *adj.* ખુશમજિાજી jocund

khyaati *n.* ખ્યાતિ renown

kidee *n.* કીડી ant

kilebandhee *n.* કલિબંધી fortification

kilebandhee karavee *v.t.* કલિબંધી કરવી embattle

killebandhee *n.* કલ્લિબંધી stockade

killebandhee karavee *v.t.* કલ્લિબંધી કરવી entrench

killo *n.* કલ્લિો fort

killo *n.* કલ્લિો moat

kimmat aankavee *v.* કમિત આંકવી value

kimmat ghataadavee *v.i.* કમિત ઘટાડવી depreciate

kimmatmaa kapaat *n.* કમિતમાં કપાત discount

kinaar *n.* કનિાર rim

kinaar *n.* કનિાર verge

kinaare utaravun *v.i.* કનિારે ઊતરવું disembark

kingalavun *v.i.* કગિલાવું gloat

kinmat *n.* કમિત price

kinnar *n.* કન્નિર eunuch

kinva rasaayan *n.* કણ્વિ રસાયણ zymurgy

kiran sanbandhee *adj.* કરિણ સંબંધી radial

kiranotsarg *n.* કરિણોત્સરગ radiation

kiranotsarjan *v.t.* કરિણોત્સરજન radiate

kishor *adj.* કશિોર juvenile

kishoraavasthaa, taarunya *n.* કશિોરાવસ્થા, તારુણ્ય adolescence

kitalee *n.* કટિલી kettle

kloroform *n.* ક્લોરોફોર્મ chloroform

kobee *n.* કોબી cabbage

kod maachhalee *n.* કોડ માછલી cod

kodh *n.* કોઢ cote

koee ek, koipan *adj.* કોઈ એક, કોઈપણ any

koee ghatanaano daakhalo *n.* કોઈ ઘટનાનો દાખલો case

koee jagyaathee door *adv.* કોઈ જગ્યાથી દૂર out

koee nahi *n.* કોઈ નહિ nobody

koee pan jagyaaman nahi *adv.* કોઈ પણ જગ્યામાં નહિ nowhere

koee vyavasaayanun *adj.* કોઈ વ્યવસાયનું professional

koee ye nahi *adj.* કોઈ યે નહિ none

koeeno aasharo levo *v.t.* કોઈનો આશરો લેવો betake

koeepan maanas *pro.* કોઈપણ માણસ whoever

kofee *n.* કોફી coffee

kogala karava *v.t.* કોગળા કરવા gurgle

kogalo karavo *v.t.* કોગળો કરવો gargle

Koh *n.* કોહ sepsis

Koi dharmsangh *v.i.* કોઈ ધર્મસંઘ secede

Koi ek *n.* કોઈ એક someone

Koi ek maanas *n.* કોઈ એક માણસ somebody

koi kaam karnaar *n.* કોઈ કામ કરનાર doer

Koi khaas kaamnaa nishnat *n.* કોઈ ખાસ કામના નષ્ણિાત specialist

Koi padaarthnee sodam *n.* કોઈ પદાર્થની સોડમ smack

koi paksha ke sampradaayano mat *n.* કોઈ પક્ષ કે સંપ્રદાયનો મત tenet

koi pana cheej *n.* કોઈ પણ ચીજ thing

Koi Vastu *n.* કોઈ વસ્તુ something

Koi vastuno bahaarno bhaag *n.* કોઈ વસ્તુનો બહારનો ભાગ surface

koi vishishta kalaa કોઈ વશિષ્ટ કળા technical

Koinee vatee bolnaar *n.* કોઈની વતી બોલનાર spokesman

koino avejee karyakar *n.* કોઈનો અવેજી કાર્યકર vicar

koipan maanas *pron.* કોઈપણ માણસ anybody

Koipan reete *adv.* કોઈપણ રીતે somehow

kokadun *n.* કોકડું skein

kokain *n.* કોકેઈન cocaine

kokal *n.* કોકલ cockle

kokaravaayun *adj.* કોકરવાયું lukewarm

kokonee bhookee *n.* કોકોની ભૂકી cocoa

kolaahal *n.* કોલાહલ din

kolaahal *n.* કોલાહલ hubbub

kolaahal *n.* કોલાહલ racket

kolaahal *n.* કોલાહલ tumult

kolaahal *n.* કોલાહલ turmoil

kolaahalabharyu *n.* કોલાહલભર્યું tumultuous

kolasaanee khaan *n.* કોલસાની ખાણ coal-mine

kolasaanee khaan *n.* કોલસાની ખાણ colliery

kolaso karavo *v.t.* કોલસો કરવો char

koleeyo *n.* કોળીયો swallow

kolera *n.* કૉલેરા cholera

koliyo *n.* કોળિયો morsel

koliyo *n.* કોળિયો mouthful

kolun *n.* કોળું calabash

kolun *n.* કોળું pumpkin

komal *adj.* કોમળ mellow

komal *adj.* કોમળ supple

komalataa *n.* કોમળતા tenderness

komodor *n.* કોમોડોર commodore

kon *pro.* કોણ who

kon, khuno, drashtikon *n.* કોણ, ખૂણો, દૃષ્ટિકોણ angle

konamaapak *n.* કોણમાપક protractor

konavaalun *adj.* કોણવાળું angular

konee *n.* કોણી elbow

koneeno halavo godo *v.t.* કોણીનો હળવો ગોદો jog

konun *pro.* કોનું whose

koochado *n.* કૂચડો brush

koodakaa *n.* કૂદકા skipping

koodako *v.t.* કૂદકો bounce

koodako, thekado *n.* કૂદકો, ઠેકડો gambol

koodavun *n.* કૂદવું leap

kookadaanee kalagee *n.* કૂકડાની કલગી cockscomb

kookadaano bol *n.* કૂકડાનો બોલ crow

kookado *n.* કૂકડો cock

kookam *n.* હુકમ fiat

kookar *n.* કૂકર cooker

koolee *n.* કૂલી coolie

koolo *n.* કૂલો buttock

koona padavun *v.t.* કૂણા પડવું relent

koonehvalu *adj.* કુનેહવાળું tactful

koonjo *n.* કૂંજો jug

kootaprashn *n.* કૂટપ્રશ્ન problem

kootaraane lagatun *adj.* કૂતરાને લગતું canine

kootaraano hadakava *n.* કૂતરાનો હડકવા rabies

kootaraanun bachchun *n.* કૂતરાનું બચ્ચું whelp

kootaro *n.* કૂતરો dog

koovo *n.* કૂવો well

koovo khodavo *v.t.* કૂવો ખોદવો bore

koparoo *n.* કોપરું kernel

kopiraait *n.* કૉપીરાઇટ copyright

koraa pagavaalu *n.* કોરા પગવાળું dry-shod

Kordaa vade fatkaarvun *n.* કોરડા વડે ફટકારવું slash

korporal *adj.* કૉર્પોરલ corporal

kosh *n.* કોષ cell

koshaadhyaksh *n.* કોષાધ્યક્ષ cashier

kosharachana karanaar *n.* કોશરચના કરનાર lexicographer

koshetaa ucher *n.* કોશેટા ઉછેર sericulture

kosheto *n.* કોશેટો cocoon

koshish *v.t.* કોશિશ endeavour

koshonun banelun *adj.* કોષોનું બનેલું cellular

kot *n.* કોટ coat

kotalaavaalun beej *n.* કોટલાવાળું બીજ nut

kotar *n.* કોતર cavern

kotar *n.* કોતર ravine

kotaravun *v.t.* કોતરવું carve

kotaravun *v.t.* કોતરવું engrave

kotaree khaavun *v.t.* કોતરી ખાવું gnaw

kotarkaam *n.* કોતરકામ fretwork

kotarkaam karavun *v.t.* કોતરકામ કરવું etch

kothaar *n.* કોઠાર barn

kothaar *n.* કોઠાર crib

kothaar *n.* કોઠાર pantry

Kothaar *n.* કોઠાર storehouse

Kothaaree *n.* કોઠારી store-keeper

kotijya *n.* કોટિજ્યા cosine

kotrelaa lakhaanvalee taktee *n.* કોતરેલા લખાણવાળી તકતી tablet

kovaaee javun *n.* કોવાઈ જવું putrefaction

kovaayelun *adj.* કોવાયેલું putrid

kovadaavavun *v.t.* કોવડાવવું putrefy

koyado *n.* કોયડો enigma

koyado *n.* કોયડો poser

koyado *n.* કોયડો quiz

koyal *n.* કોયલ cuckoo

koyal *n.* કોયલ nightingale

kraantikaarak *adj.* ક્રાન્તિકારક revolutionary

kraantivaadee *n.* ક્રાન્તિવાદી revolutionist

kram *n.* ક્રમ order

kramaanusaar *n.* ક્રમાનુસાર rotation

Kramash aavvun te *n.* ક્રમશઃ આવવું તે succession

kramavaachak (sankhya) *adj.* ક્રમવાચક (સંખ્યા) ordinal

kramik ક્રમિક gradual

kranti laavavee ક્રાંતિ લાવવી revolutionize

kreedaayudhdha *n.* ક્રીડાયુદ્ધ tournament

kreedanauka *n.* ક્રીડાનૌકા yacht

kriket *n.* ક્રિકેટ cricket

kriket ramanaar *n.* ક્રિકેટ રમનાર cricketer

kriya *n.* ક્રિયા operation

kriyaapada *n.* ક્રિયાપદ verb

kriyaapadanan kaal *v.t.* ક્રિયાપદનાં કાળ conjugate

kriyaapadanun roop *n.* ક્રિયાપદનું રૂપ copula

kriyaashakti *n.* ક્રિયાશક્તિ power

kriyaavishesan avyay *n.* ક્રિયાવિશેષણ અવ્યય adverb

kriyasheel karavun *v.t.* ક્રિયાશીલ કરવું exert

krodh *n.* ક્રોધ dudgeon

krodh *n.* ક્રોધ ire

krodh *n.* ક્રોધ wrath

krodhaavesh *n.* ક્રોધાવેશ paddy

krodhaavesh *n.* ક્રોધાવેશ rage

krodhaavesh *n.* ક્રોધાવેશ rampage

krodhee *adj.* ક્રોધી wrathful

Krodhno susvaato *v.t.* ક્રોધનો સુસવાટો snort

kroor *adj.* ક્રૂર fierce

kros saathe jadee devun te *n.* ક્રોસ સાથે જડી દેવું તે crucification

krucifix *n.* ક્રુસફિક્સિ crucifix

krumee *n.* કૃમિ fluke

krupa *n.* કૃપા boon

krupa karavee *v.t.* કૃપા કરવી vouchsafe

krupaa karavee *v.t.* કૃપા કરવી deign

krupaa kareene *int.* કૃપા કરીને prithee

krupaalu *adj.* કૃપાળુ gracious

krush *adj.* કૃશ wizen

krushi *adj.* કૃષિ agrarian

krushi *n.* કૃષિ husbandry

krutaghnata *n.* કૃતધ્નતા ingratitude

krutagn *adj.* કૃતજ્ઞ grateful

krutagnata *n.* કૃતજ્ઞતા gratitude

krutagyana *adj.* કૃતજ્ઞ thankful

krutrim *n.* કૃત્રિમ pseudo

krutrim naher *n.* કૃત્રિમ નહેર sluice

krutrim, dhongee *adj.* કૃત્રિમ, ઢોંગી affected

krutya *n.* કૃત્ય deed

ksh - kirano *n.* ક્ષ-કિરણો x-ray

kshamaa *v.t.* ક્ષમા absolve

kshamaa *n.* ક્ષમા clemency

kshamaa *n.* ક્ષમા forgiveness

kshamaa aapavee ક્ષમા આપવી absorb

kshamaa karavee *v.t.* ક્ષમા કરવી forgive

kshamaa karavee *adj.* ક્ષમા કરવી forgiving

kshamaasheelata ક્ષમાશીલતા mercy

kshamaayaachana *n.* ક્ષમાયાચના apology

kshamata *n.* ક્ષમતા ability

kshamataa *n.* ક્ષમતા capacity

kshamataa *n.* ક્ષમતા competence

kshamataavaalun *adj.* ક્ષમતાવાળું capable

kshamya *adj.* ક્ષમ્ય venial

kshan *n.* ક્ષણ moment

kshanabhangur *adj.* ક્ષણભંગુર flimsy

kshanabhangur *adj.* ક્ષણભંગુર fragile

kshanavaar *n.* ક્ષણવાર trice

kshanavaaraman - thatun *adj.* ક્ષણવારમાં – થતું instantaneous

kshanbhangur *adj.* ક્ષણભંગુર ephemeral

kshanbhar *adv.* ક્ષણભર awhile

kshaneek prakaash *n.* ક્ષણિક પ્રકાશ gleam

kshanik *adj.* ક્ષણિક momentary

kshay *v.i.* ક્ષય wane

ksheen thai javun *v.i.* ક્ષીણ થઈ જવું crumble

ksheen thavun *n.* ક્ષીણ થવું peak

kshetr *n.* ક્ષેત્ર ground

kshetr *n.* ક્ષેત્ર realm

kshetra *n.* ક્ષેત્ર sector

kshetrafal *n.* ક્ષેત્રફળ area

kshetramaapan *n.* ક્ષેત્રમાપન mensuration

kshitij *n.* ક્ષિતિજ horizon

kshobh *n.* ક્ષોભ trepidation

kshobhaman naakhavun ક્ષોભમાં નાખવું perturb

kshobhaman naakhavun te *n.* ક્ષોભમાં નાખવું તે perturbation

Kshudhaa peeditee *adj.* ક્ષુધાપીડિતી starving

kshudr *adj.* ક્ષુદ્ર petty

kshudra *adj.* ક્ષુદ્ર unsubstantial

Kshudra lekhak *n.* ક્ષુદ્ર લેખક scribbler

kshudrata *n.* ક્ષુદ્રતા pettiness

kuber *n.* કુબેર mammon

kuchaagr *n.* કુચાગ્ર nipple

kuchado *n.* કુચડો mop

kudaratanun *adj.* કુદરતનું natural

kudaratee dashaanun *n.* કુદરતી દશાનું crudity

kudaratee valan *n.* કુદરતી વલણ proclivity

Kudratnaa kaaydaathee par *adj.* કુદરતના કાયદાથી પર supernatural

kuhaadee *n.* કુહાડી axe

kuhaadee *n.* કુહાડી hatchet

kuhaadee *n.* કુહાડી woodcutter

kukhyaat *adj.* કુખ્યાત infamous

kul *n.* કુળ clan

kul jatho, parinamavun, rakam *v.* કુલ જથો, પરિણમવું, રકમ amount

kulaanushaasak *n.* કુલાનુશાસક proctor

kulamo *n.* કુલમો sausage

kulapita *n.* કુળપિતા patriarch

kulavaan maanas *n.* કુળવાન માણસ patrician

kulchinho varnavava *v.t.* કુળચિહ્નો વર્ણવવાં blazon

kuleenata *n.* કુલીનતા blueblood

kullee *n.* કુલ્લી crucible

kulo *n.* કુલો hip

kumaaree *n.* કુમારી maiden

kumaarika *n.* કુમારિકા maid

kumaarika *n.* કુમારિકા virgin

kunbhaarakaam *n.* કુંભારકામ pottery

kunbhaavavaalun *adj.* કુંભાવવાળું malicious

kuneh, chaalaakee *n.* કુનેહ finesse

kunehathee chaalavun *n.* કુનેહથી ચલાવવું contrivance

kunj *n.* કુંજ arbour

kunjo *n.* કુંજો pitcher

kunvaar *n.* કુંવાર aloes

kunvaarikaa *adj.* કુંવારિકા vestal

kunvaaro *n.* કુંવારો bachelor

kunwaaraa hovu *adj.* કુંવારા હોવું unawed

kuraan *n.* કુરાન koran

kurakuriyun *n.* કુરકુરિયું puppy

kusevaa *n.* કુસેવા disservice

kushaagrataa *n.* કુશાગ્રતા acuteness

kushaasan *n.* કુશાસન misrule

Kushal *adj.* કુશળ skilful

kushal *adj.* કુશળ skilled

kushal kaareegar *n.* કુશળ કારીગર artist

kushal parvataarohak *n.* કુશળ પર્વતારોહક mountaineer

kushal, nipun *adj.* કુશળ, નિપુણ adroit

Kushaltaa *n.* કુશળતા skill

kustee *n.* કુસ્તી boxing

kustee *v.i.* કુસ્તી wrestle

kutoohalavaalun *adj.* કુતૂહલવાળું inquisitive

kutrim *adj.* કૃત્રિમ artificial

kutrim dakko *n.* કૃત્રિમ ડક્કો. quay

kutrim hasavun *v.i.* કૃત્રિમ હસવું giggle

kutrim vaalanee topee *n.* કૃત્રિમ વાળની ટોપી wig

kutumb *n.* કુટુંબ family

kuvikhyaat *adj.* કુવિખ્યાત notorious

kvakhatanun *adv.* કવખતનું untimely

kveil *n.* ક્વેઈલ quail

kvinaain *n.* ક્વિનાઈન quinine

kvineennu jhaad *n.* ક્વિનીનનું ઝાડ cinchona

Kyaarek kyaarek *adj.* ક્યારેક ક્યારેક sometime

kyaarekanu *adj.* ક્યારેકનું unwonted

kyaarey nahi *adv.* ક્યારેય નહિ never

kyan *adv.* ક્યાં, where

Kyank *adv.* ક્યાંક somewhere

kyubit ક્યુબિટ cubit

L

laabh *n.* લાભ advantage

laabh *n.* લાભ behoof

laabh *n.* લાભ vantage

laabh levo *v.i.* લાભ લેવો avail

laabhadaayak *adj.* લાભદાયક profitable

laabhadaayee *adj.* લાભદાયી expedient

laabhadaayee *adj.* લાભદાયી remunerative

laabhakaarak *adj.* લાભકારક lucrative

laabhakaarak *adj.* લાભકારક beneficial

laabhaprad, faayadaakaarak *adj.* લાભપ્રદ, ફાયદાકારક advantageous

Laabhdaayak *adj.* લાભદાયક salutary

laadakavaayun *adj.* લાડકવાયું pet

laadavun *v.t.* લાદવું enforce

laadavun *v.t.* લાદવું inflict

laadavun *p.p.* લાદવું lade

laadeechitra *n.* લાદીચિત્ર mosaic

laadelun *n.* લાદેલું lading

laaganee *n.* લાગણી feeling

laaganee dubhavavee *v.t.* લાગણી દુભવવી. harrow

laaganeeno aaveg લાગણીનો આવેગ impulse

laaganino abhaav *n.* લાગણીનો અભાવ apathy

laaganio vinaanun *adj.* લાગણીઓ વિનાનું unnatural

Laagnee *n.* લાગણી sentiment

laagneeno sfot *n.* લાગણીનો સ્ફોટ tantrum

Laagneevash *adj.* લાગણીવશ sentimental

laagu pade evun *adj.* લાગુ પડે એવું applicable

laaindorimaan gothavaavun *v.t.* લાઈનદોરીમાં ગોઠવવું align

laakadaanan peep *n.* લાકડાનાં પીપ cooper

laakadaano kolaso *n.* લાકડાંનો કોલસો charcoal

laakadaano moto thaalo *n.* લાકડાંનો મોટો થાળો trencher

laakadaanun *adj.* લાકડાનું wooden

laakadaanun naanun ghar *n.* લાકડાનું નાનું ઘર cabin

laakadaanun paatiyun *n.* લાકડાનું પાટિયું board

laakadaanun peep *n.* લાકડાનું પીપ barrel

laakadee *n.* લાકડી baton

laakadee *n.* લાકડી cane

laakadeethee maaravun *v.t.* લાકડીથી મારવું whack

Laakdaan Vahernaar *n.* લાકડાં વહેરનાર sawyer

Laakdaanee faad *v.t.* લાકડાની ફાડ sliver

Laakdaano vaher *n.* લાકડાંનો વહેર sawdust

laakshanik *adj.* લાક્ષણિક distinctive

laakshanik *adj.* લાક્ષણિક typical

laakshanikata *adj.* લાક્ષણિકતા characteristic

laal *n.* લાળ mucus

Laal *n.* લાળ saliva

Laal *n.* લાળ sputum

laal karavun ke thavun *v.t.* લાલ કરવું કે થવું redden

laal pedaa karavee *v.t.* લાળ પેદા કરવી salivate

Laal tapkvee ke paadvee *n.* લાળ ટપકવી કે પાડવી slobber

Laal zarvee *v.i.* લાળ ઝરવી slabber

laalaash *n.* લાલાશ redness

laalach, mohakataa *n.* લાલચ, મોહકતા allurement

laalachaavavun *v.t.* લાલચાવવું lure

laalasa *n.* લાલસા cupidity

laaleem aapvee *v.t.* તાલીમ આપવી train

laalitya *n.* લાલિત્ય elegance

laalityapoorn *adj.* લાલિત્યપૂર્ણ graceful

laambee rajaa *n.* લાંબી રજા vacation

laambo dhaago *n.* લાંબો ધાગો thread

laambo saliyo *n.* લાંબો સળિયો crowbar

laambo takiyo *n.* લાંબો તકિયો bolster

laambu thai shake aevun *adj.* લાંબુ થઈ શકે એવું tractile

laanbaa thaine soovun *v.i.* લાંબા થઈને સૂવું sprawl

laanbee chees paadavi *v.t.* લાંબી ચીસ પાડવી squeal

laanbee maandagee *adj.* લાંબી માંદગી chronic

laanbo pravaas *n.* લાંબો પ્રવાસ voyage

laanbu karavun *v.t.* લાંબુ કરવું lengthen

laanbun karavun *v.t.* લાંબું કરવું protract

laanch *n.* લાંચ bribery

laanch aapavee *v.t.* લાંચ આપવી bribe

laanchakhaau *adj.* લાંચખાઉ venal

laanchhan lagaadavun *v.t.* લાંછન લગાડવું stigmatize

laanchiyun *adj.* લાંચિયું corrupt

laapee *n.* લાપી putty

laarabord *n.* લારબોર્ડ larboard

laasariyaapanun *n.* લાસરિયાપણું procrastination

laash *n.* લાશ corpse

laat maaravee *v.t.* લાત મારવી hack

laavaa *n.* લાવા lava

laavaaris *adj.* લાવારિસ unclaimed

laavavun *v.t.* લાવવું bring

laayak *adj.* લાયક good

laayak *adj.* લાયક qualified

laayak *n.* લાયક worth

laayakaat *n.* લાયકાત merit

laayakaat *n.* લાયકાત qualification

laayakaat kelavavee *v.t.* લાયકાત કેળવવી qualify

laayakaatavaalu *adj.* લાયકાતવાળું deserving

laayakee લાયકી aptness

laaykaat vinaanu *adj.* લાયકાત વિનાનું unfit

ladaaee *n.* લડાઈ combat

ladaayak *adj.* લડાયક martial

ladaayak *adj.* લડાયક militant

ladaayak *adj.* લડાયક, warlike

ladaayak svadeshaabhimaan *n.* લડાયક સ્વદેશાભિમાન chauvinism

ladanaar *n.* લડનાર combatant

ladat *v.t.* લડત conflict

ladavun *v.t.* લડવું fight

laee aavavun *v.t.* લઈ આવવું fetch

laee javu ke laavvun *n.* લઈ જવું કે લાવવું transportation

lagaam *n.* લગામ bridle

lagaam *n.* લગામ rein

lagabhag *adj.* લગભગ approximate

lagabhag *adv.* લગભગ approximately

lagabhag *adv.* લગભગ nearly

lagabhag, motebhaage *adj.* લગભગ, મોટે ભાગે almost

Lageer *adj.* લગીર slight

laghuchitr *n.* લઘુચિત્ર miniature

laghulipi lekhak *n.* લઘુલિપિ લેખક stenographer

laghulipi lekhan *n.* લઘુલિપિ લેખન stenography

laghulipino akshar *n.* લઘુલિપિનો અક્ષર stenograph

laghutaa darshak *adj.* લઘુતા દર્શક diminutive

lagn *n.* લગ્ન wedding

lagna *n.* લગ્ન espousal

lagna karavaa *v.t.* લગ્ન કરવા marry

lagnagranthi *n.* લગ્નગ્રંથિ wedlock

Lagnagranthithee jodaavun te *v.t.* લગ્નગ્રંથથિી જોડવું તે splice

lagnanee jaheraat *n.* લગ્નની જાહેરાત banns

lagnavidhinun *adj.* લગ્નવિધિનું nuptial

lagnotsav *n.* લગ્નોત્સવ bridal

lahejat *n.* લહેજત flavour

Lahejatdar *adj.* લહેજતદાર sapid

Lahejatdar *n.* લહેજતદાર savoury

laheko *v.t.* લહેકો warble

laher *n.* લહેર fad

laher *n.* લહેર whim

laherathee - niraante gaavun *v.t.* લહેરથી –નિશિતે ગાવું troll

laheratun hovun *v.i.* લહેરાતું હોવું undulate

lahereelun *adj.* લહેરીલું undulatory

lahiyo *n.* લહિયો scribe

lahoteenee ek junee ramat *v.t.* લખોટીની એક જૂની રમત taw

Laingik *adj.* લૈંગિક sexual

lajjit *adj.* લજ્જિત ashamed

lakadaano paatado *n.* લાકડાનો પાટડો beam

lakavo *n.* લકવો palsy

lakhaavelu *n.* લખાવેલું dictation

lakhapati *n.* લખપતિ millionaire

lakhavun *v.t.* લખવું write

lakkadakhod *n.* લક્કડખોદ woodpecker

lakshan *n.* લક્ષણ lineament

Lakshan *n.* લક્ષણ symptom

lakshy *n.* લક્ષ્ય goal

lalach *n.* લલચ inducement

lalachaavavun *n.* લલચાવવું alluring

lalachaavavun *v.t.* લલચાવવું decoy

lalachaavavun *v.t.* લલચાવવું entice

lalachaavavun *v.t.* લલચાવવું induce

lalachaavavun *v.t.* લલચાવવું tempt

lalachaavavun, mohit karavun *v.* લલચાવવું, મોહિત કરવું allure

lalitkalaanu shokheen *n.* લલિતકલાઓનું શોખીન dilettante

laliyun *n.* તળિયું bottom

lambaavavun *v.t.* લંબાવવું elongate

lambaavavun *n.* લંબાવવું extension

lambaroop *adj.* લંબરૂપ vertical

lambhee rajaa *n.* લાંબી રજા furlough

lananaar vyakti *n.* લણનાર વ્યક્તિ reaper

lanavun *v.i.* લણવું reap

lanbaaee *n.* લંબાઈ length

lanbaan *n.* લંબાણ protraction

lanbaanakantaalaajanak *n.* લંબાણઅકંટાળાજનક prolixity

lanbaanavaalun *adj.* લંબાણવાળું prolix

lanbaavavun *v.t.* લંબાવવું prolong

Lanee leedhelun khetar *n.* લણી લીધેલું ખેતર stubble

langadaavun *v.i.* લંગડાવું limp

langado *n.* લંગડો cripple

langadun લંગડું lame

langar *n.* લંગર shee¶anchor

langar, sthir karavun *n.* લંગર, સ્થિર કરવું anchor

langarsthaan *n.* લંગરસ્થાન berth

langotiyo mitr *n.* લંગોટિયો મિત્ર chum

lanpat *n.* લંપટ rakish

lanpatata ne lagatun *adj.* લંપટતા ને લગતું libidinous

Lapasanun *n.* લપસણું slippery

lapasee javun *v.t.* લપસી જવું slip

lasan *n.* લસણ garlic

lasaniyo *n.* લસણિયો opal

lashkaranee chhaavanee *n.* લશ્કરની છાવણી camp

lashkaree *adj.* લશ્કરી military

lashkaree adaalat *n.* લશ્કરી અદાલત courtmartial

lashkaree chhaavanee *n.* લશ્કરી છાવણી cantonment

lashkaree dal *n.* લશ્કરી દળ militia

lashkaree tukadee *n.* લશ્કરી ટુકડી battalion

lashkaree tukadee *n.pl.* લશ્કરી ટુકડી corps

lashkaree vidhyaarthee *n.* લશ્કરી વદ્યિાર્થી cadet

Lashkarno sipaai *n.* લશ્કરનો સપિાઈ soldier

lataakunj *n.* લતાકુંજ bower

latakata vaalanee lat *n.* લટકતા વાળની લટ ringlet

latakatun *adj.* લટકતું baggy

latakatun hovun *v.t.* લટકતું હોવું impend

latakavun *v.i.* લટકવું dangle

lathadavun, *v.i.* લથડવું falter

lathadiyaan khaavaa *v.i.* લથડિયાં ખાવા stagger

Lathdiyaan khaataan chaalvun *v.i.* લથડિયાં ખાતાં ચાલવું shamble

Latpatiyun *n.* લટપટિયું strop

laukik vaat *n.* લૌકિક વાત jaw

lavaad *n.* લવાદ arbiter

lavaad *n.* લવાદ arbitrator

lavaad *n.* લવાદ referee

lavaajam લવાજમ subscriben.ડ્ક

Lavaajam *n.* લવાજમ subscription

lavaaro *n.* લવારો gab

lavaaro karavo *v.i.* લવારો કરવો prate

lavaarun *n.* લવારું kid

lavacheek *adj.* લવચીક flexible

lavacheekataa *n.* લવચીકતા flexibility

laving *n.* લવિંગ clove

lay *n.* લય rhythm

lebhaagu *n.* લેભાગુ upstart

lebhaagu maanas *n.* લેભાગુ માણસ sciolist

leekh *n.* લીખ nit

leela ranganun *adj.* લીલા રંગનું green

leenbu *n.* લીંબુ lemon

leenbunun sharabat *n.* લીંબુનું શરબત lemonade

leenpavun *v.t.* લીંપવું daub

Leent *n.* લીંટ snot

Leesun *adj.* લીસું sleek

Leesun karvun *v.t.* લીસું કરવું smoothen

leetee *n.* લીટી line

leftanant *n.* લેફ્ટનન્ટ lieutenant

lekh *n.* લેખ article

lekhak *n.* લેખક author

lekhak *n.* લેખક writer

lekhakanee bhaavanaao *n.* લેખકની ભાવનાઓ lyric

Lekhan Saahitya saamgree *n.* લેખનસાહિત્ય સામગ્રી stationery

Lekhan saahitya vechnaar *n.* લેખન સાહિત્ય વેચનાર stationer

lekheet dastaavej *n.* લેખીત દસ્તાવેજ writing

lenadaar *n.* લેણદાર creditor

lenun *adj.* લેણું due

leshamaatr *adj.* લેશમાત્ર least

levadadevad *n.* લેવડદેવડ dealing

lift *n.* લિફ્ટ elevator

lijjat *n.* લજ્જત gusto

likhit maaganee *n.* લખિત માગણી requisition

lilaam karanaar *n.* લિલામ કરનાર auctioneer

lilaamee *n.* લિલામી auction

Ling *n.* લિંગ sex

livyantar karavun *v.t.* લિવ્યંતર કરવું transliterate

lobaan *n.* લોબાન benzoin

lobh *n.* લોભ avarice

lobh *n.* લોભ greediness

lobhee *adj.* લોભી avaricious

lobhee *adj.* લોભી covetous

lobhee *adj.* લોભી rapacious

lobhee *adj.* લોભી uncharitable

locho vaalavo *v.t.* લોચો વાળવો bungle

lodhun *n.* લોઢું iron

lohachunbak *n.* લોહચુંબક magnet

lohachunbakanun *adj.* લોહચુંબકનું magnetic

lohee *n.* લોહી blood

lohee choonsatun bhoot *n.* લોહી ચૂસતું ભૂત vampire

lohee ganthaai javun *n.* લોહી ગંઠાઇ જવું thrombosis

lohee ke angaara jevun *adj.* લોહી કે અંગારા જેવું red

lohee nikalavun *v.i.* લોહી નીકળવું bleed

Loheena jevun Raatu *adj.* લોહીના જેવું રાતું sanguine

loheena sanbandheeo *n.* લોહીના સંબંધીઓ kinsman

loheeno pravaahee ansh *n.* લોહીનો પુરવાહી અંશ serum

loheeva *n.* લોહીવા xenomenia

lokabolee *n.* લોકબોલી dialect

lokageet *n.* લોકગીત folksong

lokalaaganee bahekaavanaar *n.* લોકલાગણી બહેકાવનાર demagogue

lokapriy *n.* લોકપ્રિય popular

lokapriy banaavavun *v.* લોકપ્રિય બનાવવું popularize

lokapriyata *n.* લોકપ્રિયતા popularity

lokashaahee *n.* લોકશાહી democracy

lokpriyataa *n.* લોકપ્રિયતા vogue

lokshaahee *adj.* લોકશાહી demoratic

lokshaaheeno samarthak *n.* લોકશાહીનો સમર્થક democrat

lolak paranun vajan *n.* લોલક પરનું વજન bob

loochhavun *v.t.* લૂછવું wipe

loogadee *v.t.* લૂગદી paste

Loogdaaman vintvun લૂગડામાં વીટવું swathe

loont *n.* લૂંટ robbery

Loont *n.* લૂંટ spoliation

loontaaro *n.* લૂંટારો brigand

loontaaro *n.* લૂંટારો robber

loontafaat *n.* લૂંટફાટ brigandage

loontafaat karanaarun *n.* લૂંટફાટ કરનારું predatory

loontafaat karanaarun લૂંટફાટ કરનારું ravenous

loontavun *v.t.* લૂંટવું despoil

loontavun લૂંટવું ransack

loontavun *v.t.* લૂંટવું rob

loontee levun *v.i.* લૂંટી લેવું reive

loonteene laee javun *v.t.* લૂંટીને લઈ જવું plunder

loontfaat *n.* લૂંટફાટ depredation

Loontfaat karvee *v.t.* લૂંટફાટ કરવી spoliate

lootaaruvrutti *n.* લૂંટારુવૃત્તિ rapacity

lootafaat *n.* લૂંટફાટ rapine

lop paamavun *v.* લોપ પામવું vanish

lotavaalun *adj.* લોટવાળું mealy

luchchaaee *adj.* લુચ્ચાઈ cunning

luchchaaee *n.* લુચ્ચાઈ wile

luchchaaeepoorvak *adj.* લુચ્ચાઈપૂર્વક crafty

luchchee chhokaree લુચ્ચી છોકરી minx

luchchun *adj.* લુચ્ચું vulpine

luhaar *n.* લુહાર blacksmith

luhaar *n.* લુહાર farrier

Luhaarnee kodh *n.* લુહારની કોઢ smithy

lupt karavun *v.t.* લુપ્ત કરવું melt

ma chaandee padvee *v.i.* માં ચાંદી પડવી ulcerate

M

maa *n.* મા mother

maa *n.* મા mummy

maa daakhal karavun *v.t.* માં દાખલ કરવી engraft

maa kashunka bhonkaatun *v.t.* માં કશુંક ભોંકાતું tingle

maa thaine *adv.* –માં થઈને through

maachaleenee paankh *n.* માછલીની પાંખ fin

maachhalaan pakadanaar *n.* માછલાં પકડનાર angler

maachhalee *n.* માછલી fish

maachhalee ghar *n.* માછલી ઘર aquarium

maachhaleene lagatu *adj.* માછલીને લગતું finny

maachheemaar *n.* માછીમાર fisherman

maachhlaa pakadvaane jaal *n.* માછલાં પકડવાની જાળ trammel

maadak *adj.* માદક intoxicant

maadak draavan *n.* માદક દ્રાવણ tincture

maadaleeyuun, taavij *n.* માદળિયું, તાવીજ amulet

maadhyam *n.* માધ્યમ medium

maaeel, 176) vaar *n.* માઈલ, ૧૭૬) વાર mile

maaf karavun *v.t.* માફ કરવું remit

maafee *n.* માફી excuse

maafee *n.* માફી exemption

maafee *n.* માફી remission

maafee aapavee *v.t.* માફી આપવી exempt

maafee maagavaalaayak *adj.* માફી માગવાલાયક apologetic

maafee maagavee માફી માગવી apologize

maag karavee *v.t.* માગ કરવી demand

maagavun *v.t.* માગવું beg
maahitagaar *adj.* માહિતગાર aware
maahitagaar *adj.* માહિતગાર cognizant
maahitee aapvee *n.* માહિતી આપવી tele-tale
maahitee kadhavavee *v.t.* માહિતી કઢાવવી elicit
maahitee pustika *n.* માહિતી પુસ્તિકા handbook
maahiteeno bhandaar *n.* માહિતીનો ભંડાર thesaurus
maahiteepatrak *n.* માહિતીપત્રક prospectus
maakhan *n.* માખણ butter
maakhee *n.* માખી fly
maal *n.* માલ cargo
Maal *n.* માળ story
maal japt karavo *v.t.* માલ જપ્ત કરવો. distrain
maal lenaar *n.* માલ લેનાર consignee
maal utaaravo *v.t.* માલ ઉતારવો unload
maala *n.* માળા necklace
maalaano manako *n.* માળાનો મણકો bead
maalabhaadu *n.* માલભાડુ freight
maalanee japtee *n.* માલની જપ્તી distraint
maalanun utpaadan *n.* માલનું ઉત્પાદન output
maalayaadee *n.* માલયાદી inventory
maalee *n.* માળી florist
maalee *n.* માળી gardener
maalik *n.* માલિક owner
maalik *n.* મલિક possessor
maalik *n.* માલિક proprietor
maalikeenun *adj.* માલિકીનું possessive
maalikeenun hovun *v.t.* મલિકીનું હોવું belong
maalish karavun *v.t.* માલશિ કરવું knead
maalish ke chanpee *n.* માલશિ કે ચંપી massage
maalvaahak jahaaj *n.* માલવાહક જહાજ merchantman
maamalun *n.* આમળું myrobaian
maan *prep.* માં in
maan andara hovun *v.t.* માં અંદર હોવું contain
maan dakhal karavee *v.i.* માં દખલ કરવી interfere
maan ghaalavun *v.t.* –માં ઘાલવું insert
maan ghaalavun *v.t.* –માં ઘાલવું intrude
maan kaanun paadavun માં કાણું પાડવું punctur
maan khaancha paadava *v.t.* માં ખાંચા પાડવા indent
maan nihit hovun *v.i.* –માં નહિિત હોવું reside
Maan paru thavu *v.i.* માં પરુ થવું suppurate
maan praan pooravo *v.t.* માં પૂરાણ પૂરવો invigorate
maan ras dharaavanaarun *prep.* માં રસ ધરાવનારું into
maan sandovavun *v.t.* માં સંડોવવું implicate
maan vasaahat karavee –માં વસાહત કરવી populate
maanad *adj.* માનદ honorary
maanad vetan *n.* માનદ વેતન honorarium
maanadand *v.t.* માનદંડ gauge
maananeey *n.* માનનીય honourable
maanasano dekhaav *n.* માણસનો દેખાવ mien
maanasanu snaayubal *n.* માણસનું સ્નાયુબળ thew
maanasik *adj.* માનસિક psychic
maanasik asvasthata *n.* માનસિક અસ્વસ્થતા neurosis
maanasik chitr *n.* માનસિક ચિત્ર image
maanasik chitr *n.* માનસિક ચિત્ર prospect
maanasik santaap *n.* માનસિક સંતાપ pang
maanasik taan *n.* માનસિક તાણ tension
maanasik vikrutithee peedit *adj.* માનસિક વક્તિથી પીડિત mental
maanasik vyatha *n.* માનસિક વ્યથા botheration
maanasikavrutti *n.* માનસિકવૃત્તિ mentality

maanasshaastreeya *adj.* માનસશાસ્ત્રીય psychological

maanavadveshee *n.* માનવદ્વેષી misanthrope

maanavajaati *n.* માનવજાત man

maanavajaati *n.* માનવજાત mankind

maanavochit *adj.* માનવોચિત human

maanavun *v.t.* માનવું believe

maanbhang *n.* માનભંગ degradation

Maand Poortu *adj.* માંડ પૂરતું scant

maandagee *n.* માંદગી illness

maandagee *n.* માંદગી malady

maandahaasy *n.* મંદહાસ્ય chuckle

maandalun *adj.* માંદલું. morbid

Maandand *n.* માનદંડ standard

Maandgee *n.* માંદગી sickness

maandlu માંદલું unhealthy

Maandlun *adj.* માંદલું sickly

maandun *adj.* માંદું ill

Maandun *adj.* માંદું sick

maandun hovun *v.* માંદું હોવું ail

maandun padavun *v.t.* માંદું પડવું sicken

maane evun, javaabadaar *adj.* માને એવું, જવાબદાર amenable

maanee leedhelaa sidhdhaant *n.* માની લીધેલા સદ્ધિધાંત theory

Maanee leedhelee vastu *n.* માની લીધેલી વસ્તુ supposition

maanek *n.* માણેક ruby

maankan *n.* માંકણ bug

maansaahaaree praaneevarg *adj.* માંસાહારી પ્રાણીવર્ગ carnivorous

maansamachcheenu soop *n.* માંસમચ્છીનું સૂપ broth

maansanaa tukadaa *v.t.* માંસના ટુકડા fritter

maansik peedaa *n.* માનસિક પીડા distress

maanthee *prep.* માંથી from

maanthee pasaar thavun *n.* માંથી પસાર થવું undergo

maanthun *n.* માથું head

maanthun laagavun *v.t.* માથું લાગવું resent

Maanvun *v.t.* માનવું suppose

Maany *adj.* માન્ય valid

maany karavun *n.* માન્ય કરવું grant

maany thayelo namuno *n.* માન્ય થયેલો નમુનો norm

maanya karavun *v.t.* માન્ય કરવું concede

maanya karvun *v.t.* માન્ય કરવું accord

maanya raakhavun *v.i.* માન્ય રાખવું assent

maanyataa *v.* માન્યતા abjure

maanyataa માન્યતા acquiescence

maanyataa *n.* માન્યતા approbation

maanyataa *adj.* માન્યતા consider

maanyataa *n.* માન્યતા lore

Maanyataa *n.* માન્યતા validity

maanyataane yogy *adj.* માન્યતાને યોગ્ય allowable

maap *n.* માપ measure

maapadand *n.* માપદંડ criterion

maapak *n.* માપક meter

maar khaadhelun *p.p.* માર ખાધેલું beaten

maar maaravo *v.t.* માર મારવો beat

maaraamaaree, ashaanti *n.* મારામારી, અશાંતિ affray

maarano sol *n.* મારનો સોળ wale

maaravun *v.t.* મારવું hit

maaravun *v.t.* મારવું thrash

maaree *pro.* મારૂ my

maaree jaate *pro.* મારી જાતે. myself

maaree naakhavun *v.t.* મારી નાખવું kill

Maaree naakhvun *v.t.* મારી નાખવું slay

maarg *n.* માર્ગ aisle

maarg *n.* માર્ગ route

maarga *n.* માર્ગ trajectory

maargadarshak *v.t.* માર્ગદર્શક guide

maargadarshak taaro *n.* માર્ગદર્શક તારો cynosure

maargadarshak vastu *n.* માર્ગદર્શક વસ્તુ pole-star

maargadarshan *n.* માર્ગદર્શન guidance

maargasetu *n.* માર્ગસેતુ viaduct

maargasoochak stanbh *n.* માર્ગસૂચક સ્તંભ milestone

maarjarin *n.* માર્જરિન margarine

maarpeet *n.* મારપીટ batter

maarshal *n.* માર્શલ marshal
maartin pakshee *n.* માર્ટિન પક્ષી martin
maarun *n.* મારું mine
Maarvun *v.i.* મારવું smite
Maarvun *v.t.* મારવું swinge
maashook *n.* માશૂક leman
maasik *n.pl.* માસિક menses
maasik *adj.* માસિક monthly
maasik straav thavo te *n.* માસિક સ્ત્રાવ થવો તે menstruation
maateekaamanee kala *n.* માટીકામની કળા ceramics
maateena vaasan *n.* માટીના વાસણ crockery
maateenaa vaasan *n.* માટીના વાસણ earthenware
maateeno dhagalo *n.* માટીનો ઢગલો mound
maateenu *adj.* માટીનું earthen
maateenun thefun *n.* માટીનું ઢેફું clod
maatha deeth *adv.* માથા દીઠ apiece
maathaabhaare *adj.* માથાભારે insubordinate
Maathaano khodo *n.* માથાનો ખોડો scall
maathaanun darad *n.* માથાનું દરદ headache
maathaanun kavach *n.* માથાનું કવચ casque
maathe chaanyaavaalun *adv.* માથે છાંયાવાળું tented
maathe levun *n.* માથે લેવું undertake
maathee neekadavun *v.t.* માંથી નીકળવું emanate
maathun *n.* માથું noddle
maathun ane haathapaga vinaanu dhad *n.* માથું અને હાથપગ વિનાનું ધડ torso
maathun dolaavavun *v.t.* માથું ડોલાવવું nod
maatr માત્ર merely
maatruhatya *n.* માતૃહત્યા. matricide
maatrupakshanun sagun *adj.* માતૃપક્ષનું સગું maternal
maatrutv *n.* માતૃત્વ maternity
maayaalu *adj.* માયાળું friendly

maayaavee *adj.* માયાવી illusive
maayaavee *adj.* માયાવી phantastic
machchhar *n.* મચ્છર gnat
machchhar *n.* મચ્છર. mosquito
madaagaanth *n.* મડાગાંઠ impasse
madad *n.* મદદ assistance
madad *n.* મદદ help
madad karavee *v.t.* મદદ કરવી assist
Madad maate pokaar *n.* મદદ માટે પોકાર sos
madadaagaadee *n.* મડદાગાડી hearse
madadaapetee *n.* મડદાપેટી coffin
madadaneesh *n.* મદદનીશ assistant
madadaneesh *n.* મદદનીશ deputy
madh *n.* મધ honey
madhamaakhee *n.* મધમાખી bee
madhapoodo *n.* મધપૂડો hive
madhapoodo *n.* મધપૂડો honeycomb
madhapudo *n.* મધપૂડો bee-hive
madhmaakhee ucher sthal *n.* મધમાખી ઉછેર સ્થળ aplary
madhumaas *n.* મધુમાસ honeymoon
madhuprameh *n.* મધુમેહ diabetes
madhur *adj.* મધુર dulcet
Madhyaarkvalun *adj.* મદ્યાર્કવાળું spirituous
madhyabhaag *n.* મધ્યભાગ midst
madhyaga *n.* મધ્યગા median
madhyakotik *adj.* મધ્યકોટિ mediocre
madhyam kotinun *adj.* મધ્યમ કોટિનું middle
madhyam varga *n.* મધ્યમ વર્ગ bourgeoisie
madhyam vargana loko *n.* મધ્યમ વર્ગના લોકો gentry
madhyaman aavelun *adj.* મધ્યમા આવેલું medial
madhyapath *n.* મધ્યપથ gangway
madhyaraatr *n.* મધ્યરાત્ર midnight
madhyashtha *n.* મધ્યસ્થ umpire
madhyasthee karavee *v.i.* મધ્યસ્થી કરવી mediate
madhyavartee *adj.* મધ્યવર્તી cardinal
madhyaveethi *n.* મધ્યવીથિ nave
madhyayugeen gaayak *n.* મધ્યયુગીન ગાયક minstrel

madhystheethanaar *n.* મધ્યસ્થીથનાર go-between

madirapaatra *n.* મદિરાપાત્ર decanter

madyaark, madyasaar *n.* મદ્યઆરૂ, મદ્યસાર alcohol

madyarkvaalun *n.* મદ્યઆરૂવાળું alcoholic

madyatyaagee *n.* મદ્યત્યાગી teetotaller

magafalee *n.* મગફળી groun·nut

magaj *n.* મગજ brain

magar *n.* મગર crocodile

magar, susavaat *n.* મગર, સુસવાટ alligator

mahaaaparaadh *n.* મહાઅપરાધ felon

mahaaaparaadh *n.* મહાઅપરાધ felony

mahaaaparaadhee *adj.* મહાઅપરાધી felonious

mahaajan *n.* મહાજન guild

mahaakaavya *n.* મહાકાવ્ય epic

mahaamaaree *n.* મહામારી pestilence

mahaamoolun *adj.* મહામૂલું precious

mahaamushkel *n.* મહામુશ્કેલ. herculean

mahaanagarapaalikano pramukh *n.* મહાનગરપાલિકાનો પૂરમુખ mayor

mahaanibandh *n.* મહાનબિંધ thesis

mahaasaagar *n.* મહાસાગર ocean

mahaavaro paadavo *v.t.* મહાવરો પાડવો accustom

mahaavidhaala *n.* મહાવદ્યિાલય college

mahaavidhyaalayane lagatun *n.* મહાવદ્યિાલયને લગતું collegiate

mahatta vadhaaravee *v.t.* મહત્તા વધારવી glorify

mahattm *n.* મહત્તમ maximum

mahattv *v.t.* મહત્ત્વ precede

mahattv vadhaaravun *v.t.* મહત્વ વધારવું promote

mahattvaakaankshaa *n.* મહત્ત્વાકાંક્ષા aspiration

mahattvaakaankshee *n.* મહત્ત્વાકાંક્ષી aspirant

mahattvanun maanas મહત્ત્વનું માણસ personage

mahatvanun *n.* મહત્ત્વનું important

mahatvasheel *adj.* મહત્વશીલ pivotal

mahel *n.* મહેલ castle

mahemaan *n.* મહેમાન guest

Mahemaan *n.* મહેમાન sojourner

mahemaanono melaavado *n.* મહેમાનોનો મેળાવડો levee

mahenataanun *n.* મહેનતાણું remuneration

mahenataanun aapavun મહેનતાણું આપવું remunerate

mahenatanun *adj.* મહેનતનું hard

mahenatanun *adj.* મહેનતુ laborious

mahenatanun *n.* મહેનતાણુ wages

mahenun *n.* મહેણું quip

mahetal *n.* મહેતલ respite

mahilaa sangh મહિલા સંઘ sorority

mahino *n.* મહિનો month

maid geetanun sangeet *n.* મૈડ ગીતનું સંગીત chant

maithun *n.* મૈથુન coitus

maithun *n.* મૈથુન intercourse

maitreebharyun *adj.* મૈત્રીભર્યું cordial

maitreepoorvak *adv.* મૈત્રીપૂર્વક amicably

maitreevaalun *adj.* મૈત્રીવાળું nice

maja khaatar karelo pravaas *n.* મજા ખાતર કરેલો પૂરવાસ outing

majaagaraanvaalo bhaag *n.* મજાગરાંવાળો ભાગ casement

majaagaran *n.* મજાગરાં hinge

majaak karavee *v.t.* મજાક કરવી bamboozle

majaanu *adj.* મજાનું delectable

majaboot banaavavun *v.t.* મજબૂત બનાવવું embolden

majaboot pakad *n.* મજબૂત પકડ grip

majaboot pakadavun *v.t.* મજબૂત પકડવું clench

majaboot pakadavun *v.i.* મજબૂત પકડવું clip

majaboot pakadavun *n.* મજબૂત પકડવું grasp

majalo *n.* મજલો floor

Majboot vaans *n.* મજબૂત વાંસ spar

Majbootaai *v.t.* મજબૂતાઈ strengthen

majja *n.* મજ્જા marrow

majjaatantunnun darad *n.* મજ્જાતંતુનું દરદ neuralgia

majjaatantunun - sanbandhee *adj.* મજ્જાતંતુનું – સંબંધી. neural

majoor *n.* મજૂર drudge

majoor *n.* મજૂર labour

majoor mahaajan *n.* મજૂર મહાજન trade union

majooravarg *n.* મજૂરવર્ગ proletariat

makaaee *n.* મકાઈ maize

makaamataa *n.* મક્કમતા firmness

makaananee andar *adv.* મકાનની અંદર indoors

makaananee andaranun *adj.* મકાનની અંદરની indoor

makaanano khuno *n.* મકાનનો ખૂણો quoin

makaananun chhaaparun *n.* મકાનનું છાપરું roof

Makaanno mal ke majo *n.* મકાનનો માળ કે મજલો storey

makar raashi *n.* મકર રાશિ. capricorn

makkam *adj.* મક્કમ firm

makkam *adj.* મક્કમ tenacious

makkamataa *n.* મક્કમતા tenacity

malaaee *n.* મલાઈ cream

malaai utaaravee મલાઈ ઉતારવી skim

malaai utaarnaar *n.* મલાઈ ઉતારનાર skimmer

malaavarodh *n.* મળાવરોધ retention

malam *n.* મલમ plaster

malamal *n.* મલમલ muslin

malamala *n.* મખમલ velvet

malampattee *n.* મલમપટ્ટી dressing

malapaatr *n.* મળપાત્ર bed-pan

malaskun *n.* મળસકું day-break

malataapanun *n.* મળતાપણું accordance

malataavadaapanun *n.* મળતાવડાપણું amiability

malataavadun *adj.* મળતાવડું amiable

malataavadun, saujanyasheel *adj.* મળતાવડું, સૌજન્યશીલ affable

malatar *n.* મળતર emolument

malatiyo *n.* મળતિયો accessary

malatyaag karavo *v.t.* મળત્યાગ કરવો. defecate

Malkaatun *adj.* મલકાતું smiling

mall *n.* મલ્લ wrestler

mallashaala *n.* મલ્લશાળા xyst

mallashaala *n.* મલ્લશાળા xystus

Malmootra lai javaanee moree *n.* મળમૂત્ર લઈ જવાની મોરી sewer

Maltaavdun *adj.* મળતાવડું sociable

mamataa *n.* મમતા affection

man *n.* મન mind

man maarvu te *n.* મન મારવું તે self-denial

manaaee *v.t.* મનાઈ ban

manaaee *n.* મનાઈ injunction

manaaee *n.* મનાઈ veto

manaaee karavee *v.t.* મનાઈ કરવી forbid

manaaeeno hukam *n.* મનાઈનો હુકમ prohibition

manaaihookam *n.* મનાઈહુકમ embargo

manaavavun મનાવવું cajole

manaavavun *v.t.* મનાવવું propitiate

manaavavun te *n.* મનાવવું તે propitiation

manadukh *n.* મનદુઃખ resentment

manakaanee maala *n.* મણકાની માળા chaplet

manamaan saalavun મનમાં સાલવું rankle

manamaan vichaaravun *v.t.* મનમાં વિચારવું contemplate

manaman ghaolavun te *n.* મનમાં ઘોળવું તે cogitation

manaman gholya karavun *v.t.* મનમાં ઘોળ્યા કરવું revolve

manaman thasaavavun મનમાં ઠસાવવું implant

manaman utaaravun *v.t.* મનમાં ઉતારવું infuse

manamel *n.* મનમેળ reconciliation

mananee sthiti *n.* મનની સ્થિતિ mood

Mananun Saabootpanun *n.* મનનું સાબૂતપણું sanity

manapasand *n.* મનપસંદ eureka

manasvee *n.* મનસ્વી arbitrary

manasvee *adj.* મનસ્વી discretionary

manasvee *adj.* મનસ્વી imperious

manasveepanoon *n.* મનસૂવીપણું vagary

manathee vichaaronee aaple *n.* મનથી વિચારોની આપ-લે telepathy

Manch *n.* મંચ dais

manch *n.* મંચ dice

manch *n.* મંચ platform

manch *n.* મંચ tribune

mand *adj.* મંદ bovine

mand મંદ languid

Mand *adj.* મંદ sluggish

mand sameer *n.* મંદ સમીર breeze

mandabuddhi maanas *n.* મંદબુદ્ધિ માણસ dullard

mandagee, bechenee *n.* માંદગી, બેચેની ailment

mandalee *n.* મંડળી club

mandaleeno sabhy *n.* મંડળીનો સભ્ય member

mandbuddhi *adj.* મંદબુદ્ધિ subnormal

Mandbudhdhi *n.* મંદબુદ્ધિ stupidity

mandbudhhi *adj.* મંદબુદ્ધિ unapt

mandee *n.* મંદી slump

mandee *n.* મંદી tardiness

mandir *n.* મંદિર. temple

mandleema *adv.* મંડળીમાં together

mandya rahevun મંડ્યા રહેવું persist

mane *pro.* મને me

mane laage chhe ke *v.i.* મને લાગે છે કે methinks

mangalano grah *n.* મંગળનો ગ્રહ mars

mangalavaara *n.* મંગળવાર. tuesday

manjoor karanaar *n.* મંજૂર કરનાર approver

manjooree *n.* મંજૂરી approval

manjooree *n.* મંજૂરી sanction

manjooree aapatun *adv.* મંજૂરી આપતું approvingly

manjooree aapavee *v.i.* મંજૂરી આપવી give

mannee vaat kahevee *v.i.* મનની વાત કહેવી unbosom

manobala todee naakhavun *v.t.* મનોબળ તોડી નાખવું unnerve

manobhaav *n.* મનોભાવ emotion

manohar *n.* મનોહર captivating

manokaamana sevavee *v.i.* મનોકામના સેવવી aspire

manoranjak *adj.* મનોરંજક interesting

Manoranjak *n.* મનોરંજક sweets

manoranjan *n.* મનોરંજન entertainment

manoranjan *n.* મનોરંજન pastime

manoranjan karanaarun *n.* મનોરંજન કરનારું comic

manoranjan karavun *v.t.* મનોરંજન કરવું entertain

manoranjan karavun *v.t.* મનોરંજન કરવું recreate

manoranjan, aanand *n.* મનોરંજન, આનંદ fun

manovignaan *adj.* મનોવિજ્ઞાન psychology

manovikrut *n.* મનોવિકૃત aberrant

manovishleshan *v.t.* મનોવિશ્લેષણ analysis

manovishleshan karavun *v.t.* મનોવિશ્લેષણ કરવું analyse

manpasand, anukool *adj.* મનપસંદ, અનુકૂળ agreeable

mantamugdh karavun *n.* મંત્રમુગ્ધ કરવું fascination

manthee neekalavun *v.t.* માંથી નીકળવું exude

Mantree *n.* મંત્રી secretary

mantreemandal *n.* મંત્રીમંડળ cabinet

manushy vadh *n.* મનુષ્ય વધ. homicide

manushyaakruti yantr *n.* મનુષ્યાકૃતિ યંત્ર robot

manushyavadh *n.* મનુષ્યવધ murder

maraamat yogya *adj.* મરામત યોગ્ય repairable

marachun *adj.* મરચું chilli

maradana gunavaalun *adj.* મરદના ગુણવાળું manly

marado *n.* મરડો dysentery

maraghaa uchher *n.* મરઘા ઉછેર poultry

maraghaa vechavaavaalo *n.* મરઘા વેચવાવાળો poulter

maraghaannun paanjarun *n.* મરઘાંનું પાંજરૂં coop

maraghee *n.* મરઘી hen

maragheeno saad *n.* મરઘીનો સાદ chuck

maraghu *n.* મરઘું fowl

marahoom *adj.* મરહૂમ deceased

marajeethee karelun *adj.* મરજીથી કરેલું willing

maran *n.* મરણ quietus

maranaank *n.* મરણાંક fatality

marananun pramaan *n.* મરણનું પ્રમાણ mortality

maranatithi *n.* મરણતિથિ obit

maraniyo *n.* મરણિયો desperado

maraniyu *adj.* મરણિયું desperate

maraniyun *adj.* મરણિયું frantic

maranottar *adv.* મરણોત્તર postmortem

markvis *n.* માર્ક્વિસ marquis

marmabhedak મર્મભેદક poignant

marmagnya *n.* મર્મજ્ઞ connoisseur

Marmvachan *n.* મર્મવચન sarcasm

marshiyo *n.* મરશિયો dirge

marun *n.* મરૂણ maroon

maryaadaa vataavvee te *n.* મર્યાદા વટાવવી તે transgression

maryaadaabhang *n.* મર્યાદાભંગ offence

maryaadaabhang karavo *v.i.* મર્યાદાભંગ કરવો offend

maryaadaaman raakhavun *v.t.* મર્યાદામાં રાખવું confine

maryaadaao olangee મર્યાદાઓ ઓળંગી transacend

maryaadit *adj.* મર્યાદિત finite

Masaalaanee cheej *n.* મસાલાની ચીજ spice

masalat karavee *v.t.* મસલત કરવી consult

mashaal *n.* મશાલ brand

mashaal *n.* મશાલ flambeau

mashaal *n.* મશાલ torch

mashagool મશગૂલ absorbed

mashkaree *n.* મશ્કરી drollery

mashkaree *v.i.* મશ્કરી fleer

mashkaree મશ્કરી pleasantry

mashkaree karavee *v.t.* મશ્કરી કરવી. deride

mashkaree kareene cheedavvun *v.t.* મશ્કરી કરીને ચીડવવું tease

Mashkareenun *n.* મશ્કરીનું sobriquet

mashkaro *n.* મશ્કરો pantaloon

mashkaro *n.* મશ્કરો zany

mashkarun *adj.* મશ્કરું jocular

masjid *n.* મસ્જિદ. mosque

masoorano daano *n.* મસૂરનો દાણો lentil

masteekhor *n.* મસ્તીખોર imp

masteekhoree *n.* મસ્તીખોરી hilarity

mastikvidyaa *n.* મસ્તકવિદ્યા phrenology

mat *n.* મત, vote

mataadhikaar *n.* મતાધિકાર franchise

mataadhikaar raddeekaran *v.t.* મતાધિકાર રદ્દીકરણ disfranchise

matabhed *n.* મતભેદ difference

matabhed *n.* મતભેદ schism

matabhet dharaavatu *n.* મતભેત ધરાવતું dissentient

matadaan *n.* મતદાન poll

matadaar *n.* મતદાર voter

mataganak *n.* મતગણક teller

mataiky *n.* મતૈક્ય concurrence

matapatra *n.* મતપત્ર ballot

matapetee *n.* મતપેટી ballobox

matatvaakankshaa *n.* મહત્વાકાંક્ષા longing

matdaar *n.* મતદાર elector

matdaar yaadee *n.* મતદારયાદી electorate

math *n.* મઠ monastery

mathaadu aapavun *v.t.* મથાળું આપવું entitle

mathalun *n.* મથાળું caption

mathavaasee *n.* મઠવાસી. monk

Mathvun *v.t.* મથવું strive

matsy kanya *n.* મત્સ્ય કન્યા mermaid

matsyaudhog *n.* મત્સ્યઉદ્યોગ fishery

matvistaar *n.* મતવિસ્તાર constituency

maukhik *adj.* મૌખિક oral

maun મૌન mum

maun મૌન reticence

mavaalee *n.* મવાલી hooligan

mdh *n.* મધ્યમ માર્ગે viamedia

medam *n.* મેડમ ma'am

medam *n.* મેડમ madam

medavruddhee *n.* મેદવૃદ્ધિ obesity
meemaansaa *n.* મીમાંસા treatise
meen *n.* મીણ bees-wax
meen *n.* મીણ wax
meenabattee *n.* મીણબત્તી candle
meenanun banaavelun *adj.* મીણનું બનાવેલું waxen
meeniyun *n.* મીણિયું oil-cloth
meeniyun, kaapad *n.* મીણિયું કાપડ buckram
meethaaee *n.* મીઠાઈ confection
Meethaavaalun *adj.* મીઠાવાળું saline
Meethun *n.* મીઠું salt
meethun masaalo *n.* મીઠું મસાલો condiment
megaafon *n.* મેગાફોન megaphone
meghadhanush *n.* મેઘધનુષ rainbow
megnesiyam *n.* મેગ્નેશિયમ magnesium
mej ghadiyaal *n.* મેજ ઘડિયાળ timepiece
mej, teble *n.* મેજ, ટેબલ table
melavavun *v.t.* મેળવવું acquire
melavavun *v.t.* મેળવવું gain
melavavun *v.t.* મેળવવું get
melavavun *v.t.* મેળવવું obtain
melee vidya મેલી વિદ્યા witchcraft
melo *n.* મેળો carnival
melo *adj.* મેળો fair
melu *adj.* મેલું dingy
Melun *n.* મેલું sloven
Melun *adj.* મેલું sordid
Melun karvun *n.* મેલું કરવું soil
mendee *n.* મેંદી myrtle
mengeniz *n.* મેંગેનિઝ manganese
menthol *n.* મેન્થોલ menthol
Mesh *n.* મેશ soot
Meshnun ke meshnaa jevun *n.* મેશનું કે મેશના જેવું sooty
metinee *n.* મેટિની matinee
mijaaj *n.* મિજાજ temper
mijaajee *adj.* મિજાજી lofty
mijabaanee aapavee *n.* મજિબાની આપવી regale
mijabaaneene lagatu *adj.* મજિબાનીને લગતું festal
mikenik *n.* મકિનિક mechanic
milakat *n.* મલિકત estate

milakat dharaavanaar *adj.* મલિકત ધરાવનાર proprietary
minaaro *n.* મનિારો minaret
minaaro *n.* મનિારો spire
minaaro *n.* મનિારો tower
minaaro *n.* મનિારો turret
mineet *n.* મનિીટ minute
mishra *adj.* મશ્રિ composite
mishran *n.* મશ્રિણ amalgamation
mishran *n.* મશ્રિણ composition
mishran *n.* મશ્રિણ mixture
mishran karavun *n.* મશ્રિણ કરવું alloy
mishran karavun *v.t.* મશ્રિણ કરવું amalgamate
mishran karavun *v.t.* મશ્રિણ કરવું intermingle
mishran karavun *v.t.* મશ્રિણ કરવું mix
mishrita nahi tevun *adj.* મશ્રિતિ નહિ તેવું unmixed
mitaachaar *n.* મતિાચાર temperance
mitaahari *adj* મતિાહારી abstemious
Mithaaibharyu *n.* મીઠાઈભર્યુ sweetness
mithya paandity *n.* મથ્યિા પાંડિત્ય pedantry
mithyaabhimaan *n.* મથ્યિાભમિાન vanity
mithyaachaar *n.* મથ્યિાચાર hypocrisy
mitra *n.* મતિ્ર friend
mitrabhaav gumaavavo *v.t.* મતિ્રભાવ ગુમાવવો. estrange
mitrata *n.* મતિ્રતા amity
mitrataa *v.t.* મતિ્રતા befriend
mitrataa *n.* મતિ્રતા comradership
mitrataa *n.* મતિ્રતા freindship
mitrataabharyun *adj.* મતિ્રતાભર્યું amicable
mitrataanee samajootee *n.* મતિ્રતાની સમજૂતી entente
mittaahar *n.* મતિાહાર abstemiousness
mobho *n.* મોભો dignity
mochee *n.* મોચી cobbler
Mochee *n.* મોચી shoe-maker
mocheeno soyo *n.* મોચીનો સોયો awl
modee *n.* મોદી grocer

modethi, aagal jatan *adv.* મોડેથી, આગળ જતાં afterward

modhaaparano bhaav *n.* મોઢાપરનો ભાવ aspect

modu karevun *adj.* મોડું કરવું dilatory

modun *adv.* મોડું late

modun padelun *adj.* મોડું પડેલું belated

mogaree *n.* મોગરી rammer

moheet karavun *v.t.* મોહતિ કરવું enamour

mohit karavun *v.t.* મોહતિ કરવું enthral

mohit karavun *v.t.* મોહતિ કરવું infatuate

moja maate karelee musaafaree *n.* મોજ માટે કરેલી મુસાફરી tour

mojamaja *n.* મોજમજા merriment

mojamajaa karavee *v.t.* મોજમજા કરવી disport

mojanee *v.t.* મોજણી survey

Mojanno uchhalo *n.* મોજાંનો ઉછાળો surge

mojeelun *adj.* મોજીલું blithe

mojilun *adj.* મોજીલું jovial

Mojneedaar *n.* મોજણીદાર surveyor

mojun *n.* મોજું sock

mojun *n.* મોજું stocking

mojun *n.* મોજું wave

mokala mananun *adj.* મોકળા મનનું communicative

mokalaaashavaalun *adj.* મોકળાશવાળું. roomy

mokalaashavaalun, bharapoor *adj.* મોકળાશવાળું, ભરપૂર ample

mokalaashvaalun *adj.* મોકળાશવાળું commodious

mokalela paisa *n.* મોકલેલા પૈસા remittance

mokharaanee baaju *v.i.* મોખરાની બાજુ front

mokharaano bhaag *n.* મોખરાનો ભાગ facade

mokhare *adv.* મોખરે atop

mokoof raakhavun *v.t.* મોકૂફ રાખવું defer

mokt karavun *v.t.* મુક્ત કરવું liberate

mokufee *n.* મોકૂફી abeyance

mon *n.* મોં thrush

mondhu *adj.* મોંઘું expensive

monghun *adj.* મોંઘું costly

Monmaanthee laal paadvee *v.i.* મોંમાંથી લાળ પાડવી sputter

monno chaalo *n.* મોંનો ચાળો grimace

montaaj *n.* મોન્ટાજ montage

moochh *n.* મૂછ moustache

moodeerokaan *n.* મૂડીરોકાણ outlay

moodeevaad *n.* મૂડીવાદ capitalism

moodeevaadee *n.* મૂડીવાદી capitalist

moodhun *n.* મોઢું mouth

Mook, Sammati *n.* મૂક સંમતિ sufferance

mookavun મૂકવું put

mool *n.* મૂળ derivation

mool shabd *n.* મૂળ શબ્દ text

mool shodavun *v.t.* મૂળ શોધવું derive

mool sthitiman aavavun *v.t.* મૂળ સ્થિતિમાં આવવું reinstate

mool tattvo *n.* મૂળ તત્ત્વો rudiment

moola paathanu *adj.* મૂળ પાઠનું textual

moolaaranbhanun *adj.* મૂળારંભનું rudimentary

moolabhoot *adj.* મૂળભૂત elemental

moolabhoot *adj.* મૂળભૂત fundamental

moolabhoot dhatak *n.* મૂળભૂત ઘટક electron

moolabhoot siddhaant *n.* મૂળભૂત સદ્ધિાંત groundwork

moolagat *adj.* મૂળગત radical

moolamaa thato gaththo, gaanth *n.* મૂળમાં થતો ગઠ્ઠો – ગાંઠ tuber

moolanun *n.* મૂળનું native

moolavanaar *n.* મૂલવનાર appraiser

mooliyun *n.* મૂળિયું root

moolo *n.* મૂળો. radish

mooly vinaanun *adv.* મૂલ્ય વનિાનું gratis

moolya ghataadavun *v.t.* મૂલ્ય ઘટાડવું debase

moolya ghataadavun *v.t.* મૂલ્ય ઘટાડવું derogate

moolya nakkee karavun *n.* મૂલ્ય નક્કી કરવું appraisal

moolyaankan karavun *v.t.* મૂલ્યાંકન કરવું evaluate

moolyankan v.i. મૂલ્યાંકન appraise

moongu adj. મૂંગું dumb

moonjhavan n. મૂંઝવણ quandary

moorakh adj. મૂરખ crass

moorakh banaavavun v.t. મૂરખ બનાવવું befool

moorchha n. મૂર્છા coma

moorchhaa paamavee v.i. મૂર્છા પામવી swoon

Moorkh adj. મૂરખ daft

moorkh n. મૂરખ daw

moorkh n. મૂરખ fool

moorkh adj. મૂરખ witless

Moorkh adj. મૂરખ silly

moorkh maanas n. મૂરખ માણસ booby

moorkha adj. મૂરખ unwise

moorkhaamee bharelun adj. મૂરખામી ભરેલું incongruous

moorkhaameebharelun adj. મૂરખામીભરેલું rotten

moorkhaameebharyu vartan n. મૂરખામીભર્યું વર્તન tomfoolery

moorkhaameebharyun n. મૂરખામીભર્યું nonsense

moorkhamaanas n. મૂરખમાણસ jackass

moorkhamaanas n. મૂરખમાણસ ninny

moorkhataa n. મૂરખતા folly

Moorkho n. મૂરખા simpleton

Moorkhtaabharyun n. મૂરખતાભર્યું smirk

moorkhvyakti n. મૂરખવ્યક્તિ tomfool

moort roop aapavun v.t. મૂર્ત રૂપ આપવું materialize

moortakalpana n. મૂર્તકલ્પના projection

moortasvaroop n. મૂર્તસ્વરૂપ embodiment

moorti n. મૂર્તિ idol

Moorti ke baavlun n. મૂર્તિ કે બાવલું statue

moortibhanjak n. મૂર્તિભંજક iconoclast

moortimant banaavavun v.t. મૂર્તિમંત બનાવવું incarnate

Moortionun n. મૂર્તિઓનું statuary

moortipooja n. મૂર્તિપૂજા idolatry

moortipooja n. મૂર્તિપૂજા paganism

moortipoojak n. મૂર્તિપૂજક idolater

moortipoojak n. મૂર્તિપૂજક pagan

mootar n. મૂતર piss

mooth n. મૂઠ hilt

mooth n. મૂઠ knob

mootraashay n. મૂત્રાશય bladder

mootrapind n. મૂત્રપિંડ kidney

mootrapind n. મૂત્રપિંડ reins

mootrapind sanbandhee adj. મૂત્રપિંડ સંબંધી renal

Mootravrodhak n. મૂત્રાવરોધ strangury

mor n. મોર peacock

mor aavavaavaalu n. મોર આવવાવાળું efflorescence

moradee n. મોરડી halter

mota mananun adj. મોટા મનનું magnanimous

mota manapanun n. મોટા મનપણું magnanimity

motaa mananun adj. મોટા મનનું benign

motaaman moto bhaag adj. મોટામાં મોટો ભાગ. most

motaapanun n. મોટાપણું magnitude

motan mojan n. મોટાં મોજાં billow

motarasaaeekal n. મોટરસાઇકલ bike

motargaadee n. મોટરગાડી automobile

motee n. મોતી pearl

motee gaadee n. મોટી ગાડી van

motee khoondhavaalo balad n. મોટી ખૂંધવાળો બળદ zebu

motee sankhya n. મોટી સંખ્યા legion

motee sankhya n. મોટી સંખ્યા multitude

motee sankhyaaman n. મોટી સંખ્યામાં bulk

motee taanki n. મોટી ટાંકી tank

motee tukadee n. મોટી ટુકડી brigade

motee uamarnu adj. મોટી ઉંમરનું elder

moteenee chheep n. મોતીની છીપ oyster

motethee vaanchavun v.t. મોટેથી વાંચવું read

motethee, buland avaaje adv. મોટેથી, બુલંદ અવાજે aloud

moto kheelo *n.* મોટો ખીલો bolt
moto nal *n.* મોટો નળ hydrant
moto vistaar મોટો વસ્તિાર expanse
motu todu *n.* મોટું ટોળું flock
motun *adj.* મોટું big
motun chhaapelun chitr *n.* મોટું છાપેલું ચત્રિ poster
motun jahaaj *n.* મોટું જહાજ argosy
motun kabaat *n.* મોટું કબાટ wardrobe
motun khokhun *n.* મોટું ખોખું crate
motun makaan *n.* મોટું મકાન mansion
motun mojun *n.* મોટું મોજું gauntlet
motun mojun *n.* મોટું મોજું surf
motun peep *n.* મોટું પીપ vat
motun vaandarun *n.* મોટું વાંદરું baboon
mrudu svabhaav *n.* મૃદુ સ્વભાવ pliability
mrudu svabhaavanun *adj.* મૃદુ સ્વભાવનું pliable
mrugasheersh *n.* મૃગશીર્ષ orion
mrut *n.* મૃત dead
mrutdeh *n.* મૃતદેહ corpus
mrutyu *n.* મૃત્યુ death
mrutyu *n.* મૃત્યુ decease
mrutyu *n.* મૃત્યુ demise
mrutyughant *n.* મૃત્યુઘંટ knell
mrutyunondh *adj.* મૃત્યુનોંધ obituary
mrutyupatra *n.* મૃત્યુપત્ર testament
mrutyupatra karanaar *n.* મૃત્યુપત્ર કરનાર testator
mrutyupatranee saabitee *n.* મૃત્યુપત્રની સાબતિી probate
mrutyupatranu *adj.* મૃત્યુપત્રનું testamentary
mucharako *v.t.* મુચરકો recognizance
mudraalekh *n.* મુદ્રાલેખ legend
mudraalekh *n.* મુદ્રાલેખ motto
mudranakalaa *n.* મુદ્રણકલા typography
mufasil *adj.* મુફસલિ mofussil
mugat *n.* મુગટ diadem
mugat *n.* મુગટ mitre
mugdh karavun *v.t.* મુગ્ધ કરવું bewitch
mukaam *v.i.* મુકામ halt
mukaam *n.* મુકામ sojourn
mukaddamo, krutya *n.* મુકદ્દમો, કૃત્ય action

mukarar karavun *v.t.* મુકરર કરવું assign
mukhachitra મુખચત્રિ frontispiece
mukhamudra *n.* મુખમુદ્રા visage
mukhapaath karavo *v.t.* મુખપાઠ કરવો recite
mukhapatra *n.* મુખપત્ર mouthpiece
mukhavato *n.* મુખવટો visor
mukhavato utaaravo *v.t.* મુખવટો ઉતારવો unmask
mukhee *n.* મુખી headman
mukhee *n.* મુખી headman
Mukhras *n.* મુખરસ spittle
mukhy aadhaar *n.* મુખ્ય આધાર mainstay
mukhy elachee *n.* મુખ્ય એલચી consul
mukhy shaher *n.* મુખ્ય શહેર metropolis
mukhya *adj.* મુખ્ય chief
mukhya deval *n.* મુખ્ય દેવળ cathedral
mukhya janas *n.* મુખ્ય જણસ staple
mukhyatve *adv.* મુખ્યત્વે chiefly
mukhyatve *adv.* મુખ્યત્વે primarily
mukko *n.* મુક્કો punch
mukt *n.* મુક્ત devoid
mukt karavun *v.t.* મુક્ત કરવું rid
mukta vepaar *n.* મુક્ત વેપાર free trade
mukta vichaarak *n.* મુક્ત વચિારક freethinker
mukti *n.* મુક્તિ deliverance
mukti aapavee *v.t.* મુક્તિ આપવી manumit
mukya *n.* મુખ્ય major
mukya kaareegar *n.* મુખ્ય કારીગર foreman
mulaakaat *n.* મુલાકાત interview
mulaakaatee *n.* મુલાકાતી visitor
mulakee *adj.* મુલકી civil
mulatavee raakhavun *v.t.* મુલતવી રાખવું postpone
mulavanee મુલવણી valuation
munasafee *n.* મુનસફી discretion
mundana karavaanee vidhi *n.* મુંડન કરવાની વધિ tonsure
munjavan anubhavavee *v.t.* મૂંઝવણ અનુભવવી blush

munjhavanman naakhavun v.t. મૂંઝવણમાં નાખવું bemuse

murabbeevat n. મુરબ્બીવટ patronage

murkh adj. મૂરખ dumb-bells

murkha n. મૂરખ blockhead

murkhaaibharyu smit v.i. મૂરખાઇભર્યું સ્મિત simper

murkhaamee karavee v.t. મૂરખામી કરવી blunder

musaafar n. મુસાફર traveller

musaafarano saamaan n. મુસાફરનો સામાન luggage

musaafaree karavee n. મુસાફરી કરવી trek

musaafareenun bhaatun n. મુસાફરીનું ભાતું prog

musaddo n. મુસદ્દો draft

mushkel adj. મુશ્કેલ arduous

mushkel adj. મુશ્કેલ difficult

mushkelee n. મુશ્કેલી difficulty

mushkeleethee adv. મુશ્કેલીથી narrowly

mushthiyoddho n. મુષ્ઠિયોદ્ધો pugilist

mushtiyoddhaanun haathamojun n. મુષ્ટિયોદ્ધાનું હાથમોજું glove

mutaradee n. મૂતરડી urinal

muththee n. મુઠ્ઠી fist

muththee (bhar) n. મુઠ્ઠી (ભર) handful

mutsaddigeeree n. મુત્સદ્દીગીરી diplomacy

Myaan n. મ્યાન scabbard

myaanamaathee neekalelun મ્યાનમાંથી નીકળેલું unsheathe

myaano n. મ્યાનો sedan

myunisipaaliteevaalun shaher v.t. મ્યુનિસિપાલિટીવાળું શહેર borough

n gamavun v.t. ન ગમવું dislike

na viyaayelee gaay n. ન વિયાયેલી ગાય heifer

naa deva prop. ના દેવા owing

naa fala roope adv. ના ફળ રૂપે thereupon

naa jevun v.t. ના જેવું like

naa jevun hovun v.t. —ના જેવું હોવું resemble

Naa jevun ke sarkhun adj. —ના જેવું કે સરખું similar

naa jevun nahi adj. —ના જેવું નહિ unlike

naa kissaaman v.t. ના કિસ્સામાં incase

naa virodhaman mookavun v.t. —ના વિરોધમાં મૂકવું oppose

naabhi n. નાભિ navel

naabhi n. નાભિ umbilicus

naabood karavun v.t. નાબૂદ કરવું annul

naaboodee n. નાબૂદી elimination

naaboodi n. નાબૂદી annulment

naabud karvun v.t. નાબૂદ કરવું abolish

naabudi n. નાબૂદી abolition

naach n. નાચ nautch

naachavun v.i. નાચવું frisk

naadaar adj. નાદાર insolvent

naadaar banaavavun n. નાદાર બનાવવું bankrupt

naadaaree n. નાદારી bankruptcy

naadaaree n. નાદારી insolvency

naadeeno dhabakaaro n. નાડીનો ધબકારો pulse

naadurast adj. નાદુરસ્ત unwholesome

naadurast sthiti n. નાદુરસ્ત સ્થિતિ dilapidation

naadurasta tabiyataavaalun adj. નાદુરસ્ત તબિયતવાળું unwell

naagaravelanun paan n. નાગરવેલનું પાન betel

naagarik n. નાગરિક citizen

naagarikashaastr n. નાગરિકશાસ્ત્ર civics

naagarikatva n. નાગરિકત્વ citizenship

naagariktvanun adj. નાગરિકત્વનું civic

naahak maathu maarvu v.i. નાહક માથું મારવું tamper

naahavun v.t. નાહવું bathe

naahimmat karavun v.t. નાહિમ્મત કરવું daunt

naaitret n. નાઇટ્રેટ nitrate

naajuk adj. નાજુક delicate

naajuk *adj.* નાજુક frail
naajuk *adj.* નાજુક petite
Naajuk *adj.* નાજુક subtle
naajuk *adj.* નાજુક ticklish
naak *n.* નાક conk
naak *n.* નાક nose
naakaabandhee *n.* નાકાબંધી blockade
naakabul karavun *v.t.* નાકબૂલ કરવું disavow
naakabul karavun *v.t.* નાકબૂલ કરવું disown
naakabulaat *n.* નાકબૂલાત disavowal
naakanun *adj.* નાકનું nasal
naakhush *adj.* નાખુશ loath
naakhusheethee *adv.* નાખુશીથી unhappily
naalaayak *adj.* નાલાયક undignified
naalachun *n.* નાળચું muzzle
naaliyer *n.* નાળિયેર coconut
naalun *n.* નાળું channel
naalun *n.* નાળું culvert
naam નામ name
naam paadavun *v.t.* નામ પાડવું christen
naam vinaanun, nanaamun *n.* નામ વિનાનું, નનામું anonymity
naam vinaanun, nanaamun *adj.* નામ વિનાનું, નનામું anonymous
naamaankit *n.* નામાંકિત brilliance
naamaankit *adj.* નામાંકિત distinguished
naamaankit *adj.* નામાંકિત reputed
naamaavali *n.* નામાવલિ scroll
naamakaran *n.* નામકરણ nomenclature
naamanjoor karavun *v.t.* નામંજૂર કરવું disapprove
naamanjoor karavun *v.t.* નામંજૂર કરવું overrule
naamanjur karavun *v.t.* નામંજૂર કરવું disallow
naamaraashee *n.* નામરાશિ namesake
naamarajee *n.* નામરજી displeasure
naamarajeevaalun hovun *v.i.* નામરજીવાળું હોવું hesitate
naamayogee avyay નામયોગી અવ્યય preposition
naame *adj.* નામે yclept

naame karavun *v.t.* નામે કરવું denominate
naamkaranvidhi *n.* નામકરણવિધિ baptism
Naamnun paatiyun *n.* નામનું પાટિયું signboard
naamoshee lagaadavee *n.* નામોશી લગાડવી discredit
naamoshee lagaadavee *n.* નામોશી લગાડવી disgrace
naamun *n.* નામું accountancy
naana chukavanaar *n.* નાણા ચુકવનાર drawe
naana dheeranaar *n.* નાણાં ધીરનાર financier
naanaa chhod *n.* નાના છોડ underwood
Naanaa kadnu *adj.* નાના કદનું small
naanaakeey *adj.* નાણાકીય monetary
naanaakiy *adj.* નાણાકીય financial
Naanaapanun *n.* નાનાપણું smallness
naanakadee chopadee *n.* નાનકડી ચોપડી booklet
naanakadee kothalee *n.* નાનકડી કોથળી pouch
naanakadee nadee *n.* નાનકડી નદી rivulet
naanakadee sheeshee *n.* નાનકડી શીશી vial
naanakadun *adj.* નાનકડું little
naanakadun gaamadun *n.* નાનકડું ગામડું hamlet
naanakadun ghaar *n.* નાનકડું ઘર cottage
naanakadun peep *n.* નાનકડું પીપ keg
naanakdoo dhol *n.* નાનકડું ઢોલ. tabor
naanavyavathaa *n.* નાણાંવ્યવસ્થા finance
naanee dholkee *n.* નાની ઢોલકી tambourine
naanee hodee *n.* નાની હોડી skiff
naanee kataar *n.* નાની કટાર poniard
naanee khaadee *n.* નાની ખાડી creek
naanee killebandhee *n.* નાની કિલ્લેબંધી redoubt
naanee maachhalee *n.* નાની માછલી anchovy

naanee paatalee laakadee *n.* નાની પાતળી લાકડી wand

naanee pratimaa *n.* નાની પૂરતમિા microcosm

naanee pustikaa *n.* નાની પુસ્તકિ brochure

naanee sheeshee *n.* નાની શીશી. phial

naanee tolee *n.* નાની ટોળી clique

naanee unmaranun *adj.* નાની ઉંમરનું junior

Naankdee chees *n.* નાનકડી ચીસ squeak

Naankdo dhabbo *n.* નાનકડો ધબૂબો speck

naano akhaat *n.* નાનો અખાત cove

naano ghummat *n.* નાનો ઘુમૂમટ cupola

naano kheelo *n.* નાનો ખીલો sprig

naano mugat *n.* નાનો મુગટ coronet

naano taapu *n.* નાનો ટાપુ islet

naano tukado *n.* નાનો ટુકડો crumb

naano tukado *n.* નાનો ટુકડો shred

naanu *adj.* નાનું dwarfish

naanu kheesu *n.* નાનું ખીસું fob

Naanun *n.* નાનું short

naanun - sikka paadava te *n.* નાણાં - સક્કિા પાડવા તે coinage

naanun baaranun *n.* નાનું બારણું wicket

naanun chappu *n.* નાનું ચપ્પુ penknife

naanun dabalun *n.* નાનું ડબલું canister

naanun haran *n.* નાનું હરણ roe

naanun jharanun *n.* નાનું ઝરણું runlet

naanun kaanun *n.* નાનું કાણું ventage

naanun kootarun *n.* નાનું કૂતરું pug

naanun langar *n.* નાનું લંગર kedge

naanun vahaan *n.* નાનું વહાણ sloop

Naanun zarnun *n.* નાનું ઝરણું streamlet

naapasand karavun *v.t.* નાપસંદ કરવું discountenance

naapasandagee *n.* નાપસંદગી. disapprobation

naapasandagee *n.* નાપસંદગી disapproval

naapasandagee *n.* નાપસંદગી disfavour

naaraaj *adj.* નારાજ malcontent

naaraaj thavun *v.* નારાજ થવું aggrieve

naaraaja thavun *adj.* નારાજ થવું topsyturvy

naarangee *n.* નારંગી orange

Naarkee *adj.* નારકી stygian

naasabhaag *n.* નાસભાગ rout

naasabhaag karavee *v.i.* નાસભાગ કરવી stampede

naasee javun *v.i.* નાસી જવું flee

naash karavo *v.t.* નાશ કરવો extinguish

naash karavun *v.t.* નાશ કરવું destroy

naash karvo *v.t.* નાશ કરવો. exterminate

naash paamavun *v.t.* નાશ પામવું perish

naasha karvo *n.* નાશ કરવો undoing

naashavant *adj.* નાશવંત destructible

naashee javun *v.i.* નાશી જવું decamp

naasoor *n.* નાસૂર ulcer

naastaanee dukaan *n.* નાસ્તાની દુકાન cafe

naastaanee dukaan *n.* નાસ્તાની દુકાન canteen

naastik *n.* નાસ્તકિ sacrilegious

Naastik *n.* નાસ્તકિ sceptic

naastik vyakti *n.* નાસ્તકિ વ્યૂક્ત atheist

naastiktaa *n.* નાસ્તકિતા unbelief

naastiktaa *n.* નાસ્તકિત unbeliever

naastikvaad *n.* નાસ્તકિવાદ atheism

Naasto *n.* નાસ્તો snack

naataal *n.* નાતાલ christmas

naataal *n.* નાતાલ xmas

naatak *n.* નાટક drama

naatak karavun *v.t.* નાટક કરવું dramatize

naatakana kalaakaaro *n.* નાટકના કલાકારો dramatis personae

naatakashaala *n.* નાટકશાળા playhouse

naatakeey *adj.* નાટકીય dramatic

naatyagruha *n.* નાટ્યગૃહ theatre

naatyakaar *n.* નાટ્યકાર dramatist

naavik *n.* નાવકિ ferryman

naavik *n.* નાવકિ. mariner

naavya *adj.* નાવ્ય navigable

naayab નાયબ unsurpassed

naayab *n.* નાયબ vice

nabadaai *n.* નબળાઈ frailty

nabala mananun *adj.* નબળા મનનું imbecile

nabala radayvalu *adj.* નબળા હ્રદયનું weak-hearted

nabalaa manvaalu *v.i.* નબળા મનવાળું dote

nabalaaee *n.* નબળાઈ weakness

nabalaaee નબળાઈ infirmity

nabalu *adj.* નબળું dotish

nabalu *adj.* નબળું effete

nabalu *adj.* નબળું feeble

nabalun *adj.* નબળું weakly

nabalun banaavavun *v.t.* નબળું બનાવવું unman

nabalun banaavavun *v.t.* નબળું બનાવવું weaken

nabalun maanas *n.* નબળું માણસ weakling

nabhaavi levu *v.* નભાવી લેવું abide

nadaaeekhor *n.* બડાઈખોર tattler

nadatar *n.* નડતર clog

nadatar *n.* નડતર impediment

nadee *n.* નદી river

Nadee parano bandh *n.* નદી પરનો બંધ dam

nadeekaanthaano pradesh *n.* નદીકાંઠાનો પ્રદેશ riverside

nadeeno dharo *n.* નદીનો ધરો. pool

nadeeno tatapradesh *n.* નદીનો તટપ્રદેશ basin

nafarat *n.* નફરત detestation

nafarat *n.* નફરત disgust

nafarat *n.* નફરત revulsion

nafarat - tiraskaar karavo *v.t.* નફરત – તિરસ્કાર કરવો loathe

nafo karavo *v.t.* નફો કરવો profit

nagaaru *n.* નગારું drum

nagar *n.* નગર town

nagar - durg *n.* નગર – દુર્ગ citadel

nagarapaalika *n.* નગરપાલિકા municipality

nagarapaalikaanun *adj.* નગરપાલિકાનું municipal

nahaavun *n.* નહાવું toilet

naheevat *adj.* નહિવત few

naher *n.* નહેર canal

nahi *adj.* નહિ no

nahi *adv.* નહિ not

nahi jadatun *adj.* નહિ જડતું missing

nahimmat karavun *v.t.* નાહિમ્મત કરવું discourage

nahimmat karavun *v.t.* નાહિમ્મત કરવું dishearten

nahor *n.* નહોર claw

Nairutya dishaa *n.* નૈઋત્ય દિશા soutÅwest

naisargik નૈસર્ગિક idyllic

naishkapatee *n.* નિષ્કપટી sincerity

naitik adhahpaat *n.* નૈતિક અધઃપાત demoralization

naitik sinddhaant *adj.* નૈતિક સિદ્ધાન્તો ethic

naitikata *n.* નૈતિકતા morality

najaakat *n.* નજાકત delicacy

najar *n.* નજર eyesight

najar raakhavee *v.t.* નજર રાખવી supervise

najare padavun *v.t.* નજરે પડવું espy

najeek *adv.* નજીક by

najeek aavatun *adj.* નજીક આવતું oncoming

najeek mukavun *v.t.* નજીક મૂકવું collocate

najeekana sanbandhavaalun *adv.* નજીકના સંબંધવાળું near

Najeevee baabtmaan kajiyo *n.* નજીવી બાબતમાં કજિયો squabble

najeevee bhool *n.* નજીવી ભૂલ lapse

najeevee kimmata ke mahatva *n.* નજીવી કિમત કે મહત્ત્વ triviality

najeevee vastu *n.* નજીવી વસ્તુ trifle

najeevo zaghado *n.* નજીવો ઝઘડો tiff

najeevun નજીવું trifling

najiknun, adoad *adj.* નજીકનું, અડોઅડ adjacent

nakaama gapaataa maarvaa *v.t.* નકામા ગપાટા મારવા tattle

Nakaamo bakvaat *n.* નકામો બકવાટ stuff

nakaamo saamaan *n.* નકામો સામાન lumber

nakaamun *n.* નકામું futility

nakaamun *n.* નકામું spoil

nakaamun *adj.* નકામું useless

nakaamun *adj.* નકામું worthless

nakaarasoochak *adj.* નકારસૂચક negative

nakal *n.* નકલ cyclostyle

nakal *n.* નકલ skit

nakal karanaar *n.* નકલ કરનાર duplicator

nakal karavee *n.* નકલ કરવી fake

nakal karavee *v.t.* નકલ કરવી imitate

nakal karavee *v.* –નકલ કરવી quote

nakal karvee *v.t.* નકલ કરવી transcribe

nakal karvee *n.* નકલ કરવી transcription

nakalee ke takalaadee gharenu *n.* નકલી કે તકલાદી ઘરેણું trinket

nakashaapothee *n.* નકશાપોથી atlas

nakashee karavee *v.t.* નકશી કરવી emboss

nakasheedaar kaapad *n.* નકશીદાર કાપડ tapestry

nakasheekaar *n.* નકશીકાર lapidary

nakasho *n.* નકશો. map

nakha *n.* નખ nail

nakharaabaajee *v.i.* નખરાબાજી coquet

nakharaabaajee *n.* નખરાબાજી coquetry

nakharel *n.* નખરેલ coquette

nakhush karavun *v.t.* નાખુશ કરવું displease

Naklee *adj.* નકલી snide

nakshatr *n.* નક્ષત્ર constellation

nalaakaar kothee *n.* નળાકાર કોઠી cylinder

nalee *n.* નળી duct

naliyun *n.* નળિયું tile

nalnee totee *v.t.* નળની ટોટી tap

namakharaam *adj.* નમકહરામ ungraceful

namaskaar નમસ્કાર obeisance

namaskaar karava *v.i.* નમસ્કાર કરવા greet

namavun *v.t.* નમવું stoop

namavun, dholaav *v.t.* ઢોળાવ incline

namee padavun *n.* –નમી પડવું lurch

namoonaaroop *v.t.* નમૂનારૂપ typify

namoonao *n.* નમૂનો sample

namoono *n.* નમૂનો exponent

namoono *n.* નમૂનો model

Namoono નમૂનો specimen

namoono ., daakhalo નમૂનો, દાખલો exemplar

namra sevak *n.* નમ્ર સેવક vassal

namrata *n.* નમ્રતા modesty

nanaamee *n.* નનામી effigy

nanan lenaar *n.* નાણું લેનાર payee

Nanand *n.* નણંદ sister-in-law

nano jheree saap *n.* નાનો ઝેરી સાપ asp

napunsak linganun *adj.* નપુંસક લિંગિનું neuter

nar batak *n.* નર બતક drake

nar haran *n.* નર હરણ buck

nar jaati નર જાત he

nar madhamaakhee *n.* નર મધમાખી drone

narajaatinun *n.* નરજાતનું male

narajaatinun *adj.* નરજાતનું masculine

narak *n.* નરક hades

narak *n.* નરક hell

naram *adj.* નરમ flabby

Naram *adj.* નરમ soft

naram pad *n.* નરમ પડ flake

naram padavun *v.t.* નરમ પાડવું palliate

naramaansabhakshee *n.* નરમાંસભક્ષી cannibal

naramaash *v.t.* નરમાશ clem

narameen *n.* નરમીન triton

Narmaashpoorvak *adj.* નરમાશપૂર્વક softly

Narnun veerya *n.* નરનું વીર્ય sperm

nasabandhee *n.* નસબંધી vasectomy

nasakoraa bolaavavaa *v.i.* નસકોરા બોલાવવા sniff

nasakorun *n.* નસકોરું nostril

naseeb *n.* નસીબ destiny

naseeb *n.* નસીબ luck

naseebadaar *adj.* નસીબદાર fortunate

naseebadaar *n.* નસીબદાર happy

naseebadaar *adj.* નસીબદાર providential

naseebanee kasotee *n.* નસીબની કસોટી lottery

nashta karvun *v.t.* નષ્ટ કરવું undermine

natanatee *n.* નટનટી troupe

nathaarun sapanun *n.* નઠારું સપનું nightmare

nauchaalan *n.* નૌચાલન pilotage

naukaadalano khalasee *n.* નૌકાદળનો ખલાસી blue-jacket

naukaadhikari *n.* નૌકાઅધિકારી boatswain

naukaanayan *n.* નૌકાનયન navigation

naukaasainy *n.* નૌકાસૈન્ય navy

naukaayan *n.* નૌકાયન yachting

nausenaapati *n.* નૌસેનાપતિ admiral

nautaal *n.* નૌતાલ keel

nav *adj.* નવ. nine

navaaee *n.* નવાઈ wonder

navaaeenee vastu *n.* નવાઈની વસ્તુ novelty

navaganun *adj.* નવગણું. ninefold

navalakatha *n.* નવલકથા novel

navalakathaakaar *n.* નવલકથાકાર novelist

navamo (bhaag) *adj.* નવમો (ભાગ). ninth

navanirmaata *n.* નવનિર્માતા inventor

navaparineet vyakti *n.* નવપરિણીત વ્યક્તિ. benedick

navapraapt karavun *v.t.* નવપ્રાપ્ત કરવું reclaim

navapraapti *n.* નવપ્રાપ્તિ reclamation

navara besavun *v.i.* નવરા બેસવું lounge

navaraash *n.* નવરાશ leisure

navarachana *n.* નવરચના reformation

navavadhoo *n.* નવવધૂ bride

naveekaran *n.* નવીકરણ renewal

naveekaran karavun *v.t.* નવીકરણ કરવું renew

navo aakaar aapavo *v.t.* નવો આકાર આપવો recast

navun *adj.* નવું new

navun nakkor *adj.* નવું નક્કોર brand-new

navun utpann karavun *v.t.* નવું ઉત્પન્ન કરવું originate

nayaachaar *n.* નયાચાર protocol

Ne aabhaaree ganavun *v.t.* ને આભારી ગણવું ascribe

ne aanand aapavo *v.t.* –ને આનંદ આપવો please

ne aanand thavo *v.t.* ને આનંદ થવો rejoice

ne aashray aapavo *v.t.* ને આશ્રય આપવો patronize

ne badale *n.* – ને બદલે lieu

ne dagalo paheraavavo *v.i.* –ને ડગલો પહેરાવવો cope

ne dhamakaavavun *v.t.* ને ધમકાવવું threaten

ne eeja pahonchaadavee *v.t.* ને ઇજા પહોંચાડવી impair

ne ek karavun *v.t.* એક કરવું consolidate

ne gulaam banaavavun *v.t.* ને ગુલામ બનાવવું enslave

ne jaan karavee *v.t.* ને જાણ કરવી acquaint

ne khaataree karaavavee *v.t.* –ને ખાતરી કરાવવી convince

ne khabar aapavee *v.t.* –ને ખબર આપવી instruct

ne laanchhan lagaadavun *v.t.* ને લાંછન લગાડવું asperse

ne laat maaravee *v.i.* –ને લાત મારવી kick

ne lagatun *v.* ને લગતું appertain

ne maanabhang karavo *v.t.* ને માનભંગ કરવો pique

ne maate ને માટે for

Ne maate poortun hovun *v.t.* ને માટે પૂરતું હોવું suffice

ne maate taiyaaree *v.t.* –ને માટે તૈયારી provide

ne mate laayak *v.* ને માટે લાયક deserve

Ne mokalvun *v.t.* ને મોકલવું send

ne naame lakhavun *n.* ને નામે લખવું imputation

ne naame lakhavun *v.t.* ને નામે લખવું impute

ne paachhal padavun *v.t.* –ને પાછળ પડવું outdo

Ne Pavitra karvun *v.t.* ને પવિત્ર કરવું sanctify

ne raahat aapavee *v.t.* ને રાહત આપવી relieve

Ne saabu devo ke lagaadvo *n.* ને સાબુ દેવો કે લગાડવો soap

ne shaap devo *v.t.* ને શાપ દેવો imprecate

ne sonpan karavee *v.t.* ને સોંપણ કરવી confide

ne soochana *n.* –ને સૂચના notification

ne taakeed aapavee *v.t.* –ને તાકીદ આપવી notify

ne umaraav banaavavo *v.t.* ને ઉમરાવ બનાવવો ennoble

ne vishe *prep.* –ને વિશિ concerning

nedharlendanu *n.* નેધરલેન્ડનું dutch

nee aade aavavun *v.t.* ની આડે આવવું interrupt

nee aade aavavun *v.t.* –ની આડે આવવું obstruct

nee atishay preetee *v.t.* ની અતિશિય પૂરીતિ idolize

nee avaganana karavee *v.t.* ની અવગણના કરવી ignore

nee baabataman *prep.* –ની બાબતમાં regarding

nee baabataman *prep.* –ની બાબતમાં respecting

nee farate vartul *v.t.* ની ફરતે વર્તુળ environ

nee farate vartul banaavavun *v.t.* ની ફરતે વર્તુળ બનાવવું engirdle

nee fikar karanaar *adj.* – ની ફિકર કરનાર mindful

nee jagya janaavavee *v.t.* –ની જગ્યા જણાવવી locate

nee jagya laee levee *v.t.* ની જગ્યા લઈ લેવી oust

Nee Jagya levee *v.t.* ની જગ્યા લેવી supersede

Nee jagyaa levee *v.t.* ની જગ્યા લેવી supplant

nee jaroor hovee *v.t.* ની જરૂર હોવી require

nee kabajaaman - hovun *v.t.* –ની કબ્જામાં – હોવું have

nee kalpana karavee *v.t.* ની કલ્પના કરવી imagine

nee khetee karavee *v.t.* ની ખેતી કરવી cultivate

nee maalikeenun hovun *n.* ની માલિકીનું હોવું possess

nee nishaanee hovee *v.t.* ની નિશાની હોવી betoken

nee olakhaan hovee *v.t.* –ની ઓળખાણ હોવી know

nee paachhal kharch karavun ની પાછળ ખર્ચ કરવું invest

nee saathe goonthai javun *n.* ની સાથે ગૂંથાઈ જવું engagement

nee saathe sanbandhit *adj.* ની સાથે સંબંધિત relating

nee tapaash karavee *v.t.* ની તપાસ કરવી explore

nee tev - mahaavaro - paadavo *v.t.* –ની ટેવ – મહાવરો – પાડવો inure

nee upar *prep.* –ની ઉપર. upon

nee upar daam devo *v.t.* ની ઉપર ડામ દેવો cauterize

nee upar prabhutv melavavun *v.t.* –ની ઉપર પ્રભુત્વ મેળવવું overcome

nee vachche *prep.* ની વચ્ચે among

nee viruddh *v.t.* –ની વિરુદ્ધ militate

neechaa survaalun *n.* નીચા સૂરવાળું bass

neechaanavaalo pradesh *n.* નીચાણવાળો પ્રદેશ lowland

neeche *n.* નીચે below

neeche *n.* નીચે down

Neeche નીચે sub

neeche *prep.* નીચે under

neeche *adv.* નીચે underneath

neeche aavelun *adj.* નીચે આવેલું. nether

neeche karelee saheevalu *v.t.* નીચે કરેલી સહીવાળું undersign

neeche leetee dorvee *v.t.* નીચે લીટી દોરવી underline

neeche paadavun *adj.* નીચે પાડવું fell

neeche padavun *v.i.* નીચે પડવું fall

neeche padavun *v.i.* નીચે પડવું fall

neeche valavun *v.i.* નીચે વળવું droop

neechee kakshaanun *v.t.* નીચી કક્ષાનું mean

neechee khullee gaadee *n.* નીચી ખુલ્લી ગાડી trolley

neechee paayareenun *adj.* નીચી પાયરીનું ignoble

neechenaa maalanu *adv.* નીચેના માળનું downstairs

neechenee jagyaae *adj.* નીચેની જગ્યાએ downward

Neecheno thar *n.* નીચેનો થર substratum

needar *adj.* નીડર dauntless

neek *n.* નીક spillway

neelam *n.* નીલમ emerald

neelavarna *adj.* નીલવર્ણ azure

neemelun maanas *n.* નીમેલું માણસ nominee

neenavun *v.t.* વીણવું glean

neenda *n.* નિંદા calumny

neenda karavee *v.t.* નિંદા કરવી calumniate

neendan *n.* નીંદણ weed

neeraash thavun *v.t.* નિરાશ થવું disappoint

neeraash thavun *v.t.* નિરાશ થવું frustrate

neeraasha *n.* નિરાશા disappointment

neeram *n.* નીરમ ballast

neeras *n.* નીરસ drab

neeras *adj.* નીરસ prosaic

Neeravtaa. *n.* નીરવતા silence

neerbhay *adj.* નિર્ભય fearless

neerbhayataa નિર્ભયતા fearlessness

neesvaarthapanun *n.* નિઃસ્વાર્થપણું altruism

neetaravun *v.i.* નીતરવું percolate

neeti *n.* નીતિ policy

neetibhrast karavun *v.t.* નીતિભ્રષ્ટ કરવું deprave

neetimatta *n.* નીતિમિત્તા moral

neetino upadesh *v.i.* નીતિનો ઉપદેશ moralize

neetishaashtra *n.* નીતિશાસ્ત્ર ethics

netar *n.* નેતર osier

netar *adj.* નેતર wicker

netrapatal *n.* નેત્રપટલ retina

netravidya *n.* નેત્રવિદ્યા optics

nevumun, nevumo ansh *adj.* નેવુમું,

નેવુમો અંશ ninetieth

nevun *n.* નેવું. ninety

ni bhonkavun *v.t.* —ને ભોંકવું pierce

ni padakhe, baajuman *adv.* ની પડખે, બાજુમાં alongside

ni prachaar karavo *v.t.* —નો પ્રચાર કરવો propagate

nibandh *v.t.* નિબંધ essay

niche ootaravun *adj.* નીચે ઊતરવું alight

niche utaaravun *v.t.* નીચે ઉતારવું abase

nichhshit karavun *adj.* નશ્ચિત કરવું definite

nidaan *n.* નિદાન diagnosis

nidaan karavun *v.t.* નિદાન કરવું diagnose

nidar *adj.* નડિર undaunted

nidarataa નડિરતા effrontery

nidarshan *n.* નિદર્શન demonstration

nidarshan *n.* નિદર્શન parade

nidraaheen *adj.* નિદ્રાહીન restless

nigam *n.* નગિમ corporation

nigam banaavavun *v.t.* નગિમ બનાવવું incorporate

nihaarika *n.* નિહારિકા nebula

nihetu *adj.* નિહેતુ inadvertent

nikaal *n.* નકિાલ disposal

nikaal *n.* નકિાલ outlet

nikaal karavo *v.t.* નકિાલ કરવો. dispose

nikaal thaay tyan sudhee *adj.* નકિાલ થાય ત્યાં સુધી pending

nikaas *v.t.* નકિાસ export

nikaas *n.* નકિાસ shipment

nikatavartee *adj.* નકિટવર્તી imminent

nikhaalas *adj.* નખિાલસ artless

nikhaalas *adj.* નખિાલસ frank

nikhaalas *adj.* નખિાલસ ingenuous

nikhaalas *adj.* નખિાલસ open-hearted

nikhaalasata *n.* નખિાલસતા candour

nikhaalasataa *n.* નખિાલસતા frankness

nikotin *n.* નકિોટિન nicotine

nikshep *n.* નક્ષિેપ sediment

nilakanth jevun pankhee *n.* નલિકંઠ જેવું પંખી jay

nilamanee, yaakoot *n.* નીલમણિ, યાકૂત amethyst

nimanook *n.* નમિણૂક appointment

nimanook karanaar *n.* નિમણૂક કરનાર nominator

nimanook karavee *v.t.* નિમણૂક કરવી. appoint

nimanook karavee *v.t.* નિમણૂક કરવી designate

nimanook karavee નિમણૂક કરવી nominate

nimanook karavee te *n.* નિમણૂક કરવી તે nomination

nimnalikhit *n.* નિમ્નલિખિત following

ninda karavee *v.t.* નિંદા કરવી backbite

ninda karavee *v.t.* નિંદા કરવી censure

ninda karavee *v.t.* નિંદા કરવી revile

Nindaa *n.* નિંદા scandal

nindaa karavee *v.t.* નિંદા કરવી denunciate

nindaa karavee *v.t.* નિનિંદા કરવી. disparage

nindaa karavee *v.t.* નિંદા કરવી. traduce

Nindaa karnaarun maanas *n.* નિંદા કરનારું માણસ slanderer

nindaatmak *adj.* નિંદાત્મક contemptuous

nindaatmak *adj.* નિંદાત્મક reproachful

nindaatmak bhaashan નિંદાત્મક ભાષણ invective

nindaatmaka bhaashan *n.* નિંદાત્મક ભાષણ tirade

nindraa jevee avasthaa *n.* નિદ્રા જેવી અવસ્થા trance

Nindrabhraman *n.* નિદ્રાભ્રમણ somnambulism

nipajelun *adj.* નીપજેલું consequent

nipun *adj.* નિપુણ deft

niraadhaar *adj.* નિરાધાર destitute

niraadhaar *adj.* નિરાધાર penniless

niraadhaar નિરાધાર unbiased

niraadhaar *adj.* નિરાધાર unfounded

niraadhaarapanu *n.* નિરાધારપણું destitution

niraant *n.* નિરાંત quietude

niraash karavun *v.t.* નિરાશ કરવું depress

niraash karavun *v.t.* નિરાશ થવું despair

niraash thavun *v.t.* નિરાશ થવું despond

niraashaaprerak *n.* નિરાશાપ્રેરક despondent

niraashaavaad *n.* નિરાશાવાદ pessimism

niraashaavaadee *n.* નિરાશાવાદી pessimist

nirabhimabnee *adj.* નિરભિમાની unassuming

niraksharata *n.* નિરક્ષરતા illiteracy

niranaayak *adj.* નિરાણાયક final

nirankush *adj.* નિરંકુશ unbridled

nirankush raajyakartaa *n.* નિરંકુશ રાજ્યકર્તા despot

nirarthak *adj.* નિરર્થક paltry

nirarthak *adj.* નિરર્થક vain

niras *adj.* નીરસ banal

niras lakhaan *v.i.* નીરસ લખાણ twaddle

nirav *adj.* નિરવ noiseless

nirbal *adj.* નિર્બળ flaccid

nirbal *adj.* નિર્બળ unaccented

nirbal banaavavun *v.t.* નિર્બળ બનાવવું enervate

nirday *adj.* નિર્દય barbarous

nirday *adj.* નિર્દય cruel

nirday *adj.* નિર્દય grim

nirday *adj.* નિર્દય merciless

nirday *n.* નિર્દય relentless

nirdaya *adj.* નિર્દય unrelenting

nirdayata *n.* નિર્દયતા cruelty

nirdayataa *n.* નિર્દયતા brutality

nirdayataapoorvakavun *adj.* નિર્દયતાપૂર્વકનું coldblooded

nirdeshak *n.* નિર્દેશક preceptor

nirdhaar *n.* નિર્ધાર determination

nirdhaar *n.* નિર્ધાર resolution

nirdhaar karavo *v.t.* નિર્ધાર કરવો determine

nirdhaar karavo *v.t.* નિર્ધાર કરવો resolve

nirdhaaran *n.* નિર્ધારણ prescription

nirdhan *adj.* નિર્ધન penurious

nirdosh *adj.* નિર્દોષ childlike

nirdosh *adj.* નિર્દોષ innocent

nireekshak *n.* નિરીક્ષક inspector

nireekshak *n.* નિરીક્ષક supervisor

nireekshan *n.* નિરીક્ષણ supervision

nireekshan karavun *v.t.* નિરીક્ષણ કરવું
behold

nireeshvaravaad *n.* નિરીશ્વરવાદ
atache

nirgaamee નિર્ગામી emigrant

nirgaman *v.t.* નિર્ગમન emigrate

nirjana *adj.* નિર્જન uninhabitable

nirlajj *n.* નિર્લજ્જ barefaced

nirmaan *n.* નિર્માણ creation

nirmaan karavun *v.t.* નિર્માણ કરવું
construct

nirmaan karavun *v.t.* નિર્માણ કરવું
create

nirmaan karavun *v.t.* નિર્માણ કરવું
invent

nirmaan shaala *n.* નિર્માણ શાળા
manufactory

nirmaata *n.* નિર્માતા creator

nirmal *adj.* નિર્મળ undefiled

nirmam *adj.* નિર્મમ unfeeling

nirmool karavun *v.t.* નિર્મૂલ કરવું
eradicate

nirnaayaatmak *adj.* નિર્ણાયાત્મક
decisive

nirnaayak *adj.* નિર્ણાયક crucial

nirnay *n.* નિર્ણય decision

nirnay karavo *v.t.* નિર્ણય કરવો
adjudge

nirnay karavo *v.t.* નિર્ણય કરવો decide

nirogee *adj.* નિરોગી hale

nirupadravee *adj.* નિરુપદ્રવી
innocuous

nirustaah karavun *v.t.* નિરુત્સાહ કરવું
dispirit

nirutsaah karavun *v.t.* નિરુત્સાહ કરવું
deter

nirvivaad *adj.* નિર્વિવાદ undeniable

nirvivaad *adj.* નિર્વિવાદ
unquestionable

nisaaso nankhavo *v.t.* નિસાસો નાંખવો
heave

Nisaran *n.* નિઃસરણ secretion

nisaranee *n.* નિસરણી stair

Nischit *v.t.* નિશ્ચિત stipulate

Nischit swaroopnun *adj.* નિશ્ચિત
સ્વરૂપનું stereotyped

nishaachar નિશાચર nocturnal

nishaan *n.* નિશાન target

nishaan, lakshya, uddesh *n.* નિશાન,
લક્ષ્ય, ઉદ્દેશ aim

nishaanabaaj *n.* નિશાનબાજ
marksman

nishaanee *n.* નિશાની ensign

nishaanee *n.* નિશાની token

nishaanee *n.* નિશાની trace

Nishaaneevaalun *n.* નિશાનીવાળું sign

nishastra karavun *v.t.* નિઃશસ્ત્ર કરવું;
disarm

nishastreekaran નિઃસ્ત્રીકરણ
disarmament

nishchal *adj.* નિશ્ચલ motionless

nishchayaatmak *adj.* નિશ્ચયાત્મક
peremptory

nishchayaatmak *n.* નિશ્ચયાત્મક
positive

nishchayapoorvak kahevun *v.t.*
નિશ્ચયપૂર્વક કહેવું assert

nishchhtit *adj.* નિશ્ચિત decided

nishchit *adj.* નિશ્ચિત certain

Nishchit *adj.* નિશ્ચિત specific

nishchit *adj.* નિશ્ચિત sure

nishchit bindugaamee *adj.* નિશ્ચિત
બિન્દુગામી convergent

nishchitpane kahevun *v.* નિશ્ચિતપણે
કહેવું affirm

nishedh *n.* નિષેધ taboo

nishfal karavun *n.* નિષ્ફળ કરવું flunk

nishfala નિષ્ફળ unsuitable

nishfala banaavavun *adj.* નિષ્ફળ
બનાવવું thwart

nishfalataa *n.* નિષ્ફળતા shortcoming

nishkaaran *n.* નિષ્કારણ groundless

nishkalank *adj.* નિષ્કલંક immaculate

nishkalank *adj.* નિષ્કલંક taintless

nishkalank *adj.* નિષ્કલંક unblemished

nishkapat *adj.* નિષ્કપટ naive

nishkapat *adj.* નિષ્કપટ sincere

nishkarsh *n.* નિષ્કર્ષ gist

nishkarsh kaadhavo *v.t.* નિષ્કર્ષ કાઢવો
deduce

nishkriy નિષ્ક્રિય passive

nishkriya karavun *v.t.* નિષ્ક્રિય કરવું
incapacitate

nishkriyata *n.* નિષ્ક્રિયતા inertia

nishnaat *adj.* નિષ્ણાત expert

nishnaat *adj.* નિષ્ણાત proficient

Nishpaap *adj.* નિષ્પાપ sinless

nishpaksh *v.t.* નિષ્પક્ષ dispassionate

nishpakshapaat *adj.* નિષ્પક્ષપાત neutral

nishpakshapaatee *adj.* નિષ્પક્ષપાતી impartial

nishthaa *n.* નિષ્ઠા constancy

nishthaaheen *adj.* નિષ્ઠાહીન insincere

nishthur *n.* નિષ્ઠુર ruthless

nistej *adj.* નિસ્તેજ dim

nistej *n.* નિસ્તેજ dowdy

nistej *adj.* નિસ્તેજ pallid

nistej *adj.* નિસ્તેજ wan

nisyandit karavun *v.t.* નિસ્યંદિત કરવું distill

nitya *adv.* નિત્ય ever

nityasanbandhee *adj.* નિત્યસંબંધી correlative

nivaas *n.* નિવાસ habitation

nivastra karavun *v.* નિવસ્ત્ર કરવું denude

nivastraapanun *n.* નિવસ્ત્રાપણું bareness

Nivedan *n.* નિવેદન statement

nivrut *adj.* નિવૃત retired

nivrutilaabh *n.* નિવૃતિલાભ gratuity

nivrutt thavun *v.t.* નિવૃત્ત થવું resign

nivrutt thavun *v.i.* નિવૃત્ત થવું retire

nivrutta *adj.* નિવૃત્ત emeritus

nivrutti *n.* નિવૃત્તિ retirement

nivrutti vetan *n.* નિવૃત્તિ વેતન pension

Nivrutti vetan *n.* નિવૃત્તિ વેતન superannuation

nivrutti vetan paamanaar *n.* નિવૃત્તિ વેતન પામનાર pensioner

niyam *n.* નિયમ maxim

niyam *v.t.* નિયમ rule

niyam bhang *n.* નિયમ ભંગ breach

niyamabaddh karavun *v.t.* નિયમબદ્ધ કરવું regulate

niyamankaar *n.* નિયમનકાર regulator

niyamasar karavun *v.t.* નિયમસર કરવું regularize

niyamaviruddh *adj.* નિયમવિરુદ્ધ foul

niyamit *n.* નિયમિત regular

niyamit *n.* નિયમિત routine

niyamit aavjaa *v.* નિયમિત આવજા commute

niyamitata *n.* નિયમિતતા regularity

niyamo nu paalan karavun *v.t.* નિયમોનું પાલન કરવું confort

niyantrak *n.* નિયંત્રક comptroller

niyantrak *n.* નિયંત્રક master

niyantran *n.* નિયંત્રણ censor

niyantran *n.* નિયંત્રણ control

niyantran karanaar નિયંત્રણ કરનાર controller

niyantran karanaar *n.* નિયંત્રણ કરનાર controller

niyantran kshetra *n.* નિયંત્રણક્ષેત્ર fief

niyantranaman raakhavun *v.t.* નિયંત્રણમાં રાખવું check

niyantrin *n.* નિયંત્રણિ inhibition

niyat hisso *n.* નિયત હિસ્સો quota

niyat karavun *v.t.* નિયત કરવું prescribe

niyat samay pahelaanu *adj.* નિયત સમય પહેલાંનું early

niyatakaaleen *adj.* નિયતકાલીન periodic

niyatakaaleen *adj.* નિયતકાલીન periodical

niyatakaary *n.* નિયતકાર્ય role

niyatee *n.* નિયતિ fate

niyojit *n.* નિયોજિત employed

no aabhaar, -paada maanavo —નો આભાર – પાડ માનવો thank

no aagrah karavo *v.i.* —નો આગ્રહ કરવો insist

no afasos karavo *v.t.* નો અફસોસ કરવો rue

no amal karavo *v.t.* નો અમલ કરવો execute

no ant aavavo *v.t.* નો અંત આવવો expire

no apavaad karavo *prep.* નો અપવાદ કરવો except

no bhaag aapavo —નો ભાગ આપવો impart

No bhaar zilvo ke khamvo *v.t.* નો ભાર ઝીલવો કે ખમવો sustain

no bhooko karavo *v.t.* નો ભૂકો કરવો pulverize

no kabajo levo *v.t.* –નો કબજો લેવો occupy

no khoto arth karavo *v.t.* –નો ખોટો અર્થ કરવો misinterpret

no khoto uchchaar karavo –નો ખોટો ઉચ્ચાર કરવો mispronounce

no mahaavaro karavo *v.t.* –નો મહાવરો કરવો practise

no mel hovo *n.* નો મેળ હોવો chime

no praanaghaat *v.i.* –નો પ્રતૃઘાત react

no pratikaar karavo *v.t.* નો પ્રતિકિાર કરવો resist

No sankhep karvo ke hovo *v.t.* નો સંક્ષેપકરવો કે હોવો summarize

no teevr dvesh karavo *v.* –નો તીવ્ર દ્વેષ કરવો hate

no tyaag karavo *v.t.* –નો ત્યાગ કરવો quit

no vichaar karavun *v.t.* –નો વિચાર કરવું. ponder

Nokar *n.* નોકર servant

nokaradee *n.* નોકરડી housemaid

nokarashaahee *n.* નોકરશાહી bueaucracy

nokareedaataa *n.* નોકરીદાતા employer

Nokhun *v.t.* નોખું separate

Nokree *n.* નોકરી service

noliyo *n.* નોળિયો. mongoose

nondh umeravi *v.t.* નોંધ ઉમેરવી annotate

nondhanee *n.* નોંધણી. registration

nondhanee adhikaaree *n.* નોંધણી અધિકારી registrar

nondhanee kacheree *n.* નોંધણી કચેરી registry

nondhapaatr *adj.* નોંધપાત્ર notable

nondhapaatr *adj.* નોંધપાત્ર noteworthy

nondhapothee *n.* નોંધપોથી register

nondhavahee *n.* નોંધવહી record

notaree *n.* નોટરી notary

nrutya karanaar *n.* નૃત્ય કરનાર dancer

nrutya karavun *v.t.* નૃત્ય કરવું dance

nrutyakhand *n.* નૃત્યખંડ ballroom

nu banelun hovun *v.t.* નું બનેલું હોવું consist

nu jangal banaavavun *v.* નું જંગલ બનાવવું afforest

nu teevrapane soochak *adj.* નું તીવ્રપણે સૂચક redolent

nu vyasanee નું વ્યસનની addicted

nukasaan *n.* નુકસાન injury

nukasaan karavun *v.t.* નુકસાન કરવું injure

nukasaanee *n.* નુકસાની indemnity

nukashaan *n.* નુકશાન harm

nukashaan bharapaaee *n.* નુકશાન ભરપાઈ restitution

nukashaan karavun *v.t.* નુકશાન કરવું hurt

nukashaan karavun *v.t.* નુકશાન કરવું mar

nukashaanakaarak *adj.* નુકશાનકારક detrimental

nukhaso *n.* નુસખો. recipe

Nun Aagnyankit *n.* નું આજ્ઞાંકિતિ subjection

nun banelun hovun *v.t.* –નું બનેલું હોવું comprise

nun kahyun karavun *v.t.* નું કહ્યું કરવું obey

nun man saachavvun નું મન સાચવવું gratify

Nun parinam dhoi naakhvun *v.t.* –નું પરિણામ ધોઈ નાખવું stultify

nun roonee hovun *v.t.* –નું ઋણી હોવું owe

nun soochak chinh hovun *v.t.* – નું સૂચક ચિહ્ન હોવું indicate

nun varchasv hovun *n.* –નું વર્ચસ્વ હોવું predominance

nusakho *n.* નુસખો formula

nyaay viruddh *adj.* ન્યાય વરિદ્ધ illogical

nyaayaadheesh *n.* ન્યાયાધીશ judge

nyaayaadheesh *n.* ન્યાયાધીશ justice

nyaayaalay *n.* ન્યાયાલય tribunal

nyaayaalay aadesh *n.* ન્યાયાલય આદેશ writ

nyaayamandir *n.* ન્યાયમંદરિ court

nyoonata *n.* ન્યૂનતા lack

O

ochaabolu *adj.* ઓછાબોલું taciturn

Ochha mahatvnu *adj.* ઓછા મહત્ત્વનું secondary

ochhaabolun *adj.* ઓછાબોલું reticent

ochhee reete *adv.* ઓછી રીતે thinly

ochhu karavun *v.t.* ઓછું કરવું diminish

ochhu karvun *v.t.* ઓછું કરવું abate

Ochhun *adj.* ઓછું scanty

ochhun karavun *v.t.* ઓછું કરવું extenuate

ochhun karavun *v.t.* ઓછું કરવું rebate

ochintaapanun *n.* ઓચિંતાપણું abruptness

ochinto humalo *n.* ઓચિંતો હુમલો incursion

ochinto uchhaalo *v.t.* ઓચિંતો ઉછાળો. jump

Ochintu *adj.* ઓચંતું sudden

ochintun *v.t.* ઓચંતું ejaculate

odakaar khaavo *v.t.* ઓડકાર ખાવો belch

ogaadavun *v.t.* ઓગાળવું dissolve

ogalavun *v.t.* ઓગાળવું liquefy

ogalavun *v.t.* ઓગળવું thaw

oganees *n.* ઓગણીસ. nineteen

ogast mahino *adj.* ઓંગસ્ટ મહિનો august

ojaar *n.* ઓજાર bit

ojaar *n.* ઓજાર tool

ok *n.* ઓક oak

okaaree aavavee *v.t.* ઓકારી આવવી retch

oksaaid *n.* ઓક્સાઇડ oxide

oksijaneekaran *v.* ઓક્સજનીકરણ aerate

olaada *n.* ઓલાદ offspring

olakh *n.* ઓળખ recognition

olakhaan karaavavee *v.t.* ઓળખાણ કરાવવી introduce

olakhaananun prateek *n.* ઓળખાણનું પ્રતીક marking

olakhavun *v.t.* ઓળખવું identify

olakhitun maanas *n.* ઓળખીતું માણસ acquaintance

olanbaavaalee doree *n.* ઓબંભાવાળી દોરી plummet

olavavun *v.t.* ઓલવવું quench

olimpik *adj.* ઓલમ્પિક olympic

olivanun jhaad *n.* ઓલવિનું ઝાડ olive

oobha thavun *v.t.* ઊભા થવું rise

oobhaa khadak *n.* ઊભો ખડક cliff

oobharaanun *adj.* ઊભરાનું zymotic

oobharo *n.* ઊભરો ebullition

oobharo *v.t.* ઊભરો effuse

oobharo *n.* ઊભરો effusion

oobharo *n.* ઊભરો zymosis

oobhee bhekhad *n.* ઊભી ભેખડ crag

oobho doro *v.t.* ઊભો દોરો warp

oobhun karavun ઊભું કરવું raise

oochaanvalo jameenno samtal pato *n.* ઊંચાણવાળો જમીનનો સમતલ પટો terrace

oogam *n.* ઊગમ origin

oogavun *v.t.* ઊગવું grow

oojan tarike *v.t.* ઊંજણ તરીકે grease

oojavavun *v.t.* ઊજવવું celebrate

ookalatu *adj.* ઊકળતું ebullient

oolat tapaas *n.* ઊલટ તપાસ cross-examin

oolat, shighrata *n.* ઊલટ, શીઘ્રતા alacrity

oolatee karavee *v.t.* ઊલટી કરવી puke

oolatee karavee *v.i.* ઊલટી કરવી vomit

oolatee reete *adv.* ઊલટી રીતે viceversa

oolateekaarak davaa *adj.* ઊલટીકારક દવા emetic

oolatokram *n.* ઊલટોક્રમ reversal

oolatun *adj.* ઊલટું inverse

oon *n.* ઊન wool

oonanee aantee *n.* ઊનની આંટી hank

oonanun kaapad *n.* ઊનનું કાપડ tweed

oonap *n.* ઊણપ deficiency

oonapvaalu *adj.* ઊણપવાળું deficient

oonchaaee *n.* ઊંચાઈ altitude

oonchaaman oonchun bindun *n.* ઊંચામાં ઊંચું બદુિ apogee

oonchakeene laee javun *v.t.* ઊંચકીને લઈ જવું carry

oonche javun *v.t.* ઊંચે જવું ascend

oonche thekaanethee jovun ઊંચે ઠેકાણેથી જોવું overlook

oonche, tootak upar adv. ઊંચે, તૂતક ઉપર aloft

oonchee bolee lagaavavee v.t. ઊંચી બોલી લગાવવી outbid

oonchoo-neechu adj. ઊંચું-નીચું uneven

oonchun jaatanun n. ઊંચું જાતનું vintage

oonchun karavun v.t. ઊંચુ કરવું lift

oonchun pad n. ઊંચુ પદ grandeur

oondaan n. ઊંડાણ depth

oondee aah v.i. ઊંડી આહ moan

oondee kheen n. ઊંડી ખીણ canon

oondu adj. ઊંડુ deep

oondu karavun v.t. ઊંડું કરવું deepen

oonee kaapad n. ઊની કાપડ serge

oonee kaapad adj. ઊની કાપડ woollen

oonghee gayelun adj. ઊંઘી ગયેલું asleep

oonjavun v.t. ઊંજવું lubricate

oonnun jaadun kapadun n. ઊનનું જાડું કપડું baize

oont n. ઊંટ camel

oontado n. ઊંટડો jack

oontanun n. ઊંટણું ointment

oontavaidun n. ઊંટવૈદું quackery

oopaj v.t. ઉપજ yield

oopajavun v.t. ઉપજવું accrue

oopashaman karavun v.t. ઉપશમન કરવું. mollify

ootapataang ઊટપટાંગ whimsical

ootaree aavavun v.i. ઊતરી આવવું descend

op devo v.t. ઓપ દેવો glaze

oradaaono samooh pl. ઓરડાઓનો સમૂહ apartments

oradee n. ઓરડી chamber

oradee, khand, flet n. ઓરડી, ખંડ, ફ્લેટ apartment

orado n. ઓરડો hall

orado n. ઓરડો hall

orado n. ઓરડો room

Ordaa n. ઓરડા suite

osaree n. ઓસરી lobby

osaree n. ઓસરી verand

osaree janaarun adj. ઓસરી જનારું

remittent

oshikun n. ઓશકું pillow

Osree javun v.i. ઓસરી જવું subside

ot n. ઓટ oat

othonun adj. ઓઠોનું labial

ovaaro n. ઓવારો jetty

ozon n. ઓઝોન ozone

paachaa javun v.t. પાછા જવું retrace

paachak adj. પાચક digestive

paachal adv. પાછળ after

paachalanun n. પાછળનું rear

paachalnee taareekh lakhavee v.t. પાછળની તારીખ લખવી pos¶date

paachanarogee adj. પાચનરોગી dyspeptic

paachanashakti n. પાચનશક્તિ digestion

paachha hathavun v.ti. પાછા હઠવું recede

paachha javaanee vrutti v.i. પાછા જવાની વૃત્તિregress

paachhal adv. પાછળ aback

paachhal prep. પાછળ behind

paachhal laee janaarun v.t. પાછળ લઇ જનારું retrograde

paachhal padavun v.t. પાછળ પડવું pursue

paachhalaa bhaagamaan n. પાછલા ભાગમાં back

Paachhalthee adv. પાછળથી subsequently

paachhu sarakhun karavun v.t. પાછુ સરખું કરવું redress

paachhun aapavun v.t. પાછું આપવું refund

paachhun aavavun v.i. પાછું આવવું return

paachhun dhakelavun v.t. પાછું ધકેલવું repel

paachhun hatavun v.i. પાછું હટવું retreat

paachhun hathaavavun *v.t.* પાછું હઠાવવું repulse

paachhun khenchavun *v.t.* પાછું ખેંચવું retract

paachhun khenchavun *v.t.* પાછું ખેંચવું withdraw

paachhun khenchavun *v.t.* પાછું ખેંચવું withhold

paachhun khenchee lavun *v.t.* પાછું ખેંચી લેવું revoke

paachhun melavavun *v.t.* પાછું મેળવવું recover

paachun levun *v.t.* પાછું લેવું unsay

paachun melavavun *v.t.* પાછું મેળવવું regain

paada na maananaarun *adj.* પાડ ન માનનારું thankless

paadachinha *n.* પાદચિહ્ન footstep

paadaree *n.* પાદરી clergyman

paadareenee shaalaa *n.* પાદરીની શાળા seminary

paadateep *n.* પાદટીપ footnote

paadee naakhavun *v.t.* પાડી નાખવું demolish

Paadi naakhvun *n.* પાડી નાખવું shed

paadosh પાડોશ neighbourhood

paadoshanun *adj.* પાડોશનું neighbouring

paadoshee *n.* પાડોશી neighbour

paagal *n.* પાગલ bedlamite

paagal *adj.* પાગલ mad

paagalakhaanun *n.* પાગલખાનું bedlam

paagalakhaanun *n.* પાગલખાનું madhouse

paagalapanun *n.* પાગલપણું madness

paaghadee *n.* પાઘડી turban

paajaraamaa poorvun *v.t.* પાંજરામાં પૂરવું encage

Paakaa daarudiyaa jevun *adj.* પાકા દારૂડિયો જેવું sottish

paakavun *v.t.* પાકવું fester

paakavun *v.t.* પાકવું ripen

paakeet *n.* પાકીટ portmanteau

paakhandee *adj.* પાખંડી heretic

paakhandee *adj.* પાખંડી heterodox

paakhandee *n.* પાખંડી tartuffe

paako bharoso *n.* પાકો ભરોસો trust

Paako daarudi *n.* પાકો દારૂડિયો sot

paako rang devo *v.t.* પાકો રંગ દેવો engrain

paal *n.* પાળ dike

paalakh *n.* પાલખ scaffolding

paalakhee *n.* પાલખી palankeen

paalanaposhan *n.* પાલનપોષણ nurture

paalavun પાળવું domesticate

paalee *n.* પાળી coping

paanakhar *adj.* પાનખર deciduous

paanch *adj.* પાંચ five

paanchaganun *adj.* પાંચગણું quinary

paanchamu *adj.* પાંચમું fifth

paandadun *n.* પાંદડું leaf

paanditya *n.* પાંડિત્ય erudition

paandurog, raktkshay *n.* પાંડુરોગ, રક્તક્ષય anaemia

paanee *n.* પાણી water

paanee khoondataa chaalavun *v.t.* પાણી ખૂંદતા ચાલવું wade

paaneedaar *adj.* પાણીદાર plucky

Paaneedaar *adj.* પાણીદાર spirited

paaneenee taankee *n.* પાણીની ટાંકી cistern

paaneeno dhodh *n.* પાણીનો ધોધ cascade

paaneeno khalabhalaat *n.* પાણીનો ખળભળાટ ripple

paaneenun *adj.* પાણીનું watery

paaneenun paatra *n.* પાણીનું પાત્ર trough

paaneethee daazavun *n.* પાણીથી દાઝવું scald

paaneevaalun *adj.* પાણીવાળું hydrous

Paani udaadvun *v.t.* પાણી ઉડાડવું swash

paanjaraamaa pakadavun *v.t.* પાંજરામાં પકડવું entrap

paanjarun *n.* પાંજરું cage

paanjrun *n.* પાંજરું trap

paankh *n.* પાંખ wing

paankh fafadaavavee *v.t.* પાંખ ફફડાવવી flap

paankhar *n.* પાનખર autumn

paankharnun *adj.* પાનખરનું autumnal

paanpad *n.* પાંપણ eyelash

paansalee *n.* પાંસળી rib

paansaleedaar kaapad *n.* પાંસળીદાર કાપડ twill

paanurotee *n.* પાંઉરોટી loaf

Paap *n.* પાપ sin

paap karanaarun *adj.* પાપ કરનારું sinful

paap vimukti *n.* પાપ વિમુક્તિ purge

paap vimukti sthaan *n.* પાપ વિમુક્તિ સ્થાન purgatory

paapabheerun *adj.* પાપભીરૂ queasy

paapathee mukti *n.* પાપથી મુક્તિ redemption

paapavruttivaalun *adj.* પાપવૃત્તિવાળું peccable

paapman padavun *v.i.* પાપમાં પડવું backslide

paarakhavun *v.t.* પારખવું discern

paarakhee shakaay tevun *adj.* પારખી શકાય તેવું discernible

paarako *n.* પારકો outsider

paarakun *adj.* પારકું alien

paaranun *n.* પારણું cradle

paaravan *n.* પારવણ amalgam

paardarshak *n.* પારદર્શક transparent

paardarshaktaa *n.* પારદર્શકતા transparence

paaribhaashik shabdakosh *n.* પારિભાષિક શબ્દકોશ glossary

paarkaapanu *adj.* પારકાપણું alienable

paaro *n.* પારો mercury

paaro *n.* પારો quicksilver

paasadthee thavun *v.i.* પાછળથી થવું ensue

paasaport *n.* પાસપોર્ટ passport

paaseman paasenun *prep.* પાસેમાં પાસેનું next

paaseman paasenun *adj.* પાસેમાં પાસેનું proximate

Paash *n.* પાશ snare

paashavee *adj.* પાશવી bestial

paashavee *adj.* પાશવી. brutal

paashchaaty *adj.* પાશ્ચાત્ય occidental

paashchaaty *adj.* પાશ્ચાત્ય western

paashchaaty desho *n.* પાશ્ચાત્ય દેશો occident

paasu *n.* પાસું facet

paasu hatavun *v.i.* પાછુ હઠવું flinch

paatado *n.* પાટડો girder

paatadu banaavavun *v.t.* પાતળું બનાવવું emaciate

paatadu banaavavy te *n.* પાતળું બનાવવું તે emaciation

paatalaapanun *n.* પાતળાપણું thinness

paatalee *n.* પાટલી plait

paatalee lagaam *n.* પાતળી લગામ snaffle

paataloona *n.pl.* પાટલૂન trousers

paatalu *adj.* પાતળું thin

paatalu karavun *v.t.* પાતળું કરવું dilute

paatalun *adj.* પાતળું gaunt

paatalun *adj.* પાતળું tenuous

paatalun doradun *n.* પાતળું દોરડું cord

paatalun karavun *v.t.* પાતળું કરવું rerefy

paatalun patarun *n.* પાતળું પતરું plate

paateedaar *n.* પાટીદાર yeoman

paath sansodhan *n.* પાઠ સંશોધન emendation

paathabhed *n.* પાઠભેદ recension

paatharanun *n.* પાથરણું bedding

paatharanun *n.* પાથરણું carpet

paathayapustak *n.* પાઠયપુસ્તક textbook

paatiyun *n.* પાટિયું plank

Paatlee cheep પાતળી ચીપ splint

paatlee minbattee *n.* પાતળી મીણબત્તી taper

Paatlun *adj.* પાતળું slender

Paatlun *adj.* પાતળું slim

paato *n.* પાટો bandage

paatrataa *n.* પાત્રતા eligibility

paaunrotee *n.* પાઉરોટી bread

paavado *n.* પાવડો scoop

paavado *n.* પાવડો shovel

paavitry *n.* પાવિત્ર્ય chastity

paayaaroop *adj.* પાયારૂપ basal

paayaaroop *adj.* પાયારૂપ basic

paayadal પાયદળ infantry

paayadalanee tukadee *n.* પાયદળની ટુકડી platoon

paayajaamo *n.* પાયજામો pants

paayakhaanun *n.* પાયખાનું latrine

paayamaalee *n.* પાયમાલી ravage

paayaree utaar *n.* પાયરી ઉતાર reduction

paayo *n.* પાયો basis

pachaas *adj.* પચાસ fifty

pachaasamu *adj.* પચાસમું fiftieth

pachaavee paadanaara *n.* પચાવે પાડનાર usurper

pachaavee paadavun *v.i.* પચાવી પાડવું usurp

pachaavee paadavun *n.* પચાવી પાડવું usurpation

pachaneeya *adj.* પચનીય digestible

pache nahee tevu *adj.* પચે નહી તેવું undigested

pacheeno divas *n.* પછીનો દવિસ morrow

pachhaat *adj.* પછાત backward

pachhadavun *v.t.* પછાડવું slam

padaavee levun *v.t.* પડાવી લેવું reave

padabhrasht karavun *v.t.* પદભ્રષ્ટ કરવું dismiss

padabhrastha karavun *v.t.* પદભ્રષ્ટ કરવું displace

padadhaaree *adj.* પદધારી incumbent

padado *n.* પડદો curtain

padado *n.* પડદો diaphragm

padado *n.* પડદો valve

padado *n.* પડદો veil

padagho *n.* પડઘો echo

padagho *n.* પડઘો resonance

padagho padavo *v.i.* પડઘો પડવો resound

padagho padavo *v.t.* પડઘો પડવો reverberate

padak *n.* પદક medal

padakaar *n.* પડકાર challenge

padalop *n.* પદલોપ elision

padasoochak billo *n.* પદસૂચક બલ્લિો badge

padatar *n.* પડતર fallow

padatee *n.* પડતી decadence

padatu *n.* પડતું falling

padatun mukavun *v.t.* પડતું મૂકવું cast

padavee *n.* પદવી appellation

padavee *n.* પદવી degree

padaveedaan samaaranbh *n.* પદવીદાન સમારંભ convocation

padaveedarshak vastr *n.* પદવીદર્શક વસ્તર hood

padaveeghar *n.* પદવીઘર licentiate

padavruddhi *n.* પદવૃદ્ધિ promotion

padbhrashta karavun *v.t.* પદભ્રષ્ટ કરવું dethrone

Padchhaayaa jevun *adj.* પડછાયા જેવું shadowy

Padchhaayo *n.* પડછાયો shadow

paddhati *n.* પદ્ધતિ method

paddhatisaranun *n.* પદ્ધતિસરનું methodical

Paddo *n.* પડદો screen

padee baangavun te *v.t.* પડી ભાંગવું તે collapse

padee javun *v.t.* પડી જવું tumble

padeekun *n.* પડીકું packet

Padhdhateesarnun *adj.* પદ્ધતિસરનું systematic

padma *n.* પદ્મ trillion

padoshakka *n.* પડોશહક્ક easement

pag *n.* પગ foot

pag *n.* પગ leg

Pag thokvo *v.t.* પગ ઠોકવો stamp

paga ghasadatan chaalavun *v.i.* પગ ઘસડતાં ચાલવું trudge

paga mookavo *v.t.* પગ મૂકવો tread

paga vatee chalaavaatun yantra *n.* પગ વતી ચલાવાતું યંત્ર treadle

Pagaar *n.* પગાર salary

Pagaar *n.* પગાર stipend

Pagaardaar *adj.* પગારદાર stipendiary

pagadandee *n.* પગદંડી causeway

pagadandee *n.* પગદંડી footpath

pagadandee *n.* પગદંડી path

pagalaanee chhaap *n.* પગલાની છાપ footprint

pagalan bharavaan *v.t.* પગલાં ભરવા prosecute

paganee edee *n.* પગની એડી heel

paganee ghoontee *n.* પગની ઘૂંટી ankle

paganee kharee પગની ખરી hoof

pagano nalo *n.* પગનો નળો shank

pagano nalo *n.* પગનો નળો shin

paganun ke pagonun *adj.* પગનું કે પગોનું pedal

paganun laanbun mojun *n.* પગનું લાંબું મોજું hose

pagapaala paryatan *n.* પગપાળા પર્યટન hike

pagarakhaa *n.* પગરખા footwear

pagarakhaannee sagatalee *n.* પગરખાંની સગતળી rand

Pagarkhaanun taliyun *n.* પગરખાનું તળિયું sole

pagathiyan *n.* પગથિયાં stile

page chaalatun *n.* પગે ચાલતું pedestrian

page padavun *v.t.* પગે પડવું prostrate

pagerun *n.* પગેરું vestige

pagnee aanglee ke angootho *n.* પગની આંગળી કે અંગૂઠો toe

Pagrkhun *n.* પગરખું shoe

pahaadee haran *n.* પહાડી હરણ chamois

pahelaaa javee *v.t.* પહેલાં જવું forego

pahclaannce taarikh lakhavee *v.t.* પહેલાંની તારીખ લખવી antedate

pahelaannun *adj.* પહેલાંનું previous

pahelaathee chukavelun *adj.* પહેલાથી ચુકવેલું prepaid

pahelavrutti *n.* પહેલવૃત્તિ initiative

pahelee pasandagee *n.* પહેલી પસંદગી preference

pahelu *adj.* પહેલું first

paheravaano moto dagalo *n.* પહેરવાનો મોટો ડગલો. overcoat

paheravaathee jeern thayelun પહેરવાથી જીર્ણ થયેલું worn

paheravesh *n.* પહેરવેશ garb

paheravun *v.t.* પહેરવું wear

pahervesh *n.* પહેરવેશ costume

paholaa paan ni talavaar *n.* પહોળા પાનની તલવાર cutlass

paholaaee *n.* પહોળાઈ breadth

paholaaee *n.* પહોળાઈ width

paholu karavun *v.t.* પહોળું કરવું dilate

paholun *adj.* પહોળું broad

paholun *adj.* પહોળું wide

paholun karavun *v.t.* પહોળું કરવું broaden

pahonch પહોંચ counterfoil

pahonch bahaaranun *adj.* પહોંચ બહારનું inaccessible

pahonch, paavati *n.* પહોંચ, પાવતી acknowledgement

pahonchaay evun *adj.* પહોંચાય એવું approachable

paidaa uparanee vaata *n.* પૈડાં ઉપરની વાટ. tyre

Paidaano aaro *n.* પૈડાનો આરો spoke

paidun *n.* પૈડું wheel

paisa *n.* પૈસા money

paisa aapyaano daakhalo *n.* પૈસા આપ્યાનો દાખલો voucher

paisa chookavava *v.t.* પૈસા ચૂકવવા pay

paisaadaar *adj.* પૈસાદાર moneyed

paisaadaar *adj.* પૈસાદાર opulent

paisaadaar *n.* પૈસાદાર rich

Paisadaar *Adj.* પૈસાદાર substantial

pajavavun *v.t.* પજવવું assail

pajavavun *n.* પજવવું harass

pakad પકડ foothold

pakadavaanee shakti *n.* પકડવાની શક્તિ prehension

pakadavaanun ojaar *n.* પકડવાનું ઓજાર pincers

pakadee levun *v.t.* પકડી લેવું capture

pakadee levun *v.t.* પકડી લેવું catch

pakadee paadavun *v.t.* પકડી પાડવું. nab

pakadee raakhavun *v.* પકડી રાખવું hold

pakadee raakhavun *v.t.* પકડી રાખવું hug

pakhavaadiyu *n.* પખવાડિયું fortnight

Pakit *n.* પાકિટ scrip

paksh *n.* પક્ષ faction

pakshakaar, himaayatee *v.* પક્ષકાર,હિમાયતી advocate

pakshapaat *n.* પક્ષપાત predilection

pakshapaat vinaanun *adj.* પક્ષપાત વિનાનું indifferent

pakshapaatee *adj.* પક્ષપાતી one-sided

pakshapalatun *n.* પક્ષપલટું renegade

pakshapalatun *n.* પક્ષપલટું turncoat

pakshee *n.* પક્ષી bird

paksheenan peenchhan *n.* પક્ષીનાં પીછાં plumage

paksheenee paankh પક્ષીની પાંખ pinion

paksheeno maalo *n.* પક્ષીનો માળો nest

paksheenun bachchun *n.* પક્ષીનું બચ્ચું chick

paksheenun bachchun, *n.* પક્ષીનું બચ્ચું chicken

paksheenun vishraantisthaan *n.* પક્ષીનું વિશ્રાન્તસ્થાન roost

Palaalvun *adj.* પલાળવું steep

palaaneene besavun *v.t.* પલાણીને બેસવું bestried

palaayan karavun *v.t.* પલાયન કરવું scamper

palaayanayuktee *n.* પલાયનયુક્તિ elusion

palakaara maarava *v.t.* પલકારા મારવા blink

palang *n.* પલંગ bedstead

pamaanit karavun *v.t.* પ્રમાણિત કરવું certify

pan *adv.* પણ also

panakookadee *n.* પનકૂકડી teal

panchaang *n.* પંચાંગ calendar

panchakon *n.* પંચકોણ pentagon

panchano chukaado, *n.* પંચનો ચુકાદો verdict

panchano sabhy *n.* પંચનો સભ્ય commissioner

pancheekaranavidya *n.* પંચીકરણવિદ્યા ontology

Pand *n.* પંડ self

pandarmu *adj.* પંદરમું fifteen

Paneeno pravaah *n.* પાણીનો પ્રવાહ stream

panjetee *n.* પંજેટી rake

panjetee, kaansakee no daanto *n.* પંજેટી, કાંસકી, ઈ.નો દાંતો tine

pankha fafadaavavee *n.* પાંખો ફફડાવવી flutter

pankheeghar *n.* પંખીઘર aviary

pankheenun bachchu *n.* પંખીનું બચ્ચુ nestling

pankheenun viraam sthaan *n.* પંખીનું વિરામ સ્થાન perch

pankho *n.* પંખો fan

pankti *n.* પંક્તિ row

Pankti *adj.* પંક્તિ serial

panp *n.* પંપ pump

panpaadavun *v.t.* પંપાળવું fondle

panpaalavun *v.t.* પંપાળવું coddle

panpaalavun *v.t.* પંપાળવું cuddle

panpaalavun *n.* પંપાળવું pamper

panth *n.* પંથ creed

paraajay aapavo *v.t.* પરાજય આપવો defeat

paraakaashthaae pahonchavun *v.t.* પરાકાષ્ઠાએ પહોંચવું culminate

paraakaastha *n.* પરાકાષ્ઠા climax

paraakramee purush *n.* પરાક્રમી પુરુષ hero

paraane valagaadavun *v.t.* પરાણે વળગાડવું obtrude

paraavartan *adj.* પરાવર્તન reflection

paraavartan *n.* પરાવર્તન reverberation

parabeediyu *n.* પરબીડિયું envelope

paradesh *adj.* પરદેશ foreign

paradeshee naagarik *n.* પરદેશી નાગરિક burgher

paradheenataa *n.* પરાધીનતા dependence

paragaj *n.* પરગજુ complaisance

paragano *n.* પરગણું county

parahejee paalavee *n.* પરહેજી પાળવી diet

param saubhaagy *n.* પરમ સૌભાગ્ય godsend

paramaanand *n.* પરમાનંદ ecstasy

paramaanu *n.* પરમાણુ atom

paramaanun sanbandhee *n.* પરમાણુ સંબંધી molecular

paramaanune lagatun *adj.* પરમાણુને લગતું atomic

parameshvar *n.* પરમેશ્વર god

parameshvar *n.* પરમેશ્વર providence

paramiyo *n.* પરમિયો gonorrhoea

paramparaagat *adj.* પરંપરાગત traditional

paranaal *n.* પરનાળ gutter

paranavun *v.t.* પરણવું espouse

paranavun *v.i.* પરણવું wed

paranparaa *n.* પરંપરા tradition

parantuk *n.* પરંતુક proviso

parantun *adj.* પરંતુ but
parapoto *n.* પરપોટો bubble
parasevo *n.* પરસેવો. perspiration
parasevo chhootavo *v.i.* પરસેવો છૂટવો perspire
paraspar jodavun *v.t.* પરસ્પર જોડવું interlink
paraspar vinimay *v.t.* પરસ્પર વનિમિય reciprocate
paraspar virodhee *adj.* પરસ્પર વિરોધી inconsistent
parat chookavavun *v.t.* પરત ચૂકવવું repay
parat sonpavun *v.t.* પરત સોંપવું reassign
parathaar *n.* પરથાર plinth
paravaalun *n.* પરવાળું coral
paravaanagee *n.* પરવાનગી licence
paravaanagee *n.* પરવાનગી permission
paravaanagee devee *v.t.* પરવાનગી દેવી permit
paravaanagee paatr *adj.* પરવાનગી પાત્ર permissible
paravaanagi aapavi *v.* પરવાનગી આપવી allow
pardaafaash *n.* પર્દાફાશ disclosure
Pardeshee *adj.* પરદેશી strange
pardeshman *adv.* પરદેશમાં abroad
paree *n.* પરી fairy
pareeksha karavee *v.t.* પરીક્ષા કરવી examine
pareeksha levee *v.t.* પરીક્ષા લેવી catechise
pareekshaa *n.* પરીક્ષા examination
pareekshaarthee *n.* પરીક્ષાર્થી examinee
pareekshak *n.* પરીક્ષક examiner
pareevartanasheelata *adj.* પરિવર્તનશીલતા changeable
Parganun ke Jillo *n.* પરગણું કે જિલ્લો shire
paribal *n.* પરિબળ factor
paribhaashaa *n.* પરિભાષા terminology
paribhraman *n.* પરિભ્રમણ circulation
paricaanakaarak *adj.* પરિમાણકારક telling
parichaarak varg *n.* પરિચારક વર્ગ retinue
parichaarika *n.* પરિચારિકા nurse
parichaarikaa *n.* પરિચારિકા stewardess
parichit karavun *v.t.* પરિચિત કરવું familiarize
parichitataa પરિચિતતા familliarity
parigh *n.* પરિધિ circumference
parimaan *n.* પરમાણ extent
Parimaan *n.* પરિમાણ size
parimaanavaachak *n.* પરિમાણવાચક quantitative
parimiti *n.* પરિમિતિ perimeter
parinaam *n.* પરિણામ issue
parinaam *n.* પરિમાણ measurement
parinaam *n.* પરિણામ upshot
parinaamaroopee *adj.* પરિણામરૂપી resultant
parinaamasoochak *adj.* પરિણામસૂચક illative
paripakv *adj.* પરિપક્વ mature
paripakv *adj.* પરિપક્વ ripe
paripakvata *n.* પરિપક્વતા maturity
paripath *n.* પરિપથ circuit
paripoorn karavun *v.t.* પરિપૂરણ કરવું consummate
paripoorn karavun *v.t.* પરિપૂરણ કરવું fulfil
parisar *n.* પરિસર outskirt
parisar *n.* પરિસર precinct
parisar *n.pl.* પરિસર premises
parishad *n.* પરિષદ conference
parishad પરિષદ congress
parishad *n.* પરિષદ interlocution
parishad sabhya *n.* પરિષદ - સભ્ય councillor
paristhitimaan bagaado *n.* પરિસ્થિતિમાં બગાડો aggravation
paristhitine bagaadavi *v.* પરિસ્થિતિ બગાડવી aggravate
parivahan પરિવહન transport
parivardhak, dhvaneevardhak *n.* પરિવર્ધક, ધ્વનિવર્ધક amplifier
parivartan પરિવર્તન alteration
parivartan *n.* પરિવર્તન conversion
parivartan ferafaar *n.* પરિવર્તન ફેરફાર. mutation

parivartanaksham *adj.* પરિવર્તનક્ષમ convertible

parivartanasheel *adj.* પરિવર્તનશીલ mutable

parivartaneey *adj.* પરિવર્તનીય alterable

parivartanheen પરિવર્તનહીન vegetate

parivartanksham *adj.* પરિવર્તનક્ષમ reducible

parivartansheel *adj.* પરિવર્તનશીલ variable

parodh *v.i.* પરોઢ dawn

paroksh *adj.* પરોક્ષ indirect

paropakaar *n.* પરોપકાર benefice

paropakaaree *adj.* પરોપકારી. munificent

paropakaaree *adj.* પરોપકારી obliging

paropakaaree *adj.* પરોપકારી philanthropic

paropakaarita *n.* પરોપકારિતા humanity

Parpeedanvruti *n.* પરપીડનવૃત્તિ sadism

Parsevo *n.* પરસેવો sweat

Parsevo *adj.* પરસેવો sweaty

parshiano gavarnar *n.* પરશિયાનો ગવર્નર satrap

parshneeyataa *n.* પરશનીયતા tangibility

paru *n.* પરુ pus

paruvaalun *adj.* પરુવાળું purulent

parvat *n.* પર્વત mountain

parvat shikhar *n.* પર્વત શિખર alp

parvatmaanu nanu sarovar *n.* પર્વતમાંનું નાનું સરોવર. tarn

paryat *prep.* પર્યંત unto

pasand karavun *v.t.* પસંદ કરવું choose

pasand karavun *v.t.* પસંદ કરવું prefer

pasand karavun *v.t.* પસંદ કરવું select

Pasand karvun te *n.* પસંદ કરવું તે selection

pasandagee *n.* પસંદગી choice

pasandageenu *n.* પસંદગીનું favourite

pasandageepaatra *adj.* પસંદગીપાત્ર selective

paschaataapee *adj.* પશ્ચાતાપી contrite

pashchaataap *n.* પશ્ચાતાપ remorse

pashchaayaattap *n.* પૂરશ્ચાયાત્તાપ contrition

pashchim *n.* પશ્ચિમ west

pashchim tarafanun *adj.* પશ્ચિમ તરફનું westerly

pashchimaman aavelun *adv.* પશ્ચિમમાં આવેલું westward

pashendriyan, ne lagatu *adj.* પરોશેન્દ્રિયનું ને લગતું tactile

pashu *n.* પશુ beast

pashudhan *n.* પશુધન live-stock

pashunun varnan karanaar *n.* પશુનું વર્ણન કરનાર zoographer

pashurog sanbandhee *adj.* પશુરોગ સંબંધી veterinary

pashusamaan *adj.* પશુસમાન brute

pashuvaado *n.* પશુવાડો menagerie

pashuvarnan *n.* પશુવર્ણન zoography

pastaavo *n.* પસ્તાવો penitence

pastaavo karanaar *adj.* પસ્તાવો કરનાર penitent

pataaka *n.* પતાકા pennant

pataakaa *n.* પતાકા streamer

pataamanee *n.* પટામણી cajolery

pataavaalo *n.* પટાવાળો peon

Pataavat *n.* પતાવટ settlement

patan *n.* પતન ruin

patang *n.* પતંગ kite

patangiyun *n.* પતંગિયું butterfly

pathaaree *n.* પથારી bed

pathaareevash પથારીવશ bed-rid

pathadarshak paatiya *n.* પથદર્શક પાટિયા signpost

patharee *n.* પથરી gravel

pathdarshak *n.* પથદર્શક loadstar

pathikaashram *n.* પથિકાશ્રમ inn

Paththar *n.* પથ્થર stone

paththar jevun karavun *v.t.* પથ્થર જેવું કરવું petrify

paththaranee kheen *n.* પથ્થરની ખીણ quarry

pati *n.* પતિ husband

Pati athvaa patnee *n.* પતિ અથવા પત્ની spouse

patnee *n.* પત્ની, wife

patneene aadhin *adj.* પત્નીને આધનિ hen-packed

pato *n.* પટો belt

patra vyavhaar *v.i.* પત્ર વ્યવહાર correspond

patrak maa naam nodhavun *v.* પત્રકમાં નામ નોંધવું enrol

patrakaar *n.* પત્રકાર journalist

patrakaaratv *n.* પત્રકારત્વ journalism

patranaa joop maa kaavya *n.* પત્રના રૂપમાં કાવ્ય epistle

patravahevaar *n.* પત્રવહેવાર, communication

patravahevaar *n.* પત્રવહેવાર correspondence

patrika *n.* પત્રિકા pamphlet

patta vade aaveshtit *adj.* પટ્ટા વડે આવેષ્ટતિ belted

pattarano nakkar tukado *n.* પથ્થરનો નક્કર ટુકડો block

pattharanee kabar *n.* પથ્થરની કબર sarcophagus

pattee *n.* પટ્ટી batten

patto *n.* પત્તો whereabouts

pattohastarahapad *n.* પટ્ટો:સ્તર:પડ layer

pauraanik *adj.* પૌરાણિક legendary

pauraanik *adj.* પૌરાણિક mythological

paushtik *adj.* પૌષ્ટિક alimentary

pautra *n.* પૌત્ર grandchild

pavaado *n.* પવાડો ballad

pavaalun *n.* પવાલું cup

pavan *n.* પવન wind

pavanachakkee *n.* પવનચક્કી windmill

pavananee aahlaadak mand laher *n.* પવનની આહ્લાદક મંદ લહેર zephyr

pavitr *adj.* પવિત્ર. holy

Pavitra *adj.* પવિત્ર sacred

pavitra banaavavun *v.t.* પવિત્ર બનાવવું consecrate

pavitra na karelu *adj.* પવિત્ર ન કરેલું unhallowed

pavitrata *n.* પવિત્રતા holiness

pavitry *n.* પવિત્ર્ય purity

payamataavaalun *adj.* પયમતાવાળું propitious

Pech *n.* પેચ screw

peda karavun *v.t.* પેદા કરવું generate

peda karavun *v.t.* પેદા કરવું procreate

pedaa karavun *v.t.* પેદા કરવું engender

pee shakaay evun પી શકાય એવું potable

peechhethath *n.* પીછેઠઠ regression

peechho *n.* પીછો pursuit

peeda *n.* પીડા pain

peeda *n.* પીડા woe

peedh *adj.* પીઠ veteran

peedhabal *n.* પીઠબળ backing

peedhel *adj.* પીધેલ tipsy

peedit *n.* પીડિત victim

peegalelun *adj.* પીગળેલું. molten

peelaash padatun *adj.* પીળાશ પડતું yellowish

peelun *adj.* પીળું yellow

peelun chaamadun *n.* પીળું ચામડું buff

peenchhu પીછું feather

peenchhun *n.* પીછું plume

peenchhun *n.* પીછું quill

peenjaaro *n.* પીંજારો carder

peenun *n.* પીણું beverage

Peepno daato *n.* પીપનો ડાટો spigot

peevaalaayak *adj.* પીવાલાયક drinkable

peevun *v.t.* પીવું drink

peganbar *n.* પેગંબર prophet

pelee baajunun *adj.* પેલી બાજુનું yon

pelee paar *prep.* પેલી પાર beyond

pelee paaranun *adv.* પેલી પારનું yonder

pelun *pro.* પેલું that

pendant *adj.* પેન્ડન્ટ pendant

pengodaa *n.* પેગોડા pagoda

peshaab *n.* પેશાબ urine

peshaaba karavo *adj.* પેશાબ કરવો. urinary

peshabama takalif *n.* પેશાબમાં તકલીફ dysuria

peshchyuraaiz *v.t.* પેશ્ચ્યુરાઇઝ pasteurize

pestree *n.* પેસ્ટ્રી pastry

pet *n.* પેટ abdomen

pet *n.* પેટ belly

Pet *n.* પેટ stomach

peta kaayado *n.* પેટા કાયદો by-law

Petaa bhaadoot *n.* પેટા ભાડૂત subtenant
Petaabhaag *v.t.* પેટાભાગ sub-divide
petant *n.* પેટન્ટ patent
petashool *n.* પેટશૂળ colic
petee *n.* પેટી box
petne lagatun *adj.* પેટને લગતું gastric
petrol *n.* પેટ્રોલ gasolene
petrol *n.* પેટ્રોલ petrol
pichakaaree maaravee *n.* પચિકારી મારવી douche
Pichkaari maarvee ke vati chhatvun *n.* પચિકારી મારવી કે વતી છાંટવું syringe
pidavun, ribaavavun *v.* પીડવું, રબિાવવું afflict
pilchattu *adj.* પીળચટું tawny
pingalashaastr *n.* પગિળશાસ્ત્ર prosody
pint *n.* પન્િટ pint
pipet *n.* પપિટ pipette
piraamid *n.* પરિામડિ pyramid
pistan *n.* પસિ્ટન piston
pita *n.* પતિા papa
Pitaa *n.* પતિા dad
pitaa *n.* પતિા father
Pitaa *n.* પતિા sire
pitaraaee *n.* પતિરાઈ cousin
pitruhatya *n.* પતિૃહત્યા patricide
pitrupakshanun *adj.* પતિૃપક્ષનું paternal
pitruparanpara *n.* પતિૃપરંપરા paternity
pitrutulya *adj.* પતિૃ તુલ્ય fatherly
pitta *n.* પતિ્ત choler
pittaashay *n.* પતિ્તાશય liver
pittal *n.* પતિ્તળ brass
pittala jevun *n.* પતિ્તળ જેવું brazen
pittaprakop *n.* પતિ્તપ્રકોપ bile
piyaano *n.* પયિાનો piano
piyaanovaadak *n.* પયિાનોવાદક pianist
plaaneene *adv.* પલાણીને. astride
plaatone lagatun *adj.* પ્લાટોને લગતું platonic
plambar *n.* પ્લમ્બર plumber
plastik *adj.* પ્લાસ્ટકિ plastic
pletinam *n.* પ્લેટનિમ platinum
pochun karavun *v.i.* પોચું કરવું soften
pokharaaj(mani) *n.* પોખરાજ (મણ઼િ). topaz
Polaad *n.* પોલાદ steel
polaan *n.* પોલાણ cavity
polees sipaaee *n.* પોલીસ સપિાઈ police
poleesano dando *n.* પોલીસનો ડંડો truncheon
poleesano sipaaee *n.* પોલીસનો સપિાઈ copper
poleesathaanun *n.* પોલીસથાણું. police-station
polisa karmachaaree *n.* પોલીસ કર્મચારી policeman
polisano sipaaee *n.* પોલીસનો સપિાઈ constable
Polish karnaar chhokro *n.* પૉલશિ કરનાર છોકરો shoe-black
polisono ghero *n.* પોલીસોનો ઘેરો cordon
polun *n.* પોલું hollow
poochadee *n.* પૂછડી tail
poochhaparachh પૂછપરછ inquiry
poochhavun *v.t.* પૂછવું ask
poochhavun *v.i.* પૂછવું inquire
poojaapaatra *v.t.* પૂજાપાત્ર venerate
poojak, aaraadhak *n.* પૂજક, આરાધક adorer
poojavun *v.t.* પૂજવું revere
poojy *adj.* પૂજ્ય reverend
poojyabhaav *n.* પૂજ્યભાવ veneration
poolaa baandhavaa *n.* પૂળા બાંધવા stook
Poolee *n.* પૂળી sheaf
poor *n.* પૂર flood
pooran *n.* પૂરણ complement
pooratee laayakaat *adj.* પૂરતી લાયકાત competent
pooratu *adj.* પૂરતું enogh
pooratun *adj.* પૂરતું adequate
pooravanee karanaarun *adj.* પુરવણી કરનારું complementary
pooree deedhelun *adj.* પૂરી દીધેલું pent
Poorepooro naash karvo *v.t.* પૂરેપૂરો નાશ કરવો shatter
poorepooru bharelu *adj.* પૂરેપૂરું ભરેલું full
Poorepoorun bharee devun te *n.* પૂરેપૂરું ભરી દેવું તે saturation

Poorepoorun swachchh *adj.* પૂરેપૂરું સ્વચ્છ spotless

poorn bakhtaragnakavach *n.* પૂરણ બખ્તરજ્ઞકવચ panoply

poorn karavun *v.t.* પૂરણ કરવું integrate

poorn vikaas *n.* પૂરણ વિકાસ maturation

poorna karavun *v.* પૂરણ કરવું accomplish

poornaank *n.* પૂરણાંક integer

Poortun *n.* પૂરતું sufficiency

pooru paadavun *v.t.* પૂરું પાડવું furnish

poorv aadhaar *n.* પૂરવ આધાર precedent

poorv bhoomadhy pradesh *adj.* પૂરવ ભૂમધ્ય પ્રદેશ levant

poorv dishaa *adj.* પૂરવ દિશા eastward

poorv sthitie javun *v.i.* પૂરવ સ્થિતિએ જવું revert

poorva dishaanun *adj.* પૂરવ દિશાનું orient

poorva tarafanu *adj.* પૂરવ તરફનું easterly

poorvaabhaas *n.* પૂરવાભાસ premonition

poorvaapekshit baabat *n.* પૂરવાપેક્ષિત બાબત pre-requisite

poorvabhoomika *n.* પૂરવભૂમિકા background

poorvachinh *n.* પૂરવચિહ્ન precursor

poorvadhaarana પૂરવધારણા preconception

poorvagaamee *n.* પૂરવગામી predecessor

poorvagaamee *n.* પૂરવગામી progenitor

poorvagnaan *n.* પૂરવજ્ઞાન precognition

poorvagrah *n.* પૂરવગ્રહ bias

poorvagrah *n.* પૂરવગ્રહ prejudice

poorvagrahayukt *adj.* પૂરવગ્રહયુક્ત prejudicial

poorvaj *n.* પૂરવજ ancestor

poorvaj *n.* પૂરવજ forefather

poorvano maanas *adj.* પૂરવનો માણસ oriental

poorvanu *adj.* પૂરવનું eastern

poorvapakshaatmak *adj.* પૂરવપક્ષાત્મક hypothetical

poorvaprayog *n.* પૂરવપૂરયોગ rehearsal

poorvaprayog karavo *v.t.* પૂરવપૂરયોગ કરવો rehearse

poorvasoochak *adj.* પૂરવસૂચક prognostic

poorvchinha bataavavun *v.t.* પૂરવચિહ્ન બતાવવું adumbrate

poorve *adj.* પૂરવે ago

poorve *adv.* પૂરવે ere

poorveteehaas *adj.* પૂરવેતિહાસ antecedent

pop *n.* પૉપ pope

popachu *n.* પોપચું eyelid

popanun *adj.* પોપનું papal

popasamarthak *n.* પોપસમર્થક papist

'poplar' jhaad *n.* 'પૉપ્લર' ઝાડ aspen

poplin *n.* પોપલિન poplin

poro *n.* પોરો animalcule

porselin *n.* પોર્સેલિન porcelain

poshaak *n.* પોશાક attire

poshaak *n.* પોશાક raiment

poshaak utaarvaa *v.t.* પોશાક ઉતારવા unclothe

poshak tatto umeravaa *v.t.* પોષક તત્ત્વો ઉમેરવાં fortify

poshan *n.* પોષણ nutrition

poshanakaarak *adj.* પોષણકારક nourishing

poshavun *v.t.* પોષવું nourish

potaanaa hastaakshar *n.* પોતાના હસ્તાક્ષર autograph

potaane vishe *adj.* પોતાને વિષે personally

potaanee laaganee jaaher karavun *v.t.* પોતાની લાગણી જાહેર કરવું profess

potaanun *adj.* પોતાનું own

potalun *n.* પોટલું pack

potalun *n.* પોટલું package

potalun, bhaaree *n.* પોટલું, ભારી bundle

potapotaanun *adj.* પોતપોતાનું respective

pote *pro.* પોતે oneself

Pote paangreene *n.* પોતે પાંગરીને scion

potun *n.* પોતું swab

praacheen *adj.* પ્રાચીન primitive

praacheen *adj.* પ્રાચીન pristine

praacheen dantakatha *n.* પ્રાચીન દંતકથા myth

praacheen kalaakruti *adj.* પ્રાચીન કલાકૃતિ classical

praacheen, puraanun *adj.* પ્રાચીન, પુરાણું ancient

praachin dhaaraasabhaa *v.t.* પ્રાચીન ધારાસભા moot

praachin ritareevaajo *n.* પ્રાચીન રીતરિવાજો antiquities

praadeshik *adj.* પ્રાદેશિક territorial

praadhaanya *n.* પ્રાધાન્ય emphasis

praagaitihaasik *adj.* પ્રાગૈતિહાસિક prehistoric

praakakathan *n.* પ્રાકકથન prologue

praamaanik *adj.* પ્રામાણિક honest

praamaanik *adj.* પ્રામાણિક righteous

praamaanik nyaayadheesh *n.* પ્રામાણિક ન્યાયાધીશ daniel

praamaanikapanun *n.* પ્રમાણિકપણું honesty

praamaanikata *n.* પ્રામાણિકતા probity

praamaanikata *n.* પ્રામાણિકતા rectitude

praanaghaatak *adj.* પ્રાણઘાતક. mortal

praanasanchaar, jusso *n.* પ્રાણસંચાર, જુસ્સો animation

praanavaayu *n.* પ્રાણવાયુ oxygen

praanee *n.* પ્રાણી creature

praanee ke maanasana koola *n.* પ્રાણી કે માણસના ફૂલા rump

praanee rasaayanshaastra *n.* પ્રાણી રસાયણશાસ્ત્ર zoochemistry

praanee sangrahaalay *n.* પ્રાણી સંગ્રહાલય zoo

praaneejeevananan niyamo *n.* પ્રાણીજીવનનાં નિયમો zoonomy

praaneenee moonchh *n.* પ્રાણીની મૂંછ tentacle

praaneeno panjo *n.* પ્રાણીનો પંજો paw

praaneenun bachchun *n.* પ્રાણીનું બચ્ચું yeanling

praaneenun maans *n.* પ્રાણીનું માંસ meat

praaneeo sanbandheet *adj.* પ્રાણીઓ સંબંધીત zoic

praaneeshaastr *n.* પ્રાણીશાસ્ત્ર zoology

praaneesrushti *n.* પ્રાણીસૃષ્ટિ fauna

praaneevidyaashaastree *n.* પ્રાણીવિદ્યાશાસ્ત્રી zoologist

praaneevishayak vidyudaakarshan *n.* પ્રાણીવિષયક વિદ્યુદાકર્ષણ zoomagnetism

praant *n.* પ્રાન્ત province

praantik *n.* પ્રાન્તિક provincialism

praapta karavun *v.t.* પ્રાપ્ત કરવું attain

praapti *n.* પ્રાપ્તિ attainment

praapti, seeddhi *n.* પ્રાપ્તિ, સદ્ધિ achievment

praapya *adj.* પ્રાપ્ય attainable

praarabdhaavaad *n.* પ્રારબ્ધવાદ fatalism

praarabdhavaadee *n.* પ્રારબ્ધવાદી fatalist

praaranbhik taiyaaree *adj.* પ્રારંભિક તૈયારી preparative

praarthana karavee *v.i.* પ્રાર્થના કરવી pray

praarthanaageet *n.* પ્રાર્થનાગીત psalm

praasangik *adj.* પ્રાસંગિક occasional

praastaavik *adj.* પ્રાસ્તાવિક preliminary

praastaavik karavun *n.* પ્રાસ્તાવિક કરવું prelude

praastaavik sangeet *n.* પ્રાસ્તાવિક સંગીત. overture

praathamik *adj.* પ્રાથમિક elementary

praathamik saaravaar *n.* પ્રાથમિક સારવાર first aid

praayashchit *n.* પ્રાયશ્ચિત atonement

praayashchit *n.* પ્રાયશ્ચિત penance

praayashchit karavun *v.t.* પ્રાયશ્ચિત કરવું atone

prabal *adj.* પ્રબળ prevailing

prabal eechchhaa *n.* પ્રબળ ઇચ્છા ambitions

prabaleekaran *n.* પ્રબલીકરણ reinforcement

prabandhak પ્રબંધક administrator

prabha *n.* પ્રભા lustre

prabhaav ke asar પ્રભાવ કે અસર impress

prabhaav paadavo *n.* પ્રભાવ પાડવો influence

prabhaavashaalee *adj.* પ્રભાવશાળી effective

prabhaavee *adj.* પ્રભાવી awful

prabhaavee *adj.* પ્રભાવી impressive

prabhaavee *n.* પ્રભાવી magnetism

Prabhaavee *adj.* પ્રભાવી sonorous

prabhubhojan *n.* પ્રભુભોજન communion

prabhupraarthana *n.* પ્રભુપ્રાર્થના prayer

prachaalak *n.* પ્રચાલક operator

prachaar karavo *v.t.* પ્રચાર કરવો canvass

prachaarak *n.* પ્રચારક propagandist

prachaleet *adj.* પ્રચલતિ rife

prachaleet *adj.* પ્રચલતિ ruling

prachalit *n.* પ્રચલતિ prevalence

prachalit pratha *n.* પ્રચલતિ પ્રથા mode

prachand *adj.* પ્રચંડ enormous

prachand *adj.* પ્રચંડ huge

prachand pravaah *n.* પ્રચંડ પ્રવાહ torrent

prachanda *adj.* પ્રચંડ colossal

prachanda *adj.* પ્રચંડ vehement

prachandee *adj.* પ્રચંડી torrential

pracheen *adj.* પ્રાચીન. archaic

pradaan *n.* પ્રદાન bestowal

pradaan *n.* પ્રદાન. contribution

pradarshan *n.* પ્રદર્શન exhibition

pradarshan karavun *v.t.* પ્રદર્શન કરવું display

pradarshan karavun *v.t.* પ્રદર્શન કરવું exhibit

pradarshanakala *n.* પ્રદર્શનકળા window-dressing

pradashit karavun *v.t.* પ્રદર્શતિ કરવું demonstrate

pradesh *n.* પ્રદેશ region

pradesh *n.* પ્રદેશ territory

pradesha, mulaka, vistaar *n.* પ્રદેશ, મુલક, વિસ્તાર tract

pradeshnee seema *n.* પ્રદેશની સીમા bound

pradhaan *n.* પ્રધાન minister

pradhaan mandal *n.* પ્રધાન મંડળ ministry

pradhaanatattv *n.* પ્રધાનતત્ત્વ motif

pradushan *n.* પ્રદુષણ pollution

pragat eendriyagamy પ્રગટ ઇંદ્રયિગમ્ય palpable

pragat karavun *v.t.* પ્રગટ કરવું reveal

pragat thavun *v.* પ્રગટ થવું appear

pragati *n.* પ્રગતિ headway

pragati *n.* પ્રગતિ progress

pragati *n.* પ્રગતિ progression

pragatisheel *adj.* પ્રગતિશીલ progressive

Pragtimaan vighn *n.* પ્રગતમાં વિઘ્ન setback

prahasan *v.* પ્રહસન comedy

prahasan *n.* પ્રહસન farce

prajaasattaak *n.* પ્રજાસત્તાક republic

prajaasattaak *adj.* પ્રજાસત્તાક republican

prajanan *n.* પ્રજનન generation

prajananaksham avastha *n.* પ્રજનનક્ષમ અવસ્થા puberty

prakaand pandeet *adj.* પ્રકાંડ પંડતિ eruidite

prakaar *n.* પ્રકાર genus

prakaar *n.* પ્રકાર type

prakaash *n.* પ્રકાશ light

prakaash *n.* પ્રકાશ radiance

prakaashamaapak *n.* પ્રકાશમાપક. photometer

prakaashan પ્રકાશન manifestation

prakaashanun kiran *n.* પ્રકાશનું કરિણ ray

prakaashit *adj.* પ્રકાશતિ blazing

prakaashit karavun *v.t.* પ્રકાશતિ કરવું illuminate

prakaashit karavun *v.t.* પ્રકાશતિ કરવું publish

prakaashit karavun te પ્રકાશતિ કરવું તે illumination

Prakaashvun *v.t.* પ્રકાશવું shine

prakaran *n.* પ્રકરણ episode

prakhyaat પ્રખ્યાત eminence

prakhyaat *adj.* પ્રખ્યાત famous

prakrutisvabhaav *n.* પ્રકૃતિસ્વભાવ nature

prakshepaastr *n.* પ્રક્ષેપાસ્ત્ર missile

prakshubdh *adj.* પ્રક્ષુબ્ધ hectic

pralobhak પ્રલોભક tempter

pralobhan *n.* પ્રલોભન temptation

pramaad *n.* પ્રમાદ idleness

pramaad *n.* પ્રમાદ laziness

pramaad karavo *v.t.* પ્રમાદ કરવો deliquate

pramaadee *adj.* પ્રમાદી deliquate

pramaadee maanas *n.* પ્રમાદી માણસ idler

pramaan nirdhaarit પ્રમાણ નિર્ધારિત inductive

pramaanabhoot karavun *v.t.* પ્રમાણભૂત કરવું authenticate

pramaanapatra *n.* પ્રમાણપત્ર certificate

pramaanapatra *n.* પ્રમાણપત્ર testimonial

pramaanasaranun *adj.* પ્રમાણસરનું proportional

pramaanhoot *n.* પ્રમાણભૂત authoritative

Pramadee *adj.* પ્રમાદી slothful

pramey *n.* પ્રમેય theorem

pramukhapadane lagatun *adj.* પ્રમુખપદને લગતું presidential

pramukhapadanee avadhi પ્રમુખપદની અવધિ presidency

pranaalee *n.* પ્રણાલી groove

pranay kisso, eeshk *n.* પ્રણય કિસ્સો, ઈશ્ક amour

pranayacheshta karavee *v.t.* પ્રણયચેષ્ટા કરવી flirt

pranayacheshta karavee *v.* પ્રણયચેષ્ટા કરવી flirtation

pranayee, kaamuk *adj.* પ્રણયી, કામુક amative

prapanch *n.* પ્રચંડ mammoth

prapanch *n.* પ્રપંચ ruse

prasaadhan dravya *n.* પ્રસાધન દ્રવ્ય brilliantine

prasaarit karavun *adj.* પ્રસારિત કરવું broadcast

prasangaanuroop *adj.* પ્રસંગાનુરૂપ. pertinent

prasangavashaat *n.* પ્રસંગવશાત occasion

prasann *adj.* પ્રસન્ન bonny

prasann karavun *v.t.* પ્રસન્ન કરવું conciliate

prasannata *n.* પ્રસન્નતા happiness

prasansaa *n.* પ્રશંસા eulogy

prasaravun *v.t.* પ્રસરવું pervade

prasavavedanaa *v.i.* પ્રસવવેદના travail

prashaant *adj.* પ્રશાંત pacific

prashaanti *n.* પ્રશાન્તિ calmness

prashansa karavee *v.t.* પ્રશંસા કરવી belaud

prashansaa karavee *v.t.* પ્રશંસા કરવી exalt

prashansaapaatr *adj.* પ્રશંસાપાત્ર creditable

prashansaapaatr *adj.* પ્રશંસાપાત્ર meritorious

prashansaapaatra *adj.* પ્રશંસાપાત્ર admirable

prashansaatmak *adj.* પ્રશંસાત્મક laudatory

prashansak, aashik *n.* પ્રશંસક, આશિક admirer

prashasti lakhavee *v.t.* પ્રશસ્તિ લિખવી panegyrize

prashchaataap *n.* પ્રશ્ચાતાપ repentance

prashchaataap karanaar *adj.* પ્રશ્ચાતાપ કરનાર repentant

prashchaataap karavo *v.t.* પ્રશ્ચાતાપ કરવો. repent

prashn *n.* પ્રશ્ન query

prashn *n.* પ્રશ્ન question

prashn poochhanaar *n.* પ્રશ્ન પૂછનાર querist

prasiddh *adj.* પ્રસિદ્ધ celebrated

prasiddh *adj.* પ્રસિદ્ધ illustrious

prasiddh *n.* પ્રસિદ્ધિ publicity

prasiddh karavun *v.t.* પ્રસિદ્ધ કરવું promulgate

prasiddh karavun te *n.* પ્રસદ્ધિ કરવું તે publication

prasiddhino chalakaat *n.* પ્રસદ્ધિનો ચળકાટ lime-light

prasngopaat *adv.* પ્રસંગોપાત casually

prasootee pahelaanun *adj.* પ્રસૂતિ પહેલાનું antenatal

prasooti *n.* પ્રસૂતિ delivery

prasooti karaavavee *v.t.* પ્રસૂતિ કરાવવી deliver

prastaav *n.* પ્રસ્તાવ motion

prastaav *n.* પ્રસ્તાવ proposal

prastaavan *n.* પ્રસ્તાવના introduction

prastaavana *n.* પ્રસ્તાવના preface

prastaavana sanbandhee *adj.* પ્રસ્તાવના સંબંધી prefactory

prastaavanaa *n.* પ્રસ્તાવના foreword

prastut hovun *v.t.* પ્રસ્તુત હોવું concern

prastut muddo *n.* પ્રસ્તુત મુદ્દો crux

prateek *n.* પ્રતીક emblem

prateek *adj.* પ્રતીક emblematic

prateek hovun *v.t.* પ્રતીક હોવું signify

prateeksha karavee *v.t.* પ્રતીક્ષા કરવી wait

prateekul *adj.* પ્રતિકૂળ unfavourable

pratham vikray *n.* પ્રથમ વિક્રય handsel

prathamavibhaktinun *n.* પ્રથમાવિભક્તિનું nominative

pratibadhdh *n.* પ્રતિબિધ્ધ. committal

pratibadhdhata *n.* પ્રતિબિધ્ધતા. commitment

pratibandh *v.t.* પ્રતિબંધ interdict

pratibandh *n.* પ્રતિબંધ proscription

pratibandh *n.* પ્રતિબંધ restriction

pratibandh mookavo *v.t.* પ્રતિબંધ મૂકવો. restrict

pratibandhak *adj.* પ્રતિબંધક deterrent

pratibandhak *adj.* પ્રતિબંધક preventive

pratibandhak *adj.* પ્રતિબંધક restrictive

pratibandhit *adj.* પ્રતિબંધિત. contraband

pratibhaasanpann *adj.* પ્રતિભાસંપન્ન gifted

pratibhaasanpann maanas *n.* પ્રતિભાસંપન્ન માણસ genius

pratibhaashalee *adj.* પ્રતિભાશાળી talented

pratibinb paadanaarun *n.* પ્રતિબિંબ પાડનારું reflective

pratibinb paadavun *v.t.* પ્રતિબિંબ પાડવું reflect

pratigna *on* પ્રતિજ્ઞા oath

pratikaaraksham *adj.* પ્રતિકારક્ષમ resistible

pratikool *adj.* પ્રતિકૂળ averse

pratikool valan *n.* પ્રતિકૂળ વલણ aversion

pratikool, ashubh *adj.* પ્રતિકૂળ,અશુભ adverse

pratikriya *n.* પ્રતિક્રિયા reaction

pratikriya *n.* પ્રતિક્રિયા response

pratikriya aapavee *v.t.* પ્રતિક્રિયા આપવી counteract

pratikruti *n.* પ્રતિકૃતિ replica

pratikruti *v.t.* પ્રતિકૃતિ reproduction

pratikrutiroop *v.t.* પ્રતિકૃતિરૂપ duplicate

pratiksha khand *n.* પ્રતિક્ષા ખંડ waiting-room

pratikshaalay *n.* પ્રતીક્ષાલય anteroom

pratinidhimandal *n.* પ્રતિનિધિ મંડળ delegacy

pratinidhimandal *n.* પ્રતિનિધિ મંડળ delegation

pratinidhimandal *n.* પ્રતિનિધિમંડળ deputation

pratinidhitv karavun પ્રતિનિધિત્વ કરવું represent

pratipakshee *n.* પ્રતિપક્ષી opponent

pratirodhak *n.* પ્રતિરોધક buffer

pratiroop *n.* પ્રતિરૂપ twin

pratisaaraalankaar *n.* પ્રતિસારાલંકાર bathos

pratisaaraalankaar, neepaat *n.* પ્રતિસારાલંકાર, નિપાત anticlimax

pratishtha *n.* પ્રતિષ્ઠા prestige

pratishtha *n.* પ્રતિષ્ઠા reputation

pratishthit *adj.* પ્રતિષ્ઠિત demure

pratishthit vyakti *n.* પ્રતિષ્ઠિત વ્યક્તિ celebrity

pratispardhee, harif *n.* પ્રતિસ્પર્ધી, હરીફ adversary

prativaadee *n.* પ્રતિવાદી defendant

prativaadee *n.* પ્રતિવાદી respondent

pratuttar, pratibhaav *n.* પ્રત્યુત્તર, પ્રતિભાવ answer

pratyaaghaat *n.* પ્રત્યાઘાત rebound

pratyaaghaat પ્રત્યાઘાત repercussion

pratyaaghaatee vyakti *adj.* પ્રત્યાઘાતી વ્યક્તિ reactionary

pratyaavartan *n.* પ્રત્યાવર્તન refraction

pratyakshadarshee *n.* પ્રત્યક્ષદર્શી eye-witness

pratyayanu chinha *n.* પ્રત્યયનું ચિહ્ન apostrophe

pratyuttar *n.* પ્રત્યુત્તર rejoinder

pratyuttar aapavo *v.t.* પ્રત્યુત્તર આપવો rejoin

praudh *adj.* પ્રૌઢ elderly

praudh *n.* પ્રૌઢ precocious

pravaahak *adj.* પ્રવાહક confluent

pravaahee *n.* પ્રવાહી fluid

pravaahee *n.* પ્રવાહી liquid

Pravaahee e chhantvun *v.t.* પ્રવાહી ઈ. છાંટવું sprinkle

pravaaheeno nikaal *v.t.* પ્રવાહીનો નિકાલ drain

pravaas *n.* પ્રવાસ journey

pravaas *n.* પ્રવાસ travel

pravaas *n.* પ્રવાસ trip

Pravaas sharoo karvo *v.t.* પ્રવાસ શરૂ કરવો start

pravaasano maarg *n.* પ્રવાસનો માર્ગ itinerary

pravaasee *n.* પ્રવાસી passenger

pravaasee *n.* પ્રવાસી tourist

pravaasee nat *v.t.* પ્રવાસી નટ busk

pravaasnee petee *n.* પ્રવાસની પેટી valise

Pravahee padaarth par baazto mel *n.* પ્રવાહી પદાર્થ પર બાઝતો મેલ scum

pravardhan, parivardhan *n.* પ્રવર્ધન, પરિવર્ધન amplification

pravartak *n.* પ્રવર્તક motive

pravartamaan *adv.* પ્રવર્તમાન up-to-date

pravartavun *v.t.* પ્રવર્તવું prevail

pravesh *n.* પ્રવેશ access

pravesh *n.* પ્રવેશ entry

pravesh *n.* પ્રવેશ penetration

pravesh karavo *v.t.* પ્રવેશ કરવો penetrate

pravesh maarg *n.* પ્રવેશ માર્ગ orifice

pravesh na aapavo *v.t.* પ્રવેશ ન આપવો. debar

pravesh, chhoot *n.* પ્રવેશ, છૂટ admittance

praveshakhand *n.* પ્રવેશખંડ antechamber

praveshaksham *adj.* પ્રવેશક્ષમ pervious

praveshdvaar *n.* પ્રવેશદ્વાર entrance

praveshpatra paravaano *n.* પ્રવેશપત્ર પરવાનો visa

pravrutt *n.* પ્રવૃત્ત busy

pravrutt thavun *v.t.* પ્રવૃત્ત થવું rouse

pravrutti, kaaryakshetra *n.* પ્રવૃત્તિ, કાર્યક્ષેત્ર activity

pravruttinun kendr પ્રવૃત્તિનું કેન્દ્ર. headquarters

prayaas kareene praapt karavun *v.t.* પ્રયાસ કરીને પ્રાપ્ત કરવું procure

prayatna *n.* પ્રયત્ન attempt

prayatna *n.* પ્રયત્ન effort

prayatna *n.* પ્રયત્ન exertion

prayatna karavo *v.t.* પ્રયત્ન કરવો try

prayay *v.t.* પ્રત્યય suffix

prayog *v.* પ્રયોગ experiment

prayog saadhano *n.* પ્રયોગ સાધનો apparatus

prayogaatmak *adj.* પ્રયોગાત્મક tentative

prayogamoolak *adj.* પ્રયોગમૂલક empirical

prayogashaala *n.* પ્રયોગશાળા. laboratory

prayogashaalaanee baatalee *n.* પ્રયોગશાળાની બાટલી flask

prayojayataa *n.* પ્રયોજ્યતા applicability

preetibhojan પ્રીતિભોજન banquet

Prekshak *n.* પ્રેક્ષક spectator

Prekshneey *adj.* પ્રેક્ષણીય sightly

prem *n.* પ્રેમ love
prem cheshtaa karavee *v.i.* પ્રેમ ચેષ્ટા કરવી philander
premaadarapoorvak poojavun *v.t.* પ્રેમાદરપૂર્વક પૂજવું adore
premaal *adj.* પ્રેમાળ affectionate
premaandh *adj.* પ્રેમાંધ love-sick
premee *n.* પ્રેમી lover
premee, kamuk, rasik *adj.* પ્રેમી, કામુક, રસિક amorous
Prerak vastu *n.* પ્રેરક વસ્તુ spur
prerana aapavee *v.t.* પ્રેરણા આપવી inspire
preravun *n.* પ્રેરવું actuate
preravun, taakid karavee *v.t.* પ્રેરવું, તાકીદ કરવી admonish
prerit karavun *v.t.* પ્રેરતિ કરવું imbue
Prernaa *n.* પ્રેરણા stimulus
preshit karavun *v.t.* પ્રેષતિ કરવું despatch
pretaatma *n.* પ્રેતાત્મા ghost
pretaatmaane lagatun *n.* પ્રેતાત્માને લગતું spiritualism
preyasee *n.* પ્રેયસી love-lady
prinaam *n.* પરિણામ outcome
pristhitimaa privartan *n.* પરિસ્થિતિમાં પરિવર્તન vicissitude
priy *adj.* પ્રિય dear
priya *n.* પ્રિય darling
Priya athvaa pratim *n.* પ્રિયા અથવા પ્રતમિ sweetheart
priya banaavau *v.t.* પ્રિય બનાવવું endear
priya vyakti *adj.* પ્રિય વ્યક્તિ beloved
prodhyogikee *n.* પ્રૌદ્યોગિકી technology
proshaahak *adj.* પ્રોત્સાહક discouraging
protasaahit karavun *v.t.* પ્રોત્સાહતિ કરવું energize
protsaahak *adj.* પ્રોત્સાહક incentive
protsaahan *n.* પ્રોત્સાહન impulsion
Prushthvansh vinaanun *adj.* પૃષ્ઠવંશ વનિાનું spineless
pruthakkaran *v.t.* પૃથક્કરણ assay
pruthakkaran *n.* પૃથક્કરણ dissection
pruthakkaran karavun *v.t.* પૃથક્કરણ

કરવું dissect
pruthakkaranne lagatun *adj.* પૃથક્કરણને લગતું analystical
pruthavee *n.* પૃથ્વી earth
puding *n.* પુડગિ pudding
pukht vayanun *n.* પુખ્ત વયનું adult
pul *n.* પુલ bridge
punahagrahan *n.* પુન:ગ્રહણ resumption
punahaprasthaapana *n.* પુન:પ્રસ્થાપના restoration
punahasthaapana karavee *v.t.* પુન:સ્થાપના કરવી restore
punahjeevan *n.* પુન:જીવન revival
punahjeevit karavun *v.t.* પુન:જીવતિ કરવું revive
punahsansaran *n.* પુન:સંસ્કરણ redaction
punaraavartan *n.* પુનરાવર્તન repetition
punaraavartan *adj.* પુનરાવર્તન tautological
punaraavartan karavun *v.t.* પુનરાવર્તન કરવું reduplicate
punaraavrutti *n.* પુનરાવૃત્તિ recurrence
punarjeevan *n.* પુનર્જીવન regeneration
punarjeevan *n.* પુનર્જીવન resurrection
punarjeevit karavun *v.t.* પુનર્જીવતિ કરવું regenerate
punarmudran *v.t.* પુનર્મુદ્રણ reprint
punarokti *n.* પુનરોક્તિ tautology
punarrachana karavee *v.t.* પુનર્રચના કરવી rearrange
punarrachana karavee *v.t.* પુનર્રચના કરવી reconstitute
punarurachaaran પુનરુરચારણ. reiteration
punarurachaaran karavun *v.t.* પુનરુરચારણ કરવું reiterate
punarutpaadan karavun *v.t.* પુનરુત્પાદન કરવું reproduce
punarvasavaat *n.* પુનર્વસવાટ rehabilitation

punhajeevit karavun *v.t.* પુનઃજીવતિ કરવું resurrect

punhaprakaashit karavun *v.t.* પુનઃપ્રકાશતિ કરવું republish

punyaprakop paamelun te *n.* પુણ્યપ્રકોપ પામેલું તે indignation

pur avaaj *v.i.* પુર અવાજ purr

puraanavidhya *n.* પુરાણવદ્યિા mythology

puraatattvavidd *n.* પુરાતત્ત્વવદ્િ archaeologist

puraatattvavidhya *n.* પુરાતત્ત્વવદ્યિા archaeology

puraavo *n.* પુરાવો evidence

puraavo *n.* પુરાવો proof

puraskaar *n.* પુરસ્કાર award

puraskarta *n.* પુરસ્કર્તા patron

puratattvavidhya-vishayak *adj.* પુરાતત્ત્વવદ્યિા –વષિયક archaeological

puravanee *n.* પુરવણી annexe

puravatho *n.* પુરવઠો purveyance

puravo *n.* પુરાવો testimony

purohit *n.* પુરોહતિ priest

purohitana jevun *adj.* પુરોહતિના જેવું priestly

puroosho *n.* પુરૂષો men

purushaatan *adj.* પુરુષાતન virile

purushatva *n.* પુરુષત્વ virility

purushavaachak sarvanaam *pro.* પુરૂષવાચક સર્વનામ i

purva *n.* પૂર્વ east

purvaadhikaar *v.t.* પૂર્વાધકિાર prepossess

purvaastitva *v.t.* પૂર્વઅસ્તતિવ pre-exist

purvadhaarana *n.* પૂર્વધારણા hypothesis

purvadhaarnaa karavee *v.t.* પૂર્વધારણા કરવી preconceive

purvakabajo *n.* પૂર્વકબજો pre-occupancy

purvanishchit *v.t.* પૂર્વનશ્ચિતિ predetermine

purvasoochak *adj.* પૂર્વસૂચક premonitory

purvataiyaaree *n.* પૂર્વતૈયારી preparation

purvavichaar karavo *v.t.* પૂર્વવચિાર કરવો premeditate

pushachhatra *n.* પુષ્પછત્ર umbel

pushkal *n.* પુષ્કળ exuberance

pushkal *adj.* પુષ્કળ profuse

pushpadal *n.* પુષ્પદલ petal

pushpaguchchh *n.* પુષ્પગુચ્છ posy

pushpapaatra *n.* પુષ્પપાત્ર vase

pushpkosh *n.* પુષ્પકોશ calix

pusht karavun *v.t.* પુષ્ટ કરવું fatten

pushtataa *n.* પુષ્ટતા flesh

pushti *n.* પુષ્ટિ confirmation

pushti *n.* પુષ્ટિ corroboration

pushti aapavi પુષ્ટિઆપવી confirm

pushti karavee *v.t.* પુષ્ટિ કરવી substantiate

pushtikaarak *adj.* પુષ્ટિકારક tonic

pustak *n.* પુસ્તક book

pustakanun prakaran *n.* પુસ્તકનું પ્રકરણ chapter

pustakavikreta *n.* પુસ્તકવક્િરેતા bookseller

Putra *n.* પુત્ર son

putravadhoo *n.* પુત્રવધૂ daughter-in-law

pyaalo *n.* પ્યાલો brim

pyaalo *n.* પ્યાલો goblet

R

raab *n.* રાબ porridge

raacharacheelu *n.* રાચરચીલું furniture

Raad ke boom paadvee *v.i.* રાડ કે બૂમ પાડવી shout

raad paadavee *v.t.* રાડ પાડવી bawl

raadaaraad karatun *adj.* રાડારાડ કરતું vociferous

raado paadavee *v.t.* રાડો પાડવી vociferate

raaee *n.* રાઈ mustard

raag *n.* રાગ tune

raagotpaadak *adj.* રાગોત્પાદક melodious

raah jovee *v.t.* રાહ જોવી await
raahat *n.* રાહત relief
raaifal *n.* રાઈફ્લ rifle
raaj karavun *v.t.* રાજ કરવું reign
raaj pratinidhinun pad *n.* રાજ પ્રતનિધનું પદ regency
raaja *n.* રાજા king
raajaagnaa *n.* રાજાઆજ્ઞા edict
raajaanee patnee *n.* રાજાની પત્ની queen
raajaano puraskartaa *n.* રાજાનો પુરસ્કર્તા royalist
raajaashaahee *n.* રાજાશાહી monarchy
raajachinho *n.* રાજચહ્નિનો regalia
raajadhaanee *n.* રાજધાની capital
raajadoot, elachee *n.* રાજદૂત, એલચી ambassador
raajadootaalay *n.* રાજદૂતાલય embassy
raajadraahano thapako aapavo રાજદ્રાહનો ઠપકો આપવો impeach
raajahatya *n.* રાજહત્યા regicide
raajakaaran *n.* રાજકારણ politics
raajakanya *n.* રાજકન્યા princess
raajakarta *n.* રાજકર્તા ruler
raajakeey *adj.* રાજકીય political
raajakosheey *adj.* રાજકોષીય fiscal
raajakunvar *n.* રાજકુંવર prince
raajamahel *n.* રાજમહેલ palace
raajan *n.* રાજન rosin
raajaneetign *n.* રાજનીતજ્ઞ politician
raajanishth *adj.* રાજનષ્ઠિ loyal
raajanishtha *n.* રાજનષ્ઠિા loyalty
raajavee *adj.* રાજવી royal
raajaveeo *n.* રાજવીઓ royalty
Raajdand *n.* રાજદંડ sceptre
raajdoot *n.* રાજદૂત diplmat
raajdoot *n.* રાજદૂત envoy
raajdvaaree *adj.* રાજદ્વારી diplmatic
raajee *v.t.* રાજી gladden
raajeenaamun aapavun te *n.* રાજીનામું આપવું તે resignation
Raajhans *n.* રાજહંસ swan
raajkeey asantosh *n.* રાજકીય અસંતોષ disaffection
Raajkeey mataadhikaar *n.* રાજકીય મતાધિકાર suffrage

Raajneetignyataa *n.* રાજનીતજ્ઞિતા statesmanship
Raajneetiman kushal purush *n.* રાજનીતમાં કુશળ પુરુષ statesman
raajy *n.* રાજ્ય kingdom
raajy amalanun *adj.* રાજ્ય અમલનું regnal
raajy karavun *v.i.* રાજ્ય કરવું govern
raajya *n.* રાજ્ય principality
raajyaabhishekanee vidhi *n.* રાજ્યાભષિકની વધિ coronation
raajyabandhaaran *n.* રાજ્યબંધારણ constitution
raajyakraanti *n.* રાજ્યક્રાન્તિ revolution
raajyanee dhaaraasabha *n.* રાજ્યની ધારાસભા legislature
raajyapaal *n.* રાજ્યપાલ governor
raajyavyavasthaatantr *n.* રાજ્યવ્યવસ્થાતંત્ર polity
raakh *n.* રાખ ash
raakhavaanee vruttivaalun *adj.* રાખવાની વૃત્તવિાળું retentive
raakshas *n.* રાક્ષસ demon
raakshas *n.* રાક્ષસ dragon
raakshas *n.* રાક્ષસ giant
raakshas *n.* રાક્ષસ monster
raakshasee *adj.* રાક્ષસી gigantic
raal *n.* રાળ resin
raandhanakala *n.* રાંધણકળા cookery
raandhavaa maatenun *adj.* રાંધવા માટેનું culinary
raandhya vinaanun *adj.* રાંધ્યા વિનાનું raw
raaneena jevun *adj.* રાણીના જેવું queenly
Raanzan ke Ranzanee *n.* રાંઝણ કે રાંઝણી sciatica
raashichakr *n.* રાશચિક્ર zodiac
raashtra *n.* રાષ્ટ્ર nation
raashtranee maalikeenun *v.t.* રાષ્ટ્રની માલકીનું nationalize
raashtranun *adj.* રાષ્ટ્રનું national
raashtreeyata *n.* રાષ્ટ્રીયતા nationalism
raashtrirakatv *n.* રાષ્ટ્રકિત્વ. nationality

raastrasamooh *n.* રાષ્ટ્રસમૂહ commonwealth

raat *n.* રાત night

raatee *n.* રાતી hind

raatun *adj.* રાતું reddish

raavat *n.* રાવત groom

rabar *n.* રબર eraser

rabar *n.* રબર rubber

rachana *n.* રચના formation

rachanaa *n.* રચના setting

rachanaatmak *adj.* રચનાત્મક constructive

rachavun *v.t.* રચવું compose

Rachnaa *n.* રચના structure

rad karava paatr *adj.* રદ કરવા પાત્ર revocable

rad karavun *v.* રદ કરવું cancel

rad karavun *n.* રદ કરવું countermand

rad karavun *v.t.* રદ કરવું invalidate

rad karavun *v.t.* રદ કરવું reject

rad karavun *v.t.* રદ કરવું repeal

rad karavun te *n.* રદ કરવું તે revocation

rad karvun *v.t.* રદ કરવું abrogate

rada karvun *v.t.* રદ કરવું undo

radabaatal karavun *v.t.* રદબાતલ કરવું rescind

radavun *v.i.* રડવું weep

radbaatal *adj.* રદબાતલ void

radiyo *n.* રદિયો refutation

radiyo aapavo *v.t.* રદિયો આપવો refute

rafoo karavun *v.t.* રફૂ કરવું darn

raghavaayun *adj.* રઘવાયું restive

rahasmay *adj.* રહસ્યમય occult

rahasyamay *adj.* રહસ્યમય. mysterious

rahasyamay banaavavun *v.t.* રહસ્યમય બનાવવું mystify

raheesh *n.* રહીશ inhabitant

rahethan *n.* રહેઠાણ abode

rahethan badalavun *v.t.* રહેઠાણ બદલવું flit

rahevaanee jagya *n.* રહેવાની જગ્યા residence

rahevaanu makaan *n.* રહેવાનું મકાન tenement

rahevaanun ghar *n.* રહેવાનું ઘર home

rahevaasee *n.* રહેવાસી denizen

rahevaasee *n.* રહેવાસી resident

rahevun *v.i.* રહેવું dwell

railway nee shakhaa *n.* રેલવેની શાખા feeder

raj *n.* રજ ¶ittle

raj *n.* રજ whit

rajaa paravaanagee *v.t.* રજા પરવાનગી leave

rajadroha *n.* રાજદ્રોહ treason

rajakan *n.* રજકણ mote

rajakeey samiti *n.* રાજકીય સમતિ caucus

rajavaadee shamiyaano *n.* રજવાડી શમિયાનો pavillion

rajhalata loko *n.* રઝળતા લોકો riff-raff

rajhalavun *v.t.* રઝળવું rove

rajogol *n.* રજોગોલ ovum

rajoo karavun *v.t.* રજૂ કરવું cite

Rajoo karvun ke thavun te *n.* રજૂ કરવું કે થવું તે submission

rajooaat *n.* રજૂઆત representation

rakaabee *n.* રકાબી dish

rakaabee *n.* રકાબી saucer

rakaash *n.* રકાસ debacle

rakajhak karavee *v.i.* રકઝક કરવી chaffer

rakazaka karavee *v.i.* રકઝક કરવી haggle

rakhaat *n.* રખાત concubine

rakhadanaar *n.* રખડનાર nomad

rakhadanaar *adj.* રખડનાર nomadic

rakhadavun *v.i.* રખડવું roam

rakhadavun *v.i.* રખડવું wander

rakhadu *n.* રખડુ vagabond

rakhadu jaatinun maanas *n.* રખડુ જાતિનું માણસ gipsy

rakhadu jamaatanun tolun *n.* રખડુ જમાતનું ટોળું horde

rakhadun *n.* રખડું gypsy

rakhadun maanas *n.* રખડું માણસ runagate

rakhadun maanas *n.* રખડું માણસ vagrant

rakhavaalun karavun *v.t.* રખવાળું કરવું convoy

Rakhdvun *v.i.* રખડવું stray

rakhevaal *n.* રખેવાળ custodian
rakshak *n.* રક્ષક defender
rakshak *n.* રક્ષક protector
rakshak sainya *n.* રક્ષક સૈન્ય garrison
rakshan *n.* રક્ષણ defence
rakshan *n.* રક્ષણ protection
rakshan *n.* રક્ષણ rampart
Rakshan. રક્ષણ shelter
rakshan, aashray *n.* રક્ષણ, આશ્રય aegis
rakshanaatmak *adj.* રક્ષણાત્મક defensive
rakshanhin *adj.* રક્ષણહિન defenceless
rakshit *adj.* રક્ષિત sacrosanct
rakshit maanas *n.* રક્ષિત માણસ protege
rakshit raajya *n.* રક્ષિત રાજ્ય protectorate
raktapaat *n.* રક્તપાત blood-shed
raktapitt *n.* રક્તપિત્ત leprosy
raktastraav *n.* રકતસ્રાવ haemorrhage
raktastraav *n.* રકતસ્ત્રાવ hemorrhage
raktavaahinee *n.* રક્તવાહિની blood-vessel
raktavaahinee *n.* રક્તવાહિની capillary
ram *n.* રમ rum
ramakadun *n.* રમકડું plaything
raman zabhbho *n.* રોમન ઝભ્ભો toga
ramanun *n.* રમણું landing
ramat *n.* રમત game
ramat *n.* રમત play
ramatanun medaan *n.* રમતનું મેદાન playground
ramataveer *n.* રમતવીર sportsman
ramatiyaal *adj.* રમતિયાળ playful
ramatiyaal *adj.* રમતિયાળ wanton
ramatveer *n.* રમતવીર athlete
ramavaanee ek ramat *n.* રમવાની એક રમત badminton
ramooj *n.* રમૂજ jest
ramooj *n.* રમૂજ joke
ramooj pamaadavee *v.* રમૂજ પમાડવી amuse
ramoojee *adj.* રમૂજી droll
ramoojee *adj.* રમૂજી funny
ramoojee *adj.* રમૂજી quizzical
ramoojee *adj.* રમૂજી witty

ramoojee, vinodee *adj.* રમૂજી, વિનોદી amusing
Ramtiyaal *adj.* રમતિયાળ sportive
ranadveep *n.* રણદ્વીપ oasis
ranavaasee aarab *n.* રણવાસી આરબ bedouin
rang *n.* રંગ colour
rang *n.* રંગ hue
Rang bagaadvo *n.* રંગ બગાડવો stain
rang chopadavo *v.t.* રંગ ચોપડવો bedaub
rang karanaar *n.* રંગ કરનાર dyer
rang karavo *v.t.* રંગ કરવો dye
rang lagaadavo *v.t.* રંગ લગાડવો paint
rangadravy *n.* રંગદ્રવ્ય pigment
rangalo *n.* રંગલો buffoon
rangamishran paatee *n.* રંગમિશ્રણ પાટી palette
ranganee chataa ke chaayaa *v.t.* રંગની છટા કે છાયા tinge
Rangbhuminaa drashyo *n.* રંગભૂમિના દૃશ્યો scenery
Rangeelun *n.* રંગીલું sparkish
rangno thar *n.* રંગનો થર coating
ranjaadavun *v.t.* રંજાડવું victimize
ras darshaavavo *v.t.* રસ દર્શાવવો evince
rasaayanashaasrtane lagatun *adj.* રસાયણશાસ્ત્રને લગતું chemical
rasaayanashaastra *n.* રસાયણશાસ્ત્ર chemistry
rasaayano *n.* રસાયણો chemicals
rasaayanshaastree *n.* રસાયણશાસ્ત્રી apothecary
rasadaar *adj.* રસદાર juicy
Rasalvun *v.i.* રસળવું stroll
rasaviheen રસવહિીન disinterested
Rasdaar, Jaadan ane maavaavaalan paanddaanvaalee *adj.* રસદાર, જાડાં અને માવાવાળાં પાંદડાંવાળી succulent
rasee *n.* રસી gleet
rasee mukavee રસી મુકવી inoculate
raseed *n.* રસીદ receipt
raseekaran *n.* રસીકરણ vaccination
rashiyaano saamyavadee *n.* રશિયાનો સામ્યવાદી bolshevik
Raso *n.* રસો soup

rasodun *n.* રસોડું kitchen

rasoeeo *n.* રસોઈયો cook

rastaavaalee parasaal *n.* રસ્તાવાળી પરસાળ corridor

rasto *n.* રસ્તો road

rasto *n.* રસ્તો track

rasto *n.* રસ્તો way

Rasto Saaf karnar *n.* રસ્તો સાફ કરનાર scavenger

rataalu *n.* રતાળુ yam

rataashapadatun *adj.* રતાશપડતું auburn

rath *n.* રથ chariot

ratn *n.* રત્ન jewel

ratna *n.* રત્ન gem

ravaana kararu *n.* રવાના કરવુ dispatch

ravaana karelo maal *n.* રવાના કરેલો માલ consignment

ravaana thavun *v.* રવાના થવું depart

ravaangee *n.* રવાનગી transmission

Ravivaar *n.* રવિવાર sunday

razalpaat *n.* રઝળપાટ vagrancy

rechak dava *adj.* રેચક દવા purgative

rechak, aushadh *n.* રેચક ઔષધ calomel

rectar *n.* રેક્ટર rector

rediyam *n.* રેડિયમ radium

rediyo *n.* રેડિયો radio

rediyogram *n.* રેડિયોગ્રામ radiogram

reedhun *adj.* રીઢું callous

reedhun *adj.* રીઢું habitual

reedhun (maanas) *adj.* રીઢું (માણસ) incurable

reejhavavun *v.t.* રીઝવવું indulge

reetabhaat *n.* રીતભાત bearing

reetabhaat *n.* રીતભાત demeanour

reetabhaat vinaanun *adj.* રીતભાત વિનાનું unmannerly

reetabhaataman chokkas *adj.* રીતભાતમાં ચોક્કસ punctilious

reetbhaat *n.* રીતભાત etiquette

refaainaree *n.* રિફાઇનરી refinery

rejiment *n.* રેજિમેન્ટ regiment

Rekhaa *adj.* રેખા straight

rekhaa *n.* રેખા streak

rekhaachitra doravun *v.t.* રેખાચિત્ર દોરવું delineate

rekhaakrutee *n.* રેખાકૃતિ drawing

Rekhaankit *adj.* રેખાંકિત steaky

rekhaansh *n.* રેખાંશ longitude

rekheey *adj.* રેખીય linear

relamachhel karavun *v.* રેલમછેલ કરવું inundate

relamachhel karavun te *n.* રેલમછેલ કરવું તે inundation

relana paata *n.* રેલના પાટા railing

reli *v.t.* રેલી rally

relve *n.* રેલવે railway

ren karavun *v.t.* રેણ કરવું braze

ren karavun *v.t.* રેણ કરવું solder

Reshamno keedo *n.* રેશમનો કીડો silkworm

Reshamnun *n.* રેશમનું silken

Reshmee kaapad *n.* રેશમી કાપડ silk

Retee *n.* રેતી sand

reyon *n.* રેયોન rayon

rhaday *n.* હૃદય heart

rhadayaakaar *adj.* હૃદયાકાર cordate

rhadayapoorvakanun *adv.* હૃદયપૂર્વકનું wholeheartedly

rhadaynun-ne lagatun *adj.* હૃદયનું-ને લગતું cardiac

ribaavavun *v.t.* રિબાવવું crucify

rikshaa *n.* રિક્ષા ricksha

rimaand *v.t.* રિમાન્ડ remand

ringamaastar *n.* રિંગમાસ્ટર ringmaster

risaal *adj.* રિસાળ peevish

Risaal *adj.* રિસાળ spleeny

Risaayelun *adj.* રિસાયેલું sulky

rivaaj *n.* રિવાજ custom

rivet *n.* રિવેટ rivet

rivolvar *n.* રિવોલ્વર revolver

robin *n.* રોબિન robin

rochak *adj.* રોચક lovely

rodan *n.* રોડાં rubble

rodun *n.* રોડું brick-bat

rof maaravo *v.i.* રોફ મારવો flaunt

rog *n.* રોગ disease

rog avarodhak rasee mookavee *v.t.* રોગ અવરોધક રસી મૂકવી vaccinate

Rog, Dukh e thee peedit *adj.* રોગ, દુઃખ, ઈ.થી પીડિત stricken

roga mataadanaarun *adj.* રોગ મટાડનારું therapeutic

rogachaado *n.* રોગચાળો epidemic

rogana chepathee mukt રોગના ચેપથી મુક્ત immune

roganidaan *n.* રોગનદિાન prognosis

rogapratikaarakataa *n.* રોગપ્રતકિારકતા immunity

rogeene alag raakhavo *v.t.* રોગીને અલગ રાખવો isolate

rog-virodhavaad *n.* રોગ-વરિોધવાદ allopathy

rojagaaree *n.* રોજગારી employment

rojamel *n.* રોજમેળ journal

rojaneeshee *n.* રોજનીશી diary

rojano aahaar *n.* રોજનો આહાર dietary

rojanun *adj.* રોજનું wonted

rojee *v.t.* રોજી wage

rojindun kaam *n.* રોજદિ કામ job

rokad *n.* રોકડ cash

rokavun *n.* રોકવું interruption

rokavun રોકવું prohibit

Rokdaa naanaan ke sikka *n.* રોકડા નાણાં કે સક્કિા specie

rokelan naana *n.* રોકેલાં નાણાં investment

roket *n.* રોકેટ rocket

romaanch રોમાંચ horripilation

romaanchak (kalpit) ghatanao *n.* રોમાંચક (કલ્પતિ) ઘટનાઓ. romance

romano krushidev *n.* રોમનો કૃષદિવ saturn

rooaabadaar *adj.* રૂઆબદાર imposing

roodh *adj.* રૂઢ tritet

roodh, prachalit *adj.* રૂઢ, પ્રચલતિ accustomed

roodhee prayog *n.* રૂઢપ્રિયોગ idiom

roodheeprayukt *adj.* રૂઢપ્રિયુક્ત idiomatic

roodhi par aadhaarit *adj.* રૂઢિ પર આધારતિ customary

roodhichust *adj.* રૂઢચ્યિુસ્ત conservative

roodhichust *n.* રૂઢચ્યિુસ્ત tory

roodhinun paalan karavun *v.t.* રૂઢનિું પાલન કરવું conform

roomaal *n.* રૂમાલ napkin

roomaal *n.* રૂમાલ towel

roon sankhya *n.* ઋણ સંખ્યા minus

roonamukti *n.* ઋણમુક્તિ quittance

roopaalun *adj.* રૂપાળું pretty

roopaantar *n.* રૂપાંતર transmutation

roopaantar karavun *v.t.* રૂપાંતર કરવું transmute

roopak *n.* રૂપક allegory

roopakaatmak *adj.* રૂપકાત્મક allegorical

roopalun *adj.* રૂપાળું handsome

rooparekha *n.* રૂપરેખા contour

rooparekhaa *v.t.* રૂપરેખા design

roopiyo *n.* રૂપયિો rupee

rooprekhaa *n.* રૂપરેખા configuration

Ropo *n.* રોપો sapling

roset *n.* રોસેટ rosette

roshanee *n.* રોશની blaze

roshit *adj.* રોષતિ furious

rotee banaavavee *v.t.* રોટી બનાવવી loaves

rugnaalay *n.* રુગ્ણાલય hospital

rukhasad aapavee *n.* રુખસદ આપવી dismissal

runapatra *n.* ઋણપત્ર debenture

rup *v.t.* રૂપ transfigure

rushtapusht *adj.* હૃષ્ટપુષ્ટ fleshy

rutu *n.* ઋતુ season

Rutu Mosam *adj.* ઋતુ, મોસમ seasoned

ruvaateethee yukt karavun *v.t.* રૂંવાટીથી યુક્ત કરવું fledge

S

saabar *n.* સાબર elk

Saabar ke haranno nar *n.* સાબર કે હરણનો નર stag

saabit karee aapavun *v.* સાબતિ કરી આપવું verify

saabita *adj.* સાબતિ unwavering

Saaboot Mannu *adj.* સાબૂત મનનું sane

Saabu jevun *n.* સાબુ જેવું soapy

Saabudaanaa *n.* સાબુદાણા sago

saabunun feen *n.* સાબુનું ફીણ lather

Saabunun feen *n.* સાબુનું ફીણ suds

saachaapanun *n.* સાચાપણું veracity

saachavanee *n.* સાચવણી conservation

saachavavun *v.t.* સાચવવું conserve

saachesaach *adv.* સાચેસાચ truly

saachesaachun *adj.* સાચેસાચું veracious

saachun *adj.* સાચું bonafide

saachun *adj.* સાચું truthful

saachun *adj.* સાચું veritable

saachun hovaa vishe pramaanapatra aapavun *v.t.* સાચું હોવા વિષે પુરમાણપત્ર આપવું attest

saad *n.* સાદ voice

Saadaai *n.* સાદાઈ simplicity

saadhaaran *adj.* સાધારણ general

saadhaaran *n.* સાધારણ moderate

saadhaaran *adj.* સાધારણ ordinary

Saadhaaran Khaarun *adj.* સાધારણ ખારું saltish

saadhan *n.* સાધન device

saadhan *n.* સાધન instrument

saadhan સાધન means

saadhan *n.* સાધન utensil

saadhan saamagree *n.* સાધન સામગ્રી habiliment

saadhanasaamagree *n.* સાધનસામગ્રી resource

saadhanasanpann *adj.* સાધનસંપન્ન resourceful

saadhanasanpatti *n.* સાધનસંપત્તિ might

saadhuono math *n.* સાધુઓનો મઠ cloister

Saadhutaa *n.* સાધુતા sanctity

Saadhya pramaan *n.* સાધ્ય પ્રમાણ syllogism

saadrashya *n.* સાદૃશ્ય semblance

saadrashyata, anuroopata *n.* સાદૃશ્યતા, અનુરૂપતા analogy

saadun *adj.* સાદું rude

Saadun bannaavvun *v.t.* સાદું બનાવવું simplify

saaeekal *n.* સાઈકલ bicycle

saaf *adj.* સાફ unclouded

saaf *adj.* સાફ undisputed

saafa dil *adj.* સાફ દિલ unreserved

saaga *n.* સાગ teak

saahas *v.t.* સાહસ venture

saahas karavun *v.t.* સાહસ કરવું dare

saahas vruti *adj.* સાહસ વૃત્તિ daring

saahas, jokham *v.* સાહસ, જોખમ, adventure

saahasik *adj.* સાહસિક audacious

saahasik *adj.* સાહસિક bold

saahasik *n.* સાહસિક derring

saahasik vyakti સાહસિક વ્યક્તિ dare-devil

saahasikataa *n.* સાહસિકતા audacity

saahity *n.* સાહિત્ય literature

saahity sangrh *n.* સાહિત્ય સંગ્રહ anthology

saahityachoree *n.* સાહિત્યચોરી plagiarism

saahityapremee *adj.* સાહિત્યપ્રેમી literary

saahityik choree karavee *v.t.* સાહિત્યિક ચોરી કરવી plagiarize

saaiding *n.* સાઇડિંગ siding

saajaa thavun *v.t.* સાજા થવું convalesce

saajasaranjaam *n.* સાજસરંજામ kit

Saaju Narvun *v.t.* સાજું નરવું scathe

saajunsamun thavun *v.t.* સાજુંસમું થવું heal

saakad vade baandhavun *v.t.* સાંકળ વડે બાંધવું enchain

saakh સાખ credit

saaksharata *n.* સાક્ષરતા literacy

saakshee *n.* સાક્ષી witness

saakshee, puravo aapavo *v.t.* સાક્ષી – પુરાવો – આપવો testify

saalasapanu *n.* સાલસપણું docility

saalavaaree *n.* સાલવારી annals

saalavaaree *n.* સાલવારી chronology

saalo *n.* સાળો brother-in-law

saamaa thavun *v.i.* સામા થવું defy

Saamaajik jeevanpadhdhati *n.* સામાજિક જીવનપદ્ધતિ society

saamaajik shreshthata *n.* સામાજિક શ્રેષ્ઠતા gentility

saamaajik tolakee *n.* સામાજિક ટોળકી coterie

saamaan *n.* સામાન baggage

saamaan gothavavo *v.t.* સામાન ગોઠવવો stow

saamaany *adj.* સામાન્ય common

saamaany *adj.* સામાન્ય normal

saamaany arthaman *adv.* સામાન્ય અર્થમાં generally

saamaany mantavy *n.* સામાન્ય મંતવ્ય platitude

saamaany roop aapavun સામાન્ય રૂપ આપવું generalize

saamaanya maanas *n.* સામાન્ય માણસ commoner

saamaanya maanas *n.* સામાન્ય માણસ mediocrity

saamaanya maanavee *n.* સામાન્ય માનવી layman

saamaanya snaan *n.* સામાન્ય સ્નાન ablution

saamaanyapane banatun *adj.* સામાન્યપણે બનતું usual

saamaayik *n.* સામાયિક magazine

saamano karavo સામનો કરવો confront

saamano karavo *v.t.* સામનો કરવો withstand

saamant *n.* સામંત lord

saamasaama athadaavun *v.t.* સામસામા અથડાવું collide

saame *prep.* સામે afore

saame nee baaju *adj.* સામેની બાજુ fore

saamee sahee karavee *v.t.* સામી સહી કરવી countersign

saamela karavun *v.t.* સામેલ કરવું involve

saamoohik *adj.* સામૂહિક collective

saamoohik *adj.* સામૂહિક massive

Saampradaayik *adj.* સાંપ્રદાયિક sectarian

saamraagnee *n.* સામ્રાજ્ઞી empress

saamraajya *n.* સામ્રાજ્ય empire

saamraajyavaad *n.* સામ્રાજ્યવાદ imperialism

Saamrthya *n.* સામર્થ્ય strength

saamudaayik *n.* સામુદાયિક community

saamudrik vignaan *n.* સામુદ્રિક વિજ્ઞાન physiognomy

saamudrik vignyaan *n.* સામુદ્રિક વિજ્ઞાન chiromancy

Saamya *n.* સામ્ય similarity

saamyavaad *n.* સામ્યવાદ communism

saamyavaadee *n.* સામ્યવાદી communist

saanasee *n.* સાણસી pliers

saanbelun *n.* સાંબેલું pestle

saanbhalavun *v.i.* સાંભળવું hark

saanbhalavun *v.t.* સાંભળવું hear

saanbharavun *v.t.* સાંભરવું recollect

saandhaamaathee khasavun *v.t.* સાંધામાંથી ખસવું disjoint

saandhiyo *n.* સાંઢિયો lobster

saandho *n.* સાંધો jointer

saandho karavo *v.t.* સાંધો કરવો dovetail

saanj *n.* સાંજ evening

saanj *n.* સાંજ eventide

saanjanee upaasanaa, *n.* સાંજની ઉપાસના vesper

Saanjno melaavdo *n.* સાંજનો મેળાવડો soiree

saankadee galee *n.* સાંકડી ગલી alley

saankadee khaadee *n.* સાંકડી ખાડી inlet

saankadee kheen *n.* સાંકડી ખીણ glen

saankadee kheen *n.* સાંકડી ખીણ gorge

saankadee toch *n.* સાંકડી ટોચ ridge

saankado rasto *n.* સાંકડો રસ્તો lane

saankadun *adj.* સાંકડું narrow

saankal *n.* સાંકળ chain

saankdee pattee *n.* સાંકડી પટ્ટી tape

Saankdu *n.* સાંકડું strait

saanketik nirdesh *adj.* સંકેતિક નિર્દેશ allusive

saankhavun *n.* સાંખવું brook

saannidhy *n.* સાન્નિધ્ય proximity

saanpattik sthiti *n.* સાંપત્તિક સ્થિતિ circumstance

saantvan aapavun *n.* સાંત્વન આપવું pacification

Saap, *n.* સાપ snake

saapano zeree taant *n.* સાપનો ઝેરી દાંત fang

saapeksh reete સાપેક્ષ રીતે respetively

Saapnaa jevun *adj.* સાપના જેવું serpentine

saaptaahik *adj.* સાપ્તાહિક weekly

saar *n.* સાર epitome

saar kaadhavo *v.t.* સાર કાઢવો epitomize

saaraa rastaa par laavvu *v.t.* સારા રસ્તા પર લાવવું undeceive

saaraansh *n.* સારાંશ conclusion

saaragarbh *adj.* સારગર્ભ pithy

saarak (dava) *adj.* સારક (દવા) laxative

saaranagaanth *n.* સારણગાંઠ hernia

saaraneebaddh સારણીબદ્ધ tabular

saaratattv *n.* સારતત્ત્વ quintessence

saaratatv *n.* સારતત્વ quiddity

saarathi *n.* સારથિ charioteer

saaravaar *n.* સારવાર treatment

saaree abhiruchivaalu *adj.* સારી અભિરુચિવાળું tasteful

saaree haalatamaa raakhavun *n.* સારી હાલતમાં રાખવું upkeep

saaree pethe jaaneetun *adj.* સારી પેઠે જાણીતું well-known

saaree reete *adj.* સારી રીતે well-bred

saaree reete parichit *adj.* સારી રીતે પરિચિત conversant

saaree vyakti *n.* સારી વ્યક્તિ mascot

Saari pethe bheejvvun સારી પેઠે ભીંજવવું saturate

saarsoochee *n.* સારસૂચિ docket

Saartatva *n.* સારતત્ત્વ substance

saarthak *adj.* સારથક effectual

saarvajanik *adj.* સાર્વજનિક public

saarvajanika maarg *n.* સાર્વજનિક માર્ગ thoroughfare

saarvamat *n.* સાર્વમત plebiscite

saarvatrik *adj.* સાર્વત્રિક prevalent

saasun *n.* સાસુ mother-in-law

Saat *adj.* સાત seven

saatatya *n.* સાતત્ય consistence

saatatya vinaanu *n.* સાતત્ય વિનાનું desultory

saateen *n.* સાટીન sateen

saateen *n.* સાટીન satin

Saatganun *adj.* સાતગણું sevenfold

Saath (ni sankhya, 60) *adj.* સાઠ (ની સંખ્યા, ૬૦) sixty

saathamun *adj.* સાઠમું sixtieth

saathe *prep.* સાથે with

saathe chotee javun *v.t.* સાથે ચોટી જવું cohere

saathe chotee rahelun *adj.* સાથે ચોટી રહેલું coherent

saathe chotee rahevun *n.* સાથે ચોટી રહેવું coherence

saathe kaam karavun *v.i.* સાથે કામ કરવું collaborate

saathe valagee rahevun te *n.* સાથે વળગી રહેવું તે cohesion

saathee *n.* સાથી companion

saathosaath, lagolag *adv.* સાથોસાથ, લગોલગ abreast

saatmun *adj.* સાતમું seventh

saav astvyast *adj.* સાવ અસ્તવ્યસ્ત chaotic

Saav murkh *n.* સાવ મૂરખ senseless

saavachetee *n.* સાવચેતી circumspection

saavachetee *n.* સાવચેતી precaution

saavadh *adj.* સાવધ cautious

saavadh *adj.* સાવધ circumspect

saavadh *n.* સાવધ prudent

saavadh *adj.* સાવધ vigilant

saavadh karavun *adj.* સાવધ કરવું alert

saavadhaan *adj.* સાવધાન attentive

saavadhaanee *n.* સાવધાની caution

saavadhaanee *n.* સાવધાની vigil

saavadhaanee *n.* સાવધાની watch

saavadhapanun *n.* સાવધપણું alertness

saavaka bhaaee bahen *n.* સાવકા ભાઈ - બહેન half-brother

saavaranee *n.* સાવરણી broom

saavarano *n.* સાવરણો besom

Saavkaa pitaa *n.* સાવકા પિતા step-father

Saavko ke ormaan bhaai *n.* સાવકો કે ઓરમાન ભાઈ step-brother

Saavkun baalak *n.* સાવકું બાળક step-son

saayakal savaar *n.* સાયકલ સવાર cyclist

sabaath *n.* સબાથ sabbath

sabamarin *adj.* સબમરિન submarine

sabaskript *adj.* સબસ્ક્રિપ્ટ subscript

sabhaa *n.* સભા assembly

sabhaa *n.* સભા congregation

sabhaa *n.* સભા convention

sabhaa bolaavavee *v.t.* સભા બોલાવવી convoke

sabhaapati *n.* સભાપતિ chairman

sabhy *adj.* સભ્ય mannerly

sabhyata *n.* સભ્યતા politeness

sachet *adj.* સચેત conscious

sachet thavun *v.t.* સચેત થવું quicken

sachetana *n.* સચેતના cognizance

sachitr *adj.* સચિત્ર pictorial

sachiv *n.* સચિવ secretary

Sachivaalay *n.* સચિવાલય secretariate

sachot *adj.* સચોટ cogent

sachot *adj.* સચોટ persuasive

sadaachaar *n.* સદાચાર virtue

sadaachaaree *n.* સદાચારી moralist

sadaane maate *adj.* સદાને માટે everlasting

sadaane maate *adv.* સદાને માટે evermore

sadaavrat, annakshetr *n.* સદાવ્રત, અન્નક્ષેત્ર almonry

sadabhaagye *adv.* સદ્ભાગ્યે happily

sadabhaagye *adv.* સદ્ભાગ્યે luckily

sadabhaavayukt vartanavaalun સદ્ભાવયુક્ત વર્તનવાળું neighbourly

sadabhavanaavaalu *adj.* સદ્દભાવવાળું favourable

sadagaavavun *v.t.* સળગાવવું enkindle

sadantar naash karavo *v.t.* સદંતર નાશ કરવો annihilate

sadasya banaavavun *v.* સદસ્ય બનાવવું affilliate

sadavun *v.i.* સડવું decay

sadavun *v.t.* સડવું decompose

saddvyavahaar *n.* સદ્દવ્યવહાર kindness

sadelun maans *n.* સડેલું માંસ carrion

sadgrahasth *n.* સદ્દગૃહસ્થ gentleman

sadhavaalee hodee *n.* સઢવાળી હોડી yawl

sado *n.* સડો carious

sadosh nahi *adj.* સદોષ નહિ unculpable

safaaee *n.* સફાઈ cleaning

safaai *n.* સફાઈ tidiness

safal chaal *n.* સફળ ચાલ coup

safal thavun *v.t.* સફળ થવું succeed

Safaltaa *n.* સફળતા success

safarajan *n.* સફરજન apple

safed *adj.* સફેદ white

safed karavun *v.t.* સફેદ કરવું blanch

safed patthar *n.* સફેદ પથ્થર alabaster

safedikaran *v.t.* સફેદીકરણ bleach

sagaaee karavee *v.i.* સગાઈ કરવી betroth

sagadee *n.* સગડી grate

sagapan *n.* સગપણ affinity

sagarbha *adj.* સગર્ભા pregnant

sagarbha banaavavun *v.t.* સગર્ભા બનાવવું impregnate

sagarbhaavastha *n.* સગર્ભાવસ્થા pregnancy

sagavad *n.* સગવડ accommodation

Sagee bahen *n.* સગી બહેન sister

Sagee bahen jevun *adj.* સગી બહેન જેવું sisterly

sageer *adj.* સગીર minor

sageerapanun *n.* સગીરપણું minority

sago baaee *n.* સગો ભાઈ brother

sagotr *n.* સગોત્ર cognate

sagotra *adj.* સગોત્ર collateral

sagu, samaan *adj.* સગું, સમાન akin

sagun *n.* સગું relative

sagyaan *adj.* સજ્ઞાન cognizable

saha aparaadhee *n.* સહઅપરાધી accomplice

sahaadhyaayee *n.* સહાધ્યાયી class-mate

sahaanubhooti *n.* સહાનુભૂતિ sympathy

sahaanubhooti daakhavavee *v.* સહાનુભૂતિ દાખવવી condole

sahaanubhooti thavee *v.i.* સહાનુભૂતિ થવી sympathize

sahaanubhootisheel *adj.* સહાનુભૂતિશીલ congenial

sahaanubhootivaalun *adj.* સહાનુભૂતિવાળું sympathetic

sahaastitv dharaavavun *v.t.* સહઅસ્તિત્વ ધરાવવું coexist

sahaay karavee *v.* સહાય કરવી aid

sahaay karavee *v.t.* સહાય કરવી conduce

sahaay karavi *v.t.* સહાય કરવી accommodate

sahaayak *adj.* સહાયક auxiliary

sahaayakaaree *adj.* સહાયકારી helpful

sahaaykaaree *v.* સહાયકારી ally

sahachar *n.* સહચર consort

sahaj *adj.* સહજ innate

sahajaat *adj.* સહજાત connate

sahakaar *n.* સહકાર co-operation

sahakaar aapavo *v.t.* સહકાર આપવો co-operate

sahakaaryakar *n.* સહકાર્યકર colleague

sahamat *adj.* સહમત concurrent

sahamatee *n.* સહમતી agreement

sahan karavun *v.t.* સહન કરવું endure

sahana karavun *v.t.* સહન કરવું tolerate

sahanashaktee *n.* સહનશક્તિ endurance

sahanashakti *n.* સહનશક્તિ tolerance

sahanasheelata *n.* સહનશીલતા patience

sahanirdeshan *v.t.* સહનિર્દેશન co-ordinate

sahanivaas karavan *v.t.* સહનવિાસ કરવાં cohabit

sahapalaayan karavun *v.i.* સહપલાયન કરવું elope

sahapravaasee *n.* સહપ્રવાસી shipmate

sahashikshan *n.* સહશિક્ષણ co-education

sahastra *adj.* સહસ્ત્ર thousand

sahavaaras *n.* સહવારસ coheir

sahavaasee *n.* સહવાસી inmate

sahavarani karavee *v.t.* સહવરણી કરવી co-opt

sahavartee *adj.* સહવર્તી concomitant

Sahayak *adj.* સહાયક subsidiary

saheb *n.* સાહેબ sir

Sahee *n.* સહી signature

Saheesalaamat *adj.* સહીસલામત safe

saheesikkaavaalun karaaranaamu *n.* સહીસિક્કાવાળું કરારનામું indenture

sahej maandagee *n.* સહેજ માંદગી indisposition

Sahelaaithee *adj.* સહેલાઈથી simply

sahelagaa *n.* સહેલગાહ excursion

saheluu *adj.* સહેલું facile

sahetu pravaash *n.* સહેતુ પૂરવાસ expedition

sahishnutaa સહિષ્ણુતા toleration

Sahlaalintaa *n.* સહકાલનિતા synchronism

sahushnu *adj.* સહિષ્ણુ tolerant

sahya *adj.* સહ્ય bearable

sahya *n.* સહ્ય tolerable

Sai *n.* સઈ seamster

saidhaantik *adj.* સૈદ્ધાંતિક theoretical

sainor *n.* સાઈનોર signor

saitron *n.* સાઈટ્રોન citron

saja *n.* સજા punishment

saja karavee *v.t.* સજા કરવી punish

sajaa karavee *v.t.* સજા કરવી castigate

sajaa mokoofee *n.* સજા મોકૂફી reprieve

sajaamukti *n.* સજામુક્તિ impunity

sajaane paatr *adj.* સજાને પાત્ર penal

sajaateey *n.* સજાતીય congener

sajaateey *adj.* સજાતીય kindred

sajaatiy *adj.* સજાતીય homogeneous

sajaavat *n.* સજાવટ decoration

sajeev rachanaa *n.* સજીવ રચના organism

sajeevan karavun *v.t.* સજીવન કરવું enliven

sajeevan karavun *v.t.* સજીવન કરવું vivify

sajj *adj.* સજ્જ ready

sajj *v.t.* સજ્જ set

sajj karavun *v.t.* સજ્જ કરવું equip

sajjad *adj.* સજ્જડ tight

sajjada karavun *v.t.* સજ્જડ કરવું tighten

Sakaarvaalun *adj.* સકારવાળું sibilant

sakarmak *adj.* સકર્મક. transitive

Sakhat *n.* સખ્ત stern

Sakhat fatko maarvo *n.* સખ્ત ફટકો મારવો slug

Sakhat ke tang karvun સખ્ત કે તંગ કરવું straiten

sakhat mahenat karvee *v.i.* સખ્ત મહેનત કરવી toil

sakhat nindaa karavee *v.t.* સખ્ત નિંદા કરવી denounce

Sakhat reete *adv.* સખ્ત રીતે sorely

Sakhat teeka *n.* સખ્ત ટીકા stricture

sakhat thapako aapavo સખ્ત ઠપકો આપવો reprimand

Sakhat thapko aapvo *v.t.* સખ્ત ઠપકો આપવો scold

sakhat tikaa karavee *v.t.* સખ્ત ટીકા કરવી flay

sakhata banavavun *v.i.* સખ્ત બનાવવું harden

sakhata fatako *v.t.* સખ્ત ફટકો thump

sakhata sajaa karavee *v.t.* સખ્ત સજા કરવી trounce

sakhataaee *n.* સખ્તાઈ rigour

sakriya *adj.* સક્રિય active

salaad *n.* સલાડ salad

salaah aapanaar *n.* સલાહ આપનાર counsellor

salaah aapavee *v.* સલાહ આપવી advise

salaah aapavee *v.t.* સલાહ આપવી exhort

salaah, upadesh *n.* સલાહ, ઉપદેશ advice

salaahakaar *n.* સલાહકાર mentor

salaahamasalat *n.* સલાહમસલત consultation

salaahasoochan *n.* સલાહસૂચના suasion

salaahkaar *adj.* સલાહકાર advisory

Salaam *n.* સલામ salutation

salaamat *adj.* સલામત secure

Salaamatee *n.* સલામતી safety

Salaamatee *n.* સલામતી security

salagaavanaarun *adj.* સળગાવનારું incendiary

salagaavavun *v.t.* સળગાવવું ignite

salagaavavun *v.t.* સળગાવવું kindle

salagama(no chhoda) *n.* સલગમ(નો છોડ). turnip

salagatun *adj.* સળગતું burning

salagatun, jvaalaagrast *adv.* સળગતું, જ્વાલાગ્રસ્ત aflame

salagavaanee prakriya *n.* સળગવાની પ્રક્રિયા ignition

salagavun *v.t.* સળગવું burn

salekham *n.* સળેખમ catarrh

saliyo *v.t.* સળિયો spit

sama khaaine chhodavun સમ ખાઈને છોડવું forswear

samaachaar *n.* સમાચાર news

samaachaar *n.* સમાચાર tidings

samaadesh madadanish *n.* સમાદેશ મદદનીશ adjutant

samaadhaan karaavavun સમાધાન કરાવનારું concilliatory

samaadhaan karavun *n.* સમાધાન કરવું contentment

samaadhan karaavavun *v.t.* સમાધાન કરાવવું reconcile

samaadhilekh *n.* સમાધિલેખ epitaph

samaaj veerodhee *adj.* સમાજ વિરોધી anti-social

samaajabahishkaar *n.* સમાજબહિષ્કાર ostracism

Samaajmaan rahenaarun *adj.* સમાજમાં રહેનારું social

Samaajshaastra *n.* સમાજશાસ્ત્ર sociology

Samaajvaad *n.* સમાજવાદ socialism

samaalochak *n.* સમાલોચક reviewer

samaan *adj.* સમાન equal

samaan *adv.* સમાન even

samaan *n.* સમાન par

samaan dhareevaalun *adj.* સમાન ધરીવાળું coaxal

samaanaarth *n.* સમાનાર્થ equivalence

samaanaarth *adj.* સમાનાર્થ equivalent

Samaanaarthak Shabd *n.* સમાનાર્થક શબ્દ synonym

samaanataa *n.* સમાનતા equity

samaanya svabhaav *n.* સામાન્ય સ્વભાવ temperament

samaapan karavun *v.t.* સમાપન કરવું conclude

samaaptee *n.* સમાપ્તી closure

samaapti *n.* સમાપ્તિ accomplishment

samaapti *n.* સમાપ્તિ expiry

samaapti *n.* સમાપ્તિ finality

samaarakaam *n.* સમારકામ reparation

samaarakaam karavun *v.t.* સમારકામ કરવું repair

samaasamaa pelee paar *adj.* સમાસમાં પેલે પાર ultra

samaavesh *n.* સમાવેશ comprehension

samaavesh *n.* સમાવેશ inclusion

samaavesh karavo *v.t.* સમાવેશ કરવો include

samaayojan karavun *v.t.* સમાયોજન કરવું modulate

samabhuj *adj.* સમભુજ equilateral

samachoras aakaaranun *adj.* સમચોરસ આકારનું rectangular

samachoras aakruti *n.* સમચોરસ આકૃતિ rectangle

samadhaaranakaary *n.* સમધારણકાર્ય moderation

samaj shaktivaalun *adj.* સમજ શક્તિવાળું perceptive

samajaavat *n.* સમજાવટ persuasion

samajaavavun *v.t.* સમજાવવું dissuade

samajaavavun *v.t.* સમજાવવું elucidate

samajaavavun *v.t.* સમજાવવું explain

samajaavavun *v.t.* સમજાવવું illustrate

samajadaar *n.* સમજદાર rationalist

samajashaktivaalun *adj.* સમજશક્તિવાળું rational

samajavun *v.t.* સમજવું comprehend

samakaaleen *adj.* સમકાલીન coeval

samakaaleen *adj.* સમકાલીન contemporary

samakaalik *adj.* સમકાલિક synchronous

samalanbak *n.* સમલંબક trapezium

samalingakaamee *adj.* સમલગિકામી gay

samamiti *n.* સમમિતિ symmetry

Samanarthak *adj.* સમાનાર્થક synonymous

samans *n.* સમન્સ summons

samapaashrv *n.* સમપાશ્ર્વ prism

samaparimaan *adj.* સમપરિમાણ commensurable

samapramaan *n.* સમપ્રમાણ commensurate

samarpan *n.* સમર્પણ consecration

samarpan *n.* સમર્પણ dedication

samarpan karavun *v.t.* સમર્પણ કરવું devote

samarpit *n.* સમર્પિત. dedicator

samarpit *adj.* સમર્પિત devoted

samarth karavun *v.t.* સમર્થ કરવું enable

samarthak *n.* સમર્થક supporter

samarthana karavun *v.t.* સમર્થન કરવું uphold

samarthit karavun *v.t.* સમર્થિત કરવું corroborate

samasyaaroop *adj.* સમસ્યારૂપ problematic

samatal *adj.* સમતળ plane

samatolapanu *n.* સમતોલપણું equilibrium

samatulaa *n.* સમતુલા equipoise

samavaayee *adj.* સમવાયી federal

samay *n.* સમય time

samay - bindu *n.* સમય–બિંદુ juncture

samayaanuroop *adj.* સમયાનુરૂપ seasonable

samayagaalo *n.* સમયગાળો tenor

samayano golo *adv.* સમયનો ગાળો while

samayapaalan *n.* સમયપાલન punctuality

samayapatraka *n.* સમયપત્રક time-table

samayasaavadh *n.* સમયસાવધ punctual

samayasaranun *adj.* સમયસરનું timely

samayochit *adj.* સમયોચિત opportune

Samchoras *n.* સમચોરસ square

sameekaran *n.* સમીકરણ equation

sameepata *n.* સમીપતા. juxtaposition

Samgra ke aakhee vastu *n.* સમગ્ર કે આખી વસ્તુ system

samiti *n.* સમિતિ committee

samjan *n.* સમજણ understood

Samju *adj.* સમજુ sensible

Samkaalik karvun ke thavun *v.t.* સમકાલિક કરવું કે થવું synchronize

sammat na thavun *v.t.* સંમત ન થવું disagree

sammatee naa aapavee *v.t.* સંમતિ ના આપવી dissent

samooh *n.* સમૂહ mass

samoohano faanto *n.* સમૂહનો ફાંટો. firth

samoohavaachak naam *n.* સમૂહવાચક નામ vermin

samovadiyo *n.* સમોવડિયો fellow

sampaadak *n.* સંપાદક editor

sampatti, samruddhi *n.* સંપત્તિ, સમૃદ્ધિ affluence

sampoorn *adj.* સંપૂર્ણ entire

sampoorn nishfalataa *n.* સંપૂર્ણ નિષ્ફળતા fiasco

sampoorn sthirtaa *n.* સંપૂર્ણ સ્થિરતા tranquillity

Sampoorna *adj.* સંપૂર્ણ sheer

sampoorna *adj.* સંપૂર્ણ total

sampoornataa *n.* સંપૂર્ણતા totality

sampoornpane, ekandare *adj.* સંપૂર્ણપણે, એકંદરે altogether

sampradaan *n.* સંપ્રદાન dative

Sampradaay *n.* સંપ્રદાય sect

Sampramaan *adj.* સમપ્રમાણ symmetrical

sampurna *adj.* સંપૂર્ણ thorough

sampurnpane *adj.* સંપૂર્ણપણે downright

samraat *n.* સમ્રાટ emperor

samruddh *adj.* સમૃદ્ધ palmy

samruddh thavun *v.t.* સમૃદ્ધ થવું enrich

samruddhi *n.* સમૃદ્ધિ prosperity

samrudhdh , સમૃદ્ધ thriving

samrudhdha thavun *v.i.* સમૃદ્ધ થવું thrive

samudaay *n.* સમુદાય host

samudaay *n.* સમુદાય swarm

samudr kinaaro *n.* સમુદ્ર કિનારો beach

samvaad *n.* સંવાદ dialogue

samvaatan *v.* સંવાતન ventilation

samvanan *n.* સંવનન doit

Samvedanaasthaan સંવેદનાસ્થાન sensorium

Samvedankshamtaa *n.* સંવેદનક્ષમતા sensibility

Samvedansheel *adj.* સંવેદનશીલ sensitive

samvedanshoonya karavun *v.t.* સંવેદનશૂન્ય કરવું deaden

Samvednaa *n.* સંવેદના sensation

Samvednavaahak *adj.* સંવેદનાવાહક sensorial

sanaatanee *adj.* સનાતની orthodox

sanad rad karavee *v.t.* સનદ રદ કરવી disbar

sanadavaalee sansthaanun *n.* સનદવાળી સંસ્થાનું charter

sanadee vakeel *n.* સનદી વકીલ barrister

sanako *v.i.* સણકો twinge

sanasanaateebhryun *adj.* સનસનાટીભર્યું lurid

sanasanavun *n.* સણસણવું fizz

sanasanavun *v.i.* સણસણવું fizzle

sanbandh *n.* સંબંધ relation

sanbanshit સંબંધિત related

sanbhaal *v.t.* સંભાળ ward

sanbhaal levee *v.t.* સંભાળ લેવી care

sanbhaaranun *n.* સંભારણું memento

sanbhaaranun *n.* સંભારણું reminiscence

sanbhalaay nahi evun *adj.* સંભળાય નહિ એવું inaudible

sanbhavaneey *adj.* સંભવનીય potential

sanbhog *n.* સંભોગ ravishment

sanbodhan karavun *v.t.* સંબોધન કરવું address

sanbodhandhaarak સંબોધનધારક addressee

sanbodhankaarak *adj.* સંબોધન કારક vocative

sanchaalak *n.* સંચાલક director

Sanchaalan સંચાલન superintendence

sanchaanee rachana *n.* સંચાની રચના machinery

sanchaarit karavun *v.t.* સંચારિત કરવું transmit

sanchay thavo *v.* સંચય થવો accumulate

sanchit *adj.* સંચિત cumulative

sancho *v.t.* સંચો mangle

sandarbh *n.* સંદર્ભ context

sandarbh સંદર્ભ reference

sandarbh aapavo *v.t.* સંદર્ભ આપવો. refer

sandesh *n.* સંદેશ errand

sandesh *n.* સંદેશ gospel

sandeshavaahak *n.* સંદેશવાહક bearer

sandeshavaahak *n.* સંદેશવાહક messenger

sandesho *n.* સંદેશો message

sandharaajya *n.* સંઘરાજ્ય federation

sandhi *n.* સંધિ treaty

sandhiva *n.* સંધિવા gout

sandhyaakaal *n.* સંધ્યાકાળ nightfall

sandyaakaal *n.* સંધ્યાકાળ, eve

sandyaano samay *n.* સંધ્યાનો સમય dusk

sangam paamavo te *n.* સંગમ પામવો તે confluence

sangamasthaan *n.* સંગમસ્થાન junction

sangathit sanstha *n.* સંગઠિત સંસ્થા organization

sangeen *n.* સંગીન bayonet

sangeet *n.* સંગીત music

sangeet naatak *n.* સંગીત નાટક opera

sangeet nrutyanaatika *n.* સંગીત નૃત્યનાટિકા ballet

sangeetano ek soor *n.* સંગીતનો એક સૂર minim

sangeetarachanaa *n.* સંગીતરચના symphony

sangeetashaastree *n.* સંગીતશાસ્ત્રી musician

sangh *n.* સંઘ confederacy

sangh સંઘ confederation

sangh *n.* સંઘ league

sangh *n.* સંઘ syndicate

sangh *n.* સંઘ union

sangh sanstha *n.* સંઘ સંસ્થા association

sangharavun *v.t.* સંઘરવું enshrine

Sangharsh *n.* સંઘર્ષ strife

sangna *n.* સંજ્ઞા noun

sangraahak *adj.* સંગ્રાહક antiquarian

sangrah *n.* સંગ્રહ collection

sangrah karavo *v.t.* સંગ્રહ કરવો collect

sangrahaalay *n.* સંગ્રહાલય museum

sangrahasthaan *n.* સંગ્રહસ્થાન repository

sangrh karavun *v.t.* સંગ્રહ કરવું compile

sanhita banaavavee *v.t.* સંહિતા બનાવવી codify

sanjogo *n.* સંજોગો hap

sanjogovasaat સંજોગવશાત્ fortuitous

sankalanakarta *n.* સંકલનકર્તા compiler

sankalit granth *n.* સંકલિત ગ્રંથ compilation

sankalp *n.* સંકલ્પ will

sankalpashakti *n.* સંકલ્પશક્તિ volition

sankat pratibandhak *adj.* સંકટ પ્રતિબંધક prophylactic

sankelavun *v.t.* સંકેલવું furl

sanket *n.* સંકેત signal

sanketalipinun lakhaan *n.* સંકેતલિપિનું લખાણ cryptogram

sanketasthaan *n.* સંકેતસ્થાન rendezvous

Sanketchinh *n.* સંકેતચિહ્ન symbol

Sanketchinh *adj.* સંકેતચિહ્ન symbolical

sankhya vaachak *adj.* સંખ્યા વાચક numerical

sankhyaabandh *adj.* સંખ્યાબંધ many

sankhyaabandh *adj.* સંખ્યાબંધ numerous

sankhyaman chadiyaatun સંખ્યામાં ચડિયાતું outnumber

sankochaavun સંકોચાવું shrink

sankochan સંકોચન systole

sankraanti *n.* સંક્રાંતિ solstice

sankraantikaal *adj.* સંક્રાન્તિકાળ. transitional

sankshep *n.* સંક્ષેપ brevity

sankshep *n.* સંક્ષેપ compendium

sankshep *n.* સંક્ષેપ precis

Sankshep *n.* સંક્ષેપ sum

sankshepaman kahevun *v.t.* સંક્ષેપમાં કહેવું recapitulate

sankshipt *n.* સંક્ષિપ્ત abbreviation

sankshipt *adj.* સંક્ષિપ્ત compendious

sankshipt *adj.* સંક્ષિપ્ત terse

sankshipt karvun સંક્ષિપ્ત કરવું abbreviate

sankshipt roop *n.* સંક્ષિપ્ત રૂપ contraction

sankuchit *adj.* સંકુચિત narrow-minded

sanlagnataa *n.* સંલગ્નતા adhesion

sanmaan *n.* સન્માન deference

sanmaan *n.pl.* સન્માન felicitations

sanmaananeey *adj.* સંમાનનીય worthy

sanmaanavun *n.* સન્માનવું fete

sanmaanit karavun *v.t.* સન્માનતિ કરવું felicitate

sanmaanjanak khitaab *adj.* સન્માન સૂચક ખિતાબ excellency

sanmat thavun, anumati *v.i.* સંમત થવું, અનુમતિ consent

sanmati aapavee *v.* સંમતિ આપવી agree

sanmelan *n.* સંમેલન gathering

sanmishrata *adj.* સંમિશ્રિતા promiscuous

sanmohanavidhya સંમોહનવિદ્યા hypnotism

sannyaasinee (khristee) *n.* સંન્યાસિની (ખ્રિસ્તી) nun

sannyaasineeonee jamaat *n.* સંન્યાસિનીઓની જમાત nunnery

sanpaadan *n.* સંપાદન acquisition

sanpaadav karavun *v.t.* સંપાદન કરવું edit

sanpaat *n.* સંપાત equinox

sanpark *n.* સંપર્ક contact

sanpark karavo *v.* સંપર્ક કરવો. communicate

sanpark karavon *v.i.* સંપર્ક કરવો approach

sanpatti *n.* સંપત્તિ pelf

sanpatti *n.* સંપત્તિ wealth

sanpoorn *v.t.* સંપૂર્ણ complete

sanpoorn *adj.* સંપૂર્ણ plenary

sanpoorn avyavastha *n.* સંપૂર્ણ અવ્યવસ્થા chaos

sanpoorn dhovaan *v.t.* સંપૂર્ણ ધોવાણ white-wash

sanpoornabhootakaal *adj.* સંપૂર્ણભૂતકાળ pluperfect

sanpoornapane *adv.* સંપૂર્ણપણે outright

sanpoornapane *adv.* સંપૂર્ણપણે, wholly

sanpoornata *n.* સંપૂર્ણતા perfection

sanpoornataa *n.* સંપૂર્ણતા completion

sanpratibandh hareefaaee *n.* સંપ્રતિબંધ હરીફાઈ handicap

sanrakshak *n.* સંરક્ષક guardian

sanrakshak *n.* સંરક્ષક protective

sanrakshak *adj.* સંરક્ષક tutelary

sanrakshan karavun *v.t.* સંરક્ષણ કરવું preserve

Sanrakshan vyavsthaa *n.* સંરક્ષણ વ્યવસ્થા safeguard

Sansanaateevaalun *adj.* સનસનાટીવાળું spicy

sansarganishedh *n.* સંસર્ગનિષેધ quarantine

sanshay *adj.* સંશય subjunctive

sanshay pedaa karavo *v.t.* સંશય પેદા કરવો misgive

sanshayaatmak *adj.* સંશયાત્મક questionable

Sanshayaspad *n.* સંશયાસ્પદ suspicious

Sanshayvaad *n.* સંશયવાદ scepticism

sanshleshan *n.* સંશ્લેષણ synthesis

sanshodhan *n.* સંશોધન research

sanshraya *n.* સંશ્રય coverture

sanskaar *n.* સંસ્કાર refinement

sanskaaree *adj.* સંસ્કારી refined

sanskaaree banaavavun *v.t.* સંસ્કારી બનાવવું civilize

sanskaarita sanvardhak *n.* સંસ્કારિતાસંવર્ધક humane

sanskruti *n.* સંસ્કૃતિ civilization

sanskruti *n.* સંસ્કૃતિ culture

sanskrutino vaaraso *n.* સંસ્કૃતનો વારસો. heritage

sansmaraneey સંસ્મરણીય memorable

sanstha *n.* સંસ્થા institution

sant *n.* સંત saint

Sant jevun *adj.* સંત જેવું saintly

santaan jevun *adj.* સંતાન જેવું filial

santap *n.* સંતાપ anguish

santosh *n.* સંતોષ pleasure

Santosh *n.* સંતોષ satisfaction

Santoshkaarak *adj.* સંતોષકારક satisfactory

santraat *adj.* સત્રાંત terminal

Santree *n.* સંતરી sentinel

santrupt karavun *n.* સંતૃપ્ત કરવું gratification

santusht *adj.* સંતુષ્ટ glad

santusht karavun *n.* સંતુષ્ટ કરવું appeasement

santusht karavun *v.t.* સંતુષ્ટ કરવું satiate

santusht karavun *v.t.* સંતુષ્ટ કરવું satisfy

sanvedanaaheen maanav *n.* સંવેદનાહીન માનવ. boor

sanvedanaashoony *adj.* સંવેદનાશૂન્ય numb

sanveg *n.* સંવેગ momentum

sanyaasee mandal *n.* સંન્યાસી મંડળ convent

sanyaasrog *n.* સંન્યાસરોગ apoplexy

sanyaasrogavaalo *adj.* સંન્યાસરોગવાળો apoplectic

sanyaman *adj.* સંયમન austerity

sanyamee *n.* સંયમી ascetic

sanyamee *adj.* સંયમી austere

sanyamit *adv.* સંયમિત austerely

sanyog *n.* સંયોગ coincidence

sanyog *n.* સંયોગ combination

sanyog chinh *n.* સંયોગ ચિહ્ન hyphen

sanyogee *adj.* સંયોગી cohesive

sanyogee bhoomi *n.* સંયોગી ભૂમિ isthmus

sanyojak *n.* સંયોજક convener

sanyojan *n.* સંયોજન fusion

sanyukt *adj.* સંયુક્ત conjunct

sanyukt banavun *v.i.* સંયુક્ત બનવું coalesce

sapaat medaan *n.* સપાટ મેદાન esplanade

sapaatee *n.* સપાટી level

saptaah *n.* સપ્તાહ week

saptaah ant *n.* સપ્તાહ અંત week-end

Septembar mahino *n.* સપ્ટેમ્બર મહિનો september

Saptvaarshik *adj.* સપ્તવાર્ષિક septennial

saraah *n.* સરાહ sirrah

saraanano paththar *n.* સરાણનો પથ્થર rubstone

Saraansh *n.* સારાંશ synopsis

saradaar *n.* સરદાર knight

sarahad *n.* સરહદ border

saraiyo *n.* સરૈયો. perfumer

sarajanahaar *n.* સરજનહાર maker

sarakaar *n.* સરકાર government

sarakaaree amaladaar *n.* સરકારી અમલદાર officer

sarakaaree jaameenageereeo *n.pl.* સરકારી જામીનગીરીઓ consols

sarakaaree madad *n.* સરકારી મદદ subvention

sarakaaree patrak *n.* સરકારી પત્રક communique

sarakavun *v.t.* સરકવું slide

sarakhaa trana bhaagavaalun *adj.* સરખા ત્રણ ભાગવાળું triplicate

sarakhaamaneenee *n.* સરખામણી comparison

sarakhapanu *n.* સરખાપણું equality

sarakhapanu ganavun *v.t.* સરખાપણું ગણવું equate

sarakhu banaavavun *v.t.* સરખું બનાવવું equalize

sarakhun, e ja rite *adj.* સરખું, એ જ રીતે alike

sarakhun, malatun aavatun *adj.* સરખું, મળતું આવતું analogous

sarako *n.* સરકો pickle

saral *adj.* સરળ easy

saral *adj.* સરળ simple

saral *adj.* સરળ unpretending

saral bhaave *adv.* સરળ ભાવે candidly

saralataathee *adv.* સરળતાથી easily

Saranjaamdaar *n.* સરંજામદાર suzerain

saras reete *adv.* સરસ રીતે neatly

saras reete *adv.* સરસ રીતે nicely

saras!, shaabaash! *int.* સરસ! શાબાશ ! bravo

sarasenaapati *n.* સરસેનાપતિ generalissimo

Sardko bolaavvi ke bharvo *v.i.* સરડકો બોલાવવો કે ભરવો snuffle

sareraash *n.* સરેરાશ average

sarisrup *n.* સરિસૃપ reptile

sarjan karavun *v.t.* સર્જન કરવું beget

sarjanaatmak *adj.* સર્જનાત્મક creative

sarkas *n.* સરકસ circus

Sarkhaapanun *n.* સરખાપણું sameness

Sarkhun *adj.* સરખું smooth

sarmukhtyaar *n.* સરમુખત્યાર dictator

sarmukhtyaashahee *n.* સરમુખત્યારશાહી despotism

sarnjaamadaar *n.* સરંજામદાર seigneur

sarovar *n.* સરોવર loch

Sarp *n.* સરૂપ serpent

sarpaakaar dregan *n.* સરૂપાકાર ડ્રેગન wyvern

sarpil *n.* સરૂપલિ spiral

sarunun jhaad *n.* સરૂનું ઝાડ cyp ress

sarvagn *adj.* સરૂવજ્ઞ. omniscient

sarvakshama *n.* સરૂવક્ષમા amnesty

sarvamat *n.* સરૂવમત referendum

sarvanaam *n.* સરૂવનામ. pronoun

sarvasaamaanyataa *adv.* સરૂવસામાન્યતા universallity

sarvasammat સરૂવસંમત unanimous

sarvasammati *n.* સરૂવસંમતિ unanimity

sarvasattaadheesh shaasak *n.* સરૂવસત્તાધીશ શાસક monarch

sarvashaktimaan *adj.* સરૂવશક્તિમાન omnipotent

sarvashaktimaan, ateeshay *adj.* સરૂવશક્તિમાન, અતીશિય almighty

sarvashreshtha tabakko *n.* સરૂવશ્રેષ્ઠ તબક્કો, bloom

sarvashubhavaad *n.* સરૂવશુભવાદ optimism

sarvatha *adv.* સરૂવથા thoroughly

sarvatha chokkas *adj.* સરૂવથા ચોક્કસ cock-sure

sarvathaa *adv.* સરૂવથા utterly

sarvavyaapee સરૂવવ્યાપી omnipresent

sarveshvaravaad *n.* સરૂવેશ્વરવાદ pantheism

sarvochch kakshaanun *adj.* સરૂવોચ્ચ કક્ષાનું grand

Sarvoparee *adj.* સરૂવોપરી supreme

Sarvopari *n.* સરૂવોપરિ sovereign

Sarvoparita *n.* સરૂવોપરિતા sovereignty

sarvottam *adj.* સરૂવોત્તમ best

sarvottam *adj.* સરૂવોત્તમ pre-eminent

sasalaannee vasaahat *n.* સસલાંની વસાહત warren

sasalun *n.* સસલું hare

sasalun *n.* સસલું rabbit

Sasrakriya *n.* શસ્ત્રક્રિયા surgery

sastan praanee *n.* સસ્તન પ્રાણી. mammal

sastu sutarau kaapad *n.* સસ્તુ સુતરાઉ કાપડ calico

sastun *adj.* સસ્તું cheap

sastun karavun *v.* સસ્તું કરવું cheapen

satat chaalun *adj.* સતત ચાલું intermittent

satat prayaas *n.* સતત પ્રયાસ perseverance

sathee vinaa *adj.* સાથી વિના unaccompanied

satkaar *n.* સત્કાર homage

satra samaapt karavun *v.t.* સત્ર સમાપ્ત કરવું prorogue

satraant *n.* સત્રાંત terminal

satrasamaapti *n.* સત્રસમાપ્તિ prorogation

satta *n.* સત્તા authority

sattaa aapavee *v.t.* સત્તા આપવી endow

sattaa aapavee *v.t.* સત્તા આપવી atuhorize

sattaa aapavee *v.t.* સત્તા આપવી empower

sattaa rooae *v.t.* સત્તા રૂએ defacto

sattaa sonpanee *n.* સત્તા સોંપણી delegate

sattaavaar ahevaal *n.* સત્તાવાર અહેવાલ bulletin

Sattar *adj.* સત્તર seventeen

sattarmun *adj.* સત્તરમું seventieth

Satto karvo *n.* સટ્ટો કરવો speculation

sattva, tathya *n.* તથ્ય essence

satya *n.* સત્ય truth

satyaabhaasee *adj.* સત્યાભાસી glib

satyaabhaashee *adj.* સત્યાભાસી plausible

satyanishtha *adj.* સત્યનિષ્ઠા honour

satyataa *n.* સત્યતા verity

saubhaagyavaadee *n.* સૌભાગ્યવાદી optimist

saujany *n.* સૌજન્ય comity

saujany *n.* સૌજન્ય courtesy

saujanyavaalun *adj.* સૌજન્યવાળું polite

saumy *adj.* સૌમ્ય mild

saumy *adj.* સૌમ્ય placid

saumya *adj.* સૌમ્ય. genial

saumyata *n.* સૌમ્યતા mildness

saumyata *n.* સૌમ્યતા placidity

saundarya *n.* સૌન્દર્ય beauty

saundarya *n.* સૌન્દર્ય charm

saundarya shaastra *n.* સૌંદર્ય શાસ્ત્ર aesthetics

saundaryaraanee *n.* સૌન્દર્યરાણી belle

saundaryavardhak *n.* સૌંદર્યવર્ધક cosmetic

saurachikitsaalaya *n.* સૌરચિકિત્સાલય solarium

sauthee kharaab *adj.* સૌથી ખરાબ worst

sauthee mahattvanun *adj.* સૌથી મહત્ત્વનું prime

sauthee mahattvanun *adj.* સૌથી મહત્ત્વનું principal

sauthee mahatvanun *adj.* સૌથી મહત્વનું main

sauthee neeche *adj.* સૌથી નીચે undermost

savaadiyu maanas *n.* સવાદિયું માણસ epicure

savaar *n.* સવાર morning

savaar *n.* સવાર morning

savaarano naasto *n.* સવારનો નાસ્તો breakfast

savalat *n.* સવલત concession

savistaar prabandh *n.* સવિસ્તાર પ્રબંધ dissertation

savistar rajoo karavun *v.t.* સવિસ્તર રજૂ કરવું expound

seedee *n.* સીડી ladder

seedeenun pagathiyun *n.* સીડીનું પગથિયું rung

seedha dholaav jevun *n.* સીધા ઢોળાવ જેવું preciptous

seedhaa, tataar thavu *adj.* સીધા ટટાર થવું unbending

Seedhee reete *adv.* સીધી રીતે smoothly

seedheseedhu *adv.* સીધેસીધું directly

seedhu *v.t.* સીધું direct

seedhu *n.* સીધું unbend

Seedhun karvun ke thavun *v.t.* સીધું કરવું કે થવું straighten

seedhunsaamaan *n.* સીધુંસામાન ration

seel maachalee *n.* સીલ માછલી seal

seema *n.* સીમા boundary

seema *n.* સીમા frontier

seema *n.* સીમા limit

seemaachinha *n.* સીમાચિહ્ન lan·mark

seemaankan *n.* સીમાંકન demarcation

seeng *n.* સીંગ pod

seeriyaanee bhaashaa *n.* સીરિયાની ભાષા aramaic

seesaana ranganun *adj.* સીસાના રંગનું grey

seetaafal *n.* સીતાફળ custard-apple

Seevan *n.* સીવણ seam

Seevvaanaan kapdaan *n.* સીવવાનાં કપડાં sewing

selaman maachalee *n.* સેલમન માછલી salmon

selt dharmaguru *n.* સેલ્ટ ધર્મગુરુ druid

semafor *n.* સેમફોર semaphore

senaa *n.* સેના army

senaapati *n.* સેનાપતિ commander

Senetno sadsabhya *n.* સેનેટનો સદસભ્ય senator

sentigred *adj.* સેન્ટિગ્રિડ centigrade

setanee *adj.* શેતાની infernal

sevaa karavee *v.t.* સેવા કરવી serve

sevak *n.* સેવક attendant

sfatik *n.* સ્ફટિક crystal

sfatikanaa jevun svachchh *adj.* સ્ફટિકના જેવું સ્વચ્છ crystalline

sfoortilun *adj.* સ્ફૂર્તિલું quick

sfot *n.* સ્ફોટ irruption

sfot karavo *v.t.* સ્ફોટ કરવો explode

sfot thavo *v.t.* સ્ફોટ થવો burst

sfotak *adj.* સ્ફોટક explosive

sfotak padaarth *n.* સ્ફોટક પદાર્થ dynamite

shaabdik *adj.* શાબ્દિક verbal

shaabdik artha anusaar *adv.* શાબ્દિક અર્થ અનુસાર literally

shaahee *n.* શાહી ink

shaaheechoos kaagal *n.* શાહીચૂસ કાગળ blotting-paper

shaaheeno khadeeyo *n.* શાહીનો ખડીયો ink-pot

shaahudee *n.* શાહુડી. porcupine

shaakaahaaree *n.* શાકાહારી vegetarian

shaakhaa *n.* શાખા branch
Shaal odhvee ke odhaadvee *n.* શાલ ઓઢવી કે ઓઢાડવી shawl
Shaalaa *n.* શાળા school
shaalaana shikshak *n.* શાળાના શક્ષિક pedagogue
Shaalaashikshan *n.* શાળાશક્ષિણ schooling
shaamak *adj.* શામક alleviative
shaamak *n.* શામક anodyne
Shaant *adj.* શાંત sedate
shaant *adj.* શાંત silent
shaant ghodo *n.* શાંત ઘોડો palfrey
shaant karavun *v.t.* શાંત કરવું quiet
Shaant ke naram paadvun *n.* શાંત કે નરમ પાડવું soothe
shaant paadavun *v.* શાંત પાડવું allay
shaant paadavun *v.t.* શાંત પાડવું becalm
shaant paadavun *v.t.* શાંત પાડવું mitigate
shaant paadavun *v.t.* શાંત પાડવું pacify
shaant paadvu davaa aapine *v.t.* શાંત પાડવું દવા આપીને. tranquillize
shaantataavaalun *adj.* શાંતતાવાળું peaceful
shaanti *n.* શાંતિ peace
shaanti praarthanaa *n.* શાંતિ પ્રાર્થના requiem
shaantipoorvak *adv.* શાંતિપૂર્વક quietly
shaantithee *adv.* શાંતથી patiently
shaantivaachchhun *adj.* શાંતિવાચ્છું irenic
shaap *n.* શાપ curse
shaap *n.* શાપ malediction
shaapit *adj.* શાપિત cursed
shaaradee *n.* શારડી auger
shaaradee *n.* શારડી drill
shaareerik *adj.* શારીરિક bodily
shaareerik *adj.* શારીરિક carnal
shaareerik krushataa *n.* શારીરિક કૃશતા atrophy
shaasak *n.* શાસક potentate
shaasan *n.* શાસન administration
shaasanapaddhati *n.* શાસનપદ્ધતિ regime

Shaashan varchswa *n.* શાસન વર્ચસ્વ suzerainty
shaashvat *adj.* શાશ્વત eternal
shaashvatee *n.* શાશ્વતી eternity
shabaghar *n.* શબઘર morgue
shabapareekshan *n.* શબપરીક્ષણ autopsy
shabd *n.* શબ્દ word
shabd samooh *n.* શબ્દ સમૂહ phrase
shabdaalu *adj.* શબ્દાળુ verbose
shabdaandabar *n.* શબ્દાંડબર verbiage
shabdaansh *n.* શબ્દાંશ syllable
shabdaateet *adj.* શબ્દાતીત unspeakable
shabdabaahuly *n.* શબ્દબાહુલ્ય pleonasm
shabdabhandol *n.* શબ્દભંડોળ vocabulary
shabdakosh *n.* શબ્દકોશ dictionary
shabdakosh *n.* શબ્દકોશ lexicon
shabdalop *v.t.* શબ્દલોપ elide
shabdanee jaatee - ling *n.* શબ્દની જાતિ–લિંગ gender
shabdarachana *n.* શબ્દરચના wording
shabdashailee *n.* શબ્દશૈલી phraseology
shabdashlesh *n.* શબ્દશ્લેષ pun
shabdashlesh karanaaro *n.* શબ્દશ્લેષ કરનારો. punster
shahaadat *n.* શહાદત martyrdom
shahaamrug *n.* શહામૃગ ostrich
shaheed *n.* શહીદ martyr
shaher *n.* શહેર city
Shaher *n.* શહેર sewage
shaheree *adj.* શહેરી urban
shaikshanik *adj.* શૈક્ષણિક educational
shaikshanik *adj.* શૈક્ષણિક educative
shailee *n.* શૈલી fashion
shailee *n.* શૈલી style
shaishav *n.* શૈશવ babyhood
shaktiheen *adj.* શક્તિહીન powerless
shaktishaalee *adj.* શક્તિશાળી puissant
shaktithee, balajorithee *adv.* શક્તિથી, બળજોરીથી amain
shakun *n.* શકુન auspice
shakun ke apashukan *n.* શકુન કે અપશુકન portent

shaky *adj.* શક્ય possible

shaky hoy tyan sudhee *adv.* શક્ય હોય ત્યાં સુધી possibly

shakya શક્ય feasibility

shakya શક્ય feasible

shakyata *n.* શક્યતા likelihood

shakyata *n.* શક્યતા possibility

shakyata *adj.* શક્યતા potentiality

shakyata શક્યતા probability

Shamaavvun *v.t.* શમાવવું soothe

shaman *n.* શમન alleviation

shaman karavun *v.* શમન કરવું alleviate

shambumelo *n.* શંભુમેળો. farrago

shan *n.* શણ hemp

shan *n.* શણ. jute

shanagaaravun *v.t.* શણગારવું adorn

shanagaaravun *v.t.* શણગારવું beatify

shanagaaravun *n.* શણગારવું bedeck

shanagaaravun *v.t.* શણગારવું decorate

shanagaaravun *v.t.* શણગારવું emblazon

shanagaaravun *v.t.* શણગારવું garnish

shanagaaravun *v.t.* શણગારવું ornament

shanagaarelee nauka *n.* શણગારેલી નૌકા barge

shananun kaapad *n.* શણનું કાપડ linen

shanbhumelo *n.* શંભુમેળો medley

shanbhumelo *n.* શંભુમેળો. miscellany

Shanivaar *n.* શનિવાર saturday

Shanivaarnu sankshipt *p.t.* શનિવારનું સંક્ષિપ્ત sat

shaniyaano paato kaapad *n.* શણિયાનો પાટો કાપડ lint

shanka *n.* શંકા mistrust

shankaa *n.* શંકા doubt

shankaa karavee *v.t.* શંકા કરવી suspect

shankaanun nivaaran karavun *v.t.* શંકાનું નિવારણ કરવું vindicate

shankaasheel *adj.* શંકાશીલ doubtful

shankaasheel *adj.* શંકાશીલ fishy

shankaaspad *adj.* શંકાસ્પદ. apocryphal

shankaaspad *adj.* શંકાસ્પદ apprehensive

shankaaspad *adj.* શંકાસ્પદ dubiors

shankaavalu *adj.* શંકાવાળું distrustful

shankh *n.* શંખ conch

shanku *n.* શંકુ cone

shankuaakaarana falavaalun *adj.* શંકુઆકારના ફળવાળું coniferous

shankuna aakaaranun શંકુના આકારનું conical

shapath *n.* શપથ vow

sharaab khaanano nokar *n.* શરાબખાનાનો નોકર tapster

Sharam *n.* શરમ shame

Sharam aave evun *adj.* શરમ આવે એવું shameful

sharamaal *adj.* શરમાળ bashful

sharamaal *adj.* શરમાળ coy

sharamaalapanun *n.* શરમાળપણું bashfulness

sharamaavavun *v.* શરમાવવું abash

sharamaavavun *v.t.* શમાવવું assuage

sharamaavavun *v.i* શરમાવવું shy

sharamaayelun *adj.* શરમાયેલું abashed

sharamajanak *adj.* શરમજનક disgrceful

sharamata sharamata *adv.* શરમાતા શરમાતા ablush

Sharambharelu *adj.* શરમભરેલું scandalous

sharanaarthee *n.* શરણાર્થી refugee

sharat *v.t.* શરત bet

sharat *n.* શરત condition

sharat *n.* શરત wager

sharat bataavanaarun *adj.* શરત બતાવનારું conditional

sharatee sharanaagati *v.i.* શરતી શરણાગત capitulate

sharatee sharanaagati *v.i.* શરતી શરણાગત capitulation

sharatonu aakhree kahen *n.* શરતોનું આખરી કહેણ ultimatum

Sharbat *n.* શરબત sherbet

shareer *n.* શરીર body

shareer kriya vignaan *n.* શરીર ક્રિયા વિજ્ઞાન physiology

shareer parano tal *n.* શરીર પરનો તલ mole

shareeranan eendriyonun *adj.* શરીરનાં ઇન્દ્રિયોનું organic

shareeranee eendriy *n.* શરીરની ઇન્દ્રિય organ

shareeree *adj.* શરીરી corporeal

shareerna marm avayavo *n.* શરીરના મર્મ અવયવો vitals

shareernee oonchaai *n.* શરીરની ઊંચાઇ stature

shareerno baandho *n.* શરીરનો બાંધો physique

shareerrachana *n.* શરીરરચના anatomy

shareerrachanaavid *n.* શરીરરચનાવિદ્ anatomist

shareerrachanane lagatun *adj.* શરીરરચનાને લગતું anatomical

shark *n.* શાર્ક shark

Sharmaal *n.* શરમાળ sheepish

sharmindagee *n.* શરમદિગી ebmarrassment

sharmindu thaay tem karavun *v.t.* શરમદિ થાય તેમ કરવું embarrass

sharoo karavun *n.* શરૂ કરવું commencement

sharooaat *n.* શરૂઆત beginning

sharooaat *n.* શરૂઆત outset

sharooaat karavee શરૂઆત કરવી initiate

sharooaatanun *n.* શરૂઆતનું initial

shartanun kaapad *n.* શર્ટનું કાપડ shirting

Shartee *n.* શરતી saving

sharu karavun *v.t.* શરૂ કરવું, begin

shashtano maaro *n.* શસ્ત્રોનો મારો volley

shashthivibhaktinun roop *pro.* ષષ્ઠવિભિક્તનું રૂપ. his

shastraagaar *n.* શસ્ત્રાગાર armoury

shastraagaar *n.* શસ્ત્રાગાર arsenal

shastrasanranjaam *n.* શસ્ત્રસંરંજામ armament

Shastravaidak *adj.* શસ્ત્રવૈદ્ક surgical

Shastravaidhya *n.* શસ્ત્રવૈદ્ય surgeon

shastravaidyanun shastra *n.* શસ્ત્રવૈદ્યનું શસ્ત્ર lancet

shastro *n.* શસ્ત્રો fire-arm

shataabdee *n.* શતાબ્દી centenary

shataabdee utsav *adj.* શતાબ્દી ઉત્સવ centennial

shataavaree *n.* શતાવરી asparagus

shatakon *n.* ષટ્કોણ hexagon

shatravidyaano cheepiyo *n.* શસ્ત્રવૈદ્યનો ચીપિયો forceps

shatruta *n.* શત્રુતા hostility

shatrutaavaalun *adj.* શત્રુતાવાળું hostile

shatrutaavaalun *adj.* શત્રુતાવાળું inimical

shaury *n.* શૌર્ય gallantry

shaury *n.* શૌર્ય heroism

shaurya *n.* શૌર્ય valour

sheeghrata *n.* શીઘ્રતા readiness

sheekhavavun *v.t.* શીખવવું teach

sheelbhang maate lalachaavavun *v.t.* શીલભંગ માટે લલચાવવું seduce

sheengovaalun *n.* શિંગોવાળું acacia

sheershak *n.* શીર્ષક heading

sheeshunun rundan *v.t.* શીશુંનું રુંદન pule

sheetabhavan *n.* શીતભવન refrigerator

sheetal *adj.* શીતલ cool

sheexak *n.* શક્ષિક teacher

sheexak no kaam dhandho *n.* શક્ષિકનું કામ–ધંધો teaching

shekavun *v.t.* શેકવું bake

shekavun *v.t.* શેકવું foment

shekavun *n.* શેકવું fomentation

Shekee naakhvun *v.t.* શેકી નાખવું scorch

shekhachallee શેખચલ્લી fanciful

shempen *n.* શેંપેન champagne

shempoo *v.t.* શેમ્પૂ shampoo

Sherdee *n.* શેરડી sugaⷯcane

Sheree mahollo *n.* શેરી મહોલ્લો street

shero maaravo *v.t.* શેરો મારવો indorse

sheshabhaag *n.* શેષભાગ remainder

shetaan *n.* શેતાન deuce

shetaan *n.* શેતાન devil

shetaan *n.* શેતાન fiend

Shetaan *n.* શેતાન satan

shetaananu *adj.* શેતાનનું devilish

Shetaannaa Jevun *adj.* શેતાનના જેવું satanic

shetaranj *n.* શેતરંજ chess

sheth *n.* શેઠ boss

sheth *n.* શેઠ mister

shethaanee *n.* શેઠાણી mistress

shevaal *n.* શેવાળ moss

Shighra, Gati *n.* શીઘ્ર ગતિ swiftness

shikaar *n.* શકિર prey

shikaar karavo *v.t.* શકિર કરવો hunt

shikaaree *n.* શકિરી fowler

shikaaree *n.* શકિરી hunter

shikaaree kutaro *n.* શકિરી કૂતરો hound

shikaaun *n.* શખિઓ tyro

shikaree paxeeno nahor *n.* શકિરી પક્ષીનો નહોર talon

shikhaau maanas *n.* શખિઓ માણસ novice

shikhaaun શખિઓ tiro

shikhaaupanaano tabakko *n.* શખિઓઉપણાનો તબક્કો probation

shikhar *n.* શિખર acme

shikhar *n.* શિખર height

shikhar *n.* શિખર pinnacle

shikhar *n.* શિખર steeple

shikhar *n.* શિખર vertex

shikshaapaatr *adj.* શક્ષિાપાત્ર punishable

shikshaatmak *adj.* શક્ષિાત્મક punitive

shikshak *n.* શક્ષિક faculty

shikshan *n.* શક્ષિણ education

shikshan sanbandhee *adj.* શક્ષિણ સંબંધી scholastic

shikshananu pramanpatra *n.* શક્ષિણનું પ્રમાણપત્ર diploma

shikshit *adj.* શક્ષિત educated

shikshit *adj.* શક્ષિત literate

shilaachhaap *n.* શિલાછાપ lithograph

shilaalekh *n.* શિલાલેખ inscription

shilaalesh *n.* શિલાલેખ epigraph

Shilkalaa *n.* શિલ્પકળા sculpture

shilpee *n.* શિલ્પી, architect

shilpee *n.* શિલ્પી craftsman

Shilpee *n.* શિલ્પી sculptor

shingadu *n.* શિંગડુ horn

shinto anuyaayee *n.* શન્ટિો અનુયાયી shinto

shira *n.* શરિ vein

shiraaman *n.* શરિમણ lunch

shirachshed karavo *v.t.* શરિચ્છેદ કરવો. decapitate

shirastaan *n.* શરિસ્ત્રાણ helmet

shirchchhed karavo *v.t.* શરિચ્છેદ કરવો behead

shirobindu *n.* શરિોબિંદુ apex

shisht *n.* શસિત discipline

shishta *adj.* શષ્ટિ decent

shishta *adj.* અશષ્ટિ uncivil

shishtaachaar *n.* શષ્ટિાચાર deceny

shishtaachaar *n.* શષ્ટિાચાર decorum

shishtaachaar *n.* શષ્ટિાચાર manner

shishtaachaar *n.* શષ્ટિાચાર propriety

shishtapaalanane lagatu *adj.* શસિતપાલનને લગતું disciplinary

shishu (saat varasathee naanun) *n.* શશિુ (સાત વરસથી નાનું) infant

shishuno aparaadh *n.* શશિુનો અપરાધ. juvenility

shishy *n.* શષ્યિ pupil

shishya *n.* શષ્યિ disciple

shista aagrahee *n.* શસિતઆગ્રહી disciplinarian

shithil *adj.* શથિલિ lax

shithil *adj.* શથિલિ loose

shithil thavun *v.t.* શથિલિ થવું relax

shithilataa *n.* શથિલિતા laxity

Shithiltaa *n.* શથિલિતા slackness

shiyaal *n.* શયિાળ fox

shiyaal *n.* શયિાળ jackal

shiyaalo *n.* શયિાળો winter

shobhaano saajanshangaar *n.pl.* શોભાનો સાજશણગાર trappings

shobhaaspad *adj.* શોભાસ્પદ becoming

shobhaavanaar શોભાવનાર ornamental

shobhaayaatraa શોભાયાત્રા tableau

shobhaspad *adj.* શોભાસ્પદ decorous

shobhavun શોભવું beseem

shochaneey *n.* શોચનીય deplorable

shodakhol શોધખોળ exploration

shodh *n.* શોધ discovery

shodhak *n.* શોધક explorer

shodhakhol *n.* શોધખોળ quest

shodhavun *v.t.* શોધવું detect

shodhavun *v.t.* શોધવું find

Shodhvun *v.t.* શોધવું search

Shodhvun *v.t.* શોધવું seek

shok *n.* શોક grief

Shok *n.* શોક sorrow

shok karavo *v.t.* શોક કરવો bemoan

shok karavo *v.t.* શોક કરવો deplore

shokaantik naatakano abhinetaa *n.* શોકાન્તિક નાટકનો અભિનિતા tragedian

shokaantika naatakanu, -naa jevun *adj.* શોકાન્તિક નાટકનું – ના જેવું tragic

shokaatur *adj.* શોકાતુર plaintive

Shokaatur શોકાતુર sorrowful

shokagrast *adj.* શોકગ્રસ્ત woebegone

shokgeet *n.* શોકગીત elegy

shokh *n.* શોખ hobby

shokh *n.* શોખ relish

shooleee chadaavavun *v.t.* શૂળીએ ચડાવવું impale

shoony *n.* શૂન્ય cypher

shoonya *n.* શૂન્ય nil

shoonyaavakaash *n.* શૂન્યાવકાશ vacuum

shoor *adj.* શૂર brave

shorabakor *n.* શોરબકોર noise

shorabakor *n.* શોરબકોર pother

shorabakor *n.* શોરબકોર rowdism

shorabakor karanaarun *adj.* શોરબકોર કરનારું noisy

shoshan karavun *v.* શોષણ કરવું exploit

shraddhaa *n.* શ્રદ્ધા faith

shraddhaaviheen *adj.* શ્રદ્ધાવિહીન faithless

shravanendariyeey *adj.* શ્રવણેન્દ્રિયીય acoustic

shravya *adj.* શ્રવ્ય audible

shreemant *adj.* શ્રીમંત wealthy

Shrenee *n.* શ્રેણી series

shrepanel *n.* શ્રાપનેલ shrapnel

shresht *adj.* શ્રેષ્ઠ foremost

shreshthata *n.* શ્રેષ્ઠતા greatness

shreshthataa *n.* શ્રેષ્ઠતા excellence

shrotaa *n.* શ્રોતા audience

shrotaagrah, rangbhoomee *n.* શ્રોતાગૃહ, રંગભૂમિ amphi theatre

shrotaaprekshakagruh *n.* શ્રોતાપ્રેક્ષકગૃહ auditorium

shrungaarik *adj.* શૃંગારિક amatory

shrungaarik *adj.* શૃંગારિક erotic

shrunkhalun શૃંખલું barnaclen. بار

shubh *adj.* શુભ prosperous

shubh daanat *n.* શુભ દાનત bonafides

shubhechchha *n.* શુભેચ્છા. greeting

shuddh *adj.* શુદ્ધ pure

shuddh *adj.* શુદ્ધ unsullied

shuddh daanatanun *n.* શુદ્ધ દાનતનું conscientious

shuddh karavun *v.t.* શુદ્ધ કરવું purify

shuddh karavun શુદ્ધ કરવું rectify

shuddh karavun *v.t.* શુદ્ધ કરવું wash

shuddh karya vinaanun *adj.* શુદ્ધ કર્યા વિનાનું crude

shuddha bhaasaa *n.* શુદ્ધ ભાષા jargon

shuddheekaran *n.* શુદ્ધીકરણ fumigation

shuddheekaran *n.* શુદ્ધીકરણ purification

shuddhipatr *n.* શુદ્ધિપિત્ર corrigendum

Shudhdh karvun *v.t.* શુદ્ધ કરવું sublimate

Shudhdh Vivek *n.* શુદ્ધ વિવેક sobriety

shudhha chaaritryavaalu *n.* શુદ્ધ ચારિત્ર્યવાળું virtuous

shukan *n.* શુકન omen

shukrano grah *n.* શુક્રનોગ્રહ venus

shukrano taaro *n.* શુક્રનો તારો morning star

shukravaar *n.* શુક્રવાર friday

shulk *n.* શુલ્ક fee

shun *pro.* શું what

shushk *adj.* શુષ્ક dry

shushka *adj.* શુષ્ક arid

shushka શુષ્ક uninteresting

shuskataa *n.* શુષ્કતા dryness

shvaanagruh *n.* શ્વાનગૃહ kennel

shvaas levo *v.t.* શ્વાસ લેવો respire

shvaasochchhaas *n.* શ્વાસોચ્છ્વાસ respiration

shvasur *n.* શ્વસુર father-in-law

siddh karavun *v.t.* સદ્ધિ કરવું prove

siddhaant *n.* સદ્ધિાન્ત principle

siddhaant *n.* સદ્ધિાંત doctrine

siddhant shodhanaar *n.* સદ્ધિાંત શોધનાર theorist

siddhant shodhavo *v.t.* સદ્ધિાંત શોધવો theorize

sigaar *n.* સગિાર cigar

sigaaret *n.* સગિારેટ cigarette

sikka *n.* સદ્ધિ્ કા numismatic

sikkaano mukhabhaag *adj.* સફ્કિાનો મુખભાગ obverse

sikko *n.* સફ્કિો coin

Sikko *n.* સફ્કિો signet

silika *n.* સલિકિા silica

silindar aakaaranun *adj.* સલિન્ડિર આકારનું cylindrical

sinchaaee *n.* સચિાઈ irrigation

sinchaaee karavee *v.t.* સચિાઈ કરવી irrigate

sindhaaloon *n.* સધિાલૂણ rock-salt

singun foonkanaar *n.* સીંગું ફૂંકનાર trumpeter

sinh *n.* સહિ lion

sinhanun bachchun *n.* સહિનું બચ્ચું cub

sipaaee *n.* સપિાઈ flunkey

Sipaaivarg *n.* સપિાઈવર્ગ soldiery

sisaapen *n.* સસિાપેન pencil

sisakaaro karavo *v.t.* સસિકારો કરવો hiss

sismograf *n.* સીસ્મોગ્રાફ seismograph

sitam *n.* સતિમ persecution

sitee *n.* સટિી whistle

Sittermun *adj.* સત્તિેરમું seventy

sivaay *conj.* સવિાય unless

Sivvun *v.t.* સીવવું sew

sket maachalee *n.* સ્કેટ માછલી skate

slej *n.* સ્લેજ sledge

slemt maachhalee *v.t.* સ્મેલ્ટ માછલી smelt

slet *n.* સ્લેટ slate

sletar *n.* સ્લેટર slater

sliper *n.* સ્લપિર slipper

smaarak stanbh *n.* સ્મારક સ્તંભ obelisk

smaarak svaroopanun *n.* સ્મારક સ્વરૂપનું monumental

smaran karaavanaarun *v.i.* સ્મરણ કરાવનારું memorial

smaran karaavavun *v.t.* સ્મરણ કરાવવું remind

smaranakathaa *n.* સ્મરણકથા memoir

smaranashakti *n.* સ્મરણશક્તિ memory

smaranashakti *n.* સ્મરણશક્તિ rocollection

smaranasthanbh *n.* સ્મરણસ્તંભ cenotaph

smashaan સમશાન necropolis

smruti *n.* સ્મૃતિ remembrance

smruti stanbh *n.* સ્મૃતિ સ્તંભ mausoleum

smrutichinh *adj.* સ્મૃતચિહ્ન. monument

smrutichinho *n.* સ્મૃતચિહ્નો relic

smrutipatr *n.* સ્મૃતપિત્ર reminder

snaan *n.* સ્નાન bath

snaatak *n.* સ્નાતક graduate

snaayu *n.* સ્નાયુ muscle

snaayubadhdh *adj.* સ્નાયુબધ્ધ muscular

snaayunu sankochana *n.* સ્નાયુનું સંકોચન tic

sneh todavo *v.* સ્નેહ તોડવો alienate

snehapoorvak *adj.* સ્નેહપૂર્વક exanimo

snehasanmelan *n.* સ્નેહસંમેલન reunion

sneheejano *n.* સ્નેહીજનો kith

so *n.* સો hundred

sobat *n.* સોબત companionship

sobat *n.* સોબત company

sobat, gunasaadrashya *n.* સોબત, ગુણસાદૃશ્ય alliance

sobat, samaagam *n.* સોબત, સમાગમ affilliation

sobatee *n.* સોબતી comrade

Sodam *n.* સોડમ scent

sodaman rahevun *v.i.* સોડમાં રહેવું nestle

sodhee kaadhavun *v.t.* શોધી કાઢવું discover

sodiam *n.* સોડીયમ sodium

sodo *v.t.* સોદો. deal

sodo *n.* સોદો transaction

sofaa *n.* સોફા sofa

Sogan levee *v.t.* સોગન લેવી swear

sogandnaamun, pratignaalekh *n.* સોગંદનામું, પ્રતજ્ઞિાલેખ affidavit

sojo *n.* સોજો lump

sojo *n.* સોજો protuberance

Sojo *n.* સોજો swelling

sojo *n.* સોજો tumour

sol *n.* સોળ weal

Sol (ni sankhyaa 16) *n.* સોળ (ની સંખ્યા, ૧૬) sixteen

Solmun, Solmo bhag *adj.* સોળમું, સોળમો ભાગ sixteenth

sonaano dhol chadaavavo *v.i.* સોનાનો ઢોળ ચડાવવો gild

sonaanun *adj.* સોનાનું golden

sonanee lagadee *n.* સોનાની લગડી bullion

sonee *n.* સોની goldsmith

sonet *n.* સોનેટ sonnet

sonpanee *n.* સોંપણી assignment

sonpavun *v.t.* સોંપવું commend

sonpavun *v.t.* સોંપવું consign

sonpavunn *v.t.* સોંપવું commit

Sonpee devun *v.t.* સોંપી દેવું surrender

sonpelu kaam *n.* સોંપેલું કામ task

sonun *n.* સોનું gold

sooar *n.* સૂઅર hog

soochak *n.* સૂચક gnomon

soochak *adj.* સૂચક reminiscent

soochak hovun *v.t.* સૂચક હોવું denote

soochi *n.* સૂચિ list

soochit *adj.* સૂચિત implied

soochitaarth dhvanvaarth *n.* સૂચિતાર્થ ધ્વન્વાર્થ implication

soodee *n.* સૂડી nutcrackers

soog *n.* સૂગ nausea

soog - cheetaree chade evun *adj.* સૂગ–ચીતરી ચડે એવું nauseous

soojelun *adj.* સૂજેલું tumid

soojelun *adj.* સૂજેલું turgid

soojhavun *v.i.* સૂઝવું occur

sookaa ghaasano poolo *n.* સૂકા ઘાસનો પૂળો truss

sookee darakh *n.* સૂકી દ્રાખ raisin

sookee jameen *n.* સૂકી જમીન terrafirma

sooko padaarth *n.* સૂકો પદાર્થ tinder

sooksma jantun o *n.* સૂક્ષ્મ જંતુઓ bacterium

sookshmabhedak drashtee *n.* સૂક્ષ્મભેદક દૃષ્ટિ acumen

sookshmadarshak yantr *n.* સૂક્ષ્મદર્શક યંત્ર microscop

sookshmadrashti *n.* સૂક્ષ્મદરષ્ટિ insight

sookshmajeev *n.* સૂક્ષ્મજીવ germ

Sookun. *n.* સૂકું straw

soonakaar *adj.* સૂનકાર lonesome

soondh *n.* સૂંઢ snout

soonghavaanun *adj.* સૂંઘવાનું olfactory

soonghavun *v.t.* સૂંઘવું inhale

soonkaar *adj.* સૂનકાર dreary

soonkaar *n.* સૂનકાર vacuity

soony *n.* શૂન્ય nought

soony *n.* શૂન્ય zero

soopadee *n.* સૂપડી galley

Soorajmukhee fool *n.* સૂરજમુખી ફૂલ sunflower

Soorajnee jem chalktun *n.* સૂરજની જેમ ચળકતું sunshine

Soorakiran *n.* સૂર્યકિરણ sunbeam

soorano aaroh avaroh *n.* સૂરનો આરોહ અવરોહ cadence

soorano mela *n.* સૂરનો મેળ unison

soorat bagaadavee *v.t.* સૂરત બગાડવી deface

Soorokhaar *n.* સૂરોખાર saltpetre

Soorya *n.* સૂર્ય sun

sooryano vishisht kor *n.* સૂર્યનો વશિષ્ટ કોર limb

Sooryaprakaashvaalun *adj.* સૂર્યપ્રકાશવાળું sunny

Sooryasnaan karvun *n.* સૂર્યસ્નાન કરવું sun-bath

Sooryodayno samay *n.* સૂર્યોદયનો સમય sunrise

Sootar kaantvun *n.* સૂતર કાંતવું spin

sootra *n.* સૂત્ર dictum

sootra (mayakathan) *n.* સૂત્ર (મયકથન) aphorism

sootra (mayakathan) *adj.* સૂત્ર (મયકથન) aphoristic

sootramay *adj.* સૂત્રમય. laconic

sootrochchaar *n.* સૂત્રોચ્ચાર slogan

soovaanun paatiyun *n.* સૂવાનું પાટિયું bunk

Sooyanun *adj.* સૂર્યનું solar

sopaaree *n.* સોપારી betel-nut

soto *n.* સોટો pole

soviyet *n.* સોવયિટ soviet

soy *n.* સોય needle

Soyno taanko *n.* સોયનો ટાંકો stitch
spardhaa *n.* સ્પર્ધા contest
spardhaa *n.* સ્પર્ધા emulation
spardhaa *n.* સ્પર્ધા race
spardhaa karavee *v.t.* સ્પર્ધા કરવી emulate
spardhaamaa ootaravun *v.i.* સ્પર્ધામાં ઊતરવું vie
spardhaaprerit *adj.* સ્પર્ધાપ્રેરિત emulous
spardhaatmak *adj.* સ્પર્ધાત્મક competitive
sparsh rekhaa *n.* સ્પર્શ રેખા tangent
spasht *adj.* સ્પષ્ટ clear
spasht *adj.* સ્પષ્ટ distinct
spasht *adj.* સ્પષ્ટ evident
spasht *adj.* સ્પષ્ટ plain
spasht thavun *v.t.* સ્પષ્ટ થવું crystalize
spashta *adj.* સ્પષ્ટ categorical
spashtapane jaanavun *v.t.* સ્પષ્ટપણે જાણવું realize
spashtapane kahelu *adj.* સ્પષ્ટપણે કહેલું explicit
spashtataa karavee *v.t.* સ્પષ્ટતા કરવી specify
spashtataapoorvak *adv.* સ્પષ્ટતાપૂર્વક plainly
spashtavakta *adj.* સ્પષ્ટવક્તા outspoken
spashtikaran *n.* સ્પષ્ટીકરણ elucidation
spastata karavee *v.t.* સ્પષ્ટતા કરવી clarify
spenial kutarun *n.* સ્પેનીયલ કુતરું spaniel
sraddhaalu *adj.* શરદ્ધાળુ devout
staanaagr *n.* સ્તાનાગ્ર pap
staapan karvun *v.t.* સ્થાપન કરવું transplant
staarch *n.* સ્ટાર્ચ starch
stamp *n.* સ્ટમ્પ stump
stan *n.* સ્તન breast
stanbh *n.* સ્તંભ column
stanbh *n.* સ્તંભ pillar
stanbh *n.* સ્તંભ post
star *n.* સ્તર slab
starabaddh karavun *v.t.* સ્તરબદ્ધ કરવું stratify
stareekaran *n.* સ્તરીકરણ hierarchy
stavanee ek jaat *n.* સ્ટવની એક જાત primus
stediyam *n.* સ્ટેડિયમ stadium
stethoskop *n.* સ્ટેથોસ્કોપ stethoscope
sthaan *n.* સ્થાન locality
sthaanbhrasht karavun *v.t.* સ્થાનભ્રષ્ટ કરવું dislocate
sthaanbhrasht karavun *v.t.* સ્થાનભ્રષ્ટ કરવું dislodge
sthaanik *adj.* સ્થાનિક local
sthaanik svaraajasanstha *n.* સ્થાનિક સ્વરાજસંસ્થા council
sthaanika bhoogol *n.* સ્થાનિક ભૂગોળ topography
sthaapak *n.* સ્થાપક founder
sthaapan *n.* સ્થાપના installation
sthaapan karavun *v.t.* સ્થાપન કરવું constitute
sthaapan karavun *v.t.* સ્થાપન કરવું install
sthaapan karavun *n.* સ્થાપન કરવું institute
sthaapan karavun te *n.* સ્થાપન કરવું તે establishment
sthaapanaa *n.* સ્થાપના foundation
sthaapavun *v.t.* સ્થાપવું establish
sthaapavun *v.t.* સ્થાપવું found
sthaavar milakat *n.* સ્થાવર મિલ્કત property
sthaayee roop *v.t.* સ્થાયી રૂપ permanently
sthaayitv *n.* સ્થાયિત્વ permanence
sthadaantar *n.* સ્થદાંતર emigration
sthagit *n.* સ્થગતિ doldrums
sthagit karavun *v.t.* સ્થગતિ કરવું adjourn
Sthagit moodee *p.p.* સ્થગતિ મૂડી sunk
Sthagitta *n.* સ્થગતિતા suspension
sthal *n.* સ્થળ avenue
sthal *n.* સ્થળ place
sthal *n.* સ્થળ venue
sthalaantar *n.* સ્થળાંતર migration
sthalaantar *n.* સ્થળાંતર removal
sthalaantar karanaarun *n.* સ્થળાંતર કરનારું migrant

sthalaantar karavun *v.t.* સ્થળાંતર કરવું migrate

Sthayee *adj.* સ્થાયી standing

Sthir *adj.* સ્થિર stationary

Sthir aakaar *n.* સ્થિર આકાર solidity

Sthir aakaarnun *adj.* સ્થિર આકારનું solid

sthir balonun shaastra *n.* સ્થિર બળોનું શાસ્ત્ર statics

sthir karavun *adj.* સ્થિર કરવું bounden

Sthirta *n.* સ્થિરતા stability

Sthirtaa *n.* સ્થિરતા steadiness

Sthit *v.t.* સ્થિત static

sthiti *n.* સ્થિતિ position

Sthiti *n.* સ્થિતિ state

sthitisthaapak *adj.* સ્થિતિસ્થાપક elastic

sthitisthaapakata *n.* સ્થિતિસ્થાપકતા resilience

sthitisthaapakataa *n.* સ્થિતિસ્થાપકતા elasicity

sthrudataa *n.* સ્થૂળતા fatness

stree *n.* સ્ત્રી lady

stree *n.* સ્ત્રી woman

stree ane purushanee jodee *n.* સ્ત્રી અને પુરુષની જોડી couple

streedhan *n.* સ્ત્રીધન jointure

streedvesh *n.* સ્ત્રીદ્વેષ. misogyny

streeling *adj.* સ્ત્રીલિંગ feminine

streenee chaddee *n.* સ્ત્રીની ચડ્ડી knickers

streeni salaam *n.* સ્ત્રીની સલામ curtsey

streeonun vrund *n.* સ્ત્રીઓનું વૃંદ bevy

stroberi *n.* સ્ટ્રોબેરી strawberry

studiyo *n.* સ્ટુડિયો studio

stutee git *n.* સ્તુતિગીત anthem

stuti *n.* સ્તુતિ commendation

sudhaaraa rad karavaa *v.t.* સુધારા રદ કરવા stet

sudhaaraano aagevaan *n.* સુધારાનો આગેવાન apostle

sudhaaraavaadee khristee *n.* સુધારાવાદી ખ્રિસ્તી protestant

sudhaarak *n.* સુધારક reformer

sudhaarana karanaarun સુધારણા કરનારું reformatory

sudhaaravun *v.t.* સુધારવું ameliorate

sudhaaravun *v.t.* સુધારવું correct

sudhaaravun *v.t.* સુધારવું edify

sudhaaravun *v.t.* સુધારવું expiate

sudhaaravun *v.* સુધારવું improve

sudhaaravun *v.t.* સુધારવું mend

sudhaaravun *v.* સુધારવું reform

sudhaaravun *n.* સુધારવું retouch

sudhaaravun te *n.* સુધારવું તે revision

sudhaaree na shakay tevun *adj.* સુધારી ન શકાય તેવું irreparable

sudhaaree shakaay evun *adj.* સુધારી શકાય એવું corrigible

sudhaaro *n.* સુધારો amelioration

sudhaaro *n.* સુધારો amendment

sudhaaro *n.* સુધારો betterment

sudhaaro *n.* સુધારો correction

sudhaaro *n.* સુધારો rectification

sudharavun *n.* સુધરવું improvement

sudhare nahi evun *adj.* સુધરે નહઈએવું incorrigible

sudharo *adj.* સુધારો unimproved

sudhee *v.t.* સુધી till

sufiyaanu સુફિયાણું specious

sugandh *n.* સુગંધ aroma

sugandh *n.* સુગંધ fragrance

sugandh *n.* સુગંધ odour

sugandhee *adj.* સુગંધી fragrant

sugandhee padaartho *n.* સુગંધી પદાર્થો perfumery

sugandhee pravaahee *n.* સુગંધી પ્રવાહી cologne

sugandheedaar dravya *n.* સુગંધીદાર દ્રવ્ય balm

sugandheedaar parafyum *n.* સુગંધીદાર પરફ્યુમ myrrh

sugandhit *adj.* સુગંધિત aromatic

sughad *adj.* સુઘડ tidy

sughadata *n.* વ્યવસ્થિતપણું neatness

sujee javun *n.v.i.* સુજી જવું, bulge

sukaan *n.* સુકાન helm

sukaana feravavaano daando *n.* સુકાન ફેરવવાનો દાંડો tiller

sukaanee *n.* સુકાની helmsman

sukaanee *n.* સુકાની pilot

sukalakadee *adj.* સુકલકડી lank

sukhaavah *adj.* સુખાવહ blissful

sukhad ane romaanchak સુખદ અને રોમાંચક titilation

sukhadaayak *adj.* સુખદાયક comfortable

sukhakaarak *adj.* સુખકારક pleasant

sukhakaarakata, sukhasagavado *n.* સુખકારકતા, સુખસગવડો amenity

sukhasagavadavaalun *adj.* સુખસગવડવાળું luxurious

sukhee *adj.* સુખી beatific

sukshma vastu *n.* સૂક્ષ્મ વસ્તુ midget

suku ghaas *n.* સૂકું ઘાસ fodder

sulabh *adj.* સુલભ accessible

sulabh *adj.* સુલભ convenient

sulabh *adj.* સુલભ handy

suleh સુલેહ conciliation

suleh *n.* સુલેહ rapprochement

sumel *n.* સુમેળ concord

sunaavanee *n.* સુનાવણી hearing

sundar *adj.* સુંદર beautiful

sundar premikaa *n.* સુંદર પ્રેમિકા delilah

sundarata *n.* સુંદરતા prettiness

sunnat karavee *n.* સુન્નત કરવી circumcise

sunvaadi unee kaapad *n.* સુંવાળું ઊની કાપડ flannel

suparichit *adj.* સુપરિચિત familiar

surakhaab *n.* સુરખાબ flamingo

surakheedaar *adj.* સુરખીદાર ruddy

surakshit *adv.* સુરક્ષિત all right

surakshit jagyaa સુરક્ષિત જગ્યા footing

surakshit raakhavun *n.* સુરક્ષિત રાખવું preservation

surakshit raakhavun *v.t.* સુરક્ષિત રાખવું protect

suramo *n.* સુરમો antimony

surasuriyun *n.* સુરસુરિયું squib

surokhaar *n.* સુરોખાર nitre

susangat *adv.* સુસંગત according

susangat *adj.* સુસંગત compatible

susangat સુસંગત congruent

susangat *adj.* સુસંગત consistent

susangat *adj.* સુસંગત harmonious

susangat *adj.* સુસંગત relevant

susangatata *n.* સુસંગતતા relevance

susavaato *v.i.* સુસવાટો whiz

susheel *adj.* સુશીલ genteel

sushiravaady *n.* સુષિરવાદ્ય reed

sushobhan *n.* સુશોભન embellishment

sushobhit karavun *v.t.* સુશોભિત કરવું beautify

sushobhit karavun *v.t.* સુશોભિત કરવું embellish

sushobhit karavun *v.t.* સુશોભિત કરવું fret

sushupt *adj.* સુષુપ્ત quiescent

suspashtata *n.* સુસ્પષ્ટતા perspicuity

Sust *adj.* સુસ્ત stolid

Sust *adj.* સુસ્ત supine

sustee *n.* સુસ્તી languor

sustee *n.* સુસ્તી lassitude

susvaagatam *v.t.* સુસ્વાગતમ્ welcome

susvarasangeet *n.* સુસ્વરસંગીત melody

sutaarno vaansalo *n.* સુતારનો વાંસલો adze

sutar kaantanaar *n.* સુતર કાંતનાર spinner

suthaar *n.* સુથાર carpenter

suthaareenun kaam *n.* સુથારીનું કામ carpentry

suvaachy *adj.* સુવાચ્ય legible

suvaachy *adj.* સુવાચ્ય readable

suvaadavun *v.t.* સુવાડવું lull

suvaahya *adj.* સુવાહ્ય portable

suvaalu *adj.* સુંવાળું downy

suvaas *n.* સુવાસ perfume

suvarnayug સુવર્ણયુગ millennium

suvidhaa *n.* સુવિધા facility

suvidhaa karee aapavee *v.t.* સુવિધા કરી આપવી facilitate

suvikhyaat *adj.* સુવિખ્યાત renowned

suvyavasthit *adj.* સુવ્યવસ્થિત orderly

suvyavasthit સુવ્યવસ્થિત trim

suyaanee kaam *n.* સુયાણી કામ midwifery

suyogya karavun *v.t.* સુયોગ્ય કરવું standardize

suze nahee tevun *adj.* સુઝે નહીં તેવું inexplicable

svaabhaavik *n.* સ્વાભાવિક inherent

svaabhaavik reete સ્વાભાવિક રીતે naturally

svaabhimaanee *adj.* સ્વાભિમાની dignified

svaadheenata *n.* સ્વાધીનતા liberty

svaadisht *adj.* સ્વાદિષ્ટ delicious

svaadisht *adj.* સ્વાદિષ્ટ palatable

svaagatasamaaranbh *n.* સ્વાગતસમારંભ reception

svaamee *n.* સ્વામી liege

svaas *n.* શ્વાસ breath

svaasochchhaas karavo *v.t.* શ્વાસોચ્છ્વાસ કરવો breathe

svaastya sudhaaro *n.* સ્વાસ્થ્ય સુધારો convalescence

svaayatt *adj.* સ્વાયત્ત autonomous

svaayattataa *n.* સ્વાયત્તતા autonomy

svabhaav *n.* સ્વભાવ disposition

svachchh *adj.* સ્વચ્છ clean

svachchh *adj.* સ્વચ્છ neat

svachchh karanaarun *n.* સ્વચ્છ કરનારું cleaner

svachchh karavun *v.t.* સ્વચ્છ કરવું cleanse

svachchhand *n.* સ્વચ્છંદ wantonness

svachchhataa *n.* સ્વચ્છતા cleanliness

svadesh *n.* સ્વદેશ fatherland

svadesh gaman *v.t.* સ્વદેશ ગમન repatriate

svadharm tyaag *n.* સ્વધર્મ ત્યાગ apostasy

svadharm tyaagee *n.* સ્વધર્મ ત્યાગી apostate

svagatokti *n.* સ્વગતોક્તિ soliloquy

svaichchheek parityaag સ્વૈચ્છીક પરિત્યાગ renunciation

svaichchhik *adj.* સ્વૈચ્છિક voluntary

svairaachar *n.* સ્વૈરાચાર abandonment

svairapanu સ્વૈરપણું extravagance

svairavihaar karavo *v.i.* સ્વૈરવિહાર કરવો ramble

svairavihaaree *n.* સ્વૈરવિહારી loafer

svamat khandan *n.* સ્વમત ખંડન recantation

svamat khandan karavun *v.t.* સ્વમત ખંડન કરવું recant

svamataagrahee *adj.* સ્વમતાગ્રહી uppish

svapnadrashtaa *adj.* સ્વપ્નદ્રષ્ટા visionary

svar *n.* સ્વર vowel

svarg *n.* સ્વર્ગ elysium

svarg *n.* સ્વર્ગ heaven

svarg *n.* સ્વર્ગ paradise

svargasukh *n.* સ્વર્ગસુખ bliss

svargeey *adj.* સ્વર્ગીય celestial

svaroop *n.* સ્વરૂપ form

svaroop aapavun *v.t.* સ્વરૂપ હોવું embody

svaroopavaan *adj.* સ્વરૂપવાન beauteous

svasanakriya *n.* શ્વસનક્રિયા breathing

Svasantoshee *n.* સ્વસંતોષી smug

svastha *adj.* સ્વસ્થ calm

svasthachittata *n.* સ્વસ્થચિત્તતા composure

svasthataa *n.* સ્વસ્થતા equanimity

svasthataapoorvak *adv.* સ્વસ્થતાપૂર્વક calmly

svatantr *adj.* સ્વતંત્ર independent

svatantra *adj.* સ્વતંત્ર free

svatantrataa *n.* સ્વતંત્રતા freedom

svayanchaalan *n.* સ્વયંચાલન automation

svayanchaalit *adv.* સ્વયંચાલિત automatically

svayanchalan *adj.* સ્વયંચલન automatic

svayansevak *n.* સ્વયંસેવક volunteer

svayansfoorti *n.* સ્વયંસ્ફૂર્તિ instinct

svayansfoorti *adj.* સ્વયંસ્ફૂર્તિ instinctive

svedakaarak *adj.* સ્વેદકારક diaphoretic

svedakaaree *adj.* સ્વેદકારી sudorific

sveekaaranaar *n.* સ્વીકારનાર receiver

sveekaaravun *v.t.* સ્વીકારવું receive

sveekrut hakeekat *n.* સ્વીકૃત હકીકત datum

sveekrut maanyata *n.* સ્વીકૃત માન્યતા assumption

svikaar *n.* સ્વીકાર acceptance

svikaaravaa yogya *adj.* સ્વીકારવા યોગ્ય acceptable

svikaaravun *v.* સ્વીકારવું accept

svikaaravun *v.* સ્વીકારવું acknowledge

sw ankush *n.* સ્વ અંકુશ self-control

swaabhimaan *n.* સ્વાભિમાન self-esteem

Swaad *n.* સ્વાદ savour

swaad *v.t.* સ્વાદ taste

Swaadishta *n.* સ્વાદિષ્ટ dainty

swaadishta *adj.* સ્વાદિષ્ટ tasty

swaadishta koliyo *n.* સ્વાદિષ્ટ કોળિયો titbit

Swaagat karvun *v.t.* સ્વાગત કરવું salute

Swaang *n.* સ્વાંગ similitude

Swaarthee *adj.* સ્વાર્થી self-centred

Swaarthee *n.* સ્વાર્થી selfish

Swaarthpanu *n.* સ્વાર્થપણું selfishness

swaash chhodavo *v.t.* શ્વાસ છોડવો exhale

swabhaav *adj.* સ્વભાવ tempered

Swabhimaan *n.* સ્વાભિમાન self-respect

Swachcha *adj.* સ્વચ્છ shiny

Swachchh *adj.* સ્વચ્છ sanitary

Swachchh *adj.* સ્વચ્છ serene

Swachchhtaa સ્વચ્છતા serenity

Swagat bhaashan karvun *v.i.* સ્વગત ભાષણ કરવું soliloquize

swapn *n.* સ્વપ્ન dream

Swatantra astitvvaalun *n.* સ્વતંત્ર અસ્તિત્વવાળું substantive

Swayamsfoort *adj.* સ્વયંસ્ફૂર્ત spontaneous

T

Taabaamaan aanvun *v.t.* તાબામાં આણવું subjugate

taabaano mulak *n.* તાબાનો મુલક dominion

Taabadtob તાબડતોબ straightway

Taabe karvun તાબે કરવું subdue

taabe thavun *v.i.* તાબે થવું cringe

Taabe thavun *v.t.* તાબે થવું submit

taadapatree *n.* તાડપત્રી tarpaulin

taadee *n.* તાડી toddy

Taadh tadkaathee surkshit *adj.* ટાઢ તડકાથી સુરક્ષિત snug

taadhiyo taav *n.* ટાઢિયો તાવ malaria

taaipist *n.* ટાઇપિસ્ટ typist

taaj *n.* તાજ crown

taaja kalam *n.* તાજા કલમ postscript

taajagee *n.* તાજગી flush

taajagee aapanaarun *adj.* તાજગી આપનારું refreshing

taajetaranun *adj.* તાજેતરનું latter

taajetaranun *adj.* તાજેતરનું recent

taaju *adj.* તાજું fresh

taajun astitvaman aavatun *adj.* તાજું અસ્તિત્વમાં આવતું nascent

taajun karavun *v.t.* તાજું કરવું refresh

taakaat *n.* તાકાત potency

taakeed *n.* તાકીદ notice

taakeed *n.* તાકીદ urgency

taakeedanee jarooreeyaat *n.* તાકીદની જરૂરિયાત exigency

taakeedanun *n.* તાકીદનું instant

taakeedanun *adj.* તાકીદનું pressing

taakeedanun *adj.* તાકીદનું urgent

taakeede karavun *v.t.* તાકીદ કરવું expedite

taakeene jovun *v.t.* તાકીને જોવું gaze

taakid , shikhaaman *n.* તાકીદ, શિખામણ admonition

taakman rahevun *v.t.* તાકમાં રહેવું waylay

taal *n.* તાલ tempo

taalavaalun *adj.* ટાલવાળું bald

taalavaanun *adj.* તાળવાનું palatal

taalavun *v.t.* ટાળવું avert

taalavun *v.t.* ટાળવું escape

taalavun *v.t.* ટાળવું eschew

taalavun *n.* તાળવું palate

taaleem aapnaar maanas *n.* તાલીમ આપનાર માણસ. trainer

taaleemaarthee *n.* તાલીમાર્થી trainee

taaleeo *n.* તાળીઓ claps

taaleeo paadavee *v,t,* તાળીઓ પાડવી clap

taalimani sanstha *n.* તાલીમની સંસ્થા academy

taalu - kala ughaadavee *v.t.* તાળું– કળ ઉઘાડવી unlock

Taan *n.* તાણ spasm
taanavun *v.t.* તાણવું pull
taaneene khenchelun *adj.* તાણીને ખેંચેલું tense
taaneene vagaadavun તાણીને વગાડવું blare
taangavun *v.t.* ટીંગવું hang
taankanee *n.* ટીંકણી pin
taansalun *n.* તાંસળું porringer
taantav sandhi *n.* તાંતવ સંધિ suture
taapadeept *n.* તાપદીપ્ત incandescence
taapadeept *adj.* તાપદીપ્ત incandescent
taapamaan *n.* તાપમાન temperature
taapu *n.* ટાપુ island
taar *n.* તાર filament
taar *n.* તાર telegram
taar *n.* તાર wire
taar jevun *adj.* તાર જેવું wiry
taar vinaanun *adj.* તાર વિનાનું wireless
Taaraa jevun (tejswi) *adj.* તારા જેવું (તેજસ્વી) starry
Taaraaonun *adj.* તારાઓનું stellar
taaranhaar *n.* તારણહાર messiah
taarano brash *n.* તારનો બ્રશ card
taaranun goonchalun *v.* તારનું ગૂંચળું coil
taaravanee *n.* તારવણી illation
taarayantra *n.* તારયંત્ર telegraph
taareekh *n.* તારીખ date
taarkik *adj.* તાર્કિક deductive
taarkik aadhaar તાર્કિક આધાર rationale
taarnu jooth *n.* ટારનું જૂથ tetrad
taarnun *adj.* તારનું telegraphic
Taaro *n.* તારો star
taarun *pro.* તારું thine
taarun *pro.* તારું thy
taasak *n.* તાસક tray
taataalano tahevaar *n.* નાતાલનો તહેવાર yule
taatkaalik *adj.* તાત્કાલિક immediate
taatkaalik upayog maatenun *adj.* તાત્કાલિક ઉપયોગ માટેનું readymade
Taatpoortee japtee *n.* તાત્પૂરતી જપ્તી sequestration
taatvik *adj.* તાત્ત્વિક academic
taav *n.* તાવ fever

taav *n.* તાવ influenza
taavadee *n.* તાવડી fire-pan
taavadee *n.* તાવડી frying-pan
taavanaa lakshanavaalu *adj.* તાવનાં લક્ષણોવાળું feverish
taaveej *n.* તાવીજ locket
tab *n.* ટબ tub
tabadeel karavun *v.t.* તબદીલ કરવું transfer
tabadeelee *n.* તબદીલી conveyance
tabadeelpaatra *adj.* તબદીલપાત્ર transferable
Tabbe thanaarun *n.* તાબે થનારું submissive
tabeeb *n.* તબીબ doctor
Tadaavun te *v.i.* તડાવું તે stutter
tadafadeeya maaravaa *v.t.* તરફડિયાં મારવાં flounder
tadajod karavee *v.t.* તડજોડ કરવી compound
tadajod karavee *v.t.* તડજોડ કરવી compromise
tadake besavun *v.t.* તડકે બેસવું bask
tadatadavun *v.t.* તડતડવું crackle
taddan *adv.* તદ્દન quite
taddan *v.t.* તદ્દન utter
taddan *adj.* તદ્દન uttermost
taddan angat *v.t.* તદ્દન અંગત intimate
taddan baraabar *adv.* તદ્દન બરાબર exactly
taddan ena jevun ja *adj.* તદ્દન એના જેવું જ identical
taddan nirmal *adj.* તદ્દન નિર્મળ pellucid
taddan sharooaatanun *adj.* તદ્દન શરૂઆતનું primordial
tadhiyo taav, dhrujaaree *n.* ટાઢિયો તાવ, ધ્રુજારી ague
taduparaant તદુપરાંત. moreover
tafaavat તફાવત differential
tafaavat *n.* તફાવત distinction
tafaavat *n.* તફાવત gap
tafadanchee *n.* તફડંચી pilferage
tafadanchee karavee *v.t.* તફડંચી કરવી filch
tafadanchee karavee *v.t.* તફડંચી કરવી pilfer

tagaratagara jovun *v.t.* ટગરટગર જોવું goggle

tahevaar *n.* તહેવાર festival

tail chitr *n.* તૈલ ચિત્ર. oil-painting

taip raiter *n.* ટાઇપ રાઇટર type-writer

taiyaar karavun *v.t.* તૈયાર કરવું prepare

taiyaaree vinaa *n.* રૂતૈયારી વિના extemporaneous

taj *n.* તજ cinnamon

tajagya hovun *v.t.* તજજ્ઞ હોવું specialize

tajaveej karavee *n.* તજવીજ કરવી provision

tak *n.* તક opportunity

takaau *adj.* ટકાઉ durable

takaaupanu *n.* ટકાઉપણું durability

takaavaaree *n.* ટકાવારી percentage

takalaadee vastu *n.* તકલાદી વસ્તુ tinsel

takalee *n.* તકલી distaff

takanee raah jovee *v.* તકની રાહ જોવી bide

takanik *n.* તકનિક technique

takanikeevid *n.* તકનિકીવીદ્ technician

takaraarano muddo *n.* તકરારનો મુદ્દો grievance

takaraarano vishay *n.* તકરારનો વિષિય contention

takasaadhu *n.* તકસાધુ opportunist

takatak avaaj karavo *v.t.* ટકટક અવાજ કરવો click

takavun te *n.* ટકવું તે duration

takedaaree *n.* તકેદારી vigilance

takiyo *n.* તકિયો cushion

takoro *n.* ટકોરો fillip

takoro maaravo *v.t.* ટકોરો મારવો knock

taktee *n.* તકતી frame

tal *n.* તલ sesame

talaav *n.* તળાવ. lake

talaav *adj.* તળાવ mere

talaav *n.* તળાવ. pond

talabaddhata તલબદ્ધતા rhythmic

talapadun *adj.* તળપદું indigenuous

Talavaar *n.* તલવાર sabre

talavalaavavun *v.t.* ટળવળાવવું tantalize

talavun *v.t.* તળવું fry

taleem *n.* તાલીમ training

talleen *adj.* તલ્લીન rapt

tallin thavun te *n.* તલ્લીન થવું તે absorption

Talvaar *n.* તલવાર sword

Talvaar bahaadur *n.* તલવાર બહાદુર swordsman

tamaacho *n.* તમાચો buffet

tamaaku *n.* તમાકુ tobacco

tamaakunee golee *n.* તમાકુની ગોળી quid

tamaakuno vepaaree *n.* તમાકુનો વેપારી. tobacconist

tamaarun *pro.* તમારું your

tamaato *n.* ટમાટો tomato

tamancho *n.* તમંચો pistol

tamatamaat *n.* તમતમાટ piquancy

tamatamavun *v.t.* ટમટમવું flicker

Tambaanub maanas *n.* તાંબાનું માણસ stooge

tamboo *n.* તંબૂ tent

tame *pro.* તમે you

tame jaate *pro.* તમે જાતે yourself

tamenun joothanun roop *pro.* તમેનું જૂનું રૂપ ye

tammar *adj.* તમ્મર dizzy

tammarnu darad *n.* તમ્મરનું દરદ vertigo

tanaav *v.t.* તણાવ strain

tanakhaa fenkavaa *v.i.* તણખા ફેંકવા sparkle

tandraa *n.* તંદ્રા drowsiness

tandurast *adj.* તંદુરસ્ત healthy

tandurast *adj.* તંદુરસ્ત lusty

tandurastee *n.* તંદુરસ્તી fitness

tandurastee *n.* તંદુરસ્તી health

Tang *n.* તંગ straitened

tangee *n.* તંગી dearth

Tangvun ટાંગવું suspend

tankanakhaara *n.* ટંકણખાર tincal

tankankhaar *n.* ટંકણખાર borax

Tankho *n.* તણખો spark

tantrabaddh karavun *v.t.* તંત્રબદ્ધ કરવું organize

tantu *n.* તંતુ fibre

tantuvaadya *n.* તંતુવાદ્ય lute

tapaal *n.* ટપાલ mail

tapaal tikit sangrah *n.* ટપાલ ટિકિટ સંગ્રહ philatelic

tapaalanun *adj.* ટપાલનું postal

tapaalanun lavaajam *n.* ટપાલનું લવાજમ postage

tapaalee *n.* ટપાલી postman

tapaas *n.* તપાસ interrogation

tapaas *adj.* તપાસ searching

tapaas karavee *v.t.* તપાસ કરવી interrogate

tapaas karavee *v.t.* તપાસ કરવી probe

tapaas karvee, *v.t.* તપાસ કરવી enquire

tapaasavun *v.t.* તપાસવું observe

Tapaavelaa lodhaa vade daam devo *v.t.* તપાવેલા લોઢા વડે ડામ દેવો sear

tapakavun *v.t.* ટપકવું trickle

tapaku *n.* ટપકું dot

tapalee *v.t.* ટપલી flip

Tapkaanvaalun, Talkaavaalun *adj.* ટપકાંવાળું, તલકાવાળું spotted

taraad *n.* તરાડ rift

taraap maaravee *v.t.* તરાપ મારવી swoop

taraapo *n.* તરાપો raft

tarabol karavun *v.i.* તરબોળ કરવું transfuse

tarabooch *n.* તરબૂચ melon

tarabuch *n.* તરબુચ watermelon

tarachhadun *n.* તોછડું cavalier

tarachhodavun *v.t.* તરછોડવું flout

tarachodavun *n.* તરછોડવું jilt

tarang *n.* તરંગ caprice

tarang, lahereepanu *n.* તરંગ freak

tarangee *adj.* તરંગી capricious

tarangee *adj.* તરંગી eccentric

tarangitata *adj.* તરંગિતતા quixotic

taras *n.* તરસ hyena

taras *n.* તરસ thirst

tarat ja *n.* તરત જ by-end

Tarat paachhalnun *adj.* તરત પાછળનું subsequent

tarataj najare padatun તરત નજરે પડતું conspicuous

tarato barafano pahaad *n.* તરતો બરફનો પહાડ iceberg

taravun *v.i.* તરવું float

tarbain *n.* ટરબાઇન turbine

tarbol karavun *v.t.* તરબોળ કરવું drench

tarbol karvun *n.* તરબોળ કરવું transfusion

Tare tem karvun *v.i.* તરે તેમ કરવું swim

tareeke *adv.* તરીકે as

tarkana niyamonun paalan *n.* તર્કના નિયમોનું પાલન ratiocination

tarkasangat *adj.* તર્કસંગત tenable

tarkashaastr *n.* તર્કશાસ્ત્ર logic

Tarkatee *adj.* તર્કટી subtle

tarkdosh *n.* તર્કદોષ fallacy

tarpentaain *n.* ટર્પેન્ટાઇન turpentine

tarsyun *adj.* તરસ્યું thirsty

tarunee *n.* તરુણી wench

tasaveer *n.* તસવીર photograph

tasaveerakaar *n.* તસવીરકાર photographer

tatastheekrut *v.* તટસ્થીકૃત neutralize

tathaakathit *adj.* તથાકથિત ostensible

tathaastun, beshak *n.* તથાસ્તુ, બેશક amen

tatkaal *adv.* તત્કાળ forthwith

tatkaal *adv.* તત્કાળ immediately

tatkaal raju *adv.* તત્કાળ રજૂ extempore

tatkaaleen તત્કાલીન provisional

tatpar *adj.* તત્પર prompt

tattaar *adj.* ટટ્ટાર perpendicular

tattaar karavee *v.t.* ટટ્ટાર કરવું erect

tattar *n.* ટટ્ટાર erection

tattu *n.* ટટ્ટુ nag

tattu *n.* ટટ્ટુ pony

tattvagnaan *n.* તત્ત્વજ્ઞાન philosophy

tattvagnaanane lagatun *adj.* તત્ત્વજ્ઞાનને લગતું philosophic

tattvagnaanee *n.* તત્ત્વજ્ઞાની philosopher

tavaareekh *n.* તવારીખ chronicle

tavo *n.* તવો pan

te *v.t.* તે dost

te *pro* તે it

te jagyaaae *adv.* તે જગ્યાએ thither

te vakhate *adv.* તે વખતે then

teb *n.* ટેબ tab

tebal *n.* ટેબલ counter

tebal *n.* ટેબલ desk
ted *v.t.* ટેડ ted
teed *n.* તીડ locust
teeka karavee *v.t.* ટીકા કરવી criticize
teekaa karavee *n.* ટીકા કરવી commentator
Teekaa karavee *v.t.* ટીકા કરવી damn
teekaakaar *n.* ટીકાકાર critic
Teekaapaatra *adj.* ટીકાપાત્ર damnable
teekaatmak *n.* ટીકાત્મક critical
teekam *n.* તીકમ. mattock
teekam *n.* તીકમ pickaxe
teekhaash *n.* તીખાશ pungency
teekhal *adj.* ટીખળ facetious
teekhun *adj.* તીખું pungent
teekhun tamatamatun *adj.* તીખું તમતમતું piquant
Teekshan *adj.* તીક્ષ્ણ stinging
Teekshan anee *n.* તીક્ષ્ણ અણી spike
teekshana *adj.* તીક્ષ્ણ trenchant
teekshn *adj.* તીક્ષ્ણ keen
teekshna *adj.* તીક્ષ્ણ sharp
teekshna buddhivaalun *adj.* તીક્ષ્ણ બુદ્ધિવાળું brainy
teempa paadavaa *v.t.* ટીપા પાડવા drop
teenee chees *n.* તીણી ચીસ screech
Teenun *adj.* તીણું shrill
teepaa paadavaa *v.i.* ટીપાં પાડવાં drip
teepe teepe bharavun *v.t.* ટીપે ટીપે ભરવું instil
teepoy *n.* ટીપોઈ teipoy
teerachhee najare *adv.* તીરછી નજરે askew
teerandaaj *n.* તીરંદાજ archer
teerandaajee *n.* તીરંદાજી archery
teeraskaaraniy *adj.* તિરસ્કરણીય accursed
teerth *n.* તીર્થ ford
teerthayaatra *n.* તીર્થયાત્રા pilgrimage
teevr anagamo *n.* તીવ્ર અણગમો repulsion
teevr eechchha dharaavavee *v.t.* તીવ્ર ઈચ્છા ધરાવવી crave
teevr santaap *n.* તીવ્ર સંતાપ chagrin
teevra *n.* તીવ્ર tormina

teevra vedanaa *n.* તીવ્ર વેદના throe
teevrata gumaavavee *v.i.* તીવ્રતા ગુમાવવી languish
tejaab *adj.* તેજાબ acid
Tejaano ke samoohgat reete *n.* તેજાનો કે સમૂહગત રીતે spicer
tejasvee *adj.* તેજસ્વી effulgent
tejasvee *n.* તેજસ્વી luminary
tejasvee *adj.* તેજસ્વી luminous
tejasvita *n.* તેજસ્વતા refulgence
tejee *v.t.* તેજી boom
tejovalay *n.* તેજોવલય corona
Tejsvee *adj.* તેજસ્વી spirited
tekaree *n.* ટેકરી hill
tekaree *n.* ટેકરી hillock
tekaro *n.* ટેકરો bump
teko *n.* ટેકો buttress
Teko *n.* ટેકો shore
Teko *v.t.* ટેકો stay
Teko aapvo *n.* ટેકો આપવો support
tel *n.* તેલ oil
tel choline abhishek karavo *v.t.* તેલ ચોળીને અભિષિક કરવો anoint
telephone no chando *n.* ટેલિફોનનો ચંદો dial
telifon *n.* ટેલિફોન telephone
telifon *n.* ટેલિફોન phone
teligraafee *n.* ટેલિગ્રાફી telegraphy
teliprinaree *n.* ટેલપિરિનિટરી teleprintery
teliskop *adj.* ટેલસ્કોપ telescopic
tem chhataa *n.* તેમ છતાં despite
tem chhatan *adv.* તેમ છતાં nevertheless
tem chhatan *adv.* તેમ છતાં yet
temane તેમને them
temanu તેમનું their
Tenee *pr.n.* તેણી she
teneenun *pro* તેણીનું her
tenis *n.* ટેનિસ tennis
tenkar *n.* ટેન્કર tanker
tenun *pro.* તેનું its
teo *pro.* તેઓ they
tera *n.* તેર thirteen
teramun *adj.* તેરમું thirteenth
tesasvitaa *n.* તેજસ્વિતા effulgence
tev *n.* ટેવ habit
tevaaee javun *v.* ટેવાઈ જવું acclimatize

tevaayelun *n.* ટેવાયેલું wont

thaabadvun *n.* થાબડવું pat

thaak *n.* થાક weariness

thaakavun *v.t.* થાકવું tire

thaakee gayelun *adj.* થાકી ગયેલું, weary

thaakelaa hovun *adj.* થાકેલા હોવું tired

thaalee *n.* થાળી disc

thaalee *n.* થાળી disk

thaanbhalaanee kunbhee *n.* થાંભલાની કુંભી pedestal

thaanbhalo *n.* થાંભલો pier

Thaanun *n.* થાણું station

thaapaanu *adj.* થાપાનું femoral

thaapandaar *n.* થાપણદાર depositer

thaarelee doodhamalaaee *n.* ઠારેલી દૂધમલાઈ ice-cream

thaathadee *n.* ઠાઠડી bier

thaathamaath *v.t..* ઠાઠમાઠ array

Thaathmaath bataavvaa *n.* ઠાઠમાઠ બતાવવા sport

thaavakaaee *n.* ઠાવકાઈ prudery

thaayaroid *adj.* થાયરોઈડ thyroid

Thag *n.* ઠગ swindler

thag *n.* ઠગ thug

thag *n.* ઠગ trickster

thakaavat *n.* થકાવટ exhaustion

thakaavat *n.* થકાવટ fatique

thakavee naakhanaarun *adj.* થકવી નાખનારું wearisome

thakavee naakhatun *adj.* થકવી નાખતું tiring

thakavee naankhavun *v.t.* થકવી નાંખવું irk

Thal *n.* થાળ salver

thanbhaleeonee haar *n.* થાંભલીઓની હાર balustrade

thandu *adj.* ઠંડું frigid

thandun *adj.* ઠંડું chilly

thandun *adj.* ઠંડું cold

thandun karavun *adj.* ઠંડું કરવું, chill

thansavun *v.t.* ઠાંસવું guzzle

Thapaat ke tamaacho maarvo *n.* થપાટ કે તમાચો મારવો slap

thapakaapaatra *adj.* ઠપકાપાત્ર censurable

thapako *n.* ઠપકો reproof

thapako *n.* ઠપકો reproval

thapako aapavo ઠપકો આપવો chastise

thapako aapavo *v.t.* ઠપકો આપવો chide

thapako aapavo *v.t.* ઠપકો આપવો rebuke

thapako aapavo *v.t.* ઠપકો આપવો reprehend

thapako aapavo *v.t.* ઠપકો આપવો. reprove

thapako aapavo *v.t.* ઠપકો આપવો twit

thapako aapavo *v.t.* ઠપકો આપવો upbraid

Tharaav *n.* ઠરાવ stipulation

Thareethaam thavun *v.t.* ઠરીઠામ થવું settle

tharel *adj.* ઠરેલ sober

Tharel ane shaanun *adj.* ઠરેલ અને શાણું staid

tharm ekam *n.* થર્મ એકમ therm

tharmos *n.* થર્મોસ thermos

Thasso *v.i.* ઠસ્સો strut

thatharee javaaya aevo bhay *n.* થથરી જવાય એવો ભય terror

Thaththaa *n.* ઠઠ્ઠા sally

thaththaamaskaree *n.* ઠઠ્ઠામસ્કરી mock

thaumatur *n.* થૌમાતુર thaumatur

thavaa maandavun *v.i.* થવા માંડવું become

thavun *v.t.* થવું befall

thavun *v.i.* થવું betide

thavun joiye *v.t.* થવું જોઈએ should

thavun te *n.* થવું તે occurrence

Thee atyaar sudhee *adv.* થી અત્યાર સુધી since

thee door raakhavun *v.t.* થી દૂર રાખવું, avoid

thee naasee javun *v.t.* થી નાસી જવું evade

thee utarata sthane *prep.* થી ઉતરતા સ્થાને beneath

thee vadhare *n.* –થી વધારે. upwards

thee visangat hovun થી વિસંગત હોવું contradict

theegadun *n.* થીગડું patch

theejavavun *v.i.* થીજવવું freeze

theejavun *v.i.* થીજવું coagulate

theejavun *v.t.* થીજવું congeal

theeje chhe te taapamaan *adj.* થીજે છે તે તાપમાન freezing

Theek theek poshaak paherelun *adj.* ઠીક ઠીક પોશાક પહેરેલું spruce

theengoojee *n.* ઠીંગૂજી pigmy

theengoojee *n.* ઠીંગૂજી pygmy

thekadee *n.* ઠેકડી mockery

theleekaravee *n.* થેલી bag

thelo *n.* થેલો knapsack

thijaavavun *v.t.* થિજાવવું refrigerate

thikathik *adj.* ઠીકઠીક passable

thinganun *adj.* ઠીંગણું dumpy

Thingnun ane jaadun *adj.* ઠીંગણું અને જાડું stumpy

thingujee *n.* ઠિંગુજી manikin

thingujeeaone lagatu *adj.* ઠિંગુજીઓને લગતું elfin

thitih hasavvun *v.i.* ઠીઠી હસવું titter

thiyosofee *n.* થિયોસોફી theosophy

Thodaa j vakhatmaan *adv.* થોડા જ વખતમાં soon

tholakee *n.* ઢોલકી timbrel

Thoonkdaanee *n.* થૂંકદાની spittoon

thoontadaar *adj.* ઠૂંટદાર stubby

thor *n.* થોર cactus

those nun bahoovachana *pro.* those નું બહુવચન those

thoth nishaadiyo *n.* ઠોઠ નિશાળિયો dunce

tijoree *n.* તિજોરી coffer

tijoree *n.* તિજોરી exchequer

tijoree *n.* તિજોરી vault

tikaatippan *n.* ટીકાટિપ્પણ annotation

tikit *n.* ટિકિટ ticket

tikshna drushti *adj.* તીક્ષ્ણ દ્રષ્ટિ eagle-eyed

tip ket ramat *n.* ટિપ કેટ રમત tip-cat

tippanee *n.* ટિપ્પણી comment

tirango *n.* તિરંગો tricolour

tirapaayee *n.* તરિપાઈ trivet

tiraskaar *n.* તિરસ્કાર hatred

tiraskaar karavo *v.t.* તિરસ્કાર કરવો despise

tiraskaar karavo *v.t.* તિરસ્કાર કરવો. detest

tiraskaar karavo *v.t.* તિરસ્કાર કરવો disdain

tiraskaarapaatr *adj.* તરિસ્કારપાત્ર odious

tiraskaarapaatra *adj.* તરિસ્કારપાત્ર contemptible

tiraskaarapaatra *n.* તરિસ્કારપાત્ર despicable

tiraskarvun *v.t.* તરિસ્કારવું abhor

Tiraskrut *adj.* તરિસ્કૃત damned

tiraskrut *v.t.* તરિસ્કૃત spurn

Tirskaardarshak haasya *v.t.* તરિસ્કારદર્શક હાસ્ય sneer

Tirskaarvaalun *adj.* તરિસ્કારવાળું scornful

tivr anagamo, dvesh *n.* તીવ્ર અણગમો, દ્વેષ antipathy

tivra aojash *adj.* તીવ્ર ઓજાશ fulgent

tobaro *n.* તોબરો nose-bag

Tobro chadaavvo *v.t.* તોબરો ચડાવવો scowl

Toch *n.* ટોચ summit

toche *n.* ટોચે top

tochhadaaee *n.* તોછડાઈ rudeness

tochhadaaeepoorvak *adv.* તોછડાઈપૂર્વક curtly

tochhadun *adj.* તોછડું insolent

tochhadun *adv.* તોછડું off-hand

todavun *v.t.* તોડવું break

tofaan *n.* તોફાન turbulence

Tofaan machaavnaarun *adj.* તોફાન મચાવનારું stormy

tofaanee *adj.* તોફાની impish

tofaanee *adj.* તોફાની naughty

tofaanee *adj.* તોફાની riotous

tofaanee *n.* તોફાની tempestuous

tofaanee balak *n.* તોફાની બાળક urchin

tofaanee pishaach *n.* તોફાની પિશાચ goblin

tofaanee tolun તોફાની ટોળું rabble

tofanee *adj.* તોફાની boisterous

tofee *n.* ટોફી toffee

tolaa *n.* તોલા tola

tolakeeno naayak *n.* ટોળીનો નાયક chieftain

tolatappan *n.* ટોળટપ્પાં chitchat

tolateekhal *n.* ટોળટીખળ waggery

tolun *n.* ટોળું crowd

Tolun *n.* ટોળું shoal

tolun *v.t.* ટોળું throng

tonan maarava *v.t.* ટોણાં મારવા jeer

tono *n.* ટોણો taunt

Toonkaavvun *v.t.* ટૂંકાવવું shorten

toonkee drashti *n.* ટૂંકી દ્રષ્ટિ myopia

Toonkmaa *adv.* ટૂંકમાં shortly

toonko barachhat vaal *n.* ટૂંકો બરછટ વાળ bristle

Toonko hevaal *adj.* ટૂંકો હેવાલ summary

toonko kot *n.* ટૂંકો કોટ spencer

Toonko rasto *n.* ટૂંકો રસ્તો short cut

Toonku *adj.* ટૂંકું succinct

toonku jaakit *n.* ટૂંકું જાકિટ jerkin

toonkun *adj.* ટૂંકું concise

Toonkun ghaas *n.* ટૂંકું ઘાસ sward

toonkun karavun *v.t.* ટૂંકું કરવું curtail

toorkee *n.* તૂર્કી turkey

top *n.* તોપ cannon

top તોપ howitzer

topachee *n.* તોપચી gunner

topakhaanun *n.* તોપખાનું ordnance

topalee *n.* ટોપલી basket

topamaaro *n.* તોપમારો salvo

topamaaro karavo *v.t.* તોપમારો કરવો bombard

topano golo *n.* તોપનો ગોળો. projectile

topee *n.* ટોપી cap

topee utaaravee *v.t.* ટોપી ઉતારવું doff

topkhaanu *n.* તોપખાનું battery

topkhaanun *n.* તોપખાનું aritillery

topo *n.* ટોપો hat

toran *n.* તોરણ festoon

toranamaalaa *n.* તોરણમાળા arcade

torpeedo *n.* ટોરપીડો torpedo

totadun bolavun *v.i.* તોતડું બોલવું lisp

totadun bolavun *v.i.* તોતડું બોલવું stammer

totee *n.* ટોટી nozzle

Totee *n.* ટોટી spout

traajavun *n.* તૂરાજવું balance

traakomaa rog *n.* ટ્રાકોમા રોગ trachoma

traam *n.* ટ્રામ tram

traansun *prep.* તૂરાંસું athwart

traas *n.* તૂરાસ trouble

traas *adj.* તૂરાસ troublesome

traas aapavo *v.t.* તૂરાસ આપવો annoy

traas, heraangati *n.* તૂરાસ, હેરાનગતિ annoyance

traasadaayak *adj.* તૂરાસદાયક. tiresome

traimaasik તૂરૈમાસકિ quarterly

trana *adj.* તૂરણ three

trana bhaaganu banelu *adj.* તૂરણ ભાગનું બનેલું tripartite

trana naa samoohno set *adj.* તૂરણના સમૂહનો સેટ ternate

trana vaara *adv.* તૂરણ વાર. thrice

trana varase thanaarun *adj.* તૂરણ વરસે થનારું triennial

trana(ganun) *pre.* તૂરણ(ગણું) tri

tranaganun *adj.* તૂરણગણું trine

tranaganun *adj.* તૂરણગણું triple

trananu jooth *n.* તૂરણનું જૂથ trio

trananu jootha *n.* તૂરણનું જૂથ triad

transee leetee *adj.* તૂરાંસી લીટી diagonal

transship *v.t.* ટ્રાન્સશપિ tranship

transship ટ્રાન્સશપિ trans-ship

transshipment *n.* ટ્રાન્સશપિમેન્ટ transhipment

trashalaaka *n.* તૂરશલાકા catheter

trastee *n.* ટ્રસ્ટી trustee

tredmaark *n.* ટ્રેડમાર્ક trade mark

treejun *adj.* તૂરીજું third

treesa *n.* તૂરીસ thirty

treesamun તૂરિસમું. thirtieth

trevadun *adj.* તૂરેવડું treble

tribhuj *n.* તૂરિભુજ triangle

trijyaa *n.* તૂરજ્યા radius

trikona *n.* તૂરિકોણ trigon

trikonaakaar pradesh *n.* તૂરકિોણાકાર પ્રદેશ delta

trikonamiti *n.* તૂરકિોણમતિ. trigonometry

trikoneeya *adj.* તૂરકિોણીય triangular

trimiti *n.* તૂરમિતિ trilogy

Trimitidarshak *n.* તૂરમિતિદર્શક stereoscope

tripagun aasan *n.* તૂરપિગું આસન tripod

trisool *n.* તૂરશિૂળ trident

tritaal nruty *n.* તૂરતિાલ નૃત્ય waltz

trunamanee *n.* તૃણમણિ amber

tu pote *pro.* તું પોતે thyself

tuchako *n.* ટુચકો epigram

tuchako, *n.* ટુચકો anecdote

tuchchha *adj.* તુચ્છ trivial

tukadee *n.* ટુકડી detachment

tukadee *n.* ટુકડી squad

tukadee *n.* ટુકડી team

tukado *n.* ટુકડો fragment

tukado *n.* ટુકડો piece

tulana karavee *v.t.* તુલના કરવી compare

tulanaa *n.* તુલના comparative

tulanaa *n.* તુલના simile

tulaseeno chhod *n.* તુલસીનો છોડ basil

tunkaavavun *v.t.* ટૂંકાવવું abridge

Tunkdo *n.* ટૂંકડો scrap

tunkee nonth *adj.* ટૂંકી નોંધ brief

turaai *n.* તુરાઈ trumpet

turniket *n.* ટૂર્નિકિટ tourniquet

tushaarajaalak *n.* તુષારજાલક gossamer

Tushkaarvu *v.t.* તુષ્કારવું scoff

tutavun te *n.* તૂટવું તે breakage

tvachaa *n.* ત્વચા cuticle

Twaraa *n.* ત્વરા suddenness

tyaag *n.* ત્યાગ abjuration

tyaag *n.* ત્યાગ desertion

tyaag karavo ત્યાગ કરવો forsake

tyaag karavun ત્યાગ કરવું relinquish

tyaan *adv.* ત્યાં there

tyaan sudhee *prep.* ત્યાં સુધી until

tyaanthee *adv.* ત્યાંથી thence

tyajee deethelu *adj.* તજી દીધેલું forlorn

tyajee devaayelu baalak *n.* તજી દેવાયેલું બાળક foundling

tyunik *n.* ટ્યુનિક tunic

U

uanche chadaavavun *n.* ઊંચે ચડાવવું elevation

uattejanaa *n.* ઉત્તેજના elation

uattejit *v.t.* ઉત્તેજિત elate

ubaavee naakhavun *v.t.* ઉબાવી નાખવું cloy

Ubhaa hovun *v.i.* ઊભા હોવું stand

ubhaavyavee avayav *n.* ઉભયાન્વયી અવ્યય conjuction

ubharaavavun *v.t.* ઊભરાવવું teem

ubharaavun *v.i.* ઊભરાવું effervesce

ubharavun *n.* ઉભરવું emergence

ubhayjeevee *n.* ઉભયજીવી amphibian

ubhun *adj.* ઊભું upright

uchaapaat *n.* ઉચાપત peculation

uchaapaat karavee *v.t.* ઉચાપત કરવી. misappropriate

uchaapat *n.* ઉચાપત defacation

uchaapat karavee *v.t.* ઉચાપત કરવી embezzle

uchch chaaritryavaalun *adj.* ઉચ્ચ ચારિત્ર્યવાળું noble

uchch kotinun oormikaavy *n.* ઉચ્ચ કોટિનું ઊર્મિકાવ્ય ode

uchchaalak *n.* ઉચ્ચાલક lever

uchchaar karavo *v.t.* ઉચ્ચાર કરવો articulate

uchchaar karavo *v.t.* ઉચ્ચાર કરવો. enounce

uchchaaran *n.* ઉચ્ચારણ pronunciation

uchchaaran ઉચ્ચારણ utterance

uchchaarashaastr *n.pl.* ઉચ્ચારશાસ્ત્ર phonetics

uchchaaravun *v.t.* ઉચ્ચારવું pronounce

uchchaarshaastreey *adj.* ઉચ્ચારશાસ્ત્રીય phonetic

uchchapradesh *n.* ઉચ્ચપ્રદેશ plateau

Uchchattam maatranun *adj.* ઉચ્ચતમ માત્રાનું superlative

uchchhavaas *n.* ઉચ્છવાસ exhalation

uchchhedan ઉચ્છેદન extirpation

uchchhedavun *v.t.* ઉચ્છેદવું extirpate

uchheenee rakam *v.t.* ઉછીની રકમ loan

uchheenun aapavun *v.t.* ઉછીનું આપવુ lend

uchheenun levun *v.t.* ઉછીનું લેવું borrow

uchher *n.* ઉછેર breeding

uchheravun *v.t.* ઉછેરવું foster

uchheravun *v.* ઉછેરવું keep

uchit *v.t.* ઉચિત meet

uchit *adj.* ઉચિત right

uchita theravavun *v.t.* ઉચિતિ ઠેરવવું justify

udaadee devun *v.* ઉડાડી દેવું dissipate

udaaharan *n.* ઉદાહરણ example

udaaharan *n.* ઉદાહરણ illustration

udaaharan *n.* ઉદાહરણ instance

udaaharaneey *adj.* ઉદાહરણીય exemplary

udaaoo *v.t.* ઉડાઉ dissociate

udaar *adj.* ઉદાર bountiful

udaar *adj.* ઉદાર liberal

udaar *adj.* ઉદાર unsparing

udaaratan *n.* ઉદારતા generosity

udaas *adj.* ઉદાસ cres¶fallen

udaas *adj.* ઉદાસ doleful

udaas thavun *v.i.* ઉદાસ થવું mope

udaaseen *adj.* ઉદાસીન listless

udaaseen *adj.* ઉદાસીન unconcerned

udaaseen, rasaheen *adj.* ઉદાસીન, રસહીન apathetic

udaash *adj.* ઉદાસ disconsolate

udaash *adj.* ઉદાસ dismal

udaasin, chhete, alagun *adv.* ઉદાસીન, છેટે, અળગું aloof

udaata shokaantika naatak *n.* ઉદાત્ત શોકાન્તકિ નાટક tragedy

udaau *adj.* ઉડાઉ evasive

udaau *n.* ઉડાઉ extravagant

udaau *adj.* ઉડાઉ prodigal

udaau *adj.* ઉડાઉ wasteful

udaau javaab *n.* ઉડાઉ જવાબ evasion

udaau javaabo aapava *v.t.* ઉડાઉ જવાબો આપવા prevaricate

Udaau vyakti *n.* ઉડાઉ વ્યક્તિ spendhrift

udaaugeeree *n.* ઉડાઉગીરી prodigality

udabhavavun ઉદ્ભવવું emerge

udagaar ઉદ્ગાર alas

udagaar *int.* ઉદ્ગાર eh

udagaar *n.* ઉદ્ગાર exclamation

udagaar kaadhavo *n.* ઉદ્ગાર કાઢવો ejaculation

Udattata *n.* ઉદાત્તતા sublimity

uddabhavavun *p.p.* ઉદ્ભવવું begun

uddagaar *n.* ઉદ્ગાર interjection

uddghaatan *n.* ઉદ્દ્ઘાટન inauguration

uddghaatan karavun *v.t.* ઉદ્દ્ઘાટન કરવું inaugurate

uddghaatan samayanun *adj.* ઉદ્દ્ઘાટન સમયનું inaugural

uddhat *adj.* ઉદ્ધત immodest

uddhat bhaashan *n.* ઉદ્ધત ભાષણ cheek

uddipak ઉદ્દીપક stimulant

udghoshak *n.* ઉદ્ઘોષક announcer

udhaadu *adj.* ઉઘાડું flagrant

udhaaee *n.* ઉઘઈ termite

udhaaravun *v.t.* ઉઘારવું debit

udhaavavun *v.t.* ઉઠાવવું hoist

udharas *n.* ઉધરસ cough

Udhdhat *adj.* ઉદ્ધત saucy

udhyam *n.* ઉદ્યમ industry

udhyamee *adj.* ઉદ્યમી industrious

udyaan *n.* ઉદ્યાન plantation

udyamee *adj.* ઉદ્યમી assiduous

udyog saahas *n.* ઉદ્યોગસાહસ enterprise

Ugamsthaan *n.* ઉગમસ્થાન source

ugato sitaaro *n.* ઉગતો સિતારો. firmament

ughaadu paadavun *v.t.* ઉઘાડું પાડવું disclose

ughaadu paadavun *v.t.* ઉઘાડું પાડવું divulge

ughaadun *adj.* ઉઘાડું open

ugr svabhaavavaalun *adj.* ઉગ્ર સ્વભાવવાળું morose

ugra *adj.* ઉગ્ર fiery

ugrataa, kathorata *n.* ઉગ્રતા, કઠોરતા acrimony

Ugto juvaaniyo *n.* ઉગતો જુવાનિયો stripling

ujaanee *adj.* ઉજાણી festive

ujaanee *n.* ઉજાણી jamboree

ujaanee *n.* ઉજાણી junket

ujaanee *n.* ઉજાણી picnic

ujaaneeno divas *n.* ઉજાણીનો દિવસ holiday

ujjad *adj.* ઉજ્જડ barren

ujjad *adj.* ઉજ્જડ bleak

ukaalavaanun motun vaasan *n.* ઉકાળવાનું મોટું વાસણ cauldron

ukaalavun *v.* ઉકાળવું boil

Ukaalvun *n.* ઉકાળવું seethe

ukalatavaalun *adj.* ઉકળાટવાળું sultry

ukalatun raakhavun *v.t.* ઉકળતું રાખવું simmer

Ukdoon besavun *v.t.* ઊકડું બેસવું squat

ukelavun *v.t.* ઉકેલવું unroll

ukele naheen tevun *adj.* ઉકેલે નહીં તેવું illegible

ukelvun *v.t.* ઉકેલવું unfold

ukhaanun *n.* ઉખાણું charade

ukhaanun *n.* ઉખાણું riddle

Ukti *n.* ઉક્તિ saying

ulaalo *n.* ઉલાળો qualm

ulataavavun *v.t.* ઉલટાવવું invert

ulemaa *n.* ઉલેમા ulema

ulka *n.* ઉલ્કા meteor

ullaas *n.* ઉલ્લાસ jollity

ullaasee *adj.* ઉલ્લાસી joyous

ullanghan *n.* ઉલ્લંઘન contravention

Ullasvaalun *adj.* ઉલ્લાસવાળું sprightly

ullekh *n.* ઉલ્લેખ allusion

Ultee karvee ke thavee *v.t.* ઊલટી કરવી કે થવી spew

umada *adj.* ઉમદા generous

umang *n.* ઉમંગ buoyancy

umaraav *n.* ઉમરાવ aristocrat

umaraav *n.* ઉમરાવ duke

umaraav *n.* ઉમરાવ nobleman

umaraav vargnee ek padavee *n.* ઉમરાવ વર્ગની એક પદવી baron

umaraavanee padavee *n.* ઉમરાવની પદવી barony

umaraavano mobho *n.* ઉમરાવનો મોભો dukedom

umaraavo *n.* ઉમરાવો peerage

umaro *n.* ઉમરો threshold

umedavaar *n.* ઉમેદવાર candidate

umeravun *v.t.* ઉમેરવું add

umerelee vastu *n.* ઉમેરેલી વસ્તુ appendage

umero, saravaalo *adj.* ઉમેરો, સરવાળો additional

ummar, vay *n.* ઉમર, વય age

un *n.* ઉન fur

un *n.* ઉન fur

Unaalo *n.* ઉનાળો summer

Unche Udvun *v.i.* ઊંચે ઊડવું soar

unche vasavaat *n.* ઊંચે વસવાટ eyrie

Unchee bethak *n.* ઊંચી બેઠક stage

Unchee jaatnun *adj.* ઊંચી જાતનું superior

unchee kakshaanun *v.t.* ઊંચી કક્ષાનું tiptop

Unchun *adj.* ઊંચું sublime

unchun karavun *v.t.* ઊંચુ કરવું uplift

undaa avaajavaalun *n.* ઊંડા અવાજવાળું tomtom

undaan *n.* ઉડાણ flight

undar *n.* ઉંદર mouse

undar *n.* ઉંદર rat

undar nee ek jaat *n.* ઉંદરની એક જાત dormouse

undardaa *n.pl.* ઉંદરડાં mice

undhun valavun *v.t.* ઊંધું વળવું capsize

Undhun valvun ke uthlaavvun te ઊંધું વાળવું કે ઉથલાવવું તે subversion

undo khaado *v.t.* ઊંડો ખાડો trench

Undo shwaas *v.i.* ઊંડો શ્વાસ sigh

Unee swetar *n.* ઊની સ્વેટર sweater

Ungh *n.* ઊંઘ sleep

Ungh laavnaarun *adj.* ઊંઘ લાવનારું somniferous

Ungh levee *n.* ઊંઘ લેવી slumber

Ungh vinaanun *adj.* ઊંઘ વિનાનું sleepless

Unghe gheraayelun *adj.* ઊંઘે ઘેરાયેલું sleepy

unghman badbadnaar vyakti *n.* ઊંઘમાં બડબડનાર વ્યક્તિ somniloquist

Unghtun maanas *n.* ઊંઘતું માણસ sleeper

unmaargagaamee *n.* ઉન્માર્ગગામી aberrance

unmatt karavun *v.t.* ઉન્મત્ત કરવું dement

unnat karavun *v.t.* ઉન્નત કરવું meliorate

unnati, pragati *n.* ઉન્નતિ, પ્રગતિ advancement

unnnat karavun *v.t.* ઉન્નત કરવું elevate

Up samiti *n.* ઉપ સમિતિ sub-committee

Up vibhaag *n.* ઉપ વિભાગ sub-division

upaadeene laee janaar *n.* ઉપાડીને લઇ જનાર carrier

upaadelu kaam *n.* ઉપાડેલું કામ undertaking

upaahaar *n.* ઉપાહાર refreshment

upaanty *adj.* ઉપાનત્ય penultimate

upabhokta *n.* ઉપભોક્તા consumer

upachaar *n.* ઉપચાર regimen

upachaar karavo *v.t.* ઉપચાર કરવો medicate

upachaarashaastra *n.* ઉપચારશાસ્ત્ર therapy

upachhaaya *n.* ઉપચ્છાયા penumbra

upadansh *n.* ઉપદંશ pox

upadesh ઉપદેશ precept

upadeshaatmak *adj.* ઉપદેશાત્મક didactic

upadrav *n.* ઉપદ્રવ mischief

upadrav karavo *v.t.* ઉપદ્રવ કરવો infest

upadrav karavo *v.t.* ઉપદ્રવ કરવો molest

upadravakaarak maanas ઉપદ્રવકારક માણસ pest

upadravakaarak vastu *n.* ઉપદ્રવકારક વસ્તુ nuisance

upadravee *adj.* ઉપદ્રવી mischievous

upagruh *n.* ઉપગૃહ outhouse

upahaas *n.* ઉપહાસ derision

upahaas *n.* ઉપહાસ ridicule

upahaas *n.* ઉપહાસ satire

upahaas karanaarun *n.* ઉપહાસ કરનારું cynical

upahrah *n.* ઉપગ્રહ satellite

upajaavee kaadhavun *v.t.* ઉપજાવી કાઢવું concoct

upajaavee kaadhavun ઉપજાવી કાઢવું fabircate

upakaar *n.* ઉપકાર benefaction

upakaar karavo *v.t.* ઉપકાર કરવો oblige

upakaarak *adj.* ઉપકારક benignant

upakar *n.* ઉપકર cess

upakaran *n.* ઉપકરણ appliance

upakrut *adj.* ઉપકૃત indebted

upakulapati *n.* ઉપકુલપતિ vice-chancellor

upalabdh *adj.* ઉપલબ્ધ available

upalabdhataa *n.* ઉપલબ્ધતા availability

upalabdhi *n.* ઉપલબ્ધિ acquirement

upalakshan *n.* ઉપલક્ષણ metonymy

upanaam *n.* ઉપનામ pseudonym

upanaam, urfe *adv.* ઉપનામ, ઉર્ફ઼ે, alias

upanaamm *n.* ઉપનામ cognomen

upanagaraadhyaksh *n.* ઉપનગરાધ્યક્ષ alderman

upa-pramukha *n.* ઉપ-પ્રમુખ vice-president

upar *prep.* ઉપર over

upar *adv.* ઉપર up

upar *adj.* ઉપર upward

upar chadaavavun *v.t.* ઉપર ચડાવવું overlay

upar chadavun *v.t.* ઉપર ચડવું climb

upar haath mookava te ઉપર હાથ મૂકવા તે imposition

upar kaap mookavo *n.* ઉપર કાપ મૂકવો incision

upar lakhavun *v.t.* ઉપર લખવું superscribe

upar prakaashavun *v.t.* ઉપર પ્રકાશવું irradiate

Upar uparthi dekhaavu *v.i.* ઉપર ઉપરથી દેખાવું seem

uparaant *adv.* ઉપરાંત besides

uparanu *adj.* ઉપરનું upper

uparanun *adv.* ઉપરનું on

uparathee padavun *n.* ઉપરથી પડવું turnover

uparathee vahevun *n.* ઉપરથી વહેવું overflow

Uparchhallu *adj.* ઉપરછલ્લું skindeep

uparee *adj.* ઉપરી senior

uparokt geet *n.* ઉપરોક્ત ગીત repertory

upasarg *n.* ઉપસર્ગ prefix

upashaamak *adj.* ઉપશામક sedative

upashaman *n.* ઉપશમન palliation

upavaash karavun *adj.* ઉપવાસ કરવો fast

upayogee *adj.* ઉપયોગી conducive

upayogee *adj.* ઉપયોગી useful

upayogee vastu *n.* ઉપયોગી વસ્તુ commodity

upayogitaa *v.t.* ઉપયોગિતા use

upayogitaa *n.* ઉપયોગિતા utility

Updeshaatmak *adj.* ઉપદેશાત્મક suasive

Updwansh garmeevalun *n.* ઉપદંશ ગરમીવાળું syphillis

upekhaneey *adj.* ઉપેક્ષણીય negligible

upekshaa *n.* ઉપેક્ષા delinquency

upekshaa *n.* ઉપેક્ષા dereliction

upekshaa karavee *v.t.* ઉપેક્ષા કરવી disregard

uphaas karavo *v.t.* ઉપહાસ કરવો satirize

uphaaskaar *n.* ઉપહાસકાર satirist

Upnagar *n.* ઉપનગર suburb

Upnagaronun *adj.* ઉપનગરોનું suburban

Upyogee *adj.* ઉપયોગી serviceable

urachhunkhal ઉરચ્છુંખલ rampant

Urdhvapaatan *n.* ઉર્ધ્વપાતન sublimation

uropane lagatu *n.* યુરોપને લગતું. european

ushkeranee *n.* ઉશ્કેરણી instigation

ushkeravavun *v.t.* ઉશ્કેરવું arouse

ushkeravun *v.t.* ઉશ્કેરવું incite

ushkeravun *v.* ઉશ્કેરવું inflame

ushkeravun *v.t.* ઉશ્કેરવું instigate

ushkeravun *v.t.* ઉશ્કેરવું provoke

ushkervun *v.t.* ઉશ્કેરવું excite

ushmeeya *adj.* ઉષ્મીય thermal

ushnakatibandh *n.* ઉષ્ણકટિબંધ tropic

ushnakatibandheeya *adj.* ઉષ્ણકટિબંધીય tropical

ushnata *n.* ઉષ્ણતા heat

ushnataa ke garameenu *adj.* ઉષ્ણતા કે ગરમીનું thermic

ushnataamaapak *n.* ઉષ્ણતામાપક thermometer

ushnataanayan *n.* ઉષ્ણતાનયન convection

ushnataano ekam *n.* ઉષ્ણતાનો એકમ caloric

ushnataano ekam *n.* ઉષ્ણતાનો એકમ calorie

ushnataavaahak nalee *n.* ઉષ્ણતાવાહક નળી flue

ustaad *n.* ઉસ્તાદ adept

utaadan karavun *v.t.* ઉત્પાદન કરવું manufacture

Utaaree paadvun *v.* ઉતારી પાડવું snub

utaaree padavun *v.t.* ઉતારી દેવું dismount

utaaro *n.* ઉતારો caravanserai

utaaru vimaan *n.* ઉતારુ વિમાન liner

utaaval *n.* ઉતાવળ haste

Utaaval *n.* ઉતાવળ speed

utaaval karavee *v.t.* ઉતાવળ કરવી buck up

utaaval karavee *v.t.* ઉતાવળ કરવી bustle

utaaval karavee *v.t.* ઉતાવળ કરવી hurry

utaavalathee bolavun te *v.i.* ઉતાવળથી બોલવું તે patter

utaavale khaavun *v.t.* ઉતાવળે ખાવું gobble

utaavaliyun *adj.* ઉતાવળિયું cursory

utaavaliyun *adj.* ઉતાવળિયું premature

utaavalo drashtikshep *n.* ઉતાવળો દ્રષ્ટિક્ષેપ glance

utaavalun *adj.* ઉતાવળું hasty

Utaavalun *adj.* ઉતાવળું swift

utakraanti *n.* ઉત્ક્રાંતિ evolution

utakrusht *adj.* ઉત્કૃષ્ટ excellent

utapataang *adj.* ઉટપટાંગ bizarre

utaratee kakshaaman mookavun *v.t.* ઉતરતી કક્ષામાં મૂકવું relegate

Utaree gayelun *adj.* ઊતરી ગયેલું stale

uthalaavee devun *v.t.* ઉથલાવી દેવું confound

uthalaavee devun *v.t.* ઉથલાવી દેવું upset

uthalaavee paadavun *n.* ઉથલાવી પાડવું overturn

uthalapaathal *n.* ઉથલપાથલ upheaval

uthalapaathala thavee *v.t.* ઉથલપાથલ થવી upheave

uthavavun *v.i.* ઉઠાવવું bear

uthavun *v.t.* ઊઠવું wake

utkanthaa dharaavavee *v.t.* ઉત્કંઠા ધરાવવી covet

utkat eechchha hovee *v.i.* ઉત્કટ ઈચ્છા હોવી yearn

utkatata *n.* ઉત્કટતા intensity

utkrushta kalaakruti *n.* ઉત્કૃષ્ટ કલાકૃતિ masterpiece

utpaadak *adj.* ઉત્પાદક productive

utpaadan *n.* ઉત્પાદન product

utpaat *n.* ઉત્પાત cataclysm

utpaat *n.* ઉત્પાત outbreak

utpann karavun *adj.* ઉત્પન્ન કરવું production

utpann thavun *v.i.* ઉત્પન્ન થવું arise

utpati *n.* ઉત્પત્તિ genesis

utprekshaa *n.* ઉત્પ્રેક્ષા conceit

utsaaah *n.* ઉત્સાહ cheer

utsaah *n.* ઉત્સાહ ardour

utsaah *n.* ઉત્સાહ enthusiasm

utsaah *adj.* ઉત્સાહ racy

utsaah *n.* ઉત્સાહ vivacity

utsaah *n.* ઉત્સાહ zeal

utsaahabharyo aavakaar *n.* ઉત્સાહભર્યો આવકાર ovation

utsaahapoorvak aalochana *v.i.* ઉત્સાહપૂર્વક આલોચના rave

utsaahee *adj.* ઉત્સાહી enthusiast

utsaahee *adj.* ઉત્સાહી hot

utsaahee *n.* ઉત્સાહી zealot

utsaahee *adj.* ઉત્સાહી zealous

utsaahee vaktaa *n.* ઉત્સાહી વક્તા rhapsodist

utsaahi *adj.* ઉત્સાહી vivacious

utsarajan *n.* ઉત્સર્જન emission

utsarjan karavun *v.t.* ઉત્સર્જન કરવું transpire

utsuk *adj.* ઉત્સુક agog

utsuk *adj.* ઉત્સુક ardent

utsuk *n.* ઉત્સુક avidity

Utsuk *n.* ઉત્સુક solicitous

utsukataa *adj.* ઉત્સુકતા avid

uttam *n.* ઉત્તમ classic

uttar dhruvapradesh *adj.* ઉત્તર ધ્રુવપ્રદેશ arctic

uttar disha *n.* ઉત્તર દિશા north

uttaraabhimukh *adj.* ઉત્તરાભિમુખ northward

uttarajeevita *n.* ઉત્તરજીવિતા survival

uttaranun *adj.* ઉત્તરનું northern

uttarjeevee *n.* ઉત્તરજીવી survivor

Uttejak *adj.* ઉત્તેજક stirring

uttejan aapavun *v.t.* ઉત્તેજન આપવું encourage

uttejanaa *n.* ઉત્તેજના excitement

uttejit *adj.* ઉત્તેજિત heated

Uttejit karvun *n.* ઉત્તેજિત કરવું stirrup

Uttejna ke sfoorti ઉત્તેજના કે સ્ફૂર્તિ stimulation

Uttejna ke sfoorti aapvee *v.t.* ઉત્તેજના કે સ્ફૂર્તિ આપવી stimulate

Uzardan paadvaa *n.* ઉઝરડાં પાડવા scratch

vaad *n.* વાડ fence

vaad *n.* વાડ fencing

vaadaaman pooravun *v.t.* વાડામાં પૂરવું impark

vaadakavrund *n.* વાદકવૃંદ orchestra

vaadalaanthee chhavaayelun *adj.* વાદળાંથી છવાયેલું cloudy

vaadalaanthee dhankaayelun *v.t.* વાદળાંથી ઢંકાયેલું overcast

vaadalaathee chhavaayelun *adj.* વાદળાથી છવાયેલું gray

vaadalee *n.* વાદળી sponge

vaadalee ekatra karanaar *n.* વાદળી એકત્ર કરનાર sponger

vaadalee fulovaalo ek velo *n.* વાદળી ફૂલવાળો એક વેલો bugle

vaadalee rang *n.* વાદળી રંગ blue

vaadalun *n.* વાદળું cloud

vaadavivaad *n.* વાદવિવાદ controversy

vaadharee *n.* વાધરી thong

vaadhavun *v.t.* વાઢવું hew

vaadhavun *v.t.* વાઢવું shear

vaado *n.* વાડો encloseure

vaadya vagaadanaar *n.* વાદ્ય વગાડનાર fiddler

vaaee *adj.* વાઈ fit

vaaee *n.* વાઈ hysteria

vaagdatta *n.* વાગ્દત્તા fiance

vaagh *n.* વાઘ tiger

vaagolavaanee kriya *n.* વાગોળવાની ક્રિયા rumination

vaagolavun *v.t.* વાગોળવું munch

vaagolavun *v.t.* વાગોળવું ruminate

vaagolavun te *n.* વાગોળવું તે cud

vaahan *n.* વાહન vehicle

vaahanachaalak *n.* વાહનચાલક driver

vaahananee paachaalnee bethak *n.* વાહનની પાછળની બેઠક pillion

vaahava *n.* વાહવા plaudit

vaahiyaat *n.* વાહિયાત drivel

vaahiyaat vaat *v.t.* વાહિયાત વાત blether

vaahiyaat vaat *n.* વાહિયાત વાત bosh

vaai *n.* વાઈ epilepsy

vaaisaroyanun *adj.* વાઈસરોયનું viceregal

vaajaanee petee *n.* વાજાની પેટી harmonium

vaajabee *adj.* વાજબી equitable

vaajabee *adj.* વાજબી just

vaajabee tharaavavun *v.t.* વાજબી ઠરાવવું aver

vaajabeepanun વાજબીપણું justification

vaajintrno taar *n.* વાજિંત્રનો તાર catgut

vaakachhal *n.* વાકછળ quirk

vaakapatutaa *adj.* વાકપટુતા eloquent

Vaakya *n.* વાક્ય sentence

Vaakyarachnaa ke tenaa niyamo *adj.* વાક્યરચના કે તેના નિયમો synthetic

vaal *n.* વાળ hair

vaal jevee vastuvaalun *adj.* વાળ જેવી વસ્તુવાળું hairy

Vaal utaarva *v.t.* વાળ ઉતારવા shave

vaal vagaranu *n.* વાળ વગરનું depilation

vaalanee lat *n.* વાળની લટ lock

vaalanee lat *n.* વાળની લટ tress

vaaleepanun *n.* વાલીપણું tutelage

vaalo tantu *n.* વાળો તંતુ tendril

Vaalun karvun *v.t.* વાળું કરવું sup

vaaman *n.* વામન dwarf

vaanchan *n.* વાંચન reading

vaanchanapothee *n.* વાંચનપોથી reader

vaanchavano shokheen *adj.* વાંચનનો શોખીન bookish

vaandara jevu praanee *n.* વાંદરાં જેવું પૂરાણી ape

vaandaro *n.* વાંદરો monkey

vaandhaabharelun *adj.* વાંધાભરેલું objectionable

vaandhaabharelun *adj.* વાંધાભરેલું obnoxious

vaandhaspad *adj.* વાંધાસ્પદ exceptionable

vaandho *n.* વાંધો objection

vaandho વાંધો remonstrance

vaandho uthaavavo *v.t.* વાંધો ઉઠાવવો impugn

vaandho uthaavavo *v.t.* વાંધો ઉઠાવવો protest

vaandho uthaavavo *v.i.* વાંધો ઉઠાવવો remonstrate

vaandho uthaavavo te *v.i.* વાંધો ઉઠાવવો તે demur

vaando *n.* વાંદો beetle

vaaneeman ati chokhaliyun *n.* વાણીમાં અતિચોખલિયું prude

vaaneenun *adj.* વાણીનું lingual

vaanijya dootaavaas *n.* વાણિજ્ય-દૂતાવાસ consulate

vaanijyik *n.* વાણિજ્યકિ commerce

vaankavalaankavaalee aakruti *n.* વાંકવળાંકવાળી આકૃત curvature

vaankochuko rasto *n.* વાંકોચુકો રસ્તો meander

vaanku karavun *n.* વાંકું કરવું bend

vaanku karavun *v.i.* વાંકું કરવું crook

Vaanku Valvu *v.* વાંકું વળવું sag

vaankun *adj.* વાંકું crooked

vaankun *adj.* વાંકું transverse

vaankunchookun *adj.* વાંકુંચૂકું zigzag

vaankunchukun *adj.* વાંકુંચૂકું awry

vaankvaalun paatiyun *n.* વાંકવાળું પાટિયું stave

vaano *n.* વાણો weft

vaans *n.* વાંસ bamboo

vaansaanu ke tene lagatun *adj.* વાંસાનું કે તેને લગતું tergal

vaansadee *n.* વાંસળી flute

vaansalee jevun vaady *n.* વાંસળી જેવું વાદ્ય pipe

vaansanee *n.* વાંસળી fife

Vaanziyun *n.* વાંઝિયું sterility

vaaparavaanee reet *n.* વાપરવાની રીત usage

vaaparee naakhavun *v.t.* વાપરી નાખવું consume

vaar *n.* વાર yard

vaaraafaratee karanaarun *adj.* વારાફરતી કરનારું rotary

vaaraafarati thatun *adj.* વારાફરતી થતું alternate

vaaramavaar thatu *adj.* વારંવાર થતું frequent

vaaramvaar *n.* વારંવાર time-bar

vaaramvaar વારંવાર unfrequented

vaaranvaar *adv.* વારંવાર often

vaaranvaar વારંવાર repeatedly

vaaranvaar thatun *n.* વારંવાર થતું incessant

vaaras *n.* વારસ heir

Vaaras *n.* વારસ successor

vaarasaamaa avavun *v.t.* વારસામાં આવવું devolve

vaarasaaman malavun *v.t.* વારસામાં મળવું inherit

vaarasahak lai levo *v.t.* વારસહક લઈ લેવો. disinherit

vaaraso *n.* વરસો bequest

vaaraso *n.* વારસો. legacy

vaaraso *n.* વારસો patrimony

vaaro *n.* વારો innings

vaarshik *adj.* વાર્ષિક annual

vaarshik *adj.* વાર્ષિક yearly

vaarshik aavak *n.* વાર્ષિક આવક revenue

vaarshik panchhang *n.* વાર્ષિક પંચાંગ almanac

vaarshikee melavanaar *n.* વર્ષાસન મેળવનાર annuitant

vaartaalaap *n.* વાર્તાલાપ conversation

vaartaalaap *n.* વાર્તાલાપ discourse

vaartaana roopanun *adj.* વાર્તાના રૂપનું narrative

vaartaao kahenaar *n.* વાર્તાઓ કહેનાર tonguester

vaasan *n.* વાસણ pot

vaasantik *adj.* વાસંતિક vernal

vaastavalakshee *adj.* વાસ્તવલક્ષી realistic

vaastavavaad *n.* વાસ્તવવાદ realism

vaastavik *adj.* વાસ્તવિક concrete

vaastavik *adj.* વાસ્તવિક objective

vaastavik *adj.* વાસ્તવિક real

vaastavik *adj.* વાસ્તવિક tangible

vaastavik pan hakeekatamaa nhi *adj.* વાસ્તવિક પણ હકીકતમાં નહિ virtual

vaastavikata *n.* વાસ્તવિકતા reality

vaastavikpane, kharekhar *adj.* વાસ્તવિકપણે, ખરેખર actually

vaastushilp *n.* વાસ્તુશિલ્પ, architecture

vaat udaavavee *v.t.* વાત ઉડાવવી palter

vaata paadava *v.t.* વાટા પાડવા corrugate

vaataaghaat *n.* વાટાઘાટ negotiation

vaataaghaat karavee *v.t.* વાટાઘાટ કરવી negotiate

vaataaghaatpaatra *adj.* વાટાઘાટપાત્ર negotiable

vaataavaran *n.* વાતાવરણ atmosphere

vaataavaran *n.* વાતાવરણ environment

vaataavaranne lagatun *adj.* વાતાવરણને લગતું atmospheric

vaatacheet karavee *v.i.* વાતચીત કરવી converse

vaatako *n.* વાટકો bowl

vaatodiyo *n.* વાતોડિયો quidnunc

vaatodiyu *adj.* વાતોડિયું talkative

vaatodiyun *adj.* વાતોડિયું garrulous

vaatodiyun *n.* વાતોડિયું loquacious

vaavaajhodun *n.* વાવાઝોડું hurricane

vaavaazodun *n.* વાવાઝોડું tempest

vaavantol *n.* વાવંટોળ whirlwind

vaavantolavaalun *adj.* વાવંટોળવાળું windy

vaavato *n.* વાવટો banner

vaayolaano chood *n.* વાયોલાનો છોડ viola

vaayolin *n.* વાયોલિન fiddle

vaayolin *n.* વાયોલિન violin

vaayolin vagaadanaar *n.* વાયોલિન વગાડનાર violinist

vaayu *n.* વાયુ gas

vaayu pratibandhak *adj.* વાયુ પ્રતિબંધક airtight

Vaayudevtaa *n.* વાયુદેવતા sylph

vaayuroop, halakun *adj.* વાયુરૂપ, હલકું aeriform

vaayushaastra *n.* વાયુશાસ્ત્ર pneumatics

vaayuvishayak *adj.* વાયુવિષયિક aerial

vaayuyukt, vaayumishrit *adj.* વાયુયુક્ત, વાયુમિશ્રિત aerated

vachagaalaano samay *adv.* વચગાળાનો સમય meantime

vachalun *adj.* વચલું mid

vachaman *prep.* વચમાં amid

vachan *n.* વચન promise

vachanavaalun *adj.* વચનવાળું promissory

vachche *prep.* વચ્ચે between

vachche aavanaar (vastu) *adj.* વચ્ચે આવનાર (વસ્તુ) intermediate

vachhavaanaagano chhod *n.* વછનાગનો છોડ aconite

vachheree *n.* વછેરી filly

vachhero વછેરો colt

vadagan door karavun *v.t.* વળગણ દૂર કરવું disencumber

vadeelopaarjit *adj.* વડીલોપાર્જિત ancestra

vadhaaraamaan *adv.* વધારામાં too

Vadhaaraano bojo *v.t.* વધારાનો બોજો surcharge

Vadhaaraano kar *n.* વધારાનો કર surtax

vadhaaraanu *adj.* વધારાનું extra

vadhaaraanun *adj.* વધારાનું accessory

Vadhaaraanun maanas *adj.* વધારાનું માણસ super

Vadhaaranu *adj.* વધારાનું supplementary

vadhaaravun *v.t.* વધારવું augment

vadhaare *adj.* વધારે more

vadhaare bhaare hovun *v.i.* વધારે ભારે હોવું preponderate

vadhaare door *adj.* વધારે દૂર farther

vadhaare padatu *adj.* વધારે પડતું excessive

vadhaare padtu *adj.* વધારે પડતું undue

vadhaare padtun *adv.* વધારે પડતું unduly

vadhaare pramaanaman *adv.* વધારે પ્રમાણમાં increasingly

vadhaaro *n.* વધારો accession

vadhaaro *n.* વધારો increment

Vadhaaro *n.* વધારો supplement

vadhaarvun *v.t.* વધારવું enhance

vadhaavavun *v.* વધાવવું acclaim

vadhaavavun *v.* વધાવવું applaud

vadhakanee stree *adj.* વઢકણી સ્ત્રી termagant

vadhastanbh *n.* વધસ્તંભ cross

vadhastanbh *n.* વધસ્તંભ gibbet

vadhavun *v.t.* વધવું increase

vadhavun *n.* વઢવું reproach

Vadhknun *adj.* વઢકણું shrewish

vadhoono poshaak *n.* વધૂનો પોશાક trousseau

vadhu eechchhava yogy *adj.* વધુ ઈચ્છવા યોગ્ય preferable

vadhu jeevavun *v.t.* વધુ જીવવું outlive

vadhu kharaab વધુ ખરાબ worse

vadhu padatee kinmat *v.t.* વધુ પડતી કિંમત overcharge

vadhu padato bhaar *v.t.* વધુ પડતો ભાર overburden

vadhu padato upaad *v.t.* વધુ પડતો ઉપાડ overdraw

vadhu saachun kaheee to *adv.* વધુ સાચું કહીએ તો rather

vadhuma *adv.* વધુમાં further

vadhuman *prep.* વધુમાં withal

Vadhvaa maandvun *n.* વધવા માંડવું sprout

Vadhvun *v.i.* વધવું swell

vadnu jhaad *n.* વડનું ઝાડ banyan

vafaadaar *adj.* વફાદાર faithful

vafaadaar *adj.* વફાદાર staunch

vafaadaar *n.* વફાદાર trusty

vafaadaaree *n.* વફાદારી fealty

vafaadaaree *n.* વફાદારી fidelity

vafaadaaree *n.* વફાદારી troth

vafaadaari, rajya neeshtha *n.* વફાદારી, રાજ્ય નિષ્ઠા allegiance

vagadaar *adj.* વગદાર influential

vagar *adv.* વગર without

vagere *adj.* વગેરે etcetera

vahaal karavun *n.* વહાલ કરવું endearment

vahaalu *adv.* વહાલું dearly

vahaalun maanas *n.* વહાલું માણસ minikin

Vahaan *n.* વહાણ ship

vahaan *n.* વહાણ vessel

Vahaan e no. sukaanee *n.* વહાણ ઈ.નો સુકાની steersman

vahaanamaa chadaavavun *v.t.* વહાણમાં ચડાવવું embark

vahaanano moro *n.* વહાણનો મોરો prow

vahaanano veemo utaaranaar *n.* વહાણનો વીમો ઉતારનાર underwriter

vahaananun sukaan *n.* વહાણનું સુકાન rudder

Vahaanmaa musaafaree *n.* વહાણમાં મુસાફરી sailing

Vahaanna badhaa sadh *v.t.* વહાણનાં બધાં સઢ sail

vahaanvatun *n.* વહાણવટું shipping

vaheevatakartaa *n.* વહીવટકર્તા executor

vaheevatee vibhaag વહીવટી વિભાગ division

vahel maachhalee *n.* વહેલ માછલી whale

vaheliyun *n.* વહેળિયું rill

vahelo nirnay karavo *v.t.* વહેલો નિર્ણય કરવો prejudge

Vahemee *adj.* વહેમી superstitious

vahenchanee *n.* વહેંચણી distribution

vahenchanee *n.* વહેંચણી raffle

vahenchavun *v.t.* વહેંચવું dispense

vahenchavun *v.* વહેંચવુ distribute

vahenchee aapavun *v.t.* વહેંચી આપવું mete

vahetu *adj.* વહેતું effusive

Vahetun bandh hovun ke thavun *v.i.* વહેતું બંધ હોવું કે થવું stagnate

vahetun bandh karavun *adj.* વહેતું બંધ કરવું stanch

Vahetun nahi evun *adj.* વહેતું નહિ એવું stagnant

vahevaar *n.* વહેવાર relationship

vahevaaranee drashtithee *adv.* વહેવારની દૃષ્ટિથી practically

vahevaarun *n.* વહેવારું practicable

vahevun *v.i.* વહેવું flow

vahevun *v.* વહેવું pour

vahivat karavo *v.t.* વહિવટ કરવો administer

vahughelo *adj.* વહુઘેલો uxorious

vaibhav *n.* વૈભવ pomp

Vaibhav *adj.* વૈભવ splendour

vaibhavashaalee *adj.* વૈભવશાળી princely

vaid *n.* વૈદ physician

vaidak *n.* વૈદક physic

vaidakanun *adj.* વૈદકનું medical

vaidyakeey *n.* વૈદ્યકીય practitioner

vaigyaanik *adj.* વૈજ્ઞાનિક scientific

vaikalpik *adj.* વૈકલ્પિક optional

vaimaanik *n.* વૈમાનિક aviator

vaishveek *adj.* વૈશ્વીક cosmic

vaitaru, tootel chhedo *v.t.* વૈતરું તૂટેલ છેડો. fag

vaitarun *adj.* વૈતરું toilsome

vaitarun karavun *v.t.* વૈતરું કરવું moil

Vaitro *n.* વૈતરો serf

vaivaahik *adj.* વૈવાહિક conjugal

vaivaahik *adj.* વૈવાહિક connubial

vaivaahik *adj.* વૈવાહિક marital

vaividhyaheenataa *n.* વૈવિધ્યહીનતા monotony

vaividhyavaalun *adj.* વૈવિધ્યવાળું multifarious

vajan *n.* વજન weight

vajan karavun *v.t.* વજન કરવું weigh

vajanadaar *adj.* વજનદાર massy

vajanadaar *adj.* વજનદાર ponderous

vajanama vadhavun *v.t.* વજનમાં વધવું outweigh

vajankaanto વજનકાંટો steelyard

vakaro *n.* વકરો proceeds

vakatratva *n.* વક્તૃત્વ elocution

vakatratva *n.* વક્તૃત્વ eloquence

vakatrutvakala *n.* વક્તૃત્વકળા oratory

vakatrutvakalaavaan *n.* વક્તૃત્વકળાવાન elocutionist

vakeel *n.* વકીલ counsel

vakeel *n.* વકીલ lawyer

vakeel *n.* વકીલ pleader

vakeel *n.* વકીલ prosecutor

vakeel *n.* વકીલ solicitor

vakhaan - karava *v.t.* વખાણ – કરવા laud

vakhaan karavan *v.t.* વખાણ કરવાં praise

vakhaanava jog *adj.* વખાણવા જોગ praiseworthy

vakhaanavaalaayak *adj.* વખાણવાલાયક laudable

vakhaanavun *v.t.* વખાણવું admire

vakhaar *n.* વખાર depot

vakhaar *n.* વખાર godown

vakhaar *n.* વખાર warehouse

vakhatasar *adv.* વખતસર betimes

vakhatasar *adv.* વખતસર duly

vakhodavun *v.t.* વખોડવું condemn

vakhodavun *v.t.* વખોડવું decry

vakhodavun *v.t.* વખોડવું vituperate

vakhodee kaadhavun *v.* વખોડી કાઢવું deprecate

vakreebhavan karavun *v.t.* વક્રીભવન કરવું refract

vakrokti *n.* વક્રોક્તિ irony

vakshahsthal *n.* વક્ષ:સ્થલ thorax

vakta *n.* વક્તા orator

Vakyarachna ke tena niymo *n.* વાક્યરચના કે તેના નિયમો syntax

valaank *n.* વળાંક flexure

valaank devo *v.t.* વળાંક દેવો curve

valaavavun *v.t.* વળાવવું accompany

valaavavun *v.t.* વળાવવું escort

valaganamaathee mukti *v.t.* વળગણમાંથી મુક્તિ exorcize

valagavun *v.t.* વળગવું haunt

valagavun *v.t.* વળગવું obsess

valagee rahevun *v.t.* વળગી રહેવું adhere

valagee rahevun *v.t.* વળગી રહેવું cling

valan *n.* વલણ attitude

valan *n.* વલણ bent

valan *n.* વલણ inclination

valan *n.* વલણ leaning

valan વલણ propensity

valan feravavun *v.* વલણ ફેરવવું advert

valan hovun *v.t.* વલણ હોવું lean

valatar *n.* વળતર compensation

valatar *n.* વળતર recompense

valatar aapavun *v.t.* વળતર આપવું compensate

valatar, bhaththun *n.* વળતર, ભથ્થું allowance

valavun *v.t.* વળવું crouch

Vale nahi evun *adj.* વળી નહિ એવું stiff

valkenaaizanee prakriyaa *n.* વલ્કેનાઈઝની પ્રક્રિયા ebonite

valovavun *v.t.* વલોવવું churn

vamal *n.* વમળ eddy

vamal *n.* વમળ vortex

vamal *n.* વમળ whirlpool

van *n.* વન. jungle

vanaat *n.* વણાટ texture

vanaatanu *adj.* વણાટનું textile

vanakar *n.* વણકર weaver

vanaparee *n.* વનપરી dryad

vanaspatee srushtee *n.* વનસ્પતિસૃષ્ટી flora

vanaspatine lagatun *adj.* વનસ્પતિને લગતું floral

vanaspatino beejakosh *n.* વનસ્પતિનો બીજકોષ capsule

vanaspatino ek rog *v.t.* વનસ્પતિનો એક રોગ blight

vanaspatino rop *n.* વનસ્પતિનો રોપ plant

vanaspatishaastra *n.* વનસ્પતિશાસ્ત્ર botany

vanaspatishaastree *n.* વનસ્પતિશાસ્ત્રી botanist

vanaspti srushti *n.* વનસ્પતિ સૃષ્ટિ vegetation

vanavaano sancho *n.* વણવાનો સંચો loom

vanavun *v.t.* વણવું weave

vanchit *n.* વંચતિ bereavement

vanchit raakhavun *v.* વંચતિ રાખવું deprive

vando *n.* વંદો cockroach

Vankarno kanthlo *n.* વણકરનો કાંઠલો shuttle

vanmaagee *adj.* વણમાગી uncalled

Vannun *adj.* વનનું sylvan

vansh *n.* વંશ dynasty

vansh *n.* વંશ kin

vansh *n.* વંશ lineage
vansh jaatinun *adj.* વંશ જાતનું racial
vanshaanukram *n.* વંશાનુક્રમ filiation
vanshaavalee વંશાવળી genealogy
vanshaavalee *n.* વંશાવળી pedigree
vanshaj *n.* વંશજ descendant
vanshajo *n.* વંશજો posterity
vanshaparanparaagat *adj.* વંશપરંપરાગત lineal
vanshaparanparaathee malatun *adj.* વંશપરંપરાથી મળતું hereditary
vanshavruddhi karavee *v.t.* વંશવૃદ્ધિ કરવી breed
vanspati *n.* વનસ્પતિ vegetable
vantaree *n.* વંતરી beldam
vantol *n.* વંટોળ tornado
Vantoliyo *v.i.* વંટોળિયો swirl
vantoliyo *n.* વંટોળિયો typhoon
Vanvaalun *adj.* વનવાળું silvan
vaparaash *n.* વપરાશ consumption
vapraash vinaanun *adj.* વપરાશ વિનાનું unemployed
Varaal *n.* વરાળ steam
varaal *n.* વરાળ vapour
varaalanaa rupanu *adj.* વરાળના રૂપ vaporous
varaghodo *n.* વરઘોડો. procession
varakh *v.t.* વરખ foil
varanaagiyo *n.* વરણાગિયો. dandy
varanaagiyo *n.* વરણાગિયો. macaroni
varanaagiyo maanas *n.* વરણાગિયો માણસ coxcomb
varanavavun *v.t.* વરણવવું narrate
varasaad *n.* વરસાદ rain
varasaad *n.* વરસાદ rainfall
varasaadanun *adj.* વરસાદનું pluvial
varasaadee *adj.* વરસાદી showery
varasavun *v.t.* વરસવું shower
varchasv *n.* વર્ચસ્વ mastery
varchasva *n.* વર્ચસ્વ ascendancy
varchasva dharaavatu *v.t.* વર્ચસ્વ ધરાવવું dominate
varchasvavaalu *adj.* વર્ચસ્વવાળું dominant
varchasvavaalun *adj.* વર્ચસ્વવાળું commanding
varg *n.* વર્ગ category

varga *n.* વર્ગ class
vargasameekaran *adj.* વર્ગસમીકરણ quadratic
vargeekaran karavun *v.t.* વર્ગીકરણ કરવું classify
varnaatmak *adj.* વર્ણનાત્મક descriptive
varnan *adj.* વર્ણન description
varnan *n.* વર્ણન narration
varnan karavun *v.t.* વર્ણન કરવું depict
varnan karavun *v.t.* વર્ણન કરવું describe
varnapatta *n.* વર્ણપટ્ટ spectrum
varnasagaaee વર્ણસગાઈ alliteration
varnasankar *adj.* વર્ણસંકર hybrid
varnasankar santaan *n.* વર્ણસંકર સંતાન mule
varsh *n.* વર્ષ year
varshaamaapak yantr *n.* વર્ષામાપક યંત્ર raingauge
varshaamaapak yantra *n.* વર્ષામાપક યંત્ર udometer
varshaanusaar, eetihaasakaar *n.* વર્ષાનુસાર, ઇતિહાસકાર annalist
varshaasan, vaarshikee *n.* વાર્ષિકી annuity
varshamaan bevaar વર્ષમાં બેવાર bi-annual
vartamaan patr *n.* વર્તમાન પત્ર newspaper
vartan *v.t.* વર્તન conduct
vartanook *n.* વર્તણૂક proceeding
vartavun *v.i.* વર્તવું behave
vartul *n.* વર્તુળ circle
vartulaakaar binb *n.* વર્તુળાકાર બિંબ orb
varu *n.* વરુ wolf
vasaahat *n.* વસાહત colony
vasaahat sthaapavee *v.* વસાહત સ્થાપવી colonize
vasaahataman vasanaar *n.* વસાહતમાં વસનાર colonist
vasaahatee *n.* વસાહતી settler
vasantrootu *n.* વસંતઋતુ spring
vasavaat yodya *n.* વસવાટ યોગ્ય habitable

vasavun *v.t.* વસવું inhabit

vasheekaran *n.* વશીકરણ bewitchment

vasheekaran *n.* વશીકરણ philter

vashmaa karee shakaato *adj.* વશમાં કરી શકાતો tamable

vasiyatanaama dvaara aapavun *v.t.* વસિયતનામા દ્વારા આપવું bequeath

vasiyatanaamu banaavanaar *n.* વસિયતનામું બનાવનાર devisor

vasoolaat *n.* વસૂલાત recovery

vastee ganataree *n.* વસતી ગણતરી census

vastee ghataadavee *v.t.* વસતી ઘટાડવી depopulate

vasteenun pramaan *n.* વસતીનું પ્રમાણ population

vastr *n.* વસ્ત્ર garment

vastra *n.* વસ્ત્ર vestment

vastra paheravan *v.t.* વસ્ત્ર પહેરવાં clothe

vastraaharan *n.* વસ્ત્રાહરણ denudation

vastraheen *adj.* વસ્ત્રહીન bare

vastraheen *adj.* વસ્ત્રહીન naked

vastraheen *adj.* વસ્ત્રહીન nude

vastrayukt *p.p.* વસ્ત્રયુક્ત clad

vastro *n.* વસ્ત્રો apparel

vastusthiti jotan વસ્તુસ્થિતિ જોતાં whereas

vasulaatpaatra *adj.* વસૂલાતપાત્ર recoverable

vataana *n.* વટાણા legume

vataano *n.* વટાણો pea

vataavavun *n.* વટાવવું encashment

vataavee javun *v.t.* વટાવી જવું exceed

vatahukam *n.* વટહુકમ ordinance

vatalaayelo *n.* વટલાયેલો proselyte

vatemaargu *n.* વટેમાર્ગુ passer

vati *n.* વતી behalf

vayovruddh *adj.* વયોવૃદ્ધ old

vechaan *n.* વેચાણ sale

vechaan maateno maal *n.* વેચાણ માટેનો માલ ware

vechaan parvaano levo *v.t.* વેચાણ પરવાનો લેવો enfranchise

vechaanakartaa *n.* વેચાણકર્તા salesman

vechaanayogy *adj.* વેચાણયોગ્ય marketable

vechavun વેચવું vend

vechee devun *v.t.* વેચી દેવું dispose of

Vechvaa laayak, *adj.* વેચવા લાયક salable

Vechvun *v.t.* વેચવું sell

vedhashaala *n.* વેધશાળા observatory

vedho વેઢો knuckle

Vednaathee peedit *n.* વેદનાથી પીડિત sore

veejalee *n.* વીજળી electricity

veejalee dvaaraa mot *n.* વીજળી દ્વારા મોત electrocution

veejaleek *n.* વીજળીક electrical

veejaleena dabaananun maap *n.* વીજળીના દબાણનું માપ voltage

veejanee padavee *n.* વીજળી પડવી thunderbolt

veejaneeno kadaako *v.i.* વીજળીનો કડાકો thunder

Veejleenaa taar *n.* વીજળીના તાર switch

veelin *adj.* વિલીન evanescent

veemo *n.* વીમો insurance

veemo utaraavavo *v.t.* વીમો ઉતરાવવો insure

veena *n.* વીણા harp

veenaataar *n.* વીણાતાર chord

veenanti karavee *v.* વિનંતિ કરવી accost

veenash *n.* વિનાશ destruction

veenchhaalavun *v.t.* વીંછળવું rinse

Veenchhee *n.* વીંછી scorpion

Veendhvun *v.t.* વીંધવું stick

veenee kaadhavun te *v.t.* વીણી કાઢવું તે cull

veenee kaadhavun te *v.t.* વીણી કાઢવું તે pick

veenjhavun *v.i.* વીંઝવું brandish

veentadaai javun *v.t.* વીંટળાઈ જવુ entwine

veentalaaee javun *v.t.* વીંટળાઈ જવું intertwine

veentavun *v.t.* વીંટવું envelop

veentavun *v.t.* વીંટવું enwrap

veentavun *adj.* વીંટવું winding

veentavun *v.t.* વીંટવું wrap

veentee *n.* વીંટી ring
Veentee lenaarun *n.* વીંટી લેનારું surroundings
veento *n.* વીંટો twine
veeparyaay *n.* વિપર્યાય antonym
veerata *n.* વીરતા prowess
veerodh, pratipakshata *n.* વિરોધ, પ્રતિપક્ષતા antithesis
veerodhee, dushmanaavat *adj.* વિરોધ, દુશ્મનાવટ antagonistic
Veerya *n.* વીર્ય semen
veerya sanbandhee *adj.* વીર્ય સંબંધી seminal
veeryaheen *adj.* વીર્યહીન impotent
veesa *n.* વીસ twenty
veesamu *adj.* વીસમું, twentieth
veesel praanee *n.* વીસેલ પ્રાણી weasel
veeshee *n.* વીશી tavern
veesheevaalo *n.* વીશીવાળો innkeeper
veetavun *v.t.* વીતવું elapse
veetee gayelun *adv.* વીતી ગયેલું past
vefar *n.* વેફર wafer
veg *n.* વેગ velocity
vegeelo ghodo *n.* વેગીલો ઘોડો courser
vegeelun *adj.* વેગીલું rapid
velaa jevee vanaspati *n.* વેલા જેવી વનસ્પતિ trailer
velan *n.* વેલણ roller
velo *n.* વેલો creeper
velo *n.* વેલો ivy
ventiletar *n.* વેન્ટિલેટર ventilator
vepaar *v.i.* વેપાર traffic
vepaar karanaarun *adj.* વેપાર કરનારું mercantile
vepaaranee cheejavastuo *n.* વેપારની ચીજવસ્તુઓ merchandize
vepaaree *n.* વેપારી dealer
vepaaree *n.* વેપારી merchant
vepaaree *n.* વેપારી trader
Vepaaree pedheenun bhandol *n.* વેપારી પેઢીનું ભંડોળ stock
ver *n.* વેર enmity
ver *n.* વેર retaliation
ver *n.* વેર vengeance
ver levanee vruttivalun *adj.* વેર લેવાની વૃત્તિવાળું vindicative
ver vaalavun *v.t.* વેર વાળવું avenge

ver vaalavun *v.t.* વેર વાળવું retaliate
ver vikher thayelu *n.* વેર વિખ્િર થયેલું diffusion
ver, shatruta *n.* વેર, શત્રુતા animosity
vera *n.* વેર vedetta
Veraai javun *v.i.* વેરાઈ જવું straggle
veraan *v.t.* વેરાન desolate
veraan *n.* વેરાન desolation
Veraan *adv.* વેરાન stark
veraan karavun *v.* વેરાન કરવું devastate
veraan karavun te *n.* વેરાન કરવું તે devastation
verane lagatun *adj.* વેરને લગતું retaliative
veranee vasoolaat *v.t.* વેરની વસૂલાત revenge
veravikher karavun *v.t.* વેરવિખ્િર કરવું dismantle
veravun *v.t.* વેરવું strew
vero *n.* વેરો impost
vero *n.* વેરો toll
vesalin *n.* વૅસલિન vaseline
vesh *n.* વેશ guise
vesh palatavo *v.t.* વેષ પલટવો disguise
veshadhaaree *adj.* વેષધારી hypocrite
veshadhaaree *n.* વેશધારી incognito
veshadhaaree *n.* વેષધારી pretender
veshya *n.* વેશ્યા bawd
veshya વેશ્યા prostitute
veshya *n.* વેશ્યા whore
veshyaa *n.* વેશ્યા streetwalker
Veshyaa *n.* વેશ્યા strumpet
veshyaagruh *n.* વેશ્યાગૃહ brothel
veshyaavruti *n.* વેશ્યાવૃત્તિ prostitution
vetana n chookavelun *adj.* વેતન ન ચૂકવેલું unpaid
veth utaaravee *v.t.* વેઠ ઉતારવી potter
vetiyu *n.* વેતિયું elf
vevalun *adj.* વેવલું maudlin
veveeshaal karavun *n.* વેવિશાળ કરવું affiance
vibhaag *n.* વિભાગ department
vibhaagano vado *n.* વિભાગનો વડો. dean
vibhaagikaran *v.t.* વિભાગીકરણ ramify
vibhaajan *n.* વિભાજન ramification
vibhaajan *n.* વિભાજન segregation

vibhaajan *n.* વિભાજન separation

vibhaajan karavun *v.t.* વિભાજન કરવું segregate

vibhaajya *adj.* વિભાજ્ય separable

vibhaavana *n.* વિભાવના. concept

vibhaktee roopaakhyaan *n.* વિભક્તિ રૂપાખ્યાન declension

vibhakti pratyay *n.* વિભક્તિ પ્રત્યય inflection

Vichaar *v.t.* વિચાર suggest

Vichaar karaave evun *n.* વિચાર કરાવે એવું solemnity

vichaar karava jevee baabat *n.* વિચાર કરવા જેવી બાબત consideration

vichaara karavo te *n.* વિચાર કરવો તે thought

vichaarak *n.* વિચારક thinker

vichaaranaa maate mukavun *v.t.* વિચારણા માટે મૂકવું propound

vichaaraneeya *adj.* વિચારણીય considerable

vichaaravun *v.t.* વિચારવું think

vichaaree *adj.* વિચારી thoughtful

vichaaree kaadhavun *v.t.* વિચારી કાઢવું devise

vichaarpoorvak *adj.* વિચારપૂર્વક solemn

Vichaarsheel *adj.* વિચારશીલ serious

Vichakshan *adj.* વિચક્ષણ shrewd

vichchhedan *n.* વિચ્છેદન severance

vichitr *adj.* વિચિત્ર. peculiar

vichitr *adj.* વિચિત્ર queer

vichitra *adj.* વિચિત્ર exotic

vichitrata *n.* વિચિત્રતા oddity

vidaay *n.* વિદાય departure

vidaay *n.* વિદાય exit

vidaay *n.* વિદાય farewell

Vidaay *n.* વિદાય send off

vidaay *n.* વિદાય vale

vidaayavachan, saahebajee ! *n.* વિદાયવચન, સાહેબજી ! bye-bye

vidaayvelaani salaam *n.* વિદાયવેળાની સલામ adieu

videshee *n.* વિદેશી foreigner

videshee thaanu *n.* વિદેશી થાણું enclave

vidhava *n.* વિધવા widow

vidhavaa *n.* વિધવા dowager

vidhavaadaay *n.* વિધિવાદાય dower

vidhavaavastha *n.* વિધિવાવસ્થા, widowhood

vidhi *n.* વિધિ ceremony

vidhipoorvak ujavanee *v.t.* વિધિપૂર્વક ઉજવણી solemnize

vidhipoorvakanu *adj.* વિધિપૂર્વકનું formal

vidhipoorvakanun *adj.* વિધિપૂર્વકનું rituals

vidhisarnee mulaakaat *n.* વિધિસરની મુલાકાત visitation

vidhnaroope aavavun *n.* વિધ્નરૂપે આવવું supervention

vidhur *n.* વિધુર widower

Vidhvaan mahaapandit *n.* વિદ્વાન મહાપંડિત scholar

vidhvans *n.* વિધ્વંસ vandal

Vidhvansak *adj.* વિધ્વંસક subversive

Vidhvtaa *n.* વિદ્વતા scholarship

Vidhvtaabharyu *adj.* વિદ્વતાભર્યુ scholarly

Vidhyaabhyaas *n.* વિદ્યાભ્યાસ study

Vidhyaarthee *n.* વિદ્યાર્થી student

Vidhyaartheenu Daftar *n.* વિદ્યાર્થીનું દફ્તર satchel

vidhytikaran *v.t.* વિદ્યુતકિરણ electrify

vidooshak *n.* વિદૂષક clown

vidooshak *n.* વિદૂષક jester

vidooshak vedaa વિદૂષક વેડા buffoonery

vidroh *n.* વિદ્રોહ putsch

vidushakanee laakadee *n.* વિદૂષકની લાકડી bauble

vidushee *n.* વિદૂષી blue-stocking

vidvaan *adj.* વિદ્વાન learned

vidyaapeethano kulapatee *n.* વિદ્યાપીઠનો કુલપતિ chancellor

vidyaapithano adhyaapak *n.* વિદ્યાપીઠનો અધ્યાપક professor

vidyutshastree *n.* વિદ્યુતશાસ્તરી electrician

vigat aaapavee *v.t.* વગિત આપવી detail

vigatavaar kahevun *v.t.* વગિતવાર કહેવું recount

Vigatvaar varanan *n.* વગિતવાર વરણન

specification
disband

Vigatvaarnu Nondhpatrak *n.* વગિતવારનું નોંધપત્રક schedule

vighatan karavun *v.* વઘિટન કરવું disembody

vighatan karavun *v.t.* વઘિટન કરવું disintegrate

vighatit *adj.* વઘિટિત dissipated

vighnanun nivaaran *n.* વઘ્નિનનું નિવારણ clearance

vigyaan *n.* વજ્ઞિઆન science

Vigyaanshaastrano abhyaasee *n.* વજ્ઞિઆનશાસ્ત્રનો અભ્યાસી scientist

vihonun *adj.* વહિોણું wanting

vijalee *n.* વજિળી lightning

vijaleek aakraman *n.* વીજળીક આક્રમણ blitzkrieg

vijay *n.* વજિય triumph

vijay *n.* વજિય victory

vijay soochak holee *n.* વજિય સૂચક હોળી bonfire

vijayachihna *n.* વજિયચહિ્ન trophy

vijayee *adj.* વજિયી triumphant

vijayee *adj.* વજિયી unsuccesful

vijayee *n.* વજિયી victorious

vijayee thavun *v.t.* વજિયી થવું conquer

vijetaa *n.* વજિતા vanquisher

Vijyee *adj.* વજિયી successful

vikaas *n.* વકિાસ development

vikaas *n.* વકિાસ growth

vikaasano tabakko *n.* વકિાસનો તબક્કો phase

vikalp *n.* વકિલ્પ alternative

vikalp *n.* વકિલ્પ option

vikaraad *adj.* વકિરાળ ferocious

vikaraadataa વકિરાળતા ferocity

vikasavun, *v.t.* વકિસવું develop

vikasit karavun *v.t.* વકિસતિ કરવું evolve

vikendrit karavun *v.t.* વકિન્દ્રતિ કરવું decentralize

vikheraai javun *v.t.* વખિેરાઈ જવું disperse

vikheravun *v.t.* વખિેરવું diffuse

vikheree naakhavun *v.t.* વખિેરી નાખવું dispel

vikheree nakhavun *v.t.* વખિેરી નાખવું

vikhuto padelo *n.* વખિુટો પડેલો straggler

vikiran chikitsaavignaan *n.* વકિરિણ ચકિત્સિાવજ્ઞિઆન radiology

vikkretaa *v.t.* વક્રિેતા tranter

vikreta *n.* વક્રિેતા vender

vikrut *adj.* વક્રિત wry

vikrut karavun *v.t.* વક્રિત કરવું deform

vikrut karavun *v.t.* વક્રિત કરવું distort

vikrut karavun te *n.* વક્રિત કરવું તે deformation

vikrut vidamban *n.* વક્રિત વડિંબન travesty

vikrutee *n.* વક્રિતdeformity

vikruti *n.* વક્રિતdistortion

vilaano chhod *adj.* વલિોનો છોડ sallow

vilaap *adj..* વલિાપ cry

vilaap *n.* વલિાપ lamentation

vilaap *v.t.* વલિાપ wail

vilaap *n.* વલિાપ wailing

vilaap karavo *v.t.* વલિાપ કરવો. mourn

Vilaasee ane strain maanas *n.* વલિાસી અને સ્ત્રૈણ માણસ sybarite

vilaayatee daatardu *n.* વલિાયતી દાતરડું scythe

vilakshan *adj.* વલિક્ષણ phenomenal

vilakshan *adj.* વલિક્ષણ prodigious

vilakshan *adj.* વલિક્ષણ quaint

vilakshan *n.* વલિક્ષણ rummy

Vilakshan *adj.* વલિક્ષણ surprising

vilakshanata *n.* વલિક્ષણતા peculiarity

vilamaba karvo વલિંબ કરવો unfasten

vilamb *v.t.* વલિંબ delay

vilamb shulk *n.* વલિંબ શુલ્ક demurrage

vilay *n.* વલિય rescission

Vilayan *n.* વલિયન solution

vileeneekaran *n.* વલિીનીકરણ merger

vimaan *n.* વમિાન airliner

vimaan *n.* વમિાન craft

vimaan kampani *n.* વમિાન કંપની airline

vimaan, havaaee jahaaj *n.* વમિાન, હવાઈ જહાજ aeroplane

vimaanama chadavun *v.t.* વમિાનમાં ચડવું emplane

vimaanane lagatun *n.* વિમાનને લગતું aeronaut

vinaash *v.t.* વિનાશ doom

vinaash *n.* વિનાશ vastation

vinaashak *adj.* વિનાશક destructive

vinaashak *adj.* વિનાશક disastrous

vinaashak *adj.* વિનાશક pernicious

vinaashak *adj.* વિનાશક ruinous

vinaashakartaa *n.* વિનાશકર્તા destroyer

vinamra *adj.* વિનિમ્ર discreet

vinantee karavee *v.* વિનંતી કરવી appeal

vinantee karavee *v.t.* વિનંતી કરવી request

vinantee karavee *v.t.* વિનંતી કરવી urge

vinavaneethee samajaavee kakaay tevun *adj.* વિનવણીથી સમજાવી શકાય તેવું exorable

vinay *n.* વિનય civility

vinayasheel *adj.* વિનયશીલ gentle

vinayasheel *adj.* વિનયશીલ humble

vinayee *n.* વિનયી courteous

vinayee, *adj.* વિનયી bland

vinimay *v.t.* વિનિમય barter

vinimay *v.t.* વિનિમય interchange

vinimay karavo *n.* વિનિમય કરવો swap

vinod *n.* વિનોદ banter

vinod *n.* વિનોદ raillery

vinod *n.* વિનોદ recreation

vinodee વિનોદી humorist

Vintvaanee chaadar *n.* વીંટવાની ચાદર shroud

vipareet *v.t.* વિપરીત contrary

vipareet asar karavee *v.t.* વિપરીત અસર કરવી reverse

vipareetata *n.* વિપરીતતા perversion

vipul *adj.* વિપુલ abundant

vipul વિપુલ bumper

vipul *adj.* વિપુલ copious

vipul વિપુલ exuberant

vipul aahaar *n.* વિપુલ આહાર forage

vipul foolovaalu *n.* વિપુલ ફૂલોવાળું flowery

vipul hovun *v.* વિપુલ હોવું abound

vipul leelotareevaalun *n.* વિપુલ લીલોતરીવાળું verdant

Vipul paththarvaalun *adj.* વિપુલ પથ્થરવાળું stony

vipul pravaah *v.t.* વિપુલ પૂરવાહ gush

vipulata *n.* વિપુલતા profusion

vipulata *n.* વિપુલતા richness

vipulataa *n.* વિપુલતા abundance

Vipultaa *n.* વિપુલતા store

viraam *n.* વિરામ cessation

viraam *n.* વિરામ interval

viraamachinya mukavun *v.t.* વિરામચિહ્ન મુકવું punctuate

viraamchinha *n.* વિરામચિહ્ન punctuation

viral vastu *n.* વિરલ વસ્તુ rarity

viravaran *n.* વિવરણ disquisition

virodh *n.* વિરોધ opposition

virodh, dushmanaavat *n.* વિરોધ, દુશ્મનાવટ antagonism

virodhaabhaas *n.* વિરોધાભાસ contradiction

virodhee *adj.* વિરોધી opposite

virodhee, pratheespardhee *n.* વિરોધી, પ્રતિસ્પર્ધી antagonist

viroop karavun *v.t.* વિરૂપ કરવું disfigure

viruddh *prep.* વિરુદ્ધ contra

virudhha *prep.* વિરુદ્ધ versus

visamvaadee *adj.* વિસંવાદી discordant

visamvaaditaa *n.* વિસંવાદિતા discord

visangat *adj.* વિસંગત grotesque

visangat hovun *v.t.* વિસંગત હોવું contravene

visangatataa *n.* વિસંગતતા discrepancy

visfot *n.* વિસ્ફોટ explosion

visfot karavo *v.i.* વિસ્ફોટ કરવો fulminate

vish *n.* વિષ toxin

vishaad *n.* વિષાદ hump

vishaad *n.* વિષાદ melancholy

vishaal *adj.* વિશાળ immense

vishaal *adj.* વિશાળ large

Vishaal *adj.* વિશાળ splendid

vishaal *adj.* વિશાળ vast

vishaal drashy *n.* વિશાળ દ્રશ્ય panorama

vishaal pramaananun *adj.* વિશાળ પ્રમાણનું voluminous

vishaalakaay *n.* વિશાળકાય colossus

vishaanu *n.* વિષાણુ virus
vishamata *n.* વિષમતા inequality
vishamataa *n.* વિષમતા disparity
Vishambhuj *adj.* વિષમભુજ scalene
vishavidhyaa, vigyaana *n.* વિષવિદ્યા
વિજ્ઞાન toxicology
vishay *n.* વિષય content
vishay *adj.* વિષય subject
vishay *n.* વિષય topic
vishay vastu *n.* વિષય વસ્તુ theme
vishayaantar *n.* વિષયાંતર deviation
vishayaantar karavun *v.t.* વિષયાંતર
કરવું deviate
vishayaantar karavun *v.t.* વિષયાંતર
કરવું digress
vishayaantar karavun *n.* વિષયાંતર કરવું
digression
vishayaantar karavun *adj.* વિષયાન્તર
કરવું discursive
vishayasanpat maanas *n.* વિષયસંપટ
માણસ libertine
vishayasevan *n.* વિષયસેવન lust
vishayne lagatun *adj.* વિષયને લગતું
topical
vishesh *adj.* વિશેષ especial
vishesh aavadat *n.* વિશેષ આવડત forte
vishesh adhikaar *n.* વિશેષ અધિકાર
prerogative
vishesh paheravesh *v.i.* વિશેષ પહેરવેશ
suit
visheshan yukt *adj.* વિશેષણ યુક્ત
adjectival
visheshata vinaanun *n.* વિશિષતા વિનાનું
commonplace
vishisht *adj.* વિશિષ્ટ different
Vishisht *n.* વિશિષ્ટ selector
Vishisht gun ke lakshan *n.* વિશિષ્ટ
ગુણ કે લક્ષણ speciality
Vishisht praytna *v.t.* વિશિષ્ટ પ્રયત્ન
stunt
vishisht varg naa loko *n.* વિશિષ્ટ
વર્ગના લોકો folk
vishishta *adj.* વિશિષ્ટ special
vishishta aavdat *n.* વિશિષ્ટ આવડત
talent
vishishta gunn, laxan *n.* વિશિષ્ટ ગુણ –
લક્ષણ. trait

vishishta lakshan *n.* વિશિષ્ટ લક્ષણ
technicality
vishista dishaa *n.* વિશિષ્ટ દિશા trend
vishleshak *n.* વિશ્લેષક analyst
vishraanti *n.* વિશ્રાંતિ relaxation
vishraantino samay *n.* વિશ્રાન્તનો
સમય recess
vishtaa *n.* વિષ્ટા excrement
vishuvavrut *n.* વિષુવવૃત્ત equator
vishuvavruttiy *adj.* વિષુવવૃત્તિય
equatorial
vishv *n.* વિશ્વ world
vishvaas *n.* વિશ્વાસ belief
vishvaas *n.* વિશ્વાસ reliance
vishvaas mookavo *v.t.* વિશ્વાસ મૂકવો.
repose
vishvaasaghaat *n.* વિશ્વાસઘાત perfidy
vishvaasaghaatee *adj.* વિશ્વાસઘાતી
perfidious
vishvaasaghaatee *n.* વિશ્વાસઘાતી
treachery
vishvaasapaatr *adj.* વિશ્વાસપાત્ર
credible
vishvaasapaatra *adj.* વિશ્વાસપાત્ર
authentic
vishvaasapaatra *adj.* વિશ્વાસપાત્ર
trustworthy
vishvaasapaatrata *n.* વિશ્વાસપાત્રતા
credibility
vishvaasapoorn *n.* વિશ્વાસપૂરણ
confidant
vishvaash naa raakhavo *n.* વિશ્વાસ ના
રાખવો disbelief
vishvaash naa raakhavo *v.t.* વિશ્વાસ
ના રાખવો disbelieve
vishvaatghaat kare tevun *n.*
વિશ્વાસઘાત કરે તેવું traitor
vishvaatghaat karnaar *adj.*
વિશ્વાસઘાત કરનાર traitorous
vishvanaagarik *n.* વિશ્વનાગરિક
cosmopolitan
vishvasaneey *adj.* વિશ્વસનીય reliable
vishvasaneeyata *n.* વિશ્વસનીયતા
reliability
vishvavidhyaalay *n.* વિશ્વવિદ્યાલય
university

vishvavyaapee *adj.* વિશ્વવ્યાપી immanent

vishvavyapee *adj.* વિશ્વવ્યાપી worl·wide

Vishyaasakt *n.* વિષયાસક્ત sensual

Vishyasakt vruti *n.* વિષયાસક્ત વૃત્તિ sensualism

Vishyasakti *n.* વિષયાસક્તિ sensuality

vistaar *n.* વિસ્તાર span

vistaar *n.* વિસ્તાર toft

vistaaravun, prasaaravun *v.* વિસ્તારવું, પ્રસારવું amplify

vistaran *adj.* વિસ્તરણ expansion

vistaranksham *adj.* વિસ્તરણક્ષમ expansive

vistaravun *v.t.* વિસ્તરવું reach

visteerna medaan *n.* વિસ્તીર્ણ મેદાન steppe

vistirn *adj.* વિસ્તીર્ણ great

vistrut karavun *v.t.* વિસ્તૃત કરવું enlarge

vitaamin *n.* વિટામિન vitamin

vivaad *v.t.* વિવાદ dispute

vivaad karanaar *n.* વિવાદ કરનાર disputant

vivaad karavo *v.t.* વિવાદ કરવો altercate

vivaadaaspad *adj.* વિવાદાસ્પદ disputeble

vivaadaaspad *adj.* વિવાદાસ્પદ polemic

vivaadshaastra *n.* વિવાદશાસ્ત્ર dialectic

vivaahadvesh *n.* વિવાહદ્વેષ misogamy

vivaran *n.* વિવરણ exposition

vivechanaatmak nibandh *n.* વિવેચનાત્મક નિબંધ critique

vivekapoorn *adj.* વિવેકપૂર્ણ judicious

Vivekbudhdhi *n.* વિવેકબુદ્ધિ sapience

vivekbudhivaalun *adj.* વિવેકબુદ્ધિવાળું considerate

vivekee *adj.* વિવેકી reasonable

Vivekee *adj.* વિવેકી suave

vivekee *adj.* વિવેકી urbane

Vivekeepanun *n.* વિવેકીપણું suavity

vividh jaatanun *adj.* વિવિધ જાતનું miscellaneous

vividh prakaaranu *adj.* વિવિધ પ્રકારનું various

vividhataa *n.* વિવિધતા variety

viyaavun *v.t.* વિયાવું yean

vokt *n.* વોલ્ટ volt

vorabler pakshee *n.* વોરબ્લેર પક્ષી warbler

vratapaalan *n.* વ્રતપાલન rite

vruddha, gharadun *adj.* વૃદ્ધ, ઘરડું aged

vruddhi *n.* વૃદ્ધિ augmentation

vrudhdhi sahaayak *n.* વૃદ્ધિ સહાયક stepping-stone

vrudhh *n.* વૃદ્ધ dotard

vrudhhaavasthaadarshee *adj.* વૃદ્ધાવસ્થાદર્શી senile

vrukshaachchhaadit maarg *n.* વૃક્ષાચ્છાદિત માર્ગ mall

vruksharaaji *n.* વૃક્ષરાજિ grove

vrukshone lagatun *adj.* વૃક્ષોને લગતું arboreal

vrundavaadan *n.* વૃંદવાદન conductor

vruttant વૃત્તાન્ત version

vsaahatee *adj.* વસાહતી colonial

vyaabhichaaree *adj.* વ્યાભિચારી immoral

vyaaj વ્યાજ interest

vyaajavatun વ્યાજવટું usury

vyaaje paisaa dheeranaar *v.t.* વ્યાજે પૈસા ધીરનાર usure

vyaakaran anusaaranun *adj.* વ્યાકરણ અનુસારનું grammatical

vyaakaranashaastr *n.* વ્યાકરણશાસ્ત્ર grammar

vyaakhyaa *n.* વ્યાખ્યા definition

vyaakhyaa karavee *v.t.* વ્યાખ્યા કરવી define

vyaakhyaan manch *n.* વ્યાખ્યાન મંચ rostrum

vyaakhyaananun samaapan *n.* વ્યાખ્યાનનું સમાપન peroration

vyaakul karavun *v.t.* વ્યાકુળ કરવું perplex

vyaap vadhaaravo *v.* વ્યાપ વધારવો aggrandize

vyaapak *adj.* વ્યાપક comprehensive

vyaapak *adj.* વ્યાપક extensive

vyaas *n.* વ્યાસ diameter

vyaas sambamdhee *adj.* વ્યાસ સંબંધી diametric

vyaasapeeth *n.* વ્યાસપીઠ pulpit

vyaavahaarik *adj.* વ્યાવહારિક practical

vyaavahaarik drashteevaalun *adj.* વ્યાવહારિક દ્રષ્ટીવાળું pragmatic

vyaayaamne lagatun *adj.* વ્યાયામને લગતું athletic

vyaayaamshaalaa *n.* વ્યાયામશાળા gymkhana

vyabhichaar *n.* વ્યભિચાર adultery

vyabhichaar *n.* વ્યભિચાર misconduct

vyabhichaaree *n.* વ્યભિચારી adulterer

vyabhichaaree *adj.* વ્યભિચારી licentious

vyagrata *n.* વ્યગ્રતા perplexity

vyakti *pre.* વ્યક્તિ onto

vyakti *n.* વ્યક્તિ person

vyakti nirapeksh *adj.* વ્યક્તિ નિરપેક્ષ impersonal

vyaktigat *n.* વ્યક્તિગત individual

vyaktigat *adj.* વ્યક્તિગત personal

vyaktigat vishishtata *n.* વ્યક્તિગત વિશિષ્ટતા idiosyncracy

vyaktikaran *n.* વ્યક્તિકિરણ personification

vyaktionun jooth *n.* વ્યક્તિઓનું જૂથ people

vyaktitv *n.* વ્યક્તિત્વ individuality

vyaktitv *n.* વ્યક્તિત્વ personality

vyangyaatmak વ્યંગ્યાત્મક ironic

vyangyachitr *n.* વ્યંગ્યચિત્ર cartoon

vyanjan *adj.* વ્યંજન consonant

vyarth *adj.* વ્યર્થ frivolous

vyarthatha *n.* વ્યર્થતા frivolity

vyastaakshar shabd *n.* વ્યસ્તાક્ષર શબ્દ anagram

vyatpateeshaashtra *n.* વ્યુત્પત્તિ શાસ્ત્ર etymology

vyavahaaranipun *n.* વ્યવહારનિપુણ politic

vyavashit *adj.* વ્યવસ્થિત natty

vyavastha *n.* વ્યવસ્થા management

vyavasthaa *n.* વ્યવસ્થા arrangement

vyavasthaapak *n.* વ્યવસ્થાપક chamberlain

vyavasthaapak *n.* વ્યવસ્થાપક executive

vyavasthaapan karavun *v.t.* વ્યવસ્થાપન કરવું manage

vyavasthaapya *adj.* વ્યવસ્થાપ્ય manageable

vyavasthit banaavavun *v.t.* વ્યવસ્થિત બનાવવું systematize

vyavasthit karavun *v.t.* વ્યવસ્થિત કરવું arrange

vyavasthit mookavun *v.t.* વ્યવસ્થિત મૂકવું collate

vyavasthita nahi aevun *adj.* વ્યવસ્થિત નહિ એવું untidy

vyavasthitata *adj.* વ્યવસ્થિતતા. lucid

vyavsaayne lagatun *n.* વ્યવસાયને લગતું vocation

vyavsthit gothavavun *v.t.* વ્યવસ્થિત ગોઠવવું drape

vyooharachanaa *n.* વ્યૂહરચના strategy

Vyuhaatmak *adj.* વ્યૂહાત્મક strategical

vyutkram *adj.* વ્યુત્ક્રમ reciprocal

xanik *adj.* ક્ષણિક transient

yaad karavun *n.* યાદ કરવું bethink

yaad karavun *v.t.* યાદ કરવું memorize

yaad raakhavun *v.t.* યાદ રાખવું remember

yaadee *n.* યાદી Catalogue

yaadee *n.* યાદી jotting

yaadee banaavavee *v.t.* યાદી બનાવવી enlist

yaadgaar *n.* યાદગાર unchancy

yaak *n.* યાક yak

yaamyottar vrutt *n.* યામ્યોત્તર વૃત્ત meridian

yaantrik uddayan *n.* યાંત્રિક ઉડ્ડયન aviation

yaatanaa *n.* યાતના torment

yaatanaa *n.* યાતના torture

yaatanaa thavee *v.i.* યાતના થવી writhe

yaayaavar *adj.* યાયાવર migratory

yagnavedi *n.* યજ્ઞવેદી altar

yahoodee *n.* યહૂદી jew

yahoodee praarthana tanboo *n.* યહૂદી પ્રાર્થના તંબૂ tabernacle

yantr *n.* યંત્ર machine

yantrarachanaa *n.* યંત્રરચના mechanism

yantrashaastr *n.pl.* યંત્રશાસ્ત્ર mechanics

yantrashaastranun *adj.* યંત્રશાસ્ત્રનું mechanical

yantrodhyogashaastra *n.* યંત્રોદ્યોગશાસ્ત્ર technic

yathaakram *n.* યથાક્રમ ordinate

yathaarthadarshan chitr *adj.* યથાર્થદર્શન ચિત્ર perspective

yathaayogy *adj.* યથાયોગ્ય condign

yathaayogya reete *adv.* યથાયોગ્ય રીતે aptly

yauvan *n.* યૌવન youth

yoddho *n.* યોદ્ધો gladiator

yoddho *n.* યોદ્ધો warrior

yogy badalo *n.* યોગ્ય બદલો meed

yogy reete *adv.* યોગ્ય રીતે properly

yogy shiksha *n.* યોગ્ય શિક્ષા retribution

yogya *adj.* યોગ્ય appropriate

yogya *adj.* યોગ્ય apt

yogya *v.t.* યોગ્ય befit

yogya યોગ્ય felicitous

Yogya *adv.* યોગ્ય suitably

yogya reete *adv.* યોગ્ય રીતે aright

yogya reete *adv.* યોગ્ય રીતે fairly

yogyataa pramaane *adv.* યોગ્યતા પ્રમાણે deservedly

yojana *n.* યોજના idea

yojanaano amal karavo *n.* યોજનાનો અમલ કરવો implement

yojavun *v.t.* યોજવું contrive

yojavun *n.* યોજવું project

yojelo ghaat *n.* યોજેલો ઘાટ plan

Yojnaa *n.* યોજના scheme

yoonun zaad *n.* યૂનું ઝાડ yew

yootopiyaanu *adj.* યૂટોપિયાનું. utopian

yuaddh *n.* યુદ્ધ duel

yuddh *n.* યુદ્ધ war

yuddha *n.* યુદ્ધ battle

yuddhaaroodh *adj.* યુદ્ધારૂઢ belligerent

yuddhanauka *n.* યુદ્ધનૌકા galleon

yuddhanaukaaonun *adj.* યુદ્ધનૌકાઓનું naval

yuddhanee paristhiti *n.* યુદ્ધની પરિસ્થિતિ warfare

yuddhaviraam *n.* યુદ્ધવિરામ armistice

yuddhhajahaaj *n.* યુદ્ધજહાજ frigate

yudhanaukaa *n.* યુદ્ધનૌકા cruiser

Yudhdhakalaane lagtun *n.* યુદ્ધકળાને લગતું strate

yudhdhakhor *adj.* યુદ્ધખોર bellicose

yudhdhviram *n.* યુદ્ધવિરામ truce

yug *n.* યુગ epoch

yug *n.* યુગ era

yugal *n.* યુગલ dyad

yugal geet *n.* યુગલગીત duet

yukti *n.* યુક્તિ tactics

yuktibaaj *adj.* યુક્તિબાજ ingenious

yuktibaaj *n.* યુક્તિબાજ tactician

Yuktiprayukti *n.* યુક્તિપ્રયુક્તિ stratagem

yunivarsitiman pravesh *n.* યુનિવર્સિટીમાં પ્રવેશ matriculation

yurenasa *n.* યુરેનસ uranus

zaad *n.* ઝાડ tree

Zaad e no mukhya bhaag *n.* ઝાડ ઈ.નો મુખ્ય ભાગ stem

zaadanu thad *n.* ઝાડનું થડ trunk

zaadeevaalu kotar *n.* ઝાડીવાળું કોતર dell

zaadu maaravun *v.i.* ઝાડુ મારવું sweep

Zaadvun (Thad Vinaanun) *n.* ઝાડવું (થડ વિનાનું) shrub

zaakad *n.* ઝાકળ dew
zaakadabheenu *adj.* ઝાકળભીનું dewy
zaalar *n.* ઝાલર jabot
zaalar *n.* ઝાલર trimming
zaankad *n.* ઝાંકળ frost
zaankharun ઝાંખરું caper
zaankhu *v.t.* ઝાંખું feign
zaankhu ajavaalun *n.* ઝાંખું અજવાળું twilight
zaapatiyu *n.* ઝાપટિયું duster
zabakaaro *n.* ઝબકારો flash
zabakavun *v.i.* ઝબૂકવું twinkle
zabukavun *v.t.* ઝબૂકવું flare
zabunkavun *n.* ઝબુંકવું shimmer
zadapathee aagal vadhavun *v.t.* ઝડપથી આગળ વધવું scramble
zadapathee haankavun ઝડપથી હાંકવું spank
Zadpee *adj.* ઝડપી speedy
Zadpee chhabee *n.* ઝડપી છબી snap
Zagaaraa maartun *adj.* ઝગારા મારતું shinning
zagado *n.* ઝઘડો dissension
zagamagavun ઝગમગવું twinkling
zaghado *n.* ઝઘડો feud
zaghado *n.* ઝઘડો tussle
Zalhaltun *adj.* ઝળહળતું splendent
Zamvun te *n.* ઝમવું તે seepage
zankharaa *n.* ઝાંખરા heath
zankhavun *v.i.* ઝંખવું hanker

zankhu *adj.* ઝાંખું dull
zanoon, unmaad *n.* ઝનૂન frenzy
zapatun *n.* ઝાપટું gust
zaramar varasaad *v.i.* ઝરમર વરસાદ drizzel
zaran *n.* ઝરણ exudation
zaro *n.* ઝરો fount
zeenavatbharyu *adj.* ઝીણવટભર્યું elaborate
zeenee tapaas karavee *v.t.* ઝીણી તપાસ કરવી scan
zeenun kaapad *n.* ઝીણું કાપડ tissue
zeeyovaadee *n.* ઝીયોવાદી zionist
zer *n.* ઝેર venom
zer nankhavun *v.t.* ઝેર નાખવું envenom
zeree *adj.* ઝેરી venomous
zeree *n.* ઝેરી virulent
zereepanun *n.* ઝેરીપણું virulence
Zerkacholun *n.* ઝેરકચોલું strychnine
zinnu kaapad *n.* ઝીણું કાપડ lawn
zinun kaapad *n.* ઝીણું કાપડ gauze
Zinvatthi jovun ke tapaasvun *v.t.* ઝીણવટથી જોવું કે તપાસવું scrutinize
Zolee *n.* ઝોળી sling
Zonku khaavun ઝોકું ખાવું snooze
zoodavun *n.* ઝૂડવું thresh
Zoolvun *v.t.* ઝૂલવું swing
Zoompdee *n.* ઝૂંપડી shanty
zoopadapattee *n.* ઝૂપડપટ્ટી slum